2/06

GUNSMOKE

AND

SADDLE LEATHER

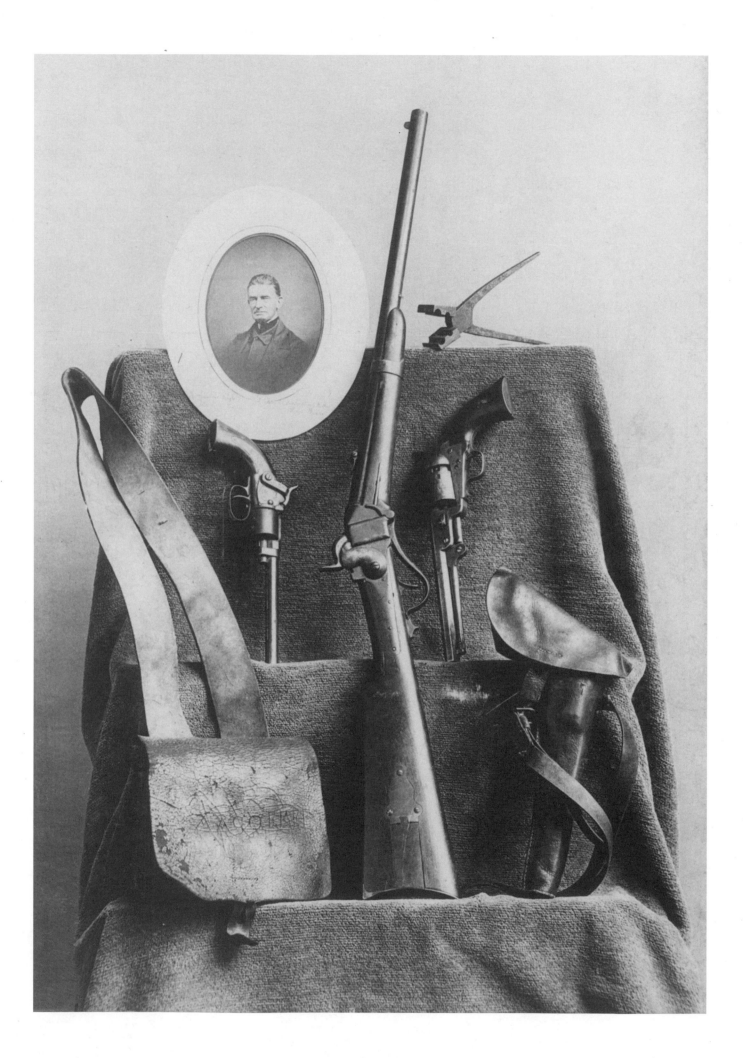

GUNSMOKE

AND SADDLE LEATHER

Firearms in the Nineteenth-Century American West

Charles G. Worman

University of New Mexico Press
Albuquerque

09 08 07 06 05   1 2 3 4 5

Library of Congress Cataloging-in-Publication Data

Worman, Charles G., 1933–
    Gunsmoke and saddle leather : firearms in the nineteenth-century American West / Charles G. Worman.
        p. cm.
    Includes bibliographical references and index.
    ISBN 0-8263-3593-4 (cloth : alk. paper)
    1. Firearms—West (U.S.)—History. I. Title.
    TS535.W67 2005
    683.4'0978'0934—dc22

                        2005014565

Book design and composition by Damien Shay
Body type is Minion 10.5/14.
Display is Mesquite and Birch.

To the memory of
those beasts of burden,
the horses, oxen,
mules, and burros,
which mutely endured
thirst, starvation, heat,
cold, and sometimes
cruelty by their owners,
but whose efforts
were essential to
westward expansion.

◆ CONTENTS ◆

✦ ACKNOWLEDGMENTS ✦

If one finds a turtle contentedly sunning itself on the top of a fence post, you know it probably had help getting up there. Like the turtle, I could not have completed this project without assistance from numerous individuals. I probably forgot a few and to those I apologize but I'm equally grateful to you, unnamed as you are. In particular I want to mention "my old saddle pard" Louis A. Garavaglia, coauthor of our previous two books on western guns, who has always been available with suggestions and encouragement. Bob Butterfield, Gary Delscamp, Norm Flayderman, William T. Goodman, Jim Gordon, Ralph Heinz, Jeff Hengesbaugh, Charles L. Hill Jr., Ron Peterson, Jerry Pitstick, Ron Paxton, and Gary Roedl have been particularly generous in making guns and/or photos available. The support of a skilled and dedicated reference librarian is indispensable, and I found such a person in Ms. Barbara Groff of the Greene County (Ohio) library system. With patience and perseverance she located some extremely useful but obscure data. No less important are the many others who have aided graciously in various ways including:

Anderson, Dale C.	Gabel, Ronald G.
Baumann, Erich	Gomber, Drew
Bertuccio, Barbara	Gross, John H.
Bowers, Carol	Gutterman, Julia and Neil
Brooks, Dennis C.	Hanson, Charles E., Jr.
Carlile, Richard	Hanson, James
Condon, David	Harmon, Dick
Cornett, Edward F.	Harpold, Donald
DeFord, Leland E., III	Hayes, John J.
Dethlefsen, Thomas	Haynes, C. Vance
DePalma, Dr. Robert A.	Henry, Paul
Dorsey, R. Stephen	Hentz, Tucker F.
Dutcher, John	Hook, Jere L.
Ellis, Richard	Houze, Herbert
Evans, Steve	Jackson, Lloyd
Fenn, H. Sterling	Kaufman, Larry
Ficken, Homer	Kinzie, Roy
Fisch, Robert W.	Kopec, John A.
Frasca, Albert J.	Kudlik, John J.

– ACKNOWLEDGMENTS –

Lecher, Belvadine

Lucas, Wade

McAulay, John D.

McNellis, Robert E., Jr.

McPheeters, Kenneth L.

McWilliams, John N.

Marcot, Roy

Martin, Greg

Mossberg, Craig

Orbelo, William R.

Palazzo, Robert P.

Pate, Charles W.

Peck, Herb, Jr.

Perry, Al

Peterson, Dale H.

Priestel, Georg

Potter, Gail

Potter, James

Prusok, Rudi

Romanoff, Steve

Rufe, Laurie

Schreier, Konrad F., Jr.

Schultz, Dr. William

Silva, Lee A.

Singelyn, Dr. Thomas

Slagle, C. W.

Smith, Rod

Snoddy, Donald D.

Spangenberger, Phil

Tarr, Blair D.

Thorn, Dave

Trevor, Thomas N.

Voliva, Robert W.

Wagner, Lewis

Ware, Donald

Wright, Mark

Zupan, James

INSTITUTIONS

Alaska State Library, Juneau

Amon Carter Museum, Fort Worth, Texas

Arizona Historical Society

Arizona Pioneers' Historical Society Library, Tucson

Austin Public Library, Texas

Bancroft Library, University of California at Berkeley

Bisbee Mining and Historical Museum, Arizona

California State Library, Sacramento

Canadian Public Archives, Ottawa, Ontario

Cheney Cowles Museum, Spokane, Washington

Chickamauga-Chattanooga National Military Park, Fort Oglethorpe, Georgia

Colorado Historical Society

Colorado Springs Pioneer Museum

Cripple Creek District Museum, Colorado

Custer Battlefield Historical and Museum Association, Montana

Daughters of Utah Pioneers Memorial Museum, Salt Lake City

Denver Public Library, Colorado

Desoto National Wildlife Refuge, Missouri Valley, Iowa

Fort Davis National Historic Site, Texas

Fort Laramie National Historic Site, Wyoming

Jim Gatchell Museum, Buffalo, Wyoming

– ACKNOWLEDGMENTS –

Henry E. Huntington Library and Art Gallery,
San Marino, California

Hubbard Museum of the American West,
Ruidoso Downs, New Mexico

Idaho State Historical Society

Institute of Texas Cultures, San Antonio

Iowa Historical Society

Kansas State Historical Society

Latter Day Saints Archives, Salt Lake City, Utah

Library of Congress, Washington DC

Los Angeles County Museum of
Natural History, California

Minnesota Historical Society

Missouri State Historical Society

Missouri State Museum, Jefferson City

Montana Historical Society

Museum of Church History and Art,
Salt Lake City, Utah

Museum of New Mexico, Santa Fe

Museum of Northern Arizona, Flagstaff

Museum of the Fur Trade, Chadron, Nebraska

National Archives, Washington DC

Nebraska State Historical Society

Nevada State Museum, Carson City

North Dakota State Historical Society

Ohio Historical Society

Oklahoma Historical Society

Oregon Historical Society

Provincial Archives of Alberta, Edmonton

Richard A. Bourne Company

Roswell Museum and Art Center, New Mexico

San Antonio Conservation Society, Texas

Simpson Confederate Research Center,
Hillsboro, Texas

Smithsonian Institution, Washington DC

Sotheby, Park-Bernet Galleries, New York

South Dakota State Historical Society

Sweetwater County Historical Museum,
Green River, Wyoming

Tombstone Courthouse State Historical Park, Arizona

US Army Military History Institute,
Carlisle Barracks, Pennsylvania

US Geological Survey, Denver, Colorado

US Military Academy, West Point, New York

Union Pacific Railroad Company, Omaha, Nebraska

University of Alaska at Fairbanks

Spencer Library, University of Kansas, Lawrence

University of New Mexico Center for
Southwest Research, Albuquerque

University of Oklahoma Library, Norman

University of Wyoming, Laramie

Utah State Historical Society

Utah State University, Logan

W. H. Over Museum, Vermillion, South Dakota

Wells Fargo Bank History Room,
San Francisco, California

Wyoming Division of Cultural Resources, Cheyenne

Wyoming State Museum, Cheyenne

Not to be ignored are Luther Wilson and his publishing staff
of the University of New Mexico Press.
I'm grateful for their patience, cooperative spirit, and goodwill.

⚞ INTRODUCTION ⚟

Beginning about 1970, Louis A. Garavaglia and I spent thirteen years researching and writing a very well-received two volume series, *Firearms of the American West 1803–1894*, also published by the University of New Mexico Press. In more than eight hundred pages of text and illustrations, we described in detail the evolution of firearms usage by civilians, the army, and Native Americans in the trans-Mississippi west. My fascination with the subject persisted and while Lou today concentrates more on modern firearms technology and design, I continued to gather additional data for another book. My primary interest has been anecdotal accounts left by the men and women who lived on the frontier rather than on the evolution of firearms technology. Lou and I had already covered that story quite thoroughly.

As any trained historian knows, personal recollections can be confused or colored by personal prejudices, fading memory, and other factors. Although they must be considered cautiously, they still can be informative and they do give us a better understanding of what life was like in another time. Also, a historian prefers to rely on original source materials, but the sheer magnitude of the task of locating the scores of nineteenth-century writings in their original form which I've cited often prevented that, and in some instances I've had to rely on the accuracy of accounts quoted by other writers. It is with these factors in mind that I've selected some personal accounts and rejected others which although entertaining were of questionable validity. In large part through the words of nineteenth-century men and women who were present on the frontier, I've sought to bring to life the role firearms played in the exploration and settlement of nineteenth-century America which lay west of the Mississippi.

Life was difficult in the west and popular history has not always been evenhanded or objective. Violence was often present but frequently has been distorted in western novels, movies, and television dramas. For example, the classic "walk down" duel between a marshal Matt Dillon and his antagonist in the middle of a dusty frontier street was a rare occurrence. In reality, history has ignored some of the most respected frontiersmen and glorified others with somewhat questionable reputations. Among lawmen, for example, "Bear River" Tom Smith, a former New York City police officer, enforced the laws in several frontier towns with fists and determination although he was murdered while serving an arrest warrant. Ex-slave Baz "Bass" Reeves was a highly respected deputy US marshal under Judge Isaac Parker for several decades but is hardly known today. Bill Tilghman of Oklahoma was described by "Bat" Masterson as "the greatest of all lawmen" and killed only two men while maintaining order. Our history books also sometimes have minimized broken treaties and other transgressions against the Native Americans committed by whites. But this volume isn't intended as a social, economic, or political history of the west. Instead its purpose is to provide additional insight into the role of firearms in settling that vast area west of the Mississippi.

Readers who compare this book with Lou's and my previous two volumes will find, with few exceptions, that text and photos between these covers do not duplicate material which we presented earlier. Instead this book is intended to expand the colorful and fascinating story of firearms on the frontier. If I've failed in this effort, the fault is entirely mine.

Charles G. Worman

Trappers, Traders, and Other Travelers

*These daring men secure to us the fur trade, while they explore
the unknown regions beyond our borders, and are
the pioneers in the expansion of our territory.*
— James Hall, 1846[1]

The fur trade in North America began along the East Coast before our Revolutionary War, and by 1800, French, British, Spanish, and Russian influence extended into the trans-Mississippi west. Americans had begun incursions into Spanish-owned Texas, hunting meat and trading for mustangs and buffalo robes with some Native American tribes by the 1790s. Following the Louisiana Purchase of 1803, Americans ventured westward toward the Rockies and the southwest in larger numbers, following game trails and those blazed by Native Americans. Trappers in search of beaver revealed the geography of the west, paving the way for others, and often served as guides for explorers, scientists, missionaries, soldiers, gold seekers, and settlers. These mountain men sometimes married into Indian tribes, establishing cultural ties. Traders, many of them men of means, provided guns, kettles, fish hooks, blankets, axes, knives, needles, and countless other goods to Native Americans, but sometimes brought debilitating whiskey and disease.

Legendary mountain man Jedediah Smith in 1827 summarized the lure the west held for some.

> Surely of all lives the hunter's is the most
> precarious, [for] we endure all the extremes
> of heat and cold, hunger and thirst, our

> lives and property are always at hazard,
> [and] when we lay down our guards must
> be placed, our rifles by our sides and our
> pistols under our heads ready to spring up
> at once from our wakeful sleep.

Despite the hardships, Smith wanted to be the first "to view a country on which the eyes of a white man had never gazed and to follow the course of rivers that run through a new land."[2]

Fur trader Manuel Lisa made thirteen trips up the Missouri River between 1807 and 1820. John Jacob Astor in 1811 founded the first major trading post at the mouth of the Columbia River, although the War of 1812 forced him to sell to the Canadian North West Company. Parties under Wilson Price Hunt and Robert Stuart in 1810–13 established the route for the Oregon Trail. William Ashley and Andrew Henry in 1822 led men up the Missouri where they did the trapping rather than trading with Indians for furs.

Ashley's 1823 expedition seemed jinxed from the start. One of two boats sprang a leak while still within sight of the St. Louis wharves, and the next day a trapper fell overboard and drowned. Three days later a cart carrying rifles, pistols, and three hundred pounds of gunpowder set out to rendezvous with the boats at St. Charles, but the

Flintlock .45 caliber iron-mounted rifle by J. J. Henry & Son (ca. early 1830s).
(Courtesy: Smithsonian Institution, Washington DC)

powder exploded killing three men. Undaunted, Ashley obtained another cart plus additional supplies on credit from gun makers Jake and Sam Hawken. Arikaree Indians later killed fifteen of Ashley's men, blocked Col. Henry Leavenworth's retaliatory military expedition, and closed the upper Missouri River to white traffic. In 1825 Gen. Henry Atkinson restored peaceful relations with most of the Indians on the upper Missouri, and Ashley revolutionized the fur trade system by establishing the summer rendezvous at which supplies were brought to gatherings of trappers and exchanged for furs. This system survived until 1840 in the face of stiff competition in the Rockies and Oregon country by the Hudson's Bay Company which was able to obtain its trade goods duty-free. Also by the early 1840s, the role of the trapper was diminishing as the trade was shifting from beaver to tanned buffalo robes.[3]

Despite the personal risks and high cost of transportation of goods, the fur trade could be quite profitable for those who undertook the hazards. Ross Cox wrote concerning 1812–13 prices for guns at the Pacific Fur Company's post at Spokane.

> Since the object of every male Indian was to obtain a gun, we played upon this desire to persuade the red men to search diligently for beavers. We made an enormous profit on the Indian trade. A good gun could not be had under twenty beaver skins; except a few small ones which we traded for fifteen. The [wholesale] price of a gun was about one pound, twenty shillings [a little less than six dollars].[4]

Another account from the same period in the Montana region indicated the sale of eight Northwest guns for 128 skins, an average of sixteen per gun, gunpowder at four skins per pound, while ten gun flints cost one skin. In 1831 Thomas Forsyth wrote from St. Louis to Secretary of War Lewis Cass and revealed that prices charged the Sauk and Fox Indians at that time were $30 for a rifle and $4 for a pound of gunpowder. Costs to the merchant were $12–13 for the rifle and only 20¢ per pound for powder.[5] European firearms and the horse affected the western Indian's culture dramatically. But to maintain perspective, it should be noted that although guns were an important element of trade and political influence, they appear to account for less than 5 percent of the total value of the trade. Even if one adds in gun-related materials such as powder, lead, etc., the total value is authoritatively estimated at no more than 10 percent.[6]

RIFLES

Most traveling west in the early 1800s carried eastern rifles, typically flintlock Kentucky (or more correctly Pennsylvania) "long rifles," usually made in Pennsylvania or Maryland. Rifles from Virginia, North Carolina, or Tennessee and weapons from makers scattered along the Ohio River added to the westward-bound inventory. John Joseph Henry of Pennsylvania was one of scores of eastern rifle makers whose guns crossed the Mississippi, a business continued by his sons. Two of the Henry family's major customers were the American Fur Company and the trading firm of Pierre Chouteau Jr. of St. Louis. Existing records of the former show orders for 1,325 Henry rifles with 42- to 44-inch barrels and calibers between .49 and .53 from 1835 until 1842.[7]

In the late 1820s and 1830s, trappers gathered at summer rendezvous sites to resupply, and eastern rifles often were included among trade goods transported there. One 1834 account listed ten iron-mounted rifles by J. J. Henry at $17.50 in addition to six iron-mounted rifles by the Hawken brothers of St. Louis at $25.[8]

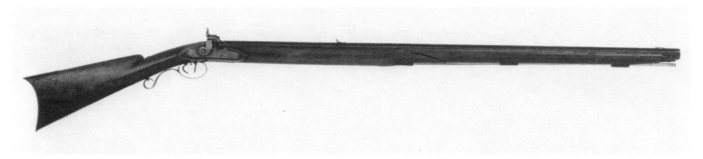

J. & S. Hawken fullstock iron-mounted rifle purchased in 1845 in St. Louis and carried to Utah by Mormon immigrant John Brown. (Courtesy: Museum of Church History and Art, Salt Lake City, UT)

William Marshall Anderson was a Kentucky lawyer who in 1834 went west with William Sublette's fur trading party to the Rockies to improve his health. He set out from Louisville "low in flesh, lower in spirits." On the trip he gained fifty pounds! His gun was "a light Tryon rifle, fifty to the pound [.45 caliber]." Rifles by Philadelphia makers George W. Tryon and later his son Edward K. under "The Sign of the Golden Buffalo," Andrew Wurfflein, and John Krider, as well as the Golcher family often went west. Another prominent maker of western rifles for both white and Indian customers was Henry Leman of Lancaster, Pennsylvania.[9]

St. Louis grew quickly from a French trading post of the mid-1760s into a major center. It became the jumping-off site for many heading west and by 1830 its population approached five thousand. Gun making and repair became an important element of the city's economy and by 1842, the St. Louis directory listed more than a dozen gunsmiths. Among the more accomplished were Jacob and Samuel Hawken. Jake arrived about 1818 and first worked with James Lakenan. Sam reached St. Louis in 1822; three years later the brothers formed a partnership.

The Hawken shop produced pistols, shotguns, and both light and heavy rifles for the local and western trade and in addition repaired guns while making such other products as axes and gun worms. In 1842 they even fitted basket handles to sixteen swords. The brothers also modified guns by other makers for western use, reboring them to larger calibers and sometimes shortening the barrel. Unlike such competitors as Horace Dimick, they produced no known target rifles. The Hawken name has gained stellar recognition among modern collectors, but the late Charles E. Hanson Jr. presented a strong argument that their prominence during the primary years of the beaver trade of the 1820s and 1830s has been exaggerated. Their fame seemingly peaked during the 1840s and early 1850s. Although their rifles were high quality, probably no more than 100–125 Hawken rifles were made in any one year beginning in the mid-1820s, and they were expensive by frontier standards, substantially more than an eastern trade rifle. Sam reported that in 1850 he had made one hundred rifles and twenty shotguns valued at $2,700.[10]

When William Ashley started for the Rockies in 1823, he later said he carried a .54 caliber rifle by Jake Hawken with a 42-inch barrel. Ashley supposedly refused a $150 offer for it in the Rockies. Known buyers of later Hawkens included Peg-Leg Smith (1838), Auguste Chouteau (1842), Jim Bridger (1842), Charles Bent (1846), Kit Carson, Tom Tobin, and in 1845 John C. Fremont purchased thirty J. & S. Hawken rifles when outfitting his third western expedition.[11]

In 1829 Etienne Provost, a French Canadian, became a partner in the American Fur Company. An entry for "2 rifles, Hawkins & Co., $50" was made against his account. This is one of the few known early references to the purchase of a Hawken rifle by a mountain man. In the same year, Kenneth McKenzie from Fort Floyd (later renamed Fort Union) asked Pierre Chouteau Jr. for two rifles "similar in all respects to the one made by Hawkins for Provost." In 1835 a listing of trade goods entrusted to Provost for delivery to the rendezvous site in the Rockies included ten steel- (iron-) mounted rifles at $17.50 each, thirty Northwest guns, three used rifles, and "6 steel mounted rifles, Hawken," at $20 each. Unfortunately there is no detailed description of these rifles. A J. & S. Hawken fullstock percussion rifle attributed to frontiersman James Clyman was described as about .52 caliber, 13 1/2 pounds, with a 38-inch barrel, and 54 inches overall with double set triggers.[12]

By the late 1830s, rifles by Jake and Sam Hawken and others making similar guns intended for the rigors of use on the plains, on the trail to Santa Fe, and in the Rocky Mountains shared certain characteristics. They typically were plain, sturdy percussion fullstocks with iron

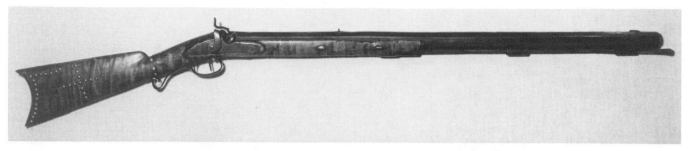

A .58 caliber Hawken halfstock rifle trimmed with brass tacks.
(Courtesy: Roswell Museum and Art Center, NM)

J. & S. HAWKEN,
MANUFACTURERS AND REPAIRERS OF

RIFLES AND SHOT GUNS,
No. 33 Washington Avenue, St. Louis, Mo.

J. & S. Hawken 1847 business card.

mountings of .45 to .54 caliber and with a barrel of less than forty inches but heavy enough to withstand a powder charge of one hundred grains or more. However, halfstock rifles by Hawken and others at this point were increasing in popularity.

Among Hawken's local competitors in the 1840s and 1850s making "Rocky Mountain" or what today are called "plains rifles" were Horace Dimick, Reno Beauvais, Thomas Albright, Hoffman & Campbell, and Frederick Hellinghaus, as well as Stephen O'Dell of Natchez, Mississippi; William Rotton of Nebraska City; Carlos Gove in Council Bluffs, Iowa; and others including some from the east such as the prolific Henry family. Kit Carson and two companions visited Harrodsburg, Kentucky, in 1842 and bought rifles made by Benjamin Mills. Not all makers, including Hawken, always made the entire rifle, and it might be composed of a barrel by Remington, a lock by Golcher of Philadelphia, and trigger guard and other fittings by Tryon.

Although the Hawken brothers produced only a modest proportion of the plains-type rifles of their era, in the 1840s and after references to rifles by Jake and Sam reflect the growing prominence of the name. Jake died of cholera in 1849, but Sam continued the business until his son William S. and Tristam Campbell took over about 1855. Sam "retired" to Denver in 1859 but set up a shop there. He returned to St. Louis in 1861 and sold out the next year to his employee, J. P. Gemmer. Almost a decade after Jake's death when William B. Parsons published his

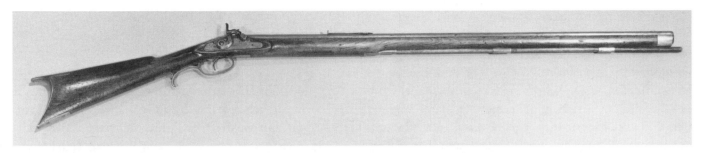

Baptiste "Little Bat" Garnier was one of the last of the famous scouts. A Mixed Blood, he and Gen. George Crook were close friends. After 1880, he spent many of his remaining years as an army scout and interpreter around Fort Robinson, Nebraska. During his earlier years as hunter and scout, he relied on this fullstock plains-type rifle of about .60 caliber by Henry Folsom & Co. of St. Louis with a lock by G. Golcher of Philadelphia. (Courtesy: Nebraska State Historical Society, neg. #7297)

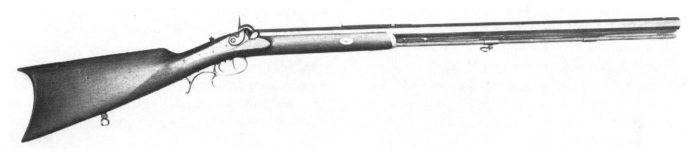

.45 percussion rifle by Augustus E. Linzell, one of the lesser known St. Louis makers, listed in business in the city between 1847 through the 1860s before relocating to Little Rock, Arkansas. The sling swivels, if original to the rifle, are an unusual feature on a civilian rifle such as this. (Courtesy: Gary Roedl)

guidebook to the gold mines of Colorado ("western Kansas" then), he recommended:

> Light sporting rifles, with fancy stocks, are not suitable to withstand the rough usage of the plains—neither should too heavy rifles be taken. One that carries about forty bullets to the pound [.49 caliber], and strongly built, is the most suitable; that known as the "Hawkins rifle" being preferable to any other.[13]

To improve his health, young William T. Hamilton in 1842 joined a party of eight free trappers for a year's hunt. He became enamored with the west and spent most of his life there. "In those days [1840s] the best rifles used were the Hawkins [sic], and they carried three hundred and fifty yards," he wrote. As late as 1866, when a desperado named Bob Jennings was captured, an account described him as "sitting by a tree, his big hocken [Hawken?] rifle leaning against the tree...and two big revolvers on the ground beside him." Two years later in 1868, the McAusland Brothers were advertising them-

selves in the Omaha city directory as "AGENTS FOR Wesson, Winchester, Lee & Hawkins [sic] Rifles." By this time, the "Hawkins" rifles may have borne the famed name but probably were made by Gemmer. (The Lee arms were .44 single-shot breechloaders produced in limited numbers by Lee's Firearms Company of Milwaukee in the mid-1860s.)[14]

Walter Cooper went west in 1858 and eventually settled in Montana where he become one of the major dealers in Sharps rifles and also developed improved gun sights. "I was for eighteen years almost constantly in camp; knew personally all the noted hunters, scouts, and mountain men from Mexico to Great Salt Lake. Kit Carson, Maxwell, Marianna, and Bridger, were among my early acquaintances." He continued:

> The Hawkins [sic] and Demmick [sic] rifles, made at St. Louis, were used almost exclusively by frontier and mountain men; these guns generally being half stock rib, single barrel, muzzle loaders, half-ounce ball, sighted usually for 200 yards point-blank, no raised [adjustable] sights were used.[15]

The early rifles carried west were flintlocks, but the percussion ignition system was becoming established in the east in the 1820s. It offered several advantages—faster fire, fewer misfires due to wind or moisture, and usually easier priming. No loss of gas through a vent also allowed use of a smaller powder charge to achieve the same velocity. One incident illustrated another drawback to the flintlock, the need to maintain a properly secured and shaped flint. Lewis Dawson, a member of an 1821–22 trading expedition to the Rockies, was being mauled by a grizzly. Trader Hugh Glenn sought to discharge his rifle to kill the angry giant, but it misfired three times before he "Sharpened [adjusted?] His flint [and] Primed His gun and Shot the Bare down."[16]

Ads in the *Missouri Republican* newspaper in 1831 made mention of both flints and percussion caps, and both were included among trade goods sent to rendezvous sites as early as 1833. In Oregon in December 1834, Nathaniel Wyeth's party "percussioned [converted] 3 Rifles our powder being so badly damaged as to render flint locks useless." He also spoke of "miserable flint guns which snap continually and afford an excuse for not killing." A member of a trapping party in 1837 "bursted the percussion tube of his rifle which obliged us . . . to make another tube." Yet in the west, the flintlock system remained in use among some into the 1840s. One reason was the greater ease of obtaining a piece of flint if far from a source of percussion caps. However to be useful any piece of flint had to be properly shaped and sharpened first. Another reason was the common reluctance of some to part with a known system. In 1838 Adolphus Meir & Company of St. Louis was advertising "1,000,000 S & B [percussion] caps in small boxes" but still was offering both flint and percussion gun locks in 1840. Henry Leman in 1852–53 sold 210 flintlock Indian rifles to Pierre Chouteau Jr. & Company Such moderately priced trade rifles met a need among whites as well as Indians. As late as 1852, Frederick Shaefer advertised in the San Joaquin (California) *Republican* "flintlocks altered to percussion."[17]

Granville Stuart of Montana recalled that as a youth in Iowa he learned to hunt with his father's two rifles.

> One was a flint-lock that he used when hunting along streams where there was timber and little wind. If the weather was cold and snow on the ground he could quickly start a fire with his flint-lock by which he would dress the deer he had killed. . . . The other gun he used while hunting on the prairies or out in the wind. It was a small-bore rifle fired with

percussion caps placed on the nipple. The cap would not blow off as did the powder in the pan of the flint-lock.[18]

Described in 1841 as "spare and gaunt," Tom Hancock was an experienced Texas frontiersman. "Tom's ordinary weapon, and the one upon which he most 'prided' himself, was a long, heavy, flint-lock rifle, of plain and oldfashioned [sic] workmanship, for he could not be made to believe in percussion caps and other modern improvements." It may have been he who advised George Wilkins Kendall, co-owner of the New Orleans *Picayune* newspaper, that one of his habits was "never to stir from my tracks, after firing, until I had reloaded."[19]

In May 1848 with six companions, George Rutledge Gibson set out from Santa Fe bound for Fort Leavenworth. "Swift has a musket, Raymond my [Hall?] carbine and Smith and myself Halls Patent Rifles." The Hall breech loading rifles were flintlocks for in anticipation of an Indian attack which didn't materialize, he wrote in his journal that "flints were screwed in, pans primed and all things made ready for a fight."[20]

Kendall, in preparing for his ill-fated journey to Texas and New Mexico in 1841, made a wise selection in his choice of a rifle.

> My rifle—short, but heavy barreled, and throwing a ball with great strength and precision, a long distance—I had purchased of the well-known [Moses] Dickson of Louisville, Ky, and a most excellent rifle it was.

His new rifle arrived in New Orleans just thirteen days after he placed the order. He later described it as "twenty four [balls] to the pound," or about .57 caliber. Such a rifle could down any large game found in the west. It was acknowledged by his companions to be "the best weapon in the command," apparently besting the Colt Paterson "repeating rifle of small bore" which a companion carried. (Colt revolving Paterson rifles and carbines were available in calibers from .34 to .525.) Kendall's rifle "would drive a ball completely through a buffalo at the distance of a hundred and fifty yards." Unfortunately he lost it when his party was captured by Mexican forces and imprisoned.[21]

One mountain man recalled that some trappers could load and fire four times a minute and he claimed to have witnessed experts who could achieve five shots, a questionable feat that if true involved loading with an undersize ball without a patch. Before the late 1830s, the

Fullstock Henry Leman trade rifle of about .50 caliber with rawhide repairs.
The rifle was once the property of Christopher "Kit" Carson.

frontiersman who wanted a multishot rifle would have had to carry a flintlock or more often a percussion gun with more than one barrel, usually a double either with both barrels rifled or one rifled and the other smooth to facilitate the use of shot. Barrels could be permanently mounted one above the other or side by side or as a swivel in which the barrels could be rotated by hand about a central pin. To have multiple shots, the tradeoffs were added weight, greater cost, and with a swivel barrel, a certain amount of fragility. Jim Bridger reportedly owned, among other guns, a swivel barrel double rifle made by John Shuler of Liverpool, Pennsylvania.

In the late 1830s, one going west also could choose a single-barrel rifle with a rotating cylinder such as made by Colt, J. & J. Miller, or William Billinghurst. John W. Cochran of New York City patented an underhammer revolving turret or radial cylinder rifle; only a few hundred were produced in the mid- to late 1830s, but some went west. Except for the Colt, each of these repeaters had a manually rotated cylinder. A Californian in April 1842 at Sutter's ranch "astonished the natives by discharging [a] Cochran's patent many chambered gun at a tree, putting six balls in a small cowpat." Josiah Gregg on his 1840 trip to Santa Fe used "one

of Cochran's nine-chambered rifles" on a buffalo hunt. He fired six shots in rapid succession and companions galloped to his aid, "not recollecting my repeating rifle, supposed I had been attacked by Indians."[22]

In the *Missouri Republican* newspaper for July 1, 1837, S. W. Meech advertised for sale one Cochran nine-shot rifle and a Cochran belt pistol. The same paper in its March 12, 1838, edition carried an ad for "Kendall's patent cast steel repeating rifle, capable of containing eight charges at one time." An early Colt Paterson rifle was offered by Thomas Jackson on May 8, 1838, "one splendid many chambered rifle, Colt patent, complete in case at $150." Another example of a rare and little used revolving rifle was mentioned in July 20, 1840, when Alonzo Child of St. Louis announced he was agent for Nichols & Child's revolving rifles. "Each cylinder contains six charges which can be discharged in the short time of twelve seconds."[23]

Nonetheless it was an uncommon frontiersman before the 1850s who didn't rely on a single-shot muzzle loading rifle. Despite having but a single shot, a resolute frontiersman when threatened by hostile Indians could sometimes defend himself by merely threatening

Egbert Johnson garbed in buckskin and perhaps photographed in the 1860s. Judging from the single front sight, his double-barrel gun is probably an over-and-under rifle-shotgun. (Courtesy: Colorado Springs Pioneers Museum, Cragin Collection)

to fire. As Capt. Randolph Marcy in his guide *The Prairie Traveler* recommended:

> If . . . Indians follow and press too closely, he should halt, turn around and point his gun at the foremost, which will often have the effect of turning them back, but he should never draw a trigger [fire] unless he finds that his life depends upon the shot; for, as soon as his shot is delivered, his sole dependence, unless he have time to reload, must be upon the speed of his horse.[24]

Rufus Sage traveled in the "far west" from 1841 until 1844 and described the buckskin-clad mountain man's equipage in this manner:

> His waist is encircled with a belt of leather, holding encased his butcher-knife and pistols—while from his neck is suspended a bullet pouch securely fastened to the belt in front, and beneath the right arm hangs a powder-horn transversely from his shoulder, behind which, upon the strap attached to it, are affixed his bullet-mould,

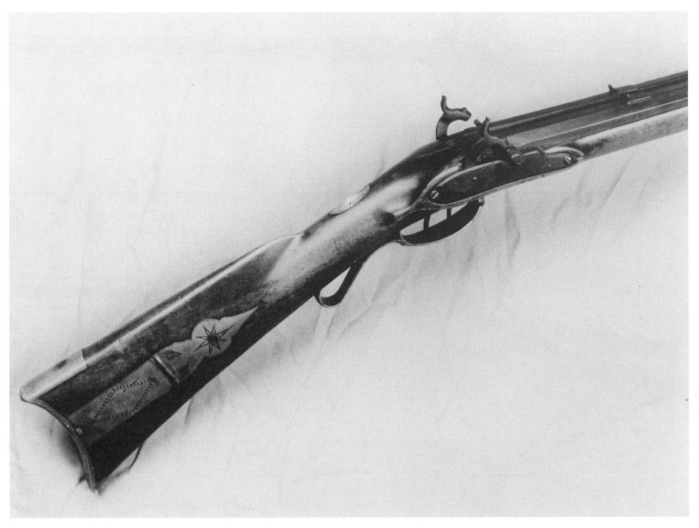

A unique percussion boxlock double rifle with the hammers mounted inside the lockplate. Each barrel is .54 caliber and the gun weighs about fourteen pounds. Unfortunately it's unsigned as to its maker, although it descended through a Texas family. (Courtesy: Frank Graves)

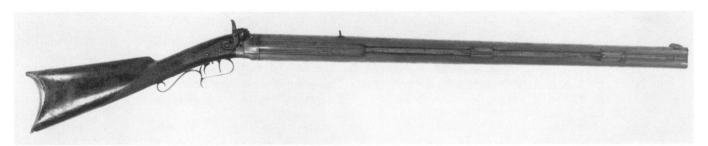

Above, a fourteen-pound double-barrel combination .50 caliber rifle and 10-gauge shotgun by Carlos Gove of Denver. Below, a Gove side-by-side .50 caliber double rifle used by Maj. D. C. Oakes in Colorado in the late 1850s. (Courtesy: Colorado Historical Society)

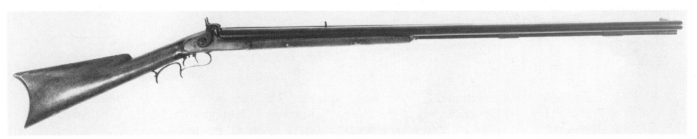

Double-barrel .50 caliber rifle by Hoffman & Campbell of St. Louis with back action locks by Tryon of Philadelphia. The barrels are marked on the underside "H&C, ST. LOUIS." The gun is a better grade weapon, with deluxe checkered wood, a cheek piece on the left, sling swivels, a rather fancy patch box cover, and an iron scroll trigger guard. (Photo by Steven W. Walenta, courtesy Mr. James D. Gordon)

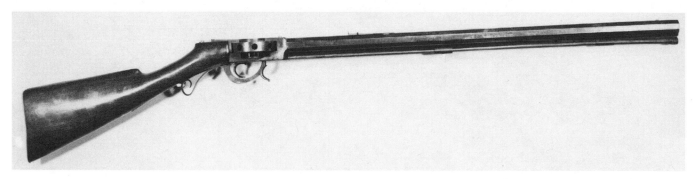

Cochran nine-shot turret rifle. (Courtesy: National Park Service, Fuller Collection, Chickamauga-Chattanooga National Military Park, Fort Oglethorpe, GA)

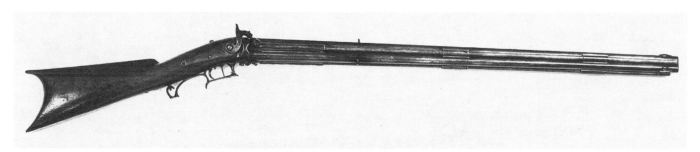

Heavy swivel-barrel rifle by M. L. Rood of Denver City, Colorado Territory, who arrived there from Michigan in 1859. Each of the three barrels is .45 caliber. It's documented as having been owned by frontiersman W. T. (Bill) Hamilton. (Photo by Steven W. Walenta, courtesy James D. Gordon)

Side-by-side double rifle by Hoffman & Campbell of St. Louis. The back action locks were made by Tryon of Philadelphia and the underside of the .50 caliber barrels are stamped "H&C, ST. LOUIS." (Photo by Steven W. Walenta, courtesy James D. Gordon)

ball-screw, wiper, awl, &c. With a gun-stick [or wiping rod] made of some hard wood, and a good rifle placed in his hands, carrying from thirty to thirty-five balls to the pound [.51 to .54 caliber] . . . [25]

Sage nicknamed his own rifle "Old Straightener" and at one stage, his party had been without food for five days when they came upon a single old bull buffalo. Fortune smiled on the famished men after first playing several cruel tricks.

I was able to approach within some sixty yards of him, when leveling, I pulled trigger,—the cap, being damp, burst without a discharge. The noise caught the quick ear of the buffalo, and caused him to look around;—however, seeing nothing to excite his alarm, he soon resumed [grazing]. . . . Having put fresh powder into the tube [nipple], and supplied it with another cap I was again raising to take aim, and had brought my piece nearly half, shoulderward, when it unceremoniously discharged itself, burying its ball in the lights of the buffalo—the very spot I should have selected had it been optional with myself. The old fellow staggered a few steps and fell dead![26]

Giving a nickname to one's gun wasn't uncommon. "Old Blackfoot" was a rifle at Bent's Fort. A trapper first had taken it into Blackfoot country where Indians killed him. Years later a white traded for the weapon and took it to the fort where it was restocked, converted to percussion, and used there as a target rifle for several years. James Josiah Webb acquired it in trade for a double-barrel shotgun, and in 1846 had it re-rifled, the forestock cut to half length, and the lock and breech plug replaced. It accompanied him on nearly all of his journeys to Santa Fe.[27]

The Franklin, Missouri *Intelligencer* in 1825 noted that shooting matches on most Saturday evenings "tend to perfect our riflemen in the use of their hair-splitting weapons. . . . Many of the most distinguished guns acquire names of the most fearful import . . . Blacksnake, Cross Burster, Hair Splitter, Blood Letter, and Panther Cooler."[28]

SMOOTHBORES

The rifle was the most important of an individual frontiersman's weapons and his life might well depend upon it.

One gets habituated to his rifle as to a trusty traveling companion. During the march the gun lies across the saddle; when one rests it is always close at hand. One never leaves camp without taking it as a cane; and at night it is wrapped in the blanket with the sleeper, to be ready for use at the first alarm.[29]

So wrote a German doctor who traveled to the Rockies in 1839.

However, shotguns played a significant if often unappreciated role in the era of the mountain man and the westward movement which followed. The versatile Northwest gun, popular with the Indian trade, could serve both as a light shotgun or, as was possible with any smoothbore, fire a snug-fitting patched round ball with success at modest ranges. Merchants found a market in the west for single- and double-barrel shotguns from the 1830s, or earlier, forward.[30]

Not only did shotguns prove useful in providing food for the cooking pot, but they offered a formidable measure of protection against Indian attacks, particularly at night. One party of trappers had "two large shotguns which we used on guard at night, as they were most effective weapons at close range." During one skirmish, "three of our men [trappers] were armed with double-barrelled shotguns, loaded with a half-ounce ball and five buckshot, deadly weapons at close range. These were now discharged and the Indians halted." Frederick Law Olmsted echoed the sentiment in the mid-1850s. "Two barrels full of buck-shot make a trustier dose . . . than any single ball for a squad of Indians, when within range, or even in unpracticed hands for wary venison."[31]

Before its versatility was more widely appreciated, the shotgun sometimes was an object of some scorn on the frontier. Washington Irving and his companions in 1832 endured "many sneers" at their double-barrel guns, and Josiah Gregg, veteran of the Santa Fe Trail, noted that nothing could persuade the frontier hunter to carry "what he terms in derision 'the Scatter gun.'" During Texas's war for independence (1835–36), the Anglo-American colonists faced a shortage of suitable firearms, and blacksmith Noah Smithwick recalled: "I fixed up many an old gun that I wouldn't have picked up in the road." One Texan said: "Our guns [were] no a count, little dobble barrels shot guns. I had a Harperferry yauger. The lock was tide on with buck skin stings, & the Mexicans had fine muskets." (The Mexican muskets generally were obsolescent surplus British "Brown Bess" flintlocks.)[32]

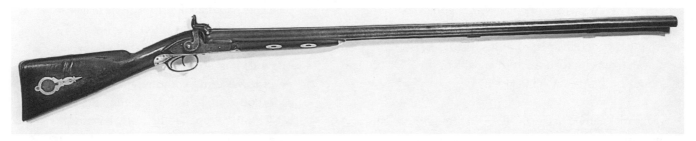

Ten-gauge double-barrel shotgun with 40-inch barrels, sold by Child & Pratt who were in business as St. Louis merchants between 1850 and 1863. A break in the wood on the underside of the wrist has been strengthened by a neatly inlaid strip of metal. (Photo by Steven W. Walenta, courtesy James D. Gordon)

Flintlock Kentucky-style pistol by Phillip Creamer. He moved from Maryland to St. Clair County, Illinois, by 1809 on the east side of the Mississippi near St. Louis and later moved across the river to the Jefferson Barracks area. As gun makers often did, he used a "ready made" lock in this pistol, one by William Ketland & Co. and imported from England. Creamer also produced good quality flintlock rifles for the local and western trade.
(Photo by Steven W. Walenta, courtesy James D. Gordon)

Sam Hawken, and presumably Jake, too, made some shotguns in addition to rifles and pistols, but these are exceedingly rare. Squire & Tyson of New York in March 1832 advertised in the *Missouri Republican* "Guns—Flint & percussion fowling pieces and ducking guns of all kinds and prices, of single and double barrel." St. Louis merchants Bentzen & Kloppenburg in November 1834 offered "25 pieces English, French and German double and single barrel guns and rifles." Mead & Adriance of St. Louis in August 1836 announced the arrival of the steamboat *Clinton*, carrying a shipment of guns which they offered: "25 fine English double and single barrel guns. 25 pair brass and iron barrel holster pistols. 75 pair fine English and German belt pistols. 250 fine English pocket pistols. 25 Bowie and Alabama hunting knives. 1 million percussion caps."[33]

James J. Webb on the Santa Fe Trail in 1844 wrote of killing a buffalo with his "double barrel shotgun carrying an ounce ball" (about .67 caliber) and mentioned that a Mexican herder had purchased a "nice double-barreled gun" in St. Louis. A year later, Lt. James Abert reported that a hunter had killed two bison on the run with a double, also firing a one-ounce round ball.[34]

Between 1850 and 1852, Pierre Chouteau Jr. & Company of St. Louis purchased fifteen doubles with 32-inch barrels and back action locks from Robert Hyslop of New York and W. Chance & Son of Birmingham, England, ten flintlock doubles, thirty percussion double-barrel shotguns with back action locks, and twenty with forward action (or bar) locks, all with 32-inch barrels. Some of these undoubtedly were sold to local customers, but some probably went west, perhaps on the Santa Fe Trail or with wagon trains bound for California or Oregon. In the 1850s, Horace Dimick of St. Louis advertised heavy shotguns suitable for buffalo running.[35]

Pair of English Hudson's Bay Company flintlock officer's belt pistols with a belt hook affixed to the left side of each. (Courtesy: Museum of the Fur Trade, Chadron, NE)

HANDGUNS

Pistols, by virtue of their short effective range, were useful only for a close encounter such as running buffalo or hand-to-hand fighting. Yet they often were part of a mountain man's equipment. After a long chase by Indians, Ross Cox and three companions in 1812 knew they could not outrun their pursuers as their jaded horses began to falter.

> I proposed that we dismount and take up
> our stand behind the horses. When the
> enemy came within range of our shot,
> each was to cover his man and fire. After
> this if we did not have time to reload, we
> could use our pistols.... The moment the
> Indians saw us dismount, they guessed
> our purpose, and wheeled about in
> retreat. We fired instantly, and two of
> their horses fell. The riders quickly
> mounted behind their companions, and
> in a short time, all had disappeared.[36]

Heading up the Missouri in 1811, Manuel Lisa's party cautiously went on shore to talk with a band of Sioux. "Each

rower had his gun by his side, and Lisa and myself besides our knives and rifles had each a pair of pistols in our belts." In describing his party of trappers (1837), "Uncle Dick" Wootton recalled that each man carried in his belt "a couple of pistols, two large knives and a tomahawk" in addition to his rifle and ammunition.[37]

A half-breed hunter and interpreter with John Jacob Astor's Pacific Fur Company, Pierre Michael, won the affection of a handsome Flathead girl of sixteen, a chief's niece. In accordance with custom, he presented her family with gifts. To his disappointed dusky rival for her affection, he gave a pistol and a dagger. Trapper Osborne Russell mentioned that during the battle with Indians at Pierre's Hole in 1834 he "kept a large German [Belgian?] horse pistol loaded by me in case they should make a charge when my gun [rifle] was empty."[38]

Depending upon one's purse and needs, the selection of handguns was extensive—flintlock or percussion, rifled or smoothbore. It might be a compact pocket size, a medium "belt size" weapon, or what was sometimes referred to as a "horse pistol," which usually meant a large and rather bulky military-style smoothbore handgun, capable of firing a single ball or several smaller ones and

Rare cutlass pistol by C. B. Allen.

usually carried by a mounted soldier in a saddle holster. Among the most handsome of pistols available were those so-called Kentucky pistols often made by the same gunsmiths who produced the Pennsylvania-Kentucky rifles. Until the late 1830s, the frontiersman's handgun would have been a single-shot unless it had more than one barrel.

In the 1830s, percussion handguns were increasingly common. Jedediah Smith was armed with a pair of percussion, belt size pistols when he was killed by Indians in 1831. Advertisements in the *Missouri Republican* by St. Louis and eastern dealers offered a variety of foreign and American handguns: "Pocket pistols of various sizes" (1834), "a few brace [pair] superior London pocket and belt pistols" (1835), "English and German pistols" (1836), and "40 prs. belt and pocket pistols of various sizes and prices, among which are the Ruggle's patent rifle pistols with cast steel barrels" (1837). The latter were underhammer "boot pistols" or "pocket rifles" of a popular style from the shops of such New England makers as A. Ruggles of Stafford, Connecticut; Gibbs Tiffany & Company of Sturbridge, Massachusetts; and D. D. Sacket of Southbridge, Massachusetts. These percussion pistols typically were .31 to .38 caliber with a barrel between three and eight inches long. Although of little use to a mountain man or hunter, these and other small size pistols were appropriate for the local trade or some westbound travelers.[39]

Most unusual was an ad in the same newspaper on December 3, 1838, in which L. Deaver of St. Louis announced: "Life Guards—Just rec'd two dozen of Elgin patent Bowie knives with pistol attached which will shoot and cut at the same time." Elgin "cutlass pistols" were the invention of George Elgin, percussion single-shots with a heavy blade mounted beneath the barrel. Also intriguing

was an 1834 advertisement: "G. & J. Erskine have 6 Lambert's Patent cane guns, 'Believed to be first of their kind offered in St. Louis.'" These unusual weapons were about .41 caliber and were invented by New Englander Roger Lambert. The wood-covered barrel served as a cane with a swivel muzzle cover. The knob handle pulled upward and swiveled to reveal the trigger and flat bar hammer.[40]

Washington Irving in 1832 participated in a mounted buffalo hunt at Fort Gibson, in what is now Oklahoma, using a pair of borrowed brass-barrel pistols.

> Pistols are very effective in buffalo hunting, as the hunter can ride up close to the animal, and fire at it while at full speed; whereas the long heavy rifles used on the frontier, cannot be easily managed, or discharged with accurate aim from horseback.[41]

Large-caliber (.54 or .69) single-shot military pistols were useful for the same purpose.

One well-known maker whose handguns reached the frontier was Henry Deringer Jr. of Philadelphia. He stated he had begun making pistols in 1825, although the fame of his small pocket pistols of the 1850s and 1860s overshadowed his earlier handguns. In contrast with his diminutive pocket guns, one of the largest Deringer pistols known is .58 caliber with a 9 1/4-inch barrel and 16 1/4 inches in overall length. His medium belt size percussion handguns became rather commonly known as Armstrong pistols in some circles as a result of a pair he made for Maj. Armstrong, agent to the Choctaw Indians during the period of their forced relocation to Arkansas and westward. Orders to Deringer sometimes mentioned "Armstrong" pistols as

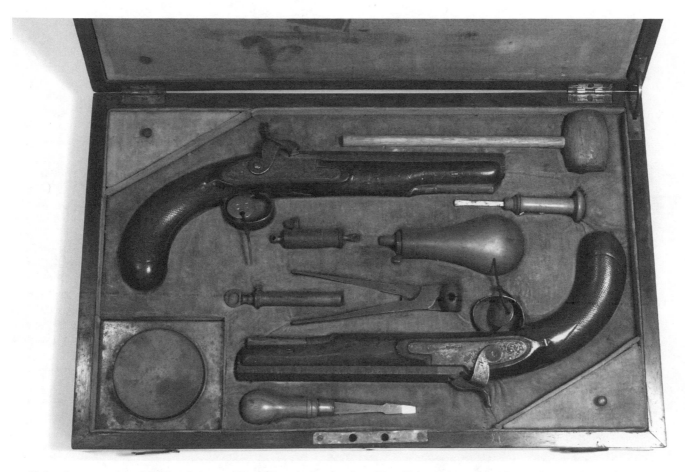

Pair of percussion 1850s vintage .60 caliber belt pistols with a 7-inch barrel by Reno Beauvais of St. Louis, cased with all necessary accessories. Reno (1820–1876) was the son of Jamien Beauvais who came to St. Louis in 1799. (Photo by Steven W. Walenta, courtesy James D. Gordon)

Peter Powell was a pioneer St. Louis gun maker, appearing in the city directory as early as 1836. Assembling this flintlock pistol, he used an 8-inch, .60 caliber brass barrel marked "London" and bearing English proofs. The lock is marked "P. POWELL & CO/ST LOUIS/WARRANTED" in three lines. (Photo by Steven W. Walenta, courtesy James D. Gordon)

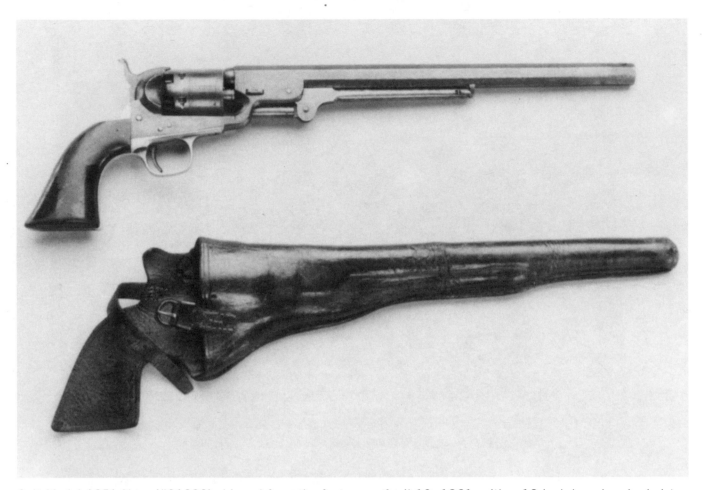

Colt Model 1851 Navy (#91833) shipped from the factory on April 19, 1861, with a 12-inch barrel and a holster. It went to B. Kittredge Arms Company of Cincinnati, a major distributor who funneled many guns to the west. (Courtesy: C. W. Slagle)

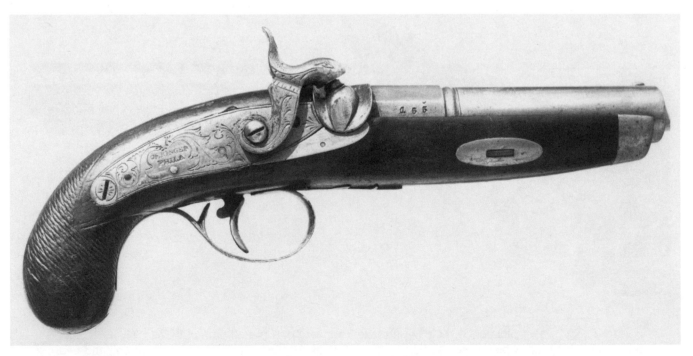

Deringer "Armstrong" pistol with a 4 1/2-inch part round, part octagonal barrel (ca. 1835). (Courtesy: Museum of the Fur Trade, Chadron, NE)

a description of the style wanted and Tryon, Son & Company, another Philadelphia maker and Deringer competitor, in 1839 in a St. Louis newspaper advertised that they "also manufacture the celebrated Armstrong Pistols."[42]

William T. Hamilton spent most of his life on the frontier, and in the late 1850s "I was presented with two beautiful, long range, Derringers [sic] by Lieut. Howard of the Third Cavalry." These obviously were belt size pistols, not pocket guns. During an 1858 trading expedition, he and his companions engaged in a fight with Blackfeet Indians near the Montana-Idaho border near the Kootenai River, and he recalled: "My revolvers being empty I next emptied my derringers, the only time I ever used them." He continued:

> We each of us had a Sharp's rifle, abundance of cartridges, and tape caps [Maynard primer rolls].... Besides this, we each had two Colts, twelve inch barrel, six shooters, with skeleton stock; these pistols would kill [at] two hundred yards. We also packed a heavy double barreled shot gun, which we used for guard at night.[43]

One may attribute Hamilton's reference to Colts with a 12-inch barrel to faulty memory. However there's a slim possibility he wasn't exaggerating. A very few Colt M1851 Navies were made on special order in the late 1850s with such a barrel length. Colt didn't receive a patent on a detachable shoulder stock until January 1859, but such an attachment could have been made by a talented gunsmith.

Several existing copies of orders for Deringer pistols from fur traders and brigade leaders in the later 1830s substantiate the demand from the west. These were usually ordered in pairs, in barrel lengths from four to seven inches and between .41 and .47 caliber. A pair of .47 iron-mounted percussion Deringer pistols with rifled 4 1/2-inch barrels was ordered in February 1835 for Hercules Dousman at Prairie du Chien in present-day Wisconsin on the east bank of the Mississippi. Each of a pair of .43 caliber pistols intended for Henry H. Sibley at Fort Snelling, Minnesota, in 1837 was to have a rifled iron barrel seven inches long with a brass plate on the wooden case inscribed "H. H. Sibley." Aeneas Mackay in an 1837 letter noted Deringer pistols as being:

> very much in use by officers, travelers & western men as belt pistols and generally known by the name of the Armstrong pistol. They are made to carry in a belt about the body or in the pocket and are seldom

put up in boxes. The pistol of 7 to 8 in. barrel..., one which he calls the dueling pistol, and made with a box, &c, will cost from $50 to $60.

William A. "Big Foot" Wallace stated he came to Texas in 1837 and "had brought with me from Virginia a good rifle, a pair of Derringer [sic] pistols and a bowie knife."[44]

The first Colt revolvers to reach the west were those various models made in Paterson, New Jersey, from about 1837 until the company failed in 1842. These ranged upward in size from the No. 1 .28 or .31 caliber "Baby Paterson." Most appropriate for use on the plains would have been a .36 caliber Belt Model or larger .36 Holster Model. All Colt percussion revolvers, except for the solid-frame Model 1855 Root side-hammer pocket model, had a common design feature, a barrel held to the frame by means of a transverse wedge. If this wedge should become dislodged, the barrel could separate from the frame. Such happened during a buffalo hunt in 1841 with a Paterson revolver.

> I still had two shots left in the [Colt] repeater, and after discharging them I intended to fall back upon the old Harper's Ferry [Model 1805 .54 pistol], and, by a well-directed shot, make a finish of the business. After firing my third shot I again crossed the path of the buffalo, and so near that my right foot nearly touched his horns.... On coming up with him a fourth time, and so near that the muzzle of my pistol was not two yards from his side, the barrel dropped off just as I was about to pull the trigger.... The chase was now up [for me] for the pistol was a borrowed one, and very valuable.[45]

Fortunately he found the lost barrel after a brief search.

Another account by William T. Hamilton described each of his 1842 trapping companions as "armed with a rifle, two pistols, a tomahawk, and a large knife, commonly called 'tooth-picker.' Besides this, two of our men had bows and arrows, and were experts with them." He later identified the pistols as Colts and described their deadly effect when Ute Indians attacked their camp. "After receiving so many shots from twenty men the Indians became panic-stricken. They had not calculated on the trappers having two pistols each—twelve shots apiece after the rifles were discharged. They had expected to exterminate us before we could reload

Pair of Blunt & Syms pepperboxes and their form-fitted saddle holsters. The holsters bear the inked name "Ceran St. Vrain," a prominent but largely forgotten trapper and trader in the southwest. In 1830 he partnered with fur trader Charles Bent and began what became one of the largest mercantile companies in the southwest. With Charles and William Bent, in 1833 he built what became known as Bent's Fort on the Arkansas River in southeastern Colorado to promote trade with trappers and Indians, primarily the Southern Cheyennes and Arapahoes for buffalo robes. For much of its sixteen-year history, the fort, one of three the company built, was the only major permanent white settlement on the Santa Fe Trail between Missouri and Mexico. The firm also had stores in Taos and Santa Fe. (Courtesy: Bob Butterfield and Charles L. Hill Jr.)

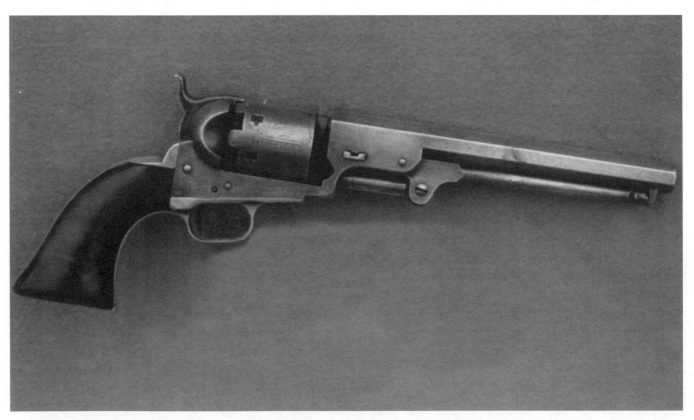

Colt M1851 #20305 obtained by Kit Carson sometime in 1853 or later. His niece sold it in 1938. (Courtesy: Ron Peterson)

our rifles." His math was incorrect since Paterson handguns were five-shooters, but the effect on their antagonists was the same.[46]

Multibarrel pepperboxes, particularly the popular double action guns by Ethan Allen, also were available from the late 1830s forward and some went west. They were less expensive than a Colt and double action specimens were faster firing, but their design made them unsuitable for any form of hunting, although they could be effective in a fight at a distance of a few feet.

The matter of carrying or handling a hand- or shoulder gun varied and depended upon such factors as convenience and comfort. John Woodland, serving with the Texas Rangers during the Mexican War, received a wound which rendered his right arm almost useless. Later he earned a living as scout, guide, and Spanish-speaking interpreter. In 1853 he recommended one practice to others.

> I've got a habit when I go to sleep to take off my Colt always and stick it under the fork of my saddle; then if it rains—'tisn't no matter how hard—there's no danger of its getting wet, and I know just where 'tis. I always sleep with my head on my saddle, and if I hear anything in the night, I can slide my hand in and get it without making any rustling, quicker than I could take it out of my belt.[47]

POWDER, LEAD, AND
RELATED ACCESSORIES

To the beaver trapper, hunter, immigrant, or other who relied on his muzzleloader, a critical component was the ramrod or "wiping stick." If it should be broken or lost, his gun was useless. It was common for a mountain man to carry a snug-fitting second ramrod in the barrel to keep it from breaking. Spare rods carried in this manner appear in drawings of frontiersmen done in the 1840s and 1850s and are mentioned in an occasional written observation. "A stick a little longer than the barrel is carried in the bore, in which it fits tightly; this keeps the bullet from moving, and in firing … they use it as a rest." So noted a British naval lieutenant who observed Capt. John Charles Fremont's party in California in 1846.[48]

On his route westward in 1841, Rufus Sage stopped in northeast Kansas to obtain hickory to make "gun sticks" (ramrods) and bows.

> Hickory is unknown in the Rocky
> Mountains, and this being the last place on

the route affording it, each of our company took care to provide himself with an extra gun-stick. Small pieces, suitable for bows, find market among the mountain Indians, ranging at the price of a robe each, while gun-sticks command one dollar apiece, from the hunters and trappers.[49]

Daniel T. Potts in a series of letters was the first in print to name the Great Salt Lake and to describe the natural wonders of what would become Yellowstone National Park. He also mentioned an accident which befell him en route up the Missouri by canoe. "On the 11th [of April 1823] I was severely wounded by a wiping stick being shot through both knees which brought me to the ground this disabled me for the spring hunt and almost forever."[50]

Also required were other accessories—a bullet mould, a ladle for melting lead, and a short needle or piece of wire used as a vent pick to clear a flintlock's touch hole or a percussion nipple. A nipple wrench if the user had a percussion rifle and a small screwdriver might also be found in the hunting or "possibles" bag along with flint and steel for starting a fire. A loading block was useful, a piece of wood with holes containing patched balls to position over the muzzle when loading to speed the process.

In 1846 Lewis Garrand began nearly a yearlong sojourn on the southwestern prairies. When one of his companions needed to cast some bullets, "in lieu of a ladle he cut a shallow place in a stick of wood—a hunter's expedient—where, laying in the lead and piling on coals, it soon melted." (In another example of expediency, Garrard, after losing his pencil, hammered out bullets—also known as "Galena pills"—and sharpened them for use as writing instruments.)[51]

Gun flints were important items of trade during the flintlock era. Merchants imported them from Europe in wooden kegs of six thousand each in the late 1700s and repackaged them in paper packs, often of five hundred. The American Fur Company sent an order dated February 25, 1839, to Hiram Cutler in England for a cask of "20M [20,000] fine black Horse pistol flints in papers of 500 each." An 1841 order to the same supplier also directed that the flints be packaged in papers of five hundred each.[52]

Lead, too, was a prominent trade commodity in the west among both whites and Native Americans. With the standardization of the Northwest trade gun, premolded bullets like bars of lead were significant trade items. Ramsey Crooks of the American Fur Company in 1847 offered to sell to the Hudson's Bay Company (HBC) three thousand pounds of trade balls, but the offer was rejected because

The prospector at right follows the wise practice of carrying a spare ramrod in the barrel of his rifle. (Courtesy: National Anthropological Archives, Smithsonian Institution, Washington DC)

the HBC could import them more cheaply. As the use of rifles by Indians developed, individual bullet molds became a necessary item.[53]

Lead mining and smelting was common along the Mississippi from Wisconsin to Missouri by 1830, and sixty-five- to seventy-pound pigs of lead were shipped to frontier posts where they were molded into trade balls or smaller bars, often of one-pound size. The first shot tower west of Pittsburgh began operation about thirty miles south of St. Louis in 1809. A substantial amount of the lead shot, round trade balls, and small bar lead used in the west from 1848 until the mid-1870s came from the St. Louis shot tower, built by Ferdinand Kennett. It was thirty-one feet in diameter at the base, seventeen at the top, and 175 feet tall. Molten lead was poured through a sieve at the top and solidified

into spheres before it reached a water bath at the bottom where the balls were graded for size and uniformity.[54]

The steamer *Bertrand* sank a few miles north of Omaha on April Fool's Day in 1865 on its maiden voyage to Fort Benton, Montana Territory. Early attempts to salvage her cargo eventually were abandoned. When the wreck of the sternwheeler was discovered in 1968–69 in what had become a cornfield, the cargo included more than two hundred one-pound bars of lead measuring 10 3/8 x 1/2 x 5/16 inches, each stamped "ST. LOUIS SHOT TOWER CO." As late as 1883, shot towers in Baltimore and St. Louis were both offering half-ounce .52 caliber balls.[55]

In 1932 a man was fly-fishing in the Wasatch Mountains of Utah when he made a startling discovery, a human skull protruding from a tall cutbank along a stream. Evidence

Twenty-five-pound shot bag and bar of lead from the St. Louis shot tower. (Courtesy: Museum of the Fur Trade, Chadron, NE)

Original paper wrapped package of five hundred black gun flints. (Courtesy: Museum of the Fur Trade, Chadron, NE)

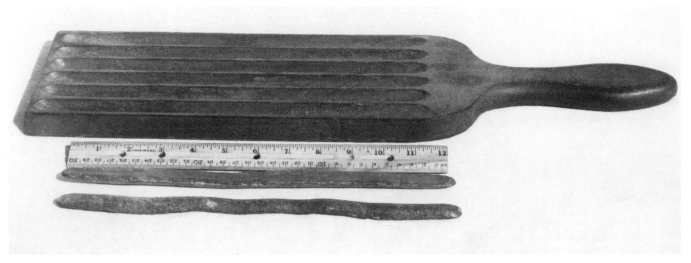

One-pound lead bars and the mold to cast them. (Courtesy: Museum of the Fur Trade, Chadron, NE)

indicated it probably was the remains of a white man who had taken shelter under the bank which had collapsed and buried him. Found with the bones were the remains of a rifle, fragments of clothing, the remains of a Bible, a bullet ladle and mould, and four one-pound St. Louis shot tower–marked bars of lead.[56]

Powder horns also were common trade items, even though an individual could make his own from the horn of a bison or steer. The Hudson's Bay Company supplied horns in the 1700s in sizes of one-, three-quarter-, and one-half-pound capacity. In February 1817 the US superintendent of Indian trade ordered from Henry Deringer ten dozen powder horns. The American Fur Company in St. Louis in 1823 sold three and one-half dozen at $7.50 to William Ashley, and the firm's inventory at Fort Union in 1832 included two hundred pure white horns. An order to Pierre Chouteau Jr. & Company in St. Louis in 1850 from Fort John (later renamed Fort Laramie) specified that horns must be well shaped "and for the right side only."[57]

Some commercial horns were of European origin, but many were made in Pennsylvania. Rifle maker Henry Leman of Lancaster offered the Bureau of Indian Affairs powder horns in nine sizes in 1839, and in 1859 he sold forty dozen each of four different sizes at between $3.88 and $6.50 per dozen. Tryon of Philadelphia in an 1839 quote to the Bureau of Indian Affairs gave a good description of what he offered. Horn No. 1 with screw top for filling, green cord, and tassels was $7 per dozen or a dollar less without cord. Size No. 2 with screw top and a screw-in bottom with a leather strap was $12 per dozen. Horn No. 3 had only a screw bottom but the price is unknown. The use of muzzle loading rifles and shotguns continued among some Americans as late as the 1880s. Jos. C. Grubb & Company of Philadelphia found

enough of a market for powder horns that in their 1885 catalog they continued to list them. They offered six models with wooden stoppers in sizes from four to twelve ounces at $1.75 to $5.75 per dozen.[58]

Horns with a small mirror inset into the wooden base plug particularly appealed to Native Americans. Oliver Wiggins told of an 1841 trading trip he made from Taos, New Mexico, to Wyoming and mentioned: "The children were intensely amused by being shown their faces reflected in a small round looking glass placed in the large end of a powder horn." Government peace commissioners in 1868 included among their gifts for the Indians three powder horns with mirrors obtained from George Kimball & Company at Fort Phil Kearny in Wyoming.[59]

Gunpowder was packed in various sizes of wooden kegs. Fifty-pound kegs often used to transport powder to western trade sites were gradually superseded by smaller size containers. Ramsey Crooks of the American Fur Company in 1835 said that twenty-five-pound kegs were common, but Indians preferred the 12 1/2- and 6 1/4-pound sizes since these later could be used as canteens. Kegs of hardwood such as oak were preferable and often were sewn in canvas bags to make them more water-resistant.[60]

There always was an element of danger associated with gunpowder. In 1832 Thomas Sarpy was operating a new trading post for the Upper Missouri Outfit near present-day Pierre, South Dakota. On the evening of January 19, a lighted candle somehow was knocked into a keg containing close to fifty pounds of black powder. The resulting explosion killed Sarpy and injured three others seriously and virtually destroyed the post.[61]

Trading posts in Indian country carried a great variety of goods and were frequented by whites as well as

Native Americans. One post with a checkered past was Fort McKenzie on the Upper Missouri River. In 1843 a band of Blackfeet killed or stole some livestock after receiving what they perceived as unfair treatment there. One white man was killed during the unrest which festered until February 19, 1844, when another band, apparently not involved in the earlier incident, was admitted to trade. Once the unsuspecting Native Americans entered the post, Chief Clerk Alexander Harvey fired on them with a cannon. Fearing retaliation, Francois Chardon moved the post to a site on the Judith River and renamed it Fort Chardon. The inventory taken there in 1844 gives an account of trade goods available to the Blackfeet and other potential customers including whites.

Blankets, scarlet cloth, ribbon, candlewick, hawk bells, awls, dried peaches, knives, and five "dragoon swords" shared the shelves with plug tobacco, suspenders, tin cups and funnels, kettles, brass thimbles, paper-covered mirrors, files, and beaver traps. Firearms-related items included the following:

7 dozen gunlocks	1 M gunflints	25 Northwest guns
512 lbs. lead in balls	839 lbs. pig lead	2 canister balls
5 50 lb. kegs gunpowder	32 cannonballs	13 powder horns

Most interesting are two "three pd. iron cannon mounted." One of these may have been used in the early massacre of the Blackfeet at Fort McKenzie.[62]

CHAPTER TWO

The Army Moves West, 1803–1865

I should like to see organized and ready for service in this country…
250 mounted rifle-men, armed with short and handy rifles, not too heavy;
one hundred well disciplined dragoons; one hundred Mexicans, armed with
lances and a pair of horse-pistols, mounted on their own native horses;
and two or three mountain howitzers, with a few men to manage them.
— Tom "Broken Hand" Fitzpatrick, 1848[1]

Despite Hollywood's stereotypical image as merely a campaigner against the Indians, the soldier's assignments and contributions throughout much of the nineteenth-century west were as varied as the climate and geography of the land. Suppressing Indian resistance to westward expansion involved protecting traders, immigrants, and frontier settlers and was a well-documented role. Not as well-known today are the army's efforts in conducting explorations and scientific surveys, building roads and bridges, undertaking agricultural experiments, assembling weather data, making harbor and river improvements, providing telegraph service, maintaining Indian rights, and eventually patrolling national parks. Civilian communities often sprang up close to military posts where the residents sometimes used army schools, chapels, and medical facilities.

With admirable foresight, Col. Zachary Taylor in 1820 observed that the ax, pick, saw, and trowel had become more the American soldier's implements than the musket, sword, or cannon. This remained often true throughout the army's participation in the exploration and settlement of the trans-Mississippi west.[2]

Trading expeditions sometimes had military escorts and in May 1849, the post commander at Fort Kearny was instructed to make surplus commissary supplies available "for the relief of emigrants broken down and returning to the states." But the commander at Fort Davis in west Texas was censured in 1856 for $42,000 spent that year to feed destitute travelers and assist in repairing their wagons. Troops at posts along mail and stagecoach routes helped protect these valuable communication and travel lines while the protection of railroad workers became a major responsibility as construction of the western railroad network expanded after civil war ended. During the pre–Civil War decade, the army's role in defending and advancing the western frontier was complicated by the politics of the era—rebel Mormons in Utah, violent partisanship in Kansas over the issue of slavery, and the growing general antagonism between north and south.[3]

EARLY INFANTRY WEAPONS

As had been true during the American Revolution, the army's regular infantry units in the west relied primarily on the smoothbore flintlock musket rather than rifles until

US Model 1795 flintlock .69 smoothbore musket. Modest improvements appeared in later models, but it was representative of the US infantry's primary type of firearm from the Revolutionary War to the 1840s. It was faster to load than a muzzle loading rifle, but striking a man-size target beyond seventy-five yards or so if loaded with a single ball was largely a matter of luck. (Courtesy: National Park Service, Fuller Collection, Chickamauga-Chattanooga National Military Park, Fort Oglethorpe, GA)

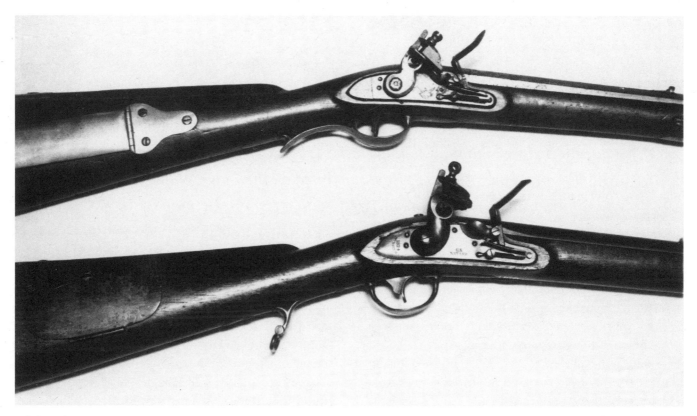

A handsome brass-mounted US Model 1803/1814 .54 rifle (above) and its successor, the sturdy iron-mounted Model 1817 "common rifle."

the 1840s. The same was true of militia of the various states and territories. Under the Militia Act of 1808, the federal government procured arms for each state, allocated in proportion to population. Theoretically arms for the federal army would be produced by the national armories at Springfield and Harpers Ferry, while those for the militia would be supplied by private contractors, but emergency needs sometimes demanded otherwise. Until the 1820s, only muskets were issued under this act, but thereafter rifles, pistols, swords, and artillery were distributed in terms of dollar equivalents to musket value.

Various models of muskets were adopted from 1795 forward with modest improvements. The later models were produced to closer tolerances and were better finished than that of 1795, but they still were a .69 smoothbore firing an undersized ball. Faster loading than a rifle, they could be fired three or four times a minute, an advantage over the rifle against massed enemy troops, but were inaccurate at much beyond seventy-five yards. However at close range they could be quite effective with an optional "buck and ball" load of a single .64 round ball plus three smaller buckshot.

The more accurate rifle was considered a specialized weapon, it being slower to load than a musket. Throughout most of the first half of the nineteenth century, rifles were acquired in lesser numbers than muskets and were issued to riflemen who often acted as light infantry supported by line infantry units. Between 1821 and 1846 there were no formal rifle regiments and such weapons were used in company size or smaller units. Following the introduction of the Model 1803 rifle and until the 1840s, the infantry adopted three other rifled long arms—the .54 model of 1814 and in larger numbers the similar Model 1817, each with a stronger full-length stock and iron mountings, and the Model 1819, a breechloader designed by John H. Hall. To differentiate between the muzzle loading M1817 and the Hall, the government applied the term "common rifle" to the former.

The Hall patent rifle, made both at Harpers Ferry and by Simeon North of Middletown, Connecticut, represented the army's initial regulation breech loading arm and was the first such gun made at a national armory. Another advance was the interchangeability of its parts between those made at Harpers Ferry and by North. Some Hall rifles in both flintlock and percussion form equipped infantrymen during the Mexican War. A few of the latter were found in Capt. Enoch Steen's Company E of the 1st Dragoons along with Hall carbines. At Buena Vista, the company's best shot downed a Mexican officer at four hundred yards using a Hall percussion rifle. Despite the Hall's innovative design, not until the late 1860s did the government adopt a breechloader as its regulation infantry arm.[4]

Each of these flintlock rifle models continued to serve federal and state militia forces in its original form or later as converted to percussion after the flintlock became obsolete. All three models equipped infantrymen in the west, but they did not immediately replace the older M1803 which could be found in use throughout the 1830s. However it was not until the 1850s that rifled arms succeeded the smoothbore musket as the primary shoulder arm in the regular infantry regiments regardless of which side of the Mississippi they were serving on.

MILITARY EXPLORATIONS

The Corps of Discovery under captains Lewis and Clark embarked on the army's first organized trans-Mississippi venture when the party headed west from St. Louis in the spring of 1804. The party's arsenal was a varied array of firearms—flintlock smoothbore muskets (probably the US Model 1795), a pair of "Horsemans Pistils," a duo of pocket pistols which Lewis later gave to Indians, two blunderbusses mounted on swivels on two of their vessels, an airgun which Indians viewed as "great medicine," and fifteen rifles prepared for the expedition at Harpers Ferry, Virginia. These latter weapons have never been identified precisely and may have been examples of flintlock Pennsylvania ("Kentucky") rifles procured from various makers under contract beginning in 1792, perhaps modified for the corps at the Harpers Ferry Armory by the addition of slings, possibly a reduction in barrel length, reboring to a common caliber, and perhaps the installation of government-furnished locks to facilitate repairs on the journey since spare gun locks were included in the expedition's equipment. They also may have been prototypes of the Harpers Ferry rifle adopted in 1803, but actual production of this model wasn't underway when the corps left St. Louis.

Even before the corps returned from the Pacific, Lt. Zebulon Pike led two expeditions westward, the first up the Mississippi and the second to the Rockies. His first party probably was equipped with Pennsylvania-style rifles, about which he complained that "our want of success [in hunting] I ascribe to the smallness of our balls, and to inexperience in following the track." He made no such complaint about the rifles carried on his second reconnaissance which began in 1806. By then Harpers Ferry Armory had begun production of the Model 1803 rifle, a handsome half-stock with brass fittings. At .54 caliber, it was sufficient for almost any western game.[5]

Maj. Stephen H. Long of the Topographical Engineers in 1819–20 led a scientific expedition which reached the foothills of the Rockies. He later characterized the central plains as the "great American desert." No detailed reports of the party's armament exist but an account stated: "We were well armed and equipped, each man carrying a yauger or rifle gun, with the exception of two or three who had muskets; most of us had pistols, all tomahawks and long knives, which we carried suspended at our belts." As did the Corps of Discovery before it, Long's company also carried an airgun.[6]

Among the best known officers who led exploring expeditions into the west was arrogant and self-promoting Capt. John C. Fremont. He made a wise choice in Kit Carson as his frequent guide, and Fremont's maps and published journals stirred the nation's imagination, stimulating western expansion. His first venture in 1842 traversed the Oregon Trail, followed by a second exploration in 1843–44. His third reconnaissance was to the southwest and began in 1845. Included in the latter party was Isaac Cooper who wrote under the name Francois des Montaignes. He made a number of sarcastic jibes at Fremont:

Capt. John C. Fremont's US Model 1842 pistol (dated 1846) by Henry Aston of Middletown, Connecticut. (Exhibited by the Arizona Historical Society, Tucson)

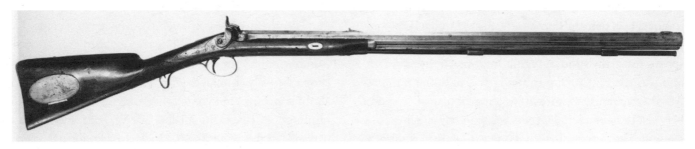

Halfstock .50 caliber percussion rifle by Joseph Cooper of New York, perhaps similar to those obtained by Fremont. (Courtesy: Museum of the Fur Trade, Chadron, NE)

Captain Fremont distributed...50 pair of tremendous horsepistols with shining barrels and rusty holsters[?]. There consequently ensued great contests as to who could hit the side of a board, with one of these formidable firearms, at 5 steps distant. The company fired some 2 or 3 hundred shot at a large box-cover...but...they could not only not make any hole in it, but couldn't even form an idea as to the probable direction which the ball may have taken.... The magnanimous and justly celebrated Commander in Chief [Fremont] however, though not larger than one of these same horsepistols [dispatched] Mesty-Woolah [his servant] for his pistols in order to show to the admiring eyes of his men, the extraordinary precision with which he could hit a board at 5 steps distance. As Bad Luck would have it however, just as the renowned Captain pulled the trigger and shut his eyes—an enormous dab of mud ploughed up by the ball in its downward course struck the center of the board and proclaimed him victor.[7]

Arms for Fremont's second venture westward included thirty-three Hall carbines and four holster pistols requisitioned from the army. In preparation for his third expedition, he purchased arms from various sources and at widely differing prices and stated: "I had procured about a dozen rifles, the best that could be found; with the object of setting them up as prizes for the best marksmen, to be shot for during the journey." He obtained a handsome cased pair of pistols for $50 and fifteen rifles in April 1845 from Joseph Cooper of New York City. Three rifles were described as having silver mountings, a hair trigger, patent breech, and a percussion bar lock. The other dozen at $20 each were less handsome with steel mountings and back action locks. These were followed by rifles from Dickson & Gilmore of Louisville—a "patent breeched half-stocked rifle" at $40, a silver-mounted specimen for $5 more, and a half dozen with iron mountings at $35 each. In St. Louis he paid $12 to $35 for nine more rifles, $8 for a pair of belt pistols, and finally from J. & S. Hawken, twenty-seven rifles at $20, one at $22, and two more for $30.[8]

THE ESTABLISHMENT OF A MOUNTED ARM FOR WESTERN SERVICE

Recognizing the need for a permanent mounted force to better deal with mobile Native Americans, Congress in 1833 authorized the creation of a regiment of dragoons. Initially the 1st Dragoons were equipped with M1803 rifles, but in 1834 they began to receive the army's first percussion arm, the Hall breech loading carbine. In 1836 the 2nd Dragoons were organized and in 1846 a regiment of mounted riflemen was added to the mix. Although the Mounted Rifles were intended to operate as light infantry, frontier conditions dictated that they, like the dragoons or "yellow legs," act more as cavalry.

John Hall's design incorporated one feature which simplified maintenance of his rifles and carbines. After the removal of a single pivot screw, the entire breech mechanism consisting of breechblock, hammer, trigger, and mainspring could be withdrawn as a single unit. A secondary but probably unplanned benefit of this feature allowed the breech mechanism when removed to be used as a crude but functioning pistol. Samuel Chamberlain of the 1st Dragoons wrote of carrying the block from his Hall carbine when he visited Mexican cantinas on leave during the Mexican War. In melodramatic style common to the era, Chamberlain described one incident:

> I thought my time had come but resolved
> not to be rubb'd out without a struggle.
> With a bound I sprang behind a large table
> used for a bar, drew the chamber of my
> Hall's Carbine (that I always carried in my
> pocket), said a short prayer and stood cool
> and collected, at bay before those human
> Tigers, guerillars.[9]

In 1843 bison stampeding through a 1st Dragoon camp tossed one of the troopers in the air.

> The joke was in the lie the tossed man
> attempted to impose upon the credulity of
> the others. It was that in the ascent and
> descent with his carbine in his hand, that
> he remembered that his carbine was capped
> and cocked, and that when he fell and
> struck the ground that the concussion
> would cause the cock [hammer] to fall, and
> so explode, that he had sufficient presence
> of mind to take off the cap, let down the
> cock, this in his journey up and down. I

suppose the truth to be that it was not cocked at all.[10]

Due in part to gas leakage at the breech, not all who received Hall carbines relished them, and there was a strong demand in some military circles for a return to a muzzle loading arm. In the early 1840s, trials of William Jenks's side-hammer breechloader and Colt repeating carbines failed to elicit Ordnance Department enthusiasm or significant orders. The result in 1847 was the adoption of a series of smoothbore .69 caliber short muskets ("musketoons") for dragoons, artillery, and miners and sappers (engineers). Hall-equipped dragoons fought gallantly during the Mexican War, but by 1850, issuance of the musketoon to the two regiments was well underway as was distribution of the four-pound .44 Colt Dragoon six-shot revolver.

The brass-mounted cavalry musketoon—the other versions of the weapon were iron-mounted—with its lack of accuracy and range proved less satisfactory than the Hall. "Worthless" was an adjective sometimes applied to it. Campaigning in 1852 with the 1st Dragoons, Percival Lowe noted they had not had fresh meat for several months "except some prairie dogs which Peel and I killed with the only rifle in the troop; no one hunted with it except us. The musketoons did not shoot accurately enough, and no one was permitted to waste ammunition."[11]

In 1853 field testing of a new breechloader began, the Sharps. Durable, accurate, and easy to operate, it received prompt and almost universal acceptance. Undoubtedly those mounted frontier troopers still relying on the Hall or musketoon as the decade progressed were envious of their comrades who were receiving the new Sharps in increasing numbers.

THE ARMY ABANDONS THE FLINTLOCK

The Hall carbine of 1833 was a percussion weapon, but not until the early 1840s did the army chose to complete its acceptance of the more reliable percussion cap. It authorized a new rifle in 1841 and percussion smoothbore models of musket and single-shot pistol the next year. Production and distribution of the new Model 1842 musket took time and some infantry regulars received flintlock muskets as late as 1848. Young lieutenant Ulysses S. Grant served with the 4th Infantry during the Mexican War and in his memoirs recalled: "The infantry under General Taylor was armed with flintlock muskets, and paper cartridges charged with powder, buck-shot and ball. At the distance of a few hundred yards a man might fire at you all day without your finding it out."[12]

In 1850 army topographical engineers, led by Lt. Israel C. Woodruff, conducted a surveying expedition of the Cherokee-Creek boundary into what today is Oklahoma. This view of their camp on the Red Fork of the Arkansas River is one of the earliest daguerreotype photos taken in the west. Standing by his horse, Davy, is S. W. Woodhouse, surgeon and naturalist. Note the saddle holsters across the pommel. In front of them is suspended what appears to be a canteen fashioned from a gourd. (Courtesy: Museum of Northern Arizona, photo #74-634, Flagstaff)

During that war, Mexican infantrymen often were relying on imported British flintlock India Pattern Brown Bess muskets as they did during the 1835–36 war for Texas independence. The Texas Army seized many of these .75 caliber smoothbores following the April 1836 battle of San Jacinto, bolstering the new Republic of Texas's store of arms which included many American-made military muskets.[13]

But whether in flintlock or percussion form, a .69 smoothbore musket had a bruising recoil. During the Civil War, Lt. Eugene F. Ware served with the 7th Iowa Cavalry and described one method of compensating.

Well, Corporal Churubusco said that what made a gun kick was—what every old Mexican [War?] soldier knew—there was space in the barrel behind the touchhole; that the fire from the cap went into the barrel too far forward. We then proceeded to fill in the barrel at the bottom, according to his suggestions. A silver dime just fitted the barrel...[and] I rammed down six of them. But the gun kicked apparently as hard as ever; and then I wanted...my money back—but that was an impossibility; the discharge had swaged the silver down and brazed it to the barrel. The gun continued to kick like "sixty."...We all named our guns; the boys generally named them after their pet girls—it was "Hannah,"

Hall-North M1843 carbine showing the breech open for loading. Until the late 1850s, US cavalry and dragoons retained various models of Halls in service and although obsolete by 1861, some served with Civil War volunteer regiments from Missouri, Kansas, and Iowa. (Courtesy: National Park Service, Fuller Collection, Chickamauga-Chattanooga National Military Park, Fort Oglethorpe, GA)

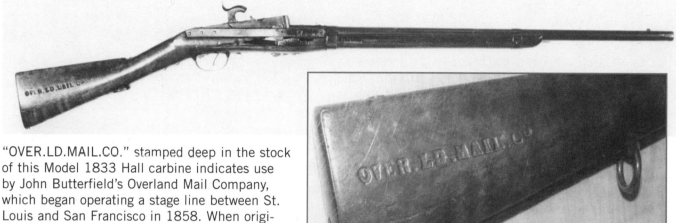

"OVER.LD.MAIL.CO." stamped deep in the stock of this Model 1833 Hall carbine indicates use by John Butterfield's Overland Mail Company, which began operating a stage line between St. Louis and San Francisco in 1858. When originally issued to the US Dragoons, both the models 1833 and 1836 Hall carbines had a sliding triangular bayonet beneath the barrel. (Courtesy: Larry T. Shelton, Missouri State Capitol Museum, Jefferson City)

or "Mary Jane," or something else. I named mine "Silver Sue."[14]

Although adopted in 1841, it required time to prepare tooling for manufacture, and production of the new .54 percussion rifle didn't begin until 1843. With brass mountings it was a handsome, sturdy, and accurate piece, and its use during the Mexican War by the red-shirted 1st Mississippi infantry regiment under Col. Jefferson Davis led to its most common nickname, the "Mississippi" rifle. It fired a round patched ball, the last US rifle to do so, and after 1855 many were modified to fire the new conical hollow-based Minie ball. Although the Regiment of Mounted Rifles was mounted for mobility, it was intended to fight primarily on foot and it received the new rifle as did other units of riflemen,

both within federal and state militia ranks. Perhaps more than one hundred thousand M1841 rifles were turned out at Harpers Ferry and by various contractors, including overruns for civilian sales.

The first soldiers that nine-year-old August Santleben ever saw, about 1854, probably were mounted riflemen. "Every soldier was armed with two holster pistols, each with a single barrel, and a Mississippi yager, both of the same caliber [.54] therefore they used the same fixed cartridges loaded with a ball and three buckshot." (He was unaware that the usual load for the Mississippi was a single round patched ball.) While his father unloaded corn at the soldiers' camp, the youth busied himself picking up playing cards scattered about. "Until then I had never seen painted pictures of any kind, and I thought the cards were the prettiest things my eyes had ever gazed upon."[15]

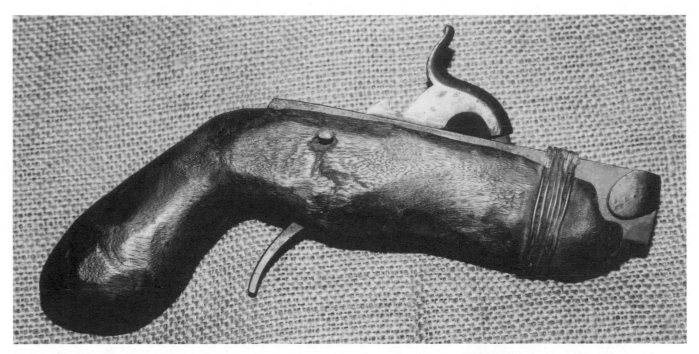

A crude muzzle loading pistol fashioned by securing a Hall breech mechanism to a rough wooden stock with a transverse pin and copper wire. It was obtained near Taos, New Mexico, and may have been an Indian gun. The author has examined two similar pistols created using a Hall mechanism.

Most Model 1841 rifles went to arm state troops, but in addition to those and the M1841s issued to the regular army's riflemen, a substantial number reached civilian hands through excess production, government sales to immigrants and others, and some by loan. On July 18, 1860, Lt. Col. C. F. Smith from Camp Floyd, Utah Territory, wrote in an only partially legible hand that in the face of Indian disturbances he had loaned the three-month-old Pony Express arms to defend their stations. These were 106 "Army Size revolvers [presumably Colt .44 Dragoons] and sixty (60) 'Mississippi' rifles and some ammunition for the same, on the condition of their being returned in good order, or paid for if [not]." Mormons, Smith noted, weren't free of suspicion of inciting the Indians to menace the Pony Express stations and run off the livestock.[16]

Smith continued, noting that the precedent had been established when his predecessor had transferred M1841 rifles on War Department authority to Messrs. Russell & Company (Russell, Majors & Waddell, government freighting contractors and later organizers of the Pony Express) to arm their employees. When no longer needed, the guns were turned in to the ordnance depot at Camp Floyd and sometimes were sold to emigrants and discharged soldiers.[17]

From Santa Fe on September 2, 1865, Brig. Gen. James H. Carleton wrote to Capt. William Shoemaker at Fort Union, New Mexico Territory. The general explained that

James Patterson was a government beef contractor and was returning to Texas for another herd. His party was not sufficiently armed to resist Indian attacks.

> Under the circumstances you are hereby authorized to loan them twelve or fifteen Sharps carbines *worn but serviceable*—if you have them to spare, or, if you have not these, twelve or fifteen Mississippi rifles.... For these they will give a receipt and bonds to a reasonable amount for their safe return.... You can let them have for *cash* a reasonable amount of ammunition.[18]

In January 1867 the government recorded the sale of what at first appear to have been Mississippi rifles to the Overland Stage Company, forty "Whitney rifles" for $15 each, probably to guard the company's way stations. But this would have been a stiff price indeed for obsolescent muzzleloaders when in the same month a batch of similar surplus Enfield rifles sold for only $3 each. These still would have been greatly overpriced if they were examples of those few Mississippi rifles converted to percussion breechloaders using the Lindner or Merrill system. Could they have been the even rarer Mont Storm conversions firing a .58 rimfire cartridge? It's unfortunate that the preparer of the listing of surplus sales didn't anticipate the

US Model 1841 .54 rifle, most popularly called the "Mississippi." Later improvements included the addition of an adjustable rear sight and various methods for attaching a bayonet. (Courtesy: National Park Service, Fuller Collection, Chickamauga-Chattanooga National Military Park, Fort Oglethorpe, GA)

US Springfield Model 1816 musket obtained in Mexico, perhaps carried south after use during the Mexican War. The under side of the forestock has been worn through to the ramrod, possibly from long-term carriage on horseback. (Photo by Steven W. Walenta, courtesy Jeff Hengesbaugh)

Pair of cut down Harpers Ferry Model 1816 muskets. The top gun's barrel at one time had been secured to the stock with rawhide and the butt stock is carved deeply "WF Co" which may represent the Western Fur Company, a nickname for the western branch of the American Fur Company. In its altered state it would have been an excellent meat gun for running bison on horseback. The bottom gun is one of three muskets cut down in similar fashion and collected in Texas, the other two being fitted with carbine slings.
They could be former Republic of Texas Army guns, perhaps "carbinized" for mounted use.
(Photo by Steven W. Walenta, courtesy Jeff Hengesbaugh)

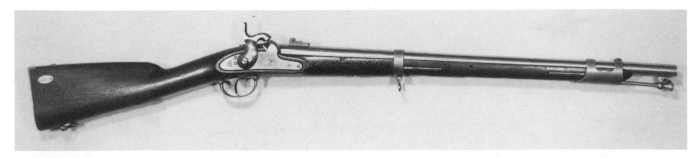

US Model 1847 .69 smoothbore musketoon, described as "worthless" by some. Specimens are found both with and without a rear sight and with either a swivel or chain securing the ramrod to the barrel. (Courtesy: National Park Service, Fuller Collection, Chickamauga-Chattanooga National Military Park, Fort Oglethorpe, GA)

question this simple entry raises for arms collectors a century and a half later![19]

Although mobility of movement was a purpose for creating the mounted regiments, Maj. Thomas Swords in his 1851 inspection report of the Quartermaster's Department of New Mexico commented: "I hope I may be pardoned for recommending as a means of rendering the mounted troops more efficient, that a lighter armament and equipment be provided. The dragoon horse carries seventy-pounds in addition to the weight of the trooper." Sgt. Frank Clarke, stationed in New Mexico in 1852, with some exaggeration as to weight described a dragoon's field kit: "[We] carry a rifle, a heavy single barreled dragoon Pistol, one of Colts Revolving Pistols [.44 Dragoon], & a heavy Dragoon sabre. The weight of a man & kit upon a horse will average 350 pounds."[20]

ARMY PISTOLS AND REVOLVERS

Handgun use within the military during much of the nineteenth century was limited to officers and mounted troops. Until the early 1840s, these were smoothbore flintlocks, .69 or .54 "rifle" caliber, most made by government contractors. Pistols usually were issued in pairs and were useful only in close hand-to-hand combat. They normally were carried in a pair of saddle holsters slung over the pommel of the saddle with covering flaps of leather, bearskin, or sealskin. Usually five round tin tubes on the front of each holster held cartridges. In 1842 the army adopted a new pistol, still a .54 smoothbore single-shot, but in percussion form for the first time.

Even while the army relied on flintlock single-shot pistols, early Colt revolvers and long arms made in Paterson, New Jersey, in the late 1830s were being subjected to scrutiny and use in modest numbers by the US Army and Navy but with little enthusiasm. Those procured by the Republic of Texas and used by its navy and later the Texas Rangers were more eagerly accepted, but nevertheless Sam Colt's Patent Arms Mfg. Co. failed in 1842.

Not long after the outbreak of war between the United States and Mexico, Capt. Samuel Walker of the US Mounted Rifles collaborated with Colt in the design of a powerful .44 six-shot revolver weighing four pounds nine ounces with a 9-inch barrel which today bears Walker's name in tribute. Walker was a former Texas Ranger and earlier had participated in the ill-fated 1842 Mier expedition into Mexico and had been captured. As a prisoner he had drawn a white rather than a black bean and thus avoided execution by a Mexican firing squad, only to be killed during the Mexican War just days after a pair of the revolvers named in his honor reached him. It was the most powerful black powder revolver ever produced, and its chambers could hold almost sixty grains of powder behind a round ball producing a muzzle velocity of almost thirteen hundred feet per second, comparable to that of a rifle. Unfortunately the cylinder couldn't always withstand the pressure produced and in service Walkers had an inordinately high rate of failure.

The government's initial order in January 1847 for one thousand of these massive handguns for the new regiment of mounted riflemen put Colt back into the gun making business, this time to stay. The army in November followed that with an order for one thousand improved Colt six-shooters, nearly a half pound lighter and with a reduced powder capacity, and known today as the Dragoon model. Ultimately almost half of the roughly twenty thousand Dragoon revolvers made until 1860 went to fill government orders for the mounted rifle and dragoon regiments as well as for militia issues. In mid-1855 the United States ordered its first Colt Model 1851 .36 caliber "Navy" revolvers for the two new regiments of cavalry organized in that year. The '51 and the Dragoon model revolvers made the single-shot pistol obsolete, but those clumsy pistols remained in use until 1858.[21]

US Model 1836 pistol carried during the Mexican War by Col. George Washington Morgan. He received a brevet as brigadier general for his performance at the battles of Contreras and Churubusco. (Courtesy: Smithsonian Institution, neg. #19742, Washington DC)

Representative of the reluctance of some to adopt the revolver were comments of Col. George Talcott of the Ordnance Department who wrote on July 19, 1858:

[Revolvers] may be used to advantage in the hands of skillful or careful men [but] it would be premature to exclude entirely the dragoon pistol.... Repeating pistols cannot be advantageously used by the mass of our private soldiers for the want of necessary discretion, coolness, and skill and ... should be furnished to them in limited numbers, only to be placed in the hands of such men as their officers may select.

Talcott preferred the Colt among the revolvers tested, and the lighter .36 Navy over the .44 Dragoon. However one reason for his opposition to widespread distribution was the cost, noting that four single-shot pistols could be obtained for the militia or regular army for every Colt.[22]

Arguments over whether the Dragoon with its heavier bullet and powder charge or the '51's lighter weight and better balance was the proper choice probably provided a topic for campfire discussions. The issue was resolved in 1861 when the army began procuring large numbers of Colt's 1860 .44 New Model Army. It weighed a pound and a half less than the Dragoon and became the most widely used Union cavalry revolver of the Civil War. By mid-1862, however, competition was growing in the form of comparable quality .36 and .44 revolvers available from the Remington Arms Company of Ilion, New York, at $10 less than the $25 Colt. Colt matched the lower price, but during the final two years of the war, after fire destroyed the Colt revolver factory in February 1864, Remington delivered more than eighty thousand revolvers to the army, mostly .44s.

Wartime demands also brought into service lesser numbers of revolvers by Starr, Whitney, North-Savage, Pettengill, Joslyn, and others plus some from Europe including the French pinfire LeFaucheux. Examples of nearly all of these revolvers reached troops serving in the west, but after 1865 the army's cavalry regiments until the early 1870s would depend primarily on .44 Remingtons and Model 1860 Colts.

The initials "WAT" for William A. Thornton are often encountered stamped on mid-nineteenth-century US martial arms including Colt Paterson revolvers, Model 1841 Mississippi rifles, and others. He spent twenty-eight years with the Ordnance Department, much of his time inspecting arms. He also served in New Mexico (1855–57) and while there and after having observed and talked with other officers prepared a detailed report in February 1856 on the various arms in the hands of mounted troops. He found that the .69

Fancy German silver grips set this .36 Allen & Thurber dragoon size pepperbox apart. They are engraved "Presented by James Milner, Esqr Buffalo, N.Y. to Alexr Hays Brevet lst Lieut. 8th Inf. U.S.A." and "Take it who can." A West Point graduate, Hays served on frontier duty in Louisiana and Texas and during the Mexican War was brevetted for gallantry at Palo Alto and Resaca de la Palma. He resigned from the army in 1848 and became a civil engineer, but served again during the Civil War attaining the brevet rank of major general before he was killed in the Wilderness campaign in 1864. (Courtesy: Norm Flayderman)

smoothbore Model 1847 cavalry musketoon, serving along with the Hall breechloader, was condemned by most of those to whom it was issued and many preferred to carry the longer and heavier Mississippi rifle.

> Although they are drilled in [the musketoon's] use, . . . they found it so severe in recoil, so inaccurate in fire, that but few men could hit an object the size of a man, at 50 paces distant, and they had therefore, lost all confidence in [it] and would, in a fight, prefer trusting solely to their revolvers. They further said, that the musketoon is with much difficulty loaded on horseback, and is oftentimes rendered useless by the loss of the ramrod, caused by the breaking of the swivel. . . . All the Officers heard from recommend the substitution of Sharps carbine, in place of the musketoon, for mounted men.[23]

Thornton noted that the "Colts heavy revolver" (.44 Dragoon) was in use, but he recommended the newly issued .36 caliber Model 1851 Navy.

The Navy size revolver is best by all means. It is less in weight, and therefore more desirable as the muzzle is not so liable to be dropped in firing. Its range is sufficiently great, and it is as formidable as the heavy pistol, for all purposes of combat. It is less cumbersome and can be carried with more convenience.

The lighter weight of the Model 1851 Colt made it practical to carry in a belt holster or "pistol case" as it was termed, rather than in saddle holsters. The latter holsters would remain in use until 1861 for larger handguns (and later by some officers), but Thornton recommended the former method so the weapon would be at hand if the soldier was dismounted. "The holster should cover the entire pistol, to protect it from the weather, and to prevent dirt from entering the muzzle. . . . Barrels have been frequently burst by a wad of mud, introduced by the wearer of the pistol, in seating himself on the ground."[24]

ADVENT OF THE SHARPS IN MILITARY SERVICE

The first Sharps breechloader to go into significant quantity production was the slant breech Model 1851, fitted with

Colt 3rd Model Dragoon (#13173) from the battlefield at Glorieta Pass, New Mexico. Here in March of 1862 Federals halted the Confederate army and forced its return to Texas, the last significant Civil War battle in the far west. (Courtesy: Ron Peterson)

This Colt 3rd Model Dragoon is inscribed "To John Charles Fremont From T. H. Benton Jr." Missouri senator Thomas Hart Benton was Fremont's father-in-law. (Exhibited by the Arizona Historical Society, Tucson)

Colt 3rd Model Dragoon (#16742), badly corroded and excavated near Hill City, Oregon. With a folding leaf rear sight and cut for a shoulder stock attachment, it was one of 940 Dragoon Model "pistol carbines" purchased by the army from Colt in the 1850s. These were issued in pairs with one detachable shoulder stock per pair.

"U.S."-marked Colt M1851 (#67933) originally purchased by the US Army, but with the Confederate inscription on the backstrap "James S. Hanks, Capt./13th Texas Cavalry." (Courtesy: Simpson Confederate Research Center, Hillsboro, TX)

Colt M1849 pocket model (#83367) bearing the name "COL. STEPTOE" engraved on the backstrap. After receiving two brevet promotions for gallantry during the Mexican War, Col. E. J. Steptoe commanded a force of US dragoons and infantry in an 1858 campaign against the Spokane, Coeur d'Alene, Palouse, and Yakima Indians in Washington Territory. (Courtesy: Charles L. Hill Jr.)

the Maynard primer and a "boxlock" with the hammer mounted inside the lockplate. The models of 1852, 1853, and 1855 followed, each with its distinctive characteristics. The army's Ordnance Department ordered modest quantities of several of these models for field testing. On February 19, 1853, Col. H. R. Craig wrote to the commanding officer of the 9th Military Department at Fort Union, New Mexico, to advise him that sixty Sharps carbines "with Maynards Lock" were being sent to him. These were to be issued to

his choice of troops for service tests. "From the preliminary trials of this arm, it is thought that it may possess advantages over the arms in service as a military weapon for mounted men," Craig wrote prophetically.[25]

Maj. Thornton spoke highly of the new Sharps breech loading carbine, available in limited numbers, although he offered suggested changes in sights, lengthening the barrel by 4 1/4 inches to increase "its sighting line," and reducing the length of the sling bar. The Maynard tape priming

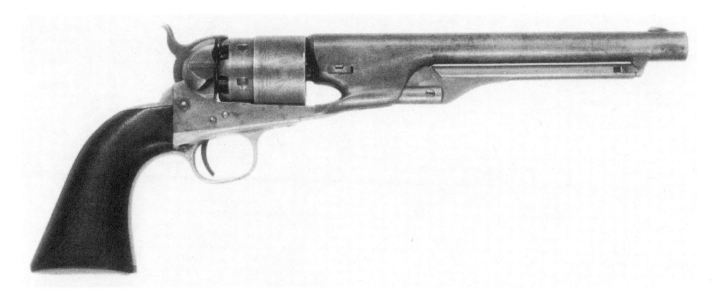

Colt Model 1860, the most widely used of the Civil War Union cavalry revolvers. This specimen is one of those refurbished after the war and reissued, often to regiments serving in the west. As these are usually found, the serial numbers are mismatched and the trigger guard is deeply stamped "US." (Courtesy: Dale H. Peterson)

mechanism on these guns came in for criticism. "I recommend that the carbine shall not be furnished with self primers; but shall be fired with the present United States percussion cap; and when so improved, that the Sharps carbine be supplied to all mounted troop, now using musketoons, or muzzle loading arms."[26]

Tom Fitzpatrick, known by many as "Broken Hand," was an experienced mountain man and guided such officers as Fremont and Col. Stephen Watts Kearny who gave him high praise. (His nickname resulted from a gun accident which injured his left hand.) He was appointed as an Indian agent in 1847, negotiated landmark treaties of 1851 and 1853, and was a strong influence with plains Indian tribes before his death from pneumonia in a Washington hotel in 1854. Although not all the tribes were within his jurisdiction, he was known to the Sioux, Cheyennes, Arapahos, Kiowas, Plains Apaches, and Comanches.[27]

His second annual report as agent for the Indians between the Upper Arkansas and Nebraska rivers (October 6, 1848) criticized the effectiveness of troops led by unskilled officers in protecting emigrants and suggested placing posts and an efficient military force on the main emigrant trails. He recommended the following:

> I should like to see organized and ready for
> service in this country [southern
> plains] . . . 250 mounted rifle-men, armed
> with short and handy rifles, not too heavy;
> one hundred well disciplined dragoons; one
> hundred Mexicans, armed with lances and

> a pair of horse-pistols, mounted on their
> own native horses; and two or three moun-
> tain howitzers, with a few men to manage
> them. Let all. . . be placed under the com-
> mand of an experienced officer, who
> understands the nature of his duty in every
> particular, who would in a short time
> accomplish the desired object.[28]

An anonymous enlisted man with the 2nd Dragoons at Camp Floyd in 1858 identified himself only as "Utah" while voicing his desire for action.

> I should like to "smell powder" in a regular
> "pitch-in," merely for the novelty of the
> thing. As yet, I have never had the pleasure
> of participating in a fight of any conse-
> quence, and I would like to see how the
> Indians would receive a charge of dragoons
> in a case where the chances were
> equal. . . . In contests with these Indians
> [Utes], the Infantry are [sic] entirely use-
> less. The natives are all well mounted, and
> scud away over the plains, to the great
> annoyance of the "double quick." The dra-
> goons can pursue them mounted, with fair
> prospects of bringing them under the sabre,
> and when they seek the shelter of the
> canons [canyons], can be speedily dis-
> mounted, and with the Sharp's Rifles

Tintype of Oliver B. Shepherd armed with a Remington New Model revolver and dressed in civilian clothing while a member of Quantrill's guerrillas. After the war he joined Jesse James's gang. Suspected of complicity in a bank robbery in Russellville, Kentucky, in March 1868, he was tracked by vigilantes to Jackson County, Missouri, and killed in a gun battle there in April. (Courtesy: George Hart)

[carbines] and revolvers do effective service on the spot, much more than can be done with the unwieldy muskets and bayonets of the Infantry.

"Utah" also wrote that desertions were quite frequent "and scarcely a night passes without one or more taking 'French leave.' They all strike for California."[29]

Col. Joseph Mansfield's inspection reports of posts in the southwest in 1853–54 offer some insight into living conditions as well as to the quality of arms in the hands of the troops. Some soldiers hadn't been paid in five months. In other instances, the government's failure to provide cloth-

ing in a timely manner forced the men to purchase socks, shirts, and shoes from the sutler at exorbitant prices "much beyond the ability of the soldier to pay." Some soldiers were immigrants who couldn't understand English when spoken to, "but it is still worse to have them near sighted, and a left handed man is quite awkward in the ranks."[30]

Mansfield, too, found the musketoon wanting.

The musketoon as an arm for the dragoon or mounted man in any way is almost worthless. The shackle that secures the ram rod to the barrel is entirely too delicate and is constantly breaking. When slung [muzzle

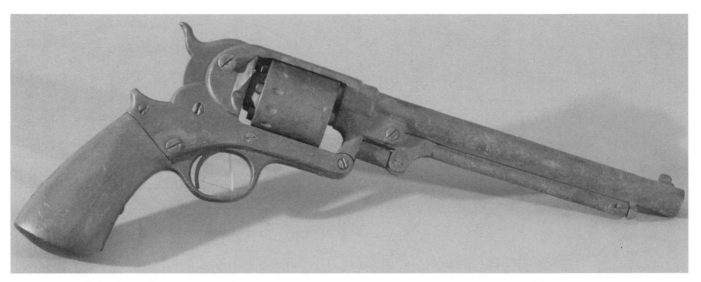

A probable participant in the Civil War struggle in Missouri, a .44 single action Starr found in its holster in a barn destroyed in a storm north of Joplin. Next to Colts and Remingtons, double and single action Starrs were the third most widely used Union handguns in the war, at almost forty-eight thousand. Withdrawing the knurled thumb screw in the frame allows the barrel to be tipped downward to remove the cylinder.
(Photo by Leland E. DeFord III, gun courtesy Edward F. Cornett)

Another Civil War revolver, a .44 Joslyn found in 1929 in woods north of Wichita Falls, Texas. The army first test-ed the Joslyn in 1859 and reportedly favorably on it, but made no purchases until 1861–62 when it obtained eleven hundred, which in service proved unreliable. (Photo by Leland E. DeFord III, gun courtesy Edward F. Cornett)

downward] it is liable to lose its ball and load. It is too light for the ball and cartridge necessary to [do] execution with it. There is no probable certainty of hitting the object aimed at, and the recoil too great to be fired with ease. There appears to be *at present* nothing better for the dragoon than the [Hall?] carbine and Sharps rifle [carbine?]. With the Sharps...the pistol and sword can

be dispensed with, whenever the horse is to be lightened and speed be necessary in the pursuit of Indians....I would recom-mend...[the] sharps short rifle carbine as the only efficient arm for the dragoons.[31]

He included in his report a tabulation of the arms and other equipment present at the various posts he visited. Within the Department of New Mexico he tallied: 1,470

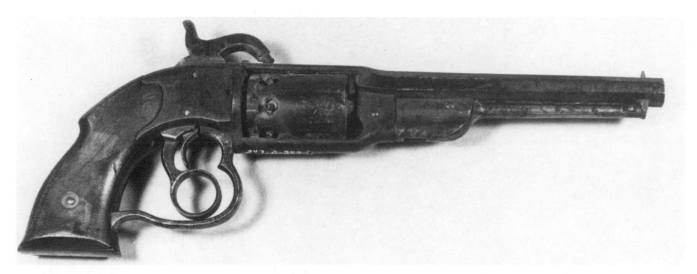

Savage-North .36 revolver reportedly taken from the body of Sam Brown, an outlaw shot in the early 1860s by Henry Van Sickle, owner of Van Sickle Station near Genoa, Nevada. Despite its unwieldy appearance, the army purchased more than eleven thousand during the Civil War and a number of Kansas and Missouri cavalry regiments were equipped with these. The ring trigger cocks the hammer and rotates the cylinder while the conventional trigger fires the piece. (Courtesy: Nevada State Museum, Carson City)

Union cavalryman with a Model 1860 cavalry saber and a twelve-millimeter (.47 caliber) LeFaucheux pinfire. Among the regiments issued this French six-shooter were ones from California, Kansas, and Missouri. (Courtesy: Herb Peck Jr.)

Members of the 21st Missouri Infantry. The revolver at left appears to be a .36 Whitney, the other is a double action Starr. Union Army purchases during the Civil War included slightly more than eleven thousand of the former and almost forty-eight thousand Starrs, the vast majority of them .44s in both double and single action models. (Courtesy: State Historical Society of Missouri)

percussion muskets, 273 flint muskets, 1,106 musketoons, 1,553 percussion rifles, 35 Sharps rifles (carbines presumably), 278 percussion carbines (probably Halls), and a total of 910 percussion pistols against only 430 Colt revolvers. The latter would have been one of the three very similar models of the .44 Dragoon since government purchases of the lighter .36 Model 1851 didn't begin until 1855. Within the Department of the Pacific, which included the ordnance depot at Benecia, he found 14,247 percussion muskets, 5,009 percussion rifles, 1,284 musketoons, 200 carbines (Halls?), 417 Colt revolvers, and 1,257 single-shot percussion pistols.[32]

Mansfield also criticized the lack of appropriate training in firing the musket.

> The practice of firing at the target with ball and buck shot is not sufficient. The mere discharge of the guard of the previous day at the target to get rid of the load is not sufficient practice, and there is not interest enough taken in it by the men to produce

any real improvement. It requires great use of the ball cartridge to make the soldier confident in what he can do with his musket. It requires a good sized cartridge to throw a ball to produce effect at long range, and light as the musket now is the soldier frequently flinches at the recoil, which practice alone can correct.[33]

Mansfield's complaint was valid. Marksmanship practice for much of the nineteenth century often was virtually ignored, in part because infantry tactics of the day relied on mass fire at close range against tight enemy formations. In 1858 the army did adopt Capt. Henry Heth's detailed course of small arms instruction but the demands of the Civil War hampered its implementation. An enlisted member of the 2nd Dragoons at Fort Bridger in 1858 noted that a dragoon "carries a Sharps rifle [carbine], as well as a sabre and a revolver." But he lamented that "for though now nearly five months wearing Uncle Sam's livery, I have

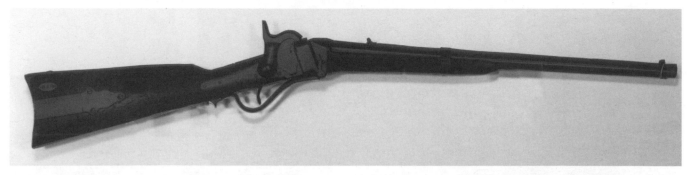

Sharps Model 1855 .52 carbine with Maynard primer. (Courtesy: National Park Service, Fuller Collection, Chickamauga-Chattanooga National Military Park, Fort Oglethorpe, GA)

but twice been at target practice, and we are not allowed to use our rifles on any other occasion—except when on guard—...without special permission."[34]

There were exceptions to this training neglect. Lt. Col. (later Maj. Gen.) E. R. S. Canby spent much of his military career in the west and in March 1856 when with the 10th Infantry helped inaugurate a training program which emphasized target practice. Earlier, during an inspection tour in the southwest, he had reported that "a vital element of [an infantryman's] efficiency is that use of his weapon which will render it most destructive to the enemy.... This necessary practical instruction cannot be said to exist in our Army." Practice often was limited to firing a single shot to clear one's weapon when coming off guard duty. Even practice with blank ammunition was rare. In his perceptive view, the effective combat infantryman needed to be drilled in estimating distances as well as sighting and aiming, and through time spent on the firing range the soldier could become familiar with his weapon and its range, effectiveness, and deficiencies.[35]

Occasionally Civil War officers in the west recognized that on the frontier Native Americans didn't fight in massed formations, requiring some individual ability on the part of the soldier. At Fort Laramie in 1864, the 11th Ohio Volunteer Cavalry practiced daily with their carbines as did the lst New Mexico Volunteer Cavalry at Fort Union.[36]

Some men did pride themselves on their ability as marksmen. Such was Lt. John Talbot serving at Fort Kearney, Nebraska, with the lst Nebraska Cavalry in 1864. Capt. Eugene Ware wrote of him:

> There was a row of telegraph poles between the Fort and Dobytown, and after we had started, this new acquaintance of mine, who had on two Colts' pistols, told me he could ride the line as fast as his horse would run, and put six bullets out of

each revolver into successive telegraph poles; that is to say, he could hit a pole with every shot. Being somewhat experienced myself from a couple of years' service in the cavalry, I did not think he could do it, but I rode along with him, and he did it with the missing of only one telegraph pole in twelve shots.... I often practiced on it myself after that, but never could quite attain so good an average."[37]

THE NEW MODEL ARMS OF 1855

In 1855 the army ceased production of smoothbores at the national armories and adopted a new series of arms—a rifle musket, a shorter rifle, and a single-shot pistol-carbine with a detachable wooden shoulder stock. Their caliber of .58 was a compromise between .54 and .69, and one other feature common to all three was the tape primer designed by Dr. Edward Maynard, a Washington DC dentist. The system used a rolled tape similar to that in a child's toy cap pistol, but it found little favor and was dropped in the Model 1861 rifle musket. As Maj. Samuel P. Heintzelman wrote in his diary for February 21, 1860, at Fort Brown, Texas: "I went this morning to see the troops fire at a target. The firing at 200 yards was pretty good. The locks of the rifle musket are not so good as the old ones & the Maynard primer missed often & sometimes the caps."[38]

These arms fired a conical projectile with a deep hollow in the base, developed by France's Capt. Claude Minie. The undersize bullet could be loaded easily except in a heavily fouled barrel and upon firing pressure expanded the base of the bullet to fill the bore and grip the rifling. Distribution of the new .58 rifles and rifle muskets in the west was underway in 1857. One other new arm adopted in 1855 but produced in limited numbers (1,026) was a rifled carbine. It was .54 caliber rather than .58 and lacked

Rolls of Maynard tape primers with one of their tin containers, recovered from the wreckage of the steamer *Bertrand*, which sank in the Missouri River near Omaha, Nebraska, in 1865. (Courtesy: Desoto National Wildlife Refuge, Missouri Valley, MO)

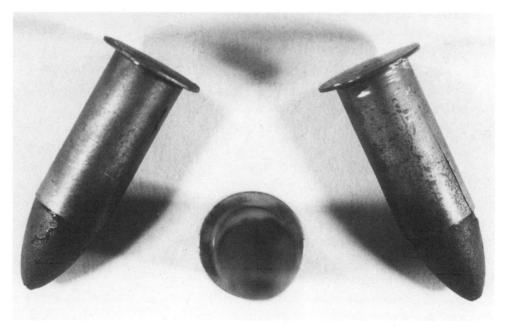

.50 caliber Maynard cartridges recovered from the sunken *Bertrand*. A hole in the base of the cartridge allows the flame from a separate percussion cap to reach and ignite the powder. (Courtesy: Desoto National Wildlife Refuge, Missouri Valley, MO)

the Maynard priming mechanism and in view of the availability of Sharps breechloaders was obsolescent at birth.

The new rifle musket of 1855 was a great improvement in range and accuracy over its smoothbore .69 predecessor. Firing tests showed it penetrated six one-inch pine boards at six hundred yards and three at one thousand yards. Although the .58 rifle musket served for little more than a decade, models of 1855, 1861, and 1863 became the army's primary infantry arm. More than 1.5 million were produced at the national armories and by various contractors who turned out many of the latter two models.

With the adoption of the Minie projectile, workers at the two national armories and Frankfort Arsenal modified thousands of existing shoulder arms to use it, including smoothbore .69 muskets which were newly rifled and fitted with a rear sight. Many .54 Model 1841 "Mississippi" rifles were rebored to .58 caliber and an adjustable rear sight added. In the late 1850s, references to "Minie rifles" usually meant the upgraded Model 1841, for by the Civil War only the regular Army Corps of Engineers and state militia units had received the new 1855 pattern rifles.[39]

Lt. Lawrence Kip of the 3rd Artillery campaigned in 1858 against Spokane Indians and their allies in Washington Territory under Col. George Wright of the 9th Infantry. The 4th, 9th, and 10th infantry regiments as well as the 3rd Artillery, Mounted Rifles, and a portion of the 1st Dragoons

US Model 1855 .58 rifle musket. The patchbox and Maynard primer were eliminated from the later models of 1861 and 1863. (Courtesy: National Park Service, Fuller Collection, Chickamauga-Chattanooga National Military Park, Fort Oglethorpe, GA)

had received the altered Mississippis. At the battle of Four Lakes, Kip observed that "minnie [*sic*] balls and long range rifles were things with which now for the first time [the Indians] were to be made acquainted."

> Strange to say, not one of our men was injured. . . . This was owing to the long range rifles now first used by our troops. . . . Had the men been armed with those formerly used, the result of the fight, as to the loss on our side, would have been far different, for the enemy outnumbered us, and had all the courage which we are accustomed to ascribe to Indian warriors. But they were panic-struck by the effect of our fire at such great distances.[40]

Former Texas Ranger John Salmon "Rip" Ford wrote that in 1858 "the rangers were armed with Minnie [*sic*] rifles, which carried an elongated ball at a range of over half a mile and they carried a ball close to the mark, when well directed. They were muzzleloaders, very long and heavy for service on horseback."[41]

In May of 1861, Texan W. N. Alexander joined the Confederate service, but one of his first engagements was against a large party of Native Americans driving a herd of stolen cattle. In the battle Capt. Davidson was killed. That evening, the Indians returned and one riding the dead captain's horse taunted the whites in Spanish from a ridge.

> I carried a Minnie [*sic*] rifle, the only long-range gun in the party, and I asked permission of Colonel Frost to take one shot at the painted scoundrel. The request being granted, I asked him to estimate the distance and his guess was about seven hundred yards. I dismounted, raised my gun-sight to five hundred yards, took good aim and cut down on him. The shot knocked up the dust almost under his horse, and Mr. big Injun heap lost no time in getting away.[42]

Attempts to find suitable arms for the mounted regiments were generally summarized in a letter of July 1858 from Col. H. K. Craig to the Ordnance Department in Washington.

> When the first regiment of dragoons was organized in 1833 they were supplied with . . . one flint-lock pistol and one Hall's carbine per man. The first change was in April, 1849, when the percussion pistol and the musketoon—one of each per man—were supplied. . . . In November, 1849, the Colt's pistol was first supplied to the regular dragoons, and this arm has gradually superseded the percussion pistol. In February, 1853, Sharp's carbines were issued to the dragoons, as experimental arms, and subsequently these arms have been supplied to the second regiment of Dragoons, and sent forward for the first regiment; those for California shipped in January and February last. Recently . . . Colt's pistol-carbines (being the pistol with a stock to be attached or removed at pleasure) were issued to five companies of the second dragoons. . . .
>
> The cavalry are armed as follows: First regiment, with Sharp's carbines and two companies with Burnside's carbines; second regiment, eight companies with rifle carbines made at Springfield Armory, muzzle

Model 1855 Springfield pistol-carbine.

loading, and two companies with Sharp's carbines. The dragoons and cavalry are both armed with the Colt's pistol, being the only fire arm (except the musketoon, no longer issued) regularly adopted for these troops in our service. While the musketoon…has gone almost entirely out of use from its short range and want of accuracy, and its manufacture has been discontinued, there has been no arm regularly adopted in its stead; but all of those which have been supplied in place of it, viz the Sharp's carbine, the cavalry rifle carbine, the Burnside's carbine, and the Colt's pistol-carbine, are…experimental arms, and there is no regularly prescribed fire arms for the dragoons and cavalry but the revolver-pistol.[43]

The new 1855 .58 pistol-carbine was intended for use by light artillery or mounted troops, either as a pistol or as a carbine with the stock affixed. When deliveries began in 1856, most went to the new lst and 2nd cavalry regiments, organized the year before and equipped with muzzle loading musketoons and rifled carbines. Capt. Richard Ewell, lst Dragoons, explained one objection to the arm. "Without the stock they are an ordinary dragoon pistol. The attach-

ment [stock] is not firm and therefore the arm is unsteady." Ewell and other dragoon and cavalry officers soon requested Sharps as replacements for the pistol-carbine, musketoon, and Model 1855 rifled carbine. By late 1859 their requests generally had been fulfilled. The urgent need for arms when civil war broke out brought some of the pistol-carbines, along with the obsolescent Hall carbine, back into service with Kansas and other state volunteer cavalry regiments.[44]

AN ASSORTMENT OF ARMS

Between 1859 and early 1861, Col. Joseph K. F. Mansfield, inspector general, and Lt. Col. Joseph E. Johnston of the lst Cavalry conducted extensive inspections of military posts in Texas and New Mexico. Their detailed reports included comments on training and small arms encountered during their assignments and reveal the continued disparity of training and equipment among frontier troops. Johnson visited Fort Garland, Colorado, in August 1859 and noted:

> The arms & accoutrements have been in use less than a year & are in good condition—except that on most of the locks "Maynard's attachment" impedes the motion of the hammer & interferes with putting the cap on the cone. Our infantry officers generally are opposed to this "attachment."[45]

At Los Lunas, New Mexico Territory, Johnston found half of the primers misfired. His negative comments on the system were echoed in other inspection reports which both he and Mansfield prepared. "The tape primer springs did not feed well. Many failed to bring out the primer and many of the caps also failed," reported Mansfield at Fort McIntosh, Texas.[46]

Johnson also noted infantrymen lacking in marksmanship ability. "Less than a seventh of the shots fired struck the target at 200 yards.... I am informed that target practice was ordered for the first time in this department, last Spring.... It is needless to add that the bayonet exercise is not taught." In practice, few Indians would ever come within range of a soldier's bayonet. "Skill with fire arms is more valuable in Indian warfare, than accuracy of movement." At the Albuquerque Depot, he found that the forty-five men of the 3rd Infantry there, too, "exhibited a decided want of skill in shooting." They were armed with .69 caliber rifled muskets, examples of the almost fifteen thousand Model 1842 smoothbore muskets which were modernized by the addition of rifling in 1855–59.[47]

At Fort Fillmore in New Mexico, Johnston inspected Company D, lst Dragoons and noted the lack of uniformity in their arms.

> All the men have sabers & Colt's
> Navy revolvers—a majority the pistol-
> carbine—some Sharps & a few, rifles
> of the cal. .54 of an inch [probably Model
> 1841].... The use of the revolver on horse
> back has not been taught yet. The shooting
> with carbines, on foot, was equal to that of
> the infantry.[48]

Johnston's reference to pistol-carbines probably referred to Model 1855s. However, in June 1858 the army ordered another form of pistol-carbine, 924 Colt .44 Dragoon six-shooters and 462 detachable wooden stocks ("breech attachments"), the .44s to be issued in pairs with one stock per pair. The 2nd Dragoons serving in California under Maj. Charles May received enough of these Colts to equip five companies beginning in early 1859.[49]

In late September of 1859, the colonel observed another company of the lst Dragoons, Company G, commanded by Capt. Richard Ewell at Fort Buchanan. Like Johnston, the captain would be wearing Confederate gray two years later.

> There is...a great variety of fire arms,
> Sharp's, Hall's [carbine] & the pistol car-
> bine, the rifle (cal. .54) [Model 1841] &
> musketoon—Colt's revolver of both sizes,
> and the old Dragoon [single-shot] pistols.
> Capt. Ewell advocates Sharp's Carbine, in
> comparison with the musketoon.... The
> Capt. has made two requisitions for car-
> bines annually for several years.[50]

At Fort Inge in Texas, Johnston found that infantrymen considered the new Model 1855 rifle musket "an admirable weapon.... The sights, however, are too coarse that at the muzzle should be of white metal—the other of blue or brown. The barrels should not be bright, their glittering prevents accurate aim & makes troops visible at great distances in sunshine & exposes sentinels by moon light."[51]

Col. J. K. F. Mansfield in 1860–61 inspected posts in the Department of Texas. In some instances his observations support Johnston's, in others they are at odds. When Company H, lst Infantry, drilled at Fort Stockton, "there were but 7 snaps of the [Maynard] tape primer out of 144." Reporting on marksmanship, he found: "At the target of 6' x 22," 48 men, one round each, at 100 yards, made 30 hits, say 62 1/2 percent; at 200 yards made 20 hits, say 40 percent, at 300 yards made 7 hits, say 14 1/2 percent." Men of the lst Artillery at Fort Duncan didn't perform as well on a target the same size. "[Thirty-nine] men one round each, at 100 yards, had 17 hits, say 43 1/2 percent; at 200 yards made 7 hits, say 18 percent; 300 yards made 5 hits, say 13 percent." He did find bayonet practice apparently was conducted more frequently in Texas and at one post, Fort Hudson, there were ten obsolete flintlock muskets used for bayonet exercise.[52]

As Mansfield concluded his tour of inspection, in January 1861 he observed two companies of the 2nd Cavalry. Company E's arms under Capt. George Stoneman included Sharps carbines, Colt "navy size" (Model 1851) revolvers, and sabers.

> The carbines were new, but the hind sights
> to some were broken off. This sight is too
> delicate for mounted men. The leaf sight is
> much more durable. The ball cartridges of
> the carbines were entirely too small by
> some mistake of the ordnance department,
> & therefore the target trial was not practi-
> cable. The pistol practice was dispensed
> with on account of the same.[53]

Company G was less well uniformly armed—"Harpers Ferry [M1841?] rifles, old, & inferior, some old [.54 M1855?]

Colt Model 1855 carbine owned by Brig. Gen. William S. Harney. As colonel of the 2nd Dragoons, in 1855 he led a combined infantry, artillery, and dragoon force against the Sioux. (Courtesy: Smithsonian Institution, Washington DC)

carbines with swivel-ram-rod, some [Colt Dragoon?] holster pistols & some Navy size."

> I could not with such arms attempt target trial even if it had the practice. I condemned all the rifles & carbines as unsuitable & to be turned in and Sharps carbines supplied in stead, but it will depend on the commanding officer of the department to say if it should be done. It is folly to put the Harpers Ferry rifle, and that worthless carbine into the hands of cavalry as an arm suitable.[54]

Mansfield concluded his report with his observations at the San Antonio Arsenal. Stores on hand included ten six-pound brass guns, a dozen twelve-pound brass howitzers, two six-pound iron guns, 862 .58 rifle muskets, 732 Harpers Ferry (1841?) rifles, eighteen Colt's navy size pistols, 385 Colt's navy size pistols, 213 Sharps carbines, seventy-eight rifle carbines, 171 horse artillery sabers, and 412 cavalry sabers. (The dual listing of Colt's navy size pistols must have included .44 Colt Dragoons).[55]

In the late 1850s, several other single-shot breech loading carbines besides those by Sharps underwent field testing, adding to the variety of arms in troopers' hands. Burnsides went to the 1st Cavalry and 1st Dragoons. When Company H of the 1st Cavalry left Fort Leavenworth in May 1857 to join Col. E. V. Sumner's campaign against the Cheyennes, the men carried Greene carbines in addition to their Springfield M1855 pistol-carbines. Maynards were tested by the 1st Cavalry and the Regiment of Mounted Rifles. Before the Civil War, the government also bought some of Sam Colt's Model 1855 revolving shoulder arms, sixty two carbines and 765 rifles. Of the latter, R. B. Marcy, anticipating a battle with the Mormons, wrote to Colt from a camp on the Green River in October of 1857.

They [Mormons] are around us on all sides and have already taken some prisoners. We are only waiting for a commander to open the ball. I expect the rifles with the commander, and I will put them in the hands of my best men who will make their marks with them. I have two which I can get from one of the other companies of my regiment, and if the ten I left with Genl. Harney do not come, I will do so.[56]

In the same letter, he candidly expressed his views on the Mormon situation.

> The Mormons are going to fight us without any doubt. Brigham Young has just come out with a proclamation in which he calls upon the people of Utah to resist the entrance of our army into the Salt Lake Valley, and he has sent a letter to the temporary commander of the [US] troops telling him to turn back and return over the same road he came or if he prefers, he can remain until spring where he is now upon condition that he delivers all his arms and ammunition to his (Brigham's) [illegible]. This is tolerably cool, and I think I see the army turning over their arms. He must be an ass to suppose he could frighten us by such tomfoolery.[57]

James Larson enlisted in the 1st Cavalry in 1860. He served throughout the Civil War and after, rising to the rank of sergeant. In July 1860 he was at Jefferson Barracks outside St. Louis and with other recruits was given a Model 1841 rifle.

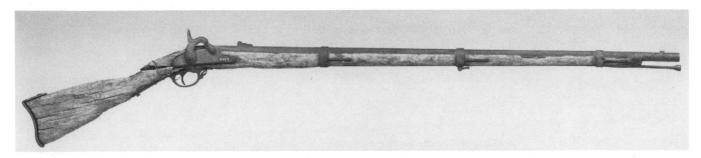

US Model 1861 .58 rifle musket made on contract by the Savage Revolving Fire Arms Company. Badly weathered after decades of exposure, it was found on Freeze Out Mountain in Wyoming about 1915. (Courtesy: Nebraska State Historical Society, acc. #24558)

We were issued a short old fashioned infantry gun, which for some reason was called the Jaeger, which was pronounced "Yoguer," presumably on account of its clumsy make. It was a muzzle loader with iron ramrod. The barrel was held to the stock by three [two] heavy brass bands and the butt end was also well covered with brass. With this shooting stick we received an infantry cartridge box full of cartridges and a small cap box also well filled. To this was added knapsack, haversack and canteen; a complete infantry outfit except bayonet on the Jaeger, but we considered ourselves well enough fitted out to fight any number of Indians. After that we received some instructions in handling the Jaeger; how to load it, but not how to fire it, as we never put a cartridge in. The manual was made as short as possible so as to get us ready for the march [westward to join the 1st].[58]

Early in September, a wagon train from Fort Leavenworth caught up with them at Fort Riley, Kansas. Now the recruits could exchange their rifles for handier Sharps carbines.

The new gun was very different from the Jaeger. It was about seven inches shorter and weighed only about half as much and could be loaded and fired very rapidly. All that was necessary was to spring the lever, insert a cartridge, close it and put on a cap.... It was the fastest firing gun in the army at that time and we carried it until, for gallant service in the Civil War... we

received the Spencer carbine.... By getting rid of the old gun [Model 1841 rifle] we also got rid of the big infantry cartridge box and received the kind intended for our branch of the service, which was much smaller and fitted better.[59]

Soon after Larson's arrival at Fort Wise, mounted drill began, at first with only a saddle blanket and no stirrups, the troopers learning to vault onto the horse's back while encumbered with waist belt, cartridge box, saber, and carbine with its shoulder sling (revolvers had not yet been issued).

The heavy carbine was attached to the sling belt by an iron swivel and hung, muzzle down, when the trooper was mounted, but when dismounted and standing to horse ready to mount, it was thrown over the right shoulder and hung down his back. The saber was attached to the waist belt by two narrow straps, one a little longer than the other and always hung loose in them except when worn on foot drill, when it was hooked up on the waist belt.

With that rig..., we stood...by our horses, ready to mount if we could.... When I stood by the side of my horse that morning looking at the long saber by my left side, the lower part of the scabbard resting on the ground about two and one-half feet behind me and the upper part of the scabbard with the hilt projecting out at least one foot in front of me, and the carbine handing down the middle of my back with the butt end just

INDEPENDENT
KANSAS
Jay-Hawkers.

Volunteers are wanted for the 1st Regiment of Kansas Volunteer Cavalry to serve our country

During the War.

Horses will be furnished by the Government. Good horses will be purchased of the owner who volunteers. Each man will be mounted, and armed with a Sharp's Rifle, a Navy Revolver, and a Sabre. The pay will be that of the regular volunteer.

Volunteers from Northern Kansas will rendezvous at Leavenworth. Those from Southern Kansas will rendezvous at Mound City. Volunteers singly, parts of companies and full companies will be mustered into the United States service as soon as they report themselves to the local recruiting officer at either of the above places. Upon arriving at Mound City volunteers will report themselves to John T. Snoddy, Acting Adjutant. Those who rendezvous at Leavenworth will report themselves to D. R. Anthony, Esq. of that place.

C. R. JENNISON,
Col. 1st Regiment Kansas Vol. Cavalry.
MOUND CITY, Aug. 24, 1861.

1861 recruiting broadside for the 1st Kansas Cavalry. "Each man will be mounted, and armed with a Sharp's Rifle, a Navy Revolver, and a Sabre." A reference to a "navy revolver" usually meant a Colt Model 1851. (Courtesy: Kansas State Historical Society)

opposite the back of my head, I wondered if it was possible....

When the command fell there followed a scramble and a terrible rattling of sabers along the line, but only a few could be seen on top of their horses when the commotion was over. The others were either lying on the ground or standing by their horses with a disgusted look on their faces, I being among the last named.... It took several days of that kind of vaulting exercise before Sergeant O'Connel allowed us to begin exercise in the riding ring. Even then we had to turn out "under arms" at every drill hour and make several vaults with the whole rig on before we were allowed to take off our belts, "stack" carbines and take the ring.[60]

CIVIL WAR WEST OF THE MISSISSIPPI

Once the Civil War broke out, Union and Confederate forces collided west of the Mississippi in major engagements at Wilson's Creek (Missouri) in 1861 and at Pea Ridge (Arkansas) the next year. Federal troops gained a significant victory when they halted a Confederate campaign in the southwest at Glorieta Pass near Santa Fe. Guerrilla-style warfare raging across Arkansas, Missouri, and Kansas continued throughout the war. However the bulk of the fighting between Federal and Confederate forces occurred east of the Mississippi.

Meanwhile, the effort to maintain peace with the Native Americans in the west during the Civil War was the responsibility of volunteer troops after regular army units were transferred east. These western volunteer regiments often were equipped with obsolescent or second class arms, particularly early in the war. Iowa received ten thousand first class British Enfield rifles in 1862, but the 24th Iowa Infantry

Iowa recruiting poster for a company in Birge's Sharpshooters, a Civil War Union regiment. The unit was armed with muzzle loading sporting rifles by Dimick of St. Louis. The Dimick revolvers mentioned actually were manufactured by the Metropolitan Arms Company of New York City and were virtually identical to Colt's Model 1851 Navy. The unit's duty was to "pick off, during an engagement, the officers and gunners of the enemy." A further inducement was the claim they would have no guard duty to perform. (Courtesy: Iowa Historical Society)

1862 Texas Ranger recruiting poster. Recruits were to provide their own firearms, preferably "double-barreled shot guns, light rifles and six-shooters." (Courtesy: Institute of Texas Cultures, San Antonio)

Colt Model 1861 .36 Navy (#5455) inscribed on the butt "Maj. R. N. McLaren/Minn. 6th." The 6th Minnesota Infantry, prior to reassignment to Arkansas in mid-1864, was assigned to frontier defense against hostile Indians in Minnesota and Dakota Territory. It lost a dozen enlisted men in combat, but four officers and 161 enlisted men died from illness, not an uncommon ratio during the Civil War. (Courtesy: Track of the Wolf via Dale H. Peterson)

reportedly paraded with wooden guns until October of that year. "A worthless lot of worn-out Belgian muskets…the caliber of which did not correspond in size with the cartridges we obtained." So a seventeen-year-old with the 6th Minnesota Volunteer Infantry described the guns issued in preparing to quell the Sioux uprising in Minnesota in August 1862.[61]

At the end of 1862, eleven regiments of Missouri mounted militia were at least partially armed with second class Austrian Jaeger short rifles. The historian for the 4th Iowa Cavalry wrote that in the spring of 1863, Austrian rifles "were still in the hands of those men who had not had the hardihood or ingenuity to 'lose them.'" Col. Patrick E. Connor in February 1863 reported on the arms of the 2nd California Cavalry at Camp Douglas in Utah Territory.

> Two companies are armed with Whitney [Model 1841 Mississippi] rifles, a very unwieldy arm and quite unsuited to cavalry service, being difficult to load or carry on horseback. Many of these are also out of repair, and some of them unfit for use by reason of long service. A large number of pistols used are also out of repair."[62]

In response to the Sioux uprising in Minnesota, the Iowa Northern Border Brigade was organized as mounted infantry, to travel on horseback but to fight on foot. Arms issued in November 1862 included 162 Austrian rifles, 40 British Enfield rifles, 20 Springfield muskets, 48 Harpers Ferry [Mississippi?] rifles, and 18 navy [Colt?] revolvers. Seven companies of the 7th Iowa Cavalry arrived in Omaha in September 1863 for duty in Indian country. "Each cavalryman had a Gallager carbine, an exceedingly inefficient weapon; a Colt's .44 caliber [probably Model 1860] revolver…, [and] a heavy dragoon sabre, which was becoming obsolete, and which subsequently before the regiment's term of service expired, was boxed up and stored," a captain in the regiment recalled.[63]

Luther North, later to gain fame with his brother Maj. Frank North and their Pawnee scouts, enlisted in the 2nd Nebraska Cavalry in the fall of 1862.

> The guns were long-barrelled muzzle loading Springfield rifles, and our revolvers were Colts, caliber .44, also muzzle loaders. Besides these firearms we wore the regulation sabre. It took a pretty expert horseman to load one of those long rifles; especially if his horse was not perfectly gentle. They tried drilling us on horseback, but the guns were so awkward that they gave us most of our drilling on foot.[64]

Pvt. Irving Howbert served with the 3rd Colorado Cavalry at the infamous slaughter of Cheyenne and

William C. Quantrill's Colt .36 Model 1862. The notorious Confederate guerrilla leader apparently enjoyed torturing animals as a youth and included among his Civil War band the James brothers and Cole Younger. (Courtesy: Ohio Historical Society)

ATTENTION!
INDIAN
FIGHTERS

Having been authorized by the Governor to raise a Company of 100 day

U. S. VOL CAVALRY!

For immediate service against hostile Indians. I call upon all who wish to engage in such service to call at my office and enroll their names immediately.

Pay and Rations the same as other U. S. Volunteer Cavalry.

Parties furnishing their own horses will receive 40c per day, and rations for the same, while in the service.
The Company will also be entitled to all horses and other plunder taken from the Indians.

Office first door East of Recorder's Office.
HAL. SAYR.

Central City, Aug. 13, '64.

An August 1864 pre–Sand Creek Colorado recruiting poster. An inducement to join was the short enlistment (one hundred days) and the spoils of war—"all horses and other plunder taken from the Indians." (Courtesy: Colorado Historical Society)

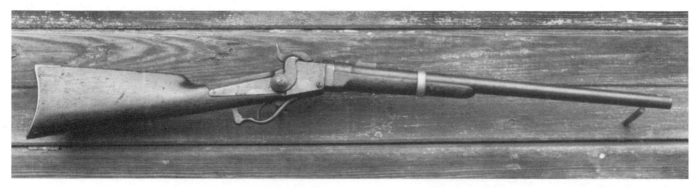

Starr percussion carbine (#4724) issued to Sgt. J. J. Brown, lst Colorado Cavalry. He was on active duty in November 1864 and probably participated in the Sand Creek affair.

Civilian-style double-barrel rifle made by Nelson Lewis of Troy, New York, and used by Hector Hutchinson at the infamous attack on the Cheyenne and Arapaho camp at Sand Creek on November 29, 1864. (Courtesy: Colorado Historical Society)

Arapaho Indians at Sand Creek in November 1864 and wrote that: "We received…old, out-of-date Austrian muskets of large bore, with paper cartridges from which we had to bite off [the] end when loading. These guns sent a bullet rather viciously, but one could never tell where it would hit."[65]

Morse Coffin of the same regiment probably was referring to the same muskets when he recalled that they were furnished with "a lot of infantry guns said to have been purchased by Fremont when he took over command in Missouri." All who could afford to do so purchased a carbine or revolver, he wrote, some of the men obtaining revolvers at $20 to $40 from teamsters delivering corn. "For Smith & Wesson [.44 Frank Wesson single-shot metallic cartridge] carbines we all paid $40 without cartridges, and the same price for navy [Colt?] revolvers." At Sand Creek, Coffin's carbine became so fouled that an empty shell casing stuck in the chamber.

> I hadn't yet learned that by wetting the
> shells in the mouth immediately before
> firing they could be easily removed with

the thumb and finger. I then used my revolver, but after several shots that was also rendered useless by a piece of the [percussion] gun cap getting down next to the lock, so it could not be cocked.[66]

His company skirmished with Cheyennes at Buffalo Springs in the fall of 1864 where the chief Big Wolf was shot. The warrior had two guns in addition to his bow and arrows—"a Lancaster [probably a Leman muzzle loading] rifle, so common among Indians, the other an army carbine, such as were used by the 7th Iowa Cavalry, some of whom were at Julesburg." The 7th was armed with Gallagher percussion breechloaders, one of the more widely procured (22,500) but only moderately successful Civil War carbines, in addition to more reliable Colt Model 1860 revolvers.[67]

As the war progressed, the shortage of first class arms in western regiments eased. By mid-1864, the seven-shot Spencer was in the hands of some units, including the 2nd Iowa Cavalry. The 12th Missouri Volunteer Cavalry had them in time for their participation in the Powder River campaign in the summer

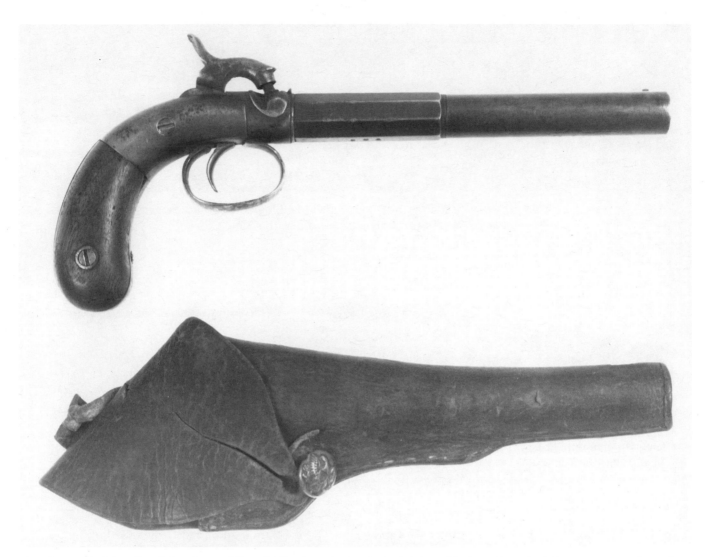

Another relic from Sand Creek, an Allen & Thurber single-shot pistol and holster found at the massacre site a few weeks after the fight, perhaps carried into battle by one of the Colorado volunteers. (Courtesy: Colorado Historical Society, neg. #F-32764)

Spencer carbine owned by Lt. Col. George A. Custer. (Courtesy: Lawrence A. Frost)

of 1865. Lt. Charles Springer commanded Company B and wrote:

> My little squad of ten men went with a yell at them, but the Indians never budged, we let a well directed volley fire at them; after the discharge a yell arose which appeared to have broke[n] loose in the infernal regions and a shower of arrows accompanied the yelling.

56

Civil War CDV of a Union cavalryman with saber and .36 or .44 Colt photographed by the Sutterley Brothers, Photographers, in Virginia (City), Nevada Territory. (Courtesy: Richard Carlile)

Brig. Gen. James H. Ford, 2nd Colorado Cavalry, "in his fighting rig" with a pair of Colts(?) worn butt forward. (Courtesy: Richard Carlile)

Probably members of one of the Colorado volunteer cavalry regiments, photographed by W. G. Chamberlain, Photographic Artist, Larimer Street, Denver, Colorado Territory. Each has a Starr percussion carbine on a carbine sling. The revolvers are a Colt .44 M1860 (left) and .44 Starr Single Action (right). (Courtesy: Richard Carlile)

I shouted "fire" and again a volley hailed against them. This appeared to astonish them; that our guns were constantly loaded, but we had to give way. . . . The Indians are brave, but they are afraid of our Spencer carabines [*sic*].

Springer in November 1865 wrote that the officers at Fort Laramie in present-day Wyoming had organized a baseball team. However there would be limited time for such recreation at many of the posts in the west during the years which followed.[68]

Across the Plains by Foot, Handcart, and Wagon

I confess to more fear from careless handling of
firearms than from an external foe.
— Anonymous, 1849[1]

The 1840s marked the beginning of emigration in substantial numbers across the Great Plains and Rockies to Oregon and California. Americans already had expanded their influence in the southwest to such settlements as Santa Fe, and the Mormons by the end of the decade were established in Utah. The reasons for this westward movement were many and included economics, the hunger for land, religion, an expansionist fervor, and the thirst for adventure. The acquisition of new lands following the Mexican War and of course the discovery of gold in California in 1848 also became major factors. But as mountain man Jim Bridger warned William Henry Gray, a lay minister, "the grace of God won't carry a man through these prairies; it takes powder and ball."[2]

Henry E. Leman of Lancaster, Pennsylvania, was one eastern gun maker who was quick to appreciate the expanding market for firearms among those moving west. In 1839 he advertised in a local newspaper: "The subscriber has constantly on hand several hundred Rifles, of every description, and particularly calls the attention of persons removing to the west. Also double and single barrel shot guns, Armstrong dueling pistols, Rifle barrels, etc., all of which are warranted."[3]

In 1841 the Bidwell-Bartelson group, guided by mountain man "Broken Hand" Tom Fitzpatrick, made the first trip to Oregon by wagon. The death of one of their

party named Shotwell (a profoundly prophetic name) was but one of the first of many resulting from firearms accidents. Between 1844 and 1848, it's been estimated that about twenty-seven hundred settlers from the east passed over the Oregon Trail, encouraged in 1846 by the settlement of the Oregon boundary dispute with Great Britain. That number jumped to an estimated thirty-five thousand in 1849. Most traveled by canvas-covered wagon but there were those who carried their possessions in a cart, wheelbarrow, or on their back. During the peak years of the gold rush (1849–52), the primary destination of most of the emigrant trains switched to the mining regions rather than the agricultural lands of the Pacific northwest, and the makeup of trains swung from family groups to a high proportion of male travelers, many of whom planned to return to the east after striking it rich and "seeing the elephant." Although the Oregon and Mormon trails served emigrants, to the south the Santa Fe Trail primarily was one of commerce.[4]

For many, the journey of almost four months across the plains and mountains to the West Coast was the experience of a lifetime. Many emigrants wrote of their experiences on the long and difficult journey and their accounts make fascinating reading. One party in 1843 chose an unusual method to select a leader. Each candidate for the office moved out in front of the company with his back to

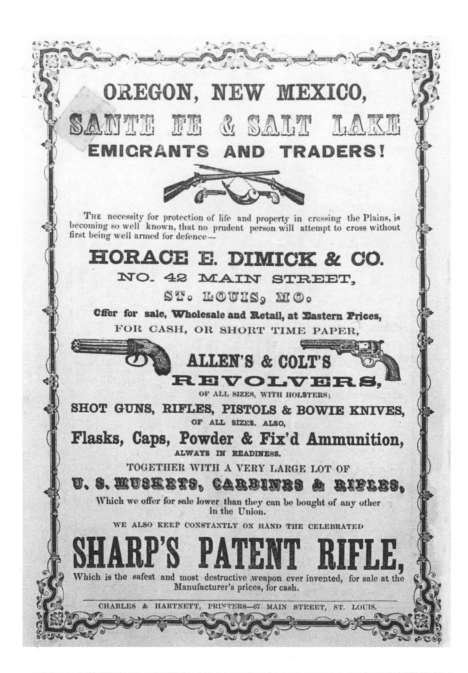

1850s advertisement by Horace E. Dimick & Co. of St. Louis promoting a variety of arms for west-bound emigrants.

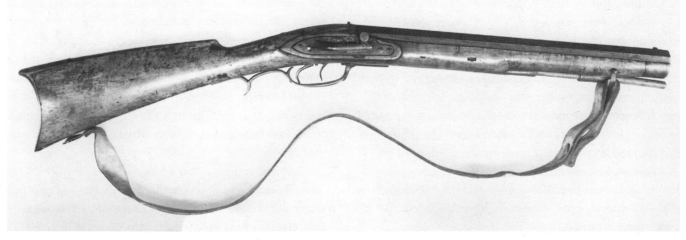

Unusual side hammer .45 carbine made by William L. Watt of St. Louis who worked for W. S. Hawken, Sam's son. A short rifle such as this would have been convenient for use on horseback. (Courtesy: US Military Academy, West Point Museum, NY)

them. At a signal, the office-seekers moved forward, followed by their backers and he with the longest "tail" was selected.

Emigrants couldn't start across the plains too early in the spring or there wouldn't be sufficient grass for livestock. Those leaving too late risked being trapped in the mountains by snow. Regardless of how well prepared a party might be, danger in various forms lay ahead. Travel conditions improved as more wagon trains passed over the established routes, but few families were immune from observing or themselves feeling heartbreaking sorrow along the way, which left lifelong scars.

One poignant account was that of the death of infant George Millington. "We gathered around his little bed in the tent to see him die." On their fourteenth wedding anniversary, the parents discussed whether to bury the child along the road or bear him onward to Carson City. They chose the latter.

> Pa, ma, and we children went to see
> George's grave about a mile from
> town.... Desolate enough but we are better
> satisfied than to have left him on Dry
> Creek.... Pa cut 20 notches on each rail
> near the head of the grave for his age—20
> months, and cut some letters and emblems
> on the board at the head and foot of the
> grave. Then we went away hoping in a year
> or so to have him sent to California.

But life had to go on, and three days after George's burial, his mother suppressed her grief long enough to bake ginger cakes for her six-year-old's birthday. When years later a family member returned to retrieve the coffin for reburial in California, all signs of the grave site had vanished.[5]

Whether for hunting or defense, firearms were among the many essential items carried westward by the emigrants, or "pilgrims" as they often were known. Item 8 in the organizational agreement signed by members of the Linn Association of Emigrants to Oregon Territory in 1844 stated that there would be included "a [firearm] and such quantity of ammunition as said committee shall think necessary" for every male person over the age of sixteen.[6]

During the early phases of travel, emigrants kept their firearms ready at hand. "The pockets of the canvas walls of the wagon held every day needs and toilet articles, as well as small fire arms. The ready shotgun was suspended from the hickory bows of the wagon." "Our men are all well armed. William carries a brace of pistols and bowie knife. Ain't that blood-curdling? I hope he won't hurt himself,"

Lucy Cooke wrote. One California-bound party of '49ers leaving from Illinois camped near Geneseo where "we spent most of the afternoon practicing with our rifles, target shooting 138 yards. Bullseye 3 inches in diameter. My ball struck 4 inches from center and was awarded the best shot."[7]

Committee members of the Jefferson County West Virginia Mining Company purchased eighty double-barrel shotguns in Baltimore, three of which were "fine" guns at $40 each. William Kelly's twenty-five-man company was armed as though going to war.

> We were well equipped, each man carrying
> in his belt a revolver, a sword, and bowie-
> knife; the mounted men having besides a
> pair of holster-pistols and a rifle slung from
> the horn of their saddles, over and above
> which there were several double and single-
> shot guns and rifles suspended in the wag-
> gons [sic], in loops, near the forepart, where
> they would be easily accessible in case of
> attack.[8]

Indians could be a nuisance for petty thievery and were a threat to run off carelessly herded livestock, and there were incidents of attack. White and Native American relations became more strained by the late 1850s, but earlier there generally was not much to fear if a party showed strength and vigilance and treated the native inhabitants with respect. Disease and accidents were greater threats to overlanders. Native Americans initially were sometimes quite generous in giving emigrants food and information and serving as guides.

Members of one wagon train were grateful to Crow Indians who in 1850 carried women and children across the Green River on their horses. Nevertheless, an 1846 guidebook warned emigrants against trading away any guns to Indians in the vicinity of Fort Hall near present-day Pocatello, Idaho, for they might be needed for their own defense. Growing antagonism on the part of the Indians was fostered by such men as Jim Kinney, an intimidating man who bragged he had "killed plenty of negroes and an Indian was no better." He captured an Indian near the fort in 1845, hitched him behind his wagon, whipped him until he felt his spirit was broken, then forced him to perform menial chores. Kinney's traveling companions were afraid to stand up to the bully, but the Indian later escaped taking his captor's prized rifle. In 1864 an emigrant train escorted by Capt. James L. Fisk laced hardtack with strychnine which killed two dozen Sioux following the loss of a dozen whites to an Indian attack.[9]

Once onto the prairie, it wasn't long before travelers encountered bison and antelope.

> This day, for the first time, we saw the antelope..., an animal somewhat resembling both the deer and the goat, but with flesh preferable to that of either. It runs with great speed.... Although a shy [animal], they are still a very inquisitive animal, and are frequently lured within gunshot by simply hanging a red handkerchief upon a ramrod or stick, and moving it aloft. The hunter keeps his body out of sight as much as possible, when the antelope, seeing nothing but the handkerchief, approached, with head erect and by slow degrees, until within rifle-shot, and then pays the penalty of its curiosity with its life.[10]

In 1846 the army organized the Regiment of Mounted Rifles to protect travelers on the Oregon Trail. Service in the Mexican War delayed its performance of this mission and it wasn't until 1849 that it conducted its first expedition along the entire length of the trail, from Fort Leavenworth to Fort Vancouver. George Gibbs accompanied the regiment as a civilian artist and naturalist and later wrote concerning emigrant parties he observed:

> It is amusing...to see men carrying on their shoulders or their saddles, in a country where there is now neither game nor enemy, the long, heavy rifles of the west and their holsters filled with pistols—each one a marching ordnance department. We see them every day roaming about the country.... The practice will probably be continued until a few are snapped [up] by some of the more western tribes. [The] Government, I learn today, has with wise liberality directed that the commissary shall hold a surplus of provisions for the relief of emigrants broken down and returning to the states.[11]

Death or injury along the emigrants' path came in many forms. Drowning during river crossings or being run over by a wagon were common. Children often were the victims of the latter tragedy. Illness, particularly cholera, mountain fever, and scurvy, caused many to suffer, both white and Indian. In 1850 an estimated five thousand emigrants died from illness, primarily cholera. (Some members of the clergy said cholera was God's retribution for greed, as in seeking gold.) The Pawnees are thought to have suffered some twelve hundred deaths in 1849 alone due to this dreaded disease.

> We are armed to the teeth but on account of the consternation among the [Pawnee] Indians because of cholera, we could hardly get a sight of them.... Our arms are useless, for we carry with us in their imagination a protection more formidable: the dread scourge which has spread among them.[12]

Another frequent cause of death or injury was the careless handling of guns by overlanders, many of whom were not familiar with their proper use. The perceived threat of Indian attack and the eager anticipation of hunting wild game prompted them to keep their guns close at hand early in the journey. One traveler noted that they were "so eager for sport that they will discharge their pieces no matter if they fire in the direction of a whole train." One party's initial encounter with bison brought injury as well as the excitement of the first hunt. "One man, in attempting to take his Rifle from the pommel, discharged it, the ball entering his shoulder; another put a ball through the neck of his horse."[13]

Withdrawing a loaded percussion rifle or shotgun muzzle first from a wagon or tent with the percussion cap in place caused many an injury, often fatal. If the hammer should snag momentarily on some obstruction, when it slipped free it could fall upon the capped nipple with sufficient force to discharge the weapon. This happened to one man who shot himself in the hand withdrawing a rifle from a guard tent. Mary Elizabeth Warren shot a lock of her hair off when she jumped onto a wagon and a gun leaning there discharged. A '49er with the Granite State Company of California-bound pilgrims dropped his rifle which discharged a ball which struck a pack mule in the knee and cut an artery. He gave up his riding horse to the mule's owner as compensation and walked the rest of the way. William Swain wrote home to his mother in June 1849 and described an accident in which a man was shot in the knee when a bundle of clothes which he threw from a wagon struck a rifle leaning against the vehicle. "His wound probably will cripple him for life."[14]

The journal kept by a traveler bound for Fort Leavenworth from Santa Fe in 1848 noted that Mr. Mace "went to untie his mule and stooping down his pistol fell

Manhattan .36 revolver carried by Samuel Hartzell across the plains to the Rockies in 1860. He later returned to Missouri and brought a herd of high grade cattle to his ranch in South Park, Colorado. (Courtesy: Colorado Historical Society)

out of his belt and struck a log and went off shooting him about 2 inches above the stomach." Another entry stated: "Maj. Singer's shot gun went off as he threw it into the wagon today but fortunately did no damage except to blow to pieces a musket."[15]

John M. Snively traveled to Oregon in 1843 and again in 1845 and as a surveyor laid out the town of Astoria. He prepared an immigrants' guide in 1846 in which he warned:

> Keep your guns in good order, but never
> have caps on them unless you are going to
> shoot; when you come in from your hunt,
> be sure to take your [percussion] cap off
> before you put your gun in the wagon.
> There are many graves along the road,
> occasioned by the accidental discharge of
> guns being put away with caps on; flint
> locks are always dangerous, and should
> never be taken along.[16]

An account of one party of gold-seeking Mormons' journey appeared in the semimonthly *Frontier Guardian* newspaper of May 30, 1849. "Near the frontier there were a few cases of cholera, but nothing very serious, except four men . . . having been accidentally shot by taking guns out of wagons with caps on them." Abner Blackburn, in the Mormon winter camp at Sugar Creek, Iowa, sustained a serious wound through the carelessness of another.

Met with a severe accident. There was a young gawkey [*sic*] fellow fooling with one of those old Flint-Lock horse pistols. It was loaded with three rifle balls [an unusual pistol load]. At the discharge of the pistol two of the balls passed through my thigh and one struck the bone. . . . They expected me to pass in my check. Brigham [Young] and Kimball were there and prayed me out of danger. My parents came . . . and by good nursing [I] came out as good as new in about six weeks.[17]

The perpetrator, Benjamin Stewart, was expelled from the camp.

> It was a palpable violation of orders for any
> man to even handle another's arms much
> less to fire one. . . . I called out all the guard
> and gave them a severe reprimand for their
> disobedience of orders & want of discipline
> and their practice of firing guns in camp
> which had been so often forbid[den].[18]

Blackburn described two more accidents, the first occurred in 1849 and the second in 1851.

> About half way down the Humboldt
> [River], I was riding along side of William

A daguerreotype, perhaps of an overlander of about 1850. He carries a cutlery handle Bowie knife and percussion rifle and fastened to his shoulder belt are a fork and a bullet mold. He wears socks for gloves. (Courtesy: John N. McWilliams)

Lane and carrying our guns across our laps when his gun went off. The bullet went through the edge of my pants, cut the stirrup leather off and went through my horse and killed him. A pretty close shave.

One of our companions was out hunting. We heard a shot and then a bellow. Went out to whear [sic] he was. He set his gun down in a bush and when he drew it out the gun went off and shot him through the bowels. We took him to camp and in the night he died.[19]

In August 1850 Daniel W. Jones was camped along the Green River when he accidentally shot himself, the ball ranging downward through groin and thigh. Standing by the side of his mule, "I was placing the pistol in the holster, after saddling up, when the hammer caught on the edge of the holster, pulling it back slightly, when it slipped and

went off." When he realized the extent of his wound, he withdrew his other pistol with the idea of ending his life. "Some good spirit told me to hold on, that I would live. Almost every one in the company expressed the belief that I would die." Despite predictions, he did survive.[20]

Improperly loading a gun also could cause an accident. A young man crossing the plains in 1849 was careless with a double-barrel shotgun and accidentally put both loads in one barrel. When he fired, the barrel burst, injuring his left hand severely. If the ball wasn't rammed all the way down the barrel and there was a gap between powder and projectile, excessive pressure could cause potentially disastrous results as Mormon '49er James S. Brown noted in his diary. "Brother Cain . . . in trying to load [his rifle] . . . had used too thick a patching, and the bullet had stuck half way down the barrel. There it was, immovable; he could neither get it up or down. Neither he nor any of the rest of us had dared to fire off the rifle for fear of it bursting."[21]

Pair of .44 saw-handle pistols reportedly given by Brigham Young to Jesse C. Little, one of the 1847 pioneers in the Salt Lake Valley. (Courtesy: Utah State Historical Society)

Gunpowder, which emigrants carried with them, also posed risks. On one occasion an overlander tried to use it as an aid when lighting a campfire. A pound and a half ignited and "like to have burnt him up. He is the worst looking pirson [sic] I ever saw," wrote one of his companions.[22]

Accidents weren't confined to the Pacific Coast–bound emigrants of the 1840s and 1850s. On the Fourth of July in 1866, a traveler on the Bozeman Trail in Montana, George W. Fox, wrote in his diary that after returning from hunting, a man in his wagon train had been wounded. "Mr Canover of Flanigans outfit. A lady handing him the pistol it went off hit his hand and went into his side they don't think he will live."[23]

In another incident on the Bozeman Trail in 1863, emigrants prepared for the arrival of a party of more than one hundred Indians. Although the presence of Native American women in the party indicated a peaceful intent, in the camp "all was bustle and confusion."

> The stock was hustled in, the corral ropes drawn and every one was out armed to the teeth. [William] Baker's wife hurriedly loaded her husband's muzzle loader which he had previously charged himself. Not seeing her act and not feeling sure of what he had done he again rammed a bullet down

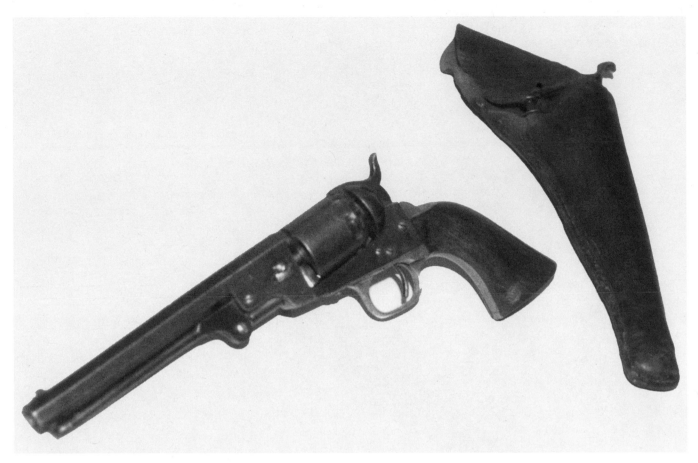

A relic of travel on the Oregon Trail, a .36 Manhattan. (Exhibited at the Scotts Bluff National Monument, NE)

the gun but discovery was later made in time to avoid a casualty.[24]

Abraham H. Voorhees, another Bozeman Trail diarist, wrote in June 1864:

> One of the guards last night through carelessness when cap[p]ing his gun let the hammer fall. His gun was fired. It was loaded with large duck shot. The contents or most of it was lodged in one of our cattles [sic] back. 22 shot holes were found through his hide.[25]

Mary Foreman Kelley in 1864 traveled with her two children to Montana to join her husband. "A Mr. Davis . . . with his wife and six children, left his rifle loaded and cocked the night he went to bed accidentally discharged it, killing him instantly. . . . We buried him near Scotts Bluff [Nebraska]."[26]

Harriet Banyard in 1869 journeyed to California from Texas by wagon and included a poignant entry in her journal.

A young man . . . accidentally shot himself with his six shooter. He was twirling it around and revolving it and it went off. The bullet went in on the right side through his breast and come [sic] out in his back on the same side. Oh how it grieves me to think that anyone should happen to have such an accident so far from home. . . . He will have the assistance of our prayers.[27]

Although they didn't happen to overlanders, several other examples of accidental shootings were reported by Kansas newspapers in 1876–79. A boy killed himself when attempting to drive a rabbit from a brush pile with the butt of his loaded gun, and a Russian immigrant leaned the muzzle of his shotgun against his body while gathering a few ears of corn when it discharged. "It is another added to the long list of those who have gone to their death through carelessness." In another shotgun accident, a man discharged one barrel to kill a rattlesnake, then while reloading, the other barrel discharged, requiring the amputation of two fingers. Perhaps with tongue in cheek, the Hays City *Sentinel* printed the following on May 11, 1878:

"One of the Austrian settlers, in attempting to shoot a snake with a six-shooter, sent a bullet through the palm of his hand.... He is offering the shooter for sale."[28]

In San Francisco in 1841, before the gold boom, Robert Davis asked William Dane Phelps, master of the ship *Alert*, to take a shot at a crow on a post.

> I took [my] rifle and wiped it out, and felt sure of there being no charge in it, on blowing into the muzzle I found there was some obstruction and put a cap on the nipple to blow it out. Mr. D[avis] took the gun in his hand to examine it and I turned the muzzle towards my own head to feel if any wind came out, and desired him to pull the trigger. Had he done so, I should have been killed instantly. As it was, he placed the rifle in my hands saying that he was unacquainted with guns and would hold his hand at the muzzle to feel if any wind came out. The first cap broke without any effect, but at the second trial the result was that a bullet passed through the middle of his right hand.

Fortunately the bullet was of a small caliber and did no serious damage. The bullet passed through a room where people were eating breakfast, directly in line with a chair, which luckily was vacant at the moment.[29]

The accidents recorded here and the warning they carry are worth noting even today. One of the author's friends lost an acquaintance who climbed a tree carrying his loaded flintlock by the muzzle. Somehow the gun discharged and later he was found dead hanging upside down from the tree.

On the plains, the sight of a herd of bison often caused great excitement. One female traveler in 1857 noted that eight or ten of the company gave chase, "some on foot, some on horseback, armed with muskets, revolvers and knives." One of the hunters crept to within sixty yards of a bull and fired a load of buckshot from a musket. The bull ran off, showing little inconvenience. A rider armed with a Sharps rifle gave chase and brought the unfortunate animal down with a single shot. Once across the central plains, the bison herds were behind and the perceived threat of Indian attacks had dissipated and guns generally were put aside.[30]

Lansford W. Hastings, a young Ohio lawyer, in 1842 with more than 150 others made the overland trip from Missouri to the Willamette Valley of Oregon, guided during the later portion of the route by mountain man Broken Hand Tom Fitzpatrick. To promote emigration to the Oregon-California region, in 1845 he published his first guidebook for those contemplating resettlement there. The volume was more a description of the California-Oregon region than a detailed guide for the journey itself, but it was among the first such guides. In recommending the equipment and supplies for the journey, Hastings dwelt at some length on firearms.

> All persons . . . should equip themselves with a good gun; at least, five pounds of powder, and twenty pounds of lead; in addition to which, it might be advisable . . . for each to provide himself with a holster [pair] of good pistols, which would . . . be found to be of very great service, yet they are not indispensable. If pistols are taken, an additional supply of ammunition should, also, be taken; for, it almost necessarily follows, that the more firearms you have, the more ammunition you will require, whether assailed by Indians, or assailing the buffalo. If you come in contact with the latter, you will find the pistols of the greatest importance; for you may gallop your horse, side by side, with them, and having pistols, you may shoot them down at your pleasure; but should you come in mortal conflict with the former, the rifle will be found to be much more effective, and terrific; the very presence of which, always, affords ample security.[31]

Members of the gold-seeking Washington City and California Mining Association elected J. Goldsborough Bruff as captain. He, too, included in his gold rush journal specific recommendations concerning firearms to others intent on crossing the plains.

> A few substantial reliable arms are all that is necessary. A U.S. per[cussion] rifle [presumably Model 1841 Mississippi], or other strong, plain good rifle, that will stand wear and tear. A brace of U.S. holster pistols—or if you do not ride a good Colt, or a pair of short, large bore, strong & plain, belt pistols. . . . Some may prefer a double barrel [shotgun]. If thick barrels, pretty long, carrying oz. [ounce] ball, and quite plain & strong, it is best for those unaccustomed to the rifle—You want no fancy rifle, full of

gingerbread work, and sundry silver fixings, with a stock so slight that it must be laid down with great care; and carrying a ball only suitable for squirreling.—No fancy pistols of the same order.... Everything for such a march, should be of the plainest & most serviceable character—made for good hard use, and fit to stand service.

For oiling guns, deer marrow from leg bones cracked and heated so the oil would run out was the suggestion. Never grease a rifle patch, he offered, but merely moisten it with your lips when loading.[32]

> Percussion caps, are, like matches, to be secured from damp. Walker's London, are undoubtedly the best, except the large Government ones;—these last are only applicable to the large cones of Government pieces—Both sorts will stand considerable damp without material injury; while common ones would be ruined. Powder, too, if exposed to damp, cakes and...is deteriorated. If you wish lead to melt quickly, place some good hot coals on it, in the ladle, which will melt it in half the time it would otherwise take. The plumb, or conical ball, called generally, by hunters, slug shot;—make a larger hole than a round one, and are therefore preferable when the latter are too small for any particular game.[33]

Through inference from Bruff's comments, both government-owned Hall and Jenks breech loading carbines may have been included among other models of surplus arms made available at low cost to emigrants. He specifically mentioned these two by name and of the Hall carbine wrote:

> An excellent and convenient cavalry gun, and handy for mere defense, for pedestrians, having a sling with spring loop, to hook into ring of [the] piece. And if tree'd by a grizzler, having one of these slung to you, with plenty of cartridges, you are safe. But for such game, they should carry an ounce ball. It is too short for deer-hunting, but about the right calabre [sic]; and regular hunters would never use it in place of a

rifle. Jenk's rifle seems to be an excellent arm, too, but those we had, carry'd too small a ball, and were too frail in stock & mountings, for service.[34]

Here it isn't clear whether Bruff referred to the Jenks Navy rifle made by N. P. Ames or the Jenks patent carbine.

His brief comment concerning Colt carbines could only apply to the Paterson revolving arms and unquestionably referred to their occasional habit of discharging more than one chamber at a time. "The danger attending them is known." Allen pepperboxes were described as: "Good for self defense in a City, or crowd."[35]

> [Flintlocks] are as good as any, till late in season, or change of climate, rendering failure weather liable. Of course, in California, during wet season, can not be depended upon. They are the cheapest arms, and the very article to trade off to Indians, along route, for horses, poneys [sic], buffalo robes, &cc. Being, with a few [powder] charges, & flints, the most valuable thing you can offer them. If you have a Government rifle, substitute a wooden ram-rod for the steel one:—lighter, & no rattling.[36]

Cartographer T. H. Jefferson may have been the child of Thomas Jefferson and the slave Sally Hemings. In 1849 he published an eleven-page guide with maps for a central route from Independence, Missouri, to San Francisco. For arms and ammunition, he suggested taking:

> [A] single-barrelled rifle. Jake Hawkins [Hawken] of St. Louis makes a good article for mountain service, price $25. Also Campbell & Hoffman, of the same place. One brace U.S. holster-pistols (percussion locks): from one to five pounds of powder, in oval or flat canisters; best split and ribbed percussion caps, [in] tin cases; bullets, bullet screw, ladle, lead;...powder-flask; oil-cloth gun case...and spy glass.... [The firm of Hoffman and Campbell may have been a Hawken subsidiary.][37]

William Swain wrote home from Buffalo, New York, on April 11, 1849, following the initial stage of his journey to the California gold fields. "I have priced all the rifles in town

Pair of US Model 1842 pistols by Henry Aston with their saddle holsters carried to the Salt Lake Valley by Dr. William Richard, a member of the initial Mormon party that crossed the plains in 1847. He had been present in the jail when the mob killed Joseph and Hyrum Smith but was not harmed. (Courtesy: Daughters of Utah Pioneers Memorial Museum, Salt Lake City)

and . . . I can get one that will answer for about $15 and good revolvers at the same price. . . . Mr. Hutchinson bought a double-barrel fowling piece for $18 to take along." During an Indian alarm, a Baptist minister with one train armed himself with a pair of dueling pistols, but seeing how nervous he was, a companion suggested he help guard the stock.[38]

Some emigrants took advantage of the War Department's February 1849 offer to sell guns and ammunition at cost to civilians bound for California and Oregon. A correspondent for the New Orleans *Daily Picayune*, John E. Durivage, wrote back to his newspaper in March 1849 as his party embarked on their overland journey, "the company was furnished with brand-new Mississippi [Model 1841] rifles and percussion-locked [Model 1842?] holster pistols from the United States arsenal at Baton Rouge[39]

Bernard Reid in 1849 contracted with the Pioneer Line for passage across the plains in a mule-drawn light wagon from Independence, Missouri, to San Francisco for $200. Other entrepreneurs made plans to transport emigrants,

but the Pioneer Line was the only one which actually completed a trip in 1849, reaching their destination a month late after much hardship. Reid was another gold seeker who outfitted himself with government arms.

> Under an order from the war department applicable to all bona fide emigrants to California or Oregon, I purchased at cost an army rifle, a brace of holster pistols, 200 rounds of ammunition and the small accessories that go with firearms. I had previously purchased a belt revolver,—an Allen five-shooter commonly called a "pepperbox."

Reid lost one of his holster pistols during a buffalo chase on horseback and on one occasion used the iron ramrod from his rifle to kill a rattlesnake. His companion also availed himself of the government's offer and purchased a rifle.[40]

On the back of this daguerreotype's case is written in ink: "Charles G. Alexander, King George County, Virginia. Taken on his way to California. April 1849." He holds a M1841 Mississippi rifle and has a pepperbox thrust in his belt. The knife is very similar to the Model 1848 Ames rifleman's knife, of which the army in 1849 received one thousand for issue to the Regiment of Mounted Riflemen. Alexander survived the trek west and during the Civil War served with a Virginia cavalry regiment. (Courtesy: Herb Peck Jr.)

Not long into the trip, Reid chose to test the accuracy of his Allen pepperbox—with an unanticipated outcome.

Pinning a paper target to a tree I stepped off twenty paces towards the camp; turned and fired. While examining the score after firing, I held the revolver muzzle downwards. This, without my knowing it, caused one of the bullets to roll down the unevenly bored barrel and lodge in the muzzle, thus leaving an air-space between powder and ball.... I fired again at the same target. Almost instantly Mr. Tiffany came galloping up from behind

me, nearly running me down with his horse, and angrily demanding why I shot at him. I assured him I had not, and pointed to the tree I had fired at in the opposite direction. Still fuming with anger he said he knew better, and that the bullet had almost grazed his face.... A look at my smoking revolver solved the mystery. The explosion of the powder in the air-space between powder and ball had burst off a longitudinal strip of the cylinder [barrel cluster] in such a manner as to hurl it directly backwards, nearly killing or wounding Mr. Tiffany, who was now profuse in his apologies for having charged me with felonious shooting. I soon after threw away the worthless cylinder, but kept the butt, which I afterwards wore for awhile in the mines, projecting from my belt as a make-believe piece of armor to conform to the prevailing custom of going armed.[41]

Before Reid discarded the Allen, he did note in a journal entry for May 25: "I tried my 'pepper-box' with effect on a rattlesnake and a moccasin." Despite their lack of accuracy, the pepper-box with its revolving cluster of barrels found favor with many individuals during the 1840s and 1850s who needed an inexpensive yet reliable weapon for possible use at close range.[42]

Young Sam Clemens, better known as Mark Twain, in describing his journey by stagecoach to Carson City, Nevada Territory, poked fun at the weapon chosen by a fellow passenger:

He wore in his belt an old original "Allen" revolver, such as irreverent people called a "pepperbox." Simply drawing the trigger back, cocked and fired the pistol. As the trigger came back, the hammer would begin to rise and the barrel to turn over, and presently down would droop the hammer, and away would speed the ball. To aim along the turning barrel and hit the thing aimed at was a feat which was probably never done with an "Allen" in the world.... She [the Allen] went after a deuce of spades nailed against a tree, once, And fetched a mule standing about thirty yards to the left of it. Bemis did not want the mule; but the owner came out with a double-barreled shotgun and persuaded him to buy it, anyhow. It was a cheerful weapon—the "Allen." Sometimes all its six barrels would go off at once, and then there was no safe place in all the region round about, but behind it.[43]

Some of the more enterprising emigrants had the foresight to bring supplies of wood with them not only to replace wagon tongues, axletrees, or wagon wheel spokes, but also for barter. Hickory, for example, was invaluable to both the white and red man.

Hickory sticks suitable for bows, are carried westward by emigrants, as they find a good market for them in wigwamland [Indian country], where they bring a buffalo robe each; "gun-sticks," as wood for gunstocks is called, bring one dollar each from Indians or trappers.[44]

The Oregon Emigrating Company reached a well-known landmark on the Oregon Trail on July 30, 1843—Independence Rock. There Jim Nesmith and other young men escorted some young ladies to the rock where several added their names in a crude paint composed of "gunpowder, tar and buffalo grease" when they found the rock was too hard to carve.[45]

A display ad in the *Missouri Republican* newspaper of November 27, 1845, by dealer and gun maker T. J. Albright of St. Louis reflected the variety of arms available to westbound and other customers.

Manufacturer of Shot Guns, Rifles and Pistols. Who has always on hand and for a large stock of Allen's 6 barrel Revolvers, of all sizes; Colt's Cylinder Repeating Pistols, Hair Trigger do., and a variety of other Pocket, Belt & Holster Pistols, also, a large stock of English, German & French twist double and single Guns, of all lengths and Calibres.[46]

Before leaving for Santa Fe in 1856, James Ross Larkin recorded in his diary an inventory of goods he purchased for the trip. Firearms and related items included:

1 Pistol Colts Army Revolver [.44 Dragoon presumably]		$29
1 " Small [.31 caliber] Pocket		17.50
1 Hawkins [*sic*] Rifle		28
1 Double Bbl Shot Gun		
1 Bullet Pouch		2.25
1 Shot do [ditto]		2.25
1 Bullet [lead] Ladle		
3 " Moulds		
1 Bdl [bundle] Bar Lead 25# 7c [cents]		1.75
1 Box Elys Per[cussion] caps W. P. [waterproof] Sm		1.40
3 " " " Large 2.25		6.75
4 Boxes Gun Wads		1.75
5 Boxes Buck Shot Cartri[d]ges		
4 Extra Nipples SG [shot gun?]		1.75
10 Pds No 5 shot		
5 " " 6 do		2.00
10 " " Goose do		

On October 23, 1856, six men, white, Indian, and Mexican, conducted a shooting match. Larkin with his St. Louis–made muzzle loading Hawken rifle "had the honor of being the best shot at the longest distance about 275 yards . . . , & third best at short distance."[47]

In 1859 a decade after the California gold rush had begun, Capt. Randolph B. Marcy published *The Prairie Traveler,* a guidebook for an overland journey.

> Every man who goes into the Indian coun-
> try should be armed with a rifle and a
> revolver, and he should never, either in
> camp or out of it, lose sight of them. When
> not on the march, they should be placed in
> such a position that they can be seized at an
> instant's warning; and when moving about
> outside the camp, the revolver should be
> worn in the belt, as the person does not
> know at what moment he may have use for
> it. Colt's revolving pistol is very generally
> admitted, both in Europe and America, to
> be the most efficient arm of its kind known
> at the present day.[48]

Not all emigrants crossing the Mississippi were bound for the far west. Despite Long's description of the central plains as "the great American desert," Iowa was organized as a territory in 1838, Kansas and Nebraska in 1854. As communities were established and people had time for social events, shooting sports became increasingly popular with rifle matches being a common holiday event. E. F. Ware was growing to manhood in Iowa in the 1850s and recalled:

> The Germans were, of all foreigners, the
> ones who seemed most devoted to shoot-
> ing, and they had their target societies that
> would compete in shooting against the
> hunters and trappers and pioneers; so that
> shooting for beef and turkeys was con-
> stantly going on. . . . If a person took a dol-
> lar's worth of shots, ten shots at ten cents a
> shot, and shot at the target, they measured
> the distance of each bullet-hole from the
> center of the target, and if the ten shots
> aggregated a distance of, say, ten inches,
> that was his "string." The person who made
> the shortest "string" got the beef. . . .
> Everyone had his own target, a board
> drawn and decorated according to the taste

of the shooter . . . [and] people had their boards as trophies. . . . Once in a while a particularly good marksman would be "barred," . . . a matter of great pride.[49]

The history of the Mormon Church in the west is not without controversy, in particular the threat of armed conflict with a federal army and church members' involvement in the infamous Mountain Meadows Massacre of more than one hundred white women, men, and children emigrants in September 1857. However Mormon settlers in Utah through common effort and irrigation changed the Salt Lake Valley into a fertile site for agriculture. In 1846 following persecution in Missouri and Illinois, the Mormons in various stages began their epochal journey to what they hoped would be their promised land along the western slopes of the Wasatch Mountains near the Great Salt Lake. The vanguard arrived in the summer of 1847 and by that fall four thousand had reached the valley. In 1856 there were twenty-two thousand Saints living in the Great Basin.

Following the murder of church leaders Hyrum and Joseph Smith in 1844, planning for a westward exodus intensified, which included the gathering of arms. Officials directed Orson Pratt to purchase guns and on October 31 of 1845 he wrote to President Brigham Young:

> I received as communication relative to
> obtaining six-barreled pistols for self-
> defense. I immediately took active measures
> to obtain them and the present prospect is
> good. I think I shall obtain several hundred
> dollars for that purpose. The six-inch pis-
> tols can be obtained at retail for twelve
> dollars. The wholesale price is ten dollars
> but by agreeing to take some thirty or
> forty they can be obtained at nine and
> one-half dollars.

In November 1845 he returned from New York with $400 worth of "Allen's revolving six-shooting pistols [pepper-boxes]." Personal weapons as well as such muskets as were church property were gathered along with four artillery pieces—two six-pounders, one three-pounder, and a twelve-pound cannon. Small arms already in the church's inventory were readied for the journey. Dances were held, the admission price being the cleaning of a gun; other church members sometimes were paid for such work.[50]

As arrangements for the move west by the first group continued, Brigham Young divided the emigrants into

Above, an Allen pepperbox with New York sales agent J. C. Bolen's name on the hammer. A silver plate inset in the handle states: "Joseph Smith held this when Martyred June 27, 1844." Smith was the founder of the Church of Jesus Christ of Latter-day Saints and was murdered while jailed in Carthage, Illinois. This Allen and the London-marked English pocket pistol below were reportedly smuggled into the jail where Joseph and Hirum Smith were held prisoner. (Courtesy: Museum of Church History and Art, Salt Lake City, UT)

military-like companies and wisely included a variety of essential occupations among the pioneers—blacksmiths, carpenters, doctors, gunsmiths, and others. The October 29, 1845, issue of the *Nauvoo Neighbor* recommended supplies for each group of five Saints crossing the plains. These included one good musket or rifle to each male over the age of twelve, one pound of gunpowder, and four pounds of lead as well as numerous other items such as cloves, dried peaches, seed, wrought iron nails, soap, and cayenne pep-

per. Included in the marching orders Young issued, he directed that "every man is to have his gun and pistol in perfect order" and that "each man is to travel with his gun on his shoulder, loaded, and each driver have his gun so placed that he can lay hold of it at a moment's warning." Safety was a concern for he added: "If the gun has a cap-lock, he should take off the cap and put on a piece of leather to exclude moisture and dirt; if a flint-lock, he must take out the priming and fill the pan with tow or cotton."[51]

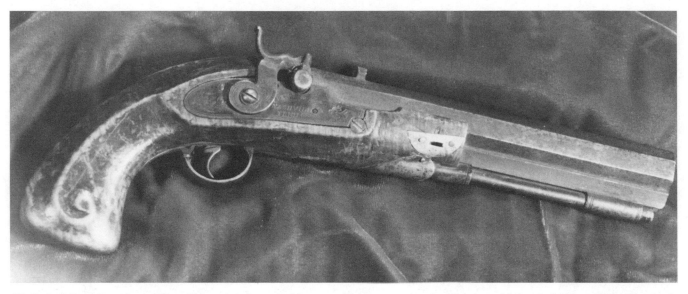

Plain but functional, a .50 caliber pistol carried by one of Mormon leader Brigham Young's bodyguards. The lock was made by John Kirkman of Nashville, Tennessee. (Courtesy: Daughters of Utah Pioneers Memorial Museum, Salt Lake City)

Among the pioneer Mormon gunsmiths was Jonathan Browning, who fathered twenty-two children, the last born when he was seventy-one. Four of his sons became gunsmiths—David, Matthew, Wesley, and the prolific John Moses Browning. Jonathan worked on Mosquito Creek, south of Kanesville, Iowa, before moving to Utah in 1852. He designed and produced hand-rotated revolving cylinder rifles and a simpler form of repeating "slide gun." He advertised the latter as "from 5 to 25 shooters, . . . not equaled this far East. . . . The emigrating and sporting community are invited to call and examine Browning's improved firearms before purchasing elsewhere." His slide gun magazine was a rectangular multichambered block of iron which was manually slid horizontally through the rifle's frame. The number of slide rifles that Browning made isn't known, but these rifles probably were those mentioned in Hosea Stout's diary, in which he wrote of an anti-Mormon mob from Carthage threatening the Mormon settlement of Nauvoo, Illinois, on June 11, 1846. "They [the mob] were met by a little band of thirty men, in ambush, commanded by Capt. William Anderson & was called the 'Spartan Band' being mostly armed with 15 shooters, who fired upon them and retreated a short distance & fired again thus retreating & firing, holding them at bay."[52]

John Doyle Lee in September 1846 was en route to Santa Fe on a mission for Brigham Young. He apparently had one of Browning's slide rifles for he noted in his diary that one morning he and his companions awoke surrounded by grazing bison. "I took [my] fifteen shooter and walked within 60 or 70 yards of them . . . and it was as much

as I could do to refrain from shooting." Yet another reference to "slide rifles" appears in a description of actions against Ute Indians by Mormons in 1850. "I [Bill Hickman] had a slide rifle; six shots in a slide, and three slides, making eighteen shots on hand."[53]

After settlement at the Great Salt Lake began in 1847, the church's arsenal gradually expanded. In June 1846 Col. Stephen F. Kearny, 1st Dragoons, had authorized the recruitment of five hundred Mormons for twelve months' service during the Mexican War with his Army of the West. They were formed into companies A through E of the Mormon Battalion and they received their arms on August 3–4, 1846, at Fort Leavenworth, Kansas. Most received a flintlock musket, a cartridge box "with heavy leather belt two and one fourth inches wide to carry over the left shoulder," a belt with bayonet and scabbard to carry over the right, and a belt "correspondingly wide and heavy all white leather" to wear about the waist. Other issue items included a knapsack for clothing "so arranged that a strap came in from each shoulder and under the arm with a long strap to reach around our bedding," a canteen, pint cup, clothing, blankets, twenty-four rounds of ammunition, and a haversack "made to swing over our shoulders also." It was "a hevy [sic] load for a Mule," Arariah Smith complained. Also distributed were "a few cap-lock yaugers [Model 1841 .54 rifles] for sharpshooting and hunting purposes." "Stand back, boys; don't be in a hurry to get your muskets; you will want to throw the d——d things away before you get to California" was Capt. James Allen's prediction.[54]

Five-shot "harmonica" rifle by an unknown maker found near the Spanish Governor's Palace in San Antonio, Texas, and photographed in 1925. (Courtesy: The San Antonio Light Collection, Institute of Texas Cultures)

The battalion's march to Santa Fe and to California involved thirst and near starvation; at one point they were reduced to eating ox guts. Some of these Mormons remained in the gold fields after their discharge; most joined their brethren in Utah. One of the conditions of enlistment was that upon discharge, the men would be allowed to retain their arms and accoutrements. Thus their flintlock muskets were added to the growing Mormon arsenal in the Salt Lake basin. An armory was established and with territorial status granted in 1850, the previously organized Nauvoo Legion continued its existence as territorial militia. This body had grown to more than two thousand in 1852 and sixty-one hundred by 1857. Public arms issued by

the federal government included a twelve-pound mountain howitzer in 1851 and almost two thousand muskets by 1855. Sharps carbines were on hand by late summer of 1852 and Colt revolvers frequently appeared on equipment rolls after 1853. There also were modest attempts within the territory to manufacture revolvers, and David Sabin in 1854 placed newspaper ads announcing he was doing so.[55]

In 1852–53 the territorial legislature encouraged the local production of gunpowder and offered $200 to the first person who produced one hundred pounds and $100 for the second one hundred pounds. Apparently no one succeeded in any attempts until the growing crisis between the federal government and the Mormons in 1857 prompted the production of modest quantities. To encourage local production of items necessary for the colony, in 1856 the Deseret Agricultural Society was formed. The list of premiums offered at its annual fair in 1860 included such diverse categories as the best five pounds of gunpowder, shovel, fire engine, bedstead, example of book binding, woolen shawl, gallon of molasses, and essay on horticulture. The list also offered $5 for the best rifle, $3 for second best, and the same amounts for the best and runner-up revolving pistols.[56]

Both David Sabin and William Naylor in 1857 were employed to produce imitation Colt revolvers, but their output was small. However world traveler Richard F. Burton when visiting Salt Lake City in 1860 noted that "the imitations of Colt's revolvers can hardly be distinguished from the originals," although he didn't identify them as to maker. Insufficient evidence exists to substantiate claims that Jonathan Browning, too, made Colt copies. Eighteen years after the Mountain Meadows incident, repentant participant Bishop Philip Klingensmith testified as to the types of arms his companions carried. "They [We] were armed with revolvers, and United States Yougers [probably M1841 Mississippi rifles]; and such guns as settlers generally have through this territory. Some revolvers, yougers, shotguns and so forth." By the late 1860s, Mormon militia returns reflected the replacement of muzzleloaders with such single-shot breechloaders as Joslyns, Ballards, Wessons, and Sharps as well as Spencer and Henry repeaters.[57]

In 1857 at the height of tension between Mormons and nonbelievers or gentiles, one band of non-Mormon immigrants sought to obtain supplies despite Brigham Young's prohibition against such trade. James Stuart and a companion went to Bishop Barnard's fort at Malad City, "as those few adobe huts were called." The travelers obtained flour, bacon, coffee, and sugar but only after they agreed to pick up their goods at midnight and drive the remainder of the night so as to be as far away as possible by dawn.

> He also sold James a small quantity of powder, lead, and percussion caps, for our muzzle loading rifles. We were also armed with the old style powder and ball Colt's navy [Model 1851] revolvers and they were mighty good weapons, too, as I often proved by killing deer, antelope, and mountain sheep, with mine at one hundred yards distance.[58]

In writing of his journey to California in 1860, Richard Burton dwelt at some length on his preparations and made suggestions to others. He carried two revolvers, probably Colts from his comments which follow. In St. Louis, he invested $25 in a "Hawkins" (Hawken) style rifle, a "long top-heavy rifle" weighing twelve pounds and about .40 caliber, "a combination highly conducive to good practice." For those who preferred a lighter weapon, he suggested a Maynard breechloader with an extra barrel for shot. "If Indian fighting is in prospect, the best tool without any exception, is a ponderous doublebarrel [sic], 12 to the pound, and loaded as fully as it can bear with slugs." Reminiscent of the Lewis and Clark expedition, he noted that "the last of the battery [presumably his] was an airgun to astonish the natives."[59]

He went on to recommend that from the time one left St. Joseph until the traveler reached Sacramento or Placerville in California,

> the pistol should never be absent from a man's right side—remember it is handier there than on the other—nor the bowie knife from his left. Contingencies with Indians and others may happen, when the difference of a second saves life; the revolver should therefore be carried with its butt to the fore, and when drawn it should not be leveled as in target practice, but directed towards the object, by means of the right forefinger laid flat along the cylinder whilst the [middle finger] draws the trigger. The instinctive consent between eye and hand, combined with a little practice, will soon enable the beginner to shoot correctly from the hip; all he has to do, is think that he is pointing at the mark, and pull. As a precaution, especially when mounted upon a kicking horse, it is wise to place the cock upon a capless nipple, rather than trust to the intermediate pins [as on a Colt].
>
> In dangerous places the revolver should be discharged and reloaded every morning, both for the purpose of keeping the hand in, and to do the weapon justice. A revolver is an admirable tool when properly used; those, however, who are too idle or careless to attend to it, had better carry a pair of "Derringers."[60]

Granville Stuart probably was unaware of Burton's recommendation of a Maynard, but in 1861 a friend from

Bible inscribed on the cover "PRESENTED BY RUS-SELL, MAJORS & WADDELL" and given to one of its teamsters in 1858. The freighting firm made a practice of giving Bibles to its employees. (Courtesy: Nebraska State Historical Society)

Fort Benton, Montana Territory, brought him a .50 Maynard, a novelty at the time, and a supply of reloadable brass cartridges. "The first lot of cartridges that he loaded he had used his powder flask and measured the powder exact, and he had been doing some remarkable shooting on his recent hunting trips and we had all been bragging... on the gun and his marksmanship." Eventually a shooting match was arranged with an old Indian named Pushigan who had a "long, heavy muzzle loading rifle of about forty caliber and on which he had a sight made of hoop iron." Betting began with modest amounts of $1 or so but the distance increased from one hundred to five hundred yards as did the wagers. "Old Pushigan began carefully manipulating his hoop iron sights and made a bulls-eye at every crack of the rifle, while Granville made but one good score. By this time our side was flat broke and afoot." The next day Stuart reloaded the brass cartridge cases, carefully measuring the forty grains of powder in each. After setting up a target,

he found he could make a bulls-eye almost every crack of the gun at two, three, five and six hundred yards. The trouble the day before was that he had loaded his shells by guess and there was too much powder in some, and in others not enough, which accounted for the bad shooting on Sunday.[61]

As communities developed in the central plains, some individuals established themselves in the gun making business there. Representative of such was William Rotton, who emigrated from England about 1850 and settled in Nebraska City, Nebraska Territory, about 1857. His selection of a site was a fortunate one since in 1858 the firm of Russell, Majors, and Waddell chose the location for their freighting depot. Gold discoveries in the Rockies in 1858–59 and in Montana in 1862 added to the city's significance as an outfitting center for miners as well as for overland freighting of civilian and military goods.

While Rotton made some rifles, the repair of guns for others constituted a portion of his business. "Repairing done neatly and promptly," he advertised. Retail sales of ready-made firearms and other goods, undoubtedly

Remington .50 1867 rolling-block pistol, reportedly used by John MacCannon of Leadville, Colorado. The town got its start in 1859–60 with the discovery of gold, but the boom was over by the mid-1860s. It wouldn't be until later that the "black stuff" that was difficult to separate from the gold was found to be lead ore bearing silver and the silver rush was on! (Courtesy: Colorado Historical Society)

George Chorpenning's Colt M1851 #65897 (ca. 1857) inscribed on the backstrap with his name and "C. & S.L. Mail" (California & Salt Lake Mail). In 1851 with Absalom Woodward he obtained a $14,000 annual government mail contract for monthly delivery by pack mule between Salt Lake City and Sacramento, an important link in transcontinental mail service. Indians killed Woodward in November 1851, but Chorpenning struggled on until William Russell acquired the contract in 1859. On several occasions in the mountains mules froze to death and Chorpenning or his men carried the letter mail on their backs to complete delivery. (Courtesy: Greg Martin)

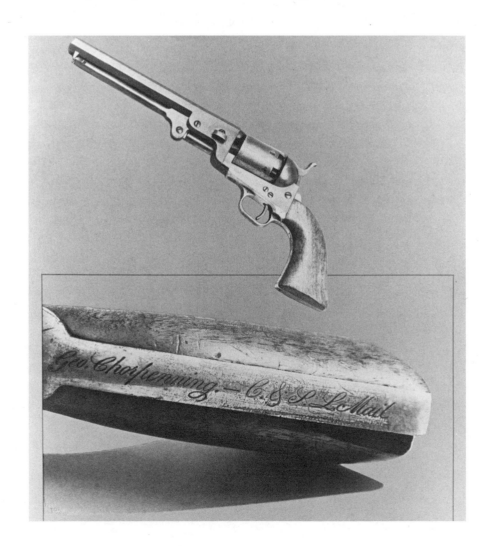

This Colt M1849 Pocket Model (#92067) bears the inscription on the backstrap "C. & S. L. Mail," representing Chorpenning's "jackass mail." (Courtesy: John G. Hamilton)

including many from the east, were also significant. As an example, the *Nebraska City News* for December 7, 1867, included a notice that the steamboat *Hensler* had brought him "a large lot of Rocky Mountain Rifles, double and single barrel shotguns, revolvers, breechloading derringers, and a large stock of sporting apparatus."[62]

Rotton had local competition in the mid-1860s from Alexander McAusland Jr. and brothers George and Frank Freund, but it was short-lived. The former returned to Omaha while the Freunds moved westward, following the construction route of the Union Pacific Railroad. By 1870 Rotton changed his newspaper ad to eliminate the words "all kinds of rifles and shotguns made to order." In their stead, he added a reference to the availability of fixed ammunition and baseballs and bats! A year later he ceased advertising himself as a gun dealer.[63]

The Wesson brothers each held a prominent place among arms makers. Daniel B. was a cofounder of Smith & Wesson, Edwin was noted for his high quality percussion target and sporting rifles, while Frank's name appears on his metallic cartridge pistols, pocket rifles, derringers, sporting rifles, and revolvers manufactured with Gilbert Harrington. It probably was one of Edwin's Massachusetts-made rifles which figured in a Texas incident reported in 1847.

A group of army officers were on a three-day hunting excursion on the Nueces River when one returned to camp with not a deer but the body of an enormous panther.

I shot a busting big buck and saw it fall about a hundred yards from me.... Knowing when "Old King Death" [the name he gave to his Wesson rifle] sends a ball that it is all up with anything it hits, I gave myself no uneasiness about the buck and was crawling upon another when I heard the d——est fuss and growling where the buck fell and concluded the wolves must have got it. I ran up and got within six feet before I saw the cause of this confusion . . . was a panther. He instantly turned towards me and prepared . . . to make another spring at me. I drew up "King Death," saying "It is you or I, old fellow," cracked away, and shot him through the center of the forehead.[64]

The discovery of gold in Montana during the Civil War soon set off another rush for riches and fostered the founding of the Bozeman Trail, a five-hundred-mile shortcut from the Platte River Road to the Montana Territory mines, named for one of its founders, John Bozeman. The trail was in use as an immigrant route for only about four years (1863–66). By the latter date, Indian resentment against white intrusions had increased the dangers of travel to the extent that it was used almost exclusively as an army supply route after that until Red Cloud's war forced the abandonment of army posts along its course. Robert Kirkpatrick's family was one of those that caught the gold fever and left Wisconsin for Montana in April 1863. As a sixteen-year-old youth, Robert kept a detailed diary.

> There were ninety people all told, a great many families among them with children. A good deal of our old train had gone on for their destinations in California and Oregon. We had three hundred shots all told including six shooters, shot guns and squirell [*sic*] rifles and a good many good breech loading rifles among us. I had a muzle [*sic*] loading rifle.[65]

Beginning in the early 1850s, breech loading Sharps rifles and carbines were available to the western traveler. The Civil War spurred development of other makes which loaded at the breech and by the mid-1860s, breechloaders including the repeating Henry and Spencer were seen in increasing numbers in emigrant hands. During the summer of 1867, the army at Fort Morgan in Colorado Territory kept track of guns carried by passing travelers and reported that about 60 percent were breechloaders. In 1865 Charles S. Stobie crossed the plains to Colorado and commented on the popularity of two competing lines of handguns. "Colt's revolvers were the favorite although many carried Remingtons."[66]

Gold Seekers: Rushes to California and Elsewhere

Pistols and knives were usually worn in the belt at the back,
and to be without either was the exception to the rule.
— J. D. Borthwick, 1851[1]

Minor gold discoveries occurred in the 1790s in North Carolina and in the 1830s in Georgia. Later rushes for gold and silver included those to the Pike's Peak region of Colorado (1859), Nevada (1860), Montana (1863–64), South Dakota (1876), Arizona (1877), Idaho (1885), and Alaska at century's end. None matched the impact of the discovery of "something shining in the bottom of the ditch" by John Marshall in a mill race where he was building a sawmill for Johann A. Sutter along California's American River in 1848. Soon the gold easily obtained by simple washing in a pan or rocking in a "cradle" had been uncovered, and from then forward successful mining resulted from efforts by organized companies with more elaborate equipment and greater capital investment.[2]

Word of the itinerant carpenter's discovery spread quickly, and the influx of gold seekers brought statehood to California in just over a decade and transformed what was a trickle of immigrants to the Pacific Coast into a torrent. Travel was accomplished overland or by one of two ways by sea—around Cape Horn or by ship to the Isthmus of Panama which was crossed on foot to secure passage on another ship up the western coast. John M. Leets in 1849 was one of those who followed the latter route and described his preparations for disembarking at the port of Chagres on the isthmus:

The revolvers, each man having at least two, were first overhauled and the six barrels [chambers?] charged. These were put in our belt, which also contained a bowie knife. A brace of smaller pistols were pocketed inside our vest; our rifles were liberally charged and with cane in hand—which of course contained a dirk—and a slung shot in our pockets, we stepped off.[3]

Most who undertook the journey to California had hopes of wealth but few achieved it. Many '49ers returned home disappointed but others remained and sometimes gained financial success not by mining but by operating businesses. One miner amassed more than $8,000 in gold before his claim was worked out. He went back to New York in 1850 but remained only six weeks. When asked why he returned to California, he explained:

I hadn't hardly landed from the steamer in N.Y., before a perfect swarm were around me, trying every means to swindle me out of . . . my dust; some of them got so very near and kind around me, that I had to draw old *sixey*, and tell them just look

African American and white miners toil at Spanish Flat, California, in 1852. (Courtesy: California State Library, neg. #918, Sacramento)

down the barrel and see if they could see anything *green* in her bottom![4]

Regardless of one's success or failure on the West Coast, the California gold rush was one of the most colorful chapters in our history. Not to be ignored, however, was the assault on California's Native American population and the land itself which resulted. It's estimated that 120,000 California Indians succumbed to disease, starvation, and massacre in 1845–60, and in 1850, the California legislature passed an act allowing Indian indenture and legalized the kidnapping of Indian children.

"Seeing the elephant" was a common expression for going to California. It is said to have evolved from the story of a farmer who longed to see an elephant and learned that

a circus was coming to town with one in its menagerie. Driving to town in his wagon loaded with goods for market, he encountered the circus on the road. His team became frightened at the sight of the elephant and bolted, upsetting his wagon and scattering his goods. "A fig for the damage," he cried, "for I have seen the elephant!"

Many '49ers who sought "to see the elephant" kept diaries or later wrote of their experiences. In reading their accounts, Colt revolvers and Allen pepperboxes figured prominently in those instances where handguns were mentioned. Merchant James Eaton advertised in the January 31, 1849, issue of the Boston *Traveller*: "FOR CALIFORNIA Both Colt's and Allen's Revolvers, and a large assortment of other Sporting Articles." Peter Decker journeyed overland in 1849 and remained in the gold mines for two years.

Before E. Deane departed for California, he had a daguerreotype of himself made, well armed with a Bowie knife in hand and a pepperbox, probably an Allen, in a simple socket holster. On the table beside him is a rifle and what may be a Colt Paterson revolver. (Courtesy: John N. McWilliams)

In his diary on February 7, 1851, he wrote: "Bot [sic] me a Colts Revolver 4 in[ch] barrel for $40.00, No. 9770." Perhaps some collector today unknowingly possesses Decker's .31 caliber Baby Dragoon revolver.[5]

To easterners who succumbed to gold fever, merchants offered various wares for their journey—jewelry, cloth, tents, portable boats, and daguerreotype images for those "desirous to leave their likeness with friends." Fletcher Westray at 71 Front Street in New York City in December 1848 advertised:

> RIFLES FOR CALIFORNIA—
> THE SUBSCRIBER OFFERS FOR
> SALE...700 of Whitney's [Model 1841]
> celebrated Rifles, with complete

equipments. These Rifles are the same kind as were used by the Mississippi regiment with so much success at the battles of Buena Vista and Monterrey."[6]

That same month, H. E. Cooper of New York offered: "CALIFORNIA—UNITED STATES RIFLES, WELL ADAPTED FOR USE in that country; also, Allen's patent six barreled Pistols, for sale singly or in quantities." A more extensive ad in April 1849 by John W. Baden & Bro. of Washington offered such arms as Colt and Allen revolving pistols, fine English double-barrel fowling pieces, Day's patent cane guns, and Jenk's patent breech loading carbines and rifles. Fayette Robinson's 1849 guidebook suggested arming oneself with "a rifle of the patent of Colt, if

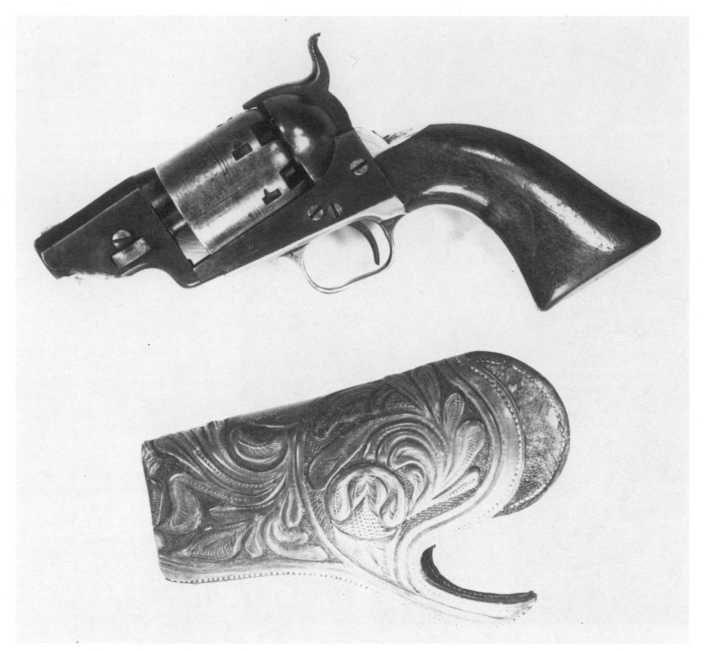

Colt Model 1851 Navy (#4998) converted to a "belly gun." The barrel was cut to a mere two inches, a blade front sight installed, and the barrel recrowned. The tooled holster bears the maker's stamp, "MAIN & WINCHESTER MAKERS SAN FRANCISCO." (Courtesy: Bob Butterfield via Charles L. Hill Jr.)

to be had; if not, the old-fashioned Yager rifle, or a long, double-barreled, smooth-bored gun."[7]

Among the early miners, crime apparently was not extensive. But by 1850, rascals were common. Practically everyone in the mines by then carried a gun, "generally a Colt's revolver, buckled behind, with no attempt at concealment," observed one Englishman. With everyone armed, "robberies are less frequent in the mines than would be expected." Said another '49er: "Arming a man's person with a Colt's revolver and a fine finished Bowie knife, is now considered a part of our toilets." Prompt justice, sometimes

at the end of a lash or even a noose, also promoted lawful behavior. "The liberal and prompt administration of Lynch law had done a great deal towards checking the wanton . . . use of these weapons."[8]

Indian threats sometimes caused alarm as noted in the May 29, 1850, *Placer Times* newspaper of Sacramento. "The Indian disturbances have raised the price of pistols. Last fall it was deemed quite absurd to take fire-arms into the diggings. Now 'Colt's' medium size command $75." The Shasta *Courier* for April 30 of 1853 reported that Capt. McDermitt and several companions had had four mules

Jasper O'Farrell surveyed San Francisco in 1846 and became an early California rancher. His revolver is an engraved Colt M1851. The daguerreotype process by which this image was produced was introduced in 1839 by Louis Jacques Daguerre in France. By a time-consuming process it produced a direct positive on a polished copper sheet. Exposure time at first was three to fifteen minutes but later this was reduced to a minute or less. Its popularity declined in the late 1850s when the less expensive ambrotype, an image on a glass plate, became available. (Courtesy: John N. McWilliams)

shot with arrows near French Gulch. Two express messengers saw fifteen to twenty Indians near the same site several days later "and accelerated their motion down the mountain by a few doses of Colt's pills."[9]

A Frenchman advised his countrymen who were considering coming to San Francisco as to what they might expect. Life was not unusually difficult; men didn't die of hunger if they were willing to work, yet many were far from well-off. A fairly good dinner with wine cost $3.50, laundresses charged $9 a dozen to launder shirts, and a musician could earn two ounces of gold (about $32) by "scraping on a squeaky fiddle for two hours every evening, or by puffing into an asthmatic flute." He warned about the "escaped bandits from Sidney [Australia]" who for a few cents would slug you and drop your body into the bay.

After eight o'clock in the evening it is hardly ever safe to walk alone on the wharves, and even if you go with a friend, you must be sure to carry a revolver. Murders are very common, and it is always unwise at night to go beyond the two or three busy streets where there is no danger.[10]

Vicente Perez Rosales, a visitor to San Francisco, observed an Oregonian approach a gambling table and wordlessly wager a sack of gold. He lost and bet again with another similar sack with the same result. He then silently removed a money belt or "snake," placed it on a card, then drew a pistol, cocked it, and aimed it at the dealer. He won!

.45 underhammer harmonica rifle by H. A. Butler, listed as being in business in Sacramento in 1852. Loads are contained in a block which is slid horizontally through the breech. (Courtesy: Bob Butterfield)

"That's certainly lucky," he said sarcastically as he gathered his winnings.[11]

Etienne Derbec, a French journalist, wrote from Mariposa, California, in 1850.

> Firearms sell readily; I have never yet seen a gun shop; only grocers sell them second hand and at a high price; especially double barrel shotguns. Even Americans obtain them; on many occasions they prefer them to their rifles which are excessively heavy, difficult to load, and with which they are unable to shoot at flocks of turtle doves or partridges which fly along the banks of the streams.
>
> Many people leave for the placers as soon as they think they have enough gold to reach them. Their first gold goes to buy a double barrel shot gun, gun powder, bullets, and large and small lead for hunting or for defending oneself if need be.... The least expensive double barrel shot gun still costs more than an ounce [of gold], and two, three, four ounces if it is decent.... Gun powder costs $3.00...; shot now costs only one. Who would believe that at one time we were forced to buy lead at four dollars or twenty francs a pound in order to make bullets? The further one gets from the cities, the higher the prices are.[12]

The Newark (New Jersey) Overland Company, led by Gen. John S. Darcy, started in the spring of 1849 with eleven wagons and enough mules and provisions for six months. "Each man is armed with a revolving pistol, double barreled gun, and a rifle." A member of the company, Charles Glass Gray, following his arrival in California decided his shotgun was superfluous to his needs and for October 30 wrote in his diary: "Met a customer for my gun & sold him the whole apparatus, shot pouch & powder and caps included for $16—& glad to get rid of all such incumbrances." A day later he regretted his decision. "I found I had sold my gun too cheap yesterday, as double guns are in demand, whilst rifles are almost given away."[13]

About 1838, Ethan Allen introduced what would be a quarter-century-long line of pepperbox revolvers, including the first double action handgun to be made in this country. Allen pepperboxes appeared in .25 to .36 caliber and incorporated a cluster of barrels, usually five or six, rotating about a center pin. In 1849 in the east, the retail list price was $9 or $11 for the larger "dragoon" size. Other makers eventually produced their own pepperboxes—Blunt & Syms, Manhattan, Robbins & Lawrence, and others—but those by Allen and his various associates predominated.

The popularity of the Allen pepperbox in California and elsewhere is reflected in writings of the day. It provided the Colt revolver with significant competition. Not only was the pepperbox less expensive, but the double action models were faster firing than Colt's single action handguns. However, once the shooter got more than a few feet from his target, the chances of hitting it diminished dramatically. Most pepperboxes were double action only and the long trigger pull, usual lack of sights, generally poor pointing characteristics, and impetus of the rotating cluster of barrels all destroyed accuracy except perhaps across a gambling table. When the term "pepperbox" came into being isn't clear, but it was in use by the time some '49ers began writing of their experiences.

The gold rush was a boon to some eastern arms makers as well as other merchants. The Norwich (Connecticut) *Courier* on January 25, 1849, carried the following:

> We doubt whether there is any branch of business in New England which has

Rusty but functional, this .31 Marston pepperbox with a bullet mold rusted shut was found in a building being torn down in Sacramento. (Courtesy: Bob Butterfield via Charles L. Hill Jr.)

received so sudden a stimulus from the California fever as the pistol making business. We were told...that our old friends, Messrs. Allen & Thurber, of Worcester, had on hand some $70,000 or $60,000 worth of their "self-cocking revolvers" [pepperboxes] upon the breaking out of the gold mania, and they were on the eve of curtailing their operations, but such had been the demand for these weapons...that the old stock had been entirely sold off, and the orders for "a few more of the same sort" were coming in so thick and fast as to render it impossible to fill them. We see it stated also that the demand for Colt's pistols has suddenly increased in the same way, and that in order to meet it he has been obliged to enlarge his establishment and greatly add to the number of workmen employed and...he is unable to do more than partially supply the markets.[14]

A Kansan in September of 1856 wrote in his diary "I will buy a pepperbox $6." About the same year a thirteen-year-old boy each evening delivered a carcass of beef from the slaughterhouse to a customer in Leavenworth, Kansas. His three-mile route took him past Curly Jack's combination saloon, gambling den, and house of prostitution on the edge of town.

Many a person went to this immoral resort and left for parts unknown, so it is told by persons who claimed to know.... It was very lonesome along there at night for a boy; however, [I] used to feel quite brave with a large bulldog on the seat with [me] and an old-fashioned pepperbox pistol in [my] hand. Often as I passed this place, I could hear screaming in the house, but I was never molested.[15]

One Allen owner was disappointed with its performance. In March 1849, Howard C. Gardiner prepared for a journey to California via the Isthmus of Panama.

I had also provided myself with a revolver— one of those newly patented pistols known as an "Allen," which for "comprehensive shooting" was truly a wonder, for no matter in what direction it was pointed, there was no telling where the bullet might strike. I took the pistol out in the yard one day for a little practice, and to say that I was astonished at its performance conveys but a faint idea of my disgust over the results of my experiment.[16]

Already accustomed to the use of firearms, Gardiner set up a target against a back fence and stepped off a dozen paces. None of his six shots struck the target and he was astonished to find there wasn't a single bullet hole in the fence. Next he aimed at a knothole in a barn door and almost missed the door but the bullet struck just under the eaves, about two feet from the end of the building. That

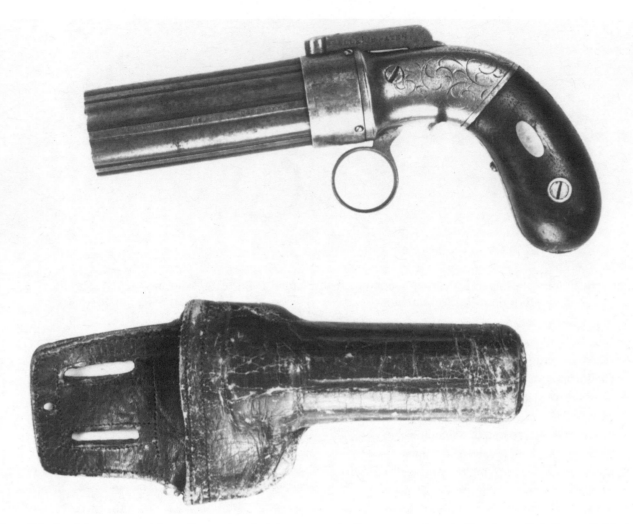

Allen .31 ring trigger pepperbox. Pepperbox holsters are not often encountered. (Courtesy: Bob Butterfield via Charles L. Hill Jr.)

was his first and last experience with the Allen, "which before leaving home I deposited in my trunk, where it remained ever afterwards, till destroyed by fire in San Francisco." His description of its loss bears recounting.[17]

Intending to give the pepperbox to an Indian who helped him build a garden fence, he decided to first unload it. Fearing to hold it, he removed the cluster of barrels, tied a string to it, and placed it in a fire while he retreated some twenty feet away.

> Of course the string burnt off and when the barrel, which I had drawn into the fire with its muzzle from me, got hot, the first explosion occurred. The barrel jumped three feet into the air and fell back with the muzzle directly toward me. As there were five more charges to go off, either of which might hit me, I threw myself flat on the ground and counted with no ordinary anx-

> iety the succeeding reports, and when the sixth charge went off, arose much relieved to find myself uninjured.[18]

Disdaining the gold mines, nineteen-year-old George Dornin was penniless when he arrived in San Francisco in 1849 after an ocean voyage around Cape Horn. With entrepreneurial spirit, he worked as a launderer, sign painter, baker, wallpaper hanger, lunch counter owner, daguerreotypist, and eventually became a state legislator and an insurance agent.

> For protection against the wild Indians and wilder Spaniards, with which imagination peopled the land [California], I provided myself with an "Arsenal" consisting of a double-barreled gun (cost $8.00) with rifled and smooth bore, an Allen's revolver of pepper-box pattern, and a bowie knife of

Allen pepperbox found in 1986 between the California gold rush towns of Georgetown and Buckeye. Three of the barrels are loaded and another has a ramrod stuck in it. (Courtesy: Charles L. Hill Jr.)

formidable dimensions. The former weapon served a useful purpose by employing my time on board ship—cleaning and oiling. The revolver was thrown away, soon after my arrival in California, as being more dangerous to the shooter than to the shot-at; the gun, which . . . I had discharged a few times only, provided me with some ready money when hard-up a few days after I landed, finding sale at $35.00 The bowie knife, alas, was reduced to the ignoble service of carving my meat.[19]

Another "Argonaut of forty-nine," David R. Leeper, was one of a party of ten prospectors with an arsenal of "two rifles, a shotgun, and perhaps a half dozen Allen 'pepperboxes.'" Despite the negative opinion some users had toward a pepperbox, a former army officer found one's presence more than comforting when in Monterey he was assaulted by one of several soldiers he had once had court-martialed. "I put a six-barreled pistol to his breast and he then concluded it was not safe to be in such close contact."[20]

Jules Francois Bekeart was the first of three generations of gunsmiths. In early 1849 he set out by ship for San Francisco and the gold fields. With him he carried an inventory of two hundred Colt revolvers and an equal number of Allen's pepperbox revolvers on consignment from dealer A. W. Spies of New York City. Bekeart set up business as a gunsmith first in Coloma in a shanty with a canvas roof, then relocated to Placerville, and in 1865 moved to San Francisco where he remained until he sold out to his son Philip in 1890.[21]

J. Goldsborough Bruff didn't include an Allen pepperbox among the belongings he carried west in 1849, but he found "1 fine Allen's Revolver" on top of Independence Rock, a famed Oregon Trail landmark in central Wyoming. Later in the California gold fields, two Indians came into camp seeking sugar and coffee. Each had a bow and arrows, but one dressed in a striped shirt, straw hat, and red ribbon also had "an Allen's revolver belted to his side."[22]

Almost the victim of an Allen pepperbox was Darius Pollock, a youthful second engineer on a Pacific mail steamer. He'd earned the rapid promotion after jumping overboard to rescue a small girl. In San Francisco he was attempting to arouse a friend one evening, rattling the door latch. A man appeared in a window above and told him to go away,

at the same time presenting a pistol—one of Allen's six-barrel pepper-boxes, as they were called, good for shooting around corners—and commenced to pop away at Pollock, who stood all the while with one arm akimbo, saying, "Look out, be careful with that d——d thing; you might hit somebody!" His voice and peculiarity of expression disclosed who he was, and the friend came down . . . and let us all in.[23]

Perhaps it was a pepperbox imported from England rather than the largest .36 caliber Allen that figured in an

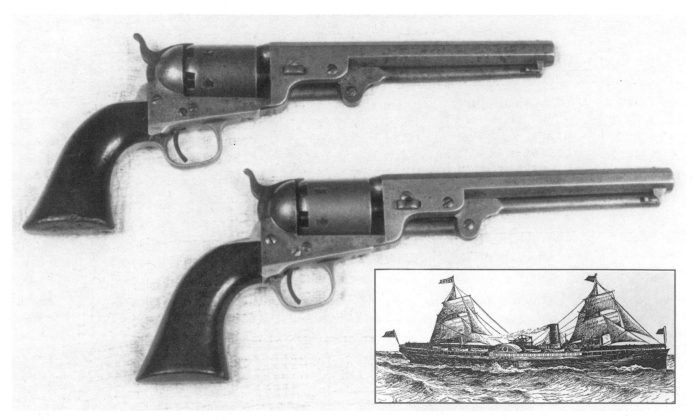

A pair of Pacific Mail Steam Ship Company Colt M1851 Navies (#165953 above, #175596 below). Both guns were manufactured about 1863 and are marked "P.M.S.S. Co." on the backstrap, but the former also is marked "St. Colorado," a steamer launched in 1864. The company began operating in 1848 between New York and San Francisco and in 1867 expanded service to include trans-Pacific sailings to Japan and China. It had a reputation for providing superior service to its passengers, in contrast to Cornelius Vanderbilt's ships which in the 1860s were characterized as "floating pig styes." The drawing is that of the steamer Colorado. (Courtesy: Lt. Col. William R. Orbelo)

altercation in Oregon. James Lemmon in 1847 traveled there to acquire land and fought against Indians in 1848–49. He and another volunteer argued as to ownership of a horse Lemmon captured.

> Father [Lemmon] was not an expert with a six-shooter, but he was a master with what was called a pepperbox, a double-action .50-caliber gun with four barrels that revolved, instead of a revolving cylinder. It had no sights, but at close range it would tear a hole in a man that you could shove a fist through. Father did not then own such a gun, but he had a friend who had loaned him one for the occasion, and he had it handy in his pocket that day. And beside his skill with the pepperbox, he was also given up to be the best wrestler and boxer in the command....

Well, Olney finally walked up, his thumbs stuck in his belt where he had two .44 Colts (army cap-and-ball six-shooters) [Colt Dragoons] and a skinning knife in a scabbard. "Jim..., I have come for my squaw's blue horse." And then he began reciting his reasons for taking the horse.

"There he is, with my saddle on him," Father said. "And it will stay there unless you are a better man than I am, which I doubt....I've seen you do some brave things...but I don't believe you have the nerve to go against a white man on an equal footing...."

He followed his speech by pulling the pepperbox and saying, "Here is a gun that goes off without cocking. I'll drop it on the ground in front of me, and you do the same with your six-shooters. At a signal from a man we'll both agree on, we grab for

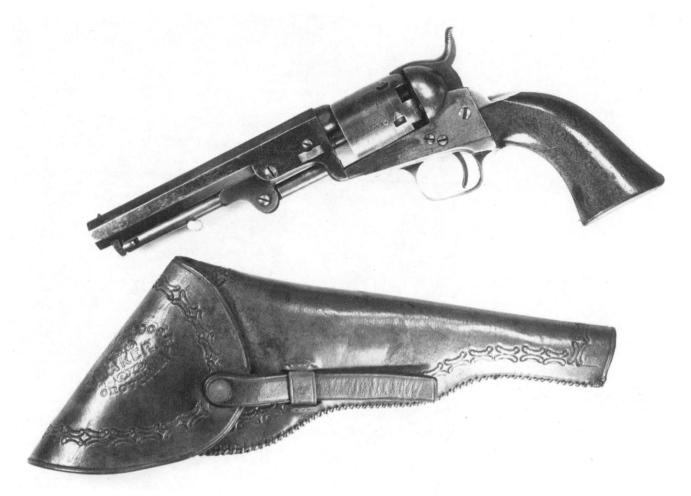

Colt Model 1849 (#50968) made in 1852 and inscribed "GEO. E. EVANS—CALIFORNIA 1853." The holster is stamped on the flap "GEORGE C. MOORE MAKER OROVILLE." (Courtesy: Bob Butterfield via Charles L. Hill Jr.)

them—and I'll fill your hide so full of holes it won't hold corn shucks. Or, if you want to leave the guns alone, I'll thrash you until your squaw won't know you." Olney heard him out, then unconcernedly turned and walked away. "Guess I barked up the wrong tree that time," he said.[24]

Meanwhile in Texas in 1850, Parker H. French, a notorious swindler, purchased a wagon train of eighteen wagons, 176 mules, two horses, and sundry goods. Included in the inventory were 120 United States rifles and 100 Allen revolvers. At that early date, the latter could only have been Allen pepperboxes, not Allen revolvers of later, more conventional design.[25]

Comparable to the Allen pepperbox in popularity in the gold country was the Colt revolver. The obsolescent Paterson-made models undoubtedly were present, but in fewer numbers than the four-pound .44 Dragoon, the medium size .36 Model 1851 Navy, or the smaller .31 cal-

iber pocket models of 1848 (the Baby Dragoon) and 1849. Historian H. H. Bancroft described 1852 as "a year prolific in pistoling" in California. In Sonora, a half dozen prominent citizens, "good men and true," often met in a secluded and unspoiled valley a quarter mile from town. Included in the group were a banker, a judge, and several lawyers. In the valley there stood a magnificent 150-foot pine tree.

> [There] we exercise our skill with Colt's Navy [Model 1851] revolver.... Practice makes perfect, and at twenty five paces it has become no great feat to cut the ace of hearts out of a card. The worst shot has to pay a fine of "Champagne Cocktails," a palatable tonic.[26]

A quarrelsome man by the name of Hayes had an argument with an elderly miner in Nevada City, California, and had threatened to shoot him on sight.

A '49er armed with a Colt
M1848 or M1849 pocket
model. (Courtesy: Bancroft
Library, University of California
at Berkeley)

When the son heard of Hayes' threat against his father, he...bought one of Colt's six-inch revolvers [.31 caliber Model 1848 or 1849 presumably], loaded it without saying a word, walked up Main street, and when he turned up Kiota street he met Hayes and shot him in his tracks....As soon as anyone heard that it was old Hayes that was killed, that was enough; the universal expression was, "Served him right." The boy had a trial that lasted about an hour, and the verdict was "justifiable homicide."[27]

A less bloody shooting in Nevada City occurred in Barker's gambling house involving two doctors.

As they met, one pulled out a pistol and told the other to draw. He threw up his hands and said he was not armed. Whereupon, the first pulled out another pistol and handed it to him, and in less than half a minute the house was clear of people—all that could get out...It was a close range struggle—pop, pop, and then a suspension for a few seconds, when I would stick my head up from behind the barrel to see if it was all over; then it would be pop, pop, and down would go my head again behind the friendly beer cask. At last each had discharged five shots and what seemed very remarkable, neither was hurt. After it was all over they shook

C. F. SCHOLL,
GUNSMITH,
COLT'S PATENT REVOLVING PISTOLS,

D Street, between Second and Third Streets,
MARYSVILLE.

All kinds of Gunsmithing done in the best style, short notice and reasonable terms. ALL WORK WARRANTED.

Revolver's loaded at short notice.— Guns and Pistols bought.

DON'T FORGET I AM PERMANENTLY LOCATED.

Christian F. Scholl repaired and sold Colts and other guns throughout the 1850s in Marysville, California, in the heart of the gold country. Note his offer to reload revolvers, a service gunsmiths and shooting galleries often provided. The firm of Wilson & Evans in their 1857–58 ad in the Sacramento Business Directory also stated: "Pistols cleaned and loaded."

hands and drank together at the bar. The whole affair was a farce. It was simply a case of two mentally diseased doctors administering to each bread pills instead of good honest lead which would have cured both at that short range.[28]

Another bloodless incident occurred in Aurora, Nevada, in 1864. Two roughnecks drinking in a saloon began arguing. As they became louder and more profane, one drew a revolver and the other fled with a crowd following. The fleeing drunk soon collapsed and his opponent prepared to settle their dispute forever—with a toy pistol. "Side-splitting laughter" ended the affair as the crowd realized they'd been duped by the practical jokers.[29]

In Hangtown, California (later renamed Placerville), a large canvas tent housed a gambling hall. One night a buckskin-clad backwoodsman, apparently drunk, entered the crowded hall carrying his rifle and a powder horn. "Boys, I have lived long enough," he shouted. He poured powder from his horn and touched it off as all watched. Suddenly he tore the horn loose and threw it inside the box stove. Without regard to money scattered about the

gaming tables, everyone stampeded to vacate the tent. There was no explosion and in the confusion the prankster slipped away. Gamblers sought him for a week, but eventually laughter replaced anger and he earned the nickname "Black Sand Jack" for that was mostly what his horn contained.[30]

Duels, sometimes formal and other times arranged on a rather casual basis, were one means of settling disputes in the gold country. Weapons of choice might include dueling pistols, rifles, Colt revolvers, shotguns, and even the popular small pocket pistols by Henry Deringer Jr. or one of his imitators, discussed in a separate chapter.

One of the more informal affairs of honor occurred behind the Quartz Hotel in Nevada City between two musicians, one a fiddler and other a vocalist. Armed with pistols, each fired on command and the bloodied singer fell to earth. Fortunately he revived quickly and was back on his feet. "The fact was, the sportive boys had loaded one pistol with powder only, and the other with a cartridge of currant jelly—hence the blood." A duel between clerks in two St. Louis drugstores in 1840 had had a similar bloodless outcome when the seconds prepared two large pills with which to load the pistols.[31]

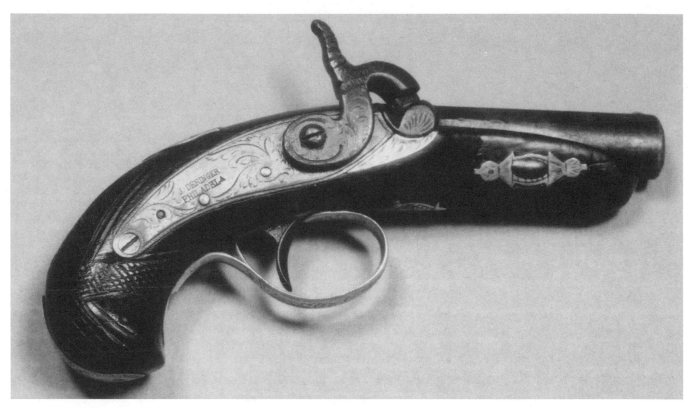

A counterfeit Deringer pistol made by Slotter but marked "J. DERINGER" on the lockplate. The barrel carries the stamp of dealer A. J. Plate of San Francisco. Henry Deringer eventually filed a lawsuit in an attempt to counter such actions.

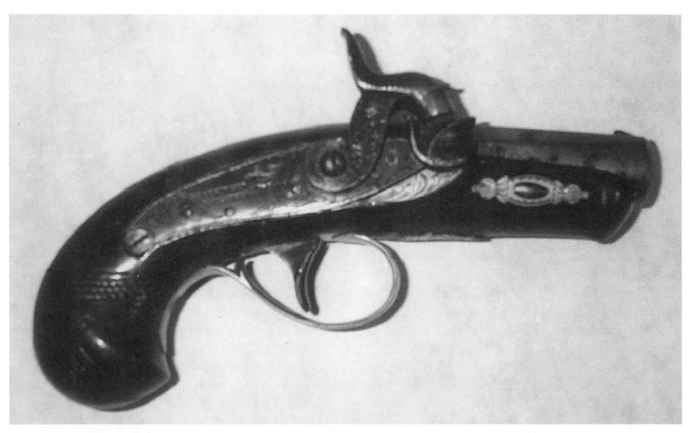

The genuine article, a Deringer sold through Charles Curry of San Francisco and marked on the barrel "C.CURRY/SAN FRANCO CALA/AGENT."

A trio of gold rush period daguerreotypes. Proportionately the Colts appear to be .31 caliber pocket models. (Courtesy: John N. McWilliams)

In a similar encounter at Chinese Camp, California, the seconds conspired to prevent bloodshed.

> The powder was covered with a wad of "tin foil," which being pressed firmly with the old style ramrod, presented the appearance of a bullet, as the concavity in the end of the rod gave the wad a globular shape so that it would deceive anyone not in the secret.... At the word, both pistols were discharged, but through the men stood only twelve paces apart neither was injured.[32]

After another discharge, one of the duelists declared the guns were not loaded with bullets, "but a sight of the four undischarged cylinders [chambers] convinced him of his error." Now Bill Saunders's second explained the whole situation and advised him to drop at the next shot. "Bill saw the point and proved himself equal to the occasion, for when his adversary blazed away the third time, Saunders dropped his weapon, threw up his hands, and fell forward with a dramatic effect that would have done credit to Edwin Forrest." Thoroughly demoralized, Tip Douglass leapt on a nearby horse and dashed through the crowd, threatening to shoot anyone who tried to stop him. When a few days later he became convinced the duel was a sham, Douglass returned to face his humiliation.[33]

The loser in one not so humorous California duel, Harry De Courcey, survived and made a rapid recovery because of careful pre-event preparations. His second, Ed Kemble, agreed to act in that capacity only if he would follow his directions precisely.

A 12-gauge double-barrel shotgun with .38 rifle barrel beneath made by John Bach, active in San Francisco from the early 1850s to the mid-1870s. This is the only known example of a drilling by Bach.
(Courtesy: Bob Butterfield)

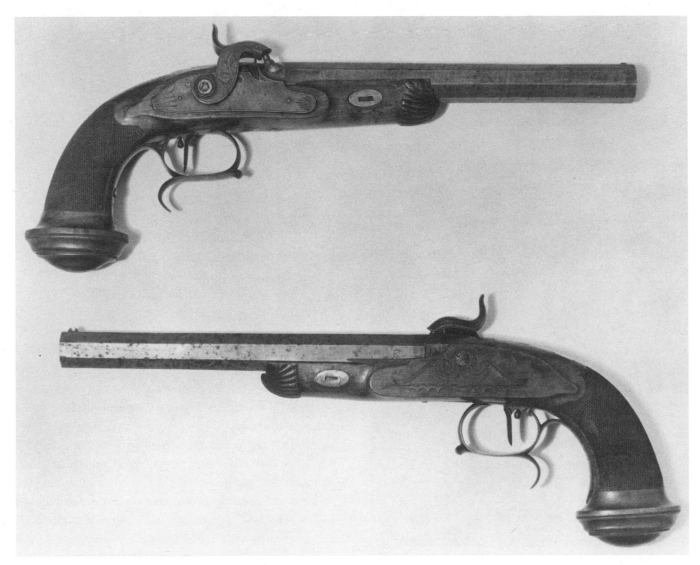

Pistols used in the famed 1859 Terry-Broderick duel in California. (Courtesy: Wells Fargo Bank History Room)

I...sparred with the other parties for time. By dilatory expedients in correspondence I delayed the meeting for three days, so as to get [De Courcey] in condition....I

confined him strictly to his room and placed him on a toast and tea diet, and not much of that. Consequently when he reached the field his stomach was empty, and when his adversary's ball perforated his bowels the flaccid intestine offered no resistance to the bullet, which passed between them and out at the other side. No vital part was affected, and as soon as the exterior flesh wounds healed he would be as sound as ever.[34]

The most publicized California duel was that in 1859 between US senator David Broderick and former California Supreme Court chief justice David Terry, conducted with handsome French single-shot Le Page dueling pistols. An eyewitness wrote later:

Two pairs of pistols were produced. One pair belonged to Dr. Aylette [Terry's attending surgeon], but had been for several months in possession of Judge Terry. The other [pair] had been brought to the field by a French gunsmith, Broderick's armorer. [Terry's second won the toss] and selected the Aylette pistols. Broderick's armorer protested... on the score of the peculiar conformation of the handles, and because the [adjustable] triggers were set to too fine a hair; but nothing came of it.

[The order to fire would be given as] "Fire—one—two," with a pause between each word, the principals to deliver their fire between the first and last words.... The word "fire" was hardly ended when Broderick commenced to raise his pistol. He had got it but partly raised when the charge went off, and the bullet entered the ground about five feet in front of him. Terry, instead of raising his pistol from his side upward, had so held it that he brought it over his shoulder and down, and before the word "two" had been pronounced, fired.... Broderick... put his hands—still holding the pistol—to his right breast, and gradually sank to the ground.... He lingered in great agony for four days, and died.[35]

The duel produced a profound effect throughout California. Many felt the terms unequal.

When McKibben [Joseph C., one of Broderick's seconds] was told by the armorer that the Aylette pistols should not be used because they were set to too fine a trigger, it was his duty to have at once insisted that the spring of the trigger should have been adjusted to an ordinary tension... The provision of the [dueling] code which provides that both parties to a dual shall be placed on a perfect equality as to weapons, was disregarded.[36]

All this mattered little to Broderick.

In flamboyant style and perhaps with tongue in cheek, a duel between Capt. J. B. Van Hagan and R. B. Moyes, both of the Nevada Rifles militia company, was recorded for future generations. The affair took place in Yuba County on June 20, 1860, with army "minnie rifles" at sixty paces.

As the combatants took their stations with anger in their eyes and rifles in their hands, the moon was smeared with blood. Both fired at the word, and upon discovering that they were still sound in body if not in mind, both champions demanded another shot. A sarcastic individual suggested that they put telescopes on the rifles, but he was quickly squelched.... Once more did tongues of flame leap from the angry rifles, and once more did the smoke lift from the field of carnage and reveal the virgin sod free from the contamination of blood. A "big talk" was then held, which resulted in an amicable understanding and both heroes were spared for future deeds of valor.[37]

The weapons used in California duels in the 1850s were as varied as the reasons behind the "affairs of honor." The following summaries reflect this:

Col. J. B. Magruder and Dr. William Osborn—derringers at 12 feet—no wounds except well placed kick from Magruder after doctor fired prematurely and missed.

California Secretary of State Gen. James Denver and newspaper editor Edward Gilbert—rifles—Gilbert fatally wounded at second shot after Denver purposely threw away his first.

Miners at work near Sugar Loaf Hill, Nevada County, in 1852. (Courtesy: California State Library, neg. #916, Sacramento)

Newspaper editor John Nugent and Alderman Cotter—pistols at ten paces—Nugent severely wounded at second shot.

John Nugent and Alderman Hayes—rifles at 20 paces—Nugent again wounded at second shot.

Robert Tevis and Charles Lippincott—double-barrel shotguns loaded with single balls at 40 yards—Tevis was shot through the heart.

Editors Judge O. P. Stidger and Colonel Richard Rust—"Mississippi yager" [Model 1841] rifles at 60 paces (first choice had been "Buckeye" rifles with set triggers but none were found)—affair was settled after two shots produced no injury.

Achilles Kewen and Col. Woodleif—Mississippi rifles at 40 paces—Woodleif was killed with shot to the head at first fire.

Philip F. Thomas and Dr. James Dixon—dueling pistols at 13 paces—latter was mortally wounded.

Capt. Frank Shaffer and James Withered—double barrel shotguns loaded with buckshot, wheel and fire—no injury.

Alfred Crane and Edward Tobey—Colt Navy revolvers at ten paces—Crane was mortally wounded.

Dubert and Ellesler—broadswords—latter severely wounded, former mortally wounded after a duel lasting almost an hour.

David C. Broderick and Judge Smith—Colt Navy revolvers at 10 paces—each fired six shots. Broderick was wounded as he was attempting to clear a jam caused by an exploded cap but bullet struck a heavy pocket watch preventing serious injury.[38]

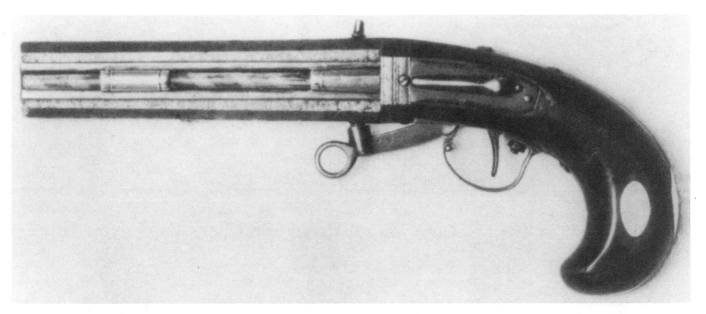

A unique underhammer double-barrel pistol by an unknown maker taken to Colorado in 1847 and on to the California gold fields in 1848. The barrels are rotated manually. (Courtesy: Herschel C. Logan)

One of the most humorous duels occurred in July of 1861 in Nevada City, California, and wasn't fought with firearms but with hydraulic hoses "from whose unerring aim there was no escape." Water was superior to blood as a cleansing agent, the parties agreed. Each combatant was armed with a twenty-five-foot hose with a quarter-inch nozzle, attached to a hydrant. Neither of the drenched but valiant duelists would submit and the affair ended only when one of the hoses "busted."[39]

By 1860 the gold rush of 1848–49 was long over for individuals, and mining was being done generally on a corporate scale. General interest in minerals persisted, however, and involved discoveries of tin, silver, quicksilver, and other valuable minerals in Nevada as well as California. The establishment of the first California geological survey included Professor William H. Brewer. He arrived in Los Angeles in December of 1860 but found that southern California was still somewhat lawless. "We all continually wear arms—each wears both a bowie-knife and [Colt Model 1851] pistol (navy revolver), while we have always for game or otherwise, a Sharp's rifle, Sharp's carbine, and two double-barrel shotguns." He described San Luis Obispo as "a notoriously hard place.... We never go to sleep without having our revolvers handy."[40]

Brewer in December 1860 was invited for dinner at the ranch and vineyard of a wealthy acquaintance.

A touch of the country and times was indicated by our rig—I was dressed in colored woolen shirt, with heavy [Colt] navy revolver (loaded) and huge eight-inch bowie knife at my belt; my friend the same; and the clergyman who took us out in his carriage carried along his rifle, he said for game, yet owned that it was "best to have arms after dark."[41]

Samuel Clemens arrived in Nevada in 1861. He noted that he never had killed anyone with his Colt Navy revolver, however he carried it "in deference to popular sentiment, and in order that I might not, by its absence, be offensively conspicuous, and a subject of remark."[42]

Harold Newmark, a Los Angeles businessman, and his wife sent out invitations on lace paper to a dinner party and dance held at his home (1858).

Men rarely went out unarmed at night, and most of our male visitors doffed their weapons—both pistols and knives—as they came in, spreading them around in the bedrooms. The ladies brought their babies with them for safe-keeping, and the same rooms were placed at their disposal. Imagine... the appearance of this nursery-arsenal![43]

Methods of carrying a revolver varied, but Ed Richardson, a robber and accused murderer, was precise in his procedure. He departed California and Nevada as an escaped fugitive and in 1863 was in Bannock, Idaho Territory,

An ad for Colt and Allen revolvers and Sharps rifles from Horner's 1859 Pike's Peak Guide.

Meyer Freide of St. Louis promoted his wares in this ad in Parker & Huyett's 1859 *Illustrated Miners' Hand-Book and Guide to Pike's Peak.*

using the alias Charley Forbes. Acquaintances described him as excelling the notorious Henry Plummer in

> quickness and dexterity at handling his revolver. He had the scabbard sewn to his belt, and wore the buckle always exactly in front, so that his hand might grasp the butt, with the forefinger on the trigger and the thumb on the cock [hammer], with perfect certainty, whenever it was needed, which was pretty often.[44]

The carrying of firearms in Los Angeles was still widespread in 1866. Rancher Robert Carlisle argued with Under Sheriff A. J. King but friends separated them. The following day, King's two brothers encountered Carlisle

The inscription on the back of this photo gives only the basic details of this well-armed band of gold seekers: "Started for Pike's Peak Feb. 16th 1859, arrived June 18th 1859, returned Nov. 8 '59," but that may say it all. All their rifles and shotguns are muzzle loaders. (Courtesy: Dr. William J. Schultz)

in the saloon at the Bella Union Hotel and a gunfight ensued. When the smoke dissipated, two combatants were dead and a third seriously wounded. One bystander was wounded in the thigh and others had their clothes pierced, "and one of the stage-horses dropped where he stood before the hotel door." Stimulated perhaps by the King-Carlisle tragedy, the Common Council in July prohibited everyone except officers and travelers from carrying a pistol, dirk, slingshot, or sword; but the measure lacked public support, and little or no attention was paid to the law.[45]

A decade after the discovery of California gold, another rush began to Colorado. Playing to New Englanders heading for the new gold diggings, William Read & Son of Boston advertised a variety of firearms in the February 28, 1859, issue of the *Boston Daily Journal.* Colt revolving pistols and rifles at reduced prices along with Sharps, Allen, Greene, and Hall breech loading rifles and carbines. "MINNIE RIFLES, all kinds; DOUBLE RIFLES; DOUBLE RIFLE AND SHOT combined. SINGLE AND DOUBLE

SHOT GUNS of every kind and description, from common iron barrel to finest laminated steel." In addition, customers could choose from "PISTOLS of every variety, single and double barrel. Allen's revolvers [pepperboxes]; Allen's breech-loading pocket and rifled-belt pistols; money belts, pocket compass; Ames' shovels, pickaxes, etc."[46]

Once in Colorado, William Larimer wrote from Denver City on January 2, 1859: "Flour sells for $20 per sack of 100 pounds, and everything in proportion. I was offered $50 for my gun, for which I paid $20 in Leavenworth. I am not a hunter, and I will sell for $60." The area prospered and twenty years later a newspaper reported that Leadville, Colorado, had nineteen hotels, forty-one lodging houses, eighty-two saloons, thirty-eight restaurants, thirteen wholesale liquor houses, twelve blacksmith shops, four theaters, four dance halls, twenty-one gambling houses, and thirty-five houses of prostitution![47]

Duels were not confined to the California mining camps. In Denver City on March 7, 1860, during the

An unusual combination of parts assembled into a crude but functioning gun that once belonged to Ludwig Schmidt, one of the discoverers of placer gold near Granite, Colorado—a barrel from a Leman muzzle loading sporting rifle plus trigger guard and 1862-dated lockplate from a British Pattern 1853 Enfield rifle or rifle musket. The stock appears homemade. (Courtesy: Colorado Historical Society, neg. #F-32799)

A Colorado prospector and his outfit, including a Colt Model 1877 or 1878 revolver. (Courtesy: Cripple Creek District Museum, CO)

Pike's Peak rush, L. W. Bliss, acting territorial governor, and Dr. J. S. Stone, a judge, met to resolve differences that resulted from a toast at a dinner. The affair was arranged in a formal manner, the choice of weapons being double-barrel shotguns loaded with ounce balls, at a distance of thirty paces.

The signal was now given and at the word "one" the doctor discharged his piece, the ball striking the ground some five feet in front of Bliss and harmlessly bounding past him.... The acting Governor raised his gun with the grace of a finished

Prospectors at Bisbee, Arizona Territory, with a string of patient but often ill-used burros. The mounted man carries his rifle in what appears to be a well-used cloth case with the end worn open. (Courtesy: Bisbee Mining and Historical Museum, AZ)

sportsman, and fired. Stone upon the instant let go his gun, gave a groan, and dropped upon the earth. The physicians were with him in a moment, and upon examination found the ball had struck him in the groin. Bliss maintained his ground until assured that Stone was satisfied, and being informed that his antagonist was not mortally hurt, exclaimed, "I thank God he is not." "Wounded honor" now restored, . . . the multitude [of spectators] dispersed.

Unfortunately some hours later the doctors pronounced Stone's wound mortal.[48]

William J. McConnell and several companions in 1863 left Portland, Oregon, for the Idaho gold fields. They were on their way before they realized they had neglected to bring any firearms! Warned that Indians along their route had been stealing horses and mules, they "concluded that it might be wise to provide at least two of our party with

guns." Merchants in a town where they stopped had none for sale, but they were able to buy two muzzle loading rifles from travelers who had passed through the danger zone and were on their way to Portland.

That afternoon, Dixon found a discarded Colt revolver in the grass. It was fully loaded but so badly rusted that the cylinder could not be rotated or the hammer cocked. After dinner, Dixon brought out his find and proposed to restore it to a condition in which it would be useful against horse thieves or others. As a first step, he intended to melt the bullets out of the cylinder.

To carry out his object he had detached the cylinder . . . and dropped it into the glowing bed of coals. The method adopted by Dixon certainly removed the bullets. The first explosion threw the cylinder several feet into the air; as it dropped back into the coals another charge exploded with similar results, until the entire six chambers were discharged. Before the last shot was

C. C. Crews was a participant in the Alaskan gold rush of 1898. The Colt is one of the improved double action models introduced in 1889 with a swing out cylinder. (Courtesy: Provincial Archives of Alberta)

exploded Porter and Dixon had rolled several rods from the fire. Fortunately they both escaped injury.[49]

One aspect of shooting black powder guns which Hollywood seldom portrays is the resulting cloud of gray smoke. Ferdinand Patterson was a sporting man drawn to Oregon in the early 1860s after discoveries of gold there and in British Columbia. A gambler by inclination, he was more than six feet tall and habitually wore an ivory handled revolver and a Bowie knife. In Oregon, he had been acquitted of murdering a ship's captain and later was released after having partially scalped a female traveling companion while attempting to cut off her hair, suspecting her of being unfaithful.

He journeyed to Boise County where Sumner Pinkham was serving as a US marshal for Idaho Territory. To enhance his reputation, Patterson determined to kill the respected lawman and followed the marshal to a warm springs spa outside Idaho City. Several of Patterson's friends accompanied him who would willingly testify on his behalf as witnesses at any trial. He was unable to provoke Pinkham into a fight in the barroom but later found him on the porch awaiting the hack that carried passengers to and from the springs.

Raising his pistol, [Patterson] said,
"Will you draw, you abolition son of a
b——?" As Pinkham turned towards
him, Patterson fired. The smoke of his

pistol partially obscured his view, and dropping on one knee, he leveled the pistol across his arm and fired the second shot. Although the first shot caused a mortal wound, both bullets took their deadly effect.

Patterson attempted to escape on horseback but soon was captured and jailed, although a large force of enraged miners had gathered and threatened to hang him. His trial ended in an acquittal.[50]

Soon after his arrival in Walla Walla in early 1866, Patterson encountered a former Portland policeman named Donohue who had arrested him for his attempted scalping of his paramour. Patterson warned him that "he would settle with him shortly." He repeated the threat when they met again so Donohue armed himself and determined to shoot Patterson on sight. Seeing his enemy in a barber's chair, Donohue approached with his revolver drawn and said, "Patterson, you must kill me, or I'll kill you." Before Patterson could move, Donohue shot him in the mouth and again as the wounded man staggered outside and into the saloon next door where he collapsed. Donohue fired twice more into the prostrate man and soon after surrendered to the sheriff.[51]

The 1850s were a decade in which the Colt revolver gained preeminence and not just in the gold camps. A Texas judge who cited it as case law in his courtroom was a former major in the Texas Rangers, R. M. "Three Legged Willie" Williamson, as related in an 1855 magazine. (The judge gained his unusual nickname because he relied on a wooden leg strapped to his crippled, natural one.) An attorney raised a point of law and the judge questioned his source, asking for book and page. The lawyer drew a pistol stating "this is my law, sir." Drawing a bowie knife, he said "this is the page," and pointed the pistol toward the court. With the utmost coolness, as the tale goes, his honor drew his six-shooter which he pointed at the attorney. "Your law is not good, sir, the proper authority is Colt on revolvers," quickly ending the discussion.[52]

Although the most dramatic of American gold rushes was over by the early 1850s, men continued to succumb to the lure of precious metals and the prospect of sudden riches. Discoveries of gold and silver ore in other parts of the west sometimes brought sudden rushes, often of brief local duration. When the earth did give up her treasure to individual prospectors, she usually did so only as a result of long and often futile searching followed by backbreaking labor with pick and shovel.

Guns and Travelers from Abroad

*If the sportsman intends to visit only the Rocky Mountains,
a shot-gun will be found an encumbrance.... Take one double-barrelled
.450 or .500 Express and one of Bland's Cape rifles.*
— William A. Baillie-Grohman, 1882[1]

The lure of adventure and the variety of game animals in the west drew many foreigners, particularly from Great Britain. One visitor was a Scotsman of whom little is known beyond a story printed in the *Sacramento Standard* newspaper in 1860.

Among the "thousand and one" articles of freight and baggage which went down to the Bay by the steamer Queen City yesterday were two old flint-lock smooth-bore rifles of the real old "Kaintuck" stripe. They were brought on board by a man who looked as weather-beaten, flinty-locked, and hard-stocked as themselves. Being curious to learn their history and who it was that possessed them, we made a few inquiries, and the owner, being mellowed by the genial influence of the corn vintage, communicated the following facts: His name was Seth Grant, a Scotchman by birth, who came to America at an early age, in the year 1819, and joined the American Fur Company.... The two rifles...were a portion of the arms of the original party, and bore the marks of

having seen long and honorable service. Mr. Grant values them highly, and, being on his way back to his own native land, intends taking them as trophies, to be hung up with the tartans and claymores of his countrymen.[2]

Contradictory as the term was, a smoothbore rifle was a compromise and not an unknown weapon of the muzzle loading era. A heavy-barreled, large-caliber smoothbore rifle could drive a patched ball with suitable accuracy for hunting at a range of at least seventy-five yards and still could handle shot while withstanding hard use.

Foreigners often brought their personal weapons with them. One was Charles Augustus Murray who visited from England in the mid-1830s. He was well armed as he prepared to meet a Pawnee chief on the Kansas prairie.

Round my waist was a strong leather belt, in which were stuck my hunting-knife and a brace of pistols in front, and at the side a short heavy iron-handled cut-and-thrust sword, such as is sometimes used in Germany in a boar-hunt, and nearly resembling the old Roman sword;...and

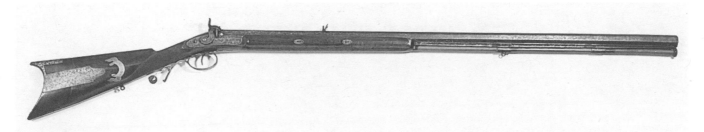

After resigning from the British Army, young George Frederick Ruxton traveled extensively in the American west in the 1840s and later wrote of his adventures in several books including the classic *Life in the Far West*. His rifle shown here was made by Thomas K. Baker, a prominent London gunsmith. Baker's address of 34 St. James Street on the barrel narrows the production date to the first half of 1846, shortly before Ruxton began a trip into the southwest and Mexico. Ruxton's name is engraved on a silver scroll inlaid in the butt stock. (Photo by Steven W. Walenta, courtesy James D. Gordon)

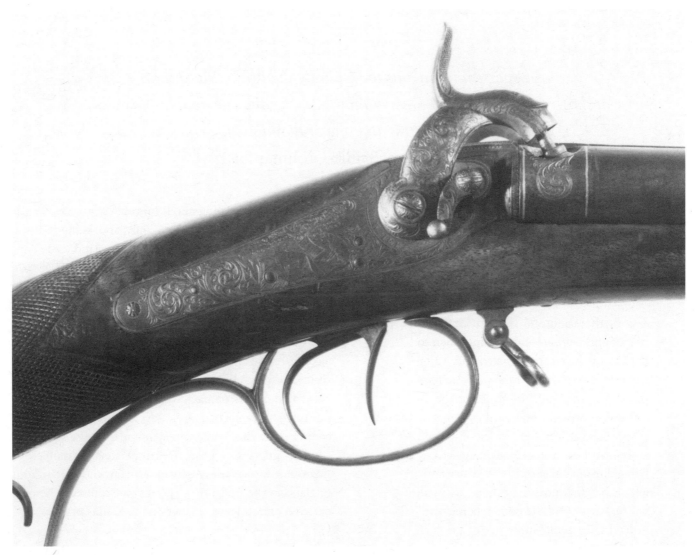

Charles Louis Ducommun, a French watchmaker by trade, traveled by foot from Fort Smith, Arkansas, to the California gold fields. For the journey he purchased this 20-gauge shotgun made by E. A. Stormer of Herzberg am Harz, Germany, and dated 1847. His vision was impaired due to a bout with smallpox which may have dictated his choice of a shotgun rather than a rifle. Ducommun was no luckier than most miners and in 1851 moved from the diggings to Los Angeles where he established a watch repair shop that expanded into a general mercantile store offering virtually anything from pistols to glass eyes and eventually becoming the city's oldest continuously operating business. (Courtesy: Los Angeles County Museum of Natural History via Konrad F. Schreier Jr.)

This London-marked English holster pistol bears the name "G. Nunez" inscribed on the barrel and may have been present at the famed battle of the Alamo. A sergeant in the Mexican Army, G. "Felix" Nunez, reportedly witnessed the killing of Davy Crockett and directed Gen. Santa Anna to the body. Nunez survived the war and died in Atascosa County, Texas, where this pistol was found, a little south of San Antonio. (Courtesy: Ronald G. Gabel)

in my right hand was my faithful double-barrelled rifle.

His rifle he later identified as made by the renowned James Purdey of London firing an ounce ball (about .69 caliber). He had a set of interchangeable smoothbore barrels for it for added utility. "Unfortunately I had mounted my shot-barrels a few hours before, in order to kill a prairie hen . . . ; and before I could replace them by the rifle barrels, the deer had taken to the bush." His choice of a double-barreled rifle was mirrored by many of the Englishmen who came to hunt.[3]

In 1840 a young British lieutenant serving in Canada, William Fairholme, had the opportunity to join six brother officers in a great adventure—a buffalo hunt to the "grand prairies of the Missouri." He didn't hesitate to accept their invitation and that summer he was able to obtain five months leave for the hunt. Each of the officers took with him a percussion double-barrel rifle plus a pair of holster pistols.[4]

Sir George Gore, a stout Irish baronet, spent $500,000 on a three-year hunting safari in Colorado, Montana, Wyoming, and the Dakotas in 1854–57. Unwilling to sacrifice personal comfort, his party at one point consisted of forty-one men with four six-mule wagons, two three-yoke ox wagons, and twenty-one red two-horse French Red River carts. One wagon carried his personal firearms—about seventy-five rifles (all muzzleloaders except for one Sharps), a dozen or so shotguns, and various pistols and revolvers, all of high quality by such makers as Purdy, Westley Richards, and Joseph Manton. Two other wagons carried Gore's fishing tackle, and one of his attendants was a skilled fly-maker who spent much of his time searching for appropriate materials for making flies. Gore rarely loaded his own gun and was described as a good shot from a rest but indifferent offhand. He estimated that he killed some two thousand bison, sixteen hundred elk and deer, and one hundred bear. Although the quantity of game animals seemed endless, such slaughter and wanton waste brought sharp criticism from Native Americans and some whites as well.[5]

In October of 1872, three Englishmen accompanied Lt. Col. Richard Dodge and another officer on a twenty-day hunt southeast of Fort Dodge, Kansas. Dodge called it "most delightful hunting." Later he unabashedly tallied the results which, excluding 11 rattlesnakes, totaled 1,251 creatures bagged including 127 bison, 11 antelope, 223 teal, 7 raccoons, 143 "meadow larks, doves, robins, &c,"—and 1 bluebird for a lady's hat! (A state law enacted in 1868 prohibited the hunting of the last four species of birds at any time.)[6]

Some men from abroad were drawn by what they perceived as economic opportunities. William Chandless fit into this category when he arrived in 1855 from England.

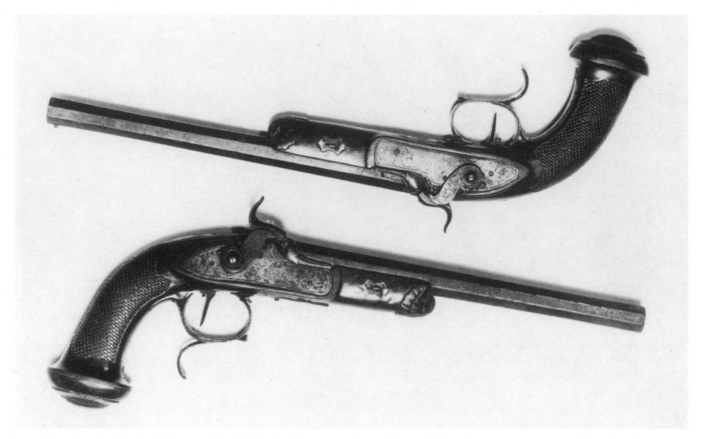

Pistols used in the February 5, 1837, duel between Gen. Albert Sidney Johnston, commanding the Texas Republic's army, and a swashbuckling Mississippi planter and slave trader, Felix Huston. After Johnston superseded Huston as commander, Huston felt his reputation had been damaged and he issued a challenge. After three exchanges of fire, Johnson was seriously wounded but months later recovered, apparently without resentment, saying he could not have commanded the army's respect if he had not met Gen. Huston's challenge. Although the author never examined the pistols, they appear to be European as were many dueling pistols used in this country. (Courtesy: Museum of New Mexico)

Tiring of $2.50 per day hotels in the east, he hired on in St. Joseph, Missouri, for $25 a month with an ox train bound for Utah Territory, inexperienced as he was as a teamster. "There was . . . a delightful novelty in working for less than a dollar a day, and mixing in a wholly untried and very miscellaneous society; one was sure to be amused, and likely to learn something too." In record time he stuffed as many useful items as he could in his bag in preparation for the next morning's departure. He included "some simple medicines, a 'Deane and Adams [revolver],' and a Bible—not a 'Beecher's Bible' (i.e. Sharp's rifle), as the collocation might suggest."[7]

Upon reaching Pawnee country, arms and ammunition were distributed.

The Pawnee have the name of being about the meanest and most rascally set of Indians in the whole country; more ready to bully than to fight, and most to pick off

stragglers; as a tribe, they are at peace with the United States. The rifles were what are called "yagers," [probably US Model 1841 rifles] but rather old ones, formerly belonging to the government; men seemed very eager to get the rifles, but not many knew how to use them: I prophesied, in case of attack, more would be killed by our own accidents than by the Indians: the supply was insufficient, and I did not get one, which I cared little about, having a D. and A. [Deane and Adams revolver].[8]

Such English revolvers as those by Robert Adams and associates and William Tranter were advertised by some American dealers in the late 1850s and into the next decade. The firm of D. Kernaghan & Co. of New Orleans in 1859 offered "Colt's, Dean & Adam's, and Derringer [sic] pistols" while Charles Kittredge of St. Louis is known to

Double-barrel pistol by William Rigby of Dublin, Ireland, owned by George Bean, a Mormon scout. (Courtesy: Utah State Historical Society)

have sold Tranter revolvers. One advantage some of these English revolvers offered over Colt and other American competitors was their self-cocking or double action mechanism. Charles Scholl of Marysville, California, in 1862 advertised, among other sporting goods, "Adam's Self-Cocking Pistols."[9]

A precursor to the use of foreign handguns by the US military during the Civil War came in June 1856 when the army agreed to purchase one hundred .36 English double action Adams revolvers. Nine months later, the chief of ordnance ordered five hundred more at $18, to be manufactured in this country by the Massachusetts Arms Company. Sam Colt, alarmed by this challenge, on April 20, 1857, wrote to the chief of ordnance offering to reduce the price of his .36 Navy revolvers to $20 or less. "I am willing to do almost anything to keep these English mad dog revolvers out of the Service."[10]

American-made pepperbox pistols, particularly those by Ethan Allen and associates, found a ready market in this country in the 1840s and 1850s. European pepperboxes were imported as well. One example of the latter is a large .50 caliber five-shot English pepperbox by J. Cogswell. A silver plate inlet into the grip is inscribed "Abel Shawk/Carondelet." Shawk, in partnership with J. K. McLanahan, about 1859 or 1860 made an estimated one hundred Whitney-style "navy sized" revolvers marked on the backstrap "Shawk & McLanahan, St. Louis, Carondelet, Mo." Another English pepperbox by Cook was found along the Oregon Trail,

badly corroded after decades of exposure. In 1856 O. H. Bogart's Sportsman's Emporium in San Francisco offered both Colt revolvers and Belgian Mariette pepperboxes for sale.[11]

Frank Marryat journeyed from Great Britain to California in 1850 and 1853 to seek adventure rather than gold. Describing preparations for a bear hunt with two Americans, he didn't mention a pepperbox but instead wrote:

> The Americans carried rifles of their own make; capital make too, though too weak in the lock on account of the cheap price at which they are supplied. The bore of their rifles seemed small for bear-shooting, carrying a half-ounce ball [.54 caliber], but they seemed to consider that their skill in shooting counterbalanced this deficiency. I carried the only rifle that I ever used on those I took out, one of German make, carrying a ball of an ounce and a half [.75 caliber]. I should say here that our rifles were often the subject of discussion with these honest fellows. I had two Rigby's with an accumulation of sights, which were perfectly useless for my work, although they were beautifully-finished weapons.... The German rifle...was rather too short, but very true within a hundred yards, and its qualities

English .50 five-shot pepperbox by J. Cogswell. It features a belt hook on the left side and a silver plate in the right grip inscribed "Abel Shawk/Carondelet." Shawk and J. K. McLanahan made a few .36 belt revolvers in Carondelet near St. Louis shortly before the Civil War. (From the collection of Steve Romanoff)

Seven-barrel pepperbox by Lewis & Tomes of London and owned by Herman H. Heiser who came to Colorado in 1863. Extra percussion caps can be stored in a small compartment in the bottom of the butt, a feature found on some of Henry Deringer's pocket pistols. The sliding safety catch behind the hammer is a fairly common feature on English pistols, but not so on those made in this country. (Courtesy: Colorado Historical Society)

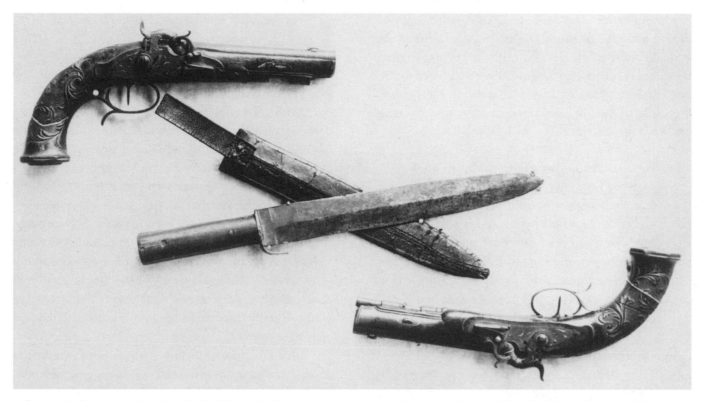

Peter H. Bell was closely allied with early Texas history. He fought as a private at the Battle of San Jacinto and remained in the Texas Army until 1839 before joining the Texas Rangers and rose to captaincy of a company. Service with the US Army during the Mexican War followed, then election as the state's third governor in 1849 and 1851. During the Civil War he fought for the Confederacy. As personal weapons at some point during his career he chose this Bowie knife and pair of European (perhaps French or Belgian) pistols. (Courtesy: Austin History Center, Austin Public Library, TX)

were expressed by its name, "Shoulder-breaker," engraved on the stock.[12]

It probably was a .44 Dragoon of which he wrote:

A Colt's revolver is invaluable to the deer-hunter, both for self-defense and killing wounded game. Perhaps the best praise I can award to this weapon is in saying that I have had mine for four years, during which time it has been much used and *more abused*, but at this moment it is perfect in every respect, and has never required repair.[13]

In 1858 Granville Stuart traded his "old reliable Kentucky rifle" for an English Westley Richards .65 rifle with 24-inch barrel when the owner complained he couldn't kill any game with it.

It had a small back action lock of exquisite finish; also a spring to regulate the trigger pull, an iron ram-rod with a screw on its end for extracting balls, and moulds for making ounce balls, and a fine sole leather case for the gun, which only weighed eight pounds. I tried the rifle and found it a fine shooter when enough powder was used, and found that Jacobs used only half enough because he feared the recoil, which was tremendous, for it would turn me half around to the right every time I fired it.[14]

Britain's J. S. Campion wrote in somewhat self-depreciating style of his hunting in the west in the 1860s, particularly in describing his initial attempts to skin a bison. He and his party of five were "a well 'healed' party, the armament being two good double-barrels [shotguns presumably], five rifles—twelve balls to the pound gauge [.73 caliber!] every one of them, not toys—and to each man a brace of six-shooters, a bowie and a tomahawk."[15]

He was visiting Denver City at a time when the city was in panic upon word of the death of two German whiskey traders a day's ride away, presumably at the hands of some of their Indian customers. His description showed the effect fear has on some. The mayor called upon all able-bodied men to assemble, gunsmiths' arms and ammunition were requisitioned, and windows of a block of brick buildings were boarded up as a refuge for women and children. One of the Englishman's own men, a youth considered courageous, was particularly affected.

> He discharged his weapon in the air, took a box of Ely's [percussion] caps out of his waistcoat-pocket—a full box—deliberately poured all the caps into his rifle-barrel, placed a greased patch on the muzzle, the ball upon it, rammed it down, withdrew the ramrod, and was pouring the powder out of his flask into the gun in a continuous stream.

Campion gave the young man a drink of brandy and calmed him. "Fortunately for him, none of the men had perceived what he had done, and I took care not to mention it . . . for his life would have been rendered unbearable by their jeers and ridicule."[16]

From England, Charles A. Messiter made three trips to North America between 1862 and 1875. During his first visit, he was preparing to unload his double rifle and carelessly fired at a crow flying overhead. "No one was more astonished than I was when it fell dead, and from that day, as I firmly refused to waste any more ammunition on crows, I found that I had gained a wonderful reputation as a shot among the Indians—hearing of what I had done many months afterwards in an Indian camp."[17]

In his descriptions of his travels, he made references to various English arms he had brought with him including a Tranter revolver and 16-bore (.66 caliber) and 12-bore (.73 caliber) double rifles. In a confrontation with Indians on one occasion, he killed an Indian's horse using one of the latter guns and a Metford exploding shell. Later they withstood a three-day attack by Comanches during his 1866 visit, but his party of six was well prepared to defend itself.

> We had nine Winchester repeating-rifles with us and three thousand rounds of ammunition for them, having brought five hundred rounds per man . . . ; then we had four double rifles and several hundred rounds of ammunition for them; and, lastly, we had a double eight-bore duck-gun, which loaded with about two ounces

of buckshot in each barrel would be grand at close quarters.[18]

Toward the terminus of the fight, they were aided by two friendly Caddo Indians who "used their Spencer carbines with great effect." When examining the body of one dead Indian, he found that "a no. 12 Medford shell had burst low down in his back, making a hole almost as large as the crown of a hat, and nearly cutting him in two."[19]

Double-barrel rifles were uncommon among Americans in the west, but in Wyoming Territory, Messiter did encounter an American meat hunter in his late twenties, Al Houston, who relied on an "over and under rifle weighing 18 pounds, which carried a ball sixty to the pound [.41 caliber]." "[He was] one of the best hunters and best shots at game with a rifle that I ever came across." Houston easily killed an average of five antelope a day and sometimes more.[20]

John Mortimer Murphy spent seven years in the American west in the 1870s and in 1880 compiled a guidebook for other wealthy English sportsmen. One warning he issued was to avoid any appearance of condescension or "high-handed dictation or any assumption of superiority" to a guide or scout. As an example, he cited the case of a party of overbearing Englishmen which for three days had not fired a single shot while following a herd of bison. When Murphy asked one of the guides the reason, he was told in vigorous language.

> [The visiting hunters] were constantly dictating to himself and his companions what they should and should not do in the most frigid and supercilious manner; that they never spoke to them except to give some command or make an impatient inquiry; that they kept entirely to themselves both in camp and on the march.

Even the servants looked upon the guides as "barbarians and mudsills." The guide explained that as long as the foreigners maintained such an attitude, he would see to it that they had no success. The guides had surreptitiously been chasing the animals away and Murphy later learned that after two weeks, the party hadn't shot a single bison.[21]

Murphy's guidelines for a hunter's weapons included a rifle with a flat trajectory and not less than .45 caliber, a breech loading shotgun, a heavy revolver, and a good hunting knife. He held a double rifle in high regard, but drew attention to one drawback of such weapons.

The double Express [rifle] has one fault . . . and that is that both barrels do not shoot with equal precision, and . . . a person sometimes forgets which barrel he is shooting; so fails to allow for its peculiarities, and the result is often a serious miss. . . . The most effective weapon that I ever used was a fifty-calibre Springfield rifle, which was resighted so that its point blank range was one hundred and fifty yards. This was almost as accurate at three hundred yards.[22]

He judged Winchester repeating rifles "very convenient for general shooting" but complained that the cartridge "would sometimes tilt as soon as it reached the breech from the magazine" requiring the shooter to clear the stoppage. Its powder charge (presumably discussing the models of 1866 and 1873) was too small for large game.[23]

Some sportsmen, he wrote, were using explosive bullets on larger game, but they could not always be relied upon to explode when wanted.

They are sometimes rather dangerous to the carrier. . . . A very good word may be said in favor of the hollow [point] bullets, as they are certainly superior to the solid in making a large wound, but they . . . lack very deep penetration unless [except] at short range and with high charges of powder, one hundred and twenty grains at least.[24]

Another Englishman, William A. Baillie-Grohman, arrived in 1880, anxious to test his hunting skills and his double rifle on big game. He described himself as very green when he first crossed the Missouri and in searching for a hunting guide, fell easy prey to men such as "Bearclaw Joe" who sought free drinks but offered little in return. One such potential guide with long greasy hair, buckskin suit, and broad Texas hat introduced himself with just that appellation.

I remarked that his sporting accoutrement was decidedly new. . . . The ponderous cartridge belt round his waist was as brand-new from the saddler's shop as his big six-shooter and Winchester rifle. . . . Nailed to the stock of his rifle were the front claws of a grizzly, and on my making some cautious inquiries respecting it, and the name by which he had introduced himself to me—"Bearclaw Joe"—he proudly informed me, that though he had that rifle but a short time, it had already annihilated the biggest bear in the Territory. . . . During the terrible combat the bear had got the stock between his jaws, and the dents the man proceeded to show me on his weapon—but which, I innocently thought, looked more like harmless hammer marks—were the result, which led his comrades to give him that name.[25]

Later the two men passed a meat shop, where the carcass of a large grizzly hung from an iron hook outside. Stopping to examine the corpse, the Englishman noted that a forepaw had been cut off. By now Bearclaw Joe appeared most anxious to pass on when the shop owner came to the door and began to berate the frontiersman.

"You cussed bull-whacking son of a dog! What in Texas did you mean cutting off that er' forepaw last night? Neighbor S. saw you do it, you Texas-begotten steer-smasher!". . . The greasy locks of the thief streaming behind him were the last I saw of noble "Bearclaw Joe."[26]

Hunting elk in the Rockies, this same Englishman encountered a lad, small for his fourteen years, gutting an elk he had killed with his "needle rifle," probably a Springfield "trapdoor."

Not unlike our Enfield rifle of prehistoric day, it was of immense bore, and decidedly a foot and a half longer than its owner was tall. The metal fastenings of the barrel to the stock [barrel bands] were gone—raw hide or "buck-string" had taken their places—and the stock was of home-made origin, studded with brass nails, and notched in the most fantastic manner. The owner . . . informed me with much pride, that he had shot already over two hundred elks and blacktails [deer] with it.[27]

Accompanying the youth to his rude family home, he found one wall held a large rack of twelve to fifteen different guns, from the Winchester repeater to "the antiquated Kentucky pea rifle." Each gun had its name. "Here was an 'Uncle Ephraim' or a 'Track-maker,' there an 'Aunt Sally' and a 'Sister Julia;' and every one had some special degree of merit and long gunning yarns attached to it."[28]

Baillie-Grohman had little use for a revolver, considering it "a most useless and cumbersome utensil for game." However he did occasionally carry a .45 Colt on which he had lightened the trigger pull and altered the sights, since small bands of Ute Indians had been stealing horses in the area. His double-barrel Express rifle often was an object of great interest to Indians. On several occasions, he allowed Indians to test fire it, but after he had adjusted it so that both barrels went off simultaneously, producing an immense recoil "sufficient to knock down a grizzly."[29]

> Both triggers could be set to hair triggers, and by firing one barrel while the other was set, the concussion would make it go off too, the lightness of the rifle and the double charge of about . . . 310 grains of powder, producing an overwhelmingly formidable recoil. Through inadvertence I tried it on myself once or twice, and it knocked me clean out of my saddle.[30]

In 1882 Baillie-Grohman published a narrative of his hunting experiences in the Rockies and included in an appendix advice on an appropriate outfit for other English sportsmen hunting in the west.

> ARMS—If the sportsman intends to visit only the Rocky Mountains, a shot-gun will be found an encumbrance. As accidents to rifles are not infrequent, especially in the case of the slender-stocked English Express, the following plan, I found, works very well. Take one double-barrelled .450 or .500 Express and one of Bland's Cape rifles (one shot, 12 bore, and one Express-barrel), and have them made, so that the stock and barrels of both arms are interchangeable, thus if you break the stock of your Express you can use the one of the Cape gun, and *vice versa*. The shot-barrel will come in useful for a change of grub in the way of grouse, though, being very tame birds, they can easily be killed with the rifle by shooting their heads off. The Express rifle should shoot a solid bullet in one barrel. For grizzlies there is nothing like a long cannelured (not patched) missile, though if made very

long it will perceptibly increase the recoil. On the whole, I think a .500 bore better than .450 for the Rockies.

> POWDER—The American powder is nearly as powerful as our best grades. For Express purposes I have found the coarse-grained *Orange Lightning* brand to answer remarkably well.

> CARTRIDGES—If a longer stay is meditated, it answers much better to take out empty cartridges and reloading tools, and load your shells yourself, or let your men do it for you. The solid-drawn straight shells of the National Arms and Ammunition Company at Birmingham are . . . decidedly superior to those manufactured by Eley Brothers. The former are more uniform in size, and their cap (containing the anvil) is better than Eley's plain cap. I have had a good many misfires with the latter, and only one with the former.

> WADS—The lubricating wad suitable for hot climates I have found to be worse than useless for the West, as somehow it seems to foul the barrels very quickly, particularly in cold weather. I always use a thick felt ungreased wad over the powder, and on it, when in the cartridge, I place a little fat, such as Elk-tallow, &c. This, I found, gave me the best results and it allows more powder.

> EXPRESS BULLETS—Ought to be taken with you.

> REVOLVER—If a revolver *must* be taken, then a small .450-Bulldog is as good a weapon as can be recommended for purposes of self-defense at close range, the disabling powers of this pistol being, on account of its large bore, of fair amount.[31]

Despite the popularity of double-barrel rifles among some foreign sportsmen, no major American maker in the metallic cartridge era produced them in any significant quantity. The Colt firm did make about forty in .45 caliber in the early 1880s at the recommendation of Sam Colt's playboy son, Caldwell Hart Colt. These resemble the Colt Model 1878 shotgun and may have been made on special order for Caldwell's hunting friends. One did go to Blair D. Taylor, an army officer stationed in the west. In addition, Lt. W. L. Scott at Fort Meade, Dakota Territory, wrote the Colt factory in early 1886 stating he had seen a double express rifle made for Gen. Randolph Marcy and asked the price of one for himself.[32]

Richard B. Townshend was twenty-three when he stepped down from the Union Pacific railcar in Cheyenne in 1869. He spent a decade in Colorado and New Mexico before returning to England and becoming assistant master at Bath College. In his writings, he made frequent mention of his experiences with firearms during his western adventures. From England, he brought a 12-bore, double-barrel muzzle loading shotgun by W. W. Greener with 30-inch barrels. Although a little heavy, he later found it worked well with round bullets as well as with small shot and buckshot.[33]

Soon after arriving in Cheyenne, he struck up a conversation with a young cowboy.

> He wore his belt slack, so that it [pistol] hung rather low on his right side; the butt...just showed at the top of the holster.... The lower end of the holster was provided with two long pieces of buckskin string, by which it was bound to his thigh.

When asked about the strings, his new friend replied they "keep it from joggling about too much when I'm riding at a lope. A gun travels better so; and if ever you want to pull it, it pulls better so.... A .44-calibre Colt is a heavish thing to tote around."[34]

Soon after, from another new friend he received hands-on advice on handling several different handguns, from a Colt .44 to a derringer. The friend advised: aim low but not too low, keep your eye on the mark more than on the sights, aim while the weapon is rising rather than wasting time by first bringing it up perpendicular and them lowering it, fire the instant you are on target, and pull with a very firm, quick squeeze of the trigger.[35]

In Denver, he struck up a friendship with famed gunsmith Carlos Gove, "an elderly man very keen on guns," from whom he bought a Colt .36 Navy revolver. He and Gove's son Tom practiced at a butt in Gove's backyard. He also loaned his Greener to the gunsmith to copy a part. His association with Carlos led him to meet Gen. McCook, Colorado territorial governor.

Gove had in his shop a Springfield rifle on which he was putting new sights.

> Every now and then, some discontented U.S. soldier would desert from Ft. Lyon, or one of the other U.S. forts...often taking with him his excellent breech-loading Government rifle, made at the U.S. armoury, Springfield, Mass. This the deserter would promptly trade off to the first ranchman he could strike a bargain with, for a suit of civilian clothes.... Often the rancher would prefer ordinary hunting sights to the Government rifle sight, and would get a gunsmith to alter them.... That is how a Springfield rifle came to be no rare object in Gove's workshop. And on such a rifle was Gove busy one day, when in came Governor McCook.... His soldierly eye spotted the Springfield rifle lying on that workbench in a moment.
>
> "Hello, Mr. Gove," he burst out, half in earnest, half jocularly, "that's Government property I see there. Guess I'll be putting in a claim for that."
>
> "Not by a jugful, you won't," Gove abruptly flung back at him. "This was put into my hands by a ranchman, and back into his hands I'll deliver it. You may be governor of this Territory alright, but you can't seize the property of no private citizen through me."
>
> I forget how they went on, but I know Gove stuck to the Springfield, and the Governor refrained from pushing his demand for it.[36]

Another new acquaintance by the name of "Wild Bill" provided the tenderfoot with added advice after Townshend expressed his desire to learn. When Wild Bill asked why he carried the Colt Navy, he replied "why...to defend myself with, I suppose. I certainly want to keep out of trouble." Bill cut in, "And you're going the very shortest way to get into it."

> Like a flash Bill's right hand went back to his hip, something clicked, and I was looking in the face of a bull-dog revolver at full cock and pointed straight at me. My hand instinctively began to move

toward my pistol. Quick as thought came the sharp command: "Don't you touch it. Don't you dare try to pull that gun, or I'll blow you through." Had the affair been in earnest, I'd be the dead man now, and Bill, with the drop, would be all alive and kicking still.

As Bill explained,

> A gun like yours if all right riding out on the range. But if you go around these yer' frontier towns with it slung to your tail, it's kind of a challenge, and some feller's liable to take you on sudden and make you look like a fool.... You put that gun away in your blankets; it's right enough for the road; but in a place like this, if you want to pack a gun around, put it somewheres where folks can't see it.[37]

By 1870 Townshend had added a .50 caliber Sharps rifle to his arsenal, describing it as "about the best rifle going in 1870." A friendly Ute named Wolf pressured him into an impromptu shooting demonstration.

> Up came the rifle to my shoulder. Quick[ly] I glanced down the sights and squeezed the trigger. Bang! The card fell off the tree and fluttered to the ground. I had driven up the nail through the middle of the spade-ace which fastened it to the tree. Wolf fairly fell upon my neck. "Oh,... you come with me. Come with me out on the Plains and kill Kiowas." That was the Ute's idea of Paradise, being able to kill Kiowas, but I hadn't lost any Kiowas.

On another occasion, a Ute warrior offered to trade his second-best wife for the Sharps.[38]

While attending a fair in Colorado Springs, word of a series of raids by renegade Cheyennes spread like wildfire. By now Townshend had acquired a ranch and was beginning to build a horse herd. His primary concern was seeing to the safety of several prized horses. Unfortunately he was unarmed, for he had loaned his Sharps to a new groom whose bride wanted some antelope meat and his Colt Navy to another friend. With no spare weapons to be found, he turned to a local restaurant owner whose wife retrieved from beneath a bed a very dusty Warner carbine, "an early

form of breechloader, rimfire, '50 calibre." More searching produced seven cartridges, "some of them a good deal bent and bulged." A cupful of petroleum, a stick, and vigorous scrubbing removed most of the rust and dirt from the bore, but an attempt to fire the Warner resulted in several misfires and a wide miss of the target, a dry goods case. The carbine was returned to its place under the bed and Townshend reached his ranch safely, though unarmed.[39]

Practice with his Navy Colt eased the rancher out of a difficult situation. He'd been warned that a man he'd hired only for the winter had threatened to "whale hell out of you" after he'd been paid. Completely outmatched in strength and size, Townshend hit on a scheme. When he and the ruffian were away from camp gathering stray cattle, they halted near a grove of cottonwood trees to rest.

> "I don't think I ever showed you how quick I could empty a six-shooter." I went to a good large tree truck close by and cut a fair-sized mark on it with my butcher-knife. I came back a few yards, looking at him, then whirled and pulled my gun as quick as I could and loosed off the six shots in pretty quick time. All hit right in the mark or close to it.
> "By God, you can shoot," said Kizer as he examined the shots, while I reloaded my pistol. "Yes... and don't you forget it." Not another word passed, but when we got [back] and I paid him off he took his money like a... man.[40]

In 1874 he arranged to sell his Colorado ranch and sought new opportunities in New Mexico. In place of his Sharps, he took with him a "16-shot Winchester [Model 1866], taking the old .44 rimfire copper cartridge" and an "up-to-date .45 Colt's pistol [Single Action Army]" in place of his percussion Colt Navy. In Santa Fe, he perhaps was a little surprised to encounter restrictions on the carrying of firearms and left his Colt at the hotel.[41]

During a hunting trip in the Sierra San Antonio, one night their camp was visited by a grizzly, or "Ephram," as hunters called the giant bears. The next morning they took up the bear's trail, but first made special preparations.

> We each of us carefully inserted fifteen cartridges in the magazines of our Winchesters, and then slipped into the firing-chamber a special cartridge that we only used upon occasion. These last carried

a bullet hollowed out at the point for a
good quarter of an inch, with an empty
closed copper tube inserted in the hole.

Although they failed to come up with the grizzly, they did use their specially prepared cartridges to kill two deer for venison. After gutting the animals, Townshend's bullet was found to have exploded while his companion's had mushroomed extensively to deal a swift death.[42]

In 1879 he gathered a herd of horses and mules in Texas and set out to drive it to the mining district of Leadville, Colorado. He nearly lost the herd to a band of four ruffians who jogged into camp at dinnertime.

Besides their revolvers they carried
Winchesters of the very newest and latest
model, and they wore two belts apiece
stuffed full of cartridges, and the biggest
of them . . . carried not one but two rifles,
a sixteen-shot Winchester for quick
shooting, and a Sharp's .45 calibre, the
famous "buffalo gun" of the plains
hunter, for long range work He was a
giant in form, with a strong, hard, cruel
face and the shifty eyes of a wolf. Never
did I see a more evil-looking man.

Eventually it became clear that the leader was a slight, boyish person, the "Kid," as his companions called him. Townshend's presentation of a note from a mutual friend improved the atmosphere of the meeting which ended with a humorous offer by the young man to take the herd "on credit." "If you see anybody along the road as wants to interfere with you, just refer 'em to Billy the Kid," said the youth as they rode off. When Townshend later heard of Billy the Kid's death, he "could not help one half sigh of regret, for Billy to me had been a mitigated [mild] ruffian."[43]

Lincoln A. Lang arrived from Ireland in 1883 at age sixteen, accompanying his father to Dakota Territory to start a cattle ranch. There they would become neighbors of Theodore Roosevelt. Not long after arriving in New York City, Lang persuaded his father to buy him a revolver.

[It] was but a little old rim-fire five-shot
affair of the type which—as I was due to
learn in good time—the cowboys were
in the habit of swallowing whole! But I

wasn't worrying a little bit about what I didn't know. What I did know was that I had a real revolver and a whole box of cartridges of my very own.[44]

Later a new friend took pity after watching him practice with his prized revolver and gave him "an old-style, long barreled, .32-calibre Smith and Wesson [S&W No. 2 Army perhaps] which shot with the precision of a rifle." Eventually the S&W was replaced with a "heavy Colt's six-shooter."[45]

The Lang ranch in 1884 hosted another Irish youth, the son of a baronet, who also wanted to learn the ranching business. Laval Nugent fit in well, being intelligent, hard working, and easygoing. On one occasion, he became the object of several drunken cowboys' humor in a bar. Just as he raised his glass to drink, several shots struck the floor almost between his feet, followed by a command to dance.

Nugent never batted an eyelash. Calmly
laying his glass down he turned toward
the pair to stand there regarding them
with a cool grin through his slightly nar-
rowed eyelids. Quickly they shot again.
Again they renewed their command.
Then, suddenly he acted. He had no gun
himself, but like a flash his hand shot forward and jerked mine from its scabbard.
Almost simultaneously he had it in action,
shooting three or four shots in quick succession into the floor right at the feet of
his baiters. He had two shots left and they
knew it. . . . [They tried] to pass it off with
a laugh as they sheepishly made their way
back to their own crowd to be received
with a chorus of jeers.[46]

Lang himself wasn't devoid of humor. In 1886 during a roundup, he and some companions rode into Glendive, Montana. Soon they were faced by the local sheriff who directed them to check their guns. They did so grudgingly. "Naturally we felt peeved. To take our guns away from us was to deprive us of our self-respect. But there seemed to be no help for it." About midnight the cowboys retrieved their guns from a saloon keeper and leaving town they passed an alley which gave access to backyards. An idea for retribution came to one of the party and quickly each had uncoiled his rope. When they left the alley, behind them lay a row of neatly upturned privies, "prone on their backs with faces turned moonward in mute appeal over the disaster that had befallen them."[47]

119

W. Koster, apparently a German cavalry officer, in 1879 included Yellowstone National Park as a stop on his trip around the world. He posed for a photo in western garb with a M1873 or M1876 Winchester, Colt Single Action on his right side and what appears to be a Smith & Wesson Old or New Model Russian. (Courtesy: Dr. Georg Priestel)

Closely connected with guns on the frontier was a pair of German-born brothers, Frank W. and George Freund. Their ancestors had made guns as early as the wheel lock era. Frank came to the United States in 1857 and obtained employment at the Remington Arms Company before enlisting in the Union Army in 1863. His brother arrived in 1865 and the two inaugurated a joint venture as gunsmiths. They followed the track of the Union Pacific Railroad as it moved slowly westward. They had shops in Nebraska City and North Platte, Nebraska; Julesburg, Colorado; Cheyenne, Laramie, Benton, Green River, Bear River, and South Pass City in Wyoming Territory; and in Utah at Corinne and Salt Lake City. When Union Pacific construction was finished, in 1869 or 1870 they transferred their business to Denver, Colorado, where they sold rifles,

shotguns, and ammunition. There Frank patented several improvements in Remington rolling-block rifle design. The gold boom in the Black Hills prompted them to sell their Denver shop to J. P. Lower and return to Cheyenne where Frank's efforts concentrated on improvements to Sharps rifles. A large sign in front of their Cheyenne "Wyoming Armory" from about 1875 advertised "500 to 1000 BREECH LOADING GUNS AND 500,000 TO 1,000,000 CARTRIDGES Furnished at any time."[48]

A most interesting patent issued to Frank Freund "of Cheyenne, Wyoming Territory," in 1876 (#183389) covers methods to modify the Colt Single Action so that it can be field-stripped without tools! Not a bad idea out there on the open plains—and an idea about twenty years ahead of its time, but one that wasn't adopted.

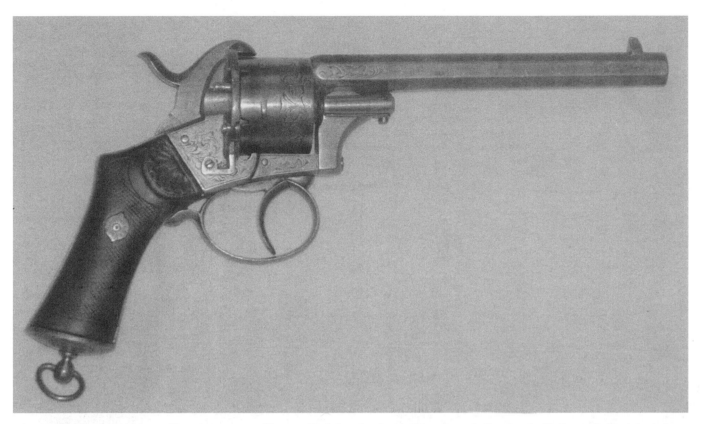

An unusual weapon for a Kansas peace officer, a Belgian twelve-millimeter pinfire by S. Holberg & Gadet. John L. "Jack" Bridges fought with Jim Lane's "Red Leg" guerrillas during the Civil War and later served as an army scout and a buffalo meat hunter. In Hays City, he was an assistant deputy US marshal under "Wild Bill" Hickok and then deputy marshal in the early 1870s. Following work as a railroad and a mine detective, he became the city marshal in Dodge City (1882) until replaced by Bill Tilghman two years later. He died in Texas in obscurity in 1915. Bridges's nephew traded the gun, badge, and image for $30 worth of grain and feed in 1910 at Nickerson, Kansas. It isn't known whether this was Bridges's primary handgun, a backup, or a souvenir.
(Courtesy: Lewis Wagner)

Even if they hadn't been skilled gunsmiths and gun designers, they would have gained recognition for between them, they obtained five patents on sights. Freund "MORE-LIGHT SIGHTS" were highly regarded by many hunters, including Theodore Roosevelt. George W. Wingate in 1886 published his account *Through the Yellowstone Park on Horseback*, and in it he devoted several pages to describing the design and use of the Freund sights mounted on his .45–75 Model 1876 Winchester. "I used the Freund sights, which I consider the best for sporting. In these, the front sight consists of a rib of tempered steel, something like the crescent sight upon an old-fashioned Kentucky rifle, but higher, and beveled at the sides so as to give the effect of a pin-head when seen from the rear." (With true entrepreneurialism, while in Denver in 1874 the Freund brothers also were operating the Hygienic Bath Establishment next to their gun store, offering Turkish baths for 75¢.) [49]

Thousands of English .577 Model 1853 Enfields as rifle muskets and shorter rifles had been imported by both sides during the Civil War. One of these muzzleloaders was still in use about 1880 by James M. Garner's cook on a horse drive. At dinner time eight to ten Indians often would arrive at the camp. Garner had his cook prepare lots of food for them, and after the meal they always wanted to shoot the cowboys' guns.

The cook became angry one day at this habit, and he filled his old Enfield rifle half full of powder and a tight wad. About this time he saw nine Indians riding up. He placed the gun against the wagon and said he would bet one Indian would not eat much dinner that day. The Indians . . . dismounted, and proceeded to wait for dinner. One of the number set up a can, took up the overloaded Enfield, squatted down and fired at the can. I think that gun flew about twenty feet in one direction and the

This 1877 exterior view of the Freund brothers' Wyoming Armory in Cheyenne shows Frank's dog, General, seated in front of the entrance. Frank once sold the dog to a friend in Denver but two weeks later the faithful animal arrived back home in Cheyenne one hundred miles away where he remained. (The man standing ninth from left holds a Sharps sporting rifle.) (Courtesy: Wyoming State Museum, Cheyenne)

Indian an equal distance in the opposite direction. Then there was a profound silence. The Indians got on their ponies and rode off, . . . thinking no doubt, the accident was the work of a ghost.[50]

Largely ignored have been the large-caliber, compact pocket revolvers imported from England, the "British Bull

Dog." The firm of Philip Webley & Son of Birmingham introduced the model about 1873 and they were offered up until the advent of World War I. The Bull Dog was a five-shot, double action weapon in .450 or .44 caliber with a short barrel and a compact, round butt. It was an easily concealed but large-caliber revolver for use at close range.

British and other European copyists, plus such American firms as Forehand & Wadsworth of Worcester,

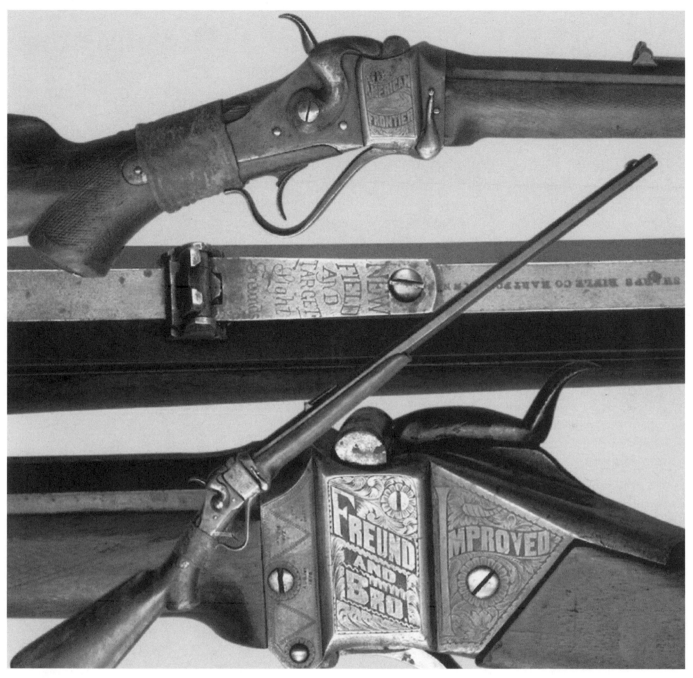

Luke Murrin, saloon owner and first elected major of Cheyenne, Wyoming Territory, in 1875 ordered from the Sharps company a "breech action in the soft state" so he could have it engraved. This .40–70, well used and repaired at the wrist, probably is the custom gun which the Freunds assembled around the action as one of their "Boss Guns." Its special features include a camming breechblock with double extractors, a trap in the butt for a cleaning rod and extra cartridge, and early Freund rear sight. The right side of the frame is engraved "AMERICAN FRONTIER" with a "smiling" rabbit and the left side "FREUND AND BRO. IMPROVED." The pistol grip is capped with a silver plate with the initials "LM" engraved thereon. (Photo by Ron Paxton, courtesy Bob Butterfield)

Massachusetts, made similar pocket guns, sometimes using a "BULLDOG" or "BULL-DOG" marking to differentiate theirs from the Webley products. The names "AMERICAN BULLDOG" and "INDIAN BULLDOG" appear on some. The E. C. Meacham Arms Company of St. Louis in their December 25, 1884, catalog advertised the .32, .38, or .44 "IMPROVED BRITISH BULL-DOG" by "F. & W." (Forehand & Wadsworth). Nathaniel Curry of San Francisco sold identical revolvers.

One of these pocket guns figured in a shooting in Las Vegas, New Mexico, in 1881. James Curry threatened Joseph Ebright, a gambler, as the two argued in Bertha's

With an eye to promoting sales on the frontier, this engraved Belgian-proofed five-shot .44 centerfire pocket revolver is marked "WESTERN BULL-DOG" on the top strap. Collectors often fail to appreciate the popularity of such foreign or similar US-made pocket guns in the west during the last quarter of the nineteenth century.

Parlor Saloon, a combination bar and brothel. After a drunken Curry drew his revolver, Ebright grabbed what was described as a British Bull Dog hidden behind the bar and fatally shot his antagonist in the head.[51]

The Bodie (California) *Morning News* of October 2, 1879, reported that the night before, John Bassett, a devoted husband and father of two, placed a British "bull dog" to his head and fatally shot himself. Other shootings in Bodie involved these pocket guns. One occurred in September 1878 when two men, each armed with a "bull dog," shot it out in a saloon over a disputed mining claim. Another took place when a husband found his wife in a hotel room with another man. In yet another lovers' triangle, one night in January 1881 Joseph DeRoche put a .38 double action Forehand & Wadsworth to the back of Thomas Treloar's head and fired one fatal shot.[52]

We don't know the nationality of the Bull Dog that figured in a shooting in 1879 in Los Angeles between William A. Spaulding, a reporter for the *Evening Express*, and Joseph D. Lynch, editor of the *Herald*. As the latter was crossing Spring Street, Spaulding "peppered away with a bull-dog pistol" but wounded a bystander instead.[53]

The son of a Methodist minister in Dodge City befriended an orphan boy named "Goodeye," who lived largely by doing odd jobs and by his quick wit. The orphan

had a .32 Bull Dog revolver, which he put in working order by making a mainspring from a piece of an old saw blade. "It was really a lady's gun, but still it would shoot through an inch board when fired at close range." He was willing to sell it for 50¢, but first the boys tested it at a target drawn in charcoal on a shed door.

> We put five bullets through the place and when we had used up all of our ammunition, the door of the shed opened and a man walked out. He had stepped in from the alley to take a fresh drink of some tonic medicine out of a bottle and he had not noticed that we were riddling the door with bullets, but he walked harmlessly away.[54]

Winchester in their 1879 catalog recognized the substantial numbers of English Bull Dogs in use in this country by advertising .32 short and long centerfire cartridges "ADAPTED TO Webley & Tranter's Double-action Pistols" as well as ammunition designated as .44 Webley and .45 Webley. In comparison with the .45 Colt cartridge with its 30 grains of powder behind a 260-grain bullet, Winchester described their .45 Webley as a 20-grain

A Webley Bulldog with ivory grips inscribed "Sheriff Nunan." The most likely namesake is Thomas Nunan who emigrated from Ireland and in 1855 went to California, attracted by the mining camps. He eventually became the owner of the Mission Street Brewery, an enterprise that suffered a $100,000 loss due to poor management! He served as sheriff of San Francisco County in 1876–77 but not without difficulty since during his tenure he was sued for $10,000 by Ho Ah Kow, a Chinese citizen whose pigtail had been cut off while in jail. Also, Nunan's property was attached after he left office to recover fees he had collected but had failed to turn over to the city. Nunan continued in the brewery business as proprietor of the Hibernia Brewery in San Francisco. (Courtesy: Lewis Wagner, biographical data courtesy Homer Ficken)

powder charge and a 230-grain bullet. The load for the .44 Webley round was slightly less, 18 grains of powder and a 220-grain bullet.[55]

The terrified yelps of his shepherd dog startled J. S. Flory from his sleep as it raced around the snowy barn yard, pursued by a large gray wolf, later found to be rabid. "In my wolf overcoat pocket at the foot of the bed was a loaded six [shot], thirty-two caliber, English revolver." He emptied the weapon, probably a British Bull Dog type, and drove the wounded animal away, but left no further description of his handgun.[56]

In the army, too, foreign-made guns sometimes appeared as privately owned officers' weapons. In September of 1872, Lt. Robert Carter's Troop E, 4th Cavalry, was ordered to Fort Sill, Indian Territory, to attend an Indian peace conference. Among those traveling with

the troopers was a "Colonel (?) McC, late of the Confederate Army (?),... a blow hard and windjammer."

> He boasted that he could drive a nail
> with his rifle off-hand shooting. It was a
> magnificent silver-mounted rifle, English
> make, with pistol [grip?] adjustable
> breech, presented to him by some
> nobleman in England, so he declared....
> On his belt... were two holsters, in
> which he carried two heavy steel-barreled
> English revolvers.

Carter later put the "colonel" in his place after he had consumed too much "tarantula juice" and began using inappropriate language in the presence of a lady. "He

Havasupai Indians in Supai Canyon in Arizona in the mid-1880s. The man at left holds what appears to be a bulldog revolver. The rifles at left and right are '73 Winchesters while the middle one may be a M1886 Winchester. (Courtesy: Museum of New Mexico, Ben Wittick photo #16246)

took it kindly. From that time his behavior was that of a little gentleman."[57]

It's generally accepted that George A. Custer at Little Bighorn carried a pair of English double action Webleys. Capt. Miles Keogh died in the same engagement and in 1877 a trader claimed he had seen an English revolver with Keogh's name on the grip in the hands of a Sioux in Canada.[58]

Sometimes foreign obsolete or surplus military arms were disposed of on the civilian American market. Such was the case with the .41 caliber repeating Swiss Vetterli rifle, adopted by the Swiss Army in 1867. A sufficient number of these apparently were imported into this country so that Winchester in 1879 began advertising .41 rimfire

bottleneck cartridges "adapted to Vetterlin [*sic*] and other Swiss Rifles."[59]

One immigrant, Jules Sandoz, brought his bolt action Vetterli with him from Switzerland in 1884. Although educated in a Swiss medical school, he abandoned medicine and came to this country. Self-reliant and sometimes brutal, he moved into a crude dugout from which he trapped and hunted. Later he became a farmer and successfully introduced fruit trees in the Nebraska sandhill country. One of his six children became the western historian and author Mari Sandoz.

In the late 1890s, the Spaulding-Haywood Arms Company of Denver was advertising other bolt action rifles, sporterized German military Mannlichers with a half

"CALIFORNIA BULLDOG" is stamped on top of the frame with the San Francisco dealer's name "Shreve & Wolf" on the side. (Courtesy: Robert P. Palazzo)

octagonal barrel, pistol grip stock with cheek piece, and frosted metal surfaces to reduce reflected light for $38. The firm offered another style of Mannlicher with fewer refinements for $28.50, still twice the price in the same catalog for a Model 1886 Winchester lever action. "Has the greatest penetration of any rifle made," boldly claimed the catalog ad for the imported rifles.[60]

F. W. Gray arrived in Canada from England in 1890 and for the next two decades sought his fortune there and in the United States and Mexico. In his memoirs he wrote in praise of Henry Burns, sheriff of Uvalde County west of San Antonio, Texas, for twenty-two years. His comments provide some insight into the mentality of handgun combat.

Henry Burns... was far from a good shot (I myself have beaten him pistol-shooting), but he was a man of wonderful nerve, which is what really counts. For a man may hit a target every shot at 30 yards, and yet cannot hit a man at 30 feet if the man is also doing some shooting. In my wanderings I have met one really wonderful shot who could, with a Colt's 44 frontier 7-inch barrel, hit a tomato can almost every shot at 40 yards. I have also known men, who were considered very good shots, stand at a distance of fifteen paces and empty their guns at one another without either getting a scratch. There is a saying throughout the South that the best weapon made is a double-barrelled shot-gun and buck-shot. I have heard and read a great deal about the wonderful pistol shots, but have, with the above exception, never met one who came up to the standards I have read of. The general advantage the bad-man had over the rest of the community was twofold: first, he practised [sic] drawing his pistol quick as a flash, and then he always knew when he intended to shoot, while the other fellow was still thinking over the pros and cons. The first shot always counts in these affrays [sic], as most of the shooting is done in a saloon or gambling-hall at a distance of a few feet when it is impossible to miss.[61]

127

Cased English Galand & Sommerville .450 self-extracting revolver presented by Lord Berkley Paget to Capt. Tom Custer in remembrance of time spent hunting bison in Kansas in 1869. Paget presented a similar cased set to Lt. Col. George Custer. (Courtesy: Col. Charles A. Custer via Custer Battlefield Historical and Monument Association, Crow Agency, MT)

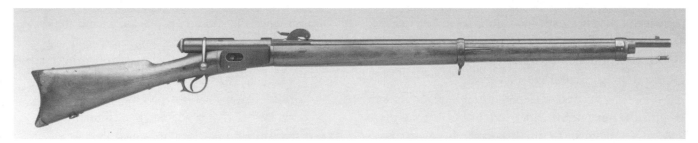

Vetterli rifle brought to Nebraska by Jules Sandoz, an immigrant from Switzerland in 1884. Its authenticity was confirmed by his daughter, author Mari Sandoz. (Courtesy: Nebraska State Historical Society)

Gray described a shooting incident in which Burns was involved.

Henry Burns was considered a good, steady shot because of his nerve, but I have seen him miss a whiskey bottle two or three times at a distance of about ten paces. He could shoot to kill, however.... Henry had put this man in jail for some offence, and the man had sworn revenge and promised to kill Henry on sight.... One day Henry...saw the man with a pistol in his hand crossing the street toward him. Henry pulled out his own gun and called to the man to halt. The man made no reply, and Henry fired and kept it up till his gun was empty, the man still advancing. When the man was

Minnesota deer hunters at the turn of the century. The man at right holds what appears to be a M1892 or M1894 Winchester while his companion is outfitted with a Swiss Vetterli, perhaps purchased from a Sears, Roebuck & Company catalog. (Courtesy: Wade Lucas)

within two or three paces of Henry he raised his pistol, pointed it at Henry, made two or three attempts to pull the trigger, and collapsed almost at Henry's feet. When they picked him up he had five 41-caliber balls through his body.... With modern weapons, such as the Colt's, Luger, or Mauser automatic pistols, shooting becomes much easier, but with the old-time Colt there were few men who could be sure of hitting their man at 25 or 30 yards.[62]

Gray also cautioned anyone who is unarmed from accepting a gun from an antagonist.

A man who will receive a gun in this manner has no chance, even if sober, unless he is like lightning, because as his hand touches the butt the other man shoots. Not necessarily because he wishes to take any advantage of the other, but because he is all keyed up and shoots involuntarily the moment he sees the other man is armed.... I saw a case in the Silver King Saloon in San Antonio one night. Two men had a row, and one slapped the other's face and then immediately drew his gun. (It is generally safer to kill a man first, and slap him afterwards.) The man who had been slapped said: "You cur, you only dare strike

129

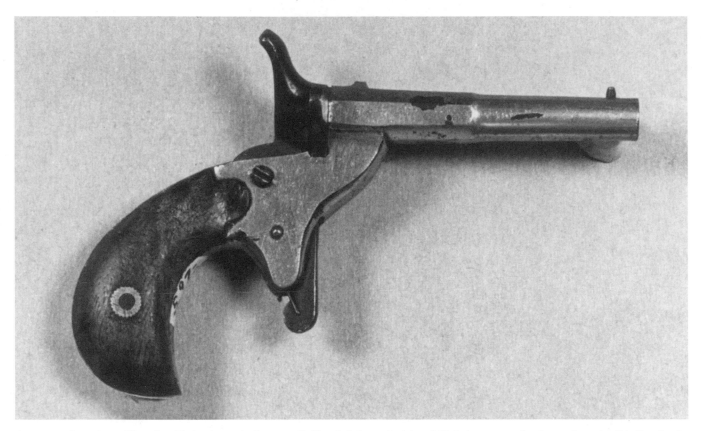

Inexpensive six-millimeter Flobert pocket or cyclist's pistol, probably of Belgian manufacture, found with the body of a man who died in the Mohave Desert. This was the smallest of a series of similar European pistols made from the mid-1880s to about 1910. (Courtesy: Nevada State Museum, Carson City)

me because I am unarmed, and you have a gun." "Don't let that worry you," said the other; "I will lend you a gun," and with his left hand he drew a second gun and offered it to the man, butt first. The other, however, was too wise even to put out his hand, and by this time the "lookouts" of the gambling hall and the barkeepers got around the armed man and hustled him out, for it hurts business to have any shooting in the house, besides the inconvenience of the trial, etc.[63]

Sharps: The "Old Reliable"

*They are the best guns for persons exposed
to the dangers of frontier life.*
— H. E. Dimick & Co., mid-1800s

Christian Sharps's patent of 1848 for a breech loading rifle led to more than three decades of arms with a strong impact on the history of the west. The arm's dependability led to the company's adoption of the trademark "Old Reliable" in 1876. Ironically, the inventor abandoned rifle-making in 1853 and concentrated on the design and production of handguns, particularly four-barrel pepperbox derringers, until his retirement to raising trout in Connecticut. Four firms bore Sharps's name—Sharps Rifle Manufacturing Company, Sharps Rifle Company, C. Sharps & Co., and Sharps & Hankins. From these firms between 1848 and 1880 emerged rifles, carbines, shotguns, single-shot pistols, pepperbox derringers, and even a few revolvers.

The Sharps rifle became a standard against which other guns were measured for power, range, accuracy, and reliability. The prominent St. Louis firm of H. E. Dimick & Co. advertised the Sharps as a gun which could be "loaded on horseback at a smart gallop, or lying down in the grass.... We will back our judgment with the 'filthy lucre'... that they are the best guns for persons exposed to the dangers of frontier life."[1]

To dispel a myth, the term "sharpshooter" had no reference to Sharps firearms. Although not the first appearance of the term, a member of Fremont's 1845 expedition referred to their "Sharp Shooters" frequently trying to bring down a fat turkey as a rarity for supper.[2]

One of the earliest accounts of Sharps in the west sprang from a journey through Texas and northern Mexico by brothers Frederick Law and John Hull Olmsted in 1852 and 1853. Frederick described the arms they chose as "a Sharp's rifle, a double fowling-piece, Colt's navy revolvers, and sheathed hunting knives." The Sharps probably was a .52 caliber Model 1851 carbine (rather than the rare Model 1850), of which only about eighteen hundred were manufactured, including 150 on army contract. The Colts were .36 caliber Model 1851s.

> The Sharp[s], in sure hands (not ours), threw its ounce ball as exactly, though far deeper, into its mark, at one thousand three hundred yards, as a Kentucky rifle its small ball at one hundred. For force, we can testify to its ball passing through a four-inch white oak fencepost; and for distance, to constantly striking a piece of water a mile and a quarter distant, with the ordinary purchased cartridge. By the inventor it can be loaded and fired eighteen times in a minute; by us, at a single trial, without practice, nine times. Ours was the

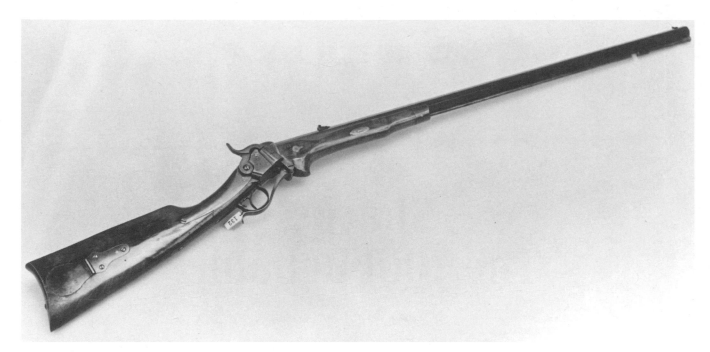

Sharps Model 1850 sporting rifle owned by John Brown Sr. of Kansas fame. (Courtesy: Richard Donaldson)

Government pattern—a short carbine, of light weight, and conveniently arranged for horseback use. Its barrel had been browned, a box made in the stock, and a ramrod added [a non-standard feature on a carbine], to which a cleaning brush could be attached. Its cost in this shape was forty dollars. We were furnished with moulds for both conical and round balls, as when cartridges fail it may be loaded at the muzzle with the ramrod, in the ordinary way. It was also fitted with Maynard's primer, a self-capping apparatus, which . . . we found so unreliable as to be useless in practice. The capsule [fulminate] never failed to fix itself in position [on the nipple], but frequently did not explode. Nothing about the piece [Sharps] during our trip gave way or got out of order.[3]

Despite Olmsted's praise for his Sharps when on a target range, he developed a certain distrust on the open prairie. Already anticipating the first venison shot by his party, he drew bead on a feeding deer "almost within pistol range."

A barrel of buck[shot] might have been a trifle safer, but . . . Sharp[s] should have the credit. . . . I [took] cool and deliberate aim (I would have staked anything on winning at a target) [and] pulled. Crack! Putting my hand to my knife, I stepped forward, to put an end to any brief misery I had created, when I saw my venison going, at a spanking rate, down the mountain, a stiff white tail, derisively hoisted . . . behind him.[4]

Another early account was that of Bill Hamilton who with a group of other mountain men had been lured to the California gold fields.

Six of us had traded out Hawkins [Hawken] rifles for Sharps rifles. . . . The barrels of the Hawkins rifles made good substitute for crowbars. These were the first Sharps rifles we had seen and we found them most effective weapons, our only criticism being that the triggers pulled too hard. We had a gunsmith resight them and fix the triggers, and securing a lot of tape caps and ammunition, we practiced for several days. They were equal in accuracy to our old rifles and far superior in effectiveness.[5]

If Hamilton's recollection of tape primers was accurate, the Sharps would have been either the rare Model 1850 or the Model 1851, the only two Sharps to use the Maynard tape primer prior to 1855.

C. SHARPS'

PATENT BREECH-LOADING AND SELF-PRIMING

Rifle, Carbine, Shot Gun, and Pistol.

MANUFACTURED AND SOLD BY SHARPS' RIFLE MANUFACTURING COMPANY.

AT HARTFORD, CONNECTICUT.

Sharps Arms combine simplicity of construction, rapidity of firing, and extraordinary range, with perfect accuracy and unequaled safety. The barrel and moving parts are of cast steel, and so wrought and finished as to insure their excellence and durability. The Arm will admit but one charge at a time, and obviates the objection to all magazine or cylinder guns. The priming magazine is charged with 50 air and water-proof pellets ready for use, but the arm is only primed when the hammer is at full cock.

To LOAD—The breech is opened by moving the lever or guard forward: the cartridge is inserted, and pressed forward smartly with the thumb, which fixes the ball in its seat; move the lever to its position, which closes the breech, and cuts off the rear end of the cartridge, exposing the powder in the line of fire communication: or insert the ball at the breech, force it to its seat with a rod and charge with loose powder.

As no patch is used, the ball should be well greased with tallow, which lubricates through the barrel and prevents leading. For warm climates, harden by mixing one-tenth bayberry tallow.

To PRIME—Cock the arm, place the thumb of the left hand on the screw head beneath the cup of the hammer and press the slide backward to a stop.

Insert the tube containing primes, in the magazine until the wooden follower lies in the side groove: holding the follower firmly in that position with the left thumb, at the same time withdraw the tube with the right hand and carefully let down the hammer, still holding the follower in the groove until the descending hammer forces it out by carrying the slide forward to position.

When the priming magazine is charged do not shove the magazine cover back so as to admit of the escape of the primes.

If by long continued firing the breech-pin becomes foul, a few drops of water, or even saliva, applied to it, and the lever moved backward and forward two or three times, will cause it to move perfectly free.

The barrel is cleaned by inserting the brush, wet or dry, at the breech, and propelling it through the bore. If any of the cartridge paper remain in the breech after the discharge, insert a cartridge and move it backward and forward once or twice and the paper will be withdrawn.

The barrel has an adjusting bushing at the breech which is fitted to the breech-pin or slide, so close as to prevent any escape.

Oil the Arms and all their parts with the best sperm oil.

JOHN C. PALMER, President.   **E. THOS. LOBDELL, Secretary.**

Sharps advertising circular from the 1850s. (Courtesy: Kansas State Historical Society)

As the presence of Sharps on the western frontier increased, so did praise for its design. Henry Skillman presumably encountered Sharps in use by members of the American Boundary Survey Commission in the southwest in 1850. He had a government contract in his pocket to carry mail between San Antonio and Santa Fe, and he chose Sharps with which to arm those men escorting his mule-drawn coaches. In June 1853 he wrote the Sharps factory from Texas:

> The ten Sharps' carbines purchased of you were all put to immediate use in arming my escort, and for range, accuracy, and rapidity of firing, they are far superior to any arm known. They have gone through what an ordnance officer would term a pretty severe field test, without the least injury.[6]

The period of their use indicates Skillman's Sharps probably were Model 1851s. During one attack on the mail by Mescalero Apaches, he demonstrated the effectiveness of the Sharps when he shot an Indian taunting the whites from what the Native American felt was a safe distance.[7]

The Olmsted brothers got a rather uncomplimentary impression of the mail train which they encountered camped along the route between El Paso and Santa Fe. The commander of the mounted six-man escort was an old Texas Ranger and the guard was composed of other former rangers. Frederick Olmsted noted they resembled "drunken ruffians" and felt no urge to join their party. He did state that they were armed with Sharps rifles [carbines] and "Colt's repeaters," presumably Colt revolvers.[8]

Another mail contractor on the San Antonio–San Diego route, George H. Giddings, also had praise for the Sharps. "I have used it for two years, a part of the time over my mail route, and it has proved a saviour to myself and my men, when any other arm would have failed me. As for killing bear, deer, &c., I will pit Sharps' rifle against all other arms known."[9]

Model 1852 Sharps carbine stamped on the barrel "ST. JOSEPH & SALT LAKE MAIL CO." The firm was only in operation in 1859–60.

Passenger service by stagecoach from San Diego to San Antonio in the 1850s was uncomfortable and hazardous, and one newspaper editor provided a list of clothes and other items to carry. Topping the list was: "One Sharp's rifle and a hundred cartridges; a Colt's Navy [Model 1851] revolver and two pounds of balls; [and] a knife and sheath."[10]

Samuel W. Cozzens in 1859 employed what probably was a pre–Model 1859 Sharps carbine with which he gained a reputation as a marksman as had Skillman. He observed a band of Apache Indians intent on running off some of the grazing stock at a stagecoach station.

> Having in my hand one of Sharp's carbines, I brought it to bear, and elevating the sight, took deliberate aim at the five Indians, who were huddled close together, and fired. I had not the slightest expectation of hitting one of them, but to my utter surprise I saw one…fall from his saddle, while the men around me uttered a shout at the success of my shot, which must have sounded to the ears of the red-skins like a yell of defiance.…They must have thought themselves far out of rifle range, and as secure as though miles away.…As for me, my unlooked-for success in bringing down this Apache gained me a most enviable reputation as a marksman along the line of the overland mail route, a reputation which I was exceedingly careful not to injure by attempting another shot.[11]

Another mail contractor, Jacob Hall, wrote in 1858 that he had used a Sharps for about four years between Independence, Missouri, and Santa Fe. He praised its reliability, accuracy, and range. He probably was writing of the Model 1852 or 1853 when he wrote: "Nor are the primers uncertain, as I have heard it sometimes asserted. I have frequently discharged a magazine of fifty primers without missing fire more than once or twice." Unlike the models of 1851 and 1855 which used the Maynard tape primers (or regular percussion caps), the two models of 1852 and 1853 could be fired using a tube of small pellet or disk primers, one of which was propelled forward over the nipple whenever the hammer fell. E. E. Cross wrote from Arizona in 1859: "Three hundred [Sharps] would sell in this territory at from $75 to $85 each." This was about triple the price in the east.[12]

Much of the early fame of Sharps arms resulted from their use during the mid-1850s era of "bleeding Kansas." The struggle between free and proslavery factions was a matter of great concern to abolitionist forces in New England. Many antislavery advocates felt that if Kansas was to remain free of slavery, immigration of free-staters there must be encouraged so their opponents could be outvoted. One of the first such groups, organized in New Haven, Connecticut, was the Beecher Bible and Rifle Colony which settled at Wabaunsee. The name resulted from the outcome of an organizational meeting in March 1856 attended by the Reverend Henry Ward Beecher. There, Professor Benjamin Stillman of Yale subscribed to the donation of a Sharps. Others followed his lead and Beecher promised that if twenty-five Sharps were given at the meeting, his Plymouth Church in Brooklyn would donate twenty-five more. In all, twenty-seven Sharps were subscribed at the gathering and within a week the twenty-five promised arrived from Brooklyn along with twenty-five Bibles.[13]

The New England Emigrant Aid Company also was prominent among antislavery organizations in the northeast. The first party of settlers which it promoted reached the site of Lawrence in August of 1854. Settlement of the towns of Topeka, Osawatamie, and Manhattan followed. Antagonism between the pro- and antislavery forces grew as did the need for arms, and in May 1855 the first lot of one hundred Sharps and ammunition was purchased by officials of the New England Emigrant Aid Company for $2,670. To avoid legal difficulties, the company invariably insisted that such weapons were furnished to free-staters by individuals rather than the company itself, although the dividing line was indeed thin. The climax came with the sacking of the town of Lawrence by proslavers on May 21, 1856. Three nights later, John Brown Sr. with his four sons and several others shot or hacked to death five proslavery men along Pottawatomie Creek.

Violence persisted and a Kansas couple writing home from Longwood in July 1856 noted:

> People…have been prevented in a great measure from getting in crops and that many have lost a great deal of private property. The only way that they had been able to do anything in the way of ploughing [sic] and putting in [crops] was to go in large companies to their fields armed with the invincible Sharpe's rifle. Mr. Stewart I have since learned is a New England Minister— but I gathered from his conversation that he thinks that here in the Territory "moral [per]suasion" will be a little better for having something like a Sharpe's rifle to stand on. He agrees with H.W.B. [Rev. Henry Ward Beecher] on that point.[14]

Antislaver Dr. John Doy wrote that at the August 30, 1856, Battle of Osawatomie, "we had Sharps rifles" but had to leave the field when their ammunition was expended. "During these troubles, the women and children made cartridges for our rifles."[15]

References to the Sharps provided to immigrants often call them "rifles," but known shipments were actually Model 1853 "32 bore" (.52 caliber) carbines. The total number shipped there by the various antislavery organizations and backers isn't known, but Sharps authority Frank Sellers estimated it to be between nine hundred and one thousand. One shipment of one hundred carbines was entrusted to David S. Hoyt for delivery. Expecting possible trouble, he removed the breechblocks from the guns and sent them by another route. As he feared, Missourians seized the guns on board the steamer *Arabia* in March 1856, but the carbines were useless in their condition. Only after three years of legal battling were the guns returned to an agent of the New England Emigrant Aid Company and their breechblocks reinstalled.[16]

One free-stater observed that "Missourians [proslavery forces] frequently break open heavy trunks or boxes to search for Sharps rifles of which they stand in great fear." In one such incident in March 1856, suspicious Missourians forced open a large crate shipped by river boat only to find it contained a piano. "A Yankee opened a box containing a cannon but closed it again before anyone noticed and said it contained cartwheels." A band of sixty-eight men, women, and children emigrating from Chicago to Kansas surrendered fifty-eight "condemned United States breach[sic]-loading Hall's rifles" and seventy-five pounds of powder when the steamer on which they were traveling was boarded by Missourians. Another group of forty men from Massachusetts lost sixty Sharps.[17]

On September 13–14, 1856, pro- and antislavery forces battled at Hickory Point. Speaking for the latter:

> We had all sorts of guns, perhaps not more than one-third of our force had Sharp's rifles. Kickapoo Stevens was armed with a Hall's breech-loading rifle and there were a good many condemned United States rifles and muskets. The rest of us were armed with sporting rifles and shotguns.[18]

Lewis Bodwell was a fiery frontier preacher, a staunch antislavery Kansan. When in December 1857 he attended a Free State meeting at Lecompton, he was described as "booted and spurred, wore a close-fitting cap, and had an Indian blanket pinned over his shoulders; under the blanket were plainly visible the muzzle of a Sharps rifle and the hilt of a Colt's revolver." Years later when traveling on behalf of the American Home Missionary Society, he always carried a revolver beneath the cushion in his buggy. "If a man carry[s] a revolver at all, it is just as well to have it handy, for…when any shooting is to be done, it makes all the difference in the world who gets the first shot." W. B. Stone arrived in Kansas in the fall of 1857 with "six wagon-loads of dry goods, which included also three dozen Sharp's rifles, or as many as we could get where we started from—central Illinois."[19]

Antislavery forces in New England also sent arms other than Sharps to Kansas, including a quantity of Colt revolvers, variously stated as five, twenty-five, or fifty dozen. The Colts were to be under John Brown's control, but were distributed to others with the understanding that Brown could request their return. Brown is thought to have carried a .31 caliber Massachusetts Arms revolver during the Kansas troubles before he headed east where he led the

Model 1853 Sharps carbine, usually found with brass barrel band and patchbox cover, is commonly known today as the "John Brown model." In appearance it differed only in minor details from its immediate predecessor, the Model 1852. (Courtesy: Kansas State Historical Society)

attack on the federal arsenal at Harpers Ferry, Virginia, in October of 1859.[20]

In its December 1, 1860, edition, the Wyandotte (Kansas) *Commercial Gazette* noted that five local residents had set out to hunt buffalo for meat. "In the way of outfit they had a tent, three Sharp's and one muzzle-loading rifle, two shotguns for small game, three Colt's revolvers, navy size."[21]

Adversity sometimes prompted ingenuity in early Kansas. Albert Morrall was caught in a snowstorm and it was a week before he could obtain medical attention for his painfully swollen, frozen feet. "When demarcation set in, I got a sharp rifle-bullet mold, and, with a file, sharpened it, and cut my toes off myself by squeezing the molds down and pulling the bones out like a tooth, one by one." He possibly used a Sharps mold, which had pincers for cutting off the excess lead or sprue from a cast bullet.[22]

Civil war intensified the factional bitterness in Kansas. One pro-Union man wrote many years later that men and women devoted more effort to practicing with firearms than to farming. His family's front gate was used as a target and often had to be replaced. Travelers were invited to stop and participate.

> They thus learned of the wonderful skill and accuracy of the settlers in the use of firearms, "sitting or on the wing." These lessons warned enemies of the danger of attack, as each cabin and stable was known to be a well-fortified fort.... The nightly occupation was molding bullets and cutting patching.[23]

The Pony Express provided mail service between St. Joseph, Missouri, and Sacramento, California, for only eighteen months, beginning in April of 1860. There is no documentation specifying what guns the young riders carried. The author has examined two Colts, a Model 1851 Navy and an 1849 Pocket Model, with authentic appearing markings representing the parent firm, the Central Overland California and Pike's Peak Express. (The name sometimes was abbreviated as C.O.C. & P.P., translated by some as "clean out of cash and poor pay.") The weight of rider and his gear was kept to a minimum, and one observer noted that riders carried only a revolver except in the mountain stretches where detours were impossible and where they could carry rifles.[24]

J. G. Kelley recalled carrying a Sharps on several rides. On one occasion, his route took him through a forest of quaking aspens where a Mexican rider had been mortally wounded two days before.

> A trail had been cut through these little trees, just wide enough to allow horse and rider to pass. As the road was crooked and the branches came together from either side, just above my head when mounted, it was impossible to see ahead more than ten or fifteen yards, and it was two miles through the forest. I expected to have trouble, and prepared for it by dropping my bridle reins on the neck of the horse, put my Sharp's rifle [carbine?] at full cock, kept both spurs into the flanks and he went through that forest like a "streak of greased lightning."
>
> At the top of the hill I dismounted to rest my horse, and looking back, saw the bushes moving in several places. As there were no cattle or game in that vicinity, I knew the movements must be caused by Indians, and was more positive of it when,

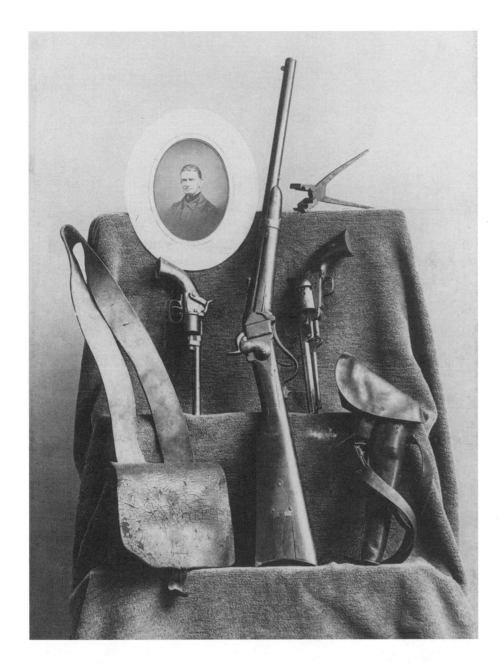

Guns attributed to John Brown Sr. From left: Massachusetts Arms Company Maynard primed .31 belt revolver, Sharps Model 1852 carbine, and Colt M1851 revolver. The former was a redesigned version of the Wesson & Leavitt revolver. A release button in front of the trigger allows the cylinder to be rotated by hand, a necessary change after the firm's loss to Colt in a landmark patent infringement lawsuit. (Courtesy: Herbert Houze)

after firing several shots at the spot..., all agitation ceased. Several days after that, two...soldiers...were shot and killed from the ambush of those bushes and stripped of their clothing.[25]

He came closer to being killed when he was almost shot by an emigrant who mistook him for an Indian as he galloped past a wagon train.

During the Civil War, the Federal government purchased almost one hundred thousand Sharps carbines and rifles, mostly the former. Many considered them the best of the single-shot percussion breech loading arms used in that conflict. Many of these Sharps went west, some sold to veterans upon their discharge from service and, later, oth-

ers disposed of by the government through surplus sales. The availability of these and other surplus arms hampered the sale of new guns. Beginning in 1867, Sharps employees for the next two years labored to convert about thirty-one thousand carbines and two thousand rifles to fire .50–70 metallic cartridges under contract for the army. Thousands of other percussion Sharps were converted for sporting use as late as the 1880s, some by Sharps and others by dealers and individuals.

The Sharps Rifle Manufacturing Company inaugurated a concerted effort to introduce a new model metallic cartridge rifle to the sporting market in 1869, producing fewer than one thousand of these rifles and carbines. But by January of 1871, production was underway of what the firm would later designate as its Model

One of approximately seventy-seven thousand Sharps models 1859 and 1863 .52 carbines purchased by the Union Army between 1861 and 1865. This M1863 (#78318) was issued to Pvt. Clark who served throughout the war with the Ist California Cavalry. The regiment operated primarily in Arizona and New Mexico. (Courtesy: John D. McAulay)

Army officers with .50–70 Sharps carbines (1873). (Courtesy: Henry E. Huntington Library and Art Gallery, San Marino, CA)

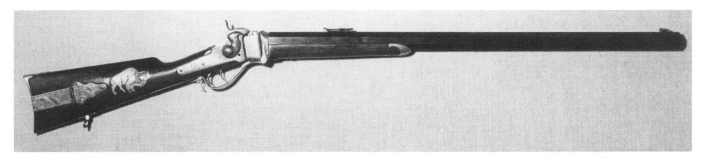

A .45 sporting rifle shipped to Sharps dealer Walter Cooper of Bozeman, Montana. The receiver, lock, and patchbox cover are engraved and the stock is inlaid with the figure of a bison. (Courtesy: Roswell Museum and Art Center, NM)

1874, turned out in numerous variations. The M1874 in the west became a workhorse among single-shot rifles. During the extermination of the bison herds during the 1870s and early 1880s, this Sharps Model 1874 became the tool chosen by the majority of professionals, a story found in another chapter. But despite the advantages of the metallic cartridge Sharps, the market for percussion guns remained among the more cost-conscious. A. J. Plate of San Francisco in 1877 wrote the Sharps factory mentioning he had two hundred Sharps "linen" or percussion carbines on hand.[26]

When James Gillett was sworn in as a Texas Ranger in June 1874, he and the other recruits received "a Sharps carbine, .50 caliber, and one .45 Colt's [Single Action] pistol. These arms were charged to us, their cost to be deducted from our first pay... of $40 per month." His recollection of the Sharps wasn't favorable, however. "These guns would heat easily and thus were very inaccurate shooters." After 1877 the rangers carried a Winchester rifle or carbine, he wrote.[27]

Many areas of the west were a hunter's paradise, whether one was seeking meat or sport, and the Sharps wasn't found wanting even if the owner encountered a grizzly. The popularity of the Sharps in Montana was representative. Walter Cooper of Bozeman became the largest Sharps dealer in Montana Territory after establishing his business in December 1868, "handling as specialties firearms, ammunition, and a general line of hunting and defensive material together with a first class gunsmith establishment." He wasn't always prompt in paying his bills and in November 1876 the president of the Sharps Rifle Company had written to him pointing out that some of his bills were as much as four years old! Yet Cooper had been a strong promoter of the Sharps and in 1872 had written the factory:

Those four guns you sent me take the eye of every one. They outshoot anything ever brought to this country. I won a bet of ten dollars the other day on penetration against an army musket [.50-70], called the Springfield Needle Gun here. Shot the same powder and shot two inches deeper into the wood.[28]

In addition to selling and promoting Sharps, Cooper's armory produced various functional and stylistic modifications including improvements in sights and a rebounding hammer which returned to half cock when fired. Andrew Garcia was a Cooper customer who already owned a Winchester Model 1873 repeater.

But [I] had to buy a buffalo gun. Like the Chinaman who took the largest size boot if it was the same price as the smaller to get more leather for the money, I bought a .45–120 caliber Sharps rifle, a buffalo gun which weighed 15 pounds and cost $75.00 although I could have had a lighter .45–90 No. 13 for the same price.[29]

Alexander D. McAusland arrived in Miles City, Montana Territory, on Christmas Eve, 1879. His arrival was embarrassing for while unloading his Sharps in a saloon it discharged, but fortunately the bullet drove harmlessly into the dirt floor. He opened the Creedmoor Armory and did a substantial gunsmithing business, often rebarreling Sharps including one which weighed twenty-six pounds when it left his shop![30]

During a range war in Arizona Territory in 1883, rancher Commodore Perry Owen was described as "carrying two six-shooters, a single-shot Sharps rifle sighted 'to shoot a mile' and a light magazine rifle for closer work" when he rode into St. Johns to rescue two African American cowboys from jail. All that was missing from

Unfortunately the archives could not provide a better quality copy, but the gun is easily identifiable in the original image as a Sharps carbine, slung from this sheepherder's saddle. (Courtesy: National Anthropological Archives, Smithsonian Institution, Washington DC)

what would have been an all-inclusive arsenal was a der-ringer and a shotgun.[31]

Dave Rudebaugh (or Rudabaugh) and five others in January 1876 made two unsuccessful attempts to rob the Santa Fe Express. After their capture, the Ford County (Kansas) *Globe* published Rudebaugh's confession includ-ing an inventory of the gang's guns. It was surprising that there wasn't a Winchester in the entire lot.

> Roark got his gun, a (45) Sharp's at Rath's sometime before.... Dan Dement had one gun, a Sharp's rifle and one six-shooter, a Colt's 45.... Thomas Gott had a 44 Sharp's and no revolvers.... Green was armed with on[e] 45 U.S. Springfield patent gun; he had [purchased?] two 45 Colt's pistols at Zimmerman's in Dodge City between the time of the first plan and before the second robbery. Ed West was armed with one United States Springfield gun and one six-shooter, Colt's 45.... I was armed with

on[e] of the Sharp's 40 calibre guns and had two Smith & Wesson pistols.[32]

When faced with unruly Brule warriors at the White Clay Agency for Red Cloud's Oglala Sioux, cowboy Edgar Beecher Bronson stood ready with several army officers, Indian agent Dr. McGillicuddy, and Indian policemen under Sword. "Time and again I caught a bead on the chief's breast with my .45–120 Sharps that easily might have sent him into permanent camp."[33]

Hiram Steward spent much of his career as a hunter in the Rockies and relied on a Sharps .44–75. In 1878 across a gambling table, Steward made a remark which a Southerner took as an insult.

> Jackson ... sprang to his feet, saying he would not be insulted by any Yankee. Drew his six-shooter, and called upon Steward to defend himself. Steward pulled open his old buckskin coat, set his slouched hat back on his head and his large, gray eyes flashed.

"Grip" the dog and his companions. Prominent in the scene are a M1874 Sharps (right) and a M1873 Winchester (center). (Courtesy: Herb Peck Jr.)

Every one thought Jackson had run a successful bluff, when Steward stood up, and, without saying a word, walked behind the counter, grasped his old Sharp's and threw in a cartridge, saying: "Jackson, I have not long to live and I know it. I am no shot with a six [gun], but just come on and we will go over the river. I will shoot it out with you now. Come on." All hands started to accompany them, and the crowd had gotten about half way down, when Jackson turned and went back to the store on the run. He never tried the bluff again, and was a laughing stock for all who had witnessed the affair.[34]

Despite the preference for the Sharps among many single-shot users, its one-shot capacity wasn't sufficient for Dan Ming. In 1887 one night at his Arizona ranch, his dogs set out after a mountain lion which had wandered into the yard. In the confusion, the lion found itself on the enclosed back porch. Ming grabbed his .44 Sharps and fired, wounding the animal slightly. Quickly he began to use the weapon as a club to stun the cougar until he was able to reload and dispatch it with another shot. Soon after the incident, he traded the Sharps for a repeating rifle. Prior to that time, he had felt repeaters were inaccurate and encouraged careless shooting.[35]

One letter to the Sharps factory came from Tom Holloway of Menard County, Texas, in January 1879, seeking .40 caliber reloading supplies. He went on to explain:

Probably a desert prospector with pick and a Sharps rifle. Its stock is the less common style with a cheekpiece and sporting butt plate, the latter with more of a crescent shape than the army or shotgun styles. (Courtesy: Herb Peck Jr.)

I should like to see more of yours [rifles] in use here & I believe they would be if there was not so much horse back traveling done when the "Winchister" is used it being a little handier to carry on the saddle than yours, but I can carry yours without any trouble, but a gun like mine 2 1/2 or 3 in. shorter & a couple of lbs lighter would beat a Winchester every way, but I am content with my old reliable as it is, at present I am foreman for Messrs. Shannon & Black stock men & the fear of the law is not half so great as the fear of a bullet with the characters we have to deal with.[36]

While Sharps rifles and carbines found much favor among western hunters, Sharps target rifles made impressive scores on the firing range at Creedmoor (New York), Walnut Hill (Massachusetts), and elsewhere in the east from 1873 forward. Until the early 1880s, matches were fired at distances of up to one thousand yards. In these long-range contests, Sharps and Remington target rifles often dominated the field among American shooters, each make with its vocal advocates. A number of westerners, too, spent long hours in perfecting their skills on paper targets.

An illuminating endorsement appeared in Sharps's 1879 catalog, a letter dated November 7, 1876, from George A. Meears of Salt Lake City, vice president of the Pioneer Rifle Club. It included the results of his club's "All Comers" match.

One must feel sympathy for the burro. Not only is the rider of ample size but he has added the weight of a heavy Sharps M1874 sporting rifle. (Courtesy: John Hartman via Gerald R. Mayberry)

Out of fourteen competitors, eleven used yours [Sharps], one a Remington Creedmoor, one Ballard, and one Spencer. During the day's shooting we had another accidental discharge with the only Remington rifle on the ground. This makes the fourth accident; one of them came near sending me to another country, the ball passing within three inches of my head.... These four accidents all occurred in about a year's time, and have completely determined me against the Remington. The rifles shoot well, but the action is not safe, no matter what the extensive advertisements may say to the contrary.... I consider your rifles absolutely safe, while I regard the Remington action as a "delusion and a snare."[37]

Apparently some accidents had occurred with the Remington rolling-block action due to the sensitive primers of that era. These were more likely to be fired prematurely as the Remington breechblock closed on them while the Sharps block closed across them.[38]

John S. Moore wrote from Galveston, Texas, on April 3 of 1875 requesting literature describing Sharps's new Creedmoor-style Model 1874 rifle. He described himself as being "passionately fond of Rifle shooting, [and I] have now a Maynard, Winchester, Spencer, two Ballards & a Wesson." His rifle club's range was "as fine a range as can be found in the U.S." He was organizing a rifle club for shorter range firing with Maynard rifles and from it would select a "long range team." His choice for the latter team would be Sharps or Remington rifles. "Although Remington's guns seem to have occasioned considerable éclat I must confess to being prejudiced in favor of Sharps though I have seen none of the Creedmoor guns of either make."[39]

Three weeks later Moore wrote to the president of the Sharps Rifle Company that he had received the literature. "Since I have tried the Remington Creedmoor I am more than ever impressed that I will decidedly prefer the Sharps. I have no fault to find with the shooting of the R[emington] but regard the action as objectionable in several

Willey Pearce with a Sharps astride an ox. (Courtesy: Arizona Historical Society Library, Tucson)

points." The Remington Creedmoor, he noted, had to be wiped clean after almost every shot and he preferred the Sharps extractor, which threw the shell clear of the gun.[40]

As the president of the Galveston Rifle Club in 1877, Moore's loyalty to Sharps rifles persisted as his February 16 letter to the company reveals:

> It has been long acknowledged by all hunters & sportsmen of Texas that for accurate & strong shooting, ease of manipulation, safety—simplicity—& strength of construction, the Sharps hunting rifle is the favorite & has no superior. We are now trying your new long range rifle & find the precision & force with which it shoots at

1000 yds perfectly surprising. As we have ground for a three mile range with the Gulf of Mexico behind it we propose to test the gun further & ascertain if possible how far it will shoot beyond the 1000 yds with accuracy. We are satisfied with the 1000 yds "the end is not yet."[41]

A member of Moore's rifle club, W. G. Morse, in March 1877 received a Creedmoor Sharps, but found it unsatisfactory.

> The Rifle ordered for me...came to hand today & is not at all satisfactory. It is nothing more in looks than one of our common

Members of a San Antonio German shooting group or *schutzen verein*. At left is a No. 5 Remington rolling block and at right a Sharps. (Courtesy: San Antonio Conservation Society, TX)

club Guns, common stock &c. &c. No special pains upon it. I wished a handsome stock rubber butt & handsome fore part. You sent Capt. Moore of this place . . . a very handsome Gun pretty Stock &c. Why should not mine be as handsome? I pay as much as he does. . . . A few more cases of this Kind will prejudice our club against Your Rifle therefore I think it will be more to your interest to be more careful with your orders.[42]

In February 1877, A. B. McDowell of Jackson County, Texas, wrote to the Sharps Rifle Company seeking a rifle for use in neighborhood shooting matches, explaining that

he had purchased two Spencer rifles, a Winchester, one Ballard, two "Rimmgtons," and a Maynard. None of these could be counted on for target shooting beyond one hundred yards although he felt the Maynard to be the most reliable. He was seeking a Sharps .40–70 sporting rifle with a 32-inch barrel. Sharps personnel probably were amused by his inquiry and what accompanied it.

The [deer] hide I send you is a fare [*sic*] sample of the lot I have. Both in size and quality, they are splendid hides, no chemicals used in dressing them. If you can engage them at $2.50 each, let me know immediately and I will forward the hides while you put me up the Rifle I order.[43]

A prospector, his burro, and a military-style Sharps rifle. (Courtesy: Colorado Historical Society, neg. #HS-12667)

With tongue firmly in cheek, another Sharps owner in Texas in 1880 wrote the factory complaining that his rifle killed game so far away that it spoiled before he got to it.[44]

Competitive shooters on the target range often scored high with Sharps and other target rifles at one thousand yards. But successful shots at a long, unknown distance were the result of a number of factors including the ability to judge distance and familiarity with one's rifle and its shooting characteristics. Luck also figured into the equation. Buffalo hunter Billy Dixon was credited with a shot that struck one of a group of Indians at a claimed measured distance of fifteen hundred yards. Jack Bean made a similar shot. In early 1874, Bean was one of a large expedition of miners and others who sought to explore the Yellowstone country of Montana. Skirmishes with Indians were frequent, but Bean made the last shot fired with hostile intent during the trip. Two Indians on a point of land

had fired on the party's corralled horses when Bean returned the compliment.

> When it was time for the bullet to get there, the Indian shot at dropped. Several who were looking at the Indian with glasses, declared that the ball had hit him. The distance between the parties must have been nearly a mile. Jack used a long range rifle (120-grain Sharp's) and had made several very effective shots during the trip.[45]

During the 1878 Lincoln County War in New Mexico Territory, a Sharps figured in one highly publicized engagement. While the Murphy-Dolan faction besieged Billy the Kid and others who took refuge in the McSween home, two snipers were firing on the house from about nine hundred

A scene at Fort Berthold photographed by F. Jay Haynes, photographer for the Northern Pacific Railroad. The rifle in the image appears to be an 1878 Sharps Borchardt. (Courtesy: South Dakota State Historical Society)

yards away. From inside the structure, Fernando Herrera reportedly silenced the snipers after only one sighting shot from his .45 Sharps.[46]

Also in 1878, the Sharps firm broke with its traditional outside hammer design and introduced a new model, the Sharps Borchardt with its distinctive hammerless action and flat-sided frame. The gun was cheaper to manufacture and while it had its converts, many customers clung to the more familiar design with an external hammer. Despite its advanced features, the Borchardt wasn't able to keep the company afloat. Military-style Borchardt rifles proved to be the best sellers with substantial numbers going to a few eastern state governments and Louisiana, and the Borchardt did have its enthusiasts among some competitive shooters.

P. H. Fagan wrote on the day before Christmas in 1880 to the Sharps Rifle Company concerning his new .45 Model 1878:

> I am very much pleased with the Express
> Rifle I purchased of you last August.... I

would not exchange it for any Rifle I ever saw.... At first I did not like it on account of it being Hammerless but now I would not have a gun with a Hammer it is much quicker and Safer I have never had it to snap.... [I] tried Several Different make[s] of Rifles Such as Winchester Ballard Spencer & Maynard, but none is as good as the Sharp. Maynard is the best of the above list.[47]

The factory's list price in January 1878 began at $16.50 for the new Borchardt in carbine length. A plain Model 1874 round barrel nine-pound .40 Hunter's rifle with single trigger was $25; $10 more could purchase a slightly heavier round barrel Business rifle in .40 or .45 caliber with double trigger. The 1874 Sporting rifle with octagonal barrel and open sights began at $38; a double trigger added $4, and any gun heavier than twelve pounds up to sixteen pounds added $1 per pound to the cost. The dedicated—and wealthy—hunter or target shooter could order an

Fortunately original factory records exist for many later model Sharps including this worn Borchardt (#9861). It was invoiced to Sharps agent William Read & Sons of Boston on December 5, 1878, as a Model 1878 carbine for $16.50. It eventually reached Colorado and fell into Indian hands, perhaps Utes. The butt plate was removed long ago, the action was rusted shut, and the stock bears many holes where tacks once decorated it. Its weathered condition indicates it may have been a burial gun, buried with its Indian owner. (Photo by Gary Roedl, courtesy William T. Goodman)

A studio portrait taken by J. T. Needles of Leadville, Colorado. The subject holds a Sharps Model 1878 Borchardt with what appear to be a Colt Single Action (left) and a Merwin & Hulbert (right). (Courtesy: Herb Peck Jr.)

An 1885 view of the interior of Freund's Wyoming Armory in Cheyenne, Wyoming. The sign on the wall promotes "SHARPS Improved Breech-Loading Sporting & Long-Range RIFLES." (Courtesy: Wyoming State Museum, Cheyenne)

engraved Long Range Model 1874 or Borchardt with various special features at up to $300, "fully tested by an expert up to 1,000 yards." Factory literature also proclaimed: "All our rifles are warranted to stand 150 grains of powder, if customers desire to use that quantity. But the *regular* charge is ample for any purpose."[48]

George Shields hunted in Montana using a .40–75 Model 1878, sometimes with Miles City photographer L. A. Huffman. "A large majority of the frontiersmen I met . . . used Sharps rifles . . . as to their effectiveness and adaptation to frontier use, they pronounced them the best arm in use." But by late 1879, the Sharps company was in serious financial difficulty. Sales were down and the ongoing work of converting percussion guns and rebarreling or repairing later guns was insufficient. As early as 1875, the Sharps company had begun a search for a repeating rifle design to manufacture. Negotiations came closest to fruition involving a bolt action magazine rifle designed by James Paris Lee, but eventually production was undertaken by Remington. In October of

1880, production of new guns at the Sharps plant ceased. Thus ended a thirty-one-year span of production of Sharps long arms which had earned a premier position among those firearms which helped settle the American west.[49]

Even though the manufacture of Sharps at the Bridgeport factory had ended, E. C. Meacham of St. Louis in that firm's 1884 catalog was advertising its own Model 1874 Sharps, assembled by the dealer's gunsmiths.

> On account of the *pressing demands* of Frontiersmen and Buffalo Hunters for Sharps' Model 1874 Rifles with heavy barrels and double triggers, we were induced to change a *limited number* at considerable expense to conform to their requirements. The barrels are of *best quality* and *workmanship*, and equal to Sharps' high standard of excellence in *every particular*. These arms are all being completed,

therefore orders varying from the following descriptions cannot be filled.

The Business-style rifle was a .45 with 28-inch round barrel at $15; the other Meachams advertised were .40 or .45 Sporting-style with a 30-inch octagonal barrel weighing 10 1/2 to 16 pounds at $16.50 to $20. Also offered were "Sharp's Long Range Creedmoor Guns, 45–105, complete sights, pistol grip, horn butt plate, wgt 10, len'th 32, List, 125 00, Net, 50 00." Also still available from Meacham were Sharps-made .45 and .50 carbines as well as .40 and .45 "Sporting Rifles" and "Saddle Rifles" from $7.50 to $10.[50]

CHAPTER SEVEN

Colts and
Their Competitors

*There are probably in Texas about as many revolvers
as male adults, and I doubt if there are one hundred
in the state of any other make.*
— Frederick L. Olmsted, 1854[1]

Handguns by Colt were the preeminent holster revolvers in the west during the last half of the nineteenth century; they were as common as spittoons in a saloon. This is true despite the availability of comparable quality arms by such makers as Manhattan, Smith & Wesson, Remington, Hopkins & Allen (Merwin & Hulberts), and others. In part it was the result of early promotional efforts by the inventor and the advantage of being first in the marketplace. Just as important, the Colt firm marketed a diverse line of reliable products.

Young Sam Colt received his first American arms patents in 1836, the year Texas achieved independence from Mexico. The inaugural production facility was in Paterson, New Jersey, where Colt produced revolving rifles and then revolvers. Word of the new arms reached Texas before large-scale production was inaugurated, as a June 3, 1836, letter from A. J. Yates to Stephen F. Austin reveals:

> I have also written to Colt of Patterson [*sic*] to inquire the prices of his ten charge [shot] rifles, carbines and pistols and want to bring out what will be most useful to the country, and dispose of it for land. . . . If horses could be promised 100

men, provided I could bring them out with the equipment and arms—I am inclined to think that 100 cavalry with Colts carbines, with spring bayonets, and pistols, will be a very powerful and efficient force. Colts carbines and pistols discharge 30 rounds in the same time that it takes to load three times.[2]

Yet it wasn't until 1839 that the debt-laden Texas republic purchased any of the new Colts, 180 .36 caliber No. 5 revolvers with a 9-inch barrel for its navy along with the same number of Colt carbines and one hundred rifles. When the Texas Rangers were reconstituted in 1844, one company was commanded by Jack Hays who obtained a quantity of used Colt revolvers from the navy depot at Galveston. These guns had their baptism of fire in ranger hands on June 8, 1844, when Hays and fifteen men, including Samuel Walker, engaged and routed a force of more than sixty Comanches. The rangers apparently were outfitted with spare cylinders for their revolvers enabling them to fire ten shots without reloading. One survivor of the battle used the phrase, "two cylinders and both loaded."[3]

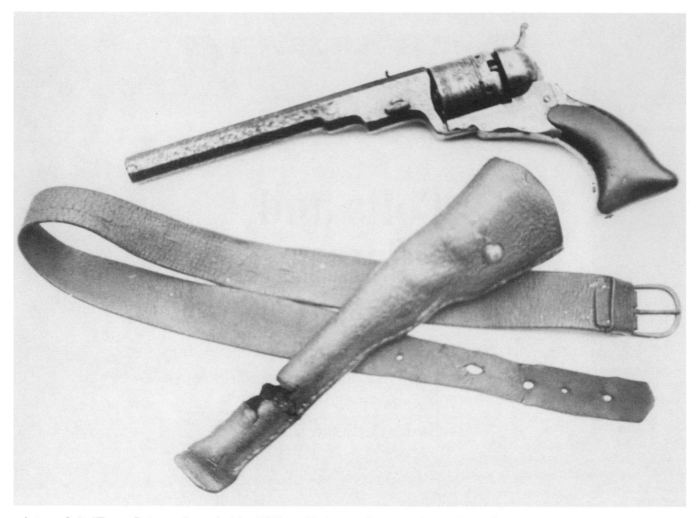

A true Colt "Texas Paterson" carried by William M. Lowe who served as a Texas Ranger under Capt. John Coffee Hays before the Mexican War. (Courtesy: Steve Evans)

William Lowe, seated with his family, fought in the Mexican War with Bell's Regiment of Texas Volunteers, journeyed to California in 1850 where he served as sheriff of Trinity County (1852–54) before returning to Missouri, and during the Civil War cast his lot with the Confederacy as captain of Company E, 11th Missouri Infantry. (Courtesy: Steve Evans)

Colt .36 Paterson found in 1929 by a well-digging crew in a collapsed adobe building northeast of Amarillo, Texas. Similar guns in "dug up" or relic condition have substantial collector appeal and their condition should be stabilized rather than attempting to clean or restore them. (Photo by Leland E. DeFord III, gun courtesy Edward F. Cornett)

During the Mexican War, Col. Ethan Allen Hitchcock described the rangers: "Their appearance [is] never to be forgotten. Not any sort of uniforms, but well-mounted and doubly well-armed: each man has one or two Colt's revolvers besides ordinary pistols, a sword, and every man a rifle. The Mexicans are terribly afraid of them."[4]

Each Paterson Colt revolver, whether one of the small .28 or .31 caliber "Baby" Patersons or the largest No. 5 .36 caliber holster model, had a five-shot cylinder capacity and a concealed trigger which popped out when the hammer was cocked. It probably was one of the larger sizes which Edwin Bryant mentioned in an account of an 1846 western journey.

> We had a shooting-match at a target,
> with a number of Sioux Indians, in
> which the bow and arrow, rifle, and pis-
> tol were introduced. These Indians shoot
> the arrow with great accuracy and force,
> at long distances. One of them handled
> the rifle with the skill of a marksman and
> hunter. The rapid repeating discharges of
> Colt's revolving-pistol astonished them
> very much. They regarded the instru-
> ment with so much awe as to be unwill-
> ing to handle it.[5]

A few years earlier in 1839, Josiah Gregg traveled to Santa Fe with a trading party. He and his brother were each provided with "one of Colt's repeating rifles, and a pair of pistols of the same, so that with extra loaded cylinders we could...carry thirty-six ready-loaded shots apiece." George W. Kendall in 1841 joined what ostensibly also was to be a trading expedition from Texas to Santa Fe, but it became clear to him that the party stood ready to raise the Texas flag over the town if rumors of widespread discontent with Mexican rule were true. The Texans relied in part on Colt hand and shoulder arms; Kendall lost the barrel of his borrowed Paterson revolver while buffalo hunting when the wedge holding barrel to frame fell out, but he recovered it.[6]

Later in the journey, Kiowas attacked a portion of the military escort, Lt. Hull and four men who were searching for water.

> Lieutenant Hull had received no less than
> thirty lance and arrow wounds before he
> fell, and the broken stock of one of Colt's
> rifles was still retained in the grasp of a
> stout man, named Mayby, plainly telling us
> that he had fought to the last, and that after
> discharging the piece he had still continued
> the combat. The heart of one of the men
> was cut out, and had not the Indians been

Colt No. 5 Texas Paterson with what may have been a fascinating yet unknown history based on the inscriptions on its ivory grips: "Texas Rangers/Mexican War/1846" and "California/1848/ Flores Expedition/1852."
(Courtesy: US Military Academy, West Point Museum, NY)

driven off the other bodies would have been mutilated in the same way.[7]

Despite praise for Colt's guns from early users, lagging civilian and military sales forced the Patent Arms Manufacturing Company into insolvency in 1842. Now the young entrepreneur busied himself in various ventures including underwater explosives, the telegraph, and tinfoil cartridges. With the outbreak of war with Mexico in 1846, Colt eagerly sought endorsements for his guns. His efforts brought a US government order on January 4, 1847, for one thousand revolvers at $25 each, the famed four-pound, nine-ounce six-shot .44 named for the gun's codesigner, Capt. Samuel H. Walker, former Texas Ranger and now with the US Mounted Rifles. These revolvers were manufactured at a factory owned by Eli Whitney Jr., but the order allowed the extroverted Colt to establish his own facility in Hartford, marking his return to the arms-making business.

The Walker was soon followed in 1847–48 by a slightly lighter (just over four pounds) series of .44 so-called Dragoons and a much smaller .31 caliber Model 1848 Baby Dragoon pocket model. This latter Colt in modified form as the Model 1849 became the most widely sold percussion revolver in this country, at some 330,000. In late 1850, a .36 caliber six-shooter appeared, commonly called the Model 1851 Navy, so named because its cylinder bore a roll engraved scene portraying an 1843 naval victory by the Texas Navy over that of Mexico. Thus by 1851, Colt was marketing a pocket size, a .36 "belt" revolver, and a heavy .44 "holster" pistol, something to fit anyone's need.

Artist George Catlin gave up his law career and turned to art and in 1830 headed west where he visited forty-eight different Indian tribes and produced 310 portraits in oil. Among his other paintings were six commissioned by Sam Colt showing a Paterson revolving rifle or a Dragoon revolver in use in North or South America.[8]

There was no agreement in the 1850s as to whether the graceful .36 Model 1851 Navy or the bulkier .44 Dragoon was the more suitable on the frontier. Each had its supporters among civilians and the military, although production of the '51 through 1859 was more than four times that of the Dragoon series (c. 90.000 to c. 20.000). As Capt. Randolph Marcy explained:

> Colt's army [.44 Dragoon] and navy sized [.36 Model 1851] have been in use for a long time in our army, [but] officers are by no means of one mind as to their relative merits for frontier service. The navy pistol, being more light and portable, is more convenient for the belt, but it is very questionable... whether these qualities counterbalance the advantages to be derived from the greater weight of powder and lead that can be fired from the larger pistol, and the consequent increased projectile force.[9]

FIFTY DOLLARS REwARD.---The undersigned will give the above reward to whoever will produce sufficient evidence to convict the person who stripped his vessel (the Alert,) of her rigging and even went so far as to pull off sheets of copper from her bottom.

April 3---3t   GEO. SIMPTON.

AT AUCTION.--Brig PENSACOLA for sale.--Will be sold at public auction, on Monday, April 5th, at 2 o'clock, P. M., on the West beach, the brig PENSACOLA, Hallett, master, her tackle and apparal: to be sold in small lots.   a3-l1p

AT AUCTION.--Brig J. PETERSON for sale.--Will be sold at public auction, on Monday, April 5th, at 2 o'clock, P. M., on the West beach, the brig J. PETERSON, Baker, master, her tackle and apparal: Her hull and apparal will be sold separately. Also---a lot of Beef, Pork, and cabin stores. By order of survey.   a3-l1p

COLTS REPEATING ARMS--Rifles, Carbines, and Pistols.--The officers of the Army and Navy are informed that these arms can be obtained until the 10th inst., at the door on the left of the gate, going out to the Wharf,

Private soldiers can be furnished when producing written permits from their immediate commanding officers.

Citizens can also be supplied upon the written permission of the Governor of the city, Major General Worth.

Vera Cruz, April 3, 1847. 3t

Mexican War ad for Colt firearms from the Vera Cruz, Mexico, American Eagle on April 3, 1847, directed at US Army and Navy officers.

A mammoth .44 Colt Walker compared with a .31 "Baby Dragoon" 1848 pocket model Colt.

The captain cited an incident in 1858 in which a dozen .36 caliber balls had failed to kill a grizzly. The wounded giant was dispatched with only two shots from a .44 Colt.

Charles Hummel, a San Antonio gun dealer, on January 2, 1854, wrote to jobber Armand Soubie of New Orleans that "Military Colts [.44 Dragoons] sell better than Navys." However on October 2, 1854, Hummel ordered two dozen each of Colt Navies and Dragoons but a week later wrote Soubie again to ask for "2 dozen Colt Navys and 1 dozen brass mounted Militarys." In another letter of September 4, 1854, he repeated the order—twenty-four .36s and twelve .44s. His letters revealed he was paying about $25 for the Navy and Dragoon but $17 to $18 for Colt .31 pocket models, although the .31s didn't sell as well.[10]

Texas Ranger John Salmon "Rip" Ford photographed in the late 1850s with a pair of .44 Colts, either Walkers or Dragoons or one of each. "Rip" sometimes was facetiously translated as "Rest In Peace." (Courtesy: John N. McWilliams)

At this time Hummel also was an agent for the sale of Whitney arms—"Mississippi rifles, revolvers, breech-loaders and ordinary carbines." Whitney-made revolvers at that time were pocket size .28 and .31 arms, produced in limited numbers. It's unknown what the breechloaders and "ordinary carbines" were that he listed but the former may have been Halls or Jenks.[11]

Whether or not the following anecdote is true, it's worth retelling. John Henry Harper of Independence, Missouri, described as "a bright fellow without character," sought the attention of teenage Fanny Owens. Her father objected and in an encounter between father and suitor, the latter threatened to commit suicide.

> Suiting the action to the words, [Harper] drew a small pocket pistol, placed the muzzle to his head and drew the trigger. It snapped. Mr. Owens coolly walked to his desk and pulled out a pair of Colts dragoon revolvers and handed them to Harper, remarking, "Try one of these, I have killed buffalo with them on the

Colt Second Model Dragoon, once the property of a Union Pacific Railroad employee. (Courtesy: Donald Snoddy, Union Pacific Railroad Company, Omaha, NE)

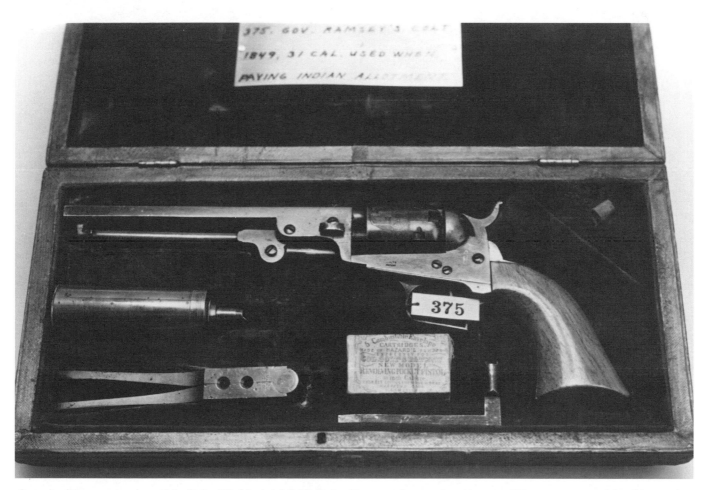

Cased with accessories, this Colt .31 Model 1848 Baby Dragoon in nearly new condition was owned by Alexander Ramsey, the first territorial governor of Minnesota (1849–53) and the second state governor (1860–63). He reportedly carried it with him when traveling by buckboard to Fort Snelling to make Indian allotment payments. Accessories include bullet mold without sprue cutter, powder flask, combination nipple wrench and screwdriver, and packet of skin cartridges. (Courtesy: Richard Donaldson)

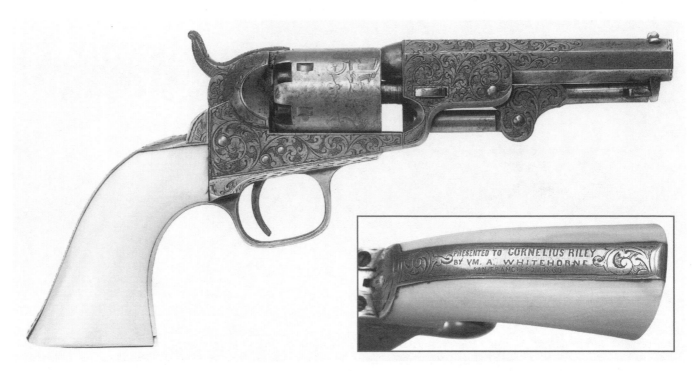

"PRESENTED TO CORNELIUS RILEY/BY VM. A. WHITEHORN/SAN FRANCISCO 1866" is the inscription on the backstrap of this Colt .31 Model 1849 (#188548). The 1866 San Francisco directory lists Riley as "Wines and Liquors and Proprietor of the Yacht Saloon. 314 & 316 Clay St. S.F." In the same volume the donor appears as Wm. A. Whitehorn, "Importer and Jobber of Guns and Sporting Material and Agent for Schuyler, Hartley and Graham N.Y. 22 Battery St. S.F.," and so would have easy access to such a handsome Colt as this. The gun was manufactured in 1860 as a six-shot variation with 4-inch barrel. Its grip is ivory and the gun is extensively engraved by Gustave Young, who engraved Colt products both in the factory and in his own shop from about 1852 until 1869. (Courtesy: Bob Butterfield)

plains, and have never known either one of them to snap yet."[12]

Frederick L. Olmsted wrote a lengthy tribute to Colts in general and the Model 1851 in particular after an 1853 trip to Texas.

Of the Colt's [sic] we cannot speak in too high terms. Though subjected for six or eight months to rough use, exposed to damp grass, and to all the ordinary neglects and accidents of camp travel, not once did a ball fail to answer the finger. Nothing got out of order, nothing required care; not once, though carried at random, in coat-pocket or belt, or tied thumping at the pummel [sic] was there an accidental dis-charge.... They simply gave us perfect satis-faction, being all they claimed to be. Before taking them from home we gave them a trial alongside every rival we could hear of, and we had with us an unpatented imita-

tion, but for practical purposes one Colt we found worth a dozen of all others. Such was the testimony of every old hunter and ranger we met. There are probably in Texas about as many revolvers as male adults, and I doubt if there are one hundred in the state of any other make. After a little practice we could very surely chop off a snake's head from the saddle at any reasonable distance, and across a fixed rest could hit an object of the size of a man at ordinary rifle range. One of our pistols was one day submerged in a bog for some minutes, but on trial, though dripping wet, not a single barrel [chamber] missed fire. A border weapon, so reliable in every sense, would give brute courage to even a dyspeptic tailor.[13]

Olmsted made reference to several means of carry-ing their Colt revolvers—in pocket, belt, or tied to the pommel of the saddle. Deep saddle holsters slung over the pommel had been the army's favored means of carrying

Capt. Leroy Southmayd was a steamboat captain before coming to Montana in 1863. He was one of the vigilantes who hanged members of the Plummer gang. He lost this Colt M1851 (#157168) when he was robbed in a stage-coach holdup but recovered it when the outlaws were captured. (Courtesy: Charles L. Hill Jr.)

Carlos Y. Velasco's Colt M1849 Pocket Model. A prominent Mexican attorney, he came to Tucson in 1862 and founded the Spanish language newspaper *El Fronterizo* which came to have a wide circulation. (Exhibited by the Arizona Historical Society, Tucson)

a pair of pistols until the mid-1850s, but they were in use by some civilians as well. John Cremony was an Arizona pioneer living among the Apaches in the 1850s and 1860s who noted that he armed himself "with four Colt's six-shooters, two in my saddle-holsters and two in my belt, with a large bowie knife." Belt holsters (pistol "cases" or "scabbards") were convenient and soon became increasingly more common with the appearance of Colt pocket models introduced in 1848 and the medium size Model 1851 Navy.[14]

Christopher "Kit" Carson was one frontiersman who chose the Colt '51 Navy in preference to the heavier .44 Dragoon. This Navy was passed down through his descendents. Carson went west as a youth and remained there for the rest of his life as trapper, scout, and later army officer. (Courtesy: Ron Peterson)

Crossing the plains in 1857, Lt. Samuel Ferguson wrote:

so frequent were assassinations that each
man traveling on the prairie,
as soon as he perceived another approaching him, slipped [loosened] his six-shooter
to have it most convenient to his hand. Of
course, the flap of the holster, placed to
protect the pistol from rain, had long
before been cut off; it was preferable to suffer a little rust on the weapon rather than
run the risk of losing a fraction of a second
in drawing it.[15]

The popularity of the Colt Model 1851 was such that the term "navy six" or merely "navy" became common. A caravan of about thirty-five freight wagons in April 1853 embarked on a journey to Santa Fe. Near the present Hutchinson, Kansas, the train was attacked by Comanches.

Outnumbered four or five to one in a
hand-to-hand fight...we soon mingled
together, but driven against the wagons, we
could dodge or parry their blows with the
tomahawk, while the rapid flashes from the
celebrated "navy" in each man's hand, was
[sic] not so easily avoided by the savage
warriors. We made the ground too hot for
them, and with yells of baffled rage, they
broke and fled.[16]

Solomon Nunes Carvalho in writing of Capt. Charles Fremont's fifth and last western exploration (1853–54) noted that each man was issued a rifle and a Colt. Later he described his preparations for a bison hunt and in doing so used the common term for the Colt of 1851. "In quick time I had my horse saddled, and, fully equipped with a rifle, navy revolver, and sheath knife, was all ready for a start." In 1860 a San Diego newspaper recommended the clothing and arms for a passenger traveling on an overland stage coach: "One Sharp's rifle and a hundred cartridges; a Colts navy revolver and two pounds of balls; a knife and sheath."[17]

In his 1859 guide to the Colorado gold fields, Dr. J. W. Reed advised travelers to supply themselves with "a good heavy rifle, navy size Colt's revolver, and butcher-knife." He also warned that wood for fuel often would be scarce and it would be necessary to rely on buffalo chips—dried manure—for cooking fires.[18]

While hunting buffalo near Dodge City, Kansas, in 1872–73, Henry H. Raymond kept a diary, sometimes mixing gunpowder and water as an ink substitute. The entry for December 15 of 1872 noted: "Bought Navy pistol of Big John for five dollars." No further description was necessary in the west to identify a Colt .36 caliber Model 1851 or perhaps the very similar but less common round barrel Colt Model 1861 Navy revolver. He often used telegraph poles as targets when practicing with the weapon, but later traded two pistols for a Smith & Wesson No. 2 .32 plus $4 to boot.[19]

John H. "Doc" Holliday, gunman, dentist, and Wyatt Earp's associate, as a youth in Georgia received a Colt

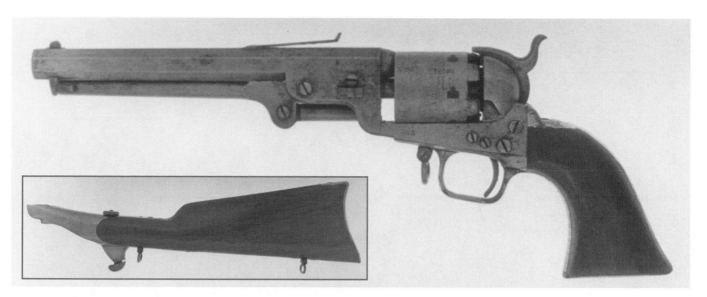

John Brown Jr.'s Colt M1851 Navy with its detachable shoulder stock, a rarely found variation. (The rear sight is of nonfactory origin.) (Courtesy: Ohio Historical Society)

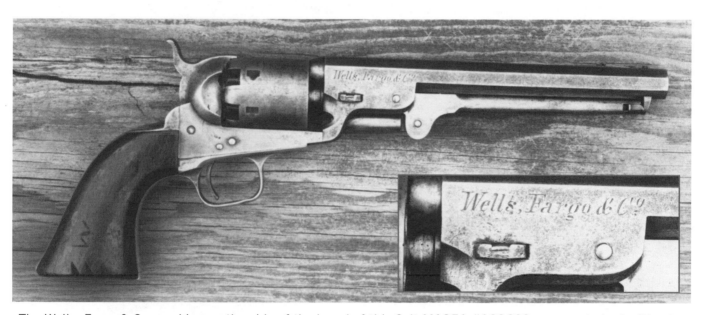

The Wells, Fargo & Co. marking on the side of the barrel of this Colt M1851 #103609 appears to be legitimate. Factory records unfortunately only show it was one of fifty guns shipped to a Rhode Island dealer before it presumably was acquired by the famed western express company.

M1851, one of four presented to family members by his uncle. While a neophyte newspaper city editor in Virginia City, Nevada Territory, with typical Mark Twain humor, Sam Clemens described himself as

> whiskered half down to my waist, and the universal navy revolver slung to my belt. . . . I had never had occasion to kill anybody, nor ever felt a desire to do so, but had worn the thing in deference to popular sentiment, and in order that I might not, by its

absence, be offensively conspicuous, and a subject of remark.[20]

Despite its weight and bulk, the four-pound Colt .44 Dragoon still found favor with some, even after the Civil War. Not long after his arrival in 1869, an English tenderfoot witnessed a hastily organized trial in the town of Evans, Colorado Territory. There he encountered "a great yellow-bearded giant in a slouch hat. He reached down to his hip, and produced an enormous revolver, one of the old dragoon Colt's, with a barrel about a foot long."[21]

161

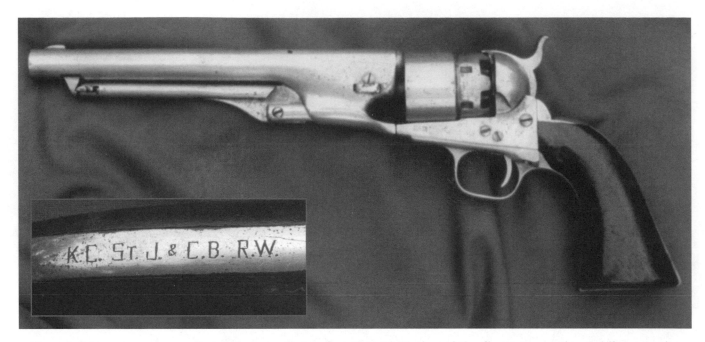

One of the many western railroads in operation before the completion of the first transcontinental line was the Kansas City, St. Joseph and Council Bluffs Railroad. Completed in 1868, it connected with the Union Pacific at Council Bluffs. Its varied freight ranged from manufactured goods bound for the mining regions of Utah, Nevada, and California to fruit to towns along the upper Missouri. The M1860 Colt (#104553) was the property of the line as its backstrap stamping indicates. (Courtesy: John J. Hays)

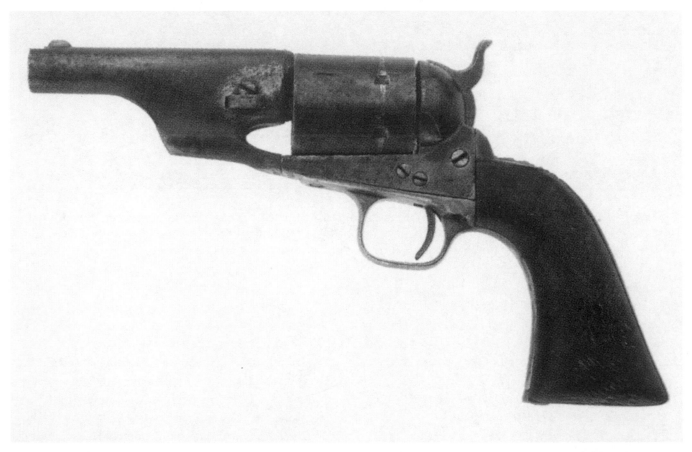

Its barrel shortened to four inches and converted to .44 rimfire, this Colt M1860 #41782 is marked on the butt "OVERLAND/STAGE L/17" indicating probable use at some time by Ben Holladay's Overland Stage Line. (Courtesy: Richard Ellis)

An aging note attached to the cylinder of the Colt M1861 Navy states it was found in a grave near Medicine Bow, Wyoming, in 1947 during road construction. (Courtesy: From Pat and Margie Free Collection via Lt. Col. William R. Orbelo)

It may have been another Dragoon, its barrel shortened, to which Dr. Henry Hoyt referred when describing an 1877 stagecoach journey to Deadwood, South Dakota. Gambler John Bull was a fellow passenger and during a brief stop in the midst of a prairie dog "village," the occupants of the coach were tempted to test their marksmanship on the unfortunate creatures. "Bull watched the scene for a time. Suddenly his hand flew to his hip; a big six-shooter of the dragoon type with a short barrel was drawn. The gun barked, and a dead dog was the result. He apparently took no aim at all."[22]

In 1860 Colt introduced an improved .44 revolver, lighter than the Dragoon, using the Navy frame adapted to accept a rebated .44 cylinder; production totaled two hundred thousand. Except for a few early guns, its grip was slightly longer than that of the '51. It had a round rather than octagonal barrel as well as a streamlined "creeping" loading lever. During the Civil War, the 1860 New Model Army was the handgun most widely used by Union forces and many went west in the hands of those who wanted a "harder shooting" Colt than the "navy six."

The Revised Army Regulations for 1861 listed the cost of a Model 1860 .44 Colt with screwdriver, spring vise, and bullet mould at $24. However the same document specified that: "Enlisted men who lose, or dispose of, the Colt's revolver pistols intrusted [sic] to their care, will hereafter be charged forty dollars in each case; that being the amount of pecuniary damage Sustained by the United States as estimated by the Ordnance Department." It's unknown how successful this was in reducing the frequency of sales of their issue Colts by soldiers on the frontier or anywhere else the guns brought an inflated price.[23]

A .36 companion piece to the M1860 appeared in 1861, a streamlined version of the earlier Navy, with round barrel and creeping lever, but it never matched the '51 in sales (39,000 versus 215,000). The popular grip shape used on both the Navies was carried over to the famed Single Action Army. Rounding out the Colt line during the Civil War years were two five-shot smaller frame .36s, the 1862 Police with a round barrel and the Pocket Navy with an octagonal barrel.

Colt applied his principles used in revolving handguns to long guns as well from the beginning at Paterson, New Jersey, in the form of rifles, carbines, and a few shotguns. In 1855 the firm introduced a new series of revolving shoulder arms featuring a solid frame and side-hammer. It may well have been some of these Hartford-made Model 1855s that Henry F. Wickersham wrote about to his parents in April 1859, "half-way to Pike's Peak" in Colorado Territory. His party of gold seekers unexpectedly drove into a camp of what he estimated at eight hundred Cheyennes and Arapahoes. The chiefs demanded sugar, coffee, and tobacco. He refused their demand, stating they had none to spare. Angered by this rejection, one of the Indians shot at but missed an ox. Wickersham ordered his men to get their guns and form a line. "When all was ready we presented a fine appearance (198 men), [and] we were capable of accommodating them with 432 shots, as we had quite a number

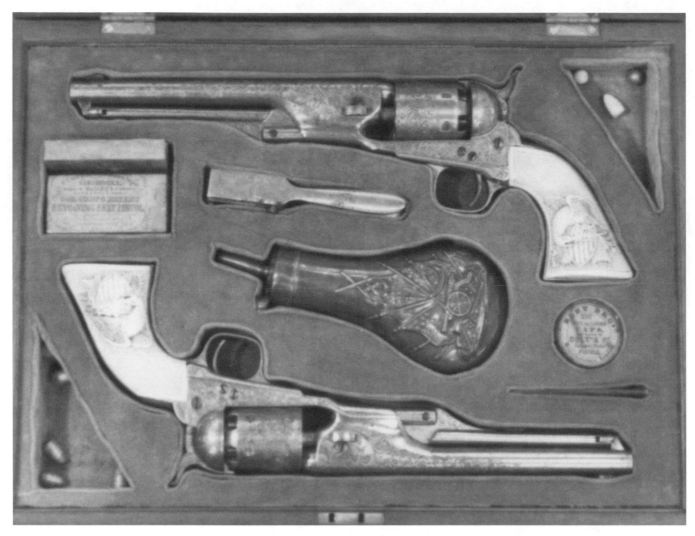

Pair of engraved Colt M1861 Navies with carved ivory grips cased in French style with accessories and presented to Gen. George A. Custer. (Courtesy: David Condon)

US Marshal A. Cutler's ivory gripped Colt M1861 Navy (#25235). He served in New Mexico Territory following his appointment by Abraham Lincoln. (Courtesy: Rod Smith)

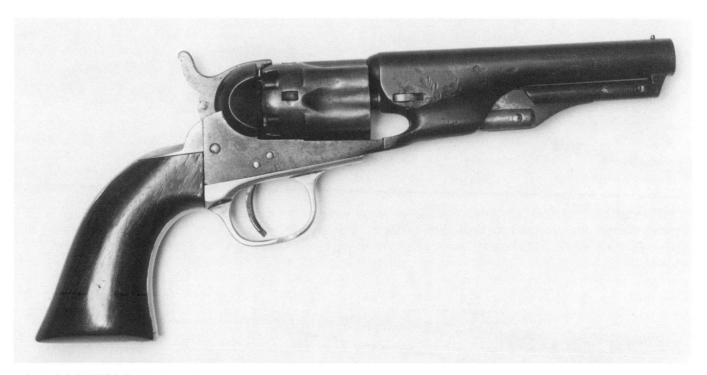

Colt .36 M1862 Police inscribed as having belonged to S. B. Reed, chief of construction and chief engineer of the Union Pacific Railroad. (Courtesy: Donald Snoddy, Union Pacific Railroad Company, Omaha, NE)

of Cots [Colts?] with us. This show of strength had the desired effect and forestalled an attack"[24]

Colt's revolving shoulder arms did achieve a modest degree of sales success despite their occasional tendency to discharge more than one chamber at a time, not a cheery occurrence if the shooter positioned his hand in front of the cylinder. During an Indian scare in the fall of 1868 in Colorado, rancher Irving Howbert borrowed a Colt's rifle, "a kind of gun that I had not seen before nor…have I seen one like it since. It was a gun built exactly on the principle of a Colt's revolver. The trouble with it was that one never knew just how many shots might go off at once."[25]

Young lieutenant J. E. B. Stuart with the 1st Cavalry wrote to Sam Colt on December 2, 1859, ordering a Model 1855 revolving rifle, but revealed his awareness of this potential problem.

> As I expect to try a campaign in the Indian Country next spring, I am anxious to equip myself with the best Rifle-arm. Judging from the reputation of your revolving Rifle that it fills the ticket, you will please send me by U.S. Express Co. to Fort Riley Kansas—one of your Revolving Rifles and all the necessary fixtures & a tolerable supply of cartridges. I want one of your own

> selection which you can warrant *not* to fire but one barrel [chamber] at a *time*.

The problem of multiple discharges could be encountered with percussion Colt revolvers as well, but in the case of young Richard Hughes, it wasn't the gun's fault. In 1876 he set out from Nebraska for the Black Hills of Dakota Territory, hoping to find gold.

> A friend contributed an old style Colt's cap and ball revolver, which was gratefully received and highly prized, though experience with it later proved it somewhat unreliable, as it developed a tendency to fire the entire battery of six shots at once. This was due to the fact that it was loaded with buckshot of more or less irregular shape, which did not completely fill the chambers and thus allowed the fire from a discharge to reach around the lead to the powder. Within a short time the old Colt's was retired from service, as of more value as a relic than as an arm of offense or protection.[26]

Stagecoaches provided transportation for passengers and mail throughout the west. The opening of a stage line

Colt Model 1839 carbine, its barrel shortened to about eight inches for convenience or following damage to the barrel. Almost one thousand of these .525 caliber six-shooters were produced and they were the best selling of the Paterson-made Colt shoulder arms. Later specimens had an attached loading lever. (Courtesy: Al Perry)

Colt M1855 revolving musket left with a family in Socorro, New Mexico, on the Rio Grande by a Texas Confederate soldier retreating after their defeat at Glorieta. He never returned and the gun remained in the family for a century. (Photo by Steven W. Walenta, courtesy Jim Gordon)

between Independence, Missouri, and Santa Fe in 1850 prompted mention in the Sacramento *Transcript*. Two stages would leave Independence on the first of each month, each drawn by six mules. The mail would be guarded by eight men.

> Each man has at his side, strapped up in
> the stage, one of Colt's revolving
> [Paterson] rifles; in a holster below, one of
> Colt's long revolving pistol; [.44
> Dragoon?], and in his belt a small Colt
> revolver [Model 1849 .31 pocket?], besides
> a hunting knife—so that those eight men
> are prepared in case of an attack, to dis-
> charge one hundred and thirty-six shots
> without stopping to load.[27]

The coaching firm of Slemmons, Roberts and Company was another one of many which obtained government mail contracts. In July 1861 one of their representatives, Andrew Stewart, shot himself when he knocked a pistol off the bureau in his hotel room in Council Grove, Kansas. We don't know whether the weapon was a percussion one with a cap in place or a new metallic cartridge arm,

but the bullet struck him in the cheek and glanced upward giving him a brain concussion. He recovered within a month or two, however.[28]

Entrepreneur that he was, Sam Colt also was a controlling stockholder in Arizona's Sonora Exploring and Mining Company. A December 31, 1857, sales order for that firm included thirty of the new solid-frame Model 1855 revolving rifles and carbines with barrel lengths from eighteen to thirty inches along with 250 Model 1851 Navy revolvers; seventy-five Model 1849 Pocket Models in 4-, 5-, and 6-inch barrel lengths; fifty Model 1855 Root pocket models with three 1/2-inch barrels; and fifty .44 Dragoons. Some of these arms may have been obtained to protect the Arizona company's property and others resold since demand for these would have been strong in that territory.[29]

Before his death in January 1862, Sam Colt was not hesitant to dispense complimentary arms, both long and short, to individuals whom he felt might be in a position to benefit him. Federal cabinet members, congressmen, general officers and admirals, newspaper editors, foreign diplomats—all were potential recipients. One of the side-hammer Model 1855 solid-frame pocket revolvers was presented and inscribed to G. Argenti, a member of the San Francisco vigilante organization of the 1850s.[30]

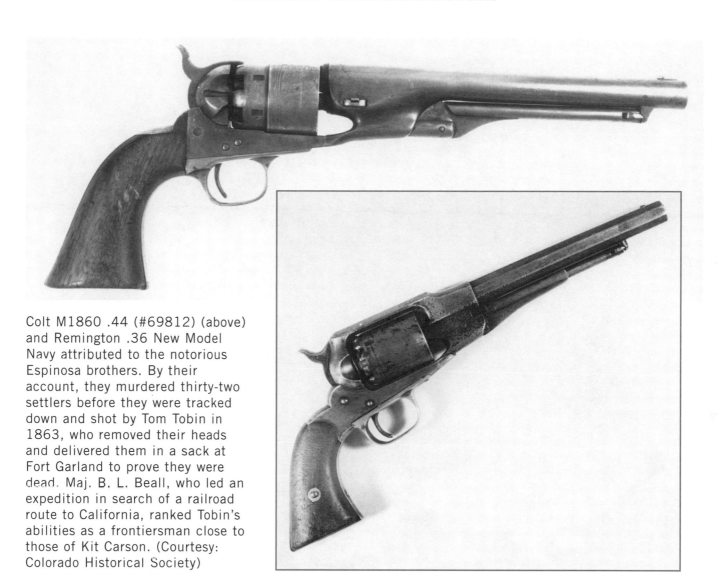

Colt M1860 .44 (#69812) (above) and Remington .36 New Model Navy attributed to the notorious Espinosa brothers. By their account, they murdered thirty-two settlers before they were tracked down and shot by Tom Tobin in 1863, who removed their heads and delivered them in a sack at Fort Garland to prove they were dead. Maj. B. L. Beall, who led an expedition in search of a railroad route to California, ranked Tobin's abilities as a frontiersman close to those of Kit Carson. (Courtesy: Colorado Historical Society)

Prior to the expiration of Sam Colt's revolver patents in 1857, his primary competition came from US makers of multibarrel pepperboxes. But once freed from legal restraints, various American makers now could offer percussion revolvers for the civilian and all too soon for the military Civil War market—Bacon, Massachusetts Arms Company, Remington, Starr, Whitney, and others. More than seventy thousand .31 and .36 pocket and navy size Colt-style handguns bore the Manhattan name.

These percussion Manhattan arms in particular caused concern to M. W. B. Hartley, secretary of the Colt firm, who wrote to Sam Colt on February 7, 1860: "If the Manhattan Company can be demoralized in any reasonable way, it should be done." Manhattan also produced very close copies of Smith & Wesson .22 pocket revolvers until halted by a lawsuit. S&W occupied a unique position, being the only firm legally manufacturing revolvers firing rear-loading metallic cartridges, although throughout the Civil War era they produced none larger than .32 caliber.[31]

Remington offered an extensive array of .31 to .44 caliber revolvers in various sizes, their primary difference from Colt-style revolvers being their solid frame with a top strap over the cylinder. Remington's big .44s during the Civil War were second only to the Colt Model 1860 in numbers purchased for use by the Union army. One of the most historically significant .44 Remingtons was that carried by William F. "Buffalo Bill" Cody during his early years as a buffalo hunter and scout. A note which accompanied the gun when in later years he gave it to an associate stated "it never failed me."

Remington .44 #111699 bears the inscription on its backstrap "CAPT. TOM JEFFORDS IND. AGT. ARIZ. TER." Thomas Jefferson Jeffords, variously a miner, scout, sheriff, and operator of a small stage line in Arizona, had earned the trust of the Apache leader Cochise. He aided in arranging Cochise's surrender in 1872 to Gen. O. O. Howard, but one condition the warrior demanded was that Jeffords be named Indian agent.

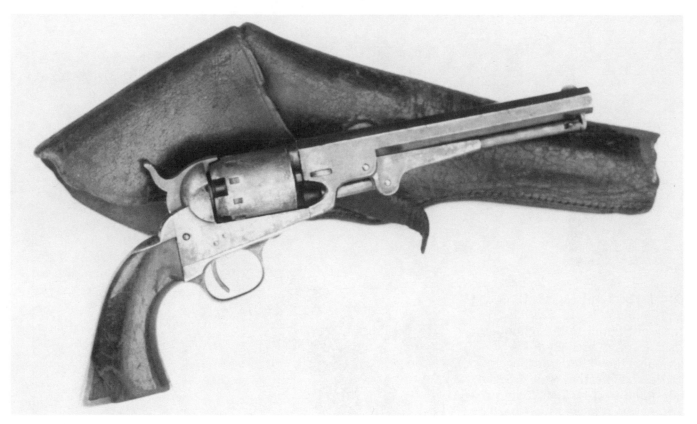

"SHERIFF A. TYNER/YUMA CO. AZ." is inscribed on the backstrap of this .36 Manhattan (#66200). He held the post in the early 1880s.

Manhattan .36 (#27942) found along an old stagecoach road near Echeta, Wyoming, and exhibited at the Jim Gatchell Museum in Buffalo, Wyoming.

Some westerners continued to rely on Remingtons, Colts, and in lesser numbers other Civil War–era percussion revolvers even after handguns converted from percussion or new models firing metallic ammunition became available in the early 1870s. A member of a mining party en route to the Black Hills in 1876 though it worthy of note that a tall, old Kentuckian who had joined them was armed with "two old-fashioned Colt revolvers, which used loose

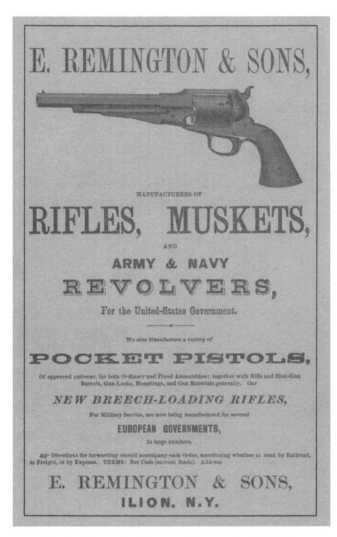

Remington advertisement from about 1868.

ammunition." Throughout the journey they knew him as nothing other than "the Old Man." Another of the prospectors was a nervous Swede, John Nelson. "His gun was what he termed a Sharps navy rifle; the only one of the kind I ever saw. The most distinguishing feature of this firearm was a leather covering that had been shrunken onto the barrel. Poor Nelson and his 'leather gun' furnished the butt of many a joke." (Nelson's gun also was of Civil War vintage, a Sharps & Hankins carbine intended for naval use, the barrel covered to minimize salt water rusting.)[32]

The continued use of outdated guns often was the result of the sale of surplus government Civil War long and short guns at bargain prices. The ad doesn't specify what handguns were offered, but a broadside for the Independence Arms Company of Independence, Kansas, in 1879 may have included surplus Civil War–era revolvers:

HO! FOR THE NEW ELDORADO! 1,400 Second-hand Six-shooters for sale. Also 1,100 Double-barrel Shot Guns, and 1,000 WINCHESTER RIFLES! As the Route from Independence to Carpenter City lies through the Cheyenne and Arrapahoe [sic] Country, it is necessary that all parties should go well armed. Special Inducements given to Outfits. A large variety of Scalping Knives at extremely Low Prices.[33]

Smith & Wesson with its control of the Rollin White patent for a rear-loading cylinder didn't bring out its first large-caliber revolver until the summer of 1870, the year after this patent expired. This S&W six-shooter officially was the No. 3, indicating its frame size, and in 1874 was designated the American Model. In addition to its larger caliber (.44), it offered several other innovations over previous S&Ws—a barrel which tipped downward rather than upward and an improved hinged frame design, plus an automatic shell extractor which threw out all empty cases when the gun was broken open for reloading.

As the first large-caliber revolver made in this country originally for metallic cartridges, the American represented a major step beyond conversions of percussion arms. Until the advent of Colt's Single Action model, its design was superior to that of any of its competitors. Production of the American ended in 1874, but it inaugurated a long line of large-frame No. 3 size S&Ws in various models which found a niche among buyers west of the Mississippi.

An uncommon accessory for the American was a detachable wooden shoulder stock, available from the factory in early 1873. Buffalo Bill Cody ordered an American so equipped and gun dealer Walter Cooper wrote the factory from Bozeman, Montana Territory, that year asking: "Do you make skeleton stocks or butt pieces to put against your shoulder like a rifle? The officers at the fort [Fort Ellis] bother me to death having them put on their pistols."[34]

The Russian government in May 1871 favored S&W with an order for twenty thousand modified No. 3s. To witness production, the Russian Grand Duke Alexis visited the S&W plant in late 1871 where he was presented with an elaborately engraved No. 3 in a handsome rosewood case, all of which cost the manufacturer $400 to prepare. The revolver accompanied him on a western tour which included a bison hunt with Buffalo Bill Cody as guide. The foreign visitor on one occasion apparently experienced only limited success with his new prize for he emptied all six rounds into one bison and failed to down the unfortunate animal.

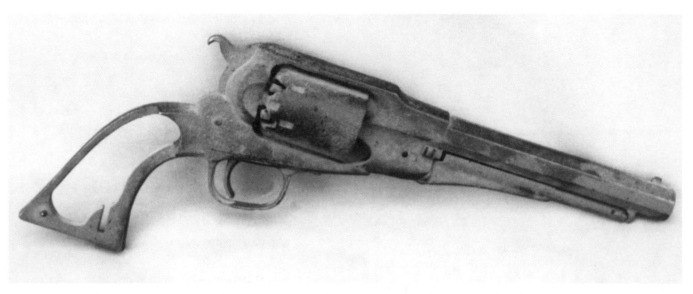

A Remington .36 Navy (#13495) found still loaded at Ice Caves near Grants, New Mexico.
(Courtesy: Ron Peterson)

Heavily encrusted with soda, this Starr single action .44 was found in 1899 at Pagosa Springs, Colorado.
(Courtesy: Colorado Historical Society)

Ultimately the Russians purchased almost 150,000 .44 S&Ws between 1871 and early 1878. Many of the changes introduced under the various Russian contracts, including grip and trigger guard shape, were incorporated in subsequent variations of the No. 3 sold commercially in this country until the early 1900s. S&W authority Charles Pate makes an interesting comparison, noting that by the end of 1879, the company had produced 215,000 of several models of No. 3 size revolvers, but most were sold abroad. Colt production of its famed Single Action didn't reach that figure until the century's end.[35]

A .44 New Model Russian was found in 1935 in southern Colorado, loaded but with the grips weathered away, and the name "Charles H. Utter Georgetown, Colerado [sic]" engraved in script on the backstrap. This S&W probably had been lost by "Colorado Charlie" Utter, one of "Wild Bill" Hickok's close friends in Deadwood, Dakota Territory. In the spring of 1876, Utter organized a large wagon train in Georgetown and set out to

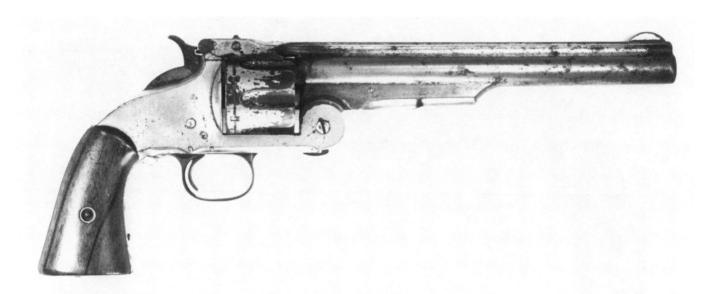

A nickeled Smith & Wesson .44 First or Old Old Model Russian owned by William Henry Holmes, artist and geologist with the US Geological Survey. He made the first recorded climb of the Mountain of the Holy Cross in Colorado and became director of the National Gallery of Art. Two mountains are named for him, one in Yellowstone National Park and the other in the Henry Mountains of Utah. (Courtesy: Bob Butterfield via Charles L. Hill Jr.)

Emilio Carrillo was an Arizona cattleman who established the Tasque Verde Ranch east of Tucson. He apparently appreciated the much better balance a shorter barrel gives a .44 Smith & Wesson No. 3 American than the 8-inch standard length. (Exhibited by the Arizona Historical Society, Tucson)

prospect for gold in the region around Deadwood. Among the passengers on the wagon train were "Calamity Jane," Madame Mustachio, and "Dirty Em" and their "girls." One of Utter's habits was a daily bath, most unusual for the era and location!

One of the more unusual requests from the west reached Smith & Wesson from Sumner "Cimmarron"

Beach. A sometime contributor to *American Sportsman,* he wrote from Ellsworth, Kansas, in May 1874 praising the No. 3.

I was told [Smith & Wessons] got out of fix too easy....I just told them that Mr. Smith & Wesson knowed what they was

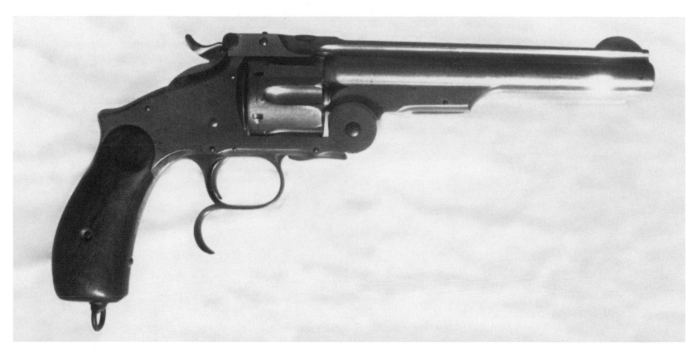

S&W .44 Third or New Model Russian dated 1874 on the butt and used on the Ralph Oppenheimer Ranch in Texas. (Courtesy: William T. Goodman and Gary Roedl)

Well-dressed Mexicans, perhaps vaqueros or cowboys, armed with Smith & Wessons in half-holsters, that on the left being either a 2nd or 3rd Model Russian with its distinctive finger spur on the trigger guard. (Courtesy: Lee A. Silva)

Standing at right is a notorious Nebraska rustler, Dick Middleton, armed with a pair of Colt Single Actions. His companion, perhaps with Smith & Wessons, is Omaha Charlie, a showman who traveled with a small group of Indians in the 1890s. (Courtesy: Dick Harmon)

doing when they made that revolver.... I have been shooting your make and find it a perfect revolver. I can kill a man at 100 yds with my revolver every time. I like all frontiersmen like the Smith & Wesson better than the Colts.

After Daniel Wesson offered to supply spare parts, Beach replied that:

I have been promised a heap of things from Eastern gentlemen whom I hunted buffalo with and sported around with, but they always seem to forget me when they go back to the States.... No buffalo hunter's outfit is considered complete until he has a Sharps rifle and two Smith & Wessons. All the notorious desperadoes

have your rev. The notorious Hurricane Bill has a pair of your revolvers.

In his next letter, Beach explained his upcoming role as guide for a wild horse hunting expedition. He dangled the bait, writing that he had only one S&W and wanted another for the journey.

I have only $225 dollars and all will have to go on the outfit.... I will have to have a Sharps Rifle which will cost $50. We use said rifle sometimes to crease a horse that we cannot take any other way. Then there is lots of Indians down there that have just went off the reservation on the war path. Now S&W, I am stylish—I want one of your Russian Model Smith & Wesson

With its shortened barrel, this Colt M1871-2 .44 Open Top is one of a number of guns in the Union Pacific Railroad's collection which were taken from criminals who "trespassed" against the firm. (Courtesy: Donald Snoddy, Union Pacific Railroad Company, Omaha, NE)

Still loaded, this Colt Model 1860 Richards conversion was found along the Mexican border south of Deming, New Mexico. (Courtesy: Ron Peterson)

Revolvers 44 calibre. For which...I will send you as fine a wild horse as we take in the herd.

At this point, the hook was set. D. B. Wesson sent the .44 but the promised horse never arrived. In 1875 when dime novelist "Buckskin Sam" Hall offered to swap the addresses of five hundred Texas frontiersmen for a revolver, Wesson's response was predictable.

We consider the names of no value whatever to us, as, nine tenths of them, were they to want a revolver, would want to purchase it upon the strength of a promise to send us a wild horse, or a buffalo, or some other promise quite as valueless, and generally never intended to be kept. We have already relied too much on these promises.[36]

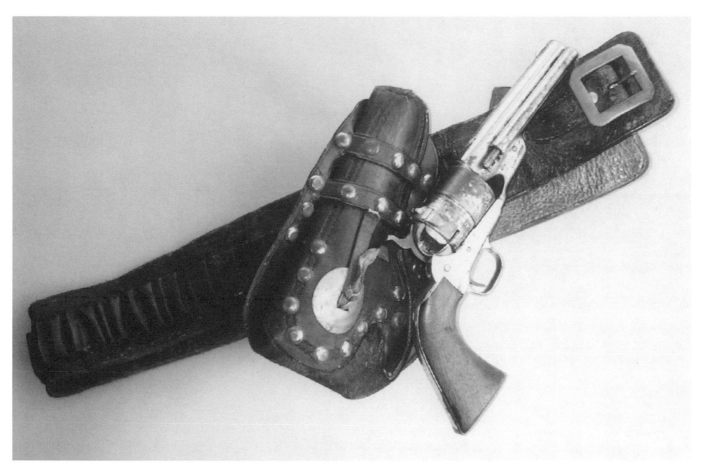

Jose Padilla probably acquired this Colt .44 Richards conversion of the Model 1860 in the early 1900s and then is known to have carried it throughout much of his life in the accompanying rig as a working cowboy on the Bell and other ranches in New Mexico. The barrel has been shortened for convenience and although its earlier history is unknown, it was well cared for and retains much original nickel finish. (Courtesy: Gary L. Delscamp)

The Colt 1871-2 .44 Open Top (#338) was not a conversion of a percussion model but was the short-lived immediate predecessor of the famed Single Action Army. Joe Parr bought this one (#338) from Freund & Brothers. Originally from Lancastershire, England, Parr went to work in the Union Pacific coal mines in Wyoming. (Exhibited by the Wyoming Historical Society, Cheyenne)

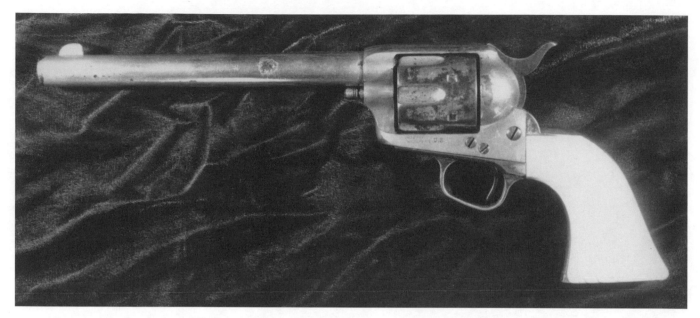

Outlaw Cole Younger's .45 Colt Single Action (#13757) taken from him after his capture following the unsuccessful Northfield, Minnesota, bank robbery attempt. The ejector housing was shot off during the fight. The backstrap is engraved with the name "C. Weidner." (Courtesy: Larry T. Shelton, Missouri State Capitol Museum, Jefferson City)

A near tragic accident with an S&W was narrowly avoided in 1876 among miners in the Black Hills. The townspeople of Custer had hired the Minute Men to provide protection against Indians. The agreed upon signal to assemble in an emergency was three rapid pistol shots and on one occasion, a tenderfoot sought to give the signal.

> He had a fine, heavy Smith & Wesson
> revolver—then coming into vogue. This
> he produced, and using both hands to
> cock the weapon, held it out at arm's
> length to discharge it. "Look out, you d—
> —d fool, you'll shoot the woman," some-
> one in the assembled crowd shouted. And
> indeed, the weapon was pointed directly
> at a woman standing in the doorway of a
> near-by cabin.[37]

Colt's attempt to circumvent the White patent with its front-loading Thuer conversions of some of its .36 and .44 percussion revolvers totaled only about five thousand guns beginning in 1869. These Colts sold slowly even though an owner could use a percussion cylinder if the special tapered metallic cartridges were unavailable. Expiration of White's patent opened the market for any maker to offer new or now obsolescent percussion models modified to fire metallic cartridges by any of a number of methods. Colt factory conversions exist in all its .36 and .44 models and

individual gunsmiths altered countless others. For Colt, its new Model 1871–72 .44 rimfire Open Top Frontier bridged the gap between conversions of its larger percussion handguns and its solid-frame Single Action Army or Peacemaker which became available in 1873. Only about seven thousand of the former model were produced, for with its open top frame it was outmoded at birth.

Production of Colt conversions of their holster size revolvers was short-lived for soon there appeared an American-made firearm which earned truly worldwide recognition, the Colt Single Action or the Model P. It also was known variously as Peacemaker or Frontier Six-Shooter (in .44–40 caliber), as well as "hog leg," "thumb buster," and other colloquialisms. On the American frontier, no handgun was as representative of the "wild west" era of the nineteenth century's last quarter. Its frequent appearance in frontier photos confirms its popularity and its status was warranted by its efficient design, comfortable handling characteristics, and durability. Production of first generation Single Actions reached almost 200,000 by 1900 and would continue until 1940 for a total of 357,000.

James B. "Wild Bill" Hickok was only one of the myriad of frontiersmen who relied on a Colt Single Action at some point. Early in his career, he is known to have favored a Colt Model 1851 Navy and at the time of his murder reportedly was armed with a Smith & Wesson .32 No. 2. However one author wrote that Colorado Charley

Manufactured in 1886, this Colt .45 (#118933) was reputed to have been left with a hardware store owner who took it in for repairs from Ben Kilpatrick, the "Tall Texan" of Butch Cassidy and the Sundance Kid's "Wild Bunch" outlaw gang. Colt introduced the eagle motif on the hard rubber grips in 1882 and continued it until 1896.
(Courtesy: Sotheby, Park-Bernet Galleries, NY)

Utter received the dead Hickok's few belongings including two Colt .45s, a needle gun (probably a Springfield), and a derringer.[38]

The Union Pacific Railroad was an early buyer of the new Colt .45. A factory letter showed that gun #14663 with a 7 1/2-inch barrel was one of ten Model Ps purchased by that firm in a January 1875 order. Initially purchasers of the Colt Single Action only could buy one with a 7 1/2-inch barrel except on special order, but in 1875 4 3/4 and 5 1/2 inch were added as standard lengths. Exotic lengths could be ordered from a mere 2 1/2 up to sixteen inches. In Arizona Territory, a messenger for a smuggler in the early 1880s rode "unarmed except for a sawed-off Colt to be carried under my arm or in my boot-leg." Most customers were satisfied with the standard combination of bluing and case hardened colors, although buyers after 1877 could select an optional nickel finish. Wood or, after 1882, hard rubber grips were the factory standards. Charles Siringo went a step beyond and in his writings made mention of his silver-plated, pearl-handled Colt .45 and his silver-mounted Winchester.[39]

Sheriff William O'Neill of Yavapai County in Arizona Territory on December 6 of 1889 sent a typewritten letter to the Colt company, incorrectly addressing it to New Haven rather than Hartford, however. He showed interest in a more ornate revolver than was standard, asking the price of a .41 Single Action "engraved, ox-head pearl handle, and extra sighted" as well as the price on a .44 and a .45. He explained: "What I want to do, is to get me a couple of real nice 'guns' for myself and perhaps some of my deputies." He went on to complain that "your '41' long cartridges do not seem to have enough powder for the amount of lead, and that they do not do as effective work at fifty and one hundred yards as your either large calibers—can this be remedied?"[40]

In June 1893, a horse race was run between Chadron, Nebraska, and the Nebraska building at the Chicago World's Fair despite efforts by various humane organizations to halt it. Each rider could use only two horses over the grueling seven-hundred-mile course. First prize was $1,500, but another prize was an engraved .44 Colt Single Action #150681 with a 5 1/2-inch barrel, described as having "ivory handle, blue steel barrel, gold plated cylinder, and upon the handle is carved a steer's head." Factory records show it was shipped on May 6, 1893, to "Harry Weir, Secretary Cowboy Race." Today it's the property of the Dawes County Historical Society Museum in Chadron.[41]

John Heath met justice at the end of a rope on February 22 of 1884. He organized a bungled robbery, which became known as the "Bisbee Massacre" after it resulted in the deaths of five citizens including a pregnant woman. Although he wasn't present at the robbery and was declared innocent of murder, a mob from Bisbee dragged him from the jail at Tombstone and hanged him from a telegraph pole on Allen Street. Public opinion supported the mob's action and the coroner listed his death as due to "asphyxiation of the lungs, brought about by great heights." The Arizona Historical Society exhibits his engraved .45 Colt Single Action with pearl grips and fitted with a belt hook on the right side of the frame. (Exhibited by the Arizona Historical Society, Tucson)

When Colt in 1878 began offering the Single Action in .44–40 caliber, it and the Model 1873 Winchester became a most convenient pair using the same cartridge. A later similar pairing between these two models occurred with the appearance of Single Actions chambered for .32–20 and .38–40 ammunition (1884). Eventually the Single Action could be purchased in a range of calibers from .22 to the British .476 Eley.

In 1882 James H. Kyner contracted to build a section of the Oregon Short Line Railroad. Concern over the number of payroll robberies caused him to purchase "a handsome single-action .44," probably a Colt, and begin to practice in private with it.

> Quickness with a revolver being essential
> if it should be of service in a pinch, I
> practiced pulling the trigger as I swung
> the gun down, and the amount of powder
> I burned in practice was enormous. From
> the commissary I obtained the circular
> pieces of cardboard that came between
> the layers of crackers in the cracker bar-
> rels, and hanging one of these on a sage-
> brush or greasewood branch, I'd pace off
> twenty or thirty steps and go to work.

As he became more proficient, he began to conduct his practice on Sundays and close enough to the construction camp where the shots might gather onlookers. He knew he had achieved his purpose when he overheard one of the construction workers say to his partner, "By God, Bill, I wouldn't want the old man to be a-shootin' at me."[42]

At age eighteen, Jeff Milton joined the Texas Rangers (1880) at which time their regulation arms were a .44 Winchester carbine and a .45 Colt Single Action. When at the Austin shop of spur-maker Petmecky, Milton found a silver-mounted .44 revolver which he purchased. "I thought I was just the king bee, .44 pistol and .44 Winchester using the same shells." His pride turned to disappointment when he fired it for the first time, for "she hung up tighter than Dick's hatband, and I had an awful time cocking it again. The next shot, the same thing. The cap [primer] would come back and stop right against the firing pin, and you could not revolve the cylinder."

He informed his fellow rangers of his problem so none would be tempted to buy and it wasn't long before he relieved himself of the gun. Batty Carr was an outlaw and gambler who rustled horses and mules along the border. He owned a .45 with the grip "like a deck of cards—spades, hearts, diamonds, and clubs cut out of silver and inlaid in the handle." When he returned to Fort Concho, Milton let

Heath suffering from "altitude sickness."
(Courtesy: National Archives, photo #111-SC-93377)

it be known he had the handsome .44 and sure enough, Carr wanted it and offered to trade his .45, an exchange to which the young lawman agreed without much hesitation.[43]

Beginning in 1894, one could order the Bisley model Colt, a variation of the Single Action designed with the target shooter in mind but marketed to all. The name came from the famed Bisley target range in England, site of numerous shooting competitions. The grip had a distinctive "humpback" shape, the hammer spur was wider and lower, and the trigger was widened and given increased curve. Like its counterpart, it could be procured in various barrel lengths and calibers.

Wyoming cowboy Frank Rollinson hired on with the M-Bar Ranch. His companion named Clark "rode a Cogshell saddle made in Miles City [Montana], and packed a gun exactly like mine—a .45 single-action Bisley model Colt."

> We all carried guns.... We all preferred the Colt single-action six-shooter. Some liked the Bisley model, others the Frontier model. Some were of different caliber, but

all were built on a .45-caliber frame. I noticed that these men carried their guns with one empty shell in the cylinder, and five loaded cartridges. This was for safety's sake. The gun was carried with the hammer on the empty shell, and, when cocked, a loaded shell was ready to fire.[44]

Not long after its introduction, Colt's Single Action Army became unquestionably the leader among western "six guns." Remington's entry into the market (exclusive of its percussion revolvers converted to fire metallic cartridges) was the Model 1875. In appearance it closely duplicated the Colt except for a slightly altered grip shape and a sloping ejector rod and cylinder pin housing beneath the barrel, reminiscent of the sloped loading lever found on many percussion Remingtons. Many of the firm's production resources and marketing efforts during the 1870s and 1880s concentrated on foreign and domestic sales of hundreds of thousands of the firm's famed "rolling block" single-shot rifles and carbines. The twenty-five thousand or so Model 1875s manufactured between about 1875 and 1889 fell far short of Colt Single Action production. The Remington was offered in three centerfire calibers, a few in .45 Colt, but the bulk of production was divided fairly equally between .44 Remington and .44–40 Winchester.

Remington never publicized the fact in their promotional materials, but one of their staunchest backers was outlaw Frank James. In October 1882, James surrendered to Missouri governor Thomas T. Crittenden. The Sedalia (Missouri) *Dispatch* for October 5 carried a lengthy account of an interview with the bandit.

> He is in perfect health for one who has been wounded seventeen times. Shot three times in the mouth, there is a slight scar on the lower lip, which a long, fair moustache hides, and he is minus some eight or nine teeth.... Governor Crittenden ... told him clearly that he had no power to either grant an amnesty or pardon, that he must go to Jackson county, be delivered there to the officers, and be subjected fully to the laws of the State.... In the meantime, [James] had unbuckled his belt, containing a Remington revolver, calibre 44, and 42 cartridges, and handing them all to Governor Crittenden, remarked: "Governor, for the first time in 21 years I now permit another

Unfortunately the subjects are unidentified but the Colt Single Action is one of the fabled "Buntline Specials" with its 16-inch barrel and nickel-plated bronze skeleton shoulder stock. In 1876 no more than two dozen of these guns were produced and most eventually were purchased by distributor B. Kittredge & Co. of Cincinnati. The claim that the colorful E. Z. C. "Ned Buntline" Judson presented five of these guns to Wyatt Earp and other Kansas lawmen has no more basis in fact than do the stories which appeared in Buntline's "penny dreadfuls" or dime novels.

On April 27, 1887, three masked men held up a Southern Pacific train south of Tucson and fled with two sacks of mail. Two of the men were caught but the third escaped and the mail was never recovered. Several years later, Sheriff Bob Underwood was called to Colossal Cave where the empty sacks and this weathered Colt Single Action were found. The Colt and one of the mail sacks are exhibited by the Arizona Historical Society, Tucson.

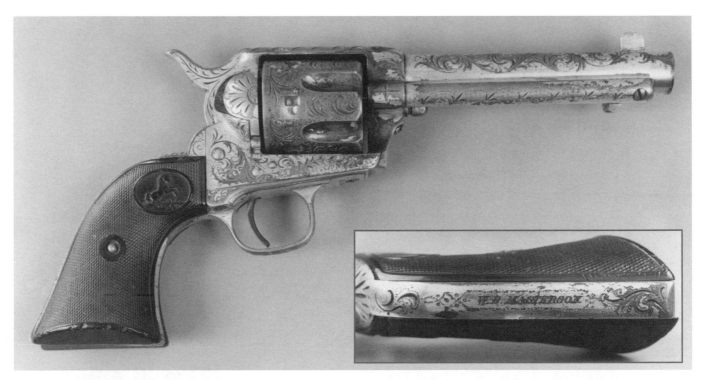

One of a number of Colt Single Actions purchased by Kansas buffalo hunter and later lawman William B. "Bat" Masterson, often as gifts for acquaintances. A factory letter confirms shipment of this single gun (#53684) on Oct. 23, 1879, in .45 caliber with "W. B. Masterson" engraved on the backstrap and silver-plated finish. The original pearl grips were damaged and replaced with ones of hard rubber. (Courtesy: Kansas State Historical Society)

man to take my pistol. It is the happiest moment of my life."

James went on to explain: "That belt was captured in open fight at Centralia. That pistol, after its owner had shot me through and through, was taken from him before I fell." The nickeled .44, #15116, remained in the Crittenden family until 1938.

Asked why he carried a Remington instead of a Colt or Smith & Wesson, he replied:

Because the Remington is the hardest and the surest shooting pistol made, and because it carries exactly the same cartridge that a Winchester rifle does [.44–40]. My armament was two Remingtons and a Winchester rifle. The cartridges of one filled the chambers of the other. You can now see why I prefer the Remington. There is no confusion of ammunition here. When a man gets into a close, hot fight, with a dozen men shooting at him all at once, he must have his ammunition all of the same kind.[45]

Although Remington sought a government contract for its Model 1875, the US Army never purchased any. Occasional blued specimens are found today with an "FR" or "JWR" inspector's cartouche in the grip and an "R" and a star on the side of barrel and frame, but these are thought to be from a contract with the Egyptian government. It is known that the US Interior Department purchased 639 nickel-plated M1875s in 1883 for use by Indian reservation police. These revolvers appear in some contemporary photos of Indian policemen.[46]

In 1888–89 Remington introduced what is sometimes called its New Model Pocket Army, identical with the Model 1875 except the ejector housing lacked the web on the underside. An 1889 catalog listed it only in .44–40 caliber and a 5 1/2-inch barrel length. Production only totaled about one thousand guns. Between about 1891 and 1896, Remington offered its so-called Model 1890. It was only available in .44–40 caliber although a customer could select either a 5 1/2-inch or a 7 1/2-inch barrel length. It, too, lacked the web and production was limited to only about two thousand guns. (Today's collectors need to exercise caution before purchasing a Model 1890 since because of its scarcity, some Model 1875s have been reworked in an effort to defraud buyers.)

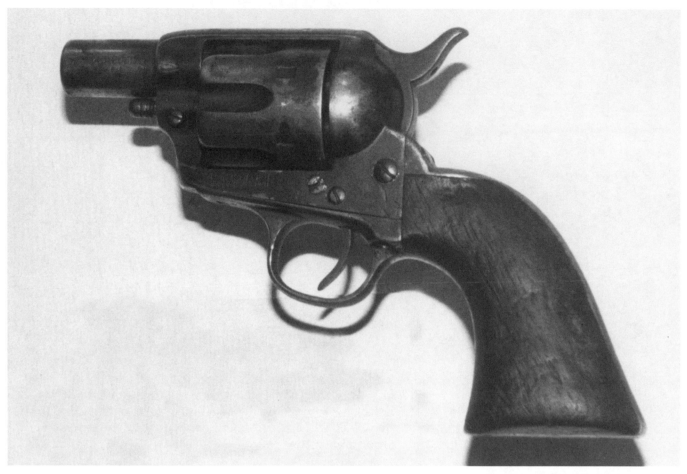

Clarence "Chappo" Beaty served as an Arizona Ranger (1902–9) and carried this Colt .45 Single Action as a "belly gun," its barrel shortened to a mere two inches. (Exhibited by the Arizona Historical Society, Tucson)

Meanwhile in Springfield, Massachusetts, Smith & Wesson was concentrating on the production of various models of their large-frame No. 3, including those to complete foreign orders. Soon after he learned of the pending introduction of the No. 3, Maj. George Schofield of the 10th US Cavalry had sought agent status to distribute them in western Kansas and Colorado. The factory sent him a sample gun and five hundred cartridges at no cost in September of 1870 and although denying his agency request, offered to sell him any number he wanted at $15 each. Eventually he ordered 111 No. 3 Americans. Schofield also recommended improvements, notably changes in the barrel latch and extractor, which he patented and S&W adopted. Two-thirds of the 8,969 .45 S&Ws made incorporating his modifications and his name went to the cavalry (6,005), plus a few more to officers, and the remainder to civilians.[47]

The express firm of Wells, Fargo & Co. purchased a number of surplus military Schofields from Schuyler, Hartley & Graham in the late 1880s and 1890s with the barrel shortened to five inches for use by guards. When

Wells Fargo agent Charles Woodward retired from the Oregon Department after forty-years service, he was presented with a gold-headed cane plus a Schofield with full-length barrel and special nickel and gold finish. One of the best known Schofields in civilian hands was #366, originally a government purchase, owned by Jesse James. The slain outlaw's widow gave the gun to Missouri's governor T. T. Crittenden. Present with Jesse at the botched Northfield, Minnesota, bank robbery was Bob Younger who reportedly surrendered a Schofield #367, its barrel shortened to about five inches, at the time of his capture two weeks after Northfield. An affidavit signed by Cole Younger's niece certified that he, too, once owned another Schofield with a shortened barrel, #2341.[48]

Bill Miner had a lengthy criminal career and his later exploits as a train robber in Canada were glamorized in the movie *The Grey Fox*, featuring the late Richard Farnsworth as Miner. The outlaw's homosexual tendencies, a subject rarely discussed in that era, weren't revealed until a 1903 Pinkerton Detective Agency wanted poster stated: "Is said to be a sodomist and may have a boy with him." A Schofield

The controversial and colorful Elfego Baca was a Mexican American folk hero in New Mexico Territory. He followed various career paths including sheriff, county clerk, private detective, real estate dealer, newspaper publisher, school superintendent, mayor, district attorney, and lawyer. Probably his closest brush with death came in 1884 as a newly appointed deputy sheriff after he arrested a drunken Texas cowboy in the town of Frisco. Soon after he was threatened by a reported eighty other Texas drovers and was forced to take refuge in a jacal or flimsy shack. He killed one Texan trying to break down the door and for more than thirty hours withstood a siege during which the mob fired hundreds of bullets into the hut as he lay on the sunken dirt floor. Eventually he surrendered to another deputy on the promise he would not be disarmed. In court he was found not guilty. Shown here is Baca's .45 Colt Single Action and sheriff's badge. (Courtesy: Ron Peterson)

he once owned is in a museum in Kamloops, British Columbia, with other Miner memorabilia. When Miner and an accomplice were arrested in 1881 for stagecoach robbery, their revolvers were the subject of an article in the Sacramento *Daily Bee.*

> The pistols, two each, taken from Miller and Miner... are handsome specimens of the Smith & Wesson brand. New, highly polished, nickel plated and self-cocking—the pattern used in the army, they are a dangerous weapon of offense or defense in the hands of an expert, and no toy to trifle with. They were admired... by old officers and men experienced in the use of arms, and pronounced to be as fine a weapon as ever defended honor or captured outlaw.

Reference to the revolvers' use by the army tended to confirm his preference for the Schofield model, although it was single rather than double action.[49]

Miner was arrested again in 1906 after having robbed a train in British Columbia, surrendering a .41 Colt Bisley Single Action and a .32 autoloading Colt pistol. One of his two accomplices, Shorty Dunn, was armed with two autoloaders, a .32 Colt and a German Luger. One of the arresting officers of the Royal Northwest Mounted Police asked if anyone knew how to unload the Luger, but Dunn's offer to do it was rejected.[50]

Early in 1878 at the request of Adams Express Company, Sheriff "Bat" Masterson in a buggy led a posse to a cattle camp fifty-five miles from Dodge City in search of two train robbers. They decoyed the suspects into a dugout where:

> Bat stood up behind a post, and came out from his concealment and presenting his pistols told the two outlaws to throw up their hands, which they did, when Kinch Riley, one of the Sheriff's posse, searched them, and took away a Colt's 45, Smith & Wesson's improved [a Schofield?].... They also had [long] guns, one a .40 Sharps

Another example of a drastically shortened Single Action is this .45 (#22124) found on outlaw Martin Mroz. He was lured across the border into El Paso and on June 29, 1895, was shot to death by US Deputy Marshal George Scarborough, former chief of police Jeff Milton, Texas Ranger Frank McMahon, and, by some accounts, Constable John Selman.

If only it could talk. Purchased by the army about 1857, this Colt M1851 Navy (#63487) eventually came into the hands of Jerry Culverhouse, a "Jehu" or stagecoach driver for Wells Fargo. Perhaps he had the barrel cut to a mere three inches for convenience. In February 1875 between Yreka and Shasta, California several robbers attempted to hold up his coach. As he whipped up the horses, a shotgun blast wounded Jerry in the shoulder and knocked out a tooth, but his heavy overcoat saved his life. This '51 was sold by Far West Hobby Shop in 1933 for $4.25. (Photo courtesy: Steve Evans)

Colt factory engraved .45 Bisley Model Single Action, one of three guns ordered by Arizona Territory sheriff Nabor Pacheco, two of which he gave to friends. (Exhibited by the Arizona Historical Society, Tucson)

sporting rifle and the other a 45 calibre Government [Springfield?] carbine.[51]

A New Model No. 3 S&W, a variation of the original American available beginning in 1878, is sometimes cited as the weapon with which Bob Ford, "that dirty little coward who shot Mr. Howard," murdered Jesse James. However in an affidavit printed in the Kansas City *Times* on May 6, 1882, Ford claimed that he had used a Colt .45 revolver #50432, a gun Jesse reportedly had given him a few days before. If that serial is correct, the gun would have been a Colt Single Action.[52]

Accepted by collectors with increasing enthusiasm in recent years have been those high quality revolvers with features designed by Joseph Merwin of Merwin, Hulbert & Co. but produced by a firm of which they were part owners, Hopkins & Allen, beginning in the mid-1870s. Despite the fact that Hopkins & Allen also produced lesser quality arms, Merwin & Hulberts were made of high quality materials, were well finished, and machined to close tolerances.

The first large-frame Merwin & Hulberts marketed were single action .44s which lacked the top strap over the cylinder, a feature introduced in 1883. Later Merwin & Hulberts appeared in both single and double action form and as both pocket and holster size weapons. All of the large-frame variations were .44s, mostly .44–40, and some bore the marking "Calibre Winchester 1873" to promote the

advantage of commonality in ammunition between rifle and handgun. A feature common to all was the advanced automatic extraction system. By pressing a release button, the barrel and cylinder could be swung a quarter turn to the side and slid forward, expelling the empty cartridge cases while leaving unfired cartridges in place. This design also allowed for easy barrel removal without tools and the interchanging of various barrel lengths depending upon the owner's need.

Not long after he shot Billy the Kid, Sheriff Pat Garrett was presented with a double action .38 Merwin & Hulbert (M&H) pocket revolver, cased, engraved, and with his name inscribed in the ivory grip. An accompanying Elgin pocket watch bore the inscription "From the Grateful Citizens of Lincoln County, September 1881. To Pat Garrett." Two other lawmen, both California sheriffs, are known to have owned M&H revolvers, J. J. Bogard and F. P. Colgan. Their guns were .44 Pocket Army models with a distinctive, rounded bird's head grip and a 3 1/2-inch barrel, although an interchangeable 5 1/2- or 7-inch barrel was available. Other frontier figures who are thought to have been M&H owners include Calamity Jane, outlaw Bob Dalton, and Texas gunmen John Wesley Hardin and Bass Outlaw. Specimens exist today with markings indicative of ownership by the Pacific Mail Steam Ship Company, the Union Pacific Railroad, and the State of Kansas. After Theodore Roosevelt purchased part

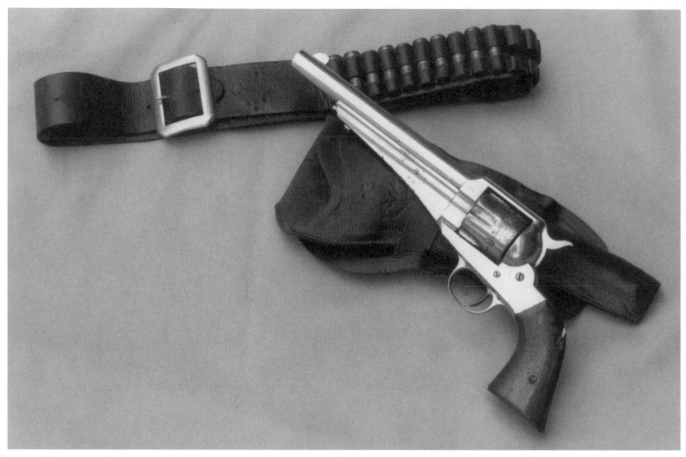

R. H. Bain joined the Alaskan gold rush and later moved to Dawson City, Yukon Territory, where he became a successful businessman. His son said he shot two claim jumpers with this Remington M1875 .44. The belt is stamped "Kennedy Hardware, Anchorage, Alas." (Courtesy: Rod Smith)

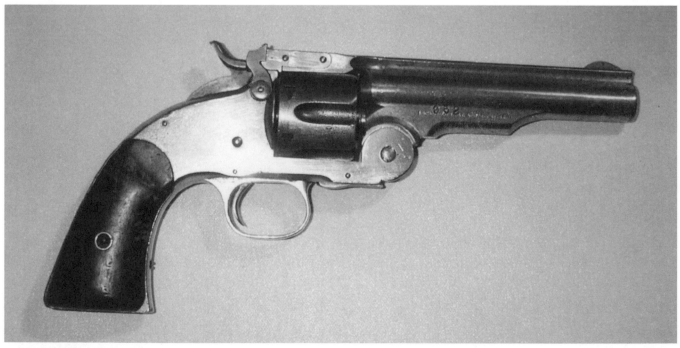

Schofield Ist Model (#952), formerly a government purchase gun, later purchased as surplus by Wells Fargo and now marked "W.F. & CO. EX. 952" on the right side of the ejector housing. Prior to about 1898 the firm's stamping was "W.F. & CO'S EX." and the number.

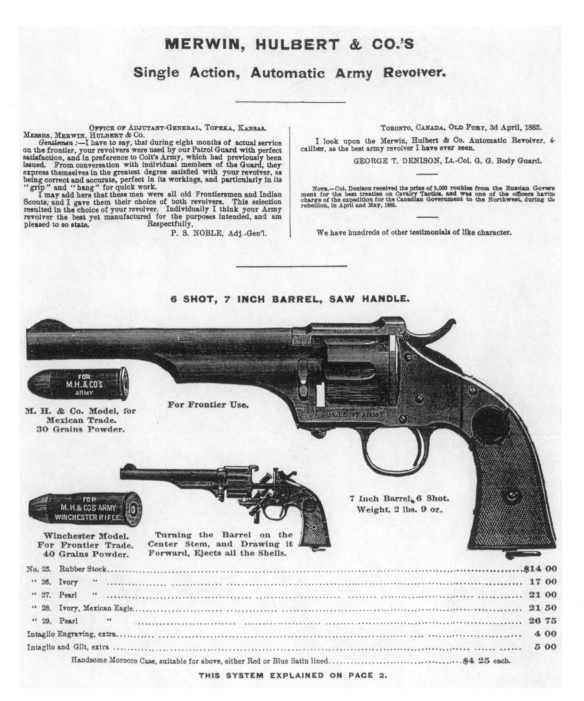

MERWIN, HULBERT & CO.'S

Single Action, Automatic Army Revolver.

OFFICE OF ADJUTANT-GENERAL, TOPEKA, KANSAS.
MESSRS. MERWIN, HULBERT & Co.
Gentlemen:—I have to say, that during eight months of actual service on the frontier, your revolvers were used by our Patrol Guard with perfect satisfaction, and in preference to Colt's Army, which had previously been issued. From conversation with individual members of the Guard, they express themselves in the greatest degree satisfied with your revolver, as being correct and accurate, perfect in its workings, and particularly in its "grip" and "hang" for quick work.
I may add here that these men were all old Frontiersmen and Indian Scouts; and I gave them their choice of both revolvers. This selection resulted in the choice of your revolver. Individually I think your Army revolver the best yet manufactured for the purposes intended, and am pleased to so state. Respectfully,
P. S. NOBLE, Adj.-Gen'l.

TORONTO, CANADA, OLD FORT, 3d April, 1885.
I look upon the Merwin, Hulbert & Co. Automatic Revolver, 4 caliber, as the best army revolver I have ever seen.
GEORGE T. DENISON, Lt.-Col. G. G. Body Guard.

NOTE.—Col. Denison received the prize of 5,000 roubles from the Russian Government for the best treatise on Cavalry Tactics, and was one of the officers having charge of the expedition for the Canadian Government to the Northwest, during the rebellion, in April and May, 1885.

We have hundreds of other testimonials of like character.

6 SHOT, 7 INCH BARREL, SAW HANDLE.

For M.H.& CO'S ARMY

M. H. & Co. Model, for Mexican Trade. 30 Grains Powder.

For Frontier Use.

For M.H.& CO'S ARMY WINCHESTER RIFLE

Winchester Model. For Frontier Trade. 40 Grains Powder.

Turning the Barrel on the Center Stem, and Drawing it Forward, Ejects all the Shells.

7 Inch Barrel, 6 Shot. Weight, 2 lbs. 9 oz.

No. 25. Rubber Stock		$14 00
" 26. Ivory "		17 00
" 27. Pearl "		21 00
" 28. Ivory, Mexican Eagle		21 50
" 29. Pearl "		26 75
Intaglio Engraving, extra		4 00
Intaglio and Gilt, extra		5 00
Handsome Morocco Case, suitable for above, either Red or Blue Satin lined		$4 25 each.

THIS SYSTEM EXPLAINED ON PAGE 2.

A page from a Merwin & Hulbert catalog showing the unique ejection system in operation.

ownership of the Maltese Cross Ranch he presented hunting companion and managing partner A. W. Merrifield with a nickel-plated and engraved .44 M&H with pearl grips as well as an 1876 Winchester.[53]

Hopkins & Allen also marketed its "X-L" models of both holster and pocket size guns under its own name—the No. 1 (.22 caliber) through No. 5 (.41 caliber), the larger .38 Navy and Police models, and the large-frame No. 8 in .44 caliber, available by the early 1880s and priced at $10, a little more than half the price of comparable Colts, Remingtons, and Merwin & Hulberts. These were more conventional in design with a swing-out ejector rod

and were less well finished than those bearing the Merwin & Hulbert marking. Competing with the X-L line in the medium price range were handguns by Forehand & Wadsworth.[54]

Double action revolvers, those which could be fired with a pull of the trigger without being thumb-cocked first, were well established in Great Britain by the 1860s. Except for Ethan Allen and other producers of double action pepperboxes, most American makers were slower to venture into that field. Colt in 1877 introduced its first double action revolver, using a smaller Single Action–style frame and a rounded bird's head grip shape. Except for a handful made

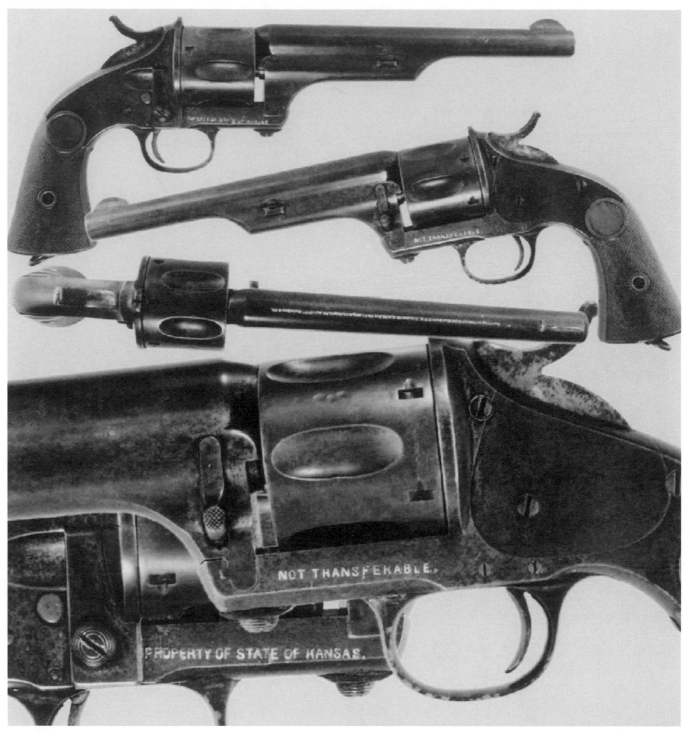

A montage of views of a .44 Merwin & Hulbert (#1924) stamped on one side of the frame "PROPERTY OF STATE OF KANSAS" and on the other "NOT TRANSFERABLE." (Photo by Ron Paxton, gun courtesy Larry Kaufman)

in .32 caliber, it was marketed as the "Lightning" in .38 caliber and the "Thunderer" in .41. It's rather surprising that production of the weapon continued until 1909 and amounted to almost 167,000 guns for its mechanism was delicate, difficult to repair, and often incapable of withstanding hard use. One June 1884 order to Colt for two dozen "Trigger Springs 41 D.A. [double action]" from Commings & Geisler of Houston, Texas, probably was to repair Thunderers.[55]

It may well have been a Model 1877 rather than the more durable Model 1878 which Corp. Thomas Schnepper with the 19th Infantry forwarded to the factory from Fort Ringgold, Texas. He'd attempted to have the .41 repaired in San Antonio but it was returned to him

An ever popular Colt Single Action at left and a holstered Merwin & Hulbert .44 single action at right.

in worse condition with the suggestion it be sent back to Colt. On Oct. 14, 1885, Schnepper sent the $1.50 to cover the cost of the repair and refinishing. (Few gunsmiths today are eager to work on a M1877, even fewer without much grumbling!)[56]

Tradition often mentions use of the Model 1877 Colt by William "Billy the Kid" Bonney (Antrim). Charlie Siringo's *History of "Billy the Kid"* is not without its errors. However he wrote that in the spring of 1882, the year after the Kid's death, Sheriff Pat Garrett auctioned off his saddle "and the blue-barrel, rubber-handled, double action Colt's 41-calibre pistol, which the 'Kid' held in his hand when killed." Siringo and the deputy county clerk, Billy Burt, were the only two bidders. Burt got it for $13.50 after Siringo dropped out of the bidding, figuring its value at only about $12. In 1920 Siringo received a letter from a man claiming to have been presented "a splendid Colt's six-shooter, forty-five caliber, seven inch barrel, and ivory handle," which was reported to have been in the Kid's hand when he died. Siringo noted that "it would be a safe gamble to bet that there are [sic] a wagon load of [Billy the Kid guns] scattered over the United States."

Siringo also for a time owned Bonney's M1873 Winchester carbine.

The Winchester rifle taken from the "Kid"
at the time of his capture at Stinking
Spring, was raffled off in the spring of 1881,
and the writer [Siringo] won it. [I] put it
up again in a game of "freeze out" poker. As

Texas Ranger Frank Hamer killed his first man with this Merwin & Hulbert .32 as a sixteen-year-old in 1900. Dan McSwain approached him and offered to pay him to kill a man. Hamer refused and told him that he planned to warn the third party. McSwain ambushed Hamer and wounded him with shotgun pellets. He recovered and purchased this .32 and a half box of cartridges for $2.50. When he confronted McSwain, there was a shootout and Hamer's bullet struck his antagonist's heart. Hamer turned himself in to the sheriff who rather than arresting him reportedly congratulated him for disposing of a troublemaker! The last two people Hamer killed were Clyde Barrow and Bonnie Parker in 1934. (Courtesy: Robert P. Palazzo)

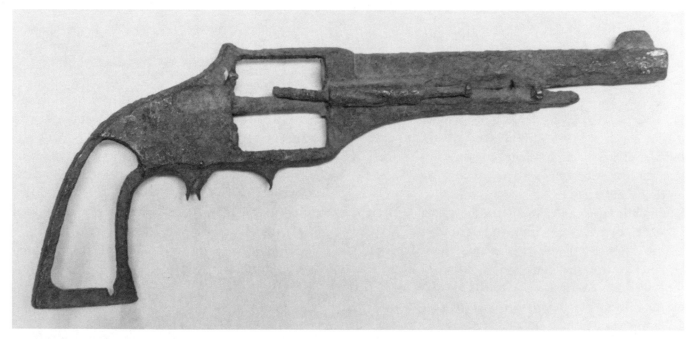

Rusted and incomplete, this Forehand & Wadsworth .44 single action New Model Army was found along the Santa Fe Trail. Production in the late 1870s and early 1880s of this and its similar predecessor isn't thought to have numbered more than one thousand of each. (Courtesy: Colorado Springs Pioneers Museum)

John Wesley Hardin's engraved Colt M1877 .41 caliber "Thunderer" (#73728), surrendered when he was arrested for displaying it openly at the Gem Saloon in May 1895 in El Paso. Three months later he was killed by lawman John Selman Sr. Hardin was considered by many to have been the deadliest of the western gunmen, but in 1894 after being released from prison he set up a small law practice. (Courtesy: Robert E. McNellis Jr.)

one of my cowboys. Tom Emory, was an expert poker player, I induced him to play my hand. I then went to bed. On going down to the Pioneer Saloon, in White Oaks [New Mexico], early next morning, the night barkeeper told me a secret, under promise that I keep it to myself. He said he was stretched out on the bar trying to take a nap. The poker game was going on near him. When he lay down all had been "freezed out" but Tom Emory and Johnny Hudgens. Just before daylight, Emory won all the chips, in a big show down, and I was the owner of "Billy the Kid's" rifle for the second time, but only for a moment, as Johnny Hudgens gave Tom Emory $20.00 for the gun, under the pretense that Hudgens had won it. Emory almost shed tears when he told me of losing rifle in what he thought was a winning hand. Of course I didn't dispute it, as I had given a promise to keep silent.[57]

George W. Coe, a participant in the Lincoln County War, described the Kid as using a "self cocker" when he killed Joe Grant in a saloon at Fort Sumner in January 1880. However, any use Bonney may have made of the Thunderer was not exclusive. A Colt Single Action is claimed to be the one taken from him when he was captured at Stinking Spring, and the only known photo of the Kid shows him with a Winchester '73 carbine and a holstered Colt Single Action. (That same image, reversed due to the photo process of the day, led rise to the false claim that Billy was left-handed.)[58]

Although not famous like the Kid, frontier doctor Henry F. Hoyt, was a satisfied Lightning owner. While operating a drug store in Bernalillo, New Mexico Territory, he had loaned his Colt .45 to a friend. A thief apparently reached through an open window and stole the gun from beneath the friend's pillow while he napped.

I felt lost without it, but regrets were useless. A few days after a traveling man from the Simmons Hardware Company of St. Louis came through and Billy presented me with a double-action Colt's thirty-eight, with a short barrel, a new model that had not been out very long and ... [which was] more suitable for me than my big forty-five. That gun has been over most of the

Two well-attired youths, perhaps ranch hands, photographed in East Las Vegas, New Mexico. The one at left carries a brace of Colt M1877 double actions, while his companion holds what appears to be a M1873, 1892, or 1894 Winchester carbine. (Courtesy: Center for Southwest Research, University of New Mexico, Albuquerque)

world with me and I still have it, apparently as serviceable as ever.[59]

Colt in 1878 began production of a larger double action, using the Single Action frame but continuing the rounded grip shape similar to that of the M1877. It eventually chambered many of the same cartridges as the Single Action including the ever popular .45 Colt and .44–40. It was more durable than its double action predecessor, but sales totaled only about fifty-one thousand. Its primary fault lay with its double action mechanism that used a fairly weak mainspring to counter a heavy trigger pull which occasionally resulted in a misfire, one reason the army rejected it.

An early purchaser of the new model was US Marshal Daniel P. Upham who served in the area administered by the

"hanging judge," Judge Isaac Parker at Fort Smith, Arkansas. Upham in the fall of 1878 was willing to pay the higher price for a M1878 than for a Single Action Colt and ordered a .45 with nickel finish and ivory grips. By the next summer, he had ordered seven more nickeled .45s, perhaps for use by others who enforced the law in what then was Indian Territory but today is Oklahoma. One of Upham's associates was George Maledon, Judge Parker's hangman, who boasted "I never hanged a man who came back to have the job done over." Maledon's M1878 is displayed at the old federal courthouse and jail in Fort Smith. Other westerners who owned Model 1878s included "Rowdy Joe" Lowe, the "poet scout" Captain Jack Crawford, and two civilians who scouted for the army during the Apache campaigns, Tom Horn and Al Sieber. Wells, Fargo & Co. also obtained a few.[60]

Trevanion Teel practiced criminal law in Texas with the enviable record of having lost only twenty of more than seven hundred cases in which he defended people accused of capital crimes. Secured in a book casing entitled High's Extraordinary Legal Remedies was his Colt M1877 .41 Thunderer (#26608) shipped from the factory in 1881. (Courtesy: Robert W. Voliva)

Buffalo Bill Cody special ordered two .45s with a non-standard 9-inch barrel in 1888, and gun dealer J. P. Lower of Denver advertised a variation of the M1878 with a 4-inch barrel length, which he designated as the "Sport's Pet." Famed Arizona lawman Jeff Milton apparently sometimes carried a M1878 .44 with a 4-inch barrel in a hip pocket leather holster. Another dedicated lawman, J. M. "Doc" Standley of California, also chose a short-barreled M1878, a .44–40 #11366. He eventually had his name engraved on the trigger guard.[61]

Customers sometimes could be very specific in their request for Colt revolvers as in a May 13, 1886, letter from Charles N. Cox, general manager of the Unaweep Stock Range Company in Colorado. It may have been the Model 1878 to which he referred when he ordered double action guns to replace "the heavy 38 cal. Pistol" he had sold to his foreman, plus two for other employees. All were to have a 6-inch barrel, two with plain blue finish and black grips and the other engraved with case hardened finish and a checkered pearl grip.

The pistols all to be the steel frame and all the full size of the 41, but bored for the 38 long cartridge and in my own I should like the fluting of the cylinder cut shorter and more shallow, so as to take less of the weight away—unless to [sic] much extra labor and expense—and the barrel left heavy as possible. The pistols all to be sighted to shoot point blank at a center, with coarse sight and made very light on trigger when cocked by the thumb.

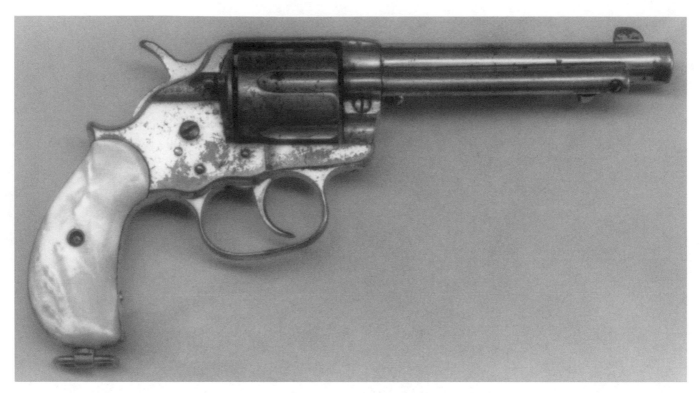

Deputy Marshal George Wellman was murdered from ambush but his suspected killer, a member of the Red Sash Gang from Wyoming's Hole In the Wall area, was never brought to trial. Wellman's nickel-plated .45 Model 1878 Double Action Frontier Colt (#10373) with pearl grips is preserved in the Jim Gatchell Museum in Buffalo, Wyoming.

A Wyoming cowboy in full regalia including a Colt M1878 double action. (Courtesy: Wyoming State Museum, Cheyenne)

A Colt M1878 double action worn butt forward with what may be a Marlin rifle in the saddle scabbard. (Courtesy: Bisbee Mining and Historical Museum, AZ)

A factory notation on the letter indicated the guns would be shipped on May 28 with the directive "make extra charge for special work on Cylinder & Barrel $5.00 [and] 1.50 for checking handles."[62]

The convenient mating of revolver and rifle firing the same cartridge was implied in an order for the 1878 Colt, the Double Action Frontier, as the factory designated the model. Joe MacDonald, superintendent of the Robinson Consolidated Mining Company at Ten Mile, Colorado, wrote in March 1881: "Please send me by express C.O.D. one pair Colts Double Action nickel plated & engraved 5 inch barrels Ivory handled and the handles carved [checkered]. With shell ejectors .44 cal. to shoot the Winchester cartridge 73 model."[63]

Many collectors are familiar with those eight hundred Colt London-made Model 1851 Navies ordered in 1855 for issue to the Canadian militia cavalry forces in Ontario (Upper Canada) and Quebec (Lower Canada). Less well-known among the American-made guns that figured in Canada's history were those 1,001 Colt Model 1878s procured in 1885 for the Canadian militia. These were .45s with a 7 1/2-inch barrel, most with nickel finish. Their intended use was to arm units organized to counter the Northwest Territory (now Saskatchewan) revolt against the government, an uprising of half-breed Metis. An "MD" stamping followed by a number found on the frame of some of these Colts is thought to represent the Canadian Department of Militia and Defence or Militia Department.

Engraved and fitted with pearl grips, this so-called Sheriff's Model ejectorless .45 Colt M1878 with a 4-inch barrel did belong to a Wyoming deputy sheriff, Les Snow. He figured prominently in the conviction of Tom Horn for the killing of young Willie Nickell. With court stenographer Charles Ohnhaus, he listened in an adjoining room as Horn confessed to the killing to Deputy Marshal Joe LaFors. Their testimony was the key element in the prosecution's case against Horn. The revolver is in the collection of the University of Wyoming's American Heritage Center in Laramie.

Some of the guns were ultimately passed to Canada's famed Northwest Mounted Police and others equipped Canadian forces during the later Boer War in South Africa.

Until 1889 Colt relied on its models of 1877 and 1878 to satisfy the needs of its customers who wanted a double action arm. In that year, the Hartford firm introduced a new model. No longer was it necessary to remove a center pin to separate frame and cylinder; the latter swung out to the left after a thumb latch was released on the side of the frame. All six of the empty cartridge cases could be extracted at once with a single push of the ejector rod at the front of the cylinder. Available in .38 and .41 like the M1877, its mechanism was a substantial improvement.

There were numerous design changes and model year designations between 1889 and 1903 and eventually Colt manufactured almost three hundred thousand of these double actions for civilian and military buyers, including the US Army, Navy, and Marine Corps as well as Wells Fargo. US Deputy Marshal Henry "Heck" Thomas's name is engraved on the backstrap of one of the Model 1889s, a .41 with a stubby 3-inch barrel. Thomas, Chris Madsen, and

Bill Tilghman in the 1890s were celebrated as the "Three Guardsmen" and were the scourge of outlaws in the more than seventy thousand square miles which comprised Oklahoma Territory.[64]

Remington produced no post–Civil War double action revolvers other than the Remington-Elliott four-barrel derringer. Not until 1881 did Smith & Wesson market a big .44 double action, another variation built on the No. 3 size frame. It somewhat paralleled the history of the Colt Model 1878 self-cocker in that it was advertised until 1913 with a production run of about seventy thousand guns.

Although lacking the glamour sometimes associated with the larger "holster" revolvers of the post–Civil War era, smaller size pocket revolvers played a significant if less publicized role in the "taming" of the west. Colt, Smith & Wesson, Remington, as well as Hopkins & Allen (many of their arms marketed by Merwin, Hulbert & Co.), Marlin, Forehand & Wadsworth, and other firearms makers included such arms in their product lines. Many of these guns could not be classed as "man stoppers" but were convenient to carry in a pocket or purse, as a lawman's or

Ben Stillman of Arizona Territory, photographed about 1900 with a M1878 Colt. (Courtesy: Bisbee Mining and Historical Museum, AZ)

outlaw's "backup" gun, or perhaps kept in a desk or bureau drawer, and some were quite inexpensive.

Competing with those pocket guns by Colt, Remington, and S&W was the compact British Bull Dog introduced about 1873 by Philip Webley & Son of England and copied by some American makers. (For a more detailed discussion of the Webley and other "bulldogs" and their use in the west see Chapter Five on foreigners and their guns.) Other pocket revolvers ranged downward in terms of quality of finish, durability, and the maker's reputation. Least expensive were those solid-frame spur (sheath) trigger guns which often bore no manufacturer's name but rather such colorful nicknames as TRAMP'S TERROR, SWAMP ANGEL, BUFFALO BILL, or EARTH-

QUAKE. These latter often are categorized today as "suicide specials." The 1884 catalog issued by N. Curry & Bro. of San Francisco priced a .32 nickel-plated single action KITEMAUG at $2.50 but a nickeled spur trigger .32 revolver by Remington at $6.50.

One suicide special that possesses greater historic significance than most is a .41 Forehand & Wadsworth "Swamp Angel" that once was the property of lawman Pat Garrett, who ended Billy the Kid's life. It was advertised for sale a few years ago and is engraved with pearl grips and gold wash and "P.F. Garrett" in script on the backstrap.

Colt between 1871 and 1877 produced almost 115,000 examples of a small .22 "open top" seven-shot weapon without a top strap. Beginning in 1871, anyone who wanted a

Cabinet card image by J. F. Standiford, "Traveling Photographer in the Indian Territory." The hunter at left carries his Colt Single Action not in a conventional holster but hung from a rare Bridgeport rig, patented by Louis S. Flatau in 1882. The revolver was suspended from a spring steel two-prong belt clip by a large button-head screw which replaced the hammer screw. The gun could be slipped free from the clip or merely swiveled and fired quickly from the hip. (Courtesy: Erich Baumann)

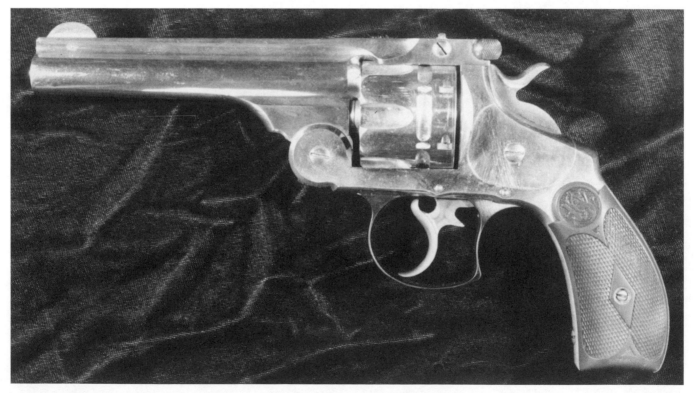

.44 Double Action Smith & Wesson, introduced in 1881, which Missouri governor Thomas Crittenden kept loaded in his desk as protection against retaliation by the James outlaw gang. (Courtesy: Larry T. Shelton, Missouri State Capitol Museum, Jefferson City)

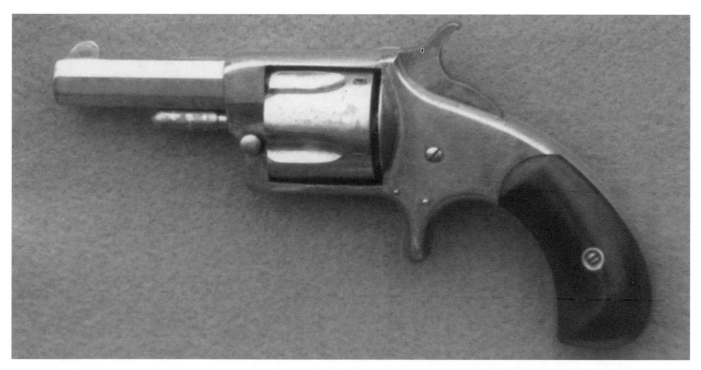

Sadie Orchard's Wesson & Harrington .38 (#440). Sadie was a madam in Hillsboro, New Mexico.
(Courtesy: Ron Peterson)

Smith & Wesson .38 Single Action 2nd Model (#286214) inscribed on the sideplate "U.S.M.H.S./1878/ DR. M. KEYES/ from/DR. WYMAN." Wyman was an assistant surgeon with the US Marine Hospital Service in St. Louis. (Courtesy: Robert P. Palazzo)

larger caliber pocket gun by Colt could choose one of the ten thousand or so .41 rimfire solid-frame Cloverleaf House Model arms, either with a five-shot round cylinder or the more common version with a four-chamber cylinder. When viewed head on, the latter cylinder did resemble a four-leaf clover and with the hammer lowered between two of the chambers it had quite a narrow, compact silhouette. From 1873 forward, Colt manufactured more than 150,000 additional solid-frame spur trigger single action revolvers in cal-ibers from .22 to .41 in their New Line, New House, and New Police series.

Colt's competition for sales of better quality single action pocket revolvers came primarily from Remington and Smith & Wesson during the 1870s and 1880s. Remington offered a series of solid-frame .30 to .41 caliber spur trigger revolvers designed by W. S. Smoot and the seven-shot .22 Iroquois. The former handguns were unusual in that the barrel, frame, and ejector housing (if present) were a

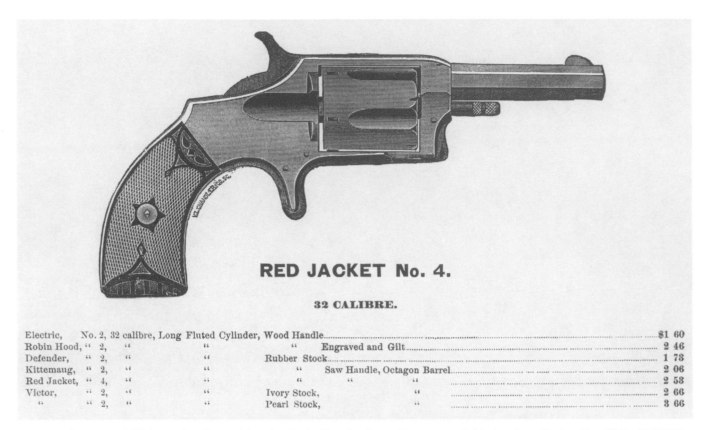

RED JACKET No. 4.

32 CALIBRE.

Electric,	No. 2, 32 calibre, Long Fluted Cylinder, Wood Handle					$1 60
Robin Hood,	" 2,	"	"	"	Engraved and Gilt	2 46
Defender,	" 2,	"	"	Rubber Stock		1 73
Kittemaug,	" 2,	"	"	"	Saw Handle, Octagon Barrel	2 06
Red Jacket,	" 4,	"	"	"	"	2 53
Victor,	" 2,	"	"	Ivory Stock,	"	2 66
"	" 2,	"	"	Pearl Stock,	"	3 66

An ad from the 1884 catalog issued by the C. J. Chapin Arms Company of St. Louis, offering the RED JACKET No. 4 and other inexpensive "suicide specials."

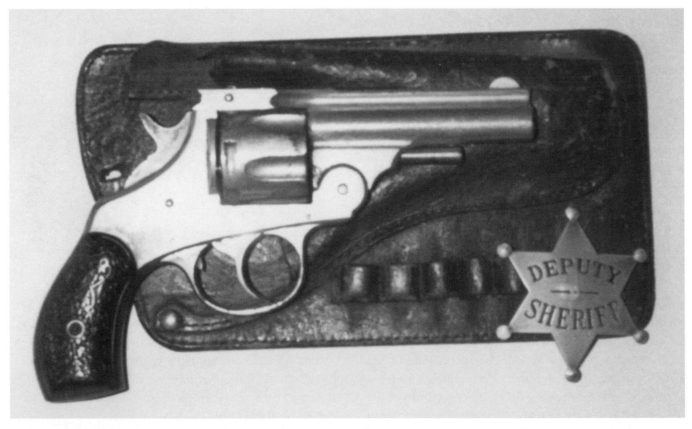

Harrington & Richardson .32 with badge and hip pocket holster, carried by Deputy Sheriff E. E. Johnston of Tombstone, Arizona Territory, in the 1890s. (Courtesy: Robert P. Palazzo)

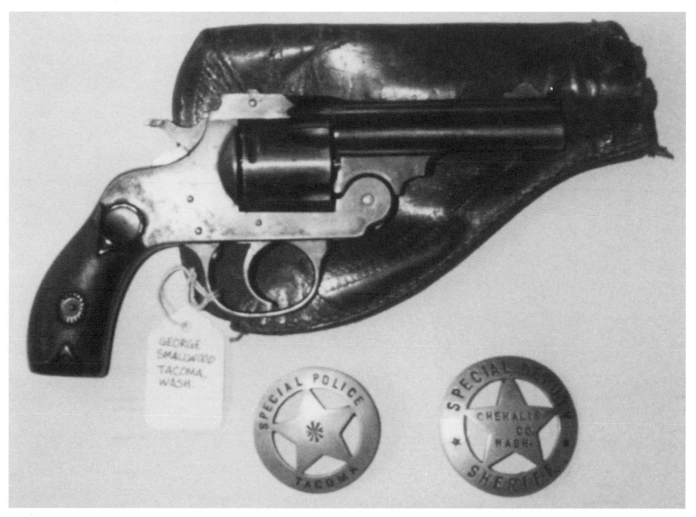

Deputy Sheriff George Smallwood of Tacoma, Washington, carried this Hopkins & Allen .38 "Secret Service Special." The company, successor to the Bacon Mfg. Co., claimed the title of being the world's largest maker of popularly priced firearms. (Courtesy: Robert P. Palazzo)

single unit. Smith & Wesson's initial competing small-frame handguns were updated round barrel versions of their Civil War–era .22s and .32s with a barrel that swung upward for cylinder removal. Beginning in 1876, a new series of .38 single action spur trigger pocket revolvers was available. The barrel swung downward instead of upward and the revolver incorporated a rack and gear extraction system which automatically ejected all the fired cartridge cases at once when the gun was broken open. Two years later a similar pocket model in .32 caliber became available, introducing an important safety feature designed by Daniel B. Wesson and James H. Bullard, a rebounding hammer which came into contact with the cartridge primer only at the instant of firing.

As early as 1875, Smith & Wesson had been receiving requests for a double action revolver, as when Sheriff Henry Morse of Alameda County, California, wrote: "[A self-cocker] would be the best weapon that a sheriff or police-

man could possibly carry and has been long looked for by the public." William C. Dodge invented a double action design and had echoed Morse's recommendation in mid-1878. "My son spent the winter at Hot Springs [Arkansas], and he says that they won't buy any pistol there that is not self-cocking.... Colt's and F & W's [Forehand & Wadsworth's] are exceedingly complicated and the former [Colt Model 1877] is very delicate."[65]

Finally in March 1880, S&W brought out its first self-cocking five-shot .38, followed later that year by a .32, and in 1881 a large-frame .44, not of pocket size. S&W pocket revolvers were compact, fast firing, and offered automatic extraction, and the public soon recognized their attributes. When production finally ended just after World War I, it had reached almost one million guns. Worthy of note when discussing these S&W pocket revolvers are the .32 and .38 S&Ws available beginning in 1887 as a model designated the Safety Hammerless or sometimes informally as "lemon

An advertising cut for Webley's "British Bull Dog."

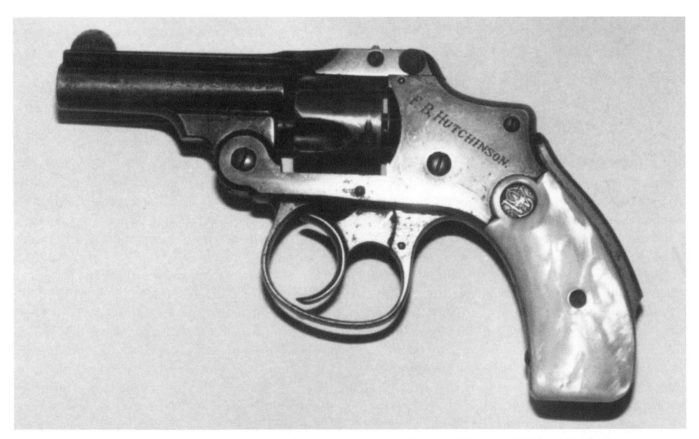

Inscribed "F. B. Hutchinson" and fitted with pearl grips, this Smith & Wesson .32 Second Model Safety (#100854) is representative of the popular S&W "lemon squeezer" pocket revolvers. Hutchinson was the manager and treasurer of Buffalo Bill's Wild West Show and later organized his own show. (Courtesy: Robert P. Palazzo)

This .38 Model 1900 Colt pistol (#2563) represents the beginning of a new era as well as a new century. The model was the first in the long line of Colt autoloading pistols and this early specimen was shipped to Omaha, Nebraska. (Courtesy: Robert P. Palazzo)

Making a tenderfoot "dance" in a staged scene in a western saloon. The bartender holds a German Mauser autoloading pistol, patented in 1897. Articles on these innovative pistols appeared in several American magazines that year and some undoubtedly had been imported by century's end. (Courtesy: Library of Congress, neg. #LC-US262-20059)

squeezer." The hammer was enclosed inside the frame and a safety lever incorporated in the grip frame precluded firing except when the handle was gripped firmly. Although it could only be fired as a double action, with no external hammer to snag on clothing it was a very practical pocket

gun and was available from the factory until just before World War II.[66]

On March 16, 1905, brothers George and Vern Gates robbed Gem Saloon patrons in Lordsburg, New Mexico Territory. Shotgun-armed lawmen later attempted to

A quartet of Texas Rangers. The only handgun visible is a German Luger autoloading pistol, being marketed in this country in 1901 by Frank A. Ellis & Son of Denver and other dealers. (Courtesy: Western History Collection, University of Oklahoma Library, Norman)

arrest them as they napped at a boarding house, awaiting a train. The thieves resisted and were riddled with buckshot. When the bloody blanket was pulled back, Vern had a .38 S&W hammerless in his hand, and an arsenal of seven other handguns lay beside the brothers. Each wore four holsters, one on each hip plus one in each hip pocket, and their overcoats were cut to give ready access to their guns.[67]

It was symbolic of the passing of an era, but when convicted killer Tom Horn broke out of jail in Cheyenne, Wyoming, in 1903, Deputy Richard Proctor wrestled with the former army scout to get control of a "Belgian revolver." A description of the incident mentioned that before Proctor relinquished the weapon, he snapped the safety on. Being unfamiliar with the pistol or not wanting to harm the officer, Horn was unable or unwilling to fire it and fled from the jail, leaving the deputy uninjured. Presumably the weapon was not a revolver but rather a semiautomatic autoloading pistol, representative of the new type of handgun that was gaining increasing popularity in the west and around the world as the new century dawned.[68]

The 1860s: A Decade of Advancing Technology

The Henry Rifle is now considered by the miners and hunters
in this country the best arm in use, and will pay more for it than any other.
— Winchester Repeating Arms Company Catalog, 1871[1]

The 1860s was a decade of technical, political, and social change. Sectional and political rivalries finally broke out in a four-year civil war, a transcontinental telegraph line was completed, passage of the Homestead Act accelerated settlement of the west with offers of free land, the first women's suffrage act in the United States was passed in Wyoming Territory, and construction of a transcontinental railroad was completed.

In firearms technology it was a decade that saw the gradual decline in popularity of the muzzle loading rifle following the appearance of the Henry and Spencer repeaters which fired metallic cartridges. Improvements in cartridge construction by the end of the decade allowed the introduction of increasingly powerful ammunition although the available repeaters couldn't handle it without major redesign. Thus a market both with civilian buyers and the government for single-shot, breech loading cartridge shoulder arms persisted into the 1870s. Meanwhile, until 1869 Smith & Wesson would control the manufacture of metallic cartridge revolvers which loaded from the rear.

HORACE SMITH AND DANIEL WESSON, A PROFITABLE PARTNERSHIP

The evolution of the Winchester began with an 1848 patent by Walter Hunt for a bullet with powder contained in the hollow base. Hunt was a prolific inventor, designing such items as a nail-making machine, lock-stitch needle, fountain pen, and the common safety pin. His gun was more complicated than practical. Lewis Jennings improved upon it as did Horace Smith and Daniel Wesson, two men who in 1854 received a joint patent on a lever action repeating pistol. Its basic features included a longitudinal sliding breech bolt locked and unlocked by a toggle linkage controlled by a finger lever, a spring-loaded tubular magazine beneath the barrel, and a vertically sliding cartridge carrier.

Smith and Wesson sold out in 1855 to the newly formed Volcanic Repeating Arms Company of which Oliver Winchester was a stockholder. The firm produced both Volcanic pistols and rifles and two years later, with Winchester at the helm, the New Haven Arms Company took over. Volcanic arms were well made and the basic design was sound. At the 1858 San Francisco Mechanics' Fair, judges called the Volcanic rifle and pistol displayed there "ingenious but rather complicated for general use." However the low-powered, hollow base "rocket ball" ammunition was a major handicap to any successful marketing effort.[2]

Meanwhile once Smith and Wesson obtained the rights to Rollin White's patent on a revolver cylinder with

S&W .22 First Model Ist Issue seven-shot revolver, sometimes sold in a gutta-percha case such as this one.

chambers which loaded from the rear, they undertook production of a diminutive seven-shot pocket revolver firing a self-contained metallic cartridge resembling today's .22 Short but with less power. The gun was a landmark in firearms development, and the venture was the genesis of a manufacturer which would gain international recognition. Full production began in 1858, followed in 1861 by the addition of a six-shot Model No. 2, a larger frame belt model in .32 rimfire caliber. These early S&Ws and their metallic cartridges offered ease of loading and durable, virtually waterproof ammunition. Demand spurred by civil war was such that S&W soon had a backlog that took them several years to fill. Not until May 1866 did they begin advertising their revolvers. Various metallic cartridge handguns such as the front-loading Moore, Pond, Prescott, and Plant appeared which avoided the White patent while such competitors as Colt, Manhattan, and Remington continued to market large quantities of

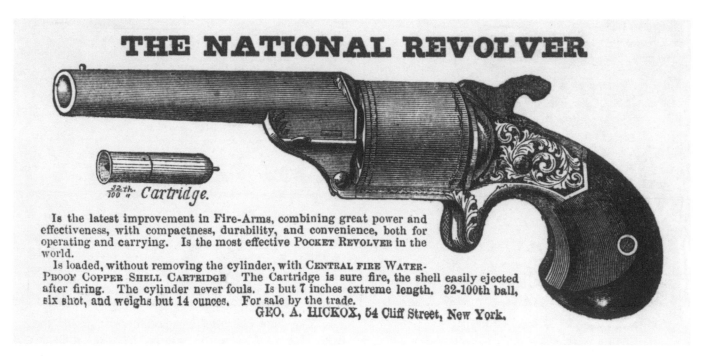

THE NATIONAL REVOLVER

32-th/100 " Cartridge.

Is the latest improvement in Fire-Arms, combining great power and effectiveness, with compactness, durability, and convenience, both for operating and carrying. Is the most effective POCKET REVOLVER in the world.

Is loaded, without removing the cylinder, with CENTRAL FIRE WATER-PROOF COPPER SHELL CARTRIDGE The Cartridge is sure fire, the shell easily ejected after firing. The cylinder never fouls. Is but 7 inches extreme length. 32-100th ball, six shot, and weighs but 14 ounces. For sale by the trade.

GEO. A. HICKOX, 54 Cliff Street, New York.

Ad for a .32 Moore "teat fire" revolver, a moderately successful front-loading evasion of the Rollin White patent. (Courtesy: Institute of Texas Cultures, San Antonio)

revolvers from pocket size to powerful .44s, but in percussion form.

Pvt. Alson B. Ostrander served with the 18th Infantry along the Bozeman Trail in 1866–67. While on furlough at Fort Laramie, he made the acquaintance of an aging frontiersman who hung around the post trader's store, Nick Janis.

> In the breast pocket of my vest, I carried a small Smith & Wesson twenty-two caliber pistol—one of those old models. Aside from the cartridges in the cylinder, I had none, One day, as my vest happened to be open, the butt of the pistol was exposed. Nick saw it and asked, "What's that?" I took the little revolver out and showed it to him. The minute he got it in his hands he just roared with laughter, and exclaimed, "Oh, look at the play toy!" Then he broke open the gun, and taking out the cylinder looked through the barrel, chuckling as he did so. Finally, handing it back to me, he said, "Boy, if you shoot me with dat and I find it out, I put acrost my knee and spank hell outen you!"

Despite the ridicule, Janis often asked to see the "play toy" and Ostrander later gave it to him as a gift.[3]

In the summer of 1865, Samuel Bowles of the Springfield (Massachusetts) *Daily Republican* newspaper with five companions journeyed to Colorado by stagecoach, armed with a No. 2 .32 S&W presented to him by the manufacturer. He wrote that "The 'noble red man'... gave us a wide berth; perhaps he had intuitive knowledge of our brave hearts and innumerable Colts,' Smith & Wessons,' Remingtons,' Ballards' and double-barreled shotguns."[4]

TYLER HENRY'S RIFLE

In October 1860 the New Haven Arms Company's plant superintendent Benjamin Tyler Henry received a patent on a new firing pin and bolt mechanism designed to load, fire, and extract a rimfire metallic cartridge of his design. The marriage of these improvements in the Volcanic with the new ammunition was a stellar event. The New Haven firm ceased Volcanic production and devoted its resources to the new rifle.

The Henry, as it was named, was mechanically very similar to its predecessor but fired a .44 200-grain bullet with twenty-eight grains of powder. Its muzzle velocity of about twelve hundred feet was more than double that of the Volcanic. Swinging the combination trigger guard and lever downward and then back extracted and ejected the empty case, fed a new round into the chamber, and cocked the hammer. The tubular magazine beneath the barrel loaded from the front by first pushing the cartridge follower to its forward limit which compressed its spring and allowed

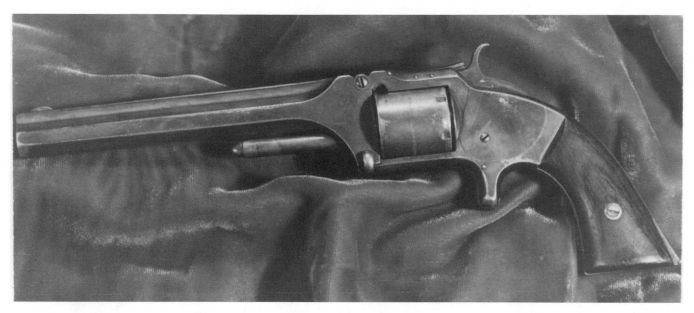

Smith & Wesson .32 No. 2 carried by a member of one of Maj. John W. Powell's exploratory trips down the Colorado River by boat. (Courtesy: Daughters of Utah Pioneers Memorial Museum, Salt Lake City)

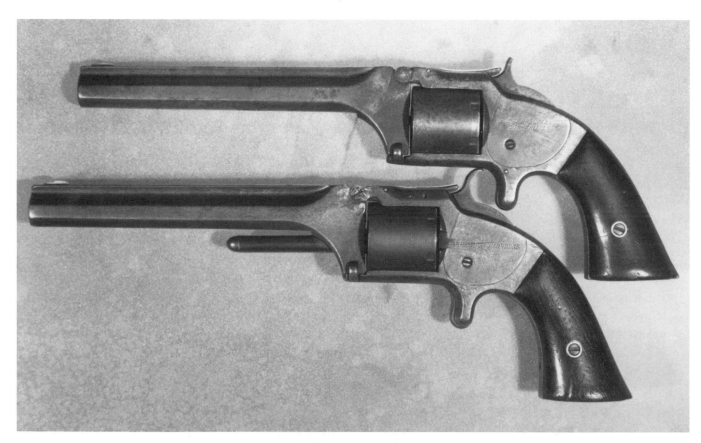

A Colorado judge's pair of S&W .32 No. 2s (#40241 and #40587). One is inscribed on the side plate "JUDGE ORSON BROOKS/DENVER, COLO." and the other merely "JUDGE ORSON BROOKS." The latter also is stamped "B. KITTREDGE & CO.," a major firearms distributor in Cincinnati. In an unusual but practical modification, the side of the recoil shield on each gun has been cut out to allow loading without removing the cylinder. Brooks served as a police judge (1869–79) and later as US commissioner for the Colorado Land & Mineral Association (1880–82). Denver's first lynching resulted after Brooks was robbed. One of the thieves was killed in a shootout in a saloon and the other was captured and convicted, but vigilantes dragged him from jail and hanged him. Each of the revolvers has been repaired at the barrel hinge, a weak point of the gun's design. (Courtesy: Norm Flayderman)

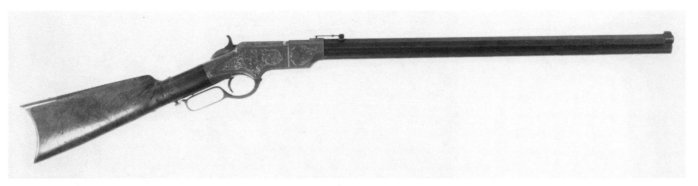

Engraved and gold washed Henry brought to Denver by Governor John Evans in the early 1860s.
(Courtesy: Colorado Historical Society, neg. #F-32798)

Henry (#729) carried by Pvt. Matthew Wilson of the 66th Ohio Volunteer Infantry during the Civil War and carried west when he homesteaded in Nebraska in the 1870s. (Courtesy: Dick Harmon)

a collar at the muzzle to be turned aside. The magazine could then be loaded with fifteen cartridges. By first inserting a round directly into the chamber, the gun became a "16 shooter." The slot along the entire length of the magazine tube through which the thumb piece for the follower moved was open. There was nothing to prevent it from accumulating mud or other debris that could hinder proper feeding. This fault was mentioned by users. "If the chamber that contains the spiral spring was closed from dust, it would be perfect," wrote one customer.[5]

About fourteen thousand Henrys were produced between 1862 and 1867 including about two hundred early ones with an iron rather than brass frame. Today's collectors prize the Henry rifle highly but it's an unfortunate fact that the handsome engraving or Civil War inscription found on some Henrys may be of recent origin! Caveat emptor—buyer beware.

The army's chief of ordnance had examined the Henry repeater in December 1861 but thought it too complicated for hard service. Another criticism of any repeater was the concern that soldiers would waste ammunition. Ultimately the Union did purchase 1,731 of these .44s and some volunteer units bought them on their own. Lt. John Brown, commanding Company C, 23rd Illinois Infantry, wrote on September 26, 1863, to the New Haven Arms Company. His letter is representative of such requests.

> I purchased one of Henry's Fifteen Shot Rifles...to practically test its value and advantages over other fire-arms. The result is such, that I have applied to Head Quarters and obtained permission for such of my company as wish to procure them, to purchase them on their own account, the Government providing the ammunition. I shall require from fifteen to twenty-five—perhaps thirty—for my company, and you will please inform me by return mail, the lowest price and terms of payment. The company wish to pay it by installments, part down and the balance in two months or next payment of the regiment.[6]

The Henry became available commercially in the east in July 1862 and through western dealers not long after. Oliver Winchester wrote in May 1863 that plain Henry rifles,

John C. Inness photographed with a Henry in Beaverhead Valley, Montana Territory, in 1865. (Courtesy: Montana Historical Society)

which retailed for $42, were selling in California for $70 to $75. M. O. Hamilton in July of 1864 asked for a price for a dozen and his letter was included in the New Haven Arms Company's 1865 catalog.

> The recent experience of my men on their journey through Sonora and Arizona armed with these weapons, gives me a high idea of their value. We have seven of them, but as our operations increase, that number will be insufficient. In the Indian country, so great is the dependence placed upon them, that none of our men care to go on escort duty unless there is one or more of these powerful and accurate weapons in the party. They are quite as fatal at 900 as 300 yards. The only addition I would suggest would be a telescopic sight, in order to cover the object at long range more perfectly.[7]

John Bach's ad in the 1868–69 San Francisco city directory advertised "Always on hand, splendid Target Rifles, Henry's Repeaters. etc." at 325 Kearny Street.

Prospector Ed Schieffelin was told all he'd find in Apache country was his tombstone. He persisted and from his discovery of gold and silver deposits the town of Tombstone, Arizona, rose. He relied on this Henry rifle for protection, exhibited with two other prospector's tools—canteen and rock hammer. (Courtesy: Tombstone Courthouse State Historic Park, AZ)

Hauling goods by wagon was essential to the economic growth on the plains before railroads. It was a dusty job and freighters weren't much higher on the social ladder than buffalo skinners. Some bullwhackers had to provide their own weapons while others were issued arms. Henry Porter, a freighter out of Denver, during Indian troubles in 1864 obtained Henry rifles for his teamsters. Nine years earlier, Alexander Toponce had been given an obsolete flintlock musket and had to pay a $15 deposit to his employer, Majors and Russell. Another Henry owner was August Santleben, an early Texas stagecoach and freighting operator, who paid the handsome sum of $95 for his from Charles Hummel of San Antonio. It was in the spring of 1867 when he first tested the gun "in battle" when eleven Indians ambushed him and his three companions, armed with two Henrys, a Colt revolving rifle, and a Spencer carbine.

> The fight only lasted about fifteen minutes, in which time about seventy-five shots were fired, and the only trophy of the battle was a dead horse!... The investigation [of the carcass] decided...who fired the fatal shot by awarding the honor to Black and his five-shot Colts rifle, because it was evident that the wound was not made by a Henry

rifle.... We were much pleased with them [Henry rifles], although we could not brag on our marksmanship.[8]

From Omaha, Nebraska Territory, Lt. W. A. Ward, 36th US Infantry, wrote to the factory in 1867:

> I have used one [Henry rifle] for the past eight months on the new route to Montana,...in several Indian fights, where rapidity of firing was an essential quality...and never knew it to fail. I have fired the whole sixteen shots nearly as fast as I could count.... The Henry Rifle is now considered by the miners and hunters in this country the *best arm in use*, and will pay more for it than any other.... In two Indian fights I owe to this rifle...my own life, and, perhaps, the lives of others.[9]

Lt. James Rothermel of the 8th Cavalry was another Henry owner, but he suffered a fatal accident with his. At Fort Boise, Idaho Territory, his gun discharged unexpectedly when he struck a rabbit with the butt.[10]

One of the classic tales of the Henry in the west concerned Stephen Venard, a city marshal in Nevada City,

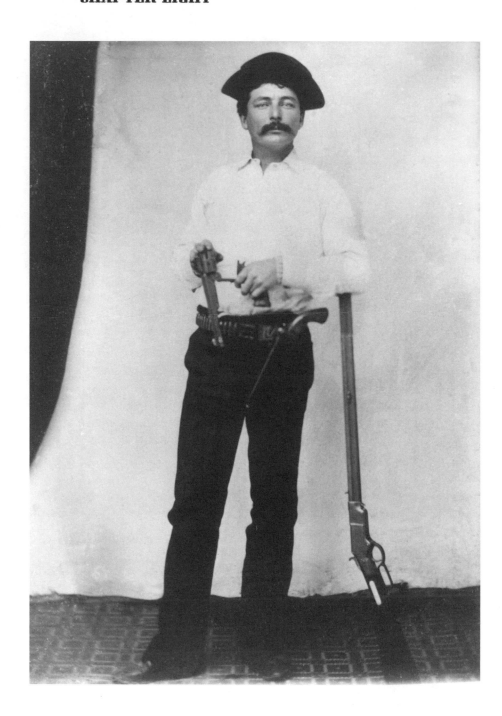

An intriguing image from a Texas album. Along with a Henry, the subject holds a .44 Smith & Wesson No. 3 American or Old Old Russian broken open as though to load it. The revolver in his belt appears to be another S&W. (Courtesy: Gary L. Delscamp)

California. Before dawn on May 16, 1866, George Shanks and two others robbed a Wells Fargo stagecoach near that town. Venard set out after them as a member of a posse, but when he came upon the outlaws he was alone. In the fight which followed, Venard killed the three with four shots from his Henry. By noon, the bandits were dead and the stolen money recovered. Wells Fargo in gratitude awarded him a new engraved Henry rifle and $3,000, which he shared with posse members.[11]

Charles Isaac Hawley admired good horses and owned one of the first Henry rifles in the vicinity of Poplar Creek, Montana. His son related that one day his father encountered an Assiniboine chief named White Dog.

Dad says to him, after showing him this gun [a Henry], "I'll give you this gun and that horse and saddle out there if you'll stand out here so far and let me shoot at you." White Dog was quite a man among his people. He had a musket he used to let them shoot at him with, and he'd show 'em the bullets come out of his mouth. Magic, you know. Of course his people didn't know this magicians' trick. . . . The musket wasn't loaded, or if it was, it was fixed so it wouldn't shoot straight. White Dog looked at him and

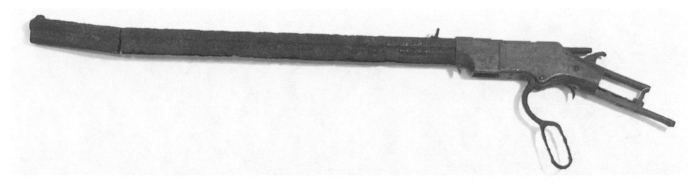

Col. N. P. Chipman of Iowa was a close personal friend of Abraham Lincoln and stood by his side at Gettysburg when the latter gave his historic address. Later Chipman was a judge at the trial of Capt. Henry Wirz, commandant of the notorious prisoner of war camp at Andersonville, Georgia. After the war, Chipman moved to Red Bluff, California, where he became a rancher and a federal judge. His ranch house burned down in the early 1900s and in 1975, a bottle collector digging in the rubble found the remains of this Henry rifle which with a little cleaning was found to have Chipman's name inscribed. (Photo by Steven W. Walenta, courtesy James D. Gordon)

said, "The white man's medicine is different from the Indian's."[12]

In the fall of 1865, Bernard Snow brought a Henry back with him to Fort Ephraim in central Utah after helping construct a government sawmill at Strawberry Valley. It caused a stir among his acquaintances and proved a wise acquisition when he used it to help repel Ute Indians who attacked a band of wood haulers.[13]

George W. Fox kept a diary of his 1866 journey on the Bozeman Trail to the gold mining country in Montana Territory. His entry for August 11 recorded that:

> I went over the bluff for buffalo shot at one
> with a Spencer but missed 6 shots hit one
> long range. afterwards took a Henry rifle
> shot a buffalo bull 130 yards & killed it.
> Shot it the second time the lst shot cut out
> the tounge [sic] let the rest lay.

An entry two days later stated: "I took my little [Henry] rifle & went ahead & killed a big bull buffalo lst shot. hit the heart. shot another & wounded him badly.... I took the buffalo tounge [sic] liver & heart & a saddle blanket off of the shoulder." Fox apparently was one of those wasteful hunters whom other immigrants sometimes criticized.[14]

Another Bozeman Trail traveler, Thomas Alfred Creigh, in 1866 was in charge of one of two divisions in a wagon train. His diary contained a description of the wagon in which he traveled.

> This wagon is also called the "Reading
> Room" having no small number of

> "Beadles" [popular paperback dime novels]
> & other interesting reading matter. We are
> not unarmed, for if we look in front of us
> we see a Spenser [sic] rifle—behind us a
> Henry rifle, on our left, strapped to the
> bows a Colts Navy & a Remingtons
> Revolver, above is tied a long knife & scab-
> bard, also pistols in pockets.[15]

In the same year, soldiers under the command of Capt. William Fetterman from Fort Phil Kearny in northern Wyoming were lured into an ambush and wiped out by Sioux Indians under Red Cloud. Col. Henry B. Carrington of the 18th Infantry in his official report described the scene.

> I found citizens James S. Wheatley and
> Isaac Fisher, of Blue Springs, Nebraska
> who, with "Henry Rifles," felt invincible,
> but fell, one having one hundred and five
> arrows in his naked body.... The car-
> tridge shells about them told how well
> they had fought.[16]

However the Henry's short .44 rimfire cartridge wasn't always up to the challenge. Hiram Upham was an Indian trader near Fort Benton in Montana in the 1860s and on one occasion spotted a large bull buffalo grazing near his trading post. He wanted the hide to cover the easy chair frame he'd completed the day before. The bullet from his Henry only wounded and angered the beast which charged. Instead of firing again, Upham dropped the rifle and dodged among the cottonwood trees in an attempt to escape. He yelled for help, but the

Even at the late date of 1894, the African American man at center right holds a Henry. There is no uniformity of long guns among these militiamen on duty during a strike in Cripple Creek, Colorado—Winchester M1886, Springfield, Ballard, Remington, and unidentifiable rifles. (Courtesy: Colorado Springs Pioneers Museum, acc. #A64-236)

spectators enjoyed the spectacle for a few minutes before one of them killed the bull with a single shot from his "long Sharps." "Sorry I couldn't have killed the bull sooner and saved you all that exercise, but I'd mislaid my cartridges and had to hunt around for them a long time." When one of the bystanders offered to skin the deceased bull, Upham told him to roll the carcass into the river. "When I want a hide for the chair I'll kill an animal myself."[17]

Luther S. "Yellowstone" Kelly purchased a Henry at Fort Berthold in 1868.

> It served me well for several years, or until
> I was able to secure a Winchester rifle.
> With the Henry and the stubby little .44
> caliber cartridge that went with it I killed
> many a buffalo, as well as other game, and
> it stood me in good hand when I was

forced to defend myself in encounters
with hostile Indians.[18]

In 1879 Camillus and Mollie Fly established a boardinghouse and photographic studio in Tombstone, Arizona, close by the entrance to the O. K. Corral. Sheriff John Behan observed the famed gunfight between the Earps and the Clanton bunch in October of 1881 from Fly's house, and Ike Clanton escaped the fight by running through the structure. Fly left the safety of the building with a Henry rifle in hand when the shooting had stopped and removed the revolver from the wounded Billy Clanton's hand. "Give me some more cartridges," Clanton reportedly requested of Fly.[19]

COMPETITION FROM THE SPENCER

The Henry's primary competing repeating rifle design in the 1860s was that of Christopher Spencer, who received patent protection in March of 1860. His rifle was somewhat

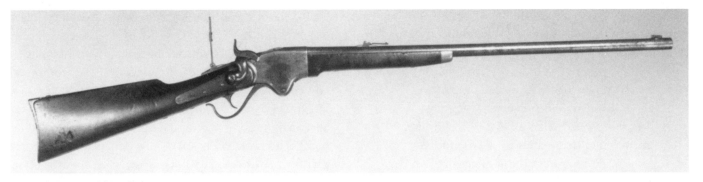

A post–Civil War Spencer sporting rifle stamped with a "reclining H," which may represent the brand of one of several Texas ranchers with the surname of Reynolds. If so, the most likely would be Samuel F. of Roanoke, a Confederate veteran of the 29th Texas Cavalry, who became a moderately wealthy cattleman. (Courtesy: John H. Gross)

less complicated and stronger than the Henry, and the spring-loaded magazine tube was completely enclosed in the hollow butt stock. Removing the tube through the butt plate allowed the shooter to load seven rimfire cartridges. As with the Henry, operating the under lever extracted the empty case and chambered a new round, but unlike the Henry action it did not cock the hammer.

Spencer initially had assembled a few small-frame sporting arms in .38 and .44 caliber, but these were unsuitable for military use. The army's chief of ordnance in December 1861 had disapproved of the Spencer as he had the Henry, but wiser heads ultimately prevailed and by the end of 1865, the government had obtained more than one hundred thousand .52 caliber Spencer rifles and carbines, primarily the latter.

Like the Henry, the Spencer was available west of the Mississippi by early 1863. One of the first to bring the Spencer to the newly established Arizona Territory in '63 was Associate Justice Joseph P. Allyn. He was enthusiastic about the weapon's features but somewhat reluctant to demonstrate it at a small town shooting match.

> The fame of my... Spencer had got ahead and they wanted to see it shoot. I didn't much like to waste ammunition when no more can be got, and to tell the truth I had no great confidence in my marksmanship to do justice to the weapon. I never fired a rifle in my life until I left the Missouri, and I never fired anything but the Spencer. This last gave me a great advantage, for the weight in the Spencer is very different from any other, and usually annoys a stranger firing it at first. I advanced into the ring, and at the first

shot had the good luck to hit the paper in the center and split the board. I concluded it was not best to try again.[20]

He felt the Spencer had no superior as a weapon for fighting Indians.

> Its seven shots can be loaded in less time than any other rifle can be loaded and capped, it can be fired more rapidly than a revolver, and re-loaded in a tenth of the time it would take to re-load a [percussion] Colt; in fact, in an Indian fight, close quarters, I think a revolver never was re-loaded. The fixed ammunition has immense advantages, as soon as it can be easily obtained, say at San Francisco even, for it never wastes and cannot be injured by transportation. So completely were the soldiers and citizens convinced of this that I could have sold a dozen on the spot with two or three hundred rounds of ammunition each, at very near a hundred dollars in gold pieces, if I had had them.[21]

Cowboy Charles Siringo in 1875 spent two weeks in Galveston, Texas, visiting his Uncle Nick. Upon leaving, "[he] presented me with a Spencer Carbine—one he had captured from a yankee while out scouting during the war. I was very proud of the gift for I had never owned a repeating rifle before."[22]

In the spring of 1868, William M. Breakenridge was managing a store in Sidney, Nebraska, when a band of six Indians ran through the edge of town and attempted to steal several horses picketed there. "Breck" grabbed a Spencer carbine and with others hurried off in pursuit. They caught up with the retreating Indians as the marauders were scrambling up a steep bank.

> I fired at one just as he reached the top of the hill and saw his horse make a plunge and disappear. I felt sure that I had hit him and tried to throw another shell into the gun, when I found that the [magazine tube] had come out and all the shells had fallen out of the gun. Fortunately, I still had my pistol in case I needed it.[23]

While operating a stagecoach between San Antonio, Texas, and Monterrey, Mexico, August Santleben assisted a man named Castro who had lost his horse. His kindness later brought immunity from robbery at the hands of the stranger's outlaw band when they met again.

> They numbered about fifteen men and all were armed with Spencer carbines and six-shooters. That pattern of rifle was the first breechloader, using metallic cartridges, introduced into Mexico.... We talked about many things, but I carefully avoided any allusion to their occupation.... Castro... assured me that I could rely on the friendship and services of himself and men at any time.[24]

Travel by coach could be hazardous to a passenger even before his journey began. On the night of July 8, 1869, David M. Mason, an employee of a stage line, hailed a coach out of San Antonio. Pvt. George Washington of Company B, 9th Cavalry, was "riding shotgun" on the driver's seat when he saw the stranger attempt to swing aboard in the darkness. A bullet from the trooper's Spencer carbine struck Mason in the chest, hurling him to the ground and wounding him mortally. Washington was exonerated.[25]

The Civil War resolved the sectional rivalry which had hindered the construction of a transcontinental railroad. Its conclusion also made available a pool of construction workers, eager for a payday and adventure. As the network of western rail lines expanded, it brought thousands of easterners and European immigrants into what once had been considered the Great American Desert but now was opened to settlement as railroad companies advertised land for sale along their routes. The Union Pacific and Central Pacific met at Promontory Point in Utah in 1869 and the Kansas Pacific opened a route between Kansas City and Denver the next year. The Southern Pacific eventually linked San Francisco and New Orleans. In 1881 the Atchison, Topeka, and Santa Fe crossed the southern plains and two years later the Northern Pacific joined St. Paul, Minnesota, and Portland, Oregon.

In 1867 construction of the Union Pacific system was advancing steadily westward despite difficulties posed by weather, terrain, and hostile Native Americans. The army gave high priority to guarding surveyors and construction workers and also made arms available to the railroads. In July 1867 the commanding officer at Leavenworth Arsenal was directed to issue thirty Model 1865 .58 Springfields to the Union Pacific and thirty more to the Western Union Telegram Company. The Kansas Pacific Railroad also received M1865 breechloaders and in June 1877 gave back 505 to the Rock Island Arsenal along with sixty-five thousand cartridges.[26]

Crossing Kansas by rail in 1868, a traveler described what at first was thought to be an Indian attack but was a herd of bison crossing the track. "In the car in which I was seated I observed twenty-five stand of arms, breech-loading rifles, and a large chest of metallic center primed needle-cartridges, provided by the railroad company, for the use of the employees to defend their trains against Indian attacks." The reference to "needle-cartridges" implies their use in Springfield rifles. In June 1870 the government sold three hundred "breech-loading muskets, caliber .58" to the Kansas Pacific Railroad for $6,000. The next entry in this listing is for thirty thousand .50 metallic cartridges sold to the railroad which raises the question of a typographical error and whether the three hundred rifles were .58 1st Model Allin conversions or later .50 caliber Allins. (The same listing also recorded the sale to Professor F. V. Hayden of the US Geological Survey "12 Springfield breech-loading muskets, '1866'" for $14.52 each and "2 Springfield breech-loading muskets, '1868'" at $18.19 plus eight unidentified revolvers.)[27]

Adolph Roenick, a Prussian immigrant, was working on the Union Pacific Eastern Division (later Kansas Pacific) line. He and six other workers comprised a section gang that was attacked by Indians. He and two companions personally owned Spencer carbines, a fourth worker had left his gun behind, and the other three were armed with company-issued "breech-loading rifles of an unusual caliber. The ammunition could not be found for sale anywhere, and it was furnished by the railroad company in such limited quantities as to allow no practice." These may have been Model 1865 breech loading Springfield 1st Model Allin conversions which chambered a .58 rimfire cartridge.[28]

In the excitement of the attack, Roenick in haste dropped eight rather than seven cartridges into the Spencer's magazine in the butt. When he reinserted the magazine tube and its follower, "I could not shut down the magazine and had to pull it [tube] out and take out one [cartridge]." Two of the section crew were shot off the handcar and killed before the others reached the safety of a dugout.[29]

Union Pacific Railroad construction efforts, guarded by armed workers, the army, and Luther North's Pawnee scouts, were harassed but not halted by hostile Indians. The Central Pacific (CP) didn't face the same degree of hostility and to facilitate its eastward move across Nevada adopted a less antagonistic attitude toward Native Americans. The CP signed treaties with the Paiutes and Shoshonis and even hired some Indian men and women to work beside the Chinese laborers. "We gave the old chiefs a pass each, good on the passenger cars and we told our men to let the common Indians ride on the freight cars whenever they saw fit."[30]

While freighting in the Black Hills, Curley Ayres found the campfire one winter night "so packed with warmers" that he couldn't get within warming distance. He reached into his pocket and gathered a handful of Spencer cartridges and tossed them in the fire.

> That widened the circle in a hurry and gave him full use of the fire.... There wasn't much danger from the explosion, unless the butt of a cartridge had happened to lodge against a log, but most of the fire circlers didn't know until afterward what caused the blast.[31]

Camped on the plains in Nebraska in July 1865, M. M. Wood of the 5th Michigan Cavalry wrote to the Spencer Repeating Rifle Company to inquire about the cost of one or a dozen sporting rifles. The Michigan Cavalry Brigade had earned an enviable reputation on the basis of its wartime service under Custer with Spencers. "I would rather have twenty-five men armed with this gun than a hundred armed with any other.... I would have rather invented the Spencer than the Electric Telegraph." Wood continued: "If I only had one of your Sporting Rifles here I think I should be perfectly happy."[32]

The Spencer company didn't begin to produce sporting rifles in earnest until after war's end. Lt. Philip Reade was commissioned in 1867 and was assigned to command Company H, 3rd Infantry. He had his name and regiment engraved on his sporting carbine which he carried during service in Kansas, Colorado, and Indian Territory where his duties included defense of wagon trains, stagecoach stations, and railroad survey parties. But despite Wood's and Reade's preference for Spencer sporters, these guns weren't a commercial success, partly because they could not be adapted to the longer and more powerful cartridges being developed. Another factor was the large number of surplus military arms on the market at greatly reduced prices. Only about seventeen hundred sporters were made before the company failed in 1868 and the Fogarty Repeating Rifle Company purchased its assets. The new ownership lasted less than a year before selling out to Winchester.[33]

Some enterprising gunsmiths and dealers converted military Spencers into sporters in various calibers. Among them was J. P. Gemmer of St. Louis, a former Hawken employee who in 1862 bought the shop from Sam and later stamped S. HAWKEN on the conversions. Other examples of Spencer conversions include a .50 rifle with 32-inch barrel marked "A.J.PLATE SAN FRANCISCO." A .44 sporting Spencer with 30-inch barrel was surrendered by the Apache Geronimo.[34]

THE FIRST WINCHESTER, THE MODEL 1866

Manufacture of the Henry repeater ceased in 1866, shortly before the demise of the Spencer. Oliver Winchester and his associates recognized the need for improvement in the Henry's magazine design. The solution was patented in May 1866 by Nelson King, a spring-tempered loading gate set in the right side of the brass frame. The new magazine tube was closed except at the rear. Loading was accomplished merely by inserting the cartridges one by one through the gate. The new lighter arm introduced another change, for on the barrel it bore the firm's new name, the Winchester Repeating Arms Company. C. S. Kingsley of Idaho City in 1871 advertised it as the "improved Henry rifle," but the designation Model 1866 was adopted once the new Model 1873 appeared.[35]

The M1866 fired the same .44 rimfire cartridge as did the Henry and used the same toggle-link action. It reportedly was nicknamed "yellow boy" in some western circles, although the author has found no nineteenth-century use of that term. It was first available in two standard models—a carbine with 20-inch barrel and a rifle with 24-inch barrel—and later in a three-band musket with a 27-inch barrel. With a round in the chamber and a fully loaded magazine, these three models held fourteen, eighteen, and eighteen cartridges, respectively. Commercial sales apparently began in 1867 and when production ended in 1898, almost 160,000 had left

Space is at a premium in this miners' log cabin cluttered with rough homemade furniture. A Spencer carbine is hung on the wall. (Courtesy: Colorado Historical Society)

the factory in New Haven. Symbolic of the future popularity of the M1866 in the west, the first two carbines were sold in August 1867 and went to H. G. Litchfield of Omaha, Nebraska, for $34 each.[36]

In tribute to B. Tyler Henry's contributions, Winchester-manufactured rimfire cartridges were marked with an "H" headstamp in the center of the base. In part to insure proper ignition of the rimfire .44 cartridge, the Henry and 1866 Winchester arms used a dual firing pin. This fact may have given rise to the application of the term "rimfire" to those western stock saddles with a double cinch about the horse's belly, while those with a single cinch were sometimes referred to as "centerfire."

Captain Henry B. Strong in 1871 wrote that he was using a Winchester (Model 1866) when he began scouting for the army in 1871. Cartridges cost him 5¢ each so

he had to be "conservative in their use." An endorsement of the new Winchester by a special agent of the Post Office Department in Texas in an official report was representative of others.

> The last serious attack was in April last [1871], upon two of the mail coaches at the head of the Concho. The Indians, some thirty or forty strong, were driven off by the persistent fighting of the guard and men led by Mr. Jas. Spear, the route superintendent, who killed three or four of the enemy, and as many of their horses, with his Winchester Rifle. The Winchester is the favorite arm on the plains. I find it everywhere.[37]

A railroad survey camp on Canada's Saskatchewan River. The man with his back against the teepee holds a Spencer carbine. Two-wheeled "Red River carts" were a rather common form of frontier transportation in parts of Canada's west. (Courtesy: Canadian Public Archives, Ottowa, Ontario)

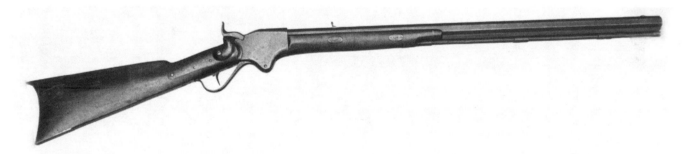

A Civil War Spencer (#47730) converted by J. P. Gemmer of St. Louis into a twelve-pound sporting rifle. (Courtesy: Gary Roedl)

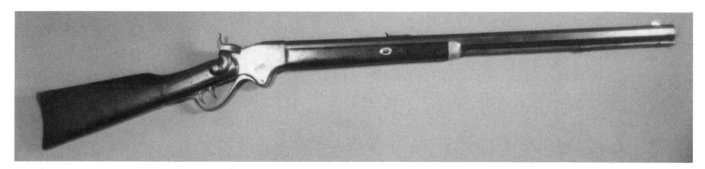

Model 1865 Spencer carbine made at war's end by the Burnside Rifle Company, rebarreled and marked "A.J. PLATE SAN FRANCISCO CAL." (Courtesy: R. Stephen Dorsey)

Model 1866 Winchester rifle, engraved and inscribed "Wichita Oct. 21, 1871 to Nehemiah Green from S.J.C. in Friendship and Gratitude." Governor Samuel J. Crawford resigned office on November 4, 1868, to assume command of the 19th Kansas Cavalry, raised to serve with the regular army against the Indians. Green, as lieutenant governor, succeeded Crawford and appointed him to command the regiment. (Courtesy: Kansas State Historical Society, acc. #1979.128)

In 1870 Yale University professor O. C. Marsh (standing fourth from right) and ten associates spent almost six months in the field collecting fossil vertebrates in Kansas and Colorado, the first Yale scientific expedition to the west. Nearly all in this scene wear holstered revolvers while several are armed with double-barrel shotguns and third from left has an 1866 Winchester carbine. Cold weather and the threat of hostile Indians ended that year's work.

Another advocate of the new Winchester was William E. Webb who journeyed across the plains in 1868.

> I became very fond of a carbine combining the Henry and King patents. It weighed but seven and one-half pounds, and could be fired rapidly twelve times [fourteen actually] without replenishing the magazine. Hung by a strap to the shoulder, this weapon can be dropped across the saddle in front, and held there very firmly by a slight pressure of the body.... So light is this ... weapon that I have often held it out with one hand like a pistol, and fired.[38]

One-armed Maj. John Wesley Powell in 1871 made his second exploratory boat trip through the rugged canyons of the Green and Colorado rivers. He explained: "Each man

Studio portrait of an unidentified Californian with a Winchester Model 1866 rifle. The converted US Model 1836 or 1842 martial pistol thrust in his belt undoubtedly is a photographer's prop, for its rammer assembly is missing. (Courtesy: California State Library, neg. #GL-4003, Sacramento)

had a rifle and some had also revolvers. Most of the rifles were [Model 1866] Winchesters. We had plenty of ammunition, and the rifles were generally kept where we could get at them quickly." Of the Winchesters, he noted: "Two were of the original Henry pattern." To satisfy a friendly Ute Indian that they had no loose gunpowder, Frederick Dellenbaugh "removed the spring from the magazine of my Winchester [Henry] and poured the sixteen cartridges out. He had never seen such a gun before."[39]

The interest and wonder Native Americans sometimes felt for these repeating rifles is reflected in a particularly intriguing Model 1866 rifle which the author examined. The gun was manufactured about 1871 and was handsomely engraved long ago by an unidentified artisan. The engraved scenes include various slain game animals and a curious Native American bent over closely examining

what clearly is intended to be a lever action Henry or M1866 held by a white man.

CONTINUED DEMAND FOR SINGLE-SHOT RIFLES

Despite the increasing availability of repeating rifles by the late 1860s, some westerners continued to rely on single-shot breechloaders firing metallic cartridges. These did offer certain advantages—simplicity, reliability, and the ability to chamber the longer, more powerful cartridges as they became available. In the 1880s, increasing numbers of repeaters firing some of the most powerful cartridges of the time were available to tempt those who swore by single-shots. Most popular single-shot arms were those by Sharps, Remington, and Ballard, and those military Springfields that reached civilian hands. Other

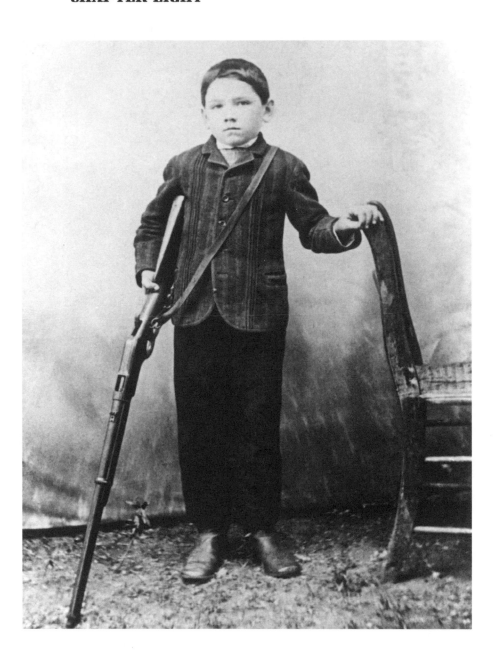

Young Joseph William Petty of Lipan, Texas, wasn't much taller than this M1866 Winchester carbine when he was photographed about 1870. (Courtesy: Phil Spangenberger)

early single-shot metallic cartridge rifles of lesser prominence in the west included such as Peabody, Phoenix, Wesson, and Whitney. Winchester, too, entered the single-shot market, but not until 1885

The ready availability and low prices of surplus Civil War arms sold by the government attracted many buyers. Between 1866 and 1869, F. S. Hodges kept a journal of his surveying trips for the Union Pacific along the proposed route of the railroad. A January 1868 inventory of the party's arms included his own Ballard rifle, a shotgun, and a dozen "Jocelyn" carbines. This undoubtedly was a misspelling of "Joslyn," one of the many models of Civil War breech loading single-shots. These may have been loaned or given to the Union Pacific by the army or they may have been purchased as surplus by the railroad. Civil War veterans sometimes also took advantage of the opportunity to purchase

their arms upon discharge as did several members of the lst Oregon Cavalry in January 1866. "They took their arms & accoutrements at the government price of eight dollars each for the revolver and carbine & three dollars for the sabre & belt."[40]

One of the least common single-shot rifles of the period was a .44 rimfire designed by the Howard brothers of Detroit but manufactured under contract by the better known Whitney Arms Company of Connecticut. Nicknamed the Thunderbolt, production was limited in all of the three versions—rifle, carbine, and shotgun. John C. Anderson made a round-trip journey from St. Louis to Virginia City, Montana, in 1866 and took a Howard Thunderbolt with him which he found suited his needs. One of his journal entries mentioned: "Today I shot off a Snipe's head [at] about 90 yards with my 'Howard Rifle.'"

Engraved Model 1866 Winchester rifle (#38586) owned by stagecoach king Ben Holladay. The M1851 Colt belonged to expressman George Chorpenning. (Courtesy: Greg Martin)

Later he had the chance to compare the relative merits of his Howard against a Spencer during a buffalo hunt. "'Spencer' rifles will shoot hard—but not straight. I got out my 'Howard' and tried the relative merits of each for distance. I beat the 'Spencer' very badly—and then mine will shoot with some accuracy."[41]

On his return trip, he related his firearm preferences in some detail.

> A person learns a great deal from experi-
> ence. Of all patent breech loading guns I
> prefer a "Henny" [Henry] rifle—after that
> a "Howard"—but of all the guns in the
> world I would prefer a muzzle loading rifle
> of about 30 to the pound [.54 caliber].
> That is the gun for service. The breech
> [loader] will shoot a great deal harder and
> a great deal quicker and oftener and can
> be used in wet weather as the metallic car-
> tridge is water proof but the muzzle loader
> will shoot with accuracy which cannot be
> attained by any patent [gun] now in exis-

> tence and will shoot far enough for any
> ordinary purpose. During my whole trip I
> killed only one animal that was beyond
> the range of a good muzzle loading rifle
> but on the other hand I missed dozens and
> dozens with my patent [Howard?], that I
> could have certainly killed with the other.
> Of all pistols, I decidedly prefer Colts Navy
> Revolver. Some other pistols are good but
> this is in my opinion the best. A good shot
> gun too is a very good thing to have on
> such a trip as this has been.[42]

His preference for a muzzle loading rifle in the mid-1860s was not unique. Samuel Houston of Texas, one of a party of prospectors headed for the Black Hills in 1877, was described as "a grizzley bear in the fight, always ready with his old Hawkins [Hawken muzzle loading] rifle, which never left his side."[43]

Far more popular than the Howard was the rifle designed by Charles H. Ballard which first appeared in the spring of 1862. Early models, both civilian and those

Rarely found in photos of civilians is this pair of Smith breech loading carbines of Civil War vintage, perhaps purchased as surplus. The man at left has a percussion Remington revolver thrust in his belt. The tintype image (which is reversed) may have been made in Platte City, Missouri.

produced on contract for Civil War use, were chambered for rimfire ammunition with its inherent pressure limitations. A useful accessory for civilian purchasers of a Ballard was a steel chamber insert patented in January 1864, allowing the use of loose powder and ball if metallic ammunition was unavailable.

In November 1865 a writer for *Harpers New Monthly Magazine* journeyed by stagecoach through Kansas to Colorado. He and his three fellow passengers "each . . . had provided himself with a Ballard rifle and a pair of [Colt?] navy revolvers." The coach preceding them was attacked by Cheyennes at a way station where a Negro blacksmith and several other men took refuge in a buffalo wallow.

When the blacksmith stood up to fire, he was shot in the head and collapsed. A passenger rolled what they thought was his lifeless body to the rim of the wallow as a breastwork and proceeded to use the blacksmith's Ballard to help stand off the attackers. Later the "corpse" surprised his companions by regaining consciousness and returned to the safety of the wallow.[44]

The Woodmansee Brothers advertised in a Salt Lake City newspaper in the fall of 1867 that they had "14 cases Ballard Rifles with fixtures all complete to exchange for stock-cattle." Two months earlier, the Denver *Rocky Mountain News* carried an advertisement by sales agents Merwin & Bray of New York directed at "plainsmen and

Percussion .47 target bench rifle by Carlos Gove with a Malcolm scope. The 34-inch barrel is marked "C. GOVE/Bluff City/Iowa" indicating manufacture before he moved to Denver in the early 1860s. The gun weighs forty-two pounds, the bench rest another twenty. (Courtesy: Colorado Historical Society, neg. #F-6083)

A false muzzle partially in place on the Gove rifle. Loading through a false muzzle starts the bullet into the rifling without deformity and also reduces muzzle wear. It's removed before firing. (Courtesy: Colorado Historical Society, neg. #F-11743)

sportsmen" offering for the first time "Ballard Rifles and Carbines of larger caliber, as follows, 44–100, 46–100 and 50–100. This want has long been felt." The ad reminded potential buyers that the Ballard was "the only breech loader that can be loaded with loose ammunition as [well as] with copper cartridges." Ballard popularity increased in the west as chamberings for more powerful cartridges became available, but so did competition from such makes as Sharps and Remington.[45]

In 1872 Henry Shane, operator of a sheep camp, was placing a board in the fork of a tree as a shelf. His wagon was parked a dozen yards away while his riding mule grazed nearby. When confronted unexpectedly by a band of Comanche Indians, he dashed for the wagon and grabbed a "Mississippi yager" (US Model 1841 rifle) and shot one Indian's horse with the only load he had for the muzzle-loader. His other gun was a new, single-shot Ballard rifle. When he left home that morning, he carelessly had left his

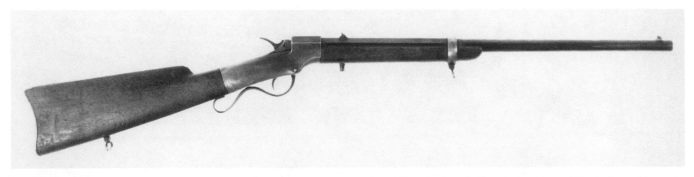

Ballard carbine used to guard machinery owned by the Gregory Mine in Leadville, Colorado, while being shipped by wagon train. (Courtesy: Colorado Historical Society, neg. #F-32793)

full cartridge belt behind. He had only two cartridges for the Ballard, one in the chamber and the other in his pocket. He held his fire until he risked one of his cartridges in a shot which mortally wounded one of his attackers intent on cutting his mule's tether. Fortunately for Shane, his attackers eventually slipped away, unwilling to expose themselves to his fire.[46]

The muzzle loading Model 1841 Mississippi military rifle, which Shane was still using in 1872, had been a fairly common and popular weapon in civilian hands. In another incident in Texas in 1867, three men were cutting grass with which to roof a house when they had a skirmish with Indians. "[Servier] Vance had a Mississippi rifle and six-shooter, Joe Decker had a Mississippi rifle, and Charley [Decker] a Spencer carbine."[47]

As construction work on the Union Pacific Railroad progressed westward in the late 1860s, settlements sprang up along the route. Some were mere tent cities, rowdy and temporary, but others became permanent towns. One such latter community was Cheyenne, Wyoming. Early inhabitants, consisting of "military Officers, with 350 rank and file, Government Directors, and civil Engineers of the Union Pacific Railroad and their friends," drew up a "declaration of independence" describing how they planned to conduct themselves in the "goodly city of Cheyenne." Among their listed complaints about the rules of eastern society were "extravagant dress, requiring one to two changes of linen each day" and "too much Newport, Saratoga and Long Branch." Privileges that they claimed for themselves and their posterity included "the most simple dress, consisting of flannel shirt, overalls, blouse, top boots with spurs, and slouch hat" and "protecting ourselves from hostile Indians, by our own Henry and Ballard rifles and Colt's revolvers."[48]

Trailing Cattle

If you ever have a youngster
And he wants to follow stock,
The best thing you can do for him
Is to brain him with a rock.
— Anonymous[1]

The fictionalized cowboy in novels by Zane Gray and others and on the television or movie screen often was portrayed as a western hero. In truth, he was a dirty, dusty laborer who worked long hours for modest wages. There was little glamour in his job.

The cattle industry in Texas reportedly began with a bull and six heifers brought by Spaniards in 1521. Throughout the eighteenth and nineteenth centuries, cattle were a major source of wealth in Texas. In the twenty years before the Civil War with increasing industrialization in the east came a growing demand for hides and tallow as well as meat, and Texas cattle were shipped by steamboat to New Orleans or were trailed to other ports on the Mississippi. St. Louis and Kansas City were marketing sites along the Shawnee Trail, and some herds were driven on hoof as far as Chicago. During those years it's been estimated that perhaps two hundred thousand cattle were driven overland to Missouri alone, although not without difficulties. Cattle drives north through the Indian nations sometimes were charged a toll. Armed bands of "border ruffians" sometimes extracted payment by threat and as early as 1851 Missouri placed an embargo on Texas cattle, fearing the spread of the tick-borne Texas fever. Kansas in 1867 would establish a quarantine line east of which Texas herds were banned.[2]

Hispanic influences on the cattle industry in the southwest were strong and not merely in terminology. Texas beef was of Spanish origin and was "long of horn and legs, variegated in color, and belligerent of disposition." The Mexican War increased the demand for beef and following the discovery of gold in California, longhorns costing $14 in Texas were marketed for as much as $100 to miners. In 1853 a traveler described a California-bound herd of about four hundred head. Most of the twenty-five drovers were young men headed for California, glad to have their expenses paid for their services. "They were all mounted on mules, and supplied with the short government rifle [possibly US Model 1841 Mississippi rifles] and Colt's repeaters. Two large wagons and a cart, loaded with stores, cooking utensils, and ammunition, followed the herd."[3]

Despite Texans' prominence in the cattle trade prior to the Civil War, they didn't have a monopoly. The cattle industry was well established in California by the 1830s, often employing Native American and Mexican or Spanish drovers. But California ranchers weren't able to meet the increased demand for beef generated by the discovery of gold in 1848, and Mormon cattle drives from Utah were common throughout the 1850s. Beef also was being raised in Oregon as early as the 1850s. "Road ranches" operated

A cow puncher with Henry rifle in hand. (Courtesy: George Jackson)

by livestock traders sprang up along the Oregon and California trails in the 1840s which provided immigrants with fresh beef as well as replacements for worn out oxen, proving that cattle could winter successfully on the northern plains.[4]

A drover, a term seemingly used more frequently than "cowboy" before 1880 or so, found that a cattle drive was difficult and dangerous. An 1854 issue of the San Diego *Herald* printed the epitaph of a Texan, perhaps a drover:

Here lies the body of Jeems Hambrick who was accidentally shot on the banks of the pacus [Pecos] river by a young man. He was accidentally shot with one of the large colt's revolver[s] with no stopper for the cock to rest on. It was one of the old fashion kind brass mounted and of such is the kingdom of heaven.[5]

Civil War veterans returning to Texas after the Civil War found their land hadn't been fought over and devastated as in the east, but the state was in financial ruin. Hundreds of thousands of half-wild longhorn cattle roamed the plains and brush country. The east was hungry for beef, but there was the continued resistance to drives through Missouri and eastern Kansas in the form of quarantine laws and on occasion armed mobs, sometimes using Texas fever merely as an excuse for demanding ransom. Some Texans by now claimed there was nothing in Kansas but three suns—sunshine, sunflowers, and sons of bitches.

Joseph G. McCoy in 1867 persuaded the skeptical president of the Eastern Division of the Union Pacific Railroad (later the Kansas-Pacific) to give him favorable freight rates and at the hamlet of Abilene, Kansas, McCoy bought land and constructed cattle pens. Col. O. O. Wheeler delivered the first herd from Texas to Abilene in late summer, after hiring about fifty cowboys and arming them with Colt revolvers and Henry repeating rifles. An estimated thirty-five thousand longhorn cattle were driven to Abilene during the first season, short as it was, and sold at an average figure of $14 per head. The town would become an island in a sea of cattle.[6]

In the decade that followed, other Kansas towns served as major shipping points—Wichita, Ellsworth, Newton, Dodge City, and eventually Caldwell, all of which became well-known in western lore. The business the drovers brought to these towns was substantial and in the April 28, 1877, edition of the Dodge City *Globe* the paper noted that the town was preparing for the seasonal cattle trade. "Places of refreshments are being gorgeously arrayed in new coats of paint and other ornaments to beguile the festive cowboy."[7]

A correspondent for the New York *Daily Tribune* in a November 1867 article described the Texas drovers he encountered in Abilene.

> And here are the drovers, the identical chaps
> I first saw at Fair Oaks, and last saw at
> Gettysburg. Every man of them unquestion-
> ably was in the Rebel army. Some of them
> have not yet worn out all of their distinctive
> gray clothing—keen-looking men, full of
> reserved force, shaggy with hair, undoubt-
> edly terrible in a fight, yet peaceably great at

cattle-driving, and not demonstrative in their style of wearing six-shooters.[8]

Abilene was incorporated in 1869 and ordinances against carrying firearms were passed and posted, but rowdy drovers shot up the signs and tore down the almost completed jail. Locals who were hired to enforce the law failed but "Bear River" Tom Smith became town marshal and maintained order more often with his fists than his gun before he was murdered.

Other Texas herds were driven to New Mexico, Colorado, and Utah or to populate the northern ranges in Wyoming, Montana, and the Dakotas where soon Texas speech was heard commonly. It's been claimed that an average of 350,000 cattle were driven out of Texas each year from the late 1860s to the 1890s. Substantial numbers of cattle were trailed eastward from Oregon and Washington in the 1870s, and many of the cowboys who made these latter drives were experienced Texas drovers.[9]

During the early post–Civil War cattle drives from Texas, Indians were a threat to herds and cowboys. A veteran of an 1867 drive, W. H. Boyd, recalled that he saw many fresh graves "that had never been rained upon." Later a Texas Ranger, James B. Gillett, recalled that when he was herding cattle in 1871 in Texas, "every cowboy of that day and time carried either a six-shooter or a Winchester.... They had to... for self-protection as Indians hung on the flanks of all cow outfits... just watching for a chance to steal horses or kill a cowboy." (Not all who drove cattle appreciated the term "cowboy" or "cowpony." "Hell, man, they were horses and men," exclaimed Jim Shaw who trailed cattle from Texas to Wyoming.)[10]

Young Joe Horner (he later assumed the name Frank Canton after serving jail time) in 1869 joined a crew driving a herd from Texas to Kansas. The drovers were not well-prepared for what lay ahead. While gathering plums, he spotted two painted Indians watching him and spurred back to the herd with a warning.

> We... gathered what few guns we had
> and found that they were very rusty
> from the wet weather and in no condi-
> tion for service. We had brought
> along... some old Henry rifles, which
> were rim fire and not much good, but we
> all had good six-shooters with plenty of
> ammunition. We had scarcely got our
> guns cleaned. and loaded when about
> twenty-five mounted Indians came gal-
> loping down towards the herd.... Each

The Spartan interior of bunkhouse at a ranch on the Powder River. (Courtesy: Montana Historical Society)

They weren't cowponies and cowboys, challenged one drover, "Hell, man, they were horses and men." (Courtesy: Colorado Springs Pioneers Museum)

A southwestern drover riding a double-cinch "rimfire saddle" with a Colt Single Action on his hip.
(Courtesy: Center for Southwest Research, University of New Mexico, Albuquerque)

Indian had a bow and quiver of arrows with steel-tipped heads, and they were also armed with good rifles and apparently had plenty of ammunition.[11]

Soon after, the Indians stampeded the herd and during the excitement ran off all the drovers' horses except for the night herders' picketed mounts. "There was nothing for us to do but drive on foot in the daytime, as we could not buy horses any place along the trail. Then commenced the hardest trip of my life."[12]

An actual incident of the Texas cattle drives was one Larry McMurtry used as the basis for the climax of his classic western novel *Lonesome Dove* in which co-hero Capt. Augustus McCrae receives a wound that later takes his life. Oliver Loving had trailed cattle to Illinois from Texas in '58 and in 1866 joined Charles Goodnight for a drive to Denver. Their route through New Mexico and into Colorado became known as the Goodnight-Loving Trail. Goodnight invented the chuck wagon for use on the trail as a mobile kitchen. Like many drovers, he developed hemorrhoids and had his own home remedy—a suppository made of salt and buffalo tallow.

They were pushing another herd up the trail in 1867 when Loving and Bill Wilson moved on in advance toward Fort Sumner, New Mexico, where they had a contract to provide beef for reservation Indians. Attacked by Native Americans, they took refuge along a riverbank where a bullet wounded Loving in the hand and side. Wilson later recorded: "The Indians at this time made a desperate charge, and after I had emptied my five-shooting Yarger, I picked up Mr. Loving's gun and continued firing." Wilson offered no further details of his "Yarger" other than to indicate it didn't use metallic cartridges. A five-shot Colt Model 1855 .56 caliber revolving rifle or carbine does fit such a description.[13]

The cattlemen's plight had become desperate by nightfall. Wilson eased Loving's fever with water he retrieved from the river in a boot, but the Indians remained close at hand. At Loving's insistence, Wilson set out for help, drifting downriver in the darkness.

> He [Loving] insisted that I take his gun [Goodnight later identified it as a Henry], as it used metallic cartridges and I could carry it through the water and not dampen

Charles Goodnight's well-used Henry rifle, with the initials "CG" stamped in the wrist of the stock.
(Photo by Steven W. Walenta, courtesy James D. Gordon)

the powder. Leaving him with all of my pistols and my rifle, I took his gun and with a handclasp told him goodbye.... The river was quite sandy and difficult to swim in, so I had to pull off all of my clothes except my hat, shirt and breeches. The gun nearly drowned me,... so I got out and leaned it up against the bank of the river, under the water, where the Indians would not find it.... Then I made a three days' march barefooted. Everything in that country had stickers in it.[14]

Trailed by wolves and suffering from hunger and exhaustion, Wilson finally gave out and sought refuge in a cave along the anticipated route the herd would follow.

When he was found, Goodnight and about fourteen of his men rode in search of Loving. They located the battle site and the Henry cached in the river, but Loving was gone and was assumed dead. Two weeks later, word reached Goodnight that his partner was in Fort Sumner. He, too, had evaded the Indians by floating down the river and then had lain for five days along a road until a group of Mexicans found him. Goodnight and Wilson hastened to Fort Sumner.

As soon as we beheld [Loving's] condition, we realized the arm would have to be amputated. The doctor [who had never amputated any limbs] was trying to cure it without cutting it off. Goodnight started a man to Santa Fe after a surgeon, but before he could get back mortification set in, and we ... prevailed upon the doctor to cut off the affected limb. But too late. Mortification went into his body and killed him. Thus ended the career of one of the best men I

ever knew. Mr. Goodnight had the body of Mr. Loving prepared for the long journey and carried it to Weatherford, Texas, where interment was made.[15]

Not all encounters between cowboys and Native Americans were of a hostile nature. Doc Barton's wife accompanied him on a trail drive in the late 1870s, driving a spring wagon by herself. In Colorado a band of Cheyennes suddenly surrounded her after the wagon became stuck in mud. Her husband was too far away to give immediate assistance. In amazement, he watched the braves slip off their mounts and heave the wagon back onto solid ground before starting to ride off laughing. Barton cut out a thin heifer and signaled the Indians to take the animal, which they quickly killed and butchered.[16]

Cowboys' clothing and horse gear varied by region and personal preference, and there was variety among the guns which they carried. Prior to the early 1870s, the choice for a revolver usually was a large-frame percussion Colt or Remington in .36 or .44 caliber. In the mid-1860s a few .36 Manhattans, Whitneys, double or single action Starrs, and undoubtedly even a limited number of Confederate-made revolvers probably could have been found in Texans' holsters, but not in any significant quantities. While some drovers favored the solid-frame Remington, it is the Colt that appears more often than any other make in writings of the period.

Hiram G. Craig recalled difficulties sometimes encountered with percussion handguns.

It would not be amiss to state what our artillery consisted of at that time. We used a long and trusty cap and ball rifle, familiarly known as "Long Tom." Then the old cap and ball sixshooter, sometimes called "outlaws." At times they

Jim Philbrick of the Pot Hook Ranch in Colorado pauses before a crude shack. He carries what appears to be an ivory-handled Colt Single Action in a double loop holster and wears "woolies" or Angora goatskin chaps, popular for cold weather wear on the northern plains. (Courtesy: Erich Baumann)

would behave and fire one shot, and again they would fire two, three, or possibly all six chambers at one time.[17]

It probably was a Colt or similar design that figured in another incident on the trail when a Texas drover got into a row with a Mexican whose herd kept crowding that from Texas.

I was riding a fiery gray horse and the pistol I had was an old cap and ball, which I had worn out shooting on the trail. There was so much play between the cylinder and the barrel that it would not burst a cap and fire unless I held the cylinder with one hand and pulled the trigger with the other. I made several unsuccessful attempts to shoot the advancing Mexican from my horse but failed. I then got down and tried to shoot and hold my horse, but failed in that, too. Jim Clement shouted at me to "turn that horse loose and hold the cylinder." I did so and fired at the Mexican, who was only ten paces from me. I hit him in the thigh and stunned him a little.[18]

To keep a six-gun from being dislodged from its holster, a thong sometimes was slipped over the hammer. Evidence in a murder trial in New Mexico included the observation that the deceased's gun "was securely tied into his scabbard with a hard knot and not the usual slip-knot which cowboys used to prevent its jumping out when riding on the range."[19]

For a long gun, one had the option of a muzzleloader or, beginning in the early 1850s, a breechloader such as the Sharps. Colt revolving rifles and carbines found favor with some, either early specimens made in Paterson, New Jersey, between 1837 and 1841 or the more common solid-frame Model 1855 Hartford-made shoulder arms. The 1860s marked the availability of metallic cartridges in larger calibers and brought the .44 lever action repeating Henry rifle and its successor, the popular brass-framed Model 1866 Winchester, as well as the seven-shot Spencer, and various single-shot Civil War–era carbines such as the Starr, Burnside, Wesson, and Maynard to the western market.

Ben Drake was sixteen when he first trailed cattle out of Texas in March of 1871. His outfit included $14 custom-made boots, "a pair of bell spurs, a Colt's cap and ball six-shooter, and a rim-fire [Model 1866] Winchester, as well as a pair of leather leggings which cost $12.00. This was the first time in my life that I had been rigged out,

The revolver may be a Remington M1875, more commonly found with a lanyard ring in the butt than a Colt Single Action. (Courtesy: Wyoming Division of Cultural Resources)

and you bet I was proud." That summer, nineteen-year-old Charles W. Allen signed on with a trail herd of one thousand Texas cattle on the way to a sheep and cattle ranch in Wyoming. "I had been furnished with a good Winchester [Model 1866] rifle and ammunition, as everyone carried a gun at this time."[20]

After 1869, large-frame revolvers in the form of the .44 Smith & Wesson No. 3 and conversions of percussion Colts, Remingtons, and a few other makes became available for customers who wanted a handgun firing metallic cartridges. By the late 1870s, just like Arbuckle coffee and a hat by John B. Stetson, the famed Colt Single Action Army revolver and the Model 1873 Winchester rifle or carbine were becoming and remained the primary weapons of choice among many cowboys until the late 1890s, after the Winchester models of 1892 and 1894 appeared. Irrefutable evidence of the popularity of the Colt Single Action and the '73

Winchester appears in nineteenth-century photos. It's also confirmed by written accounts despite the appearance of the double action Model 1877 and the larger frame Model 1878 Colts; the availability of high quality revolvers by Smith & Wesson, Remington, and others; and the arrival of lever action Marlin repeating rifles in 1881. Throughout the 1870s and well into the 1880s, the Sharps remained a favorite single-shot rifle over the Ballard and Remington's rolling-block rifles for anyone who demanded a powerful arm, although production of Sharps ended in 1880.

Regardless of the gun a cow puncher chose, there were many potential dangers facing him on the trail in addition to those posed by Native Americans and rustlers. Swollen rivers, stampedes, severe weather, and injuries or illness far from adequate medical treatment all were hazards. A rattlesnake bite, although not always fatal, was another risk. In the early 1870s an African American horse

Studio cabinet card from Abilene, Texas. The carbine is a Whitney-Kennedy repeater. (Courtesy: George Jackson)

wrangler named Nigger Dick returned to camp with a badly swollen hand and arm, sucking his thumb. A cowboy took a knife and cut the thumb around the fang marks. Then he broke open a revolver cartridge, poured the powder on the wound, and lit it with a match. The inflammation went no further and Dick made a quick recovery—from both wound and treatment![21]

Informal shooting matches momentarily relieved monotony on the trail, sometimes with unanticipated results. In 1868 J. L. McCaleb found a five-dollar bill on the trail, the first he'd ever seen. The foreman assured him it was good.

> One day at dinner the Negro cook offered to bet me a two-year old heifer... against my five dollars that he could beat me shooting, only one shot each. I was good

with a pistol, but I knew the cook was hard to beat.... One of the boys got a little piece of a board, took a coal out of the campfire, made a black spot about the size of a twenty-five-cent piece, stepped off fifteen steps and yelled, "all ready, shoot." I was to shoot first. I jerked my old cap and ball [Colt?] Navy out and just about one second before I pulled the trigger I saw the heads of six Indians just over a little rise...coming toward the camp. This excited me so that I did not hit the spot, only about one-half of my bullet touched the board just to the right of the target. I yelled to the Negro, "Shoot quick! Look at the Indians!" By that time we could see them plainly on top of the rise. He fired, but never touched the

Preparing to mount, carrying the ever-popular Colt Single Action. (Courtesy: Montana Historical Society)

board. So six big Osage Indians saved me my valuable find—the five-dollar bill.[22]

Until recently, the role of the estimated five thousand or more African American cooks, wranglers, and others who trailed cattle often has been ignored as has been the role of Native American drovers. Although black cowboys might encounter hostility in towns or when the drive was over, demands of the trail usually transcended prejudice.

Charles A. Siringo, cowboy and later Pinkerton detective, on several occasions was saved from death or serious injury by black compatriots. A Negro cowboy named Williams gained fame as a horse gentler, not a bronc buster, a nineteenth-century "horse whisperer" it seems. He worked for one of Theodore Roosevelt's South Dakota neighbors, Lincoln A. Lang, who called him "the first to introduce sane horse breaking in our section of the country." Thornton Biggs of the Two Bar Ranch gained the reputation as being "the best top hand ever to fork a horse or doctor a sick cow on the Laramie Plains" of Colorado and

Wyoming. Nepture Holmes, noted for his skill with a revolver, for more than thirty years was a close companion to Shanghai Pierce after the latter established his El Rancho Grande in Texas.[23]

An ex-slave, Bose Ikard, worked for such prominent cattlemen as Oliver Loving, John Chisum, and John Slaughter. He rode with Charles Goodnight from 1866 until 1869 who said of him "I have trusted him farther than any living man." When Ikard died in 1929, Goodnight paid this tribute.

> Served with me four years on the
> Goodnight-Loving Trail, never shirked
> a duty or disobeyed an order, rode with
> me in many stampedes, participated in
> three engagements with Comanches,
> splendid behavior.[24]

Larry McMurtry made use of this additional fragment of Texas history in his novel *Lonesome Dove*.

Cowboys appropriately dressed for their picture in Rock Springs, Wyoming. Their Colt Single Actions have a 4 3/4- or 5 1/2-inch barrel length, available beginning in 1875 as alternatives to the initial 7 1/2-inch length. The young man second from left carries a Colt double action Model 1877 or 1878. (Courtesy: Sweetwater County Historical Museum, Green River, WY)

Following the death of the loyal but fictional Negro Deets, Captain Call carved these words in the rough board grave marker:

> JOSH DEETS: SERVED WITH ME 30 YEARS. FOUGHT IN 21 ENGAGE-MENTS WITH THE COMMANCHE AND KIOWA. CHERFUL IN ALL WEATHERS, NEVER SHIRKED A TASK. SPLENDID BEHAVIOR.[25]

Greenhorns on the trail often had to endure their share of harassment and practical jokes, sometimes of a potentially dangerous nature. Such was the case with B. D. Lindsay. Also on the drive was another "tenderfoot," weighing 230 pounds, too heavy for such work on horseback and someone the crew wanted to get rid of.

The boys began to carry news to him of talks I had made about him, and from him they brought yarns to me. Of course neither of us had said anything about the other. We all carried the old style cap-and-ball [Colt] navy pistols, as was the custom in those days. One evening while I was holding the cattle, the evening relief came out and this big 230-pounder made straight toward me, saying that I had talked about him long enough and he was going to put a stop to it. I had been told by the other boys that the trouble was coming, and to open up on him when it started, which I proceeded to do. I shot at him six times . . . aiming at his paunch, but he did not fall. Now mind you, the boys had previously extracted the bullets from my pistol, and I was shooting only wads, but I did not know it. The wads set his clothing afire, and also the sage grass, and it took us several hours to put out the prairie fire. The "wounded" man ran off, left his horse, went to camp, got his time, and quit, just what the bunch wanted him to do. The boys told me I would be arrested when we got to Fort Worth, and advised me to go to the boss and get a horse and leave the herd, scout along in the neighborhood for a few days, and fall in again. I took it all in like a sucker, until I asked Sam Driskill for the horse. Sam told me that it was all a put-up job, and to pay no attention to them. From that time on I got along very well.[26]

Then as today, there sometimes was a fine line between humor and harassment. Frontier photographer Solomon Butcher wrote of an incident involving a part-time outlaw whom he called Dick Milton. It inspired Butcher to stage a similar event which he photographed.

Dick Milton was at a cattle ranch one day and he noticed a cluster of laughing cowboys by the barn [where] a cowboy was making an old man dance by shooting at his feet. Every time the old man would stop and beg to sit down, the young cowboy would shoot at his feet again. It was clear that the old man was exhausted and frightened. Dick Milton looked on for a few minutes and decided to join in. He drew his gun and told the old man to step aside, and then he asked the cowboy to show what skill *he* had as a dancer. The cowboy laughed, thinking it was a joke, and then with a loud ringing shot, the dirt at his feet was plowed up. He began to dance. None of the cowboys were laughing anymore. But this one danced until he dropped in a heap from exhaustion. Only then did Dick Milton put his gun away. He warned the young man to pick on someone his own size next time.[27]

At the end of a long, dusty cattle drive, it wasn't unusual for a cowboy to spend some of his pay on new clothes and

pose for a photo, sometimes wearing his revolver or one borrowed from the proprietor of the photo gallery. Such photos today are prized by collectors.

Before I went home...I stopped in North Platte where they paid us off, and [I] bought some new clothes and got [my] picture taken. I had a new white Stetson hat that I paid ten dollars for and new pants that cost twelve dollars, and a good shirt and fancy boots. They had colored tops, red and blue, with a half-moon and star on them. Lord, I was proud of these clothes! They were the kind of clothes top hands wore, and I thought I was dressed right for the first time in my life. I believe one reason I went home was just so I could show them off. But when I got there and my sister saw me, she said: "Take your pants out of your boots and put your coat on. You look like an outlaw." I told her to go to hell. And I never did like her after that. Those were the first store clothes I had ever bought myself.[28]

Not infrequently at the end of a hard drive cowboys overindulged in alcohol and fought, but sometimes tempers flared while still on the trail. One such 1884 incident was recorded by Laban S. Records, who was a cowboy in the Cherokee Outlet area of Kansas and Indian Territory. John Potts didn't work long at any cow camp for he was surly and became abusive when drinking. He began quarreling with another drover, Ben Franklin, and wanted to shoot it out.

Ben told him he was drunk and to wait until morning when it would be settled. In the morning they met and Ben asked Potts if he had sobered up. Potts said he had. Franklin then said, "You owe me an apology for the things you said last night." Potts said that he did not apologize to anybody; he would back up what he had said last night. Both had six-shooters and Ben told Potts if he didn't apologize, they would shoot it out. Potts was a quick fellow to draw but he fired before he aimed and missed. Ben was a little more deliberate and dropped Potts with the first shot. He lived only several hours. There was

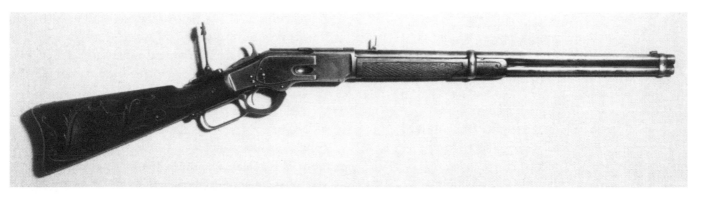

Winchester .44 M1873 carbine (#66208), unusual with a rear tang sight. It was owned by Willis Everette who joined Company A of the Texas Rangers in 1882. (Courtesy: Roswell Museum and Art Center, NM)

another fellow in the camp who had known Potts in Texas [where he reportedly had killed a man]. Potts told him to tell their acquaintances there that he had died gamely with his boots on. He was buried on a little sand hill close to the ranch house, and four posts were placed around it with three or four strands of wire stretched around.[29]

Another gunfight involved what the owner called "an unlucky gun," a Colt Single Action.

Ike Low… practically died in my arms after a gun duel in a roundup camp one morning. On his deathbed he asked us not to prosecute his killer, Charley Ensley, since he [Ike] had brought on the fight. When fighting the duel, Ike was using my pearl-handled Colt .45. A few weeks later I sold the gun to a fellow named Oscar Phoebus. Shortly afterward, while flourishing the gun in Sidney [Nebraska], Oscar, who was somewhat lushed up, accidentally shot it off and killed himself.

That seemed to be an unlucky gun. I got it in Fort Sidney [Sidney Barracks] from an army officer who had ground the U.S. off [the frame] and nickled [sic] over the place before selling it to me. At the coroner's inquest over Oscar it was discovered that the U.S. was ground off, though the number was still plain. It was through the number that the gun was traced to the fort, where it was still on record. I was told the officer nearly got

court-martialed for its disappearance, and that if it had been traced to me I might have been in trouble for buying government property. I could have pled ignorance, and like I could've made it stick, as I was so young.[30]

Walt Coburn of the Circle C Ranch in Montana provided a detailed description of a cowboy's common choice of a sidearm from the mid-1870s forward, the ubiquitous Colt Single Action.

The early-day cowpuncher wore a filled cartridge belt that carried his holstered Colt .45 six-shooter. The cartridge belt was slanted and the holster tied down by a whang leather string around the thigh. But in my time, which was the generation of the pioneer sons, the wearing of cartridge belts and holstered guns ceased. The cowhand usually owned a single-action Colt six shooter, but he wore it tucked inside the waistband of his pants, the flange of the cylinder [loading gate] swung out to keep the gun from sliding down the pants' leg. The heavy six-shooter carried in this manner put a callous on the hipbone of the gun toter.[31]

Edgar Beecher Bronson, a nephew of abolitionist minister Henry Ward Beecher, served his apprenticeship on a ranch before establishing his own north of the Platte River in 1878 in Nebraska. Not yet age twenty-one, he stepped down from a train in 1875 in Cheyenne, Wyoming, where he was met by a family friend.

Before leaving the train, I had prudently strapped to my waist a new... 45 Colt six-shooter, that looked and felt a yard long.... Until I learned its tricks, the recoil at each discharge gave me a smash in the forehead from hammer or barrel, that made me wish I had been the target instead of the marksman. The rig I had taken so much time in selecting and felt so proud of he [his friend] quickly consigned to the scrap heap—lace boots, little knee leggings, short hunting spurs, little round soft hat; everything... except my pistol. And even the pistol had to be stripped of its flap holster and rehabited in the then new décolleté Olive scabbard.[32]

At age sixteen, Lincoln A. Lang in 1883 emigrated from Ireland with his father to operate a cattle ranch in Dakota Territory. Upon their departure from Jersey City, New Jersey, Lang's father bought him a revolver and a box of cartridges. "The revolver... was but a little old rim-fire five-shot affair of the type which—as I was due to learn in good time—the cowboys were in the habit of swallowing whole." Later a new friend took pity on him and gave him "an old-style, long-barreled, 32-calibre Smith and Wesson [No. 2 Army perhaps], which shot with the precision of a rifle." This, too, eventually was replaced, with "a heavy Colt six shooter."[33]

Economics sometimes dictated a cowboy's choice of a handgun. The June 19, 1884, edition of the *Bad Lands Cow Boy* carried an ad for J. Slatcher's Golden Gun Armory in Dickinson, Dakota Territory. It offered Colt .45 six-shooters for $14, about half a month's wage for a typical cow puncher, .45–60 rifle cartridges at $2.75 per hundred, a pound of gunpowder for 40¢, and loaded shotgun shells at $4 per hundred.[34]

One tenderfoot drover named Payne found that metallic ammunition for his new revolver was too expensive so he bought an obsolescent percussion revolver merely for practice. On one occasion before setting out to ride the line, he left his "white-handled six-shooter" on his bunk in the line cabin and thrust the cap and ball revolver in his new scabbard on his new cartridge belt. Later he was accosted by a half-dozen roving Indians coming from his shack and carrying various items they had taken from there. They surrounded him and one of them jerked Payne's revolver from his holster and shot him in the neck and arm before stealing his horse. A few moments later as Payne regained consciousness, he saw the Indians returning.

Anticipating that they wanted the belt with its cartridges for his new revolver they had stolen from his cabin, he shifted his position on the ground so the buckle was in plain view. He played dead as one of the Indians dismounted, yanked the belt free, then rode off.[35]

Reloading metallic cartridges was one cost-saving procedure, but two cowboys almost came to grief when doing so while winter trapping in 1879. Kept indoors by bad weather, Frank Tracy spread a blanket smooth and poured several pounds of gunpowder on the bunk. Prying the exploded primers from the cartridge cases with his knife was slow work so he attempted a novel method.

I sat on the edge of the bunk between the fire and the pile of powder but took no notice. Suddenly there was a terrible explosion. Fire, smoke, and dust filled the dugout; coals of fire hit me. I jumped to my feet, shook off the coals, and saw the coals burning a hole in the blanket all around the powder. We got the fire off the bunk first. Tracy had filled two shells with water and had put them in the fire to blow out the caps by the force of accumulated steam. The caps were not loosened and the empty shells were ruined.[36]

In 1886 J. M. Custer was the trail boss on a cattle drive from Las Vegas, New Mexico, to Nebraska. He killed a Mexican in a shooting scrape during the drive, but he held his ground against any retaliation. "If [something] didn't go right, we always had a machine to make it go right. The... machine the cow-puncher had was sometimes called a 'cutter,' and sometimes it was called a 'hog-leg,' but it was better known as a six-shooter gun, and we frequently had a use for it, for it was a 'friend in need' in those days."[37]

As to the matter of the two-gun cowboy, E. C. Abbott, better known as "Teddy Blue," came up the trail from Texas to Montana with the herds driven there to stock the northern ranges. He worked cattle in Montana in the 1870s and 1880s and married a daughter of Montana pioneer stockman Granville Stuart. In his autobiography, Abbott noted:

I punched cows from '71 on, and I never yet saw a cowboy with two... six-shooters. Wild Bill [Hickok] carried two guns and so did some of those other city marshals, like Bat Masterson, but they were professional gunmen themselves, not cowpunchers. The

Being photographed was a frequent occurrence for drovers at the end of a trial drive. These youths display a variety of shirt styles and the cowboy seated at center wears lace-up shoes rather than boots. (Courtesy: Wyoming Division of Cultural Resources)

others that carried two guns were Wes Hardin and Bill Longley and Clay Allison and them [sic] desperadoes. But a cowboy with two guns is all movie stuff, and so is this business of a gun on each hip. The kind of fellows that did carry two would carry one in the scabbard and a hide-out gun down under their arm.[38]

Abbott made a confusing statement when he recalled that the "old twelve-inch barrel Colt pistol was cut down to a six- and seven-and-a-half inch barrel, with black rubber, ivory, or pearl handle." Colt Single Action Army revolvers with barrels longer than 7 1/2 inches were rare and available only on special order.[39]

Another longtime cowboy supported Abbott's view.

As to the fiction writer's favorite, the two-gun man—well, I never saw a two-six-shooter man who could use both at once and be accurate. Many could use first one and then the other, but not both at once. And even one gun could be dangerous in the hand of a greenhorn. Back in 1906 I was on my way to Chicago from Kansas City in a sleeping car. A young fellow on the same coach had spent most of the day fooling with a gun. Early the next morning I got up and dressed [and] a little later I heard the gunman slip out of his berth and cross over to the empty seat behind me. About a minute later the gun, a Colt's .45, went off, almost deafening me.

The greenhorn had placed the Colt beneath his pillow the night before. When the porter pulled the blankets off the berth to make it up, the gun fell and struck the seat, discharging the live round beneath the hammer and mortally wounding the tenderfoot in the belly. "I knew that damn gun would get him into trouble, He handled it like a kid."[40]

Tom Bendy, an El Paso policeman who had served with John Selman as a police officer and often shot with him, in a 1921 interview made a comment which tended to discredit another myth that sometimes appears in western gun lore. Speaking of Selman, he stated: "He was the only man I ever knew who indulged in the practice so often related in western stories—notching his gun." Bendy thought Selman was a glory seeker and recalled that Selman's gun "had at least seven and perhaps nine notches."[41]

A drover's proficiency with a revolver or shoulder gun depended upon his aptitude and the amount of time and powder he was willing to spend practicing. The average cowboy was no gunfighter, yet there were exceptions.

> The man that had charge of that Circle Diamond wagon, or that part of the outfit that year [ca. 1896] was Win Cooper. He came from Jack County, Texas, and was a wonderful cowboy. He used to carry a 45 Colts six-shooter and had the trigger filed so it wouldn't stand cocked, but [he] fanned the hammer with his thumb. He told me the reason he had his gun fixed that way was for quick action. He could fill the chamber [cylinder] with bullets and start a tomato can rolling and keep it going until his gun was empty. He used to tell me about the gun fights they had in Texas a long time ago...and I think he sometimes got lonesome for those old feuds and would like to go back and have a little excitement.[42]

Another exception was Commodore Perry Owens, named for Commodore Oliver Hazard Perry, victor on Lake Erie against the British in 1813. An Arizona cowboy described him as being a two revolver man "and [he] could draw either with his right hand or his left with wonderful speed. Several times at round-ups I had seen him stand twenty feet from an empty tomato-can and keep it rolling and jumping with alternate shots from his two guns until it was torn to pieces."[43]

Thomas E. Crawford may have "stretched the blanket a little" when relating stories of his life as a cowboy and saddle tramp in the 1880s, but his comments warrant reading. Before he left home in Ohio, as a youngster he had become proficient with "a .44 rimfire, brass breech, Winchester [Model 1866]" given to him by a hardware dealer. With it, he won his share of turkeys at holiday shoots against "gray-haired old fellows who shot old muzzle-loader rifles, with set triggers and all kinds of fancy sights, wind gauges, etc."[44]

His mother forwarded his '66 Winchester to him after he headed west. "This little rim-fire had its advantages, and I would not have traded it for any make of rifle that I knew of at that time." It was a carbine, for he wrote:

> It was very short and light, and I could shoot it with accuracy by holding it free from the body with one hand, like shooting a pistol. I made a scabbard out of cowhide for it, and hung it from the horn of my saddle. The barrel went between the stirrup leathers; it was not noticeable because of its shortness, and it was not in the way of either roping or riding. I carried this little rifle with me for a good many years.[45]

He added a Colt .45 revolver to his outfit and became proficient with it as well. "I always kept the dogs of a six-shooter filed down until they were about a hair trigger. You cannot do good work with a hard-pulling gun. I was never very good at fanning, but shot very well from the hip with either hand." Fanning a single action revolver involved bracing the gun at waist level, holding the trigger back, and then with the side of the other hand cocking the hammer rapidly in a downward striking motion and allowing it to slip free. Similarly, a slightly slower procedure was "slip shooting" in which the trigger was held back and a thumb cocked the hammer, allowing it to slip free. Each was a fast way to empty a revolver but could be effective only at close range.[46]

Fanning probably was used in a gunfight far less often than Hollywood "horse operas" would indicate. However reporter Richard Harding Davis in 1892 along the Rio Grande camped with a company of Texas Rangers under Capt. J. A. Brooks. They breakfasted on bacon and coffee and then he witnessed a shooting exhibition. "The Rangers... could shoot as rapidly with the revolver as with the rifle, and had become so expert with the smaller weapon that instead of pulling the trigger for each shot, they would pull steadily on it (holding it back) and snap the hammer until the six shots were exhausted."[47]

Although the Colt and Remington large-frame single actions could be fanned or fired by slip shooting, the

Commodore Perry Owens of Arizona with a double belt of rifle and revolver cartridges. The rifle, quite possibly a photographer's prop, is a Springfield "trapdoor." (Courtesy: Arizona Pioneers' Historical Society Library, Tucson)

hammer spur on similar S&Ws was too small and the mechanism of Merwin & Hulberts (made by Hopkins & Allen) didn't allow it. However George W. Cilley, a Hopkins & Allen mechanic, in 1886 patented an improvement in single action lockwork which in part specified: "when it is desired to fire rapidly, by drawing the trigger clear back and then firmly holding it, while the other hand may be used in drawing back the hammer and

allowing it to fall without engaging at all with the trigger, which action can be repeated with great rapidity." The feature apparently wasn't incorporated by Hopkins & Allen, probably due to the increasing availability of double action handguns.[48]

Returning to Crawford's recollections, in the late 1880s and into the 1890s, he was living in Jackson Hole, Wyoming. While there:

The drover with his back to the camera carries his Colt M1878 butt forward.
(Courtesy: Montana Historical Society)

I found it necessary to wear at least one six-shooter where it could not be seen; for while it sometimes seemed to me to be a bit cowardly to do so, self-preservation is the first law of nature. I packed a sawed-off .45 in a light scabbard, inside my shirt in front at the belt-buckle location. The shirt was split down the front to give easy and quick access to the gun, and the scabbard was sewed to my underwear. It was quite common among gunmen and sheriffs as that time to carry one pistol upside down in a scabbard under the arm, with the gun hanging by the front sight. There was no drawing to it. You simply reached under your coat, flipped out your pistol, and fired from your stomach. It was all very quickly done. I seldom wore a coat; hence, the split shirt. There were no shirts on the market in those days open in front all the way down. The idea was my own.

When you have gained a reputation, whether you deserve it or not, guilty or not guilty, very often some rattle-brained fellow, especially when he is drinking, will get it into his head that he wants to kill you. At the least provocation he will start a quarrel, thinking, I presume, that the quarrel justifies his act. Now when you see that the fellow has nothing in his mind except to murder you and the psychological moment has arrived, you beat him to the draw by a fraction. That is my only excuse for being here and able to tell you this tale. Anyway, by carrying one concealed gun I saved at least two men from being shot. By beating them to the draw, I was able to talk them out of the idea of shooting me. A fraction of a second sometimes separates us from his life and eternity.

I liked the five-and-one-half-inch [barrel] gun. It could be drawn quicker from the scabbard on the belt. Any gun of a smaller caliber than a .44 will not knock a man down when he is drinking or in anger. If you shoot a man with a

Cowboys from Col. Jesse Ellison's Q Ranch near Globe, Arizona. (Courtesy: Bisbee Mining and Historical Museum, AZ)

small-caliber pistol he will keep on coming and probably shoot you.[49]

Pete Steckels had been a top cowhand but near the turn of the century he was perhaps sixty years old and had assumed a role as a stock detective in Wyoming.

It was said by some of the old-timers that he was as fast a man with a six-gun as ever was known. He had a crippled hand from a gunshot wound and he walked with a limp from a bullet.... A couple of us were shooting at a target, ... a gallon bucket on a low post, about fifty yards away. [Steckels] watched us awhile as we would draw and fire as quickly as possible. We could hit the can by slow aiming, but missed it when we fired from a quick draw. [Pete advised:] "Boys, try doing that draw this way: as the hand comes up from the holster or belt, with the gun, the thumb cocks it. Continue to raise the gun to the level of the eye ... and as the gun levels to the target,

squeeze—don't jerk—the trigger," and without changing his position on his horse, continued, "See-like this," and almost before our eyes could follow his lightning-like move, the gallon can jumped off the post.... Later I did learn that Pete's manner of drawing and firing was the faster way, and I always used it.[50]

How one carried a revolver varied with personal preference. It's not known whether there was any validity to the observation reporter Richard Harding Davis made about 1891, but it's worth noting.

Of the many compliments I have heard paid by officers and privates and ranch-owners and cowboys to [artist] Mr. Frederic Remington, the one which was sure to follow the others was that he never made the mistake of putting the revolver on the left side. But as I went North, his anonymous admirers would made this same comment, but with regret that he should be guilty of such an error. I could not understand this at first until I found that the two sides of the shield lay in the Northern cowboy's custom of wearing his pistol on the left, and of the Texan's of carrying it on the right. The Northern man argues... that the sword has always been worn on the left, that it is easier to reach across and sweep the pistol to either the left or right, and that with this motion it is at once in position. The Texan says this is absurd, and quotes the fact that the pistol-pocket has always been on the right, and that the lasso and reins are in the way of the left hand. It is too grave a question of etiquette for any one who has not at least six notches on his pistol-butt to decide.[51]

Davis participated in a shooting match with Texas Ranger captain Brooks to see who could be first to put eight rifle shots from a Winchester into a board.

> Captain Brooks, as far as I could make out from the sound, used only one movement for his entire eight shots.... When I had put two shots into space, the captain had put his eight into the board. They sounded, as they went off, like fire-crackers well started in a barrel, and mine, in comparison, like minute-guns at sea. The Rangers... could shoot as rapidly with a revolver as with a rifle, and had become so expert with the smaller weapon that instead of pressing the trigger for each shot, they would pull steadily on it, and snap the hammer until the six shots were exhausted.[52]

Jeff Milton, a respected lawman, called badman John Wesley Hardin "the fastest thing he'd ever seen with a gun." Others whose life depended upon a revolver did become skilled although few men of that period sought or achieved the gun handling abilities one sees on the television or movie screen. They were hampered by the cost of ammunition for extensive practice as well as limitations of the mechanics of the guns available then. But in the 1930s, a portly, unimposing exhibition shooter named Ed McGivern amazed spectators with his speed and accuracy with handguns of his era. It must be remembered that he wasn't confronting an opponent determined to end his life, nor did he perform in the smoky confines of a frontier saloon

where senses might be dulled by alcohol and visibility reduced by the heavy gray smoke produced by the black powder ammunition of the nineteenth century.

Taking these factors into account, he did demonstrate what could be done by someone who practiced extensively and perhaps was aided by a certain degree of natural ability. Most of his shooting was done with modern double action Smith & Wessons, but among his various feats, he consistently fired five shots from a Colt Single Action in less than 1 1/5 seconds by "fanning" and kept the shots in groups that could be covered by one's hand. Other demonstration shooters have followed his path and have performed similarly amazing feats.[53]

A revolver sometimes was useful for more than defending one's self, as a means of relieving boredom. Stewart Edward White wrote of stopping at the Circle I Ranch and while awaiting supper, he lounged on his back in the bunkhouse. There he counted 362 bullet holes in the ceiling. "They came to be there because the festive cowboys used to while away the time lying as I was lying while waiting for supper, in shooting the flies that crawled about the plaster." A ranch hand near Trinidad, Colorado, joined in the boisterous bunkhouse fun one evening, shooting at magazine pictures pasted on the walls. One of the first shots struck Benjamin Franklin directly in the eye and later shots cut off the end of a pretty girl's nose, which one drover felt was a little too long.[54]

Hospitality among cowboys including a spot at the cooking fire or a bunk for the night was expected and usually given readily. Oliver Nelson served as a cook, freighter, cowboy, and rancher in the Neutral Strip or Oklahoma panhandle. He recalled that in 1883 four cowboys traveling from Dodge City southward to participate in a roundup stopped at his camp for the night.

> In the morning one of our boys asked one of them for twelve .45 pistol cartridges and paid him twenty-five cents for them. Another of the four found out about the transaction, and asked their pard if he took pay for the cartridges. He said, "Yes, I did. They cost *me* twenty-five cents. What of it?" The other said, "Nothing, only you're goin' to get a damn good lickin'. We stay here all night free, and then you won't give him a few cartridges. We'll learn you." They stretched him across the hind hound [?] of the wagon, and hit him about twenty times with a two-inch cinch strap. I went out and said, "You fellows

Little has changed in these two views at the Sawtell Ranch in Idaho in 1872, except someone made a gargantuan effort to locate an impressive array of firearms to mount above the fireplace, including Remington and Colt revolvers, Spencer and Sharps carbines, plus miscellaneous other weapons. (Courtesy: U.S. Geological Survey)

ought to be ashamed to whale that poor devil that way." One said, "*He* ought to be ashamed." They gave him a little more, and told him to pull back up the line to home camp—over a hundred miles.[55]

In the fall of 1902, a tramp enjoyed the "hospitality" of a group of cowboys returning home after having delivered a herd of cattle to a shipping point. The tramp was invited to share their evening meal and their night camp. As the crew and guest relaxed, two of the drovers slipped away and removed the bullets from cartridges in their revolvers and substituted chunks of soap instead. Returning to the fire, they seated themselves on either side of the vagabond and soon began to argue, then drew their guns and began firing at each other, although aiming at the tramp. The poor fellow bolted toward the reservoir and dove in.

Another returning beef outfit had camped on the opposite side of the reservoir and dragged him out of the water despite his pleas that they allow him to remain hidden from the cowboys who had shot him and were still on his trail.

> The tramp said he had dived into the water, which was rimmed with wafer ice, to cover his blood-spattered trail and throw them off his track. He swore he'd been shot in at least ten places and was bleeding to death. The boys pulled down his trousers to see where he'd been shot, but all they found were plenty of black and blue spots.... When they finally made him understand a joke had been played on him, he declared he'd have no more of the West, or cowboys, but was heading straight off for the East and his old home of peace, if not plenty.[56]

As towns grew in size the civilized elements moved in; usually it wasn't long before townspeople tired of cowboys' boisterous antics. The editor of the Caldwell (Kansas) *Commercial* happily reported on August 24, 1884: "Civilization is advancing in the west, particularly in ... Caldwell. Any for why? Because the Winchester and self-cocker have given place to nature's arms, good 'bunches of fives [fists]' and perhaps a stick."[57]

Sometimes a farmer didn't object when a trail herd rested overnight on his land for in the morning he'd have an ample supply of cow chips which when dry could serve as fuel where wood was scarce. But in its issue for September 20, 1884, the *Arizona Champion* newspaper expressed some citizens' views of cowboys. "They are bragging, whiskey drinking bummers who delight in six-shooters, fine horses, saddles and fast women. Their aim in life seems to be to have a good time. They delight in disconcerting the eastern tenderfoot. Nearly all die with their boots on, and no one mourns their death."[58]

The same paper in an 1886 issue described the cowboy's disdain for a citified tenderfoot. The newcomer drew a small .22 revolver on a cowboy who had been taunting him in a saloon. The latter's response was to draw his .45 revolver and order, "Here, bring that damn thing over and let it suck."[59]

Ed Lemmon spent more than fifty years in Nebraska and the northern plains, herding cattle and later operating a sheep ranch. In 1902 he managed a fenced pasture on the Standing Rock Indian Reservation that was larger than the state of Rhode Island. The town of Lemmon, South Dakota, would be named in his honor. About 1871 when he was only fourteen, he was playing baseball when a citified sixteen-year-old asked to join the game.

> The dude then stepped over to a pile of ball clubs, unbuckled a brand-new Remington revolver, belt and all, and laid it on a bench. During an inning when I wasn't at bat I went over to the bench, took the gun out of the scabbard and was admiring it. The dude came right over and took the gun, saying it was not a nice plaything for little boys. I ... gave him a cool stare, for I was thinking, "Why you big stiff! I'll bet that is your first gun, and right now I could almost make one like it, as well as I know guns and how they work." A few years later [I learned] it really was his first gun and right then he couldn't hit a block of barns with it, while I had been carrying and using one since I was nine.[60]

One example of the "civilizing" of the boisterous cow towns in Kansas was the creation of the Dodge City Cowboy Band. Details of the unit's history are sketchy and contradictory, but C. M. "Chalk" Beeson often is credited as the founder, sometime between 1879 and 1881. The band gained considerable local support and eventually a national reputation. Throughout the 1880s at least and perhaps a decade later, the band gave concerts at state fairs, cattlemen's conventions, and other gatherings as far away as

Dodge City Cowboy Band with their array of musical instruments—and Colt Single Actions. In addition to performances in front of the Long Branch and Opera House, they played in St. Louis, Denver, Chicago, and in President Benjamin Harrison's inaugural in Washington. (Courtesy: Kansas State Historical Society)

Washington DC. Beeson always claimed that each band member was or had been a cowboy, but the professional quality of their music made this claim rather dubious.

The *Missouri Republican* newspaper of November 18, 1884, described their appearance at the national stockmen's convention in St. Louis as "gorgeous."

> The inseparable gray slouch hat with a band inscribed "Cowboy Band of Dodge City, Kansas" and bearing also the picture of a steer, each hat having a different brand.... A flannel shirt, leather leggings of a conventional type, bandana handkerchief around throat, belt with a six-chambered ivory handled revolver and fierce spurs complete the genuine cowboy outfit.[61]

However not all the delegates viewed the musicians favorably. As a Texas cattleman objected: "They parade the streets with the handles of their revolvers protruding from their hip pockets and their leader keeping time with one." A delegate from Colorado also complained about the impression the band's appearance made.

> We feel that the cowboy band is out of place as long as they persisted in making a parade of their leggings and revolvers.... People in the East have been led to believe that a greater portion of cattlemen ... are as a rule desperate characters and that we roam about over the prairies armed to the teeth with knives and revolvers. We want to dispel this idea.... Years ago when likely to meet a

bunch of Indians, we were required to go heavily armed when we followed our cattle. Times have changed and...on many ranches cowboys are not allowed to carry revolvers. Today the average cowboy is as good an average American citizen as can be found anywhere.[62]

A photo of the band shows their revolvers to be Colt Single Action Army revolvers.

Author Charles Siringo described himself as having spent fifteen years on the "hurricane deck" of a Spanish pony. In the spring of 1876 while herding cattle near Galveston, Texas, he encountered an 1871 Texas law prohibiting the carrying of pistols and which carried a fine of $25 to $100. "They socked a heavier fine on me than I was able to pay; but I found a good friend...who loaned me the desired amount." The law presumably had little effect since it exempted many people including travelers, those who feared personal attack, and those in certain counties designated by the governor as "frontier counties."[63]

Despite his encounter with this law, Siringo a decade later still advised newcomers to buy a revolver, a "most important ornament."

If you are foolish enough to go without the latter [a revolver], the cooks at the different ranches where you happen to stop will not respect you. Instead of putting the handle to your family name, they will call you the sore-footed kid, old man Nibbs, or such names as these. We know from experience that the pistol carries much weight with it, and therefore especially advise the young "tenderfoot" to buy one, even if he has to ride barebacked [for lack of money].[64]

Legislation restricting the use of firearms appeared rather early in the west, although it would intensify in the 1880s as the era of the unfenced open range ended. The newly organized town of Burlington, Iowa, in 1837 passed an ordinance prohibiting anyone "except in defense of his person or property" from discharging a firearm under threat of a fine of between $5 and $10. The *New Orleans Bee* of August 10, 1835, observed that "the law is tolerably strong relative to carrying dirks, pistols or other weapons of assault. Why is it not enforced?" Local and state laws in the west often restricted the carrying of firearms, but these sometimes were ignored or

applied only in certain circumstances As early as 1849, a sign posted on the Commerce Street bridge in San Antonio, Texas, warned "NO SHOOTING ALOUD In The City Limits." Fourth of July celebrants apparently riddled the sign with their bullets judging from a daguerreotype reportedly taken on July 5 and sketched in an account of one man's travels.[65]

Nebraska law in 1867 decreed that anyone convicted of carrying "any pistol, gun, knife, dirk, bludgeon, or other offensive weapon with intent to assault any person" could be fined up to $100 and jailed for up to three months. In July 1871 legislation was passed in Dallas, Texas, making it unlawful to carry a concealed weapon with the intent of doing harm.[66]

Abilene, Kansas, had a reputation as being "wild and wooly" but the *Chronicle* for May 12, 1870, reported in detail new city ordinances prohibiting carrying deadly weapons openly or concealed, discharging a firearm within town limits, gambling, or maintaining a "house of ill-fame." The same paper on June 8, 1871, reported: "The Chief of Police has posted up printed up notices, informing all persons that the ordinance against carrying fire arms or other weapons in Abilene, will be enforced. That's right. There's no bravery in carrying revolvers in a civilized community." Not all abided by the restriction for on June 22 the *Chronicle* described a shooting after two men exchanged harsh words as they passed on the street.

One drew his revolver, and No. 2 remarked "you know you have got the advantage of me." No. 1 then put back his weapon, whereupon No. 2 drew a Derringer and fired at No. 1 who also managed to draw his six-shooter. Each fired two shots, one was hit in the wrist and the other in the shoulder. The police were promptly on hand and arrested the parties.[67]

Wichita's city council on June 28, 1871, approved and formally accepted the newly constructed jail and instructed City Marshal Mike Meagher to: "Procure at the expense of the City two pine boards 3 x 4 feet and have the following inscribed thereon: 'NOTICE. All persons are hereby forbidden the carrying of firearms or other dangerous weapons within the city limits of Wichita under penalty of fine and imprisonment.'" The mayor was empowered to appoint toll keepers as special police on the bridge into town who were to collect firearms. The mayor also could purchase fifty brass, copper, or tin checks to be exchanged for guns surrendered upon entering town.[68]

Permit to Carry Concealed a Deadly Weapon.

State of California,

CITY AND COUNTY OF SAN FRANCISCO.

Under the provisions of Order 1,226 of the Board of Supervisors of said City and County, PERMISSION is hereby granted by the POLICE COMMISSIONERS of said City and County, to Wilson S. Edwards a peaceful person residing at 24th & Dolores. Street, by occupation or profession a Reporter Com'l Agency to carry concealed a Deadly Weapon, to wit: a Pistol in said City and County, for his own protection, for the period of One Y'r year from the date hereof.

This permission is granted and accepted subject to revocation by a majority of said Police Commissioners, and must be carried by the grantee, and exhibited to any police or peace officer on his demand.

Dated this 11th day of November 1879

Richd P. Hammond PRESIDENT.
Robt. J. Tobin
William Alvord
POLICE COMMISSIONERS.

John [illegible] CHIEF OF POLICE.

Register 7953. Alfred Clarke Clerk.

By John W. Moffett Deputy Clerk.

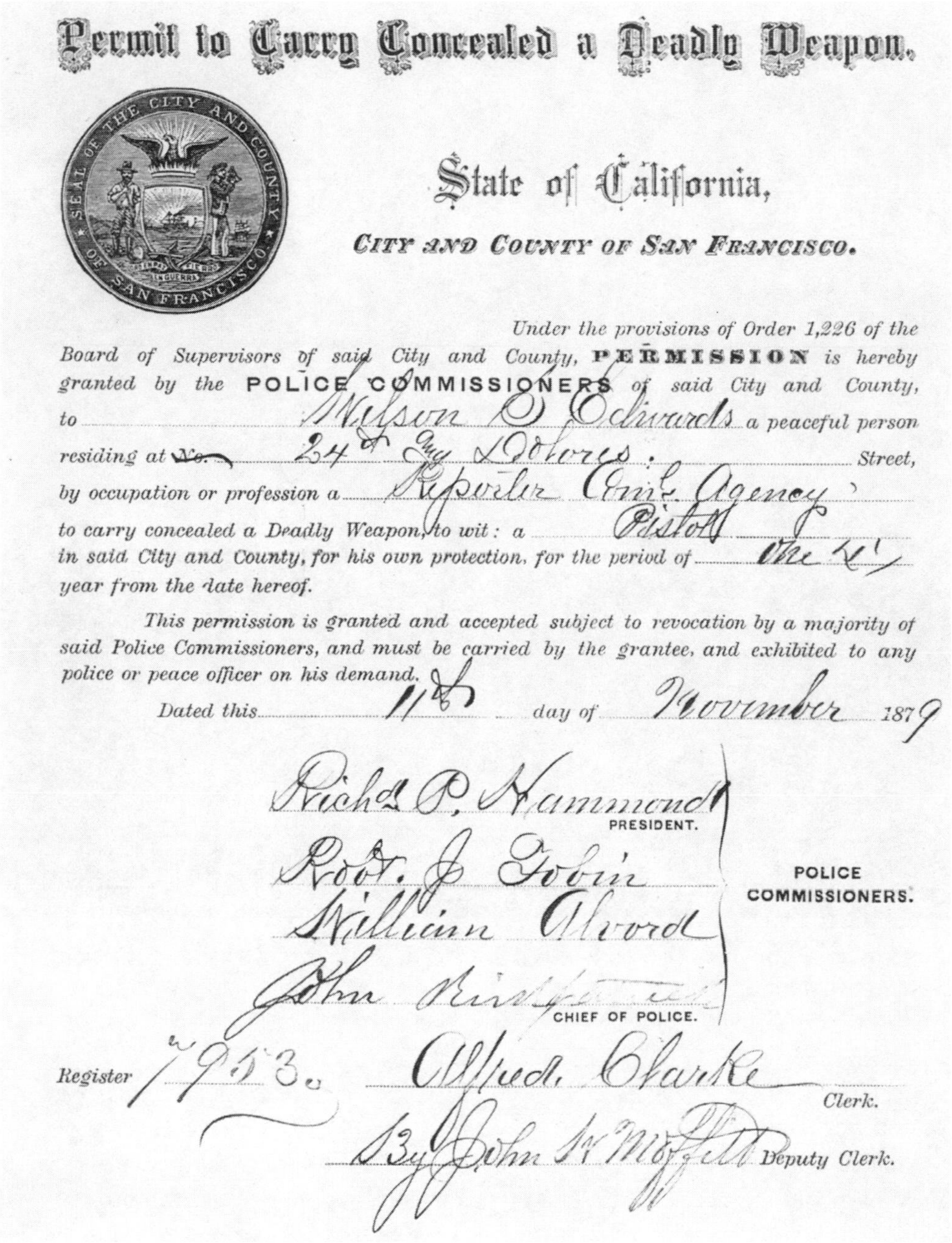

Permit issued on November 11, 1879, to Wilson S. Edwards, a reporter, permitting him "to carry concealed a deadly weapon" in the city and county of San Francisco.

In December of 1875, Dodge City residents formed a city council. As in Abilene and Wichita, the body passed a law prohibiting the wearing of firearms within the town limits. Guns had to be checked at stores, saloons, and elsewhere upon arrival. No guns would be returned to drunks. Other prohibitions included cruelty to animals, the carrying of knives, the firing off of firecrackers, and public profanity. Off-duty soldiers were forbidden from wearing "drinking jewelry," a nail bent into the shape of a ring. A veteran cowboy, Andy Adams, warned:

> I've been in Dodge every summer since '77, and I can give you boys some points. . . . Don't ever get the impression that you can ride your horses into a saloon, or shoot out the lights in Dodge; it may go somewhere else, but it won't go there. . . . You can wear your six-shooters into town, but you'd better leave them at the first place you stop. . . . Most cowboys think it's an infringement on their rights to give up shooting in town, and if it is, it stands, for your six-shooters are no match for Winchesters and buckshot; and Dodge's officers are as game a set of men as ever faced danger.[69]

This 1903 photo shows that some cow punchers still carried a sidearm, in this case a Colt Single Action. The armed cowboy at left wears what appears to be a Sears, Roebuck & Co. "Chief Moses" hat. (Courtesy: Wyoming State Museum, Cheyenne)

To help keep the peace, in May 1876 Dodge's city fathers hired Wyatt Earp as deputy city marshal. Cowboy Pink Simms didn't have a high opinion of Earp and the city's policemen in general.

I knew [him] and have seen him shoot a revolver and he was not a peerless performer with one by a long shot—and I never knew a man I was less afraid of, though he hated cowboys in general.... [Dodge officials] would get a law passed prohibiting a cowboy from packing a pistol and then proceed to take his money; they couldn't lose. An old timer told me they controlled the liquor, gambling and everything else. If the cowboy gets boisterous and objects to the manner in which he lost his money, he is pistol-whipped and if he returns armed, is cut

down with shotguns. The badges [lawmen] wore were the variety that today's [1935] honkey-tonk operators get to protect their places so they can keep a pistol under the counter.[70]

Six months before the famed gunfight near the O. K. Corral in Tombstone, Arizona Territory, on April 19, 1881, a seemingly ambiguous city ordnance took effect concerning the carrying of concealed weapons. "It is hereby declared to be unlawful for any person to carry deadly weapons, concealed or otherwise (except the same be carried openly in sight, and in the hand) within the limits of the City of Tombstone." The prohibition didn't apply to those entering town who were on their way to depositing their weapons.[71]

In October of 1876, the board of health in Deadwood, Dakota Territory, passed an ordnance stating that "no person shall fire or discharge any cannon or gun, fowling piece, pistol, or fire-arm of any description" without the mayor's consent. Although it prohibited miners and others from firing, it did not restrict carrying firearms. George Stokes, a Deadwood merchant, advised: "I have known localities where the blue barrel of a pistol would catch the eye of people taking chances with the rights and properties of others in a way that the law would not.... In a new camp, a 'six gun' takes the place of courts, judges, and jury." More than a quarter century later in 1909 a visitor to Custer, South Dakota, rented a room over a bar and found a protective sheet of boiler plate beneath his bed to protect the occupant from bullets fired by boisterous patrons below.[72]

Despite the increasingly frequent prohibitions against carrying or discharging a firearm within a town, violations continued. During the 1880 cattle season from mid-April to mid-October, 207 arrests were recorded in the Caldwell, Kansas, police docket. Prostitution or keeping a bawdy house counted for 62, drunkenness and causing a disturbance totaled 53, gambling resulted in 31 arrests, and fourth most common was carrying or firing a weapon with 26 arrests.[73]

One of Caldwell's police officers, Daniel W. Jones, suffered a major indignity when he accidentally was locked in a restroom in one of the town's fashionable hotels. The incident as described in the local *Post* of September 25, 1879, brought added renown to the recently appointed deputy marshal.

> There is a seat in the room just opposite
> the door upon which Dan sat himself
> down, put his feet against the door, and
> with Heenan like strength pushed the
> door asunder, and at the same instant
> back went Dan's revolver, down to the
> bottomless—after which a light was
> brought into requisition—it was fished
> up, a tub of water, barrel of soft soap and
> scrubbing-brush were readily used up
> and the pistol looks as natural as ever,
> and if the street gossip don't [*sic*] men-
> tion this we will never say a word about
> it to Dan.[74]

In an unusual arrangement in 1879, the Texas state house in Austin was financed in an exchange with a Chicago firm for three million acres of land in the virtually uninhabited Texas panhandle. Those acres became what probably was the largest cattle ranch in the west, the XIT, eventually enclosed by miles of barbed wire. At one time, between 100 and 150 cowboys tended some 150,000 cattle grazing on that unspoiled land. The XIT ranch hands lived and worked under a lengthy and strict set of rules. Those guidelines as of January 1888 included prohibitions on gambling and drinking intoxicating beverages. Abusing or neglecting any mule, horse, or cattle would not be tolerated and any employee doing so would be discharged. Rule number eleven specified the following concerning concealable weapons:

> No employee of the Company, or of any
> contractor doing work for the Company,
> is permitted to carry on or about his
> person or in his saddle bags, any pistol,
> dirk, dagger, sling shot, knuckles, bowie
> knife, or any other similar instruments
> for the purpose of offense or defense.
> Guests of the Company, and persons not
> employees of the ranch temporarily stay-
> ing at any of its camps, are expected to
> comply with this rule, which is also a
> State law.[75]

John Southerland was not a drover but an emigrant who ran afoul of the law in Boynton, Missouri, in 1885. En route westward with a group who planned to settle in Oregon, he walked into a store and almost was arrested for carrying a revolver.[76]

In 1890 nearly all the states had some laws on the books relating to the "carrying or drawing" of weapons, presumably applied generally in cities and towns. Nebraska law carried a jail sentence of up to thirty days or a fine of up to $100; in Texas it was imprisonment of between ten and thirty days and a fine of $25 to $200; Utah law called for jail time of up to six months and/or a fine of not less than $300; and if convicted in Oregon, one faced five to one hundred days and/or a fine of $10 to $200. In some instances, the lesser penalty was applied if one merely was carrying a concealed weapon, a higher sentence was applied if one actually drew a dangerous weapon. The penalties under the laws of states east of the Mississippi for similar offenses were no more severe than in the less populated west. Ohio law, for instance, called for up to thirty days in jail or a fine not exceeding $200.[77]

Among cowboys by the 1880s, the practice of carrying a revolver was not universal although some clung to the habit. "We carried pistols because everyone else did, not because we needed them particularly, but because of the sense of security and almost companionship." So wrote Benjamin S. Miller describing range conditions in

1880. "The Colt's '45,' with its scabbard and belt of car-tridges, was a cumbersome affair, but so used did we become to it that we did not mind the extra weight and felt lost without it. Weapons of light caliber were an uncommon quantity in cow-land." Miller also voiced a Texan's opinion that in some circumstances is applicable in today's society. When asked about the practicality of carrying a revolver, he said "One might carry a gun for ten years and never need it at all; then, again, he might need it like hell." In contrast, J. L. Hill, driving cattle from San Antonio to Dodge City in 1883, noted that "Driscoll would not allow any of the boys to have a six-shooter, though he carried one himself. We did not like that very well, but agreed to it, and left our guns behind."[78]

The risk of accidental shootings was one reason some cattle bosses limited access to firearms among their employees. James C. Shaw in 1879 became bored with trailing cattle and with a friend set out to hunt buffalo for their hides.

> We were getting along good until one day one of those bad men came along and wanted to throw in with us. He had money and some horses and we let him in, but he would never lay off that six-shooter, but would play with it from morning until night, turning it on one finger and cocking it as it went over. One day he let it off and [nearly?] shot out my eye, and I have had no use for those six-shooter men since. Last week there was one of them standing in the door of the hotel, turning the pistol the same way. An army officer came out and told him there were women and children in the hotel who would not like to see that, but the fellow never stopped. He said that a little six-shooter bullet would not hurt anyone. The next day he was doing the same thing when the gun went off. The bullet went down his side and he hollered so loud that everybody in town heard.[79]

James H. Cook encountered a similar situation with a fancy gun handler when herding cattle. He remedied the situation before an accident happened.

> [Jack Harris] had been having fun at my expense all along the trail. Every chance he could get he would ride up to me, sud-denly draw his six-shooter, cock it, and aim it at me, saying, "Are you the sheriff that is looking for me?" Generally he would wind up this little act by taking his revolver by the barrel, his finger on the trigger guard, and reaching the butt toward me, and saying, "I'm tired of fight-ing; take my gun." Allowing some imagi-nary sheriff time to reach for it, he would reverse the weapon quick as a flash, cock it again, and aim straight for my face. All this, he said, was "just for practice." I think it was, for later I found out that he could be a bad man in some places. One day before we reached Fort Griffin [Texas], he played his gun game on me once more. After he had put up his revolver, I said, "Jack, don't practice on me any more." "Why not?" "Because it would be dangerous for you," I replied. "If this sort of thing goes on, it will be only a matter of time before you will let your thumb slip, and I might go dead. Then you'd be sorry. I would rather be killed purposely than by accident. If you ever aim a gun at me again, you'd better shoot, for I will surely kill you if I can."[80]

In the 1880s, a Crooked L cowboy named Arnold admired another hand's ivory-gripped revolver and asked to look at it. Arnold began to repeatedly twirl and holster the weapon but caught his thumb on the ham-mer and somehow caused the gun to discharge, seriously wounding himself. It was a black day for one novice gun handler and an unfortunate horse as the Tombstone, Arizona, *Epitaph* reported: "A tenderfoot from New Jersey named Markley while playing cowboy at Crittenden a few days since, undertook to show his skill with a pistol. The result was that he shot the horse he was riding through the neck, killing it, and in falling it broke Markley's leg."[81]

One caution against the accidental discharge of a sin-gle action revolver was expressed by various westerners—always load only five cartridges in a six-shot revolver and allow the hammer to rest on the empty chamber. "Five beans in the wheel," was a colloquialism for this safety measure. Such advice applied to almost any single action revolver of that era, even if the gun's hammer had a "safety" notch. That notch might fail if the revolver was dropped from a sufficient height, allowing the hammer

254

An essential vehicle on any cattle drive was the chuck wagon, developed by Charles Goodnight. Nate Champion (third from right) was killed in the Johnson County War in 1892. (Courtesy: Wyoming State Museum, Cheyenne)

to strike the live round beneath it and discharge the weapon. Smith & Wesson in 1878 introduced its New Model No. 3 revolver with a rebounding hammer, which reduced the chance of an accidental discharge in such a situation, but neither Colt nor Remington adopted this feature in their single action revolvers.[82]

Carelessness prevented the apprehension of several rustlers as cowboys stealthily approached their camp.

> Crawling along the edge of the bluff, [Sam Tate's] . . . revolver slipped out of the holster and fell some four feet below him; the hammer struck on a rock and a cartridge exploded. I had cautioned him several times on the trip never to carry more than five cartridges in the cylinder of his revolver, so that the hammer would always rest on an empty chamber, but he would not take my advice until this last accident.

> He got a . . . bullet through the brim of his Stetson hat, which I think taught him a lesson that he will never forget.

The thieves jumped on their horses and disappeared safely into the hills.[83]

Rancher Edgar B. Bronson later became a proficient writer and in describing a confrontation with Oglala Sioux at the White Clay Agency wrote:

> Acting almost in unison, . . . several of us proceeded to take on a bit of extra insurance by slipping spare cartridges into the "hammer chamber" of our pistol cylinders, usually carried empty for purposes of better safety against accidental discharge. I am sure I should have been glad to have a pistol into which I could have emptied the entire contents

of my full belt, for the odds against us looked rather long.[84]

In 1881 William H. Breckenridge was appointed as a deputy sheriff of Cochise County, Arizona Territory, by Sheriff John H. Behan. The two men were seated in the office in Tombstone when a shot was fired so close to Breckenridge "that a grain of powder struck my temple and set the blood running freely." The bullet lodged in a stack of papers in a pigeonhole in the desk.

> I thought the shot had come from out-doors, and had been fired in an effort to rescue the prisoner [being held for rob-bing a stagecoach]. I jumped to the door with a loaded shotgun that was standing next to the desk, but could see no one. I then saw what had happened. Behan's pis-tol had dropped from his belt and fallen on the floor and accidentally discharged. When the excitement was over, I took a cartridge from my pistol and placed the hammer on an empty chamber, and never carried but five shots in it from that time. I was always careful to see that the ham-mer was on an empty chamber whenever I put the gun on.[85]

An incident in 1887 between two employees of the RL Ranch in Montana illustrates another reason why some employers placed restrictions on firearms.

> George's story was that him [sic] and Matt were playing poker single-handed that day and got into a dispute over a pot. George [Sheperd] said [John] Matt tried to steal a twenty dollar gold piece out of the pot. They got into an argu-ment over it. They both had guns (all cowboys wore guns those days)—Matt reached for his gun but George beat him to it and killed him right there at the poker table. Finally the boss got George to give himself up and the fact that no one saw the shooting and George's testi-mony was all there was, he got clear on the grounds of self defense.[86]

A plea for restrictions on cowboys carrying firearms appeared in the *Texas Live Stock Journal* in February 1882.

The day of the Winchester rifle, ivory-handled pistol and cartridge belt belongs in the past—it is gone never to return, and with it should go every man who can-not discharge his duties on the ranch without being thus accoutered.... Ranchmen should no longer make proficiency in handling firearms the req-uisite qualification to employment.... This wholesale arming of cowboys is a disgrace to stock raising, injurious to the business, provocative of lawlessness and crime, and should be prohibited by the laws of the State, the rules of the associa-tion and by the owners of the ranches.[87]

At the stockmen's convention in Caldwell, Kansas, in April of 1882, attendees adopted a resolution that

> the six-shooter is not an absolutely neces-sary adjunct to the outfit of a cowboy working on the ranges of the association and we deprecate its use except in extreme cases of necessity...and further we con-demn the habit of the carrying of six-shooters by cowboys or by others especially while visiting any of the towns along the border.

Early the following year, Wyoming ranchers adopted a sim-ilar resolution.[88]

Entering the fray with pen and wit, a humorist for the Laramie, Wyoming, *Boomerang* countered:

> This new departure may tickle the stock-men, and not be objectionable to the cow-boy, but it knocks the romance out of the latter individual.... No more will the fes-tive cowboy, loaded to the muzzle with tarantula juice, caper up and down the streets, yelling like a Comanche and bid-ding defiance to the city marshal. No more will he help the coroner by shooting a half-dozen companions in a drunken row. No more will he ride into a gin-mill, and with his cannon pointed at the dia-mond stud on the barkeeper's shirtfront, order up drinks for all the hands, then shoot out the lights and three or four spectators' gizzards.

Disarm the cowboy? Take his pop from him and bring him down to the level of a common man? Ye Gods, no! In the name of 10,000,000 eastern readers of fiction—no! Let our young bloods wear skintight pants and Seymour coats; let fried shirts and paper collars become the rule; let the electric light and telephone plant themselves right in our midst, as they have already done, but touch not the cowboy and his revolver.[89]

Despite such growing opposition to indiscriminate wearing of firearms by cowboys, the practice persisted among some, including Teddy Blue Abbott.

Along about the nineties a lot of people out here [Montana] began to quiet down and start leaving off their guns. The country was getting so thickly settled then and the houses was [sic] so close together they figured they didn't need them any more. But I wouldn't give mine up. A six-shooter's an awful lot of company. Suppose you break your leg, you can signal. If you're caught afoot, you can shoot a jack rabbit. If you're held up, you can defend yourself. And then, too, six-shooters were a great thing for keeping the peace. You wouldn't have any of this calling names and brawling and fighting, where every man was wearing a deadly weapon in plain sight. And as for that expression about a son of a b., I never heard it said with a smile, as they say, before the nineties. In the early days men were soft-spoken and respectful to each other, because it didn't pay to be anything else. It's not like that now. But we were a prehistoric race. We were way behind.[90]

Continuing Abbott's narrative:

I would like to say more about this business of gun fights because so much has been written about it in fiction, and it is nearly all exaggeration as far as this part of the country [Montana] is concerned. I worked up here from 1883 on and I saw a lot of hard work on the range but very

little shooting. In fact, from '85 on, until it quit being a range, there was never but one shooting scrape here in the Maginnis district, and then nobody got killed; and over on the Judith and the Moccasin, which were the next ranges, they never had one.[91]

A lot of this shooting you hear about was just crazy high spirits. You'd be standing up to the bar with a pipe in your mouth, and bang! The pieces would fall on the floor. Somebody took a shot at it. But it was all in fun. . . . There was a fellow that used to be around Miles City [Montana], by the name of Tom Irvine, who was the best shot I ever saw. One night . . . in the saloon, Louis King, a [deputy], was standing there with a cigar in his mouth, and Tom pulled his six-gun out and shot the end off. Louis never budged. He just stuck his face out a little further and Tom clipped another half inch off the cigar so it was down to a little stub. Still Louis never moved, but only stood there with it held out between his lips as though he was daring Tom to come on and shoot again. Tom said: "You go to hell," and shoved his gun back in the scabbard.[92]

Charles Siringo supported Blue's observations. He believed that the "fast draw," quicker than the eye could follow, was more a fiction of writers of western tales than reality.[93]

By the 1880s, the day of the open range was disappearing. Barbed wire, invented in 1873 by Joseph Glidden, fenced thousands of acres and the role of the cowboy with a $10 horse and a $40 saddle was changing. In some areas including Oklahoma's panhandle, ranchers and Texas trail herds sometimes came into conflict. The fear of tick fever was still present and trail bosses were "encouraged" to follow clearly defined specific trails northward. Trail boss Ab Blocker recalled:

The cow outfits . . . had organized to fight rustlers and to keep their stock from mixing with trail herds. We heard about this down the trail, even before we got to Fort Worth, and we found that these men meant business. It looked like every man

Representative of the beginning of a new era, an African American cowboy poses with what appears to be a .38 Colt M1902 autoloading pistol. (Courtesy: George Jackson)

had a Winchester rifle in his saddle boot and a six-shooter or two strapped on him. And even the boys were dressed that way! The way I remember it was that it looked like a place where the kids teethed on forty-five caliber cartridges.

But the day of the long trail drives to market had passed its zenith and the introduction of such new cat-

tle breeds as Herefords, Shorthorns, and Aberdeen Angus not only had improved the quality of beef sent to market, but these animals were more docile and required less space per animal when transported by train than did Texas beeves with their long horns. While cattle production still was an important aspect of Texas's economy, more herds were being grazed on the central plains, and other western states were becoming major beef producers.

Harry Campbell cleans a Marlin rifle at a crude line camp on the Matador Ranch in Texas at the turn of the century, illustrating that life on the range often lacked comforts! (Courtesy: Amon Carter Museum, Fort Worth, TX)

I believe the day is not far distant when cowboys will be armed with prod poles— to punch the cattle out of the way— instead of fire-arms. Messrs. Colt and Winchester will then have to go out of business, or else emigrate to "Arkansaw" and open up prod-pole factories.

So predicted Charles Siringo, only somewhat tongue in cheek.[94]

Where once the old six-shooter spoke
The copper's billy swings;
The glamour of the past is broke
By laws an' rules an' things,
What once was roarin' dance-halls
A deadly silence wraps—
Since punchers took to overalls
Instead of spurs an' chaps.
— Barton Braley[95]

Small but Deadly:
Derringers and Other
Pocket Protectors

We pack six shooters and derringers
for fear of the knaves.
— George A. Whitney, 1863[1]

Compact flintlock and later percussion pistols sized conveniently for a man's pocket or lady's purse or muff were available since the later years of the eighteenth century. Many of European origin, often English or Belgian, were imported into this country, competing with those of American make. But it wouldn't be until the 1850s that the term "derringer" became common, referring to small, easily concealed pistols.

Henry Deringer Jr. of Philadelphia (1786–1868) succeeded his father as a gun maker about 1806. The son became a prolific producer of both military and civilian rifles, muskets, and pistols as well as Northwest guns and rifles for the Indian trade. He stated that he made his first pair of pistols in 1825, but it apparently was about 1852 that he began to produce the distinctive, small pocket pistols which would put his name in the dictionary as a noun and which, like the Pennsylvania-Kentucky rifle, were distinctly American in style and origin.

Deringer's early pistols were larger holster or belt size. One of the largest known is .58 caliber with a single-set trigger, 9 1/4-inch barrel and an overall length of 16 1/4 inches, contrasting sharply with the pocket pistols that eventually

would ensure his fame. Dimensions for diminutive "Deringers" would vary from .33 to .50 caliber and barrel lengths beginning as short as about an inch, but about .41 caliber and a 1 1/2-inch to 2-inch barrel length were fairly typical. These pistols were particularly popular in the south and west, and in 1866, two years before his death at age eighty-two, he stated that in just the previous ten years he had sold 5,280 pairs.[2]

Copyists in this country and Europe made thousands more, some of which went west, often unmarked but sometimes stamped "Deerringer" or "Deringe" to confuse potential buyers. Some makers in the east such as Richard P. Bruff, Tryon, John and Andrew Wurfflein, John Krider, and George Gillespie were more straightforward and marked those from their shops with their names. Slotter & Co. of Philadelphia sometimes marked their pistols "J. Deringer," after having hired a tailor by that name to legalize the deception. Some of these copies were equal to the genuine Deringer in quality and some considered those by Slotter to be superior since they used a steel barrel.

Horace Dimick of St. Louis, Glassick & Schneider of Memphis, and Louis Hoffman of Vicksburg, all on the

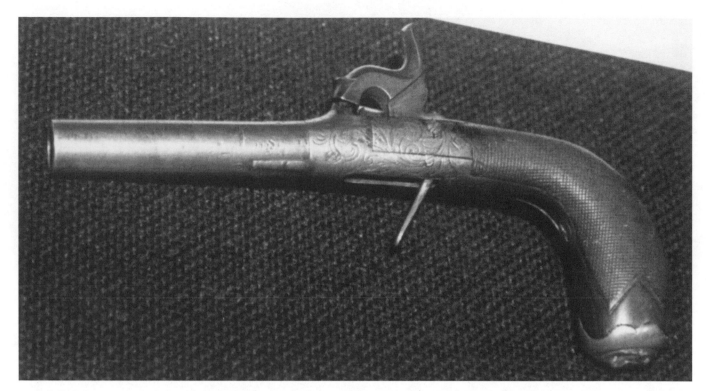

.36 Belgian pocket pistol given to Mrs. Jesse Benton Fremont about 1850 by her father, Senator Thomas Hart Benton. (Exhibited by the Arizona Historical Society, Tucson)

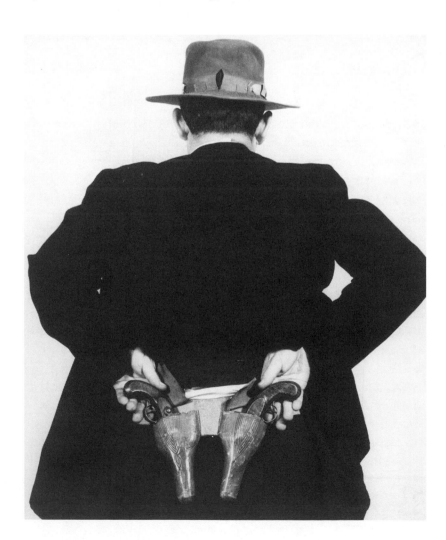

Unusual pair of percussion pistols made by a member of the famed Drepperd family of gun makers of Lancaster, Pennsylvania in their original holsters. The .36 caliber 4-inch brass barrels and the locks are marked "Drepperd— Lancaster." The holsters can be fastened to suspenders and worn in the small of the back, hidden perhaps beneath a gambler's vest or frock coat. (Courtesy: Norm Flayderman)

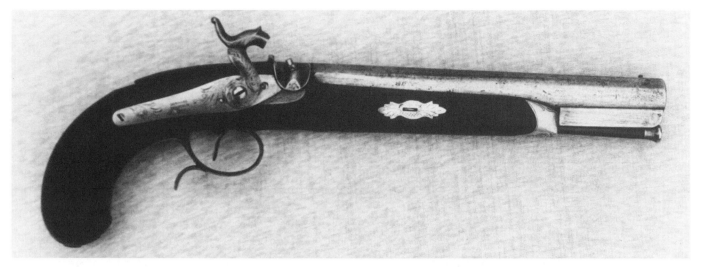

One of the largest Henry Deringer pistols known, .52 caliber with a 9-inch barrel.

Mississippi River, were in prime locations to cater to gamblers and others in the riverboat trade and to provide anyone westbound with Deringer-type pistols of their own or other make. Only rarely encountered are pistols with the names of J. P. Lower (Denver), L. J. E. Beardon (Galveston, Texas), and Gustav Erichson or E. Schmidt & Co. of Houston, Texas, representative of a sprinkling of western gunsmiths who probably marked only a handful of guns that they perhaps retailed rather than produced.

Several dozen merchants, some of them jewelers, are known to have advertised and sold the genuine Deringer pocket pistol. Their names sometimes appear on the barrel. Many of these agents were located in such southern cities as Memphis and New Orleans, but in San Francisco W. C. Allen, the Curry brothers, R. Liddle & Co., and A. J. Taylor were representative. Adolphus J. Plate, a Prussian immigrant, came to San Francisco during the gold rush and sold genuine Deringers as well as counterfeits, including those by Slotter & Co. This latter venture brought him into legal difficulties when in 1863 Henry Deringer sued him for trademark infringement in a celebrated lawsuit which dragged on until 1870. Taylor operated a shooting gallery and also loaded derringers and other pistols for customers. He was fatally shot in the head in 1858 when a customer accidentally discharged a Colt revolver in his shop.[3]

A pair of pocket pistols, perhaps Deringers, prevented a robbery or worse in San Francisco in 1853. As John Steele walked along a busy street, a stranger crowded him against a door and suddenly shoved him inside.

> Instead of the usual revolver, I carried two
> single shooters in a place prepared inside
> my coat; and, while with my right hand
> trying to prevent his shutting the outside
> door, with my left hand I cocked one,
> drew it, but just then saw another man
> standing in a side door, and as I raised the
> pistol he disappeared and shut the
> door.... I drew the other pistol with my
> right hand, when the man who had
> pushed me in disappeared through a door
> on the opposite side and it was
> shut.... On regaining presence of mind,
> [I] saw that the room was only about six
> feet square, but containing three
> doors.... The fact that I had been pursued
> by a robber became apparent, and only
> instant resort to the pistols saved
> me.... The room into which I was so sud-
> denly pushed was evidently a prepared
> trap, into which the victims who could
> not be decoyed might be forced.[4]

California deputy sheriff John C. Boggs in 1858 showed more persistence than good sense when he attempted to arrest "Rattlesnake Dick" and another highwayman armed only with handcuffs, an arrest warrant, and a derringer of unspecified origin. He halted the stagecoach as they rode on top and when they opened fire on him, he fired back. Fortunately for him, they leaped to the ground and ran into the brush. Later in his lengthy career as a peace officer, Boggs called his action "childish" and the incident a "stupid effort."[5]

The number of existing Deringer-type pistols with known frontier association, other than those bearing a western maker or dealer's name, is small. Probably the best

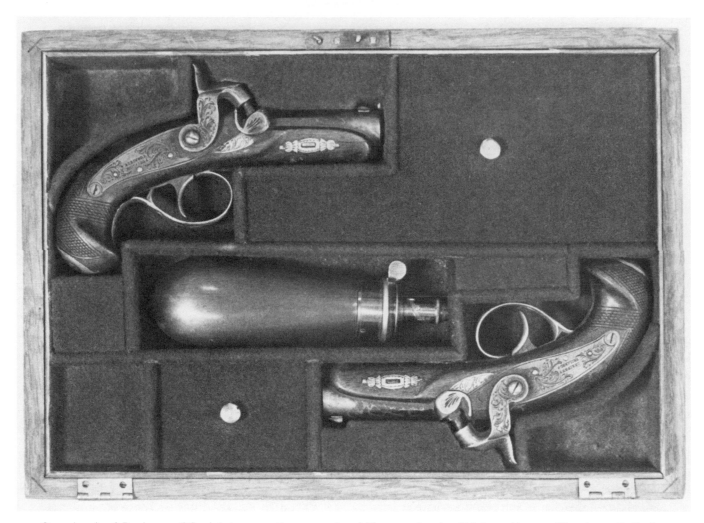

Cased pair of Deringer .36 pistols once the property of Mormon leader Brigham Young. (Courtesy: Sotheby, Park-Bernet Galleries, NY)

known is a pair of genuine Deringers with "W. F. Cody/1865" engraved on the nickel-silver escutcheon plates, the owner presumably being Buffalo Bill Cody.

Other competitors to Deringer's pocket pistols, although they didn't look like the genuine article, were the small, inexpensive single-shot percussion pocket or boot pistols by such makers as Ethan Allen, Bacon & Co., Blunt & Syms, and others, usually of .31 to .36 caliber. The steamer *Arabia* sank in 1856 after hitting a snag in the Missouri River when bound for Council Bluffs, Iowa. Included among the artifacts recovered when she was excavated in 1988 were fourteen such pistols by W. W. Marston of New York (Washington Arms Company), as well as forty-eight Belgian Northwest trade guns, thirty-one brass powder flasks, nine powder horns, fourteen bullet molds, five hundred pounds of lead shot, and three shotguns.[6]

Clarence King at age twenty-one in 1863 began a career as a geologist and western explorer. Professor William H. Brewer of the Geological Survey of California described an incident:

> In those days, most of the men of the California mountain camps posed as desperados, and went about burdened with a more or less heavy assortment of firearms, the tenderfeet and bluffers by preference sporting the more conspicuous six-shooter, while one or more of the vest or trousers pockets of the really ready and artistic life-takers was sure to hold a short Derringer pistol, which was often, on due emergency, fired from within the pocket. On one occasion, when in the joint bar and office of a small mountain hotel, King was unavoidably drawn into an argument with a bitterly aggressive advocate of secession, which finally became so heated that King's

Derringer made by Stephen O'Dell of Natchez, Mississippi. He also sold genuine Henry Deringer pistols. (Photo by Steven W. Walenta, courtesy James D. Gordon)

Deringers such as these, owned by Salt Lake City publisher T. B. H. Stenhouse, usually were sold in pairs although not always cased in this manner. (Courtesy: Utah State Historical Society)

Kansas free-staters who rescued Dr. John Doy (seated) from proslavers. Among the various weapons displayed, the man second from right has a small double action single-shot pocket pistol, probably an Allen or a Marston, hung from his neck by a string. (Courtesy: Kansas State Historical Society)

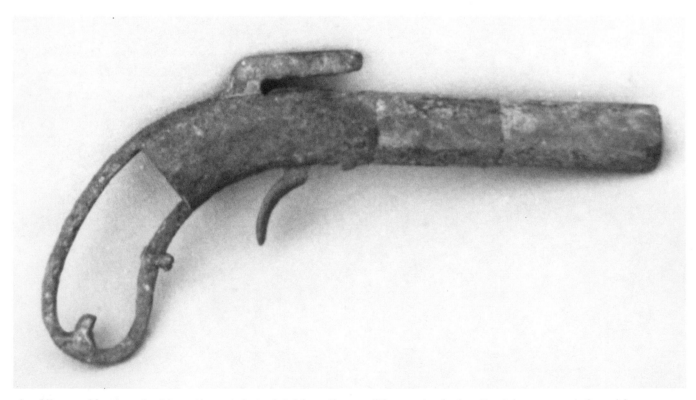

An Allen or Marston double action pocket pistol in relic condition and missing the trigger guard, found in a sewer in Santa Fe. (Courtesy: Ron Peterson)

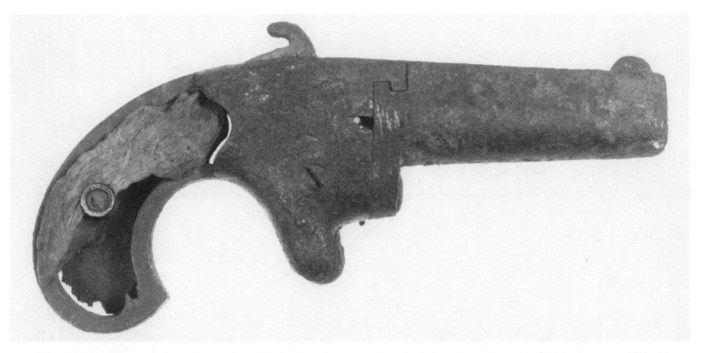

National Arms Company second model .41 rimfire derringer found at the site where N. C. Meeker was killed by Ute Indians in 1879. (Courtesy: State Historical Society of Colorado)

adversary dropped his hand on his six-shooter. But he never drew it. King was entirely unarmed; but, standing at the moment with his right hand in his trousers pocket, at the first hostile move he stuck forward his thumb until it looked like the muzzle of a pistol and then snapped a quill toothpick that fortunately happened to be in the same pocket, the sound of which was so much like the muffled click of a pistol lock, that his adversary promptly bolted through the door. King observed: "... in this country there are not many wolves in sheep's clothing, but there are a lot of sheep in wolves' clothing."[7]

"We pack six shooters and derringers for fear of the knave." So wrote George A. Whitney, a miner and hay rancher, to his brother in Iowa in 1863 from Aurora in present-day Nevada.[8]

Among today's arms collectors, it's common to use the terms "derringer" or "deringer" when writing of pocket pistols made by others than the namesake, referring to genuine examples as "Deringers." But testifying in 1866, H. H. Wilson of the San Francisco firm of Wilson & Evans stated: "All these short pistols are called Deringer pistols without regard to the maker." Deringer-type pistols came in many forms and from various firms. Unfortunately they rarely

appear in nineteenth-century western photos and only occasionally are mentioned by name in nineteenth-century accounts, yet they were popular with lawmen, gamblers, legislators, prostitutes, genteel ladies, and others in the west.[9]

By the early 1860s, new and improved derringers accepting metallic cartridges were entering the market to challenge the earlier percussion types. Again referring to testimony in the *Deringer v. Plate* trial, dealer Charles Kaeding of San Francisco stated: "The demand of [percussion] Deringer pistols has been decreasing. It has to compete with breech-loaders, and the demand for the latter is twenty to one for Deringer muzzle loaders. Very many other pistols of the Deringer style have been thrown into the market." "The laws of California against carrying concealed weapons, have also caused sales [of derringers] to fall off," added John R. Evans.[10]

Among the single-shot breech loading derringers, a .41 rimfire cartridge became the frequent standard. With a few exceptions, multishot derringers were of lesser caliber. One of the more practical of the breech loading derringers for its time was the single-shot model designed by David Williamson, patented in 1866 and manufactured by both the Moore and National firearms companies. The barrel slid forward to load the single .41 cartridge, but insertion of an auxiliary chamber containing a percussion nipple allowed the gun to be loaded with loose powder and ball if fixed cartridges weren't available. Wild Bill Hickok reportedly owned a pair of these pistols.[11]

Three "hard cases," that at left holding a Remington Vest Pocket derringer. (Courtesy: Herb Peck Jr.)

The Remington company in Ilion, New York, beginning in the early 1860s produced a wide variety of pistols that by their size fall into the derringer category. Best known is the Model 95 Double Deringer. Even though the firm's name changed several times over the years, the basic design of the Model 95 didn't. Its two superposed ("over and under") barrels swung upward to load and the firing pin alternated between them when the hammer was cocked. The estimated 150,000 produced over a span of almost three quarters of a century (1866–1935), all chambered for the same stubby .41 rimfire cartridge, was a sign of the practicality of William H. Elliott's design.

Joseph Rider designed Remington's No. 1 size derringer, the diminutive and aptly named single-shot Vest Pocket. Advertised at a base price of $3.25, in .22 caliber it measured only four inches overall and weighed but 8 1/2 ounces, small enough to conceal almost anywhere about one's person. It probably was one of these Vest Pocket .22s about which Elizabeth Bacon Custer wrote.

One of our ladies [army wives] . . . had a little of the Molly Pitcher spirit. She had shot at a mark, and she promised to teach us to put in the cartridges and discharge the piece. We were filled with envy because she produced a tiny Remington pistol that heretofore she had carried in her pocket when traveling in the States. It was not much larger than a lead pencil, and we could not help doubting its power to damage. She did not insist that it would kill, but . . . we had to laugh at the vehement manner in which she declared that she could disable the leg of an enemy.[12]

Remington also produced a larger Saw Handle Deringer in .30, .32, and .41 calibers as well as a compact .41 single-shot with a rounded bird's head grip, another of Elliot's designs. Another popular pocket pistol from Remington was what was termed its New Repeating Pistol

Remington .32 Elliott pepperbox inscribed on the backstrap "JUDGE JAMES KELLY/CALDWELL KANSAS."
James D. Kelly Sr. was first elected as Caldwell's police judge in August 1879. (Courtesy: Jerry Pitstick)

(Elliot's Patent) No. 1 in .22 caliber or the more common No. 2 in .32 rimfire caliber. The gun was of pepperbox design, consisting of a stationary cluster of five (.22) or four (.32) barrels with a revolving firing pin and a ring trigger. Total production including both calibers is estimated at around twenty-five thousand beginning about 1863.

Competition to the Remington pepperbox pistol came from the thousands of four-barrel pocket pistols by C. Sharps & Co. and Sharps & Hankins in .22, .30, and .32 caliber, first patented in 1859. Although there were numerous variations, all were designed around a block of four barrels which slid forward to load. The firing pin rotated a quarter turn each time it was cocked. Similar in appearance but with a barrel cluster which tipped downward was the four-shot .32 rimfire Starr, patented in 1864.

The New York firm of Schuyler, Hartley & Graham in their 1864 catalog of arms and military goods listed a handful of small American derringers, indicative of what was available on the market at that time. Offered but unmarked as to price were the .41 Moore all-metal 1st Model, a per-

cussion "Deringer" (maker not specified as Henry himself), and an unnamed single-shot in .22, .30, or .32 caliber with a side-swinging barrel, perhaps made by Bacon or Prescott. The four-barrel Sharps and .32 Remington Elliott pepperboxes also were included.

Simplest of the pocket guns were the percussion pistols made by Manhattan and its successor, the American Standard Tool Company, in the late 1860s and early 1870s. Some were unmarked and others were stamped "Hero" with or without the maker's name. They were simple in design but adequate for the purpose with no trigger guard, forged brass frame, grips held with a simple wood screw with no escutcheon plates, and an unrifled .34 screw-off barrel. Priced at $1 or even slightly less, they were a true "poor man's derringer."

The purchaser who wanted a derringer by Colt had to wait until 1870 when the Hartford firm bought out Daniel Moore's National Arms Company. Introduced as Colt's No. 1 and No. 2 derringer, each was a single-shot .41 in which the barrel was tilted to the side to load. Each was a direct

Remington derringers, clockwise from I o'clock: .41 Double Derringer, .22 five-shot Elliott, .32 four-shot Elliott, and .22 Vest Pocket single-shot.

descendent of the almost identical National Arms Company's pistols. The No. 1 was of all-steel construction and shaped so it also could be used rather effectively in striking a blow with the fist. The No. 2, similar in appearance, had wooden grips. Added to the line about the same time was the Colt 3rd Model, in which the barrel pivoted horizontally. It was designed by F. Alexander Thuer, better known for his system of converting percussion Colt revolvers to fire a front-loaded metallic cartridge. It proved to be by far the most popular of the three Colt derringer designs and was marketed until 1912.

Joe Horner lived as a fugitive from the law in Texas in the 1870s but changed his name to Frank M. Canton and later served as a lawman in Wyoming, Indian Territory, and Alaska. (He also was accused of the ambush slaying of sev-

eral homesteaders during Wyoming's Johnson County War.) In 1894 as a deputy marshal in Oklahoma Territory he arrested a murder suspect in a bunkhouse. "I had a heavy pocket derringer that I usually carried in my hip pocket when in town. It was a forty-one-caliber Colt. I thought it was a good one, but had never tried it out." McCool objected to the arrest, slapped Canton, and reached into his hip pocket.

> I pushed him [McCool] away from me
> and at the same time drew my derringer
> and fired at his head. The bullet struck
> him in the forehead just over the left eye.
> He fell on his back, and I supposed from
> the appearance of the wound that he was

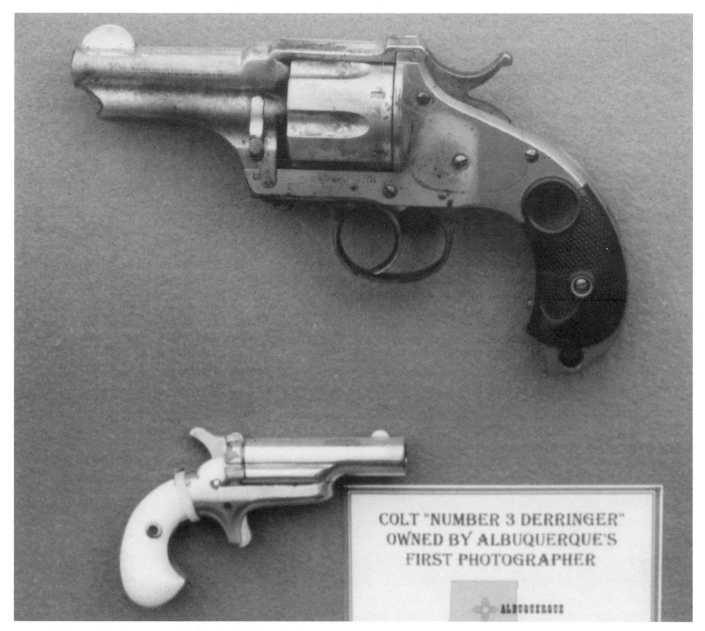

Colt No. 3 derringer (below) and Merwin & Hulbert .44 Pocket Army revolver, both owned by Albuquerque's first professional photographer, William Henry Cobb. (Courtesy: Ron Peterson)

shot square through the head.... When the doctor examined the wound in Lon McCool's head, he found that the bullet had not penetrated his head, but had glanced around the skull under the skin, and come [*sic*] out at the back of his head. He was unconscious for twelve hours, then commenced to improve.... I threw away this derringer that I had and have never carried one since.[13]

Canton's pistol could have been either of the three Colt models of derringers, but the incident illustrated the lack

of punch the .41 rimfire cartridge had, yet Colt, Remington, and others chambered many of their pocket pistols for it.

In 1866 George W. Fox traveled the Bozeman Trail to the Montana gold mines and kept a diary of the expedition. "This evening [June 24] while after the cattle I saw a jack rabbit fired 6 shots at it with a navy [probably Colt] revolver & killed it with a vest pocket pistol."[14]

George D. Freeman was a blacksmith by trade and a local lawman in Kansas in the 1870s and 1880s. In 1872 an armed mob seized a horse thief in his custody, Tom Smith, and lynched him. In explaining the situation later, Freeman noted that "the shining barrels of the shotgun [pointed at him] looked as large as stovepipes,

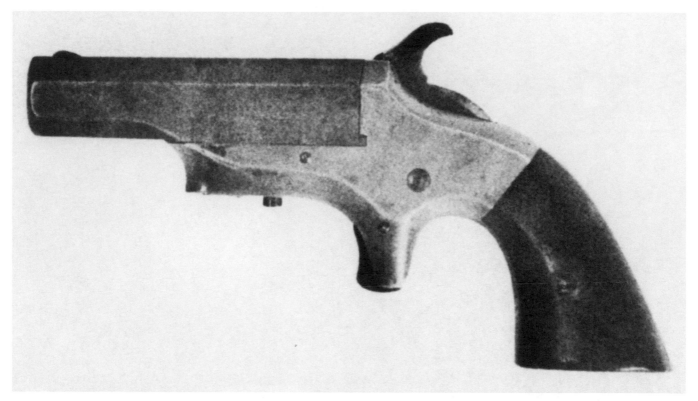

Texas Ranger captain Neal Coldwell's .41 Southerner derringer. He served with the agency for almost a decade (1874–83).

so I concluded it was safer to keep quiet." Later the thief's brother, Charlie, threatened to kill Freeman on sight and that meeting came about when both men were judges at a horse race.

> I looked around and saw Smith coming [toward me] with his hand in his pocket. I drew my revolver from the scabbard and held it in my hand near my side. As he came near I heard the click of the hammer of his derringer, as he raised it preparatory to shooting and I watched his arm, and the first movement he gave I intended to shoot him. He approached and stood within a few feet of me for several moments, but the suspense made the moments seem like hours, and I drew a long sigh of relief when he turned and entered a saloon. The saloon proprietor had been watching and . . . said, "you coward why didn't you shoot him?" Smith's reply was that he only had one load in his derringer, and if it by chance refused to fire or if his aim was not true, I would have the drop on him.[15]

A derringer in his pocket didn't prevent the death of Judge John P. Slough in the lobby of the original La Fonda Americana Hotel in Santa Fe. In his role as territorial chief justice, Slough apparently could be abrasive. An argument developed when a territorial legislator, W. L. Rynerson, accused the judge of having called him a liar and a thief. Rynerson waved a Colt revolver menacingly, but the judge thrust his hand into his pocket and told him to "shoot and be damned." The single shot fired proved mortal to Slough who as he fell dropped a derringer on the floor. Rynerson was tried but after a change of venue was acquitted on a plea of self-defense.[16]

In Tucson, Arizona Territory, in 1870, an ex-US marshal named Duffield served as US mail inspector. He was a tall, powerfully built and sometimes quarrelsome man. A drunken tough named "Waco Bill" confronted Duffield who knocked him to earth with one blow.

> No sooner had he [Waco Bill] touched Mother Earth than . . . his hand sought his revolver, and partly drew it out of [his] holster. Duffield . . . did not raise his voice above a whisper the whole time that his drunken opponent was hurling all kinds of anathemas at him; but now he saw that

something must be done. In Arizona it was not customary to pull a pistol upon a man; that was regarded as an act both unchristian-like and wasteful of time— Arizonanas [sic] nearly always shot out of the pocket without drawing their weapons at all, and into Mr. "Waco Bill's" groin went the sure bullet of the man who, local wits used to say, wore crape upon his hat in memory of his departed virtues.[17]

Local dances in Tucson were affairs to which most people went "on a peace footing... that is to say, all the heavy armament was left at home, and nothing taken along but a few Derringers, which would come in handy in case of accident." In a room adjoining the long saloon where a dance was being held, some of the ex-marshal's friends persuaded him to produce some if not all of his weapons. "He drew them from the arm-holes of his waistcoat, from his boot-legs, from his hip-pockets, from the back of his neck, and there they all were—eleven lethal weapons, mostly small Derringers, with one knife."[18]

Judge John Titus had only contempt for Duffield and sought to put down even the least semblance of lawlessness. The day after the dance, he had Duffield arrested and brought before him for carrying a concealed weapon. The judge asked the first witness to demonstrate how Duffield had drawn his revolver. Matching action and word, the witness drew his own revolver from its holster on his hip. There was a ripple of laughter in the courtroom as people at once saw how absurd it was to hold one man responsible for a misdemeanor of which a whole community was guilty, and the matter was quickly dropped.[19]

Smith & Wesson's .22 lst Model revolver, although not classified as a derringer, was representative of pocket revolvers small enough for easy concealment and despite the diminutive cartridge it fired, found favor with many as a weapon for pocket or purse. Preparing for a journey across the plains by stagecoach, Sam Clemens readied himself for any eventuality.

> I was armed to the teeth with a pitiful little Smith & Wesson's seven-shooter, which carried a ball like a homoeopathic pill, and it took the whole seven to make a dose for an adult. But I thought it was grand. It appeared to me to be a dangerous weapon. It only had one fault—you could not hit anything with it.[20]

Lt. Robert G. Carter in September 1870 was newly graduated from West Point and just married. His bride accompanied him on the journey to his assignment with the 4th US Cavalry in Texas. Lt. William A. Thompson, a member of the escort party to Fort Concho, was a tease.

> He delighted to ride up to the ambulance and with mischief lurking in his eyes... tell the brides that near a certain tree we were now passing, only a few weeks ago, "a whole stageload of people had been massacred by Indians, scalped and mutilated," which would cause them to cry out and grasp with nervous strength one of the smallest sized Smith and Wesson pistols with which one of them had armed herself at the beginning of the journey and which would not bruise a man at fifteen feet.[21]

As early as February of 1860, M. W. B. Hartley, secretary of the Colt company, urged Sam Colt to challenge the popularity of such metallic cartridge pocket guns.

> Large numbers of small pocket pistols made by Smith and Wesson and also by Sharp have been sold. They are mere toys fired with a loaded cap and if you got out a small size it would at once supercede them. Say, stocked like the smallest sized deringer, of black composition, a short cylinder loaded with a bulleted cap and a short stumpy barrel, put up in a neat case.

Colt couldn't comply with the suggestion without infringing on the Rollin White patent, however.[22]

Sometimes the size of a handgun didn't matter in the outcome of a confrontation. In Las Vegas, New Mexico Territory, in 1880, a group of drunken railroad workers were causing a disturbance. Their boss Joe Castillo was called to the dance hall to quiet them down.

> Castillo was about to do so when the new peace officer, Dave Mathers (better known as "Mysterious Dave"), appeared on the scene and started making arrests. Not knowing that Mathers was an officer, Castillo resented what he took to be arbitrary interference. Hot words were bandied...; then Castillo pulled out a small pocket pistol of only .22 caliber, thinking it

Almost a derringer, a Colt Model 1862 .36 Police revolver skillfully modified to serve as an easily concealed yet effective "belly gun." The loading lever has been removed, the barrel shortened, and the reshaped butt reduced in size. Examples of similarly modified M1862 Colts can be found in several western museums. (Courtesy: Los Angeles County Museum of Natural History, CA)

might serve to intimidate Mathers. But . . . Mathers pulled his gun and fired, killing young Castillo instantly. Young Castillo had not intended to shoot anyone, but under the code of the time the display of even so harmless a weapon as a .22-caliber gun was enough to warrant the other man's firing. This left no other course open to the jury . . . than to render the verdict that it was homicide in self-defense.[23]

Two of the more unusual pocket revolvers of the day occasionally were offered by frontier dealers. One of these was the Protector "palm pistol," somewhat reminiscent of a large pocket watch. Jacque Tarbiaux of Paris, France, took out European patents, and American patents were granted him in 1883. Two firms produced these unusual "squeezer" pistols in the United States in the 1890s, the Chicago Firearms Company and the Minneapolis Firearms Company. To load with .32 extra short cartridges, one

removed a side plate and took out the flat turret cylinder. The weapon was held in the palm of the hand with the barrel protruding between the third and fourth fingers. Squeezing the hand compressed the lever at the rear and fired the pistol in double action fashion.

Equally as distinctive in shape were the My Friend "knuckle-duster" pocket revolvers in various styles, most with an all-metal frame shaped conveniently to strike a blow in a hand-to-hand scuffle. Produced by James Reid of Catskill, New York, from the late 1860s to the early 1880s, most were .22 caliber, a lesser number .32, and perhaps 150 or so .41s. Most recognizable are those Reids with no barrel as such, the bullet exiting directly from the chamber.

Neither derringer, fish, nor fowl were compact alarm or burglar guns, designed to discharge either a ball or at least a blank cartridge to make a loud report when a door or window was opened. Such a device was the primary element in a practical joke Miguel Otero and another young man working in a Colorado supply house played in 1877. They resented the fact that one of the clerks had a key to the store, which allowed him to return to his lodging there late at night.

None of us had been accorded this privilege save Collier and that fact rankled in our bosoms. As the door Collier entered was directly under Mr. Sellar's room, we decided to make the latter aware of what Collier was up to. We had recently secured one of the contrivances known at that time as "burglar pistols," a device that screwed into the door frame and, by the means of a still spring, held a pistol in such a position that anyone opening the door would find the barrel pointing directly at his face. There was also a lever that would cause the pistol hammer to fall and fire the load. We loaded the old pistol with plenty of powder and paper wads and hid ourselves near the door to see the fun. Shortly after midnight, Collier entered the office and tiptoed to the door. As he quietly opened the door, the spring flew back, and off went the pistol with a report loud enough to wake the dead. Before the others came to see what it was all about, Kelly and I removed the pistol and no one could discover how it all happened.[24]

Earlier when Otero was only a boy of ten or eleven he suffered a serious gunshot wound. One night he released the family dog, which was barking excitedly. Quickly the canine grabbed the leg of a boy named Turner, son of a saloon owner, who was attempting to steal from the woodpile. Miguel called the dog off and Turner hurdled the fence and escaped. He got his revenge a few days later. Otero and a few friends had been practicing with revolvers and were cleaning them with several boxes of cartridges lying open nearby when Turner approached.

In view of what happened, Turner must have succeeded in slipping a cartridge from one of the boxes and inserting it into my brother's pistol. Pointing the gun directly at me, Turner said: "Here, take this," and, suspecting nothing, I at once grabbed the barrel in my hand. Instinctively, I turned the pistol away from my stomach, and well for me that I did, for Turner pulled the trigger and the next second my right hand was literally torn to pieces.

A doctor worked diligently to repair the damaged hand and fortunately the wound finally healed almost without a scar.[25]

However size often did matter in the west and small pocket guns sometimes were ridiculed as one westerner recalled.

My uncle...had a wealth of stories, but I remember only one of them, a story having to do with the contempt of the Westerner for "the parlor" or anything but "a man's size gun."...One day on an overland train the porter, while cleaning out the smoking compartment, stooped over and dropped a derringer from his hind pocket. My uncle, darting upon it, had traded a ten-dollar bill for the privilege of throwing the filthy thing out of the window. This tradition concerning "the parlor gun" still persists. To the Far Westener there is nothing so humiliating as to be threatened with or shot by a small caliber revolver.[26]

The Slaughter
of the Bison

There ... in my plain sight grazed the entire buffalo army of Southern Kansas.
As far as the western horizon the whole earth was black with them.
The desire to shoot, kill or capture utterly passed away.
I only wished to look, and look till I could realize or find
some speech for the greatness of nature that silenced me.
— Anonymous, 1872

It's been estimated that in the early 1800s there were between sixty and seventy-five million bison grazing on the plains of North America. The herds seemed endless, but by 1900 there would be fewer than one thousand wild bison remaining. In 1868 while campaigning in Oklahoma, Gen. Phil Sheridan asked ten of his officers to estimate the number of bison they had seen during that single day. The average estimate was 243,000. These herds not only provided an abundant source of meat and other products, but the Plains Indians established a lucrative trade in tanned bison robes which by the early 1840s overshadowed the beaver skin as a prime commodity in the western fur trade. While the Native Americans were sometimes wasteful in their hunting of the bison, it was during the period from about 1871 to the mid-1880s that the destruction of the gigantic herds by white hunters took place.[1]

At Fort Pierre in Sioux country, Pierre Chouteau Jr. & Co. in 1843 was purchasing about seventeen thousand robes per year, paying $2 to $4 for bison hides painted by Indian women, $2.50 to $3.25 for "seasonal" (winter) robes,

$1.50 to $3.00 for summer robes, and $3 to $6 per dozen for bison tongues. The previous year an employee wrote: "Our beaver returns are small, say about seven packs [of sixty to eighty skins per pack]." Chouteau reportedly brought forty-five thousand bison robes to St. Louis in 1839 and sixty-seven thousand in '40. The St. Louis market would grow to ninety thousand annually in the 1840s and one hundred thousand in the next two decades in addition to growing sales of buffalo tongues and other meat. Typical retail prices for trade items, which included hundreds of different products, in the early '40s at Fort Pierre were $1 per pound for coffee, sugar, or flour; $8 to $12 for Northwest trade guns; gunpowder 26¢ per pound; 50¢ for a powder horn; and $1 for a tomahawk.[2]

George Wilkins Kendall described buffalo hunting on the southwestern plains in 1841:

The whites have two ways of hunting these animals. One is to creep up within a short distance, and shoot them with a rifle carrying a heavy ball, or with a musket—a mode of hunting seldom resorted to except by those who are in want of meat. The other way is to sally out after them on horseback, armed with heavy holster-pistols, run alongside, while under full speed, and shoot from the saddle. Of all hunting in the world this is probably the most exciting, at the same time involving the sportsman in no little danger.[3]

As he prepared for a buffalo hunt on horseback, he described himself as including in his saddle holsters "a bell-muzzled affair which was loaded with two or three balls, and some twenty-five or thirty buckshot" in addition to a five-shot Colt Paterson revolver and a "heavy Harpers Ferry [.54 caliber Model 1805] dragoon-pistol, throwing a large ball with great force and accuracy."[4]

George Andrew Gordon was educated at Miami University in Ohio and Wabash College, Indiana. He was admitted to the bar in 1844 but poor health prompted him to visit the central plains. On a whim in February 1846, he agreed to join four others on a meandering bison hunt. Two were gray-haired French Canadians who for years had hunted and trapped in the northwest. His other two companions were from Arkansas, one being a young doctor.

These men were each armed with a flint-lock rifle and a huge bowie knife. One of the graybeards also had a small ax hung to his saddle.... I had no weapon more dangerous than a penknife, but one of the graybeards offered to loan me a rifle if I would join them. I accepted the offer.... The gun given me was a long-barreled heavy rifle, that shot an ounce ball [.54 caliber].... I named the gun "Long Tom," as I believed a gun in the navy was known by that name. It would not pay to shoot small birds with Long Tom, but if a ball from him struck a buffalo on the side near the termination of the long hair, his days were numbered.

We killed many buffalo that we did not use even so much as the tongue. Such a "slaughter of the innocents" appearing to me inhuman, if not criminal, I proposed that we kill no more than we needed for food. This meant the killing of at least one buffalo a day, as we had fresh meat every night, but could not incumber

[sic] ourselves with any unnecessary weight during the day.[5]

Writing of his time in the west in the early 1840s, Rufus Sage recommended:

A gun, suitable for killing this kind of game [bison], should never carry to exceed forty balls to the pound [.49 caliber]—a lesser bore would be almost entirely useless. The distance generally required for a shot, the smallness of the ball, its liability to variation from the wind, and its failure to "hold up" and retain its force, contribute to render the use of such a piece little else than idle waste of ammunition.[6]

To many, hunting bison from horseback was exhilarating. In 1857, newly graduated from West Point, Lt. Samuel W. Ferguson joined the 2nd Dragoons, a component of Albert Sidney Johnston's expedition against the Mormons in Utah Territory. He and Lt. Marmaduke set out on a buffalo chase near Fort Kearny and he quickly found himself overtaken with excitement and dispensed with caution.

I never was so excited in my life, and blazed away, first at one, then at another, and when the loads in one pistol were exhausted I drew another, until it also was emptied. Then I drew rein and remembered the caution to look out for Indians. Making haste to reload, I found that I had lost my brand-new navy [Model 1851] Colt from its scabbard, and that I had even fired my Sharps carbine—which I had firmly intended to hold loaded in reserve.[7]

Thrilling as a chase might be, it was dangerous to both rider and mount. One's horse or mule might shy at a gun's discharge, stumble, or step in a prairie dog hole and throw its rider into the path of the herd. Occasionally a maddened bison turned on its pursuer and hooked horse or rider with a horn. A hunter named McCarey suffered a serious accident of another form in 1834.

He had been running a buffalo, and was about reloading the gun which he had just discharged. when the powder in his horn was ignited by a burning wad remaining in the barrel; the horn was burst to fragments,

"A Buffalo Hunt," a drawing by Theodore R. Davis, many of whose western scenes appeared in *Harper's Weekly* in the 1860s and 1870s.

the poor man dashed from his horse, and his face, neck and hands, [were] burnt in a shocking manner.[8]

A similar accident befell a hunter on the South Saskatchewan River north of the Montana border in 1857, running buffalo with his pipe in his mouth.

> He . . . commenced to reload . . . in the ordinary manner, by pouring out powder from his horn into the palm of the left hand, when a spark fell from his pipe and set the powder alight; the fire jumped to the powder-horn and blew it to pieces. The man, astonishingly, escaped without a serious burn, but lost his whiskers, eyebrows, and eyelashes. The Peacemaker [a Cree chief], too, ran buffalo that morning. He killed a good cow, but complained of having lost his ramrod. He went back some distance to look for it. When at length he abandoned

his search and returned to cut up his animal, he found the remains of his ramrod in its body. He had loaded with the ramrod and, in the excitement of the chase, had forgotten to withdraw it before firing.[9]

During a buffalo hunt in 1846, Frances Parkman's mule was startled by a rabbit which sprang up almost under its hooves. Parkman was thrown and his percussion rifle discharged when it struck the ground.

> Soon recovering myself, I arose, [and] picked up the rifle. . . . The stock was cracked, and the main screw broken, so that the lock had to be tied in its place with a string; yet happily it was not rendered totally unserviceable. I wiped it out, reloaded it, . . . and mounted again.[10]

On his third western exploring expedition, Capt. John C. Fremont almost became a fatality due to his own carelessness during a buffalo chase when one of his pistols fired unexpectedly and the ball barely missed his head. "My holster pistols were a hair-trigger pair," he explained.[11]

Another participant in Fremont's third expedition in 1845 decried the waste which wanton hunting involved.

> Many a veteran bull fell beneath our rifles and the savage people of these desert and untillable tracts can not be censured for detesting the whitefaces, who pass through the only pastures with which nature has provided him, & slay his cattle which feed therein & which form his only means of subsistence.[12]

Among the most colorful of the early non-Indian buffalo hunters in the southwest was the Mexican *cibolero*. Josiah Gregg left a description of one he encountered.

> We observed a horseman approaching, who excited at first considerable curiosity. His picturesque costume, and peculiarity of deportment, however soon showed him to be a Mexican *Cibolero* or buffalo-hunter. These hardy devotees of the chase usually wear leathern trousers and jackets, and flat straw hats; while, swung upon the shoulder of each hangs his *carcage* or quiver of bow and arrows. The long handle of their lance being set in a case, and suspended by the side with a strap from the pommel of the saddle, leaves the point waving high over the head, with a tassel of gay parti-colored stuffs dangling at the tip of the scabbard. Their fusil, if they happen to have one, is suspended in like manner at the other side, with a stopper in the muzzle fantastically tasseled.[13]

In 1874 John R. Cook found Mexican lancers in New Mexico still hunting bison from horseback and joined in one of their hunts.

A participant in Fremont's 1853–54 exploration described a more unusual hunting method.

> A Delaware Indian, in hunting buffaloes, when near enough to shoot, rests his rifle on his saddle, balances himself in his stirrup on one leg; the other is thrown over the rifle to steady it. He then leans on one side, until his eye is on a level with the object, takes a quick sight, and fires while riding at full speed, rarely missing his mark, and seldom chasing one animal further than a mile.[14]

During the construction of the Union Pacific and Kansas Pacific rail lines after the Civil War, as workers sang such songs as "Whoops Along, Luiza Jane" and "Brinon on the Moor," the companies hired hunters to provide meat for their messes. Young William F. Cody in October of 1867 went to work for the Goddard Brothers who had a contract to feed Kansas Pacific workers. Cody received $500 a month to provide a dozen bison per day— "twenty-four hams and twelve humps, as only the hump and hindquarters of each animal were utilized," he later wrote. He went on to kill 4,280 bison for his employer. His choice of a rifle was a .50–70 Springfield which he described as "my celebrated buffalo-killer, 'Lucretia Borgia,'—a newly-improved breech-loading needle gun, which I had obtained from the government." A ditty concerning Cody's hunting prowess circulated among the construction workers.

> Buffalo Bill, Buffalo Bill
> Never missed and never will;
> Always aims and shoots to kill
> And the company pays his buffalo bill.[15]

It was while hunting for the Kansas Pacific that Cody engaged in a shooting contest with guide and scout, Billy Comstock. "We were to hunt one day of eight hours, beginning at eight o'clock in the morning. The wager was $500 a side, and the man who should kill the greater number of buffaloes from horseback was to be declared the winner. Incidentally my title of 'Buffalo Bill' was at stake." Cody rode his favorite, "Brigham," which he considered to be the best buffalo horse in the country. He also felt his .50 caliber Springfield was an added advantage. "Comstock's Henry rifle, though it could fire more rapidly than mine, did not . . . carry powder and lead enough to equal my weapon in execution." When the day ended, Cody was the undisputed winner, with sixty-nine kills versus Comstock's forty-six.[16]

The railroads also took commercial advantage of the bison herds before they were wiped out. The Union Pacific and Kansas Pacific promoted excursions to bring hunters to participate in the slaughter. One advertised excursion from Leavenworth, Kansas, left on Tuesday,

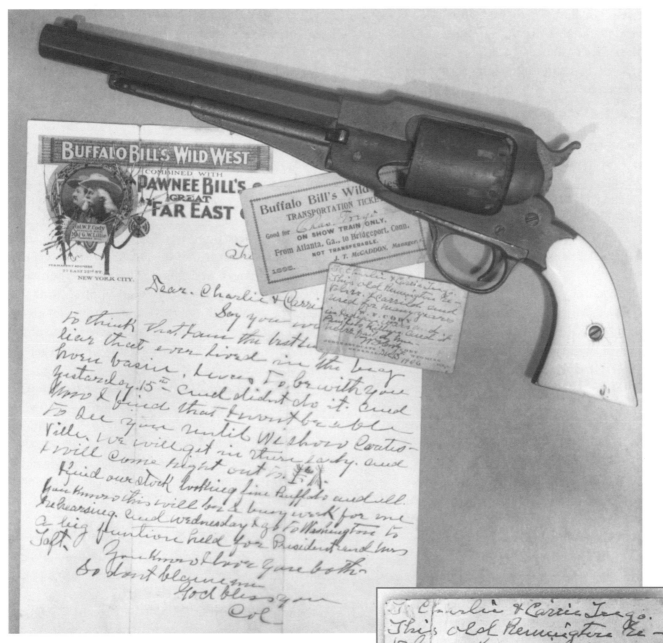

Well known to the world as a buffalo hunter was William F. "Buffalo Bill" Cody. His .50 caliber Springfield "trap-door" rifle "Lucretia Borgia" was paired with a .44 Remington revolver. In 1906 the handgun was sent to his close friend and business associate Charles Trego and his wife, Carrie, with a card which read: "This old Remington revolver I carried and used for many years in Indian wars and buffalo killing and it never failed me. W. F. Cody." (Courtesy: Charles Trego Family via Norm Flayderman)

October 27, 1868, and would return the following Friday for a roundtrip fare of only $10. "Ample time will be had for a grand Buffalo HUNT ON THE PLAINS. Buffaloes are so numerous along the road that they are shot from the cars nearly every day. On our last excursion our party killed twenty buffaloes in a hunt of six hours."[17]

Before scheduled timetables were established, Kansas Pacific engineers sometimes slowed or stopped their trains to allow passengers to shoot at passing herds. John Putnam, an attorney from Topeka, Kansas, wrote in 1868: "We failed to bag a buffalo. I did not shoot, having ill defined ideas as to hunting rifles, which end you

put the load in and which end you let it out at."
Nevertheless, Putnam's excited shouting mingled with
that of the other passengers.[18]

The practice of shooting from moving trains continued even when it was not practical to stop and recover
the meat.

> A most cruel and foolish fashion prevails
> on these trains, of shooting the poor animals from the cars . . . for the mere pleasure
> of killing. Of course, many more are missed
> than hit but when they are wounded there
> is no means of stopping to dispatch them;
> so they die in misery along the line.[19]

Similarly, in 1868 en route by train to Fort Hays, Kansas,
a passenger was startled by shots from a forward car. In the
car in which he was riding, he saw twenty-five breech loading rifles and a large chest of "metallic center primed needle-cartridges [probably for .50–70 Springfield rifles],
provided by the railroad company, for the use of the
employees to defend . . . against Indian attacks." Several of
the train crew rushed into his car and grabbed rifles and
handfuls of cartridges.

> I re-examined my own rifle, buckled on a
> pair of pistols, slung my cartridge box over
> my shoulder and started forward. . . . At this
> moment a shout "Buffalo crossing the
> track," was heard and bang! bang! bang!
> simultaneously went several pieces. Poking
> my head out of the car window I observed
> a small herd of six buffalo bulls running at
> full speed parallel with the train, about a
> hundred yards ahead and not more than
> sixty feet from the track.

Eventually two of the unfortunate animals fell to the fusillade of bullets. "After cutting out the tongues and a few
strips of 'hump' the rest of the two immense carcasses were
left as a dainty and abundant repast for the wolf."[20]

In the words of one observer in 1872:

> A needle-gun [Springfield .50–70] or [an
> imported English] Wesley Richards rifle
> are the best to use for buffalo shooting, on
> account of carrying a heavy ball; they are
> very tenacious of life, and as many as
> twenty-five bullets have been known to
> hit one before bringing him down. . . .

> Parties [of hunters] may get off [the
> train] at almost any station beyond Ellis
> [Kansas] . . . and get good shooting at
> these noble beasts.[21]

While Col. George Custer was stationed at Fort Hays,
Kansas, large numbers of dignitaries from the east and
abroad arrived by train to hunt bison with him. In the fall
of 1870, his wife, Libbie, complained in a letter to her cousin:
"We had so many buffalo hunts this summer for strangers
who came with letters to Autie [Custer], that it is such a
bore to us."[22]

In 1870 there were several main herds on the Great
Plains, extending from the Montana-Canadian border into
Texas, their ranges overlapping. Commercial hunting for
meat and hides for robes and "sport hunting" had persisted for decades, but only had modest impact on the
herds. Yet their extermination took little more than fifteen
years after professional hunting for hides began in
earnest in Kansas in 1871.

Meat either salted, dried, smoked, or fresh was an
important commodity, particularly in winter when
spoilage wasn't a problem. Even during the hide-hunting
era, the Cator brothers reportedly in one year made $800
more selling meat at 2¢ a pound than they did from hides.
But the primary impetus for the slaughter was the development of a process to convert the hides into high-grade
industrial leather, such as machinery drive belts. According
to Col. Richard Dodge's estimates, the railroads—principally the Atchison, Topeka & Santa Fe, the Union Pacific,
and the Kansas Pacific—in the three years of 1872–74 had
transported 1,378,359 untanned "flint" hides, 6,751,200
pounds of buffalo meat, and 32,380,050 pounds of bones,
and he felt these figures may have been conservative. In
the winter of 1872–73, just the firm of Charles Rath and
his associates shipped by rail two hundred carloads of
bison hindquarters, two carloads of tongues, and one hundred thousand hides out of Dodge City. Any numbers for
hides shipped represented only a portion of the animals
killed, for some hides were ruined by careless skinning or
by insects and others were transported by wagon rather
than railroad.[23]

The Wichita *Eagle* for November 7 of 1872 estimated
there were between one and two thousand hide hunters
working just in the vicinity, each man killing an average
of fifteen per day. Faced with the increasing scarcity of bison
in Kansas, J. Wright Mooar and John Webb in July of 1873
journeyed south into Texas, each with "200 rounds of
ammunition, big 50 [caliber] guns, and a pocket full of salt."
They encountered large numbers, but the land between was

A bison hunters' camp in Texas with hides pegged out on the ground and tongues and other meat hung up to dry. (Courtesy: Western History Collection, University of Oklahoma Library, Norman)

considered unsafe since it was Indian territory, controlled by Kiowas, Comanches, and Cheyennes who had been granted hunting rights there by the Medicine Lodge Treaty of 1867. Upon their return to Kansas, Mooar and another hunter approached the commandant at Fort Dodge asking what his policy would be if they were to cross the neutral strip to hunt in Texas. "Boys, if I were a buffalo hunter, I would hunt buffalo where buffalo are," was Col. Dodge's response. That sealed the fate of the Texas herd as Kansas hunters prepared to move south.[24]

Col. Richard I. Dodge recorded what he observed as a typical professional hunter's outfit.

> The most approved hunting party consists of four men, one shooter, two skinners and one man to cook, stretch hides and take care of camp. Where buffalo are very plenty the number of skinners was increased. A light wagon, drawn by two horses or mules, takes the outfit into the wilderness, and brings into camp, the skins taken each day.

> The outfit is most meager, a sack of flour, a side of bacon, five pounds of coffee, ten of sugar, a little salt, and possibly a few beans is a month's supply. A common or A tent furnishes shelter, a couple of blankets for each man is bed. One or more of Sharp's or Remington's heaviest sporting rifles and an unlimited supply of ammunition is the armament, while a coffee pot, dutch oven, frying pan, four tin plates and four tin cups, constitute the kitchen and table furniture. The skinning knives do duty at the platter, and "fingers were made before forks." Nor must be forgotten one or more ten gallon kegs of water, as the camp may of necessity be far away from a stream.[25]

Indians in the region resisted with force, and the slaughter of the bison was a major cause of the Red River War of 1874. A trading post established at a site known as Adobe Walls about fifty miles northeast of Amarillo

An octagonal-barrel Remington No. 2 sporting rifle in .50–70 caliber. (Courtesy: Ed Curtis via Roy Marcot)

Rath & Wright's hide yard. (Courtesy: National Archives, National Park Service photo #79-M-4)

became the scene of an historic encounter between twenty-nine white civilians (including one woman) and four hundred to six hundred Comanches, Kiowas, Cheyennes, and Arapahoes on June 27 of 1874. Fortunately for the besieged whites, Billy Dixon, Bat Masterson, and perhaps seven other buffalo hunters were present and their prowess with their Sharps rifles was a vital factor in the outcome of the day-long stand. It was fortunate for Dixon, who had lost his .50 Sharps in the Canadian River, that there was a new .44 Sharps on hand at Rath & Wright's store which had not been picked up yet by the intended buyer. Dixon obtained a case of ammunition for it but during the fight was able to exchange the .44 for his preference, a "big 50" Sharps.[26]

One particularly tragic episode occurred several days after the actual battle. Hanna Olds, the only woman present, had come with her husband Billy to establish a restaurant. As her husband was climbing down a ladder from a lookout position with rifle in hand, the gun somehow discharged, blowing the top of his head off. Hanna came into the room just as her husband fell dead, last of the four white men killed there.

Another historic incident occurred about the same time, Billy Dixon's controversial "long shot." After the battle, a party of about fifteen Indians appeared on a bluff overlooking Adobe Walls Creek and someone suggested that Dixon try his "big 50" Sharps. He did so, and an Indian fell from his horse. Dixon described the distance of the shot

Bison slaughtered for their hides. A Sharps has been leaned against one carcass.

as "not far from seven-eights of a mile" or about fifteen hundred yards. Dixon was skilled, well versed in estimating distance, and knew the capabilities of the rifle. "I was admittedly a good marksman, yet this was what might be called a 'scratch' [lucky] shot." Modern tests showed that a bullet from a .50 Sharps retained sufficient energy and velocity to kill at that range and considering that Dixon was firing at a group of men, the shot was definitely possible even though it has been questioned.[27]

As hunters moved south from Kansas, Fort Griffin, west of Fort Worth, became the supply and marketing center of the Texas hide trade during the decimation of the southern herd. Twenty-year-old Joe McCombs led one of the first hunting expeditions out of the fort on Christmas of 1874, while the army was still mopping up from the Red River campaigns against Indians of the region. The firm formed by Frank Conrad and Charles Rath became the largest of the outfitters in the town of Griffin and their magazine reportedly contained thirty tons of lead and five tons of gunpowder. They also had a hide lot of about four acres. Shipping hides was a simpler operation after a railroad reached Fort Worth in mid-1876.[28]

One who visited Griffin in January 1877 described their store as:

> An immense house of rooms, crowded to
> their utmost with merchandise, with forty
> or fifty wagons waiting to be loaded and
> perhaps a hundred hunters purchasing
> supplies. I was told that yesterday Mr.
> Conrad's sales amounted to nearly $4000,
> about $2500 of which was guns and
> ammunition just received.[29]

An area known as the Flat grew up near the fort and became a notorious center of recreation for buffalo hunters and skinners as well as drovers and others. A newcomer from Missouri in the fall of 1876 was surprised

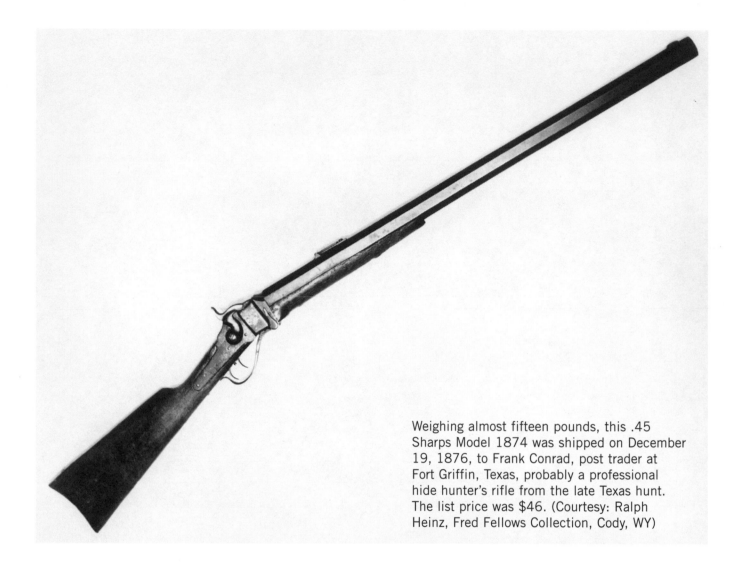

Weighing almost fifteen pounds, this .45 Sharps Model 1874 was shipped on December 19, 1876, to Frank Conrad, post trader at Fort Griffin, Texas, probably a professional hide hunter's rifle from the late Texas hunt. The list price was $46. (Courtesy: Ralph Heinz, Fred Fellows Collection, Cody, WY)

when in one of the dance halls, "I saw men and women dancing without a stitch of clothing on." Another man observed a buffalo hunter who marketed his season's hides for $1,500 and the next day had to borrow money for breakfast.

> The gamblers had gotten all of it. The ordinary fellow did not have the ghost of a show in those gambling halls. Most all of the games were crooked and if they could not get it one way, they would another. Frequently they would get their victims drunk and "roll" them and take it away from them in that way.[30]

In December 1876 P. C. Bicknell wrote from a camp on the North Concho River in Texas by the light of a "bitch" or a piece of cotton cord in a plate filled with buffalo tallow. He informed his friend he had traded a horse for a Sharps .50 caliber carbine and fourteen or sixteen cartridges. With no more cartridges, he skinned, staked out the hides to dry, and cooked while his partner hunted.

> My partner shoots a Maynard 40 cal-ring ball 70 gr. Powder 340 gr. lead.... The Maynard seems to do as good work as the .44-cal. Sharps. The only objection my partner has to it is that it ought to shoot a patch ball. Shooting 20 or 30 shots inside of half an hour leads the gun & probably wears it out sooner. That .40 cal. Sharps must be the Boss gun. You see it shoots the same amount of powder as the .44 with a longer ball. The Winchester is a laughing stock among these men—they would not take one as a gift if they had to use it.[31]

In Texas in late '74, John R. Cook joined the slaughter, first as a skinner at 30¢ per hide. He was "promoted" after he killed two bison with an Enfield "needle gun,"

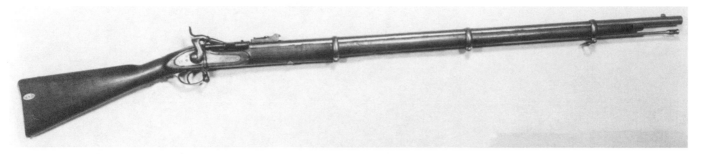

British Enfield .577 rifle musket converted to a breechloader by the system adopted by England but designed by an American, Jacob Snider. (Courtesy: National Park Service, Fuller Collection, Chickamauga-Chattanooga National Military Park, Fort Oglethorpe, GA)

Although not mentioned nearly as frequently in nineteenth-century writings as the Sharps, the Remington enjoyed some popularity among the professional hunters, such as this No. 1 in .45–70 caliber fitted with a scope sight. (Courtesy: Roy Marcot)

probably a British Enfield rifle musket of Civil War vintage converted to a breechloader by the Snider system. His employer remarked: "Well, I'll be darned! I've threatened to throw that old gun away several times, but I'm glad . . . I didn't." Soon after, Cook upgraded his equipment.

> I was fortunate enough to buy . . . a Sharp's 44-caliber rifle, reloading outfit, belt, and 150 shells. The man had used the gun only a short time, and seventy-five of the shells had never been loaded. I got the gun and his interest in the entire buffalo range for thirty-six dollars, he having met with the misfortune of shooting himself seriously, but not fatally, in the right side with the same gun. . . . It was an elegant fine-sighted gun, with buckhorn sights.[32]

On New Year's Day 1875, he and his five companions set out with provisions for three months. "We had 250 pounds of St. Louis shot-tower lead in bars done up in 25-pound sacks; 4000 primers, three 25-pound cans of Dupont powder, and one 6-pound can." Before leaving

Fort Elliott, he made the rounds of the garrison with a sack gathering all the newspapers and magazines he could beg. In the fall of 1876, he bought a .45 Sharps Creedmore at the fort.

> Most of the old hunters were now using that caliber. They were long-range guns, and by continuous practice most hunters had become good judges of distances and had learned to shoot pretty accurately by raising the muzzle of the gun, without raising or lowering the rear graduated sights.[33]

One hunter Cook encountered was "Arkansas Jack" Greathouse whose Sharps is illustrated here. Napoleon Bonaparte Greathouse had been clawed by a cougar in Arkansas and bore the scars of the encounter. "And a horrible-looking wound it had been. Commencing at the collar-bone, and running to the lower end of his ribs, were unmistakable marks of all the claws of one foot of the animal he had battled with." One of Cook's hunting companions also had a close call with a cougar he cornered in a gulch alone with old "Once-in-a-while." "This was the name

Luther S. Kelly, better known as "Yellowstone Kelly," was a professional hunter, guide, and army scout in the 1870s. After adventures in Alaska and the Philippine Islands, he became an Indian agent at the San Carlos Apache Reservation in Arizona before retiring to a fruit ranch in California. There is strong evidence that this six-teen-pound deluxe .44–90 Sharps Sporting Rifle (#C53209) with scope sight was his. The first time it was broken at the wrist it was repaired with two German silver inlaid strips; the second break was remedied with a rawhide wrap covering the entire wrist. (Photo by Ron Paxton, courtesy Bob Butterfield)

of an old army needle-gun [Springfield?] whose firing pin was so worn that one would have to snap it three or four times before it would explode the primer. Some shells it would not fire at all, and again others would go at first trial. Hence, we named that gun 'Once-in-a-while.'"[34]

By 1879 the Texas herd was largely gone, leaving forlorn bands of orphaned calves. One of the last Texas hunts was conducted by four hunters out of San Angelo in November 1879. They found that bones littered the plains where thousands of bison once had grazed. The party saw only twenty-two bison and killed twelve of those, then poisoned and trapped more than six hundred coyotes. They sold the bison hides for $5 each and the coyote skins for 50¢ apiece.[35]

Corp. E. A. Bode served between 1877 and 1882 with the 16th Infantry and in all his travels in Indian Territory (Oklahoma), Kansas, and Texas, to his knowledge he never saw a genuine wild buffalo. "Had it not been for the cavalry who killed a few in Texas and brought some of the meat home I never would have had an opportunity to taste buffalo meat."[36]

The final extermination of the northern herd came later, but by 1884 it had been largely killed off as the bison fell to the hunters' rifles in Montana. Existing game laws enacted as early as 1878 were ignored and in the spring of 1882, eighty-two thousand hides reportedly were shipped out of Miles City, Montana, alone, piled high on the decks of the riverboats. The following year, the

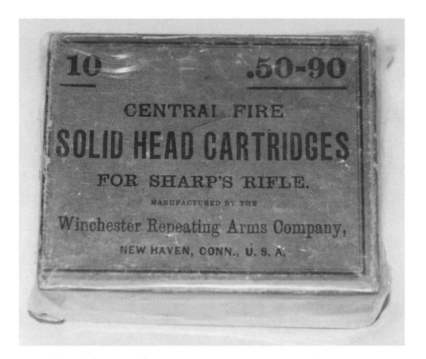

The label on this box of ten Winchester .50–90 cartridges is marked "FOR SHARP'S RIFLE." Hunter Jack Greathouse's "big fifty" Sharps (#C53401) was shipped to Frank Conrad at Fort Griffin, Texas, in 1876. The heavy (fifteen-pound) pullover-style buffalo hide coat is photographed with a cartridge belt marked "Denver Mfg. Co." with loops for .50 caliber cartridges. (Courtesy: Lewis Wagner)

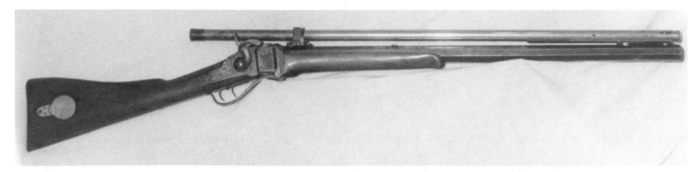

A '74 Sharps with telescopic sight invoiced to Cheyenne, Wyoming, dealer P. Bergersen. (Courtesy: Dennis Brooks)

Sign advertising the services of P. Bergersen, gunsmith and dealer in Cheyenne. (Courtesy: Wyoming State Museum, Cheyenne)

number of hides shipped had dwindled to only eight thousand or so. The quantity of hides hauled by the Northern Pacific Railroad dropped dramatically as well, although in 1884 the railroad carried a single load of bones weighing six hundred tons.[37]

A number of prominent westerners at one time were buffalo hunters—famed lawmen Bill Tilghman, Ed and Bat Masterson, and Wyatt Earp, as well, of course, as Buffalo Bill Cody, Billy Dixon, and others. Frank Freund, one of the premier frontier gunsmiths,

also hunted "the big woolies." Perhaps his hunting experience prompted his improvements on the Sharps action which he did by designing double bilateral extractors. He also redesigned the breechblock to provide a camming action to increase leverage when loading a cartridge into the chamber.

The hide-hunting profession has a somewhat romantic image today among some, but it was a hard, dangerous, and bloody undertaking. A cowboy from the northern plains had a strong opinion on the subject:

Fortunately original Sharps factory shipping records exist for many Model 1874 rifles. These records indicate this sporting rifle (#162075) was shipped to Conrad & Rath at Fort Griffin, Texas, on October 29, 1877, as a .45 with 30-inch octagonal barrel and double set triggers. The weight was fifteen pounds, nine ounces and cost $46. "The Flat," a settlement close to the fort, was said to have "a man for breakfast every morning." (Photo by Gary Roedl, courtesy William T. Goodman)

Leather scabbard, handmade ripping knife, and butcher's sharpening steel thought to have belonged to a Miles City, Montana, bison hunter. (Courtesy: Ralph Heinz, Fred Fellows Collection, Cody, WY)

Cowpunchers and buffalo hunters didn't mix much, and never would have even if the buffalo hunters hadn't went [*sic*] out of the picture when they did. The buffalo hunters was [*sic*] a rough class—they had to be, to lead the life they led.... All this slaughter was a put-up job on the part of the government, to control the Indians by getting rid of their food supply. And in a way it couldn't be helped. But just the same it was a low-down dirty way of doing the business, and the cowpunchers as a rule had some sympathy with the Indians. You would hear them say it was a damn shame.

The buffalo hunters didn't wash, and looked like animals. They dressed in strong,

John Leasure, a 7th Cavalry trooper, sold this percussion Sharps Model 1853 sporting rifle about 1878 when he ordered a metallic cartridge Sharps, planning to hunt bison professionally following his discharge. Frank Mista purchased it for his use, unable to afford any other Sharps. Long after the destruction of the northern herd, Mista became a wrangler with Buffalo Bill's Wild West Show (1906–16). (Photo by Gary Roedl, courtesy William T. Goodman)

heavy, warm clothes and never changed them. You would see three or four of them walk up to a bar, reach down inside their clothes and see who would catch the first louse for the drinks. They were lousy and proud of it.[38]

The wanton slaughter of the bison herds shocked many people. Texas lawmakers in 1875 considered a bill that would have provided some protection for the beasts, but Gen. Phil Sheridan argued vehemently against it. Instead, he argued, the hunters should be given medals, one side showing a dead bison and a sad Indian on the other.

[Hunters] have done more in the last two years, and will do more in the next years, to settle the vexed Indian question, than the entire regular army has done in the last thirty years. They are destroying the Indians' commissary.... Send them powder and lead, if you will, but for the sake of a lasting peace, let them kill, skin, and sell until the buffaloes are exterminated. Then your prairies can be covered with speckled cattle and the festive cowboy, who follows the hunter as a...forerunner of an advanced civilization.[39]

The bill failed.

One of Sheridan's fellow officers, Lt. Col. A. G. Brackett of the 2nd Cavalry, disagreed with his commander. "The wholesale butchery of buffaloes upon the plains is as needless as it is cruel. Hundreds and hundreds of them have been killed in the most wanton manner, or for their tongues alone."[40]

In the same tone, the Hutchinson (Kansas) *News* as early as August 1, 1872, expressed concern for wasteful killing. A party of twenty-three men, women, and boys spent almost a week south of the Arkansas River where they found thousands of bison.

[They] had a good time shooting at them. They secured four very fine ones and wounded several others that got away. Miss Ninde shot a very large animal and her little brother 11 years old sent a bullet into another with such force as to knock him down although he afterwards escaped. Notwithstanding the success of their expedition, [they] express the intention to kill no more buffalo until cold weather. This is in consequence of all the meat secured...spoiling. We hope they will stick to their determination, and that their example will be followed by the rest of the people of the Arkansas Valley. The wanton and wholesale destruction of buffalo is outrageous and we would be glad if the U.S. Congress would pass a law restraining the above.[41]

A writer for the same paper in October of 1872 observed that:

Some of the hunters are in quest of meat, but a very large majority hunt to kill for

Dealer F. C. Zimmerman of Dodge City, Kansas, received this rifle (#C52860) in a shipment of twenty such .50–70 military-style M1874 Sharps, shipped in February of 1873. The price to Zimmerman was $20, substantially less than the typical Model 1874 sporter. "Ft. Union" is carved in the stock. (Photo by Gary Roedl, courtesy William T. Goodman)

the mere sport of the thing. Experiments to see how much "lead" a certain buffalo bull can get away with are of common occurrence. This sort of sport seems to us the very acme of human cruelty and should be discouraged.[42]

In 1861, the year of Kansas statehood, the legislature passed one of its first game laws, prohibiting the taking of prairie chickens, quail, wild turkeys, partridges, and deer between April and September. Probably enforcement was rare. A bill introduced in 1872 to protect bison was vetoed by the governor; the economic gains to railroads and others from the sale and transportation of hides and meat was too great. William T. Hornaday, taxidermist for the Smithsonian Institution in 1889, wrote of the professional hunters: "If they could have obtained Gatling guns with which to mow down a whole herd at a time, beyond a doubt they would have gladly used them."[43]

Guns used during the post–Civil War slaughter were as varied as the backgrounds of the men who hunted—from former Civil War arms to the latest commercially marketed sporting rifles. The .50–70 Springfield "trapdoor." military rifle was the early choice of many; including Henry H. Raymond who hunted with the Masterson brothers—Ed, Jim, and Bartholomew ("Bat")—out of Dodge City in 1872–73. Others favored the Remington "rolling block" as it became available in various styles and calibers and single-shot Maynards or Ballards sometimes could be found in hunters' camps. No make was as frequently mentioned as the Sharps in hunters' accounts, however.

Not all hunters were professionals, able to afford the most effective rifles. Some were farmers or others seeking to supplement a meager income. They might be forced to rely on guns such as a surplus military Spencer rifle or carbine more appropriate for their purse. However without

question, the Sharps rifle, particularly the so-called Model 1874 (actually introduced in 1871), became the arm preferred by the majority of professional hunters.

Hunters purchased the 1874 Sharps in various styles and chose barrel length, sights, and weight based on personal preference whether it be the round barrel Hunter's Rifle (1875) or Business Rifle introduced in 1876, or the heavier octagonal barrel Sporting Rifle that is most often regarded as the typical Sharps "buffalo gun." Sharps factory records for 1871–73 show sales of 286 Sporting Rifles from the plant at Hartford directly to individuals and dealers in Kansas, southern Nebraska, and Kit Carson, Colorado, (less than fifty miles from the Kansas line). Although additional Sharps reached the western killing grounds through other distributors in the east and elsewhere, these records show that buyers' preferences were for .44 and .50 caliber rifles, usually with double set triggers. Most had either open or globe and peep sights; a dozen or so were sold with telescopic sights. F. C. Zimmerman was a major purchaser, first in Kit Carson and then in Dodge City, Kansas, where he advertised himself as a dealer in firearms, ammunition, hardware, tinware, groceries, grain, and lumber and as an agent for Sharps sporting rifles and Oriental powder.[44]

However according to these same records, even more (309) of the Model 1874 rifles shipped to Kansas-area dealers in these years were .50 military style, priced at about $20 compared to twice or more that figure for a sporter. These guns had a 30-inch barrel held to the full-length stock by three barrel bands. They were lighter than many of the sporting rifles and their military-style sights could be altered to suit the owner's preference. One buyer of a military model added a screw in the stock between the trigger guard and lockplate by which tension on the sear could be altered, thus creating a cheap form of set trigger.[45]

Ed Burton sent the Sharps firm a testimonial from Ellis, Kansas, in August 1872.

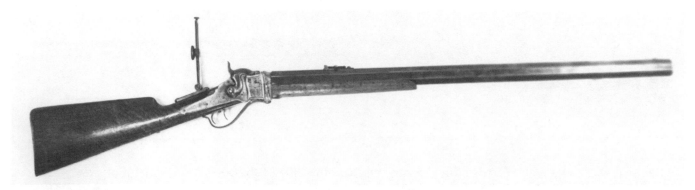

A true Texas bison hunter's rifle, a .45 M1874 Sharps with 30-inch barrel, double set triggers, and weighing just under sixteen pounds. It was invoiced to Conrad & Rath at Fort Griffin at $46. (Courtesy: Bob Butterfield)

My Partner... sent for a 44–100 Caliber Sporting Rifle last spring, and as he has retired from hunting life afterward, I took the Rifle, and have used it with the greatest satisfaction now, for sometime, Buffalo and Antelope hunting. I have used the Maynard, Peabody, Ballard, and the Government Springfield Needle Gun, but none equaled the arm manufactured by you for accuracy and especially for long range.[46]

Some hunters used sporting Sharps weighing as much as eighteen pounds, although such were tiring to carry on extended hunts. J. Wright Mooar claimed he killed sixty-five hundred bison with his fourteen-pound Sharps and fourteen thousand with his lighter eleven pounder. The former Sharps was a .50 x 2 1/2 inch with a part round/part octagonal barrel, double set triggers, and open sights shipped to dealer F. C. Zimmerman of Dodge City on August 3, 1874.

Mooar in 1871 with a party of five hunted on the Arkansas River near Fort Dodge, Kansas.

We used the Springfield Army rifle, a center fire cartridge, 70 grains of powder, a swadge ring ball 50 caliber. In 1872 the hide market was established and the Sharps Rifle Mfg. Co. developed the big 50 rifle, 90 grains of powder, a slug ball ... with paper patch, the weight of the gun was from 12 to 16 pounds.[47]

This marked the genesis in mid-1872 of the Sharps "big 50." Popular with early professional buffalo hunters, the .50–90, with ninety grains of powder in a 2 1/2-inch case, was a gun in which the .50–70 government cartridge also

could be fired. Hunter Billy Dixon used a big 50 in 1872–73 and had a Sharps .44 at the Adobe Walls fight in 1874, a gun he described as "next best" to the .50. As reported by the late Charles E. Hanson Jr., archeological studies at the site of Adobe Walls revealed that all fired rifle cartridge cases found where Hanrahan's saloon stood were either .50–70, .50–90, or .44–77. Bob Cator arrived at Adobe Walls on June 28 and stated that one of the .50–70s used there was his Remington rolling-block sporting rifle. An experienced hunter could recognize the different sound of various caliber guns. "We heard the sound of the big fifties and the more rifle-like crack of the 44's."[48]

One confusing aspect of the various .40, .44, .45, and .50 caliber Sharps metallic cartridge sporting rifles was the numerous cartridges for which they were chambered. As the late Sharps enthusiast Jerry Mayberry pointed out, whether the cartridge case was straight or bottlenecked, cases could vary in length or the same case could be loaded with various powder charges and bullet weights. An example was the .44 2 1/4-inch bottleneck cartridge, often called the .44/77, a popular load. First loaded by Sharps with seventy grains of powder, it was increased to seventy-five and when loaded by the Union Metallic Cartridge Company (UMC) and Winchester contained seventy-seven grains. Adding to the confusion, many Model 1874 Sharps were rechambered or even rebarreled later by dealers and gunsmiths for another cartridge.[49]

George W. Brown first hunted bison in 1870 for meat, which he sold initially at Fort Wallace, Kansas. It wasn't until about May of 1871 that he learned from other hunters that W. C. Lobenstein of Leavenworth, Kansas, was buying hides. Brown continued in the bloody business until 1876.

I had a big 50-caliber rifle, weighing 16 pounds with a 32-inch octagonal barrel. It used 120 grains of powder and bullets an

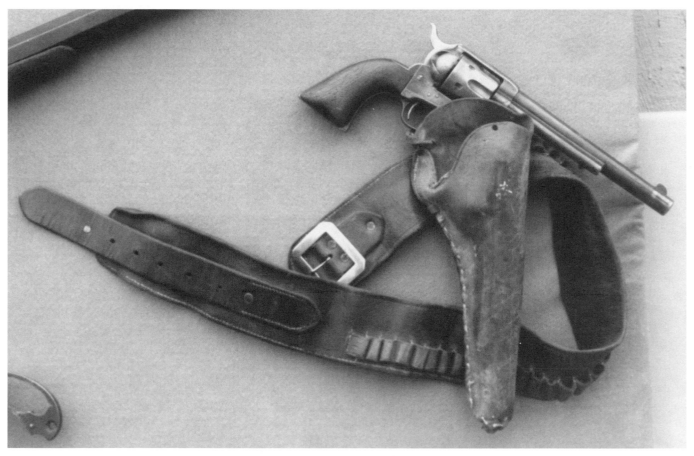

Colt Single Action (#68031) and rig owned by Benito Ortega, who used his profits from hunting bison to buy a ranch near Taos, New Mexico. (Courtesy: Ron Peterson)

inch and a quarter long. Sometimes when I was out in the main herd of buffalo with it, I would wear two belts of cartridges, each holding 42 of these big loads, and I often carried a bottle of water to pour through the barrel when it got too dirty to shoot straight.[50]

He recalled paying 50¢ per hide to have them hauled by mule train and received $2 each for cow hides and $3 each for bull hides. During the earlier Indian trade in tanned robes, a prime cow hide had brought the higher price, but in the 1870s the hunters were supplying the leather market as well and bull hides sold higher.[51]

Oliver Perry Hanna and Jim White hunted together in Montana in 1878–80 and used sixteen-pound .50 caliber Sharps. "The reason we had such heavy guns was because...when we would get what we called a 'stand' on them, the small [lightweight] guns would get so hot in a short time they would be useless."[52]

A few years earlier in Kansas, a group of entrepreneurs in Wichita got together and formed a "buffalo pool." Ben

Lampton was one of the men they hired, paying him board and 30¢ for each hide.

He started walking southwest from Wichita with a forty-five Sharpe's square-barrel [octagonal] gun and 200 rounds of cartridges in his belt. His knapsack was filled with a small frying pan, ground coffee, bacon, flour, salt, and matches. The company sent teams and wagons too later to haul supplies and hides. The drivers listened for the gun report to find him, located their camp near fuel and water, and began skinning buffaloes.[53]

It was most economical and convenient for a hunter and his skinners if he could establish a stand, doing the killing in one spot rather than scattering the carcasses over the prairie. Brown killed thirty-five in one stand.

What we called a stand is when we killed a buffalo [preferably the leader, usually a

1876 sales promotional flyer by a New York dealer in tanned buffalo robes.

cow] the first shot, the others would smell the blood and begin to hook the dead one and paw the earth. Then we would shoot the outside ones [that appeared ready to move away], and the more blood there was scattered around the better they would stand. I have often shot two belts of cartridges away at one stand. Each one of those belts would hold forty-two cartridges. My gun weighed fourteen pounds; the gun and those two belts of cartridges made quite a load to carry around over those prairies.[54]

Brown could skin a carcass in fifteen to twenty minutes, but Bill Hillman set a record by skinning and pegging out seventy buffalo hides in less than ten hours.[55]

George W. Reighard hunted from the fall of 1871 until the spring of 1873, killing more than five thousand bison. In his first big stand he dispatched sixty-eight.

I had two big .50 Sharps rifles with telescopic sights, using a shell three and a half inches long...with 110 grains of powder. Those guns would kill a buffalo as far away as you could see it, if the bullet hit the right spot.... Usually I carried a gun rest made from a tree crotch, which I would stick in the ground to rest the gun barrel upon.[56]

His biggest kill came as he lay on a ridge one hundred yards from a herd of a thousand bison at rest after drinking. The barrel of his Sharps became overheated after he had shot twenty-five.

A bullet from an overheated gun does not go straight, so I put that gun aside and took the other one. By the time that one became hot, the other had cooled, but the powder smoke in front of me was so thick that I could not see through it. There was

In the 1870s, seventy-two Native American warriors, mainly Kiowas, Cheyennes, and Arapahoes, were sent to Fort Marion in Florida as hostages. While they were confined there, Lt. Richard Pratt encouraged their education and some produced small books of drawings, which they sold to St. Augustine tourists as souvenirs, often sending the money home to help support their families. This sketch from a Kiowa album shows a Native American shooting bison using a stick rest. (Courtesy: Oklahoma Historical Society)

not a breath of wind to carry it away, so I had to crawl backward, dragging my two guns in order to work around to another position on the ridge. From there I killed 54 more. In one and a half hours I had fired 91 shots, as the count of the empty shells showed afterwards, and I had killed 79 buffalos. We figured that they all lay within an area of about two acres of ground. My right hand and arm were so sore...that I was not sorry to see the remaining buffalos start off on a brisk run that soon put them beyond range.[57]

Other hunters killed even more in a single stand. Tom Nixon in September 1872 boasted in Dodge City that he would set a record. In front of witnesses, he killed 120 in forty minutes in a single stand and later broke his own record with a stand in which he made 204 kills.[58]

The practice of killing from a stand was not unique to the professional hunters of the post–Civil War years. One of Fremont's subordinates during his third western exploration (1845), Lt. James W. Abert, described this method of hunting.

When a hunter succeeds in approaching a herd undiscovered he can often kill as many as 10 or 15 without "raising" the band. They pay very little attention to their fallen companions, unless an unsuccessful shot strikes and wounds one that communicates his fright to the rest of the band.[59]

By necessity, Indians in the 1840s and 1850s often had limited access to rifles and relied on the lance, bow and arrow, and short-range smoothbore guns and so were forced to use the less efficient method of hunting bison from horseback.

During the later years of the slaughter, .40 and .45 caliber Sharps rifles predominated as the quarry became more wary and fewer in number and shots often had to be taken at longer ranges. In its January 1877 price list, the Sharps Rifle Company announced it was discontinuing its .44 and .50 caliber rifles except on special order. That summer a hunter from Kansas wrote to the company at its new factory in Bridgeport, Connecticut, asking about the cost of a twelve-pound .50–105 rifle noting that "the Big Fiftys are [an] out of date thing in the East I suppose, but they are yet a good Buffalo gun."[60]

Sharps round barrel Business Rifle captured from Cheyennes on Antelope Creek, Nebraska, in 1879. Originally it may have been taken from a Kansas buffalo hunter. (Courtesy: Smithsonian Institution, neg. #93-4875, Washington DC)

A pile of bison bones gathered in preparation for shipment east. (Courtesy: Montana Historical Society)

Amidst the continuing boom of the hide hunters' rifles, thousands of bison carcasses soon littered the plains. After the wolves, coyotes, buzzards, and other scavengers had picked them clean, bare skeletons were all that remained. A market for these sun bleached bones existed in the east and many a poor farmer gathered them to help his family survive difficult times. Prices varied, but bones were worth about $7 a ton in Dodge City in 1879. The Hutchinson (Kansas) *News* of January 23, 1873, reported: "A large part [of the bones] have gone to Wilmington, Delaware, where the best are selected for combs, knife handles, &c., the next best are . . . ground into dust and used in refining sugar; and the refuse is ground into meal for fertilizing purposes."[61]

While the bone market was an economic blessing for some, others viewed it otherwise, as reported in the Kingsley (Kansas) *Graphic* of August 3, 1878.

Within twenty rods of the *Graphic* office, almost in the center of town, one hundred and twenty tons of buffalo bones and refuse lie piled and sweltering in the torrid heat of the August sun, to the great annoyance of our citizens who reside to the windward. We insist upon our dealers having this nuisance abated. Pile your ossified nuisance at the stock yard switch.[62]

Such was the ignoble end to the free roaming bison herds. When in 1886 William T. Hornaday went west to acquire a few bison to mount for the Smithsonian Institution, he estimated that perhaps only three hundred remained in the wild. The following year he pleaded that only by saving the bison could Americans in a small way "atone for the national disgrace that attaches to the heartless and senseless extermination of the species in a wild state."[63]

The demise of the bison and increasing scarcity of other game animals was partially responsible for the growth of hunting clubs throughout the country and by 1891 there were at least 103 in the west. Among them was the Boone and Crockett Club founded by Theodore Roosevelt in 1887. The efforts of such groups to promote the protection of vanishing wildlife for their continued pleasure undeniably was self-serving. Yet their calls for game laws to protect bison and other threatened species and for the establishment of wildlife preserves and national parks joined the demands from Hornaday, George Bird Grinnell, the New York Zoological Society, and others. These voices finally were heard and in 1902 Congress appropriated $15,000 to help rebuild Yellowstone National Park's bison herd.[64]

Many a veteran bull fell beneath our rifles and the savage people
of these desert and untillable tracts can not be censured
for detesting the whitefaces, who pass through
the only pastures with which nature has provided him,
& slay his cattle which feed therein & which
form his only means of subsistence.
— Anonymous, 1845[65]

CHAPTER TWELVE

Shotguns, Versatile and Deadly

The mouth of the Sutro tunnel is like a nailhole
in the Palace Hotel compared to a shotgun.
— Anonymous stagecoach driver[1]

Smoothbores occupied a significant but sometimes overlooked niche on the western frontier. Within limits, they were a more versatile weapon than rifle or handgun. Of course they could be used for their intended purpose, the discharge of a number of pellets, but depending upon their construction, they could fire a single naked or patched ball with some accuracy at moderate ranges against larger game such as bison or humans. Frederick L. Olmsted, a Texas traveler in 1853–54, wisely noted: "Two barrels full of buck-shot make a trustier dose, perhaps, than any single ball for a squad of Indians, when within range, or even in unpracticed hands for wary venison."[2]

During the 1700s, many French "fusils de chasse" or hunting guns were shipped to New France where they served voyageurs, Indians, and other woods runners. Like the Northwest gun, which succeeded them, they were light smoothbores, iron mounted, capable of firing shot or ball. Heavier military-style muskets found favor with some. British forces serving in America relied on the .75 caliber smoothbore Brown Bess musket, Britain's primary infantry weapon from before the French and Indian War of the 1750s until after the War of 1812. Originally fitted with a 46-inch barrel, the length was reduced to forty-two

inches in subsequent models and before 1800 to thirty-nine inches. Balls from these muskets produced substantial shocking power, but their accuracy at one hundred yards in one test produced only 40 percent hits on a target about twelve feet square. However Manuel Lisa reportedly carried an example of the sturdy brass-mounted Brown Bess when he journeyed up the Missouri in 1807 and Solomon Juneau, one of the first permanent traders in the Milwaukee area, relied on one as well. Some individuals preferred higher grade single-barrel fowling pieces or double-barrel shotguns.[3]

The bell-mouthed blunderbuss, a form of shotgun, was utilized in various capacities and sizes in the west, sometimes as a handheld weapon or just as often in larger size as a swivel gun mounted on a boat or wagon. Firing tests have discredited the theory that its flared muzzle distributed its shot in a wide pattern. More likely its configuration was intended to facilitate loading in the rigging of a swaying ship or on a bouncing mail coach. Undeniably the gaping muzzle also may have had a strong psychological effect on anyone at whom it might be pointing.

Lewis and Clark's Corps of Discovery carried at least two blunderbusses part of the way on their monumental journey, and John Jacob Astor's inventory of goods turned

Inset in the stock of this 12-gauge shotgun by C. F. Scholl of Marysville, California, is a silver medal stating the gun was awarded in 1858 by the California State Agricultural Society to O. Wood for the best saddle mule. The locks are engraved with dogs and game animals. Wood may have been the owner of Woods Yuba Express Company or a large sheep rancher in Marysville. (Courtesy: Bob Butterfield and Charles L. Hill Jr.)

An Arkansas traveler with fiddle and percussion double-barrel shotgun. Necessary accessories are the leather shot bag and powder flask hanging from the wall. (Courtesy: National Anthropological Archives, Smithsonian Institution, Washington DC)

Percussion 10-gauge double-barrel shotgun sold by Child & Pratt, St. Louis merchants between 1850 and 1863. (Photo by Steven W. Walenta, courtesy James D. Gordon)

over to the British in 1813 in Oregon listed five of these weapons with a brass barrel and seven with an iron barrel. On Manuel Lisa's second voyage up the Missouri in 1811, two brass-barrel blunderbusses were carried in the boat's cabin. At Astor's trading outpost at Astoria in 1811, the accidental discharge of a blunderbuss tore a corner of a Chinook chief's robe. Fearing the accident was an assassination attempt, the Indians armed themselves before two Astorians eased the tense situation.[4]

Shotguns were sometimes selected by trappers for night guard duty against marauding Indians. In the 1850s, a Mr. Bowles of Sabinal, Texas, was concerned about Indian raids and one night stood guard near his house with a double-barrel shotgun heavily loaded with buckshot. He hadn't waited long before he saw three Indians approaching on foot in single file. When they were in range, he fired both barrels simultaneously. The gun's recoil threw him to the ground on his back and the gun flew out of his hands. Later investigation revealed that all three Indians had received mortal wounds.[5]

Then as now, tragic accidents sometimes occurred with shotguns as well as other firearms, usually from carelessness. In 1873 a homesick eighteen-year-old en route to San Antonio attempted to secure a rope which was attached to his saddle. It was after dark and he overlooked a shotgun which also was fastened to his saddle. When he pulled the rope, it somehow discharged the shotgun sending a fatal load of buckshot into his stomach. A Kansas farmer when plagued by blackbirds in the spring of 1878 strapped a shotgun to his plow. "Unfortunately for the young inventor, the muzzle of the gun pointed toward the plow handles, and in drawing the gun from its place, . . . the fowling-piece was discharged, lodging a load of shot in [his] shoulder, badly mangling it." In an incident in 1876, a boy killed himself when he attempted to drive a rabbit out of a brush pile with the butt of his loaded gun.[6]

Another tragic accident was described in rather lurid detail in the Hays City (Kansas) *Sentinel* of September 12, 1879. A Russian immigrant hunting rabbits with a single-barrel shotgun carelessly placed the butt of the gun on the ground, leaned the muzzle against his body, and began to gather a few ears of corn.

> In some unexplainable manner the gun was discharged; the entire load passing through his body and heart. He made a few steps toward the house, and fell. A little daughter, who witnessed the accident, hastened to him; but his form was already rigid in death when she reached him. He was taken to the house and cared for by kind neighbors; the simple funeral taking place the next day. It is another added to the long list of those who have gone to their death through carelessness.[7]

A potentially tragic but comic misadventure occurred when a preacher near Dodge City fenced off a portion of his land through which a former trail passed. The gate offended some townspeople, one of whom galloped up to the house and demanded that the fence be removed. A hearted argument arose, viewed by the minister's two sons who were watching from upstairs where they were readying guns for a goose hunt. One of their borrowed guns was a "drilling," a double-barrel shotgun with a third rifled barrel.

> Having this three-barreled heavy duty weapon at my shoulder, my brother looked out of the partially raised window, pointing the muzzle at the ground, but as he protruded the gun through the window, just to be doing so, the top of the hammers accidentally scraped upon the bottom of the sash rail. "Bang, bang," went the heavy reports.

Sand and perhaps some goose shot struck the visitor's horse in the hocks.

A trio of Kansas hunters. The two at left may be holding imported French pinfire LeFaucheux breechloading shotguns. (Courtesy: James Zupan)

That mustang jumped out from under his rider like an antelope.... The man fell into the huge bed of prickly pear cacti, gorgeous in the spring of the year, but...in no sense a comfort to lie down in.... As he slowly arose,...he was begging for his life. He was expecting to be shot.... He would leave the fence question alone for good, so he agreed. Father picked up the man's gun for him, shook the cartridges out of it and handed it back to him, whereupon he instantly disappeared toward his pony.[8]

Shotguns took their toll on game for the cooking pot, but were employed in organized shooting contests as well.

In late May of 1876, a live pigeon shoot took place in Salina, Kansas. The unfortunate birds were released at specific distances from the gunners who attempted to shoot them within specified boundaries. Only eight birds were killed. In preparation for an October 1879 tournament in Saline County, Kansas, the organizer of the event purchased in Chicago thirty-five hundred pigeons trapped in Wisconsin and Michigan. Far more humane was a series of matches held in Ellis and Hays City, Kansas, in the same year, in which the sportsmen attempted to break glass balls thrown into the air.[9]

Capt. Edmund Kirby Smith, later a Confederate general, was reassigned from teaching mathematics at West Point to duty with the 2nd Cavalry in Texas, taking with him "books, a lamp, bedstead, keg of gun powder, six-shooter, knife and double-barrel shot gun." In a letter to his mother in 1856 he described his "scouting costume."

> Mounted on my mule—(the dearest, gentlest, and most intelligent brute . . .) [I wore] corduroy pants; a hickory or blue flannel shirt, cut down in front, studded with pockets and worn outside; a slouched hat and long beard, cavalry boots worn over the pants, knife and revolver belted to the side and a double barrel gun across the pommel.[10]

To the military as well as civilians, the shotgun was useful for other than hunting purposes. About 1868 a severely undermanned 6th Cavalry outpost in Texas was threatened by a night Indian attack. Mike Kelly had been sick in quarters and had loaned his Spencer repeater to another man. He obtained a shotgun and took up a position at the corral gate. When approached by his sergeant, he warned him:

> "Sergeant, if I let this off, I wouldn't advise ye to be too near, for I know she'll bust, but I'll make a scatteration among thim red devils whin I shoot her." Taking the ramrod, he showed me that it projected about nine or ten inches out of the barrels, and informed me he had put forty buckshot in each barrel! Mike surely would have blazed away had the Indians attacked us, which fortunately for him and them they did not do.[11]

Famed Indian fighter Gen. George Crook wasn't traveling in style when he arrived at Fort Apache, Arizona Territory, in September of 1882.

> I will never forget my thrill at the first sight of this famous soldier. . . . At the head of the line rode Crook on a large, gray mule, his usual mount. A yellow canvas coat and a pair of blue soldier trousers, much the worse for wear, was his uniform. On his head he wore one of those white East Indian pyramidical hats. . . . At the pommel of his saddle he carried a double-barreled shot-gun—his favorite weapon. He had a rather full, grizzly beard, and his hair was long. A most unmilitary figure, indeed![12]

A "scattergun" in the hands of an express company guard or messenger was a potent threat to potential robbers. As one observer wrote:

> Next to the old-time stage drivers, the famous messengers or guards employed by the Wells Fargo Express Company to protect their treasure boxes from robbers were perhaps the most picturesque, colorful figures of stage days. The Tombstone [Arizona Territory] Stages, both in- and out-bound, carried one on each coach. . . . Every messenger sat on top of his coach, generally right beside the driver, six-shooter at hip (sometimes one on each hip), a repeating rifle or sawed-off shotgun resting in the hollow of his arm. Usually his feet rested on the iron-bound treasure box which lay under them.[13]

J. Morley drove a Wells Fargo stagecoach in the late 1870s and remembered: "We stage drivers were furnished . . . sawed-off shotguns especially made in the East for the company. The shot-gun barrels were charged with 7 1/2 grams [115 grains] of powder and loaded with 16 buck shot in four layers, with four shot to the layer."[14]

In the 1870s a passenger complained to the driver of the stagecoach that the coach hadn't been dusted out, "He turned upon me with a look of profound contempt and muttered something about my being the worst 'tenderfoot' . . . he ever saw, quietly entered the stage, and with his ugly, sawed-off, double barrel shot-gun, placed himself so as to occupy the entire front seat."[15]

One young messenger in the early 1880s chose a different approach.

> Occasionally, I guarded Wells Fargo treasure out of Globe [Arizona Territory], crouching with a sawed-off shotgun in the rear boot of the coach instead of beside the driver. The bandits shot some good men off the high seat without warning, but they quit [harassing] the Dripping Springs line after they had been given a salute from the great leather boot at the rear.[16]

In 1882 Lt. Thomas Cruse, 6th Cavalry, was traveling with his wife on a Santa Fe railroad construction train that was carrying some $30,000 consigned to Winslow,

Cut down Remington 10-gauge with a copper plate in the stock marked "Property of U.S. Marshal, Carson City, Nevada." (Exhibited at Nevada State Museum, Carson City)

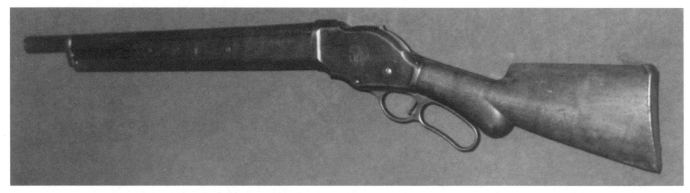

On February 15, 1900, five members of the Stiles-Alvord gang attempted to rob a Southern Pacific train at Fairbanks, Arizona Territory. Although twice wounded in the gun battle that followed, famed lawman Jefferson (Jeff) D. Milton shot "Three Finger" Jack Dunlop with this 10-gauge Model 1887 Winchester shotgun. Despite the popularity of Winchester's lever action rifles, its M1887 "scattergun" met with only modest success in the face of increasing competition from Winchester's own and other makers' pump or slide action repeating shotguns. (Exhibited by the Arizona Historical Society, Tucson)

Arizona Territory. Masked bandits had stolen a payroll only two weeks before without firing a shot.

> From Dodge City, they sent some of their "detectives" to guard subsequent shipments—gunmen of killing records.... In the caboose rode several of the guards. When the train stopped at McCarthy these men dropped off and made a quick, practiced examination of the *jacales* [shacks] and the train and the country about. We went into the eating shack and sat down at a rough plank table. Two of the guards came in. One sat down beside Mrs. Cruse and leaned his sawed-off shotgun against the table. When he began calmly to eat his meal we noted that he wore two revolvers—strapped to his wrists!... In my western experience I had met a few of the genus Bad Man but one who strapped his six-shooters to his forearms was a novelty, even though each gunman I ever saw had some special and peculiar way of carrying his weapons.[17]

A shotgun could be equally as intimidating if held by a highwayman, recalled a stagecoach driver, or "Jehu" as drivers sometimes were called.

> Until you have been suddenly called upon to look down the opening of a double-barreled shotgun, which has a road agent with his hand on the trigger at the other end you can have no idea how surprised

you are capable of being. I have had a six-shooter pulled on me across a faro table. I have proved that the hilt of a dirk can't go between two of my ribs; I have seen four aces beaten by a royal flush; but I was never really surprised until I looked down the muzzle of a double-barreled shotgun in the hands of a road agent. Why, my friend, the mouth of the Sutro tunnel is like a nailhole in the Palace Hotel compared to a shotgun.[18]

A story of perhaps questionable authenticity is told of a stagecoach driver called "Dutch Jake" who in 1863 after being robbed several times rejected the offer of a guard and instead rigged a shotgun in the driver's seat and selected a team of lively mules for a trip on which he was carrying gold bullion. Several hours out of Aurora, Nevada Territory, he reputedly was stopped by two road agents, one of whom grabbed the bridles of the lead mules. As the other bandit approached the driver, Jake fired the shotgun and the mules bolted, leaving one highwayman trampled and the other kicked into the brush. Unfortunately the lead mules had their inner ears shot off.[19]

The presence of robbers might justify a fusillade of shots from stagecoach passengers. However an 1877 issue of the Omaha (Nebraska) *Herald* warned: "Never attempt to fire a gun or pistol while on the road [in a stagecoach]. It may frighten the team and the careless handling and cocking of the weapon makes nervous people nervous."[20]

Throughout most of the 1880s, Fred J. Dodge served as an undercover agent for Wells Fargo in Arizona Territory and in Tombstone was closely allied with Wyatt Earp. In Dodge's memoirs, he makes frequent mention of his reliance on his "Short Wells Fargo Double barrel Shot Gun." One night in 1885 outside Tombstone he went to the home of Jim Burnett to serve an arrest warrant. He had been warned that Burnett had threatened to kill him and had a trap gun set, a shotgun strapped to a log with a string attached to the door.[21]

Jim was in the bedroom—this room had a window facing the east. I was close to the door where the trap gun was and I said to Jim, "All right, Jim, I am going to break this door down and come and get you," (just what Jim wanted) but instead I stepped to the window and could see Jim plainly—and I just shoved my short

double barrel shot gun right through the window and I had Jim covered. . . . I made him move to the center of the room and then I called Charley Smith who broke out some more of the window and went in. I kept Jim covered and Charley put the handcuffs on him and gathered up the guns—1 shotgun and 2 sixshooters— then I went in and Charley and I unstrapped the shotgun from the log.[22]

Bill Thompson, "a tin horn by trade, and a desperado by pretence," was the brother of Ben Thompson, a well-known man-killer from Texas. He insulted a lady to whom Jim Tucker was partial and was "called down" for his indiscretion. Perhaps driven by what he felt his brother would have done to protect his image, Bill brooded and waited his opportunity. That evening he stepped inside the bar where Tucker was drinking and fired a quick snapshot at him.

The ball cut off three of Tucker's fingers and the tip of the fourth, and, the bar being narrow, spattered us with his blood. Tucker fell, momentarily, from the shock. Supposing from Tucker's quick drop he had made an instant kill, Bill stuck his pistol in his waistband and started leisurely out of the door and down the street. But no sooner was he out of the house than Jim sprang up, seized a sawed-off ten-gauge shotgun, ran to the door, leveled the gun across the stump of his maimed left hand, and emptied into Bill's back, at about six paces, a trifle more No. 4 duck shot than his system could assimilate.[23]

In the mining town of Aurora, Nevada Territory, William Carder was a feared gunman. The *Esmeralda Union* described him as "probably more expert [with deadly weapons] than any other man on the Pacific Coast. . . . His quickness and proficiency . . . were almost beyond belief, and his remarkable coolness and bravery rendered him the terror of the community." On December 10, 1864, he "went on a tear" and attempted to provoke fights with several townspeople, including Moses Brockman whom he threatened to kill. Fearing for his life, Brockman waited in a doorway with a double-barrel shotgun and loosed both loads of buckshot into Carder's neck when the ruffian emerged from a saloon, tearing "a most

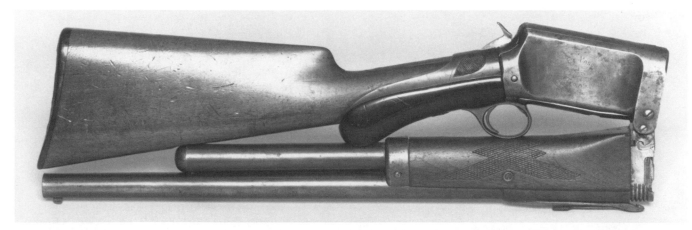

Unusual in design and historical in association, this 12-gauge Burgess folding shotgun (#3019) was patented in 1894 by Andrew Burgess, who designed lever action rifles for both Colt and the Whitney Arms Company. It was promoted in advertising literature as being well suited for law enforcement personnel, easily carried slung in a scabbard beneath a coat. This specimen is engraved "ROBERT G. ROSS CAPTAIN POLICE" and "EL PASO TEXAS." Ross was a newspaperman who turned to law enforcement after moving to Texas to ease his tuberculosis. After his death from peritonitis in 1899, the Burgess passed to Pat Garrett, famed as Billy the Kid's killer, who served as US customs collector in El Paso (1901–5). Garrett had this gun with him when in 1908 he was gunned down by one of his tenants, Wayne Brazel, while standing beside a buggy. His shotgun shells were loaded with #8 shot, indicating Garrett probably was hoping to shoot small game rather than anticipating any trouble that day. (Courtesy: Mark Wright)

shocking hole" and killing him instantly. In view of Brockman's reputation as a sober, peaceful miner, the coroner's jury ruled the killing justifiable.[24]

Granville Stuart, a leader in early Montana history, in 1861 traveled briefly with two strangers, one of whom identified himself as Henry Plummer. He had a damaged double-barrel shotgun

> which he had broken off at the grip, coming through the timber from Elk City. Reece forged four strips of iron about five-eights in[ches] wide and three and one-half in. long and Granville set them into the gunstock on top and bottom of the grip, and screwed them down solid so that the gun stock was stronger than before it was broken.[25]

Plummer became a notorious outlaw and eventually was hanged for his misdeeds.

At a trading post along the Platte River in 1862, Dan Slade, a rowdy, bullying division agent for the Overland Stage Company, while half drunk attempted to hit John Y. Nelson with a whiskey bottle. "At the same time I stooped down, and with my right hand clutched an old double-barrelled shot-gun, which had the butt-end of the stock sawn off, and was a sort of an elongated pistol. This I cocked as I brought it up, and presenting it at [Slade's] head, fired." One of Slade's men knocked the barrel up so the shot missed, then others calmed the combatants.[26]

Sometimes progress didn't keep pace with crime. In 1866 J. H. Pulley was serving as deputy sheriff in Burlingame, Kansas. There being no jail yet, he was holding a burglar named Bates in his home, shackled and cuffed and chained to a wall, while awaiting a trial. When Pulley and his wife wanted to go into town, his father agreed to guard the prisoner with a double-barrel percussion shotgun if the deputy would remove the chain and cuffs. As Pulley's daughter later recounted, Bates somehow distracted the older man and seized the gun.

> A scuffle followed. Bates bit Grandfather's thumb off. The gun was broken in two, Grandfather getting the stalk [stock] and the piece with the hammers on and Bates the parts [barrels] with the caps on. Grandfather did not think he could shoot with that part. But Bates took a rock and hit the caps, shooting Grandfather. Grandfather lived three weeks.

Bates cut his shackles with an axe and escaped but was recaptured and later was hanged.[27]

Upon arriving in Cheyenne, Wyoming Territory, in 1869 from England, R. B. Townshend was taken under the wing of a Mr. Crocker who sought to inaugurate the tenderfoot into frontier ways. When Townshend informed his new friend that he indeed did have a gun, a muzzle loading 12-gauge double-barrel shotgun by W. W. Greener of Birmingham, England, Crocker explained: "Very good thing to have too sometimes, but a shotgun's not very handy at close quarters, unless it's a sawed-off. For fighting in a barroom . . . or on top of a stage-coach, they like to cut the barrels off a foot in front of the hammers, so the gun handles more like a pistol."[28]

While ascending the Upper Missouri to Fort Benton in a twenty-four-foot rowboat in 1872, Thomas P. Roberts and seven companions encountered no Indians. However "two Henry rifles and a Greener breech-loading shot-gun were convenient to the 'quarter-deck,' constantly loaded, but never fired except to replenish the larder."[29]

Western arms dealers offered a multitude of breech loading shotguns in the century's last quarter. Among the top of the line choices were a Charles Daly "Diamond Quality" hammer gun advertised for $200 by J. C. Chapin Arms Company of St. Louis in 1884. Prices from E. C. Meacham in St. Louis the same year for a hammerless double with laminated steel barrels by Harrington & Richardson began at $100. Remington had entered the market in 1874 with its first breech loading double-barrel hammer gun. Colt followed four years later with its more expensive Model 1878, roughly two decades after the firm had failed to generate much interest in its percussion Model 1855 revolving shotgun. Colt's Model 1883 was one of the first American-made hammerless doubles. It could be carried safely loaded with the action broken open, but it was ready to fire the instant it was closed. Winchester beginning about 1879 added their name to thousands of double guns they imported from England while the Sharps Rifle Company in 1878–80 engraved their name on several hundred 10- and 12-gauge guns made by England's Philip Webley & Co. Among the best known of American-made double-barrel shotguns were those produced in numerous grades by the Parker brothers of Meriden, Connecticut, from about 1869 until World War II.

To those homesteaders and others in the 1880s who could not afford a double-barrel shotgun by Parker at $55 or a Remington priced at $10 less or even a double by William Moore & Co. for only $17.33, there was an inexpensive alternative. That was a single-barrel, former military, smoothbore muzzle loading musket or rifle musket with the rifling bored out to make it suitable for firing shot. The C. J. Chapin Arms Company in their fall 1884 catalog advertised their No. 42, a smoothbore US Model 1842 percussion musket for $2.33 or No. 57, a "cut down Springfield, Model 61 [1861 rifle musket]" for $4.00. The illustration for No. 57 showed a Springfield rifle musket with a drastically shortened forestock and a ramrod mounted beneath the barrel held by two thimbles.

From the same year's Meacham catalog, one could order the Zulu 12-gauge single-shot breechloader for $2.75, "an admirable Boy's or Farmer's gun." These were Belgian conversions of former French muzzle loading muskets fitted with a hinged breechblock designed by Jacob Snider Jr. of Philadelphia, producing a true poor man's shotgun. J. F. Schmelzer & Sons of Kansas City, Missouri, in their catalog for 1903–4 was still promoting former US Army muskets as "the biggest shot gun bargain ever offered" at $3.50. "A Knock-about Gun for the Farm, a Rabbit Gun for the Boys; Safer than Half the Guns Costing Ten Times as Much," the ad proclaimed.

Howard Ruede lived in a Kansas dugout in 1877–78 and on December 6, 1877, wrote to his family in Bethlehem, Pennsylvania: "I am going to trade the revolver for an old musket if I can, as the revolver is not much account for rabbits, being unfit to use shot." His other letters home reflected the monotony and hard life he endured as a homesteader.[30]

What might appear to be genuine Springfield Armory–manufactured breech loading shotguns were marketed to civilians by some western dealers beginning in the mid-1880s. For $7.50, E. C. Meacham of St. Louis was selling such single-barrel 16- or 20-gauge shotguns which from the illustrative cut appeared to be a Model 1881 Springfield, but these were described as "Springfield System." Actually the guns were assembled using obsolete

A frontier family poses in front of their house, constructed of blocks of sod. The shotguns provided food and protection against "varmints." Sod houses, common on the treeless plains, were rather well insulated against winter's cold and summer's heat. (Courtesy: Utah State University, neg. #A-0500, Logan)

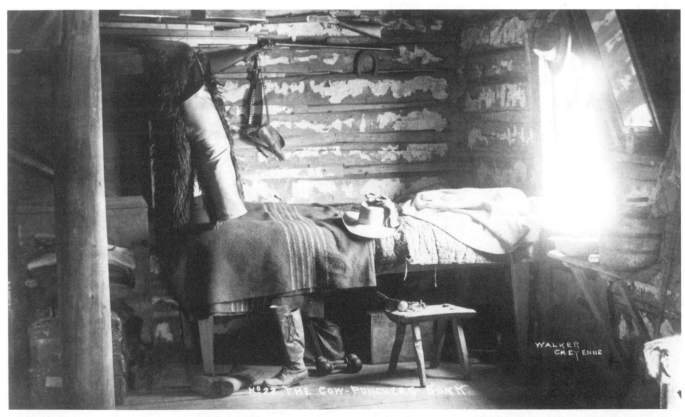

A Wyoming cow puncher's bunk. Mounted on the wall are (from top) a Winchester M1873 rifle, a double-barrel shotgun, and a holstered Colt M1878 revolver. A pair of hand weights on the floor beside the boots indicates the owner must have been health conscious, but the horseshoe is hanging with the open end downward, which traditionally would have allowed the good luck to fall out. The wall once was covered with newspaper or other material to keep out the wind. (Courtesy: American Heritage Center, University of Wyoming, Laramie)

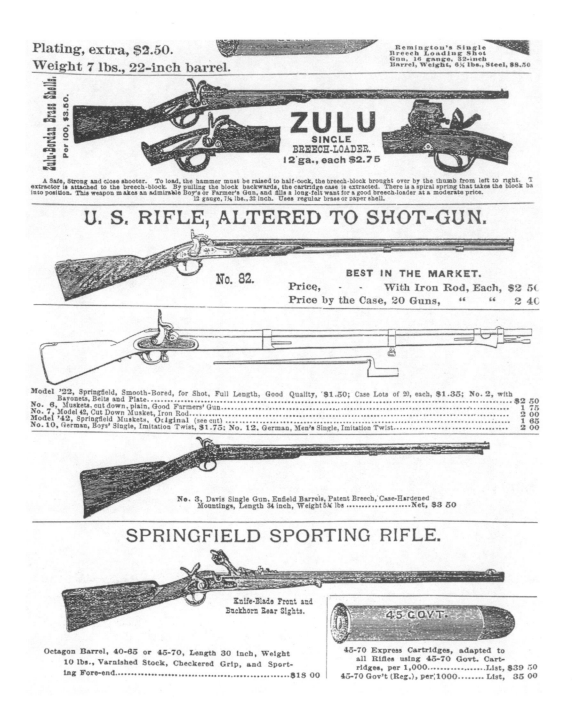

Plating, extra, $2.50.

Weight 7 lbs., 22-inch barrel.

Remington's Single Breech Loading Shot Gun, 16 gauge, 32-inch Barrel, Weight, 6¾ lbs., Steel, $8.50

Zulu-Berdan Brass Shells.
Per 100, $3.50.

ZULU
SINGLE
BREECH-LOADER.
12 ga., each $2.75

A Safe, Strong and close shooter. To load, the hammer must be raised to half-cock, the breech-block brought over by the thumb from left to right. T extractor is attached to the breech-block. By pulling the block backwards, the cartridge case is extracted. There is a spiral spring that takes the block ba into position. This weapon makes an admirable Boy's or Farmer's Gun, and fills a long-felt want for a good breech-loader at a moderate price.
12 gauge, 7¼ lbs., 32 inch. Uses regular brass or paper shell.

U. S. RIFLE, ALTERED TO SHOT-GUN.

No. 82.

BEST IN THE MARKET.

Price, - - With Iron Rod, Each, $2 50
Price by the Case, 20 Guns, " " 2 40

Model '22, Springfield, Smooth-Bored, for Shot, Full Length, Good Quality, $1.50; Case Lots of 20, each, $1.35; No. 2, with
  Bayonets, Belts and Plate..$2 50
No. 6, Muskets, cut down, plain, Good Farmers' Gun...................................... 1 75
No. 7, Model 42, Cut Down Musket, Iron Rod... 2 00
Model '42, Springfield Muskets, Original (see cut).................................... 1 65
No. 10, German, Boys' Single, Imitation Twist, $1.75; No. 12, German, Men's Single, Imitation Twist.......... 2 00

No. 3, Davis Single Gun, Enfield Barrels, Patent Breech, Case-Hardened
Mountings, Length 34 inch, Weight 5¼ lbs.....................Net, $3 50

SPRINGFIELD SPORTING RIFLE.

Knife-Blade Front and
Buckhorn Rear Sights.

45 GOVT.

Octagon Barrel, 40-65 or 45-70, Length 30 inch, Weight
10 lbs., Varnished Stock, Checkered Grip, and Sporting Fore-end..$18 00

45-70 Express Cartridges, adapted to
all Rifles using 45-70 Govt. Cartridges, per 1,000.................List, $39 50
45-70 Gov't (Reg.), per 1000........List, 35 00

A page from an 1884 catalog by E. C. Meacham of St. Louis offering the inexpensive ZULU breech loading shotgun as well as muzzle loading shotguns made from former US military muskets.

parts being sold by the national armory since the Model 1881 government forager gun was only produced in 20 gauge and at that time none were being sold as surplus. N. Curry & Bro. of San Francisco in their 1884 catalog offered the same gun in either gauge for $12 and used the same illustration. This catalog also reflected the continued use of percussion shotguns and rifles by some at this relatively advanced date. It carried four pages of illustrations of powder flasks in eight-, twelve-, or sixteen-ounce capacity, some of copper and others covered with hogskin. Five additional pages displayed leather shot pouches in 2 1/2- to 5-pound sizes and shot belts with double or single chargers.

In almost any situation involving possible short-range gunplay, the shotgun held an advantage. Jim Redfern described a saloon he visited in Virginia City, Montana Territory, while herding cattle in 1885. Gaming tables, he recalled, customarily were watched over by a lookout seated on a small, raised platform in a swivel chair, holding a sawed-off shotgun across his knees. "A man of proven alertness was generally selected for this job, and if he had no shotgun we knew he was armed with a Colt single-action .44 or .45 six-shooter. We knew he was picked for the job because he was almighty fast on the draw, and a sure shot as well."[31]

Chairs do double duty as a bachelor prepares a meal. Although the date is 1886, the double-barrel shotgun is an older percussion arm. (Courtesy: Nebraska State Historical Society, Solomon D. Butcher Collection, neg. #B983-2401)

Swift action with a shotgun probably saved an American family's lives when in 1899 saloon owner Jim Herron traveled into Mexico with his wife and children to appear in court to recover illegally seized horses. Below the border he was accosted by Yaqui Indian soldiers who claimed to have been sent as an escort. The suspicious situation grew more tense. Soon after, Herron's bartender Harry Ramsey joined the party with a warning that a rumor was circulating that the Americans would never reach their destination alive. "Harry had our double-barrel, sawed-off backbar shotgun tied to his saddlehorn with a thong, ready for business."

> The lieutenant barked an order in Spanish and started to draw his revolver. Harry's shotgun roared and the lieutenant dropped from the saddle, dead. The sergeant had ridden up with his rifle drawn, and Harry

> cut him down with the other barrel.... The remaining soldiers turned tail and fled.

Subsequent events proved concerns about the family's safety were justified.[32]

US Marshal Bill Tilghman traveled to Eureka Springs in Arkansas in January 1896 where he'd heard the outlaw Bill Doolin had been seen. The lawman was prepared to use a shotgun but it proved unnecessary. Upon his arrival, "I went to a carpenter and ordered a box made in which I could carry a loaded shotgun, determined to disguise and, carrying the box under my arm, walk about until I met him again, the box being arranged so that with a slight movement of the thumb it would drop, leaving the gun in my hand ready for action." As the carpenter was making the box, Tilghman elected to take a mineral bath. There he unexpectedly encountered Doolin in the lounge reading a newspaper. Tilghman got

In front of a photographer's painted backdrop, youths pose with (from right) a breech loading shotgun, a holstered Colt M1877 double action, and a small-frame top break revolver. (Courtesy: Idaho State Historical Society, neg. #1085-D)

A shotgun-armed herder guards sheep at a water hole with the help of his shepherd dogs. (Courtesy: Wyoming State Museum, Cheyenne)

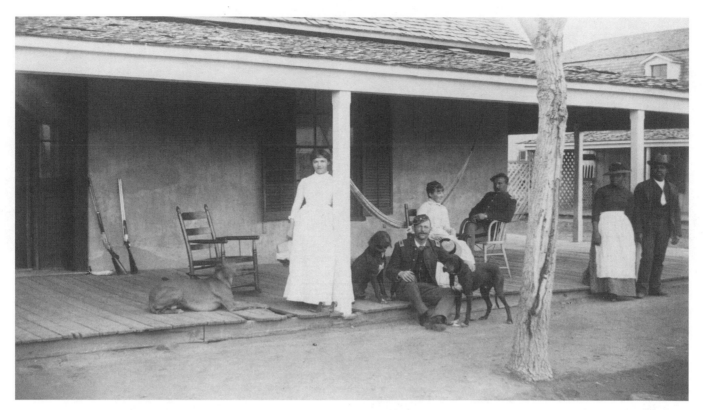

Officers and ladies relax on the porch of the Bachelor Officers' Quarters at Fort Verde, Arizona Territory, in the mid-1880s, perhaps in anticipation of a hunt with dogs and the Winchester M1873 rifle and double shotgun against the wall. (Courtesy: Library of Congress, neg. #LC-US262-105868)

the drop on the outlaw with his revolver and made the arrest without a struggle or the need to use the clever ruse he had planned.[33]

One day in 1882, Nate Priest, the town marshal of Medicine Lodge, Kansas, received word that cowboys were planning to shoot up the town that night. He sent a warning by way of a drover who was returning to camp. "You know all of the boys from the Strip, and I want you to tell 'em I've organized a gun club of twenty-five businessmen. If they start shooting up the town tonight, we'll be right there with twenty-five breech-loading shotguns, loaded with buckshot."[34]

Necessity sometimes caused westerners to take unusual measures. Such was the case when Ira Norton was harassed one night by several drunken rowdies who proceeded to ride around his sod house while firing into its walls. Norton had a percussion double-barrel shotgun but lacked any

shot. As the harassment continued, he beat a lime-encrusted cast iron teakettle into small bits with a hammer and loaded his scattergun with the fragments. His first shot knocked one man from his horse, dead. The second trespasser received the contents of the other barrel and departed quickly, wounded in the neck and shoulders. Some years later, the second man's body was exhumed and given to a young physician in need of a skeletal specimen. The bones were found to be peppered with small bits of lime-encrusted cast iron.[35]

One of the few guns on a Wyoming ranch in the 1880s was a 10 gauge that the rancher bought from a drunk who had rammed the muzzles into the mud, then tried to fire it. "That cracked the barrels nearly half-way up. After the barrels were sawed off it made a dandy prairie-chicken gun, but kicked like a mule." It was representative of the many well-used shotguns present on the frontier.[36]

Pistols and Petticoats: Women as Shootists

I had firm hold of a revolver, and felt exceedingly grateful all the time that I had been taught so carefully how to use it, not that I had any hope of being able to do more with it than kill myself, if I fell in the hands of a fiendish Indian.
— Mrs. Frances Roe, 1872[1]

Isolated as they sometimes were on the western frontier, women could be forced to manage for themselves when the men were away, when traveling alone, or if they should be widowed or otherwise on their own. In addition to tending to children, they might perform those chores necessary to keep the family farm or ranch operating, whether it be splitting firewood, plowing, hunting, taming horses, branding cattle, or any other tasks which might be considered men's work. Defending themselves and children against predatory animals or two-legged marauders sometimes was their responsibility as well. It was a burden not to be taken lightly.

Ann McAdams's husband served with Capt. Jack Hays's Texas Rangers before the Civil War. Whenever he was away from home, she dressed in men's clothing with a revolver belted about her waist and a gun over her shoulder to deceive any reconnoitering Comanche Indians into thinking her husband was at home. Mary Ann "Molly" Goodnight, wife of Texas cattleman Charles Goodnight, not only was recognized as an accomplished rifle shot but also as an astute businesswoman. Her kindness and generosity

to others made her a favorite among those who knew her. However one Arizona woman fired through her cabin door at an "Indian" but wounded a neighbor's burro, for which her husband had to pay $2 in damages. Ella Bird-Dumont took aim at what she perceived to be an approaching Indian, only to discover that she had almost shot her own husband.[2]

In the summer of 1871, Sam Heaton filed claim on land in Kansas and left his wife alone when he drove his oxen and wagon to a sawmill four days away for more lumber. Envious of the land, a man named Soaper with several companions moved all the Heatons' household goods except their tent onto an adjacent claim, but "Mrs. Heaton stood in the door of her tent with a Smith & Wesson revolver in her hand, and refused to budge." The Heatons' claim later was upheld in court, but Mrs. Heaton had shown typical frontier pluck.[3]

Marilla Washburn Bailey was one of those brave women emigrants who journeyed by covered wagon to the Pacific coast via the Oregon Trail. On the way or soon after her arrival she learned to handle firearms and shot grouse, pheasants, and even deer and bears. "[I]

A frontier home might be little more than a hole in the ground and greased paper or parchment might serve as window glass. Grasshoppers in Kansas in 1884 were so thick they beat like hail on buildings and some even ate window curtains, hardly an appealing environment for most frontier women in which to raise a family. (Courtesy: Cunningham-Prettyman Collection, University of Oklahoma Library, Norman)

became so expert with a revolver that at 50 to 100 feet I could beat most men." A diary kept by Jane Gould Tourillott of her journey by wagon train from Iowa to California contained this entry. "Friday, May 30 . . . Lou and I shot at a mark with a revolver. The boys said we did first rate for new beginners." Seventeen-year-old Eliza McAuley crossed the plains with her older brother and sister in 1852 and helped herd cattle. Early in the venture she learned how to handle a pistol. "April 19th: This morning Tom made me practice target shooting with his pistol. I was very expert at missing the mark, but managed to hit the tree three times out of five." Hardly into her journey to California, in May of 1853 Lorena L. Hays was witness to a near accident. A man was holding a pistol when it discharged. The ball passed through another's hat and the powder burned his face. "I hope it will learn them to be more careful about loaded guns and pistols."[4]

The presence of a woman in a wagon train bound for Fort Union, New Mexico, in 1859 caused some concern.

Even though the party consisted of fifty men armed with Sharps and revolvers, after they passed a large number of Cheyenne and Arapaho Indians on the trail they confined Julia Anna Archibald to her husband's wagon, out of sight. Eventually her presence became known, however.

> Though there was not a shadow of danger in such a company as ours, as many of us well knew at the time and as many experienced men have since informed us, it is very true that the red men have an unaccountable fancy for white women. My husband received several very flattering offers for me. One Indian wanted to trade two squaws for me, who could probably perform four times the physical labor that I could. Others, not quite so timid, approaching the wagon made signs for me to jump up behind them on their ponies, but I declined the honor.[5]

Ernest Valeton deBoissiere (with white beard) and members of the French communal colony at Silkville, Kansas, in 1869. Cheap foreign competition forced the colony to turn from silk culture to dairying. The only armed people in the scene are women, two with double-barrel shotguns. (Courtesy: Kansas State Historical Society)

Hallie Riley Hodder in 1863 traveled by "steam car" to Kansas and then by stagecoach to Denver where she spent a year and a half before returning east. Indians at this time were unpredictable and before leaving Denver, her cousin "provided me with a small revolver, and taught me how to use it. It was loaded and I had taken it from the holster at my belt, so I presume I was ready to use it on myself if we were captured."[6]

Life on the frontier could be particularly hard on women if isolated from neighbors. One desperately lonely farmer's wife in Kansas sometimes sat among their sheep merely to feel the presence of other living creatures. Another Kansan, Mrs. B. L. Stotts, arrived in the newly established town of Garden City in 1881. She later recorded that she missed the trees familiar to her in Colorado and the only shade, slight as it was, came from soap weeds. The blazing sun created tempting mirages of lakes and groves of stately trees when she didn't feel a drop of rain for nine months.

> The awful monotony was killing. There was nothing to do, nothing to see and no where to go, and should we have attempted to go anywhere we would only have become lost,

for there were only a few dim trails leading to the claims of a few settlers, so we women crept about from house to house.

Life became a little easier as other families arrived in the new settlement and within two years the population grew to four hundred people.[7]

An English sportsman in 1879 visited a small settlement of eight or nine families in the Rockies only a day or two after news had reached them of an uprising by Ute Indians. The men of the town were away on a cattle drive, but the women were prepared to defend their homes and families. As he approached the first cabin, he was stopped by a boy of eleven or twelve who rested a "needle-rifle" (probably a Springfield "trapdoor") on a fence rail. The youngster described himself as "the boss in this yer camp" and removed a plug of tobacco from his pocket and took a substantial bite. The lad directed the stranger into the cabin "where mam oughter be cooking dinner." Inside, he found the mother "prepared for squalls—a well-filled cartridge-belt girthed her waist, a long six-shooter in its sheath being attached to it, while a Winchester rifle was leaning against the stove ready for

A trio of young huntresses at Stone Ranch in Wyoming. Even the youngest, with revolver in hand, presumably added to the family's meat supply. (Courtesy: Wyoming State Museum, Cheyenne)

immediate action." After dinner, the boy's sentry duties were taken over by a neighbor's daughter.[8]

An ex-slave, "Stagecoach" Mary Fields at six feet tall and more than two hundred pounds could not be called petite. After leaving employment at an Ursuline convent in Toledo, Ohio, she went west to Montana where she was recognized as a skilled horsewoman as well as a skilled teamster. She reportedly seldom went outdoors without a Smith & Wesson revolver on her person. Her generosity caused her to fail in the restaurant business before she obtained a government contract to deliver mail. She was held in such high regard by the folk in Cascade, Montana, that for years her birthdays (twice yearly due to the uncertainty of the actual date) were school holidays before her death in 1914. In one photo of her, she holds a Model 1876 Winchester carbine.

Life in town could have its dangers as well as that afield. In 1875 an army major and his wife spent the night in a Dodge City hotel. They described the manager who showed them to their room as a six-foot woman with a bowie knife and a revolver in her belt. Their room was directly above a saloon and later that night when shoot-

ing broke out downstairs, they prayed no bullets would come through the floor.[9]

Army wives endured much the same hardships as did their husbands, whether married to officers or enlisted men. Most written accounts came from the former group. Many officers' wives came from sheltered eastern families and the transition to frontier life was a rude shock. Some of these wives were forced to live in tents during some phase of their frontier experience. The searing heat and sandstorms of Arizona, the bitter winters in the Dakotas, the isolation of many posts, the added difficulties of childbirth and raising children under harsh conditions, plus the threat of Indian hostilities were but some of the hardships these women faced.

One army wife, Eveline Alexander, experienced an attack while at lunch in camp at Fort Stevens, Colorado, in October 1866 as Indians unsuccessfully sought to drive off the horse herd. She rushed to her tent and "buckled on [her] revolver that was lying ready loaded on the table" before taking refuge with another wife behind boxes and flour sacks in a small tent.[10]

Martha Summerhayes journeyed with her husband to his new station in Arizona with the 8th Infantry in 1874. She eventually accepted her life as an army officer's wife despite its burdens. On one matter she was steadfast. "It was never my good fortune to meet with an Indian Agent who impressed me as being the right sort...to deal with...the Indians. [Indians] know and appreciate honesty and fair dealing, and they know a gentleman when they meet one."[11]

In the spring of 1875, her husband was promoted to first lieutenant and transferred from Camp Apache to Camp MacDowell. Speaking of the escort party, she wrote:

> Six good cavalrymen galloped along by our side,...with two ambulances, two army wagons, and a Mexican guide.... The drivers were all armed, and spare rifles hung inside the ambulances. I wore a small derringer, with a narrow belt filled with cartridges. An incongruous sight...it must have been. A young mother, pale and thin, a child of scarce three months in her arms, and a pistol belt around her waist![12]

The unanticipated threat posed by roving Apaches made the journey memorable for the young mother. In preparation for a possible ambush in a pass, Lt. Summerhayes instructed his wife to lie in the bottom of the ambulance.

> I took my derringer out of the holster and cocked it. I looked at my little boy lying helpless there beside me...and wondered if I could follow out the instructions I had received [from my husband]. "If I'm hit, you'll know what to do. You have your derringer; and when you see that there is no help for it,...don't let them get...either of you alive."[13]

Fortunately there were no Apaches waiting in ambush.

Frances Roe, wife of an infantry officer, adapted rather quickly to frontier life, although she remained aloof to African American soldiers and to Indians. She learned to ride the army way, "tight in the saddle" without posting at the trot, and advanced to jumping hurdles and ditches as well. Her husband felt it essential in Indian country that she learn to handle firearms. Her instruction began soon after arriving at Fort Lyon in Colorado Territory in late 1871.

It was hard work at first, and I had many a bad headache from the noise of the guns. It was all done in a systematic way, too, as though I was a soldier at target practice. They taught me to use a pistol in various positions while standing; then I learned to use it from the saddle. After that a little four-inch bull's-eye was often tacked to a tree seventy-five paces away, and I was given a Spencer carbine to shoot...and many a time I have fired three rounds, twenty-one shots in all, at the bull's-eye, which I was expected to hit every time, too....I obligingly furnished amusement for [husband] Faye and Lieutenant Baldwin until they asked me to fire a heavy [.50 caliber?] Springfield rifle—an infantry gun. After one shot I politely refused to touch the thing again. The noise came near making me deaf for life; the big thing rudely "kicked" me over on my back.[14]

Mrs. Roe had reason to appreciate her firearms training the following year after reassignment to Camp Supply, Indian Territory. Sentries' warning shots aroused the garrison one night, alarmed by an effort by Indians to steal horses. Mrs. Roe and another wife for two hours sat on the porch steps wearing raincoats over their nightgowns "ever listening for the stealthy tread of a moccasined foot at a corner of the house."

> I had firm hold of a revolver, and felt exceedingly grateful all the time that I had been taught so carefully how to use it, not that I had any hope of being able to do more with it than kill myself, if I fell in the hands of a fiendish Indian. I believe that Mrs. Hunt...was almost as much afraid of the pistol as she was of the Indians.[15]

During the 1880s as enthusiasm for marksmanship training within the army blossomed, wives sometimes could be found on the practice ranges. Like their mothers, sons of frontier soldiers—and presumably daughters as well—often became familiar with firearms at an early age. Fiorello La Guardia wrote that youngsters at Fort Huachuca, Arizona Territory, in the late 1880s were taught to shoot "even though they were so small that the gun had to be held for them by an elder."[16]

Studio cabinet card by a Sacramento, California, photographer. The rifle appears be a Remington No. 4, available in .22, .25, and .32 calibers. Remington rolling-block sporting rifles were offered in various frame sizes from the No. 1 (.40 to .50 caliber) down to the No. 7 (.22 and .25) with numerous variations and features. (Courtesy: James Zupan)

Civilian farm women, like Mrs. D. Homer Jennings of Kansas, sometimes played the role of defender of the chicken flock as well as of the family, as the *Russell County Record* described on October 14, 1875.

> Having lately lost several fine chickens by hawks, [she] determined to try her skill as a shootist, and while at dinner, yesterday, an opportunity presented itself. The old rooster gave warning that the enemy was approaching, and Mrs. J. took down the [shot?]gun and walked to the door. There was fire in her eye as she stepped out and beheld his hawkship hovering over a group of her choice houdans. She quickly brought the gun to her shoulder and fired, and

> down came the hawk, as dead as a mackerel; and now his carcass hangs at the top of a high pole as a warning to any of his tribe which may chance this way.[17]

The presence of women in the west was a stabilizing and civilizing influence. Schools, churches, and culture followed in their wake. There were exceptions, however. Calamity Jane (born as Martha Jane Cannary or Canary) was an exception to what was considered "feminine behavior," certainly not representative of the genteel lady. She supported herself on various occasions as a prostitute, mule skinner, stagecoach driver, and apparently did serve for at least a short time as an army scout since her name appeared in the pay rosters at Fort Saunders in Wyoming in 1872. Her exploits, real and imagined, appeared in some

Lady hunters presumably bagged this deer or antelope with the M1886 Winchester in the scene.
(Courtesy: Amon Carter Museum, Fort Worth, TX)

of the dime novels of lurid western adventures first published by Ernest Beadle in 1866. She probably exaggerated the extent of her affair with Wild Bill Hickok. She joined Buffalo Bill Cody's wild west show in 1893 but was discharged for excessive drinking.

Pvt. John Burkman of the 7th Cavalry served as Custer's personal orderly or striker for nine years and had a rather uncomplimentary recollection of her during the 7th's expedition to the Black Hills in 1874.

> Calamity Jane hung 'round our camp, pestering us considerable. She dressed in men's clothes and was allus beggin' some one fur a drink. We didn't like her. She was dirty. She was lousy. The men wouldn't have nothin' to do with her. Some of 'em hired her to wash their clothes, payin' her in whiskey.[18]

Some frontier women existed on the fringe of the law and others crossed the line entirely. Prostitutes formed one element of female society found in almost any town. Their social standing often depended upon their degree of beauty and charm and the class of customers they served. They ranged from the madam of a high class bordello offering fine wine along with other services downward to the alcoholic or drug-addicted, unfortunate wretch who serviced all comers in a tiny "crib" or shack.

Ella "Cattle Kate" Watson, a prostitute, sometimes accepted cattle in payment for her favors. In 1888 she homesteaded in Wyoming with her common-law husband James Averill. However, both were lynched during the opening days of the 1892 Johnson County war between large cattlemen and "nesters." In 1897 Cora Hubbard with two male companions robbed an Arkansas bank but later she was apprehended and jailed.

Belle Starr, born Myra Belle Shirley, attended a ladies' "finishing school" in Missouri before marrying outlaw Jim Reed in 1866. She reportedly accompanied him on some of his robberies before he was shot to death in 1874. She married or lived with various other unsavory characters including Blue Duck and Sam Starr and rode with

Calamity Jane with a Stevens pocket rifle with detachable skeleton stock. (Courtesy: Western History Collection, University of Oklahoma Library, Norman)

the latter on horse stealing and cattle rustling forays and eventually served six months in jail. A shotgun blast in the back ended her life in 1889.

For decades, women in the west sometimes hunted game to help feed their families. Martha Maxwell, known as the "Colorado Huntress," went beyond this point. Educated at Oberlin College in Ohio, she and her husband moved to Colorado in 1860 where she developed her interests as a hunter, taxidermist, and naturalist. At the 1876 Centennial Exhibition in Philadelphia, the Colorado-Kansas entry was a prize winning diorama of mounted game animals which she had shot.[19]

Although not a westerner by birth (Greenville, Ohio), Annie Oakley, "Little Sure Shot," was a star per-

former with Buffalo Bill Cody's wild west shows from 1885 until 1901, touring in this country and abroad. She perhaps was the inspiration for a Union Metallic Cartridge Company calendar for 1889 showing a young lady resembling her loading a shotgun in preparation for a hunt, one of the first ads featuring women and guns. One of her feats was firing twenty-five shots from a Model 1891 Marlin lever action .22 rifle in a mere twenty-seven seconds in 1893, all bullet holes touching at a range of twelve yards. Her marksmanship, combined with her feminine grace, undoubtedly was an encouragement to other ladies to develop an interest in firearms. Other women, too, including May Lillie and Lillian Smith, were demonstrating their skills as sharpshooters. By the mid-1890s,

Manhattan .36 revolver (#40307) similar to one attributed to outlaw Belle Starr. (Courtesy: Larry T. Shelton, Missouri State Capitol Museum, Jefferson City)

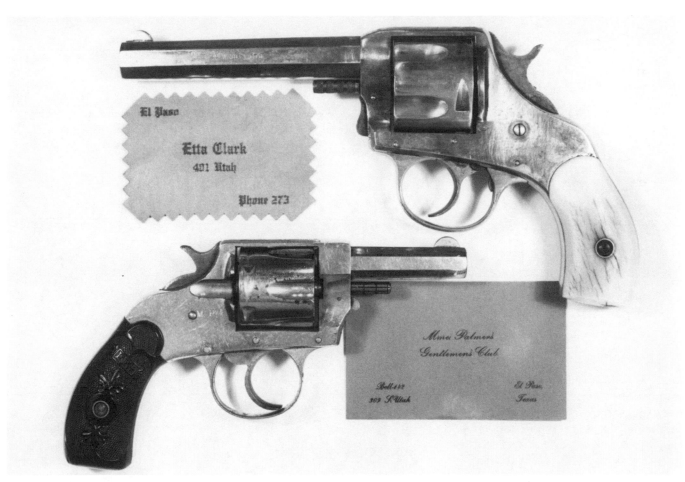

Two El Paso prostitutes' guns. Above, a .44 Hopkins & Allen "American Bulldog" used in an 1886 shooting affair between Alice Abbott and Etta Clark, madams whose brothels were across the street from each other. A newspaper reporter wrote that Alice had been shot in the "public arch," perhaps a typographical error which should have read "pubic arch." It was more appropriate as printed, however, and Alice survived. Below is a Forehand & Wadsworth .32 double action owned by May Palmer, who moved to El Paso in 1889 and opened her own brothel in 1898. (Courtesy: Robert E. McNellis Jr.)

44 Merwin & Hulbert Pocket Army revolver taken from lady stagecoach bandit Pearl Hart by Sheriff W. C. Truman in 1899. (Exhibited by the Arizona Historical Society, Tucson)

Mrs. M. A. Maxwell, a taxidermist in Boulder and Denver, Colorado, whose work was exhibited at the 1876 Centennial Exposition in Philadelphia. Her rifle is one of perhaps twelve thousand or so produced in the 1870s by the Evans Repeating Rifle Company of Mechanic Falls, Maine, in rifle, musket, and carbine models. Its revolving magazine, loaded through the butt, held up to thirty-eight .44 cartridges, depending on model. (Courtesy: James Zupan)

Maude Stern Mortensen hunting in the Sierra Nevada about 1900. (Courtesy: Nevada Historical Society)

women performers in various wild west shows and rodeos were entertaining crowds not only with gun handling ability but with their skill as trick riders, ropers, and in other acts. Many of these women had learned their skills while actually working on farms or ranches.[20]

In 1885 a member of a hunting party passing through Yellowstone Park "took along a little .22 calibre rifle for the ladies to shoot with, which we frequently found quite handy in shooting birds and small game." About the same time, Harold J. Cook was growing up on a ranch in Nebraska and observed his mother's interest in sport shooting.

> Father loved shooting so much that he installed in a pit on the island across the pond from the house a machine that released tin birds. Among the army officers at Fort Robinson there were many good marksmen. The tin birds were a patented device that could be used over

and over. Ammunition was bought by the case, and thousands of rounds were shot over those traps. Mother often joined in the shooting. She was also a good game shot. It was my job to release the tin birds from the machine.[21]

By the 1890s, an increasing proportion of guns manufactured in this country were intended strictly as sporting arms. At this time, too, women were assuming new roles in society, gaining greater access to higher education, and striving for suffrage (Wyoming Territory in 1869 became the first to give women the vote) and increased employment opportunities. In 1900 roughly a quarter of Winchester employees were women, although they often held lower paying positions producing ammunition.[22]

At century's end, women were ever more actively involved in shooting sports. Arms and ammunition

Annie Oakley in front of a painted western backdrop with an 1892 or 1894 Winchester.

A rare view of what appears to be a French pinfire LeFaucheux revolver (at left), probably a photographer's prop (ca. 1900). Civil War purchases of these military size twelve-millimeter (.47 caliber) Model 1853 pinfires included almost thirteen thousand by the North plus an unknown number by the Confederacy. The women may be performers in a wild west show. (Courtesy: Herb Peck Jr.)

This 1884 Worcester Excursion Car Company hunting party at Fargo, Dakota Territory, includes two women, obviously not reluctant hunters. (Courtesy: Montana Historical Society)

This lady's accessories include a knife, Colt Single Action revolver, and a Winchester Model 1895. (Courtesy: Archives Division, Texas State Library, Austin)

makers soon began portraying females in advertising posters and calendars promoting firearms sales to sportswomen for hunting and target shooting. In such ads, women were shown as active shooters, rather than mere adornments in a passive role. Marlin, for example, adver-

tised its Model 1892 .22 lever action rifle as being "a ladies' rifle without equal, owing to the attractiveness of its appearance, the convenience and cleanliness of loading and manipulating, and the feeling of security and confidence that the solid top affords." Trapshooting had

In this late nineteenth-century scene, the lady seated in the center cradles what appears to be a Stevens Ideal single-shot rifle sold in .22, .32, 38, or .44 caliber, inappropriate for the longer cartridges in her belt. Her revolver is a double action, perhaps an Iver Johnson. If so, its grips probably bear a distinctive owl head design, a trademark of the firm. (Courtesy: Cheney Cowles Museum, Eastern Washington State Historical Society, neg. #L83-113.69, Spokane)

Junction City, Kansas, "soiled doves." (Courtesy: Kansas State Historical Society)

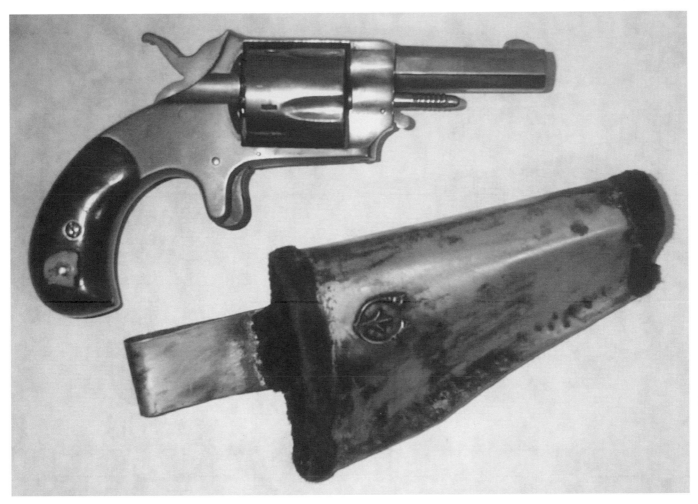

A nineteenth-century Denver madam's .38 rimfire Forehand & Wadsworth "BULL DOG" (#10126). The grip has a piece of turquoise stone inlaid and the tin holster is lined with red velvet. These guns in .32 caliber are often marked "TERROR," "BULL DOG" or "BULL DOZER" in .38, and "SWAMP ANGEL" in .41 caliber.
(Courtesy: Jerry Pitstick)

been introduced into this country in 1831, and George Ligowski in 1880 invented the clay pigeon and a device by which it could be thrown. Gradually these targets replaced live birds and by 1900 women were being drawn in growing numbers into the sport, in part because it did not involve the killing of living creatures.[23]

From "Trapdoor" to Krag: The Post–Civil War Army

[I] mounted the men, cautioned them to keep well deployed,
to cut off the magazines of their Spencer carbines, reserving them until
the last moment, and to commence falling back—using single shots—
turning to fire, but on no account to turn and run until they got the word.
— Lt. Robert Carter, 1871[1]

During the quarter century after the Civil War, the army's chief responsibility in the west was to subjugate the estimated 270,000 Native Americans living there, of whom 100,000 were considered warlike. By mid-1866, the army had dwindled to thirty thousand and in July, President Andrew Johnson signed an act establishing its strength at ten regiments of cavalry, forty-five of infantry, and five of artillery to occupy the former Confederate states, protect our national borders, and pacify the western Native Americans. Those regiments that went west usually were substantially under authorized strength and in 1865 130 of its 169 active posts were beyond the Mississippi. Spread as thin as the army was in the west, by necessity the tactical unit often was a company of fifty to one hundred men.[2]

Army life on the frontier before and after the Civil War could be difficult for both enlisted man and officer. Monotony, separation from family and society, frequent civilian prejudice against soldiers (particularly enlisted men), harsh weather, low pay, and a rigid caste system between officers and subordinates all were factors. So were strict discipline, in some instances a questionable degree of available medical care, and a diet which often consisted of flour, hardtack, coffee, bacon, salt pork (dubbed "Cincinnati chicken"), and a few other staples plus whatever fresh meat hunters could provide or a soldier could afford to purchase from the sutler or elsewhere. At many posts it was not possible to maintain vegetable gardens, which would have added variety and nutrition to the menu.

One day in June 1877, a 7th Cavalry recruit encountered a hardship he probably hadn't anticipated, a swarm of grasshoppers so thick that they clouded the sun for almost an hour. As they covered the ground, "they chewed holes in our tents, blankets, overcoats, etc., and one of the men lost thirty rounds of ammunition, and when questioned as to what had become of it, he said that the grasshoppers had eaten it, brass shells and all."[3]

Reasons for enlisting were many—a desire for adventure, an escape from poverty or the law, or in the case of immigrants, an opportunity to learn the language and customs of their new land. Enlisted men found some of their officers to be efficient and concerned for their welfare, but

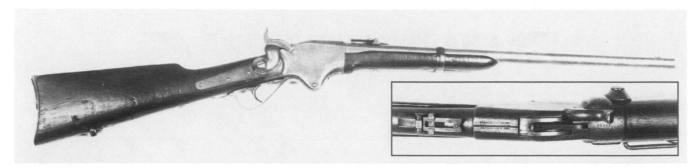

Gen. Edward S. Godfrey's distinguished army career began as a private in the Civil War. Later after graduation from West Point, he was assigned to Custer's 7th Cavalry and fought at the battle on the Washita in 1868 and survived the Little Bighorn fight. He received the Medal of Honor for gallantry against the Nez Perces at Bear Paw Mountain in Montana where he was wounded severely. He probably had this M1860 Spencer carbine (#30313) with him on the Washita and perhaps as well on the later Yellowstone and possibly Black Hills expeditions with the 7th. It was passed down through his family. The view of the gun's top surface shows a narrow sighting groove filed in the receiver, perhaps as a temporary replacement for a missing rear sight which couldn't be replaced in the field. (Courtesy: Dale C. Anderson)

others indifferent, harsh, cruel, or drunkards. In fact, drunkenness among officers and enlisted men and desertion were common problems throughout most of the nineteenth century. A 7th Cavalry private who joined in 1876, too late to fight at the Little Bighorn, blamed desertions largely on "the manner in which many of the harsh officers treat enlisted men."

> As a rule an army officer does not mix with or recognize the fact that enlisted men have any rights or attributes to be respected. There is, socially, an impassable gulf between enlisted men and their officers—I qualify this broad statement by adding, "with rare exceptions." General George A. Custer was one of the *rare exceptions.*[4]

Army life in the post–Civil War west was not one of continual campaigning against Native Americans. In Texas in the early post–Civil War years, for example, the army fought the problem of cattle and hide rustling and sometimes provided escorts for herds. It was possible for a soldier, particularly an infantryman, to go through a five-year enlistment with little actual combat against Native Americans, even though he might spend much time in the field on exhausting marches or guarding water holes.

Sgt. John Cox of the 1st Infantry described his army experience as "so 'tame' as to not be worth relating." Yet he participated in long marches, witnessed a horse stealing raid by the Sioux on the Ponka reservation, and was present when the army had the hazardous duty of disarming the Sioux at the Standing Rock Agency in 1876. The army listed

938 engagements with Native Americans between 1865 and 1898, many being small unit affairs. Total army casualties were recorded as 919 killed and 1,025 wounded, roughly one killed and one wounded for each encounter.[5]

CAVALRY SPENCERS AND SHARPS

The seven-shot war-tested Spencer and the single-shot Sharps .50–70, the latter converted from percussion, were the two primary cavalry carbines of the post–Civil War decade. Despite its rapid fire capability, the Spencer was inferior in range to the Sharps and its ammunition brought some criticism. However, Spencers served regular cavalry regiments as well as some militia units including those of Kansas, Colorado, and Oregon. After retirement a 6th Cavalry sergeant wrote: "The 'Spencer carbine' with which the cavalry was armed in my time [1866–71] has long since been replaced by other arms, but it had many good features, among which its strength and durability were prominent."[6]

Although providing two different types of ammunition meant added work for supply officers, on at least one occasion this was fortunate. During the Modoc War in 1872–73 in California, a company of the 1st Cavalry encountered a defective lot of Spencer ammunition. "Several men…told me that the failure of so many cartridges almost caused a panic…had it not been that other troops with them had Sharp's carbines that never missed fire."[7]

Indian depredations beginning in mid-1868 kept Kansas in an uproar. Under Gen. Phil Sheridan's orders, the army retaliated. In September Maj. George A. Forsyth led fifty frontiersmen recruited as scouts on the trail of a large Sioux and Cheyenne war party. The brevet colonel's

A railroad survey crew in Kansas. Although the infantry escorts' guns can't be identified, a Spencer carbine is in the right foreground. (Courtesy: Kansas State Historical Society)

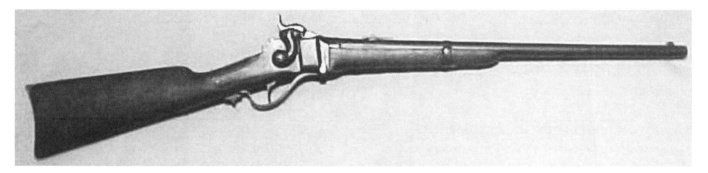

A M1868 .50 Sharps carbine issued to the 3rd Cavalry. (Courtesy: Kenneth L. McPheeters)

company was an interesting mixture. His first sergeant, William H. H. McCall, had been brevetted a brigadier general during the Civil War and Forsyth recalled that a number of his scouts were college graduates. He described their arms as "a Spencer rifle [carbine?] . . . a Colt's revolver, army size [.44 Model 1860], and 140 rounds of rifle and 30 rounds of revolver ammunition per man—this carried on the person." Four pack mules carried four thousand extra rounds of ammunition plus other gear.[8]

The pursued turned on their pursuers in what became known as the Battle of Beecher's Island in eastern Colorado. It undoubtedly was due in part to their fast-firing Spencers that Forsyth's men were able to withstand numerous attacks against their island position. The siege

lasted almost a week before their first rescuers arrived, men of the black 10th Cavalry. By then, Forsyth's scouts had been reduced to eating their dead horses and mules, liberally sprinkled with gunpowder to mask the taste and odor of rotting flesh.

Although most of the men carried Spencers, there were one or two Henry repeaters in the party along with three Springfield longer range rifles, probably Model 1866 .50–70s. On the third day, a portly naked Indian placed himself beyond what he felt was rifle range and began taunting the scouts. Forsyth directed the men with Springfields to "sight them at their limit . . . and aim well over the sight, and see if . . . we might not stop the antics of this outrageously insulting savage. At the crack of the three rifles he

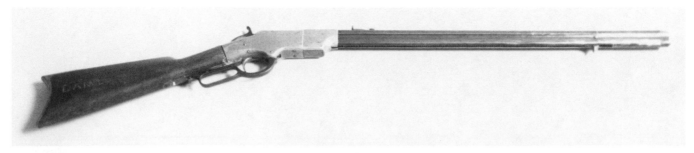

Henry rifle (#6913) used by Louis A. McLaughlin, one of the survivors of the Beecher's Island fight. It remained in the family until 1907. (Courtesy: Kansas State Historical Society)

sprang into the air with a yell of...surprise and anguish, and rolled over stone dead."[9]

David L. Spotts enlisted in the 19th Kansas Cavalry in 1868 in time to participate in the Washita campaign under Custer. On November 4 the regiment drew Spencers and twenty rounds of ammunition. "They are carried on horseback by a strap over the shoulder that holds them diagonally across our backs, making them easy to carry and not in the way while riding. No sabers or revolvers were issued."[10]

Then-lieutenant Robert Carter of the 4th Cavalry offered an opinion based on firsthand experience with the Spencer. On October 10 of 1871, the 4th engaged Comanches under Quanah Parker at Canyon Blanco in Texas. Carter and five men of G Troop found themselves cut off and far from an arroyo which would offer them cover. Carter recalled:

> [I] mounted the men, cautioned them to keep well deployed, to cut off the magazines of their Spencer carbines, reserving them until the last moment, and to commence falling back—using single shots—turning to fire, but on no account to turn and run until they got the word.... The Indians were poorly armed with muzzle-loading rifles and pistols, lances, and bows. We commenced moving to the rear, bending low on our horses, several of which were struck with arrows. We faced about as often as possible to fire and check them, hoping every moment to see the head of [Colonel Ranald] Mackenzie's column come out of the adjacent valley.... When we finally faced the leading warriors, a bullet struck Downey in the hand, cutting two fingers, as he was in the act of working the lever of his carbine.

> With his hand streaming blood, his efforts seemed useless. The shell would not eject. "Lieutenant, what shall I do?" I shouted, "Use your hunting knife, and eject the shell with it!" The brave man did it with his wounded hand, and firing a moment later..., dropped an Indian out of the saddle. They were still afraid of our carbines. Using them up to the last moment as single shooters, I shouted, as we neared the arroya: "Now, men, unlock your magazines, bunch your shots, pump it into them, and make a dash for your lives!" The Indians recoiled as we delivered this volley, and several going off their ponies caused some confusion, as we made the run. Thank God for those Spencers! My affection for them has never changed. It was not necessary that they should carry one thousand or twelve hundred yards, but kill at from five hundred down to twenty or thirty yards.

Carter mentioned his own vain attempt to save Lt. Gregg's life with fire from his Smith & Wesson, undoubtedly a .44 No. 3. His men's post–Civil War Spencers were those fitted with the Stabler magazine cut-off device, a button in front of the trigger which could limit downward movement of the lever and allow the rounds in the magazine to be held in reserve while using the weapon as a single-shot.[11]

Although not a criticism of the Spencer design, the inability of soldiers in the field to reload its rimfire cartridges in July 1865 added to the critical situation of soldiers immediately prior to the Platte Bridge Battle at present-day Casper, Wyoming. Skirmishing with Indians in the vicinity had been heavy and rains had delayed the delivery of ammunition and other supplies by wagon. Troopers of the 11th Ohio Cavalry were low on Spencer cartridges and the "galvanized

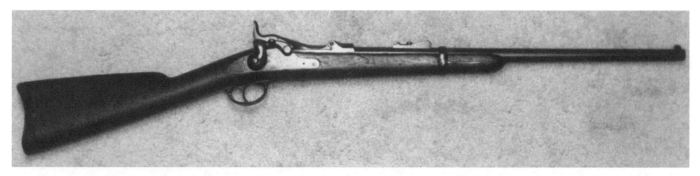

Undoubtedly one of the earliest M1873 Springfield carbines known, #36. Markings on the trigger guard plate indicate it was issued to Company A of the African American 10th Cavalry. (Courtesy: R. Stephen Dorsey)

Yankee" infantrymen (Confederate prisoners of war who volunteered to serve in the west) were armed with muzzle loading rifle muskets. Men of the 11th Kansas Cavalry had fewer than twenty rounds each for their breech loading percussion Smith carbines; no ammunition had been sent them since their departure from Fort Riley the winter before. Some of the men began to cast bullets and make cartridges for the Smith carbines.[12]

A Spencer-armed sentry survived nature's fury during a Texas thunderstorm when his carbine was struck by lightning. He was knocked to the ground and at first was thought dead.

> On examination, the lightning appeared to
> have struck the muzzle of the gun, about
> two inches of which was fused into a shape-
> less mass, as if a stick of sealing wax had
> been subjected to a flame; passed down the
> barrel, burning off the hammer and part of
> the lock, down the man's leg, and through
> his right foot into the ground.... His hand
> was badly burned, also his foot, and he was
> stunned, remaining unconscious for hours,
> but was in a few days fit for duty. The car-
> bine is now in the military museum at the
> city of Washington, it being a curiosity, on
> account of the way in which the muzzle was
> fused off, and, furthermore, the car-
> tridges ... were none of them exploded.[13]

The African American 9th Cavalry was armed with Spencers until they were replaced with .45 Springfield Model 1873 carbines. In more than one engagement the repeater was a factor in the outcome, as Sgt. Jacob Wilks reported.

> In 1873 I was sent with a detail of twelve
> men ... to carry the mail to Fort Bliss

> [Texas]. Each man carried a mail sack
> strapped to the cantle of his saddle, and we
> were armed with seven-shooting Spencer
> rifles [carbines?]. At Eagle Springs we were
> attacked by about one hundred Apaches.
> The fight lasted several hours, during which
> the Indians made repeated charges. We
> were on an open plain without any protec-
> tion whatever, but we dismounted, held our
> horses by the halter-reins, kept close
> together, and withheld our fire until the
> Indians charged up within close range. Our
> rapid fire from long range guns wrought
> such havoc that in the evening they drew
> off, after killing one of our men [who
> against orders had mounted and charged in
> among the Indians]. During the fight they
> made six charges, and it was after a repulse
> of one of these charges that our man
> Johnson was killed.[14]

The army wasn't the place to look for angels, and black units like others had some discipline problems, but generally they served with distinction in the west and usually with lower rates of desertion and drunkenness despite the prejudice often shown against them. African American soldiers were excluded from service with ordnance, artillery, engineer, or signal corps units as being beyond their ability. Custer refused to serve with them and rejected a colonelcy in the black 9th Cavalry. In contrast, Col. Benjamin Grierson, commanding the 10th Cavalry, respected his men and argued vehemently with a colonel of the white 3rd Infantry at Fort Leavenworth when the latter ordered the 10th's "nigger troops" not to parade close to his men.[15]

Equally as disgraceful was the harassment of black cadets at West Point. Of twenty cadets in the nineteenth

Canada's "49th Rangers," mixed blood scouts for the North American Boundary Commission with Spencer carbines. (Courtesy: Royal Canadian Mounted Police, National Archives of Canada, Ottowa, Ontario)

century, only three graduated. In one incident, Cadet Johnson C. Whittaker in 1880 after two years at the school was found tied to his bed with his ears slashed and his hair cut off. He was dismissed after a board found him guilty of inflicting the injuries on himself and falsely accusing others.[16]

In 1872 a joint American-British expedition began to survey that portion of the boundary between the United States and Canada, the 49th parallel, from the Lake of the Woods in Minnesota westward to the crest of the Rockies. Most of the fieldwork was completed by 1874. The British officers and men were armed with their nation's Adams cartridge revolvers and single-shot breech loading Snider rifles, but American-made Spencer carbines were issued to the troop of thirty mixed breed Metis scouts, designated as the 49th Rangers and recruited to serve as guides, hunters, and herdsmen. Serving as escort for the American force of surveyors, topographers, and other personnel during the first season were a company of the 20th Infantry and two companies of the 7th Cavalry commanded by captains Thomas B. Weir and Myles W. Keogh, with Maj. Marcus A. Reno of the 7th in overall command of the escort.[17]

The presence of other American arms within Canada's military forces is revealed by a September 1, 1879, ad by the Department of Militia & Defense requesting bids on surplus arms. Those guns specified by make included 107 Spencer carbines, 5 Spencer rifles, 2,033 Peabody rifles, 226 Starr carbines, 176 Colt (Model 1851?) revolvers, and 34 Allan's [sic] pistols, along with 1,840 muzzle loading Long Enfield rifles, and 187 muzzle loading Short Enfield rifles. The "Allans" probably were Allen & Wheelock revolvers.[18]

INTRODUCTION OF THE "TRAPDOOR" SPRINGFIELD

The army had shown no reluctance to equip its mounted troops with breechloaders just before the Civil War, but that conflict delayed efforts to replace the infantry's muzzleloaders. In January 1865 an ordnance board convened at Springfield to examine what eventually totaled sixty-five breech loading designs. The system selected used a breechblock hinged at its upper forward corner with features patented by Springfield master armorer Erskine Allin. Initially five thousand .58 rifle muskets were converted to fire a .58 rimfire cartridge using Allin's system, inaugurating a progression of Springfield single-shot breech loading arms. These often were referred to as "needle guns" because of the long firing pin extending diagonally through the entire length of the breechblock; a modern nickname is "trapdoor." The metallic cartridge held primer, powder, and projectile in one

US .58 lst Model Allin 1865 Springfield conversion with the breechblock swung upward for loading. The stock marking "BAGGAGE 24" may indicate use by the Kansas Pacific or Union Pacific railroad. Another M1865 is known marked similarly "BAGGAGE 20."

Sharps New Model 1863 carbine (#71068) converted from percussion to .50–70 and bearing F Company, 10th Cavalry, markings.

loader, and could load in a concealed prone position. With this advance in the infantry's primary weapon came a change in tactics from several ranks standing shoulder to shoulder to a single rank an arm's length apart.

A change to a faster firing breechloader couldn't come too soon for infantrymen facing Native American foes. Gen. Philip St. George Cooke in 1866 reported that a cattle guard had refused to fire on threatening Indians because their rifle muskets were muzzleloaders and if they fired a volley, they'd be at the mercy of their attackers.[19]

Additional consideration of more than forty designs beginning in early 1866 resulted in the continued dependence on the Allin system, but with modifications including an improved extractor and a reduction to .50 caliber using a barrel liner. This Model 1866 or Second Model Allin conversion used a .50–70 centerfire cartridge which produced about 1,250 feet per second of velocity at the muzzle. Professional bison hunters in the early 1870s downed many of the shaggy mammals using Springfields and civilian rifles chambered for this cartridge.

The arrival of M1866s in July 1867 at forts C. F. Smith and Philip Kearny on the Bozeman Trail proved critical in the outcome of two dramatic encounters. On August 1, a party of twenty soldiers of the 27th Infantry and six civilians cutting hay successfully withstood a day-long series of attacks by Sioux in what became known as the Hayfield Fight. Capt. T. B. Burrowes credited with new rifles with their survival. "The confidence which the new arms' firing rate and accuracy gave the men, tends to keep them calm, composed and confident under fire."[20]

almost waterproof unit, not prone to damage as was the fragile paper percussion cartridge with its separate percussion cap primer. Equally as important was the fact that the soldier in the confusion of battle couldn't load his breechloader improperly, as often was the case with a percussion muzzle-

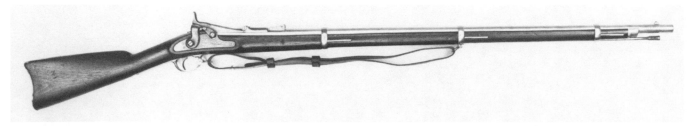

US .50–70 Springfield M1866, also known as the 2nd Model Allin conversion.

Smith, a topographer with an 1871 western geological survey party, with a sporterized halfstock .50 Springfield "trapdoor" secured to his saddle in a leather socket. (Courtesy: US Geological Survey, W. H. Jackson neg. #590)

The following day twenty-six infantrymen of the 27th from Fort Philip Kearny and a handful of civilian wood-cutters were attacked by hundreds of Sioux. The whites were doubtful of their survival and were prepared to take their own lives rather than endure capture and the torture they were sure would follow. When the attacks began, Sgt. Samuel Gibson already had removed his shoelaces and made loops in them to reach the trigger to facilitate his suicide. A private recalled that the smoke from their guns was so thick that they seldom could see farther than a few rods, but the volume of firepower from the new breechloaders surprised the attackers and eventually they withdrew, allowing the whites to survive the Wagon Box Fight.[21]

Infantrymen and artillerymen continued to carry the M1866 and subsequent model Springfield .50 rifles of 1868 and 1870. However the army persisted in its pursuit of the most practical design for an infantry rifle, conducting various board studies and 1871–73 field trials. With economy in mind, testing culminated in the adoption of the Springfield No. 99, a Model 1870 with a .45 caliber barrel. Designated as the Model 1873, with various modifications it would remain the US Army's standard rifle—and in carbine length for cavalry—for the next two decades. The .45–70 rifle cartridge—the carbine load was a lighter 55-grain powder charge—became one of the more popular civilian rounds with Sharps, Remingtons, Ballards, Marlins, Winchesters, and other arms chambered for it.

Deliveries of the new .45 Springfields to regiments on the frontier began in early 1874, but the replacement of obsolescent arms, particularly in remote areas, took several years to accomplish. By mid-1875 all regular army units had at least a few '73s on hand, but dissemination to the militia received lower priority. The African American 10th Cavalry in Texas was the first regiment to receive large numbers of the '73 carbine. In mid-1875 there were still some .50 carbines in service—Sharps plus a limited number of Ward-Burtons and Model 1870 Springfield carbines that had been issued for field trials. The Spencer, with its inferior range, by then was largely gone from service. For example, ordnance returns for the 7th Cavalry as of June 30, 1876, only days after the Little Bighorn fight, showed 639 .45 Springfield carbines, 639 Colt .45 revolvers, 2 Springfield .50 Model 1870 carbines, 14 .50 Sharps carbines, and 3 Remington .50 single-shot pistols on hand.[22]

In 1901 on the twenty-fifth anniversary of the Custer defeat, the H. J. Heinz Company wrote to the War Department explaining they had on exhibition in Atlantic City, New Jersey, a twenty-two-foot painting entitled "Custer's Last Rally" and they wanted to display appropriate firearms with it. The reply included a tabulation by troop presumably before the battle. Carbine totals were 872 .45 Springfields, 15 .50 Springfields, 8 .50 Sharps, and 1 .50 Remington plus 3 .45 Springfield rifles and 1 .50 rifle of unspecified make. Colt .45 revolvers numbered 831 plus 3 .44 (percussion?) Remingtons and 3 Remington .50 single-shot pistols.[23]

At least one Spencer carbine is known to have been present with the 7th Cavalry at the Little Bighorn, in a civilian's hands. Among the bodies found near Custer Hill was that of Mark Kellogg, who accompanied the column as a special correspondent for the Bismarck *Tribune*. Sgt. John Ryan later reported: "[Kellogg] carried a Spencer carbine with him, and rode a small mule. He wore a peculiar shaped boot, we knew him by that."[24]

Soon after completing a cattle drive to Wyoming in 1871, Charles W. Allen found himself "inducted into the Ancient Order of Mule Skinners—which . . . means simply mule drivers." Business was brisk, whether the cargo was wood, logs, hay, or freight. One load was unusual and involved a certain degree of risk.

> All the western military posts, when supplied with improved firearms, sold their old muzzle-loading Springfield rifles and their cap and ball ammunition. A large quantity of these paper, powder and ball cartridges had been sold by the Government to various traders throughout the country. They were easily disposed of to the Indians, trappers and hunters for their powder and lead, which they could remold and shape to fit their rifles of various calibers. It seems that our employers had about two wagon loads of boxes containing this kind of goods and had received a tip that there was a plot hatching among the Indians to seize this lead and powder when the village went to hunt, for at that time they were poorly supplied with modern guns. . . . While we ate breakfast the force about the store began loading into our wagons the small lead-colored boxes, about eighteen inches by twelve by ten, all branded "U.S.I.C." [US inspected and condemned] and provided with slotted handholds.[25]

As the new .45 Springfields reached units in the field, many obsolescent arms were turned in. The post commander at Fort Sully in Dakota Territory, for example, in early 1875 requested authority to turn in to the nearest arsenal 65 Spencer .50 carbines, 108 .44 Colt revolvers, 104 .50 Springfield rifles, 29,000 rounds of .50 Sharps carbine ammunition, and 82,000 .50–70 Springfield rifle cartridges which had been issued for the Model 1866 and Model 1868 Springfield rifles in use by the 22nd Infantry in prior years there. However, General Order No. 103 of August 5, 1874, allowed each infantry company to retain five .50 caliber rifles for hunting and target practice and some continued in service in the hands of civilian army employees and Indian scouts throughout the decade. As late as 1880, one hundred Model 1866s were issued at Fort Union, New Mexico Territory, probably to such individuals. State and territorial militia units were slower to replace their .50 rifles.[26]

Throughout the life of the .58, .50, and .45 Springfield breech loading rifles, the army supplied reconditioned Civil War triangular bayonets. In lesser numbers, ten thousand combination bayonet and trowel-like entrenching tools were issued beginning in October 1874 for field trials, and in 1888 a slender rod bayonet mounted beneath the barrel was adopted. None of these appendages proved of significant value in the field. One doughboy with the 16th Infantry spoke of bayonets doing service as candlesticks in camp, a long-practiced tradition in the army.[27]

"Doughboy" was a term used frequently when referring to a US World War I infantryman, but the word's origin went back to pre–Civil War days. It may have been a reference to the adobe dust which a soldier endured on a long march in the southwest, but the term persisted. Pvt. W. E. Smith, 4th Cavalry, referred to "doe boys" in describing an 1876 incident. Earlier, Col. Richard Irving Dodge in his journal entry for May 31, 1875, in the Black Hills noted a midnight shot alerted the camp to possible trouble with the beef herd. But there was no cause for concern, "a 'Doboy' recruit having got scared at a loose horse, & fired to give the alarm."[28]

During the service life of the "trapdoor," the army tested other arms including designs by Remington, Sharps, Peabody, Whitney, and others. The single-shot .50 Ward-Burton was one of the first bolt action arms the army examined and it was made in limited numbers at the Springfield Armory in 1871. One complaint was that the gun was automatically cocked when the bolt was shoved forward to chamber a cartridge. A few of these bolt action rifles did see combat against the Modoc Indians in 1873.

In the fall of 1871, Gen. Philip Sheridan hosted a group of eastern "sportsmen" on a ten-day hunting trip. The party, with Buffalo Bill Cody as a guide, covered almost two hundred miles, leaving behind "a trail of empty champagne bottles and animal carcasses from Fort McPherson, Nebraska to Fort Hays, Kansas." They slew more than six hundred bison plus hundreds of elk, antelope, and other game. One participant later wrote of his experience and noted:

> One party of eight [bison] crossed our path about two hundred yards in advance of us, and gave General Sheridan an opportunity of testing the value of a new gun he had with him of the Ward Burton pattern. With two shots he knocked over the two leading animals of the herd, killing each dead with a single shot.[29]

The expedition was the preliminary to an even more extravagant hunt conducted by Sheridan and Cody the following year for the Grand Duke Alexis of Russia.

The new Model 1873 Springfield caught the attention of a correspondent for the Bismarck (Dakota Territory) *Tribune* covering the preparations for the army's foray into the Black Hills in 1874 under Lt. Col. George A. Custer. Problems in securing the new weapons caused Custer some concern in making ready.

> [The expedition] is armed with the new Springfield arm just adopted for the army. Gen. Taylor, who was president of the commission which adopted the arm, declares it the most perfect breech-loading gun yet manufactured. It was submitted to all the known tests, and was adopted after a year's investigation. General [Alfred] Terry says that on one occasion, five shots made at five hundred yards could have been covered by a man's hand. The calibre is reduced from 50 to 45, the ball more elongated, the charge of powder heavier [not so], giving longer range and greater accuracy.[30]

In the hands of the 7th Cavalry troopers, the expedition provided a testing ground for the eagerly anticipated new Springfield carbine but their tardy delivery delayed the start. The guns hadn't arrived as of May 19 and Custer was increasingly concerned.

> I desire to call particular attention to the failure of the forwarding officers to send to this post the ordnance stores including arms and ammunition required for, invoices of which have been received as long ago as in December. We cannot move without these stores. . . . I desire, and all the company commanders concur in the desire to obtain revolvers for this command, Smith & Wesson's or Colt's improved pattern preferred. Four-fifths of our carbines are unserviceable, hence the importance of tracing up the stores enroute.[31]
>
> . . . Brevet Major General [Custer] commanding is in receipt of an official telegram from Department Headquarters informing him that Springfield carbines Cal. 45 have been ordered for this command. This will necessitate a change in the waist belts already prepared to carry cartridges of 50 caliber. All Springfield muskets, and the various patterns of carbines now in the

hands of the men belonging to the cavalry companies of this post, will be stored at this post, until the return of the expedition.[32]

In his diary, Lt. James Calhoun noted for July 1: "The new Springfield arms and ammunition were issued to the command today. They seem to give great satisfaction. In fact this Expedition is so thoroughly equipped as to render it one of the most complete that has ever moved west." Colt .45 revolvers, too, had arrived. However orders restricted any temptation to test the new arms indiscriminately. "As a pistol or rifle shot will be the signal of danger, the discharge of fire arms within or near the lines by day or night is strictly prohibited. Firing at game from the column or from the vicinity of camp is prohibited except under circumstances warranting special permission." Despite such orders, Calhoun noted that some of the men "were very careless in shooting across the column" at antelopes which sometimes approached to within twenty-five yards of the command.[33]

In general, the two-month expedition went smoothly. The press played up the confirmation of the discovery of gold, which soon led to a rush into the Black Hills by eager miners, despite half-hearted efforts by the military to keep them out of the Indian lands. Two soldiers under Custer's command died of disease and one was murdered in the finale to a lengthy quarrel between two troopers, privates William Roller and George Turner. The former, one morning, found his horse had been cross hobbled, which prevented the animal from moving without falling. Roller swore he would whip the perpetrator whomever it was, and Turner accepted the challenge. He reached for his revolver on his right, forgetting he had moved his holster to his left side just that morning. Responding to Turner's move, Roller drew his own Colt and mortally wounded his antagonist.[34]

The .45 "trapdoor" carbine with its 22-inch barrel and 55-grain powder charge lacked the range and accuracy of the rifle, although it surpassed the Winchester Model 1873 repeater in these areas. In some instances, cavalrymen fired the 70-grain rifle cartridge in their carbines to extend range, despite the increased recoil. As the Battle of the Little Bighorn neared its conclusion on Reno Hill in June of 1876, several Indians were annoying the exhausted 7th Cavalry troopers, firing from beyond the range of their carbines. Capt. Thomas French, commanding Company M, turned to 1st Sgt. John Ryan who in 1909 described the situation:

> I possessed a seventeen pound Sharp's telescope rifle, made for me in Bismarck, which cost me $100. I used infantry ammunition,

70 grains of powder, which I procured from First Sgt. Wm. F. Bolton of Co. G, 17th Infantry, before going out on this trip. I gave him some of our carbine ammunition in place of it. I told Captain French I would see what I could do.... I raised the sight of my gun, and the first shot that I fired fell a little short, as I could see by the dust that it raised. I fired again and got the range of those Indians. I immediately put in half a dozen shots in rapid succession as quickly as I could fire, and those Indians scampered from that bluff.[35]

Ryan's second enlistment was nearing its end when the 7th returned to Fort Abraham Lincoln. "I raffled that gun [Sharps] off... and received $100 for it. Sgt. Charles White... was the lucky one to receive it."[36]

Complaints about the carbine's limited range, one ordnance officer felt, were largely due to improper instruction in sighting. But perhaps prompted by that incident on Reno Hill, on March 27, 1877, Rock Island Arsenal was directed to forward 120 Springfield rifles to the 7th, ten per company, to compensate for the carbine's shorter range. The regiment spent almost eight hard months in the field in 1877 and when these rifles were inspected later, "they were almost all unserviceable by reason of abrasions, loss of parts, or accumulation of rust. They had generally been carried on the pommel, and the stocks in some cases were worn down to the barrel by constant friction against the saddle."[37]

Capt. J. W. Reilly, ordnance chief for the Division of the Missouri observed:

> The Indians do possess a rifle here and there, possibly one in ten of their armament, that exceeds it [Springfield carbine] in range and accuracy at long range. To overcome this advantage, the method in use in the 5th Cavalry, giving to each company five Springfield rifles for selected marksmen, and in the 7th Cavalry, giving ten rifles per company for the same purpose, seems to answer.... Aside from the companies of the 4th Cavalry serving in the Department of Missouri, which were ordered to be armed with the Springfield rifle, and companies K and M, 3rd Cavalry, which must have been for some time so armed, none of the companies of cavalry serving in the division have

Tintype image of a trooper holding a M1873 Springfield carbine and two belts of .45 rifle ammunition. The date of the image is 1882 or later since production of a 500-grain rifle bullet rather than the shorter 405-grain slug began in that year. The carbine load continued to be a 405-grain bullet. (Courtesy: Herb Peck Jr.)

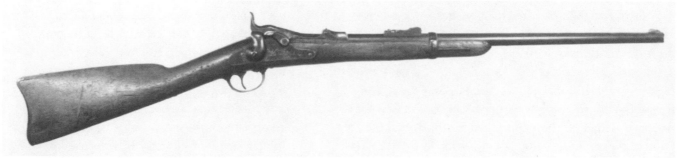

Springfield M1873 carbine (#20140) identified with a cartridge found about four hundred yards east of "Last Stand Hill" on the Custer Battlefield by an archeological team in 1984. It had been owned by a Montana family since 1900 or earlier. It has a sear let-off screw and a replaced front sight blade that are thought to represent simple improvements made by armorers at western posts, probably for men designated as "sharpshooters."
(Courtesy: Ralph Heinz)

A 6th Cavalry trooper "stands to horse" in the 1880s with Colt Single Action and Springfield carbine, the latter carried in the carbine boot which covered the entire breech area. Earlier the carbine was held in a short leather socket of Civil War vintage. (Courtesy: Fort Davis National Historic Site, TX)

availed themselves of the permission granted by the General of the Army [Sherman] to exchange their carbines for rifles. The only inference from this is that a large majority of cavalry still have faith in the carbine.[38]

Within Col. Eugene Carr's 6th Cavalry, some company commanders preferred the carbine because of the convenience of carrying on horseback, others opted for the longer range accuracy of the rifle. Carr eventually left the choice up to company commanders but on February 12, 1881, issued printed instructions for handling rifles which in part specified: "In using the Springfield rifle mounted, until some other sling or holster be adopted, or until further orders, the rifle will be slung across the

back by its own gun sling, from the right shoulder to the left side, muzzle up."[39]

The concept of supporting carbines with rifles was not a new one. During the Mexican War, Hall rifles had been issued to dragoons in limited numbers for hunting and long-range shooting. Similarly after the adoption of the short-range smoothbore Model 1847 cavalry musketoon, it appears it was common for one percussion rifle to be issued to each dragoon company for hunting.[40]

The M1873 carbine also came under some criticism after the battle on the Little Bighorn for failure to extract fired cases. Careful analysis by army ordnance captain O. E. Michaelis laid the blame for any such difficulties on the ammunition rather than the gun's design. He found that there were few if any similar complaints about the rifle and no carbine extraction criticism during the 3rd Cavalry's

Casually uniformed members of the 3rd Cavalry in the early 1880s equipped as unofficial mounted infantry with Springfield rifles and Smith & Wesson Schofield revolvers. (Courtesy: Thomas N. Trevor)

engagement on the Rosebud only days before Custer's defeat. Ammunition carried in the field for months sometimes became dirty and dented. If carried in a leather cartridge belt, tanning acids caused the formation of verdigris on the case which could cause it to stick in a chamber when fired. As Indians threatened Gen. Crook's camp near the Bighorn Mountains in August 1876, Sgt. George Howard of the 2nd Cavalry remembered that "the men went to cleaning cartridges."[41]

Michaelis also found that ammunition manufactured at Frankfort Arsenal was being improperly gauged and often was not within proper tolerance. Regardless of the problem's cause, it was of sufficient significance that beginning in January 1877 a headless shell extractor was issued for emergency use, carried with the three-piece cleaning rod in the carbine's butt stock while infantrymen carried the tool in a pocket. The introduction of a "prairie" cartridge belt with a leather body but loops of cotton or canvas, the

use of an ammunition gauging machine after March 1877, and finally in 1888 the change from copper to tinned brass cases made at Frankfort Arsenal followed. The entire question of the adequacy of the .45 carbine was fast becoming less relevant since except in the southwest, the intensity of Indian warfare by 1880 had diminished.[42]

Despite the army's continued reliance on the single-shot "trapdoor" carbine, Col. Ranald Mackenzie commanding the 4th Cavalry in the summer of 1876 sought to have his regiment supplied with faster firing Winchesters. His request was denied, but the army did acquire at least one of these repeaters. Capt. O. E. Michaelis on July 9, 1876, was authorized to purchase one Winchester rifle at $60 which was issued to C. R. Morris, a civilian scout carrying messages through Sioux country. At that price, the gun would have been a new Model 1873 .44.[43]

As the army's experience with the new Springfields increased, one frontier officer criticized the "trapdoor" in

The Model 1890 sight protector barrel band on this M1884 carbine dates the photo, taken in Winfield, Kansas. The protector was developed in response to complaints of damage to the sight leaf when the carbine was inserted into the carbine boot. The carbine sling by which the weapon was secured to the trooper is the Model 1885, narrower than the Civil War version in use until that time.

general not for its overall design but rather for its trigger pull and sights.

> I have frequently cocked a U.S. rifle musket, turned it muzzle downward, and dangled it, the whole weight of the gun being on the trigger resting on my finger without pulling it off. With such a weapon and great economy in the expenditure of cartridges, it is little wonder that the majority of the Army are as poor shots as can be found. The system on which even the little practice that soldiers have is conducted, is as absurd as can well be imagined. To put a recruit to firing off hand at a target three hundred yards away, when he cannot with a rest, hit a cracker box at twenty paces, is as ridiculous a performance as could well be devised....
>
> There is no sort of excuse for such sights as are put on the rifle musket. The apology for the hard trigger is that men would be more likely to shoot each other if the triggers were easy, a most weak and frivolous pretense... [for] a breech-loader is never charged [loaded] until wanted for use, and that when not actually at the "ready," the gun stands at the half cock notch, which may be as hard as they please to make it. Old men are nearly always opposed to innovation.[44]

An infantryman who served in the late 1870s and early 1880s observed that the regulars generally didn't take much interest in anything they were compelled to do, except

Troop C, 3rd Cavalry, in the field near Fort Davis, Texas, about 1885. A trooper standing at center right holds a Smith & Wesson Schofield revolver in his right hand. It is unusual to see sabers carried in the field since by this date they were shown to be more of a noisy inconvenience that of any benefit in Indian warfare. (Courtesy: Fort Davis National Historic Site, TX)

training for combat. "Every man would take pride in drill so long as it was useful skirmish drill accompanied by the manual of arms. But when it came to the bayonet and saber exercise—the infantry not using the bayonet and the cavalry [not using] the saber in the field—then a man [would] lose interest." Both of these edged weapons, particularly the saber, often were left behind when campaigning after the early 1870s. The infantryman's full field equipment in 1877, including rifle, sixty rounds of ammunition, five days' rations, overcoat, blanket, etc., totaled forty-two pounds or more. Tom Horn served for a while as a scout for the army. He opined that "[a belt full of] .45–70 cartridges weighs eleven pounds when you first put [it] on, and at the end of twenty days...about as much as a small sized locomotive."[45]

Another distressing aspect of a soldier's life was the general lack of continuing target practice, a situation which carried over from pre–Civil War days. Maj. William A.

Thornton in a May 1856 letter from Santa Fe to Col. H. K. Craig had recommended that each man be given the modest number of ten ball cartridges per week along with careful instruction. Ammunition should also be provided for hunting to hone shooting skills as well as to provide experience in scouting. The best shots would be rewarded with a gill of whiskey, he proposed. To bolster his position, he cited his experience the previous summer when he observed 160 musket shots fired from seventy yards at a two-foot-square target. "Only five balls and a few buck shot struck the square." The blame for such a poor showing could not be levied entirely on the inaccuracy of the smoothbore musket itself. "I saw men aim carefully, and then turn their faces to the rear and fire."[46]

At Fort C. F. Smith in Montana Territory, General Order No. 9 dated April 2, 1868, specified that three rounds of ammunition per day would be allowed for use during daily drill. Two weeks later, in the face of prevailing Indian

Members of Company B of the African American US 25th Infantry in dress uniforms with bayoneted Springfield "trapdoor" rifles at Fort Snelling, Minnesota (ca. 1883). (Courtesy: Minnesota Historical Society)

Troop A of the black 10th Cavalry at Fort Apache, Arizona Territory, March 1887. (Courtesy: Fort Davis National Historic Site, TX)

Rifle team representing the Department of the Platte (1887).

unrest, the order was revoked and the garrison would be given target practice twice daily, at 10 a.m. and 2 p.m. "Company commanders will exercise economy in the expenditure of ammunition at target practice."[47]

Custer was an exception to the often overlooked matter of marksmanship training. Prior to the 7th Cavalry's winter campaign in 1868, his men practiced daily for a month with their .50 Spencer carbines. Their enthusiasm was bolstered by his formation of an elite forty-man company under Lt. W. W. Cooke consisting of the best shots and which would march separately and be excused from guard details.[48]

The post–Civil War army faced a severe shortage of funding. In part due to the increased cost of metallic ammunition, General Order No. 50 of May 12, 1869, allowed only ten ball cartridges per month to each soldier for target practice with the new breechloaders (increased to twenty rounds per month in late 1876). While frontier soldiers might be encouraged to hunt game for fresh meat, General Order No. 103 dated August 5, 1874, specified they had to pay for the ammunition they used at the rate of 2 1/2¢ for .45 carbine cartridges and 3¢ each for rifle ammunition! In a letter dated June 7, 1873, Maj. S. V. Benet replied on behalf of the chief of ordnance to a request by Gen. John Schofield to increase this allowance.

[General Order No. 50] permits an expenditure of 120 ball cartridges a year to each soldier, or a total of 3,600,000 ball cartridges for the Army of 30,000 men, besides the blank cartridges for recruits, that may increase this total to 4,000,000 a year expended in target practice.

The appropriations for metallic ammunition to supply the entire Army has averaged during the past 3 years less than $125,000 a year, enabling the Department to supply less than 5,000,000 cartridges annually. If . . . 4,000,000 be used in target practice, but 1,000,000 will remain for military operations. . . . It is not seen in view of our limited appropriations how the allowance of cartridges . . . can be properly increased.[49]

Where soldiers were given target practice, good performance sometimes was rewarded with relief from guard duty as in March 1867 at Fort Kearney in Nebraska. While recovering from a back injury, A. F. Mulford, 7th Cavalry, wrote of his rather brief army career and included a description of revolver practice as conducted in Company M.

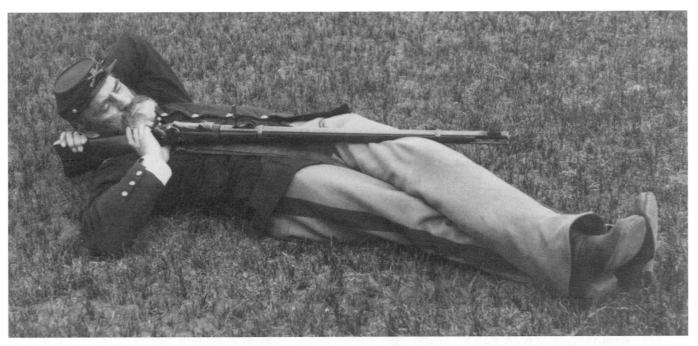

The so-called Texas position, popular in the army for long-range target shooting in the 1880s. (Courtesy: Colorado Historical Society, neg. #35888)

Mounted target practice is fascinating. The target is made from pieces of hard-tack boxes shaped to resemble a man standing erect. The company is formed in a right front into line, and then the men file off from the right of the line, with horses at a walk. They do not stop their horses, but as they pass the target they try to see how many bullets they can put through the tack man, firing from the shoulder; that means having the muzzle of your revolver held on a level with the shoulder, and then firing as soon as the arm is extended. As soon as the men get so that they can hit the target with their horses on a walk, at thirty paces from it, they go at a trot, then lope, and at last as fast as their horses can run. It is very exciting, both to man and beast, and it is considered good shooting to hit a target and load and hit it again, in a distance of not more than forty yards, and your horses on a dead run all the time.[50]

One night in 1874 Indians intent on stampeding cavalry horses during a Texas campaign by Col. Ranald Mackenzie failed when troopers guarding the herd unleashed a hail of gunfire. One participant bemoaned the fact that "but for the total lack of target practice in those days [we] would have emptied many [Indian] saddles." The situation finally was beginning to change by the late 1870s. A manual for marksmanship training developed by Col. T. T. S. Laidley was adopted (1879) and was followed in 1885 by one written by Capt. Stanhope Blunt, instructor of rifle practice for the Department of Dakota. As in the civilian community, interest in target shooting was growing with greater emphasis placed on such instruction within the army. With the army's adoption of rifle ammunition with external primers, it was possible to reload fired cartridge cases as an economy, a task sometimes assigned within a company as a form of punishment or as a regular rotating detail. Frankfort Arsenal in 1879 began issuing reloading kits and a light "gallery load" of only seven grains of powder now allowed economical practice at ranges of less than one hundred feet and indoor practice in bad weather.[51]

Some soldiers relished the competitive environment of greatly expanded marksmanship training of the 1880s. Three army teams participated in the international matches at Creedmoor in 1879, but in 1881 as a cost-saving measure the army inaugurated annual matches rather than attendance at Creedmoor. The three winners in each division—Atlantic, Missouri, and Pacific—received special "trapdoor" Marksman Rifles as prizes. However, medals were awarded instead beginning the next year. Although cavalrymen could compete in rifle matches, their greater familiarity with the carbine put them at a disadvantage with infantrymen and it was not until 1890 that separate

Distinguished marksmen in 1887 wearing their various shooting medals. Standing center is Sgt. John Nihill, Company F, 5th Cavalry, wearing the Medal of Honor awarded him for distinguished service in the Whetstone Mountains of Arizona on July 13, 1872. (Courtesy: Guy V. Henry Collection, US Army Military History Institute, Carlisle Barracks, PA)

Carbine practice with Springfield "trapdoors." (Courtesy: Latter Day Saints Archives, Salt Lake City, UT)

Medal inscribed on the obverse "THIRD CLASS PRIZE ARMY DIVISION MARKSMANSHIP" and on the reverse "WON BY Sgt. F. W. Weeks Co. 'E' 6th INFTY. AT DIV OF MISSOURI Rifle Competition Sept. 5th, 7th, 9th & 11th 1885." (Courtesy: Gary L. Delscamp)

matches for the two branches were initiated. Mounted practice for cavalrymen previously had been scant, but in the decade of the '80s it, too, was promoted with both revolver and carbine. It was not until about 1890, however, that increased official attention was paid to instruction in firing at moving targets and at stationary targets scattered at unknown distances.[52]

Soldiers found that a lengthy session on the firing range could be bruising. A 7th Ccavalryman in 1887 noted that soldiers:

> had sockets to put over the butt of the carbine, and on top of that we were glad to put paper or anything we could get to keep it from the shoulder. I was black and blue all over the shoulder and down into my chest. I got so I couldn't help flinching and I didn't make a very good score.

One soldier with the 13th Infantry used two pairs of socks to dampen the recoil during extended practice. Nevertheless, the Fourth of July events at Fort Yates, Dakota Territory, in 1879 included a rifle match between five enlisted men and five officers as well as horse and foot races and a baseball game between officers and their men.[53]

In 1885 Maj. Andrew Burt of the 8th Infantry stood as one of the army's top marksmen. Stationed at Fort Bidwell,

California, almost on the Oregon and Nevada borders, he drilled the men of his command on the target range. In August 1885 he competed with a Mr. Brown, a bookkeeper for a local merchant, in a match in which each fired a string of fifteen shots at distances of two, three, and six hundred yards for a purse of $50. Burt won easily, even though he fired several of his shots at six hundred yards standing.[54]

A rifle match was part of the Christmas Day activities in 1884 at Fort Bidwell with five teams participating: Company F, 8th Infantry with a final score of 224; Citizens, Fort Bidwell (223); Independents (221); Troop C, 2nd Cavalry (215); and Pah-Ute Indians (180). As reported in the *Army-Navy Journal*:

> The shooting was pretty close between the two leading teams, so much so that the winning of the prize depended on our commanding officer, Major Burt, who shot last in the infantry team. The excitement was quite tense between the time he fired his last shot and when the result became known; had it been a "magpie" [middle scoring ring] the citizens of Bidwell would have carried off the coveted prize, but when the four disk loomed up close to the bull's–eye, quite a relief was experienced by the boys of the 8th Foot.[55]

Sgt. Max Simon of Troop H, 6th Cavalry, wearing a silver 3rd Class Medal (1886) and Distinguished Marksman badge (1887). (Courtesy: Thomas N. Trevor)

On the target range and in the field, the regular army was relying on the Springfield, but civilians hired by the army at $30 to $50 a month as teamsters or to handle pack animals ("packers") sometimes carried obsolescent government arms such as Sharps .50 carbines. Their role in the success of a campaign was usually unsung except in one poem written from the packers' point of view. As the last stanza revealed:

> When you're stationed in the firin' line
> along a rocky crest,
> And you're diggin' like a gopher in
> the dirt,
> When the chunks of lead are comin'
> like a hummin' hornets' nest,
> And you're tyin' up your wounded
> with your shirt;

> When you've searched the dead for
> ca'tridges and shot 'em all away.
> And you feel yourself beginnin'
> to despair,
> Then you yell for ammunition—oh,
> you needn't holler twice,
> For you bet you'll find the pack-
> train there![56]

Corp. E. A. Bode never fired his Springfield at an Indian or was fired upon during his service in the west with the 16th Infantry (1877–1882). Yet he described one near accident supporting the safety admonition to always treat any gun as being loaded. While waiting to be relieved from guard duty, another corporal playfully raised his rifle and aimed at a white horse grazing about forty feet away. Remarking that he could hit the horse right in the eye, there

TARGET YEAR OF 188*7.*

SHARPSHOOTER'S CERTIFICATE, No. *74*

Headquarters Department of *Texas,*

OFFICE OF THE INSPECTOR OF RIFLE PRACTICE,

*San Antonio, May 16" , 188*7.

Reinhard Miller, Pvt. of Tp. "D," 3d Regiment of Cavalry , having made, under the regulations prescribed in the "Instructions in Rifle and Carbine Firing for the United States Army," the scores necessary for qualification as a SHARPSHOOTER, *is graded as such for the target year of 188*7.

Inspector of Rifle Practice, Department of *Texas*

APPROVED:

Brig. Genl. U.S.A. Commanding.

QUALIFYING SCORES:

RANGE.	SCORES.				TOTAL.	RANGE.	SCORES.				TOTAL.
200 yds	77	73	77	74	91	600 yds	70	71	77	74	87
300 yds	71	77	77	75	90	800 yds	18	77	73	74	87
500 yds	71	77	73	74	90	1,000 yds	19	19	77	70	80

GRAND TOTAL OF SCORES *525*

Sharpshooter's Certificate awarded to Pvt. Reinhard Miller, 3rd Cavalry, in 1887. (Courtesy: Thomas N. Trevor)

was great astonishment at the report and smoke rising from the muzzle of his rifle. "All eyes directed to the horse, but he looked unconcerned, continuing his meal to the great relief of the sharpshooter. Strange to say nothing was done to him [the corporal] for his carelessness, which should have been severely punished."[57]

Bode later was almost the victim of an accident. He prepared to fire at a wolf and retrieved his rifle which had been lying on some sacks of corn. The animal disappeared in some trees before he could fire.

> On my return to the wagon I took the cartridge from the chamber, noticing a few grains of corn rolling out. Examining the barrel I saw it was stocked with corn up to the muzzle. What a narrow escape! Had I fired the barrel would have exploded and

blown my head off, and made a cornfield of a wolf's hide.[58]

On a lighter note, darkness and a broom saved Bode from punishment. While asleep and clothed at the guardhouse awaiting his turn to go on duty, he was startled awake by the order to call out the guard for the officer of the day. Half asleep and unable to find his rifle, which someone had kicked under his bunk, he grabbed a broomstick and took his place. The officer passed down the line but failed to detect Bode's ploy. "I returned to the [guard]room with a much lighter feeling, thanking my lucky star and the darkness to pass inspection undetected with a broom."[59]

Bode was not above exaggeration when he described another incident. Traveling through the woods in a wagon in 1878, a corporal's rifle was caught between two trees and bent "almost forty five degrees."

Army pack mules and their packers, armed with Springfield carbines, near the Mexican border in 1883. (Courtesy: National Archives, photo #111-SC-89096)

Pistol grips on their carbines sets apart this scene of 6th Cavalry troopers in New Mexico in the mid-1880s. Detachable wooden grips were offered on the Officer's Model rifle beginning in 1877, metal grips two years later. Such attachments were sometimes used on long-range rifles. (Courtesy: Thomas N. Trevor)

The gun was a supernumerary one issued to him for the trip to save his own from wear and exposure of the weather. That evening the gun was straightened again between some trees and given to a civilian, who claimed to be a good shot, for practice. As might be expected the ball went way off its mark and somewhere around the corner.[60]

On one occasion in 1878, a cooking fire caught the prairie grass on fire. It was extinguished but not before an officer's tent and its contents—including five thousand rounds of ammunition packed in wooden boxes—were ablaze.

Shells and bells went whizzing past our heads, sounding as if the Indians had attacked and were giving us a shower of blue-beans. We succeeded at last by throwing enough water on them to save most of the cartridges, putting a stop to the unwelcome "whizzers" who…endangered our precious lives for a while.[61]

"TRAPDOOR" VARIATIONS

A specialized variation of the "trapdoor" was a sporting-style rifle intended for sale to officers. The Springfield Armory prior to 1875 had assembled customized rifles and several carbines on special order for individual army officers, priced according to features. Gen. Grenville Dodge, chief engineer of the Union Pacific Railroad construction project, paid $70 for his M1868 .50 sporter. George Armstrong Custer was an ardent hunter during his service on the plains and from the armory purchased a M1866 sporter with a halfstock and double set triggers. By 1873 he had added a commercial Remington rolling-block No. 1 .50–70 sporting rifle to his hunting arsenal, an arm that seemingly became his favorite and fell with him at the Little Bighorn. In an October 1873 letter to the editors of *Turf, Field and Farm*, Custer signed himself as "Nomad" and with ill-concealed pride mentioned forty-one antelope he had killed during a three-month expedition. "My score was made with a Remington hunting rifle, caliber .50; cartridges containing 70 grains of powder. I seldom killed at a less distance than 150 yards, running up…to 630 yards.[62]

Maj. George W. Schofield, known for the Smith & Wesson revolver model bearing his name, in May 1874 requested a Model 1873 carbine with apparently rather minor modifications for the cost was only $19.25. Among the more unusual requests came from Lt. E. H. Townsend at Sioux City, Iowa, with the 13th Infantry. He offered to pay $50 for only a barreled action which he planned to have stocked and sighted to resemble a Ballard. The .50 barrel was to be octagonal and four feet long [!] and the action was to have a double extractor.[63]

In response to continuing requests such as these from officers, the Ordnance Department in May 1875 decided to standardize the design of an Officer's Model .45–70 rather than continue the annoyance of special orders. Between July 1, 1875, and June 30, 1885, the national armory produced 477, many of which were delivered to purchasers stationed in the west. Features included a half-length stock with checkered wrist and forearm, wooden cleaning rod mounted beneath the barrel, adjustable tang sight, set trigger, and engraved hammer, lockplate, breechblock, and receiver. Among those listed as purchasers of Officer's Models are Lt. Gen. P. H. Sheridan (1876), Col. Benjamin H. Grierson (1878), Lt. Charles B. Gatewood (1880), Lt. Col. George A. Forsyth (1880), Col. John Gibbon (1884), and Capt. Arthur McArthur Jr. (1885).[64]

Although the handsome Officer's Model was available for purchase, some other single-shots as well as repeaters served as officers' privately owned arms. Lt. Thomas Cruse commanded a company of Indian scouts and served against the Apaches with the 6th Cavalry after graduating from West Point in 1879. He mentioned his Marlin repeater, which would have been a Model 1881, probably a .45–70 to allow use of government ammunition. Another officer who participated in campaigns against the Apaches and owned a M1881 Marlin was Gen. George Crook, as well as Mickey Free, an Indian scout and interpreter. John L. Bullis, then a lieutenant with the black 24th Infantry in Texas, on August 24, 1878, wrote the Sharps factory: "What price do you ask for your very best target rifle, with implements for loading &c. Model of 1878 [Borchardt], globe and peep sights, set trigger, Long range." (Bullis also is listed as having purchased an Officer's Model in February 1878.)[65]

In 1881 Springfield Armory inaugurated production of a 20-gauge "trapdoor" shotgun, using some obsolete components such as stocks and bored out .58 rifle musket barrels. The intent was to issue two per company at western posts for use by hunters and scouts to take small game. Armory personnel turned out 1,376 of these smoothbores between 1881 and 1885. The army earlier in the mid-1870s procured imported foreign as well as American-made Parker 10-gauge double-barrel guns for use by guards at the federal prison at Leavenworth, Kansas. Additional 10-gauge doubles were issued to army payroll escorts, including at least sixteen Parkers in the Department of Texas

Members of the geological survey team of 1871 breaking camp with a customized .50 Springfield in the foreground. The rifle has a civilian-style trigger guard and double set trigger. (Courtesy: US Geological Survey, W. H. Jackson neg. #1638)

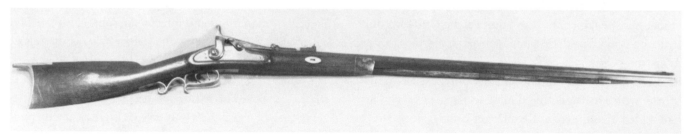

"LONESOME CHARLEY REYNOLDS from GEORGE A. CUSTER" is inscribed on the plaque set into the stock of this customized M1866 .50–70 Springfield sporting rifle. Reynolds was a civilian scout for the 7th Cavalry and had warned Custer of the overwhelming force of Indians camped along the Little Bighorn. Reynolds is said to have anticipated his possible death and gave away many of his possessions before the battle. He lost his life during the retreat of the companies commanded by Maj. Marcus Reno to what today is known as Reno Hill. (Courtesy: Norm Flayderman)

where they saw heavy use until withdrawn in 1882. Another known US-procured specimen the author examined was a 10-gauge double by J. P. Clabrough & Bros. of San Francisco with a Springfield inspector's stamp and acceptance date of 1887 in the stock.[66]

Army officers who wanted a shotgun for their personal use found that the Colt firm, at least in the 1880s, apparently routinely offered a 25 percent discount to them. Capt. Leonard Y. Loring, an assistant surgeon, in May 1882 from Fort Dodge, Kansas, took advantage of this offer when he

Sporterized Springfield M1873 rifle owned by civilian chief of scouts Al Sieber who served under Gen. Crook in the 1870s and early 1880s. (Exhibited by the Arizona Historical Society, Tucson)

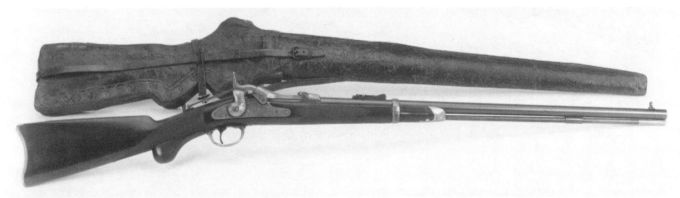

A Springfield Officer's Model identified as to its original owner is a particular prize. Such is this example, which belonged to Lt. John Murphy, 14th Infantry. An Irish immigrant, he enlisted in the artillery in 1858 and served as a sergeant with the 5th US Artillery throughout the Civil War. He received his commission in 1867 and served for the next thirty-two years with the 14th. He campaigned against the Sioux in 1876, participating in the Battle of Slim Buttes and marching with Gen. Crook's force on the ill-famed "starvation march" in pursuit of Chief Crazy Horse. A marksman and a hunter, Murphy was the range officer at Fort Vancouver Barracks in the late 1880s and was captain of the Department of the Columbia's rifle team. His rifle is the second type, produced in 1877 with detachable wooden checkered pistol grip and a round base variation of the tang sight secured with a single screw which, when loose, allowed it to rotate. The custom leather case protected the rifle through his many western travels and bears his name and regiment. (Courtesy: Roy Kinzie)

Gen. Phil Sheridan's Springfield Model 1873 (#41083) customized by Carlos Gove of Denver. (Courtesy: Roswell Art and Museum Center, NM)

A sporterized Springfield Model 1870 .50–70 rifle musket. The barrel retains a stamping "Co H 3d INFTY" indicating earlier use by that company which was stationed at Fort Dodge, Kansas, between 1867 and 1870. A silver plaque in the left side of the butt is inscribed "L. B. WHEAT/Leavenworth City. Kan./1871." Lysander Wheat was a prominent Leavenworth attorney and the rifle may have been a gift to him from an army officer. A possible connection with George A. Custer exists. In January 1868 Custer was charged in civil court with the murder of a private soldier attempting to desert. One of Custer's attorneys was E. N. O. Clough, brother of Wheat's senior law partner. (Courtesy: C. Vance Haynes Jr.)

Lt. Patrick Henry Ray ordered this Sharps Model 1874 .45 sporting rifle (#161269) in 1878. The price was $59.95 and included 100 bullets, 100 cartridges, and 250 primers. Ray served as an enlisted artilleryman during the Civil War and after being commissioned in 1867, served at various posts in the west with the 8th Infantry. He retired as a brigadier general in 1906. (Courtesy: Bob Butterfield via Charles L. Hill Jr.)

ordered a 10-gauge Model 1878 double-barrel hammer gun with a half-grip checkered stock and a line-engraved rebounding lock for $75 minus his discount. Col. L. Wheaton from Fort Assiniboine, Montana Territory, on April 6, 1886, used this discount and ordered a 12-gauge double with 30-inch barrels with "length of stock and drop suitable for medium sized man. Gun to make good target with No. 6 shot." It isn't clear whether he ordered a M1878 or a top of the line Model 1883 hammerless gun but the $65 list price would indicate the former. One officer who did

order the more expensive Model 1883, a heavy 12-gauge for $100, was Lt. C. H. Rockwell with the 5th Cavalry at Fort McKinney, Wyoming Territory, in 1885. He noted he had been using a Colt 12-gauge hammer gun for several years and was pleased with it.[67]

Other specialized Springfield arms included long-range and match rifles, and continuing efforts to improve the weapon resulted in many experimental pieces throughout the years of "trapdoor" production. The 1872–73 Ordnance Board had stated that the

Lt. Henry D. Styer, 21st Infantry, relaxed against a rotting cabin near Fort Steele, Wyoming. The gun is a Springfield M1881 shotgun. (Courtesy: Fort Laramie National Historic Site, WY)

adoption of a repeating magazine gun for the army was only a matter of time. Even as the typical frontier soldier of the early 1880s was campaigning with his Springfield, some units in the west received Winchester-Hotchkiss, Remington-Lee, and Chaffee-Reese .45 bolt action repeaters for field trials. Despite the advanced features these arms offered, it was not until 1892 that the army finally abandoned the .45 Springfield for the Norwegian-designed Krag-Jorgensen, a five-shot bolt action repeater firing a smokeless powder .30–40 cartridge. Sizeable issues of this new rifle didn't begin until late 1894, followed the next year by the introduction of the Krag carbine. Although the Springfield .45 would serve longer with state troops and Spanish-American War volunteers, the regular army's reliance on single-shot black powder rifles and carbines had ended, just as a new century loomed on the horizon.

IN SEARCH OF A REVOLVER

In the immediate years after Lee's surrender at Appomattox, Colt Model 1860 and Remington .44s plus a lesser number of Colt Model 1851 .36s and a sprinkling of single action .44 Starrs and .36 Whitneys were the hand weapons of the frontier cavalryman. But as Capt. William Thompson of the 7th Cavalry pointed out, the difficulty of reloading a percussion revolver while in an engagement on horseback made the gun, once emptied, "of little use to a trooper mounted." Any practical effort to update these arms to fire metallic cartridges were stymied prior to 1869 by Smith & Wesson's control of the rights to the Rollin White patent. However in 1870 an ordnance board met in St. Louis and from its review of various handguns offered for consideration came a decision to request authority to obtain one thousand each of two entries—a sturdy .50 caliber single-shot Remington pistol using the familiar rolling-block action and a newly designed .44 self-extracting S&W six-shooter. For a reason lost to history, Remington had declined an army request that they submit a proposal for a revolver.[68]

The Remington pistols were acquired not through purchase but by exchange with the manufacturer—five thousand pistols in return for an equal number of unused army .44 percussion Remingtons. Their .50 caliber cartridges were loaded with thirty grains of powder behind a 320-grain bullet. Like the other handguns undergoing field testing, some were scattered throughout

The only identification of this image is that the soldier's name was Powers from Fort Halleck. Nevertheless, he has a Colt Single Action thrust into his cartridge belt and he holds a scarce M1881 Springfield shotgun. (Courtesy: Nevada Historical Society)

the various cavalry regiments, but their service life in competition with available revolvers was short.

Of the S&Ws the army received, two hundred were nickel plated and the remainder blued to compare these finishes. Known as the No. 3 and later as the American Model, these .44s reached the civilian market that same summer. Col. Ranald Mackenzie sought to equip his entire 4th Cavalry with the new revolvers. Capt. Myles

Keogh of the 7th Cavalry would lose his life at the Little Bighorn in June 1876. Earlier in March 1874 he reported unfavorably on the .44 No. 3 American after observing its performance in the field. "The pistols are too complicated and constantly out of repair, necessitating replacement of portions of mechanism of the lock and ejector."[69]

Nevertheless a substantial number of officers serving in the west ordered No. 3s as personal sidearms. Smith &

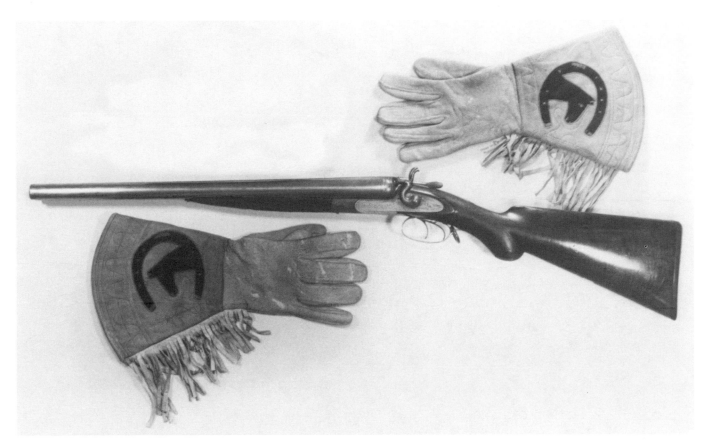

Gen. Ranald S. Mackenzie's buckskin gauntlets and 10-gauge Clabrough & Bros. shotgun. A small German silver escutcheon in the stock is engraved "R.S.M. 4th U.S. Cav." The barrels show substantial use and have been cut to about twenty inches in length and a saddle ring was added behind the trigger guard. Family records indicate the gun and a saber were presented to Mackenzie by Gen. George Crook in appreciation for then colonel Mackenzie's service under Crook during the Powder River Campaign. In what otherwise was a lackluster campaign, Mackenzie defeated the Northern Cheyennes at the Dull Knife Battle in November 1876. (Courtesy: Tucker F. Hentz)

A unique Springfield pattern rifle with 32 1/2-inch barrel fitted with a fourteen-hundred-yard adjustable rear sight. The butt plate is stamped "US" plus "BY ORDER OF COL. BENTON FEB. 18, 1881." The gun probably was the prototype made up at the Springfield Armory when the Model 1881 marksman's rifle was developed. (Photo by Hugo Poisson, courtesy Richard Bourne Co.)

Wesson authority Charles W. Pate in gathering data for a book on No. 3s found that among the West Point class of 1873 graduates, at least fifteen purchased S&Ws from the factory. One was William H. Carter, whose performance with the 6th Cavalry at Cibicu Creek in Arizona in 1881 brought him the Medal of Honor. Another was Edward H. Casey, chief of scouts at Wounded Knee.

Other officers who owned examples of the big .44s included captains Robert H. Young, assigned to the 7th Cavalry at one time; William B. Wetmore of the 6th

Their .30 Krag rifles stacked, men of the 22nd Infantry break for coffee beside a bridge over the Powder River east of Miles City, Montana (1896). (Courtesy: John D. McAulay)

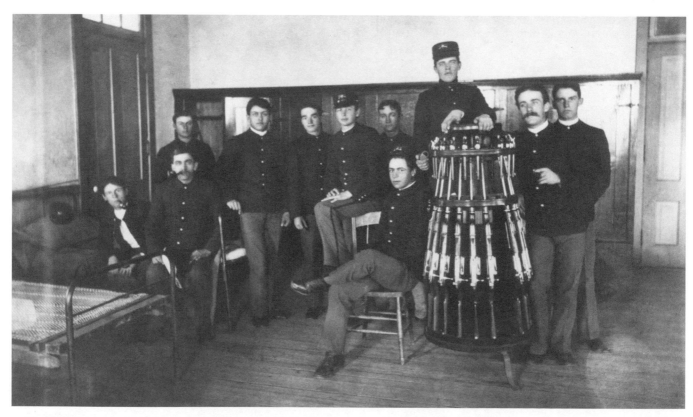

Barracks scene at Fort Riley, Kansas, in 1901. The arms rack holds Colt .38 double action revolvers and Krag .30–40 carbines. (Courtesy: Pennell Collection, Spencer Library, University of Kansas, Lawrence)

Gen. Nelson A. Miles's deluxe Winchester Model 1895 carbine (#22417) made in 1899. Miles's name is inlaid in gold on the right side of the frame and a silver plaque inset in the left side of the butt is inscribed "MAJOR GEN- ERAL NELSON A. MILES/FROM HIS FRIEND/CAPT. J. R. HEGEMAN." The gun being .30–40 caliber, Miles could use standard army ammunition issued for the newly adopted Krag repeater. (Courtesy: Norm Flayderman)

Winchester .45–70 lst Model Hotchkiss carbine (#745), one of 160 sent to Dakota Territory and Texas for field trials in 1879. (Photo by Gary Roedl, courtesy William T. Goodman)

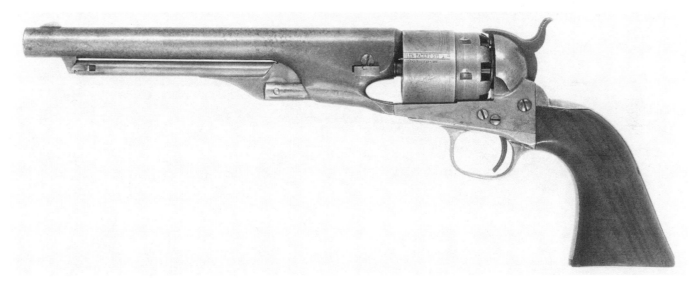

Model 1860 .44 Colt (frame #72361), which was refurbished after the Civil War, reassembled without regard to matching serial numbers, and stamped "US" on the trigger guard. These Colts often seem to have been issued to cavalry regiments in the west. (Courtesy: Track of the Wolf via Dale H. Peterson)

Cavalry, who paired his with two Winchester .44 carbines, a Model 1866 and later a Model 1873; and Louis Carpenter of the black 10th Cavalry. The latter received the Medal of Honor for his forced march to relieve the beleaguered survivors of the 1868 Battle of Beecher's Island in eastern Colorado. Maj. Frank North, who led a battalion of Pawnee scouts for a dozen years, owned a pair of No. 3s and in shooting contests with Wild Bill Hickok and others demonstrated his skill. He also was an outstanding horseman and his brother Luther recalled that during "one run after buffalo, he killed 11 with the 12 shots from his two Smith & Wesson revolvers."[70]

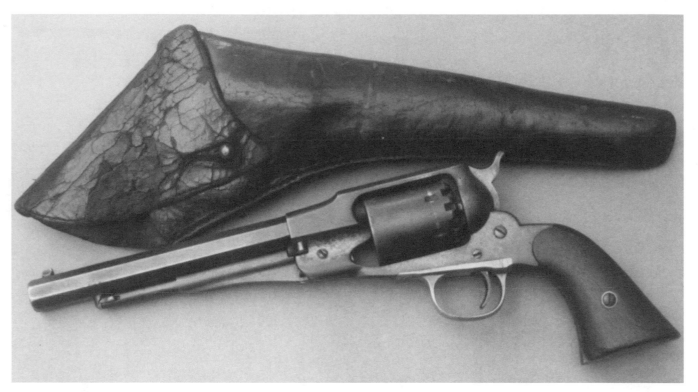

Pvt. George App served with the 3rd Infantry in Indian Territory and Montana during his enlistment (1874–78). This New Model .36 Remington with its Civil War–style holster was his personal weapon, which he found more convenient to carry than a rifle while assigned to duty as an army "mule skinner" out of Fort Supply, Indian Territory. (Courtesy: Jerry Pitstick)

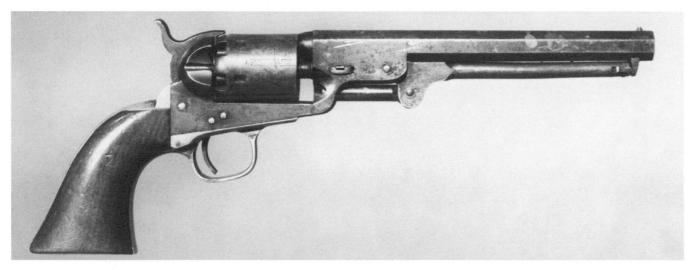

"H. B. Carrington Col. 18th Inf. U.S.A." engraved on the backstrap identifies this M1851 Colt Navy. Col. Carrington laid out the Bozeman Trail defensive line of forts in Montana Territory in 1866—Reno, Philip Kearny, and C. F. Smith. These were later abandoned under the Fort Laramie Treaty of 1868. (Courtesy: Norm Flayderman)

The Colt company was not to be left out of the competition. The army had shown no interest in the front-loading Thuer conversion of percussion Colts, but in 1871 the government ordered one thousand .44 Colt M1860s to be converted to centerfire metallic ammunition using C. B. Richards's design and eventually obtained just over twelve hundred of them. In March 1871 all .36 Colt Navies remaining on hand were recalled. However after that point and until 1873, a cavalry trooper on the frontier might be armed with a percussion .44 Colt or Remington or either

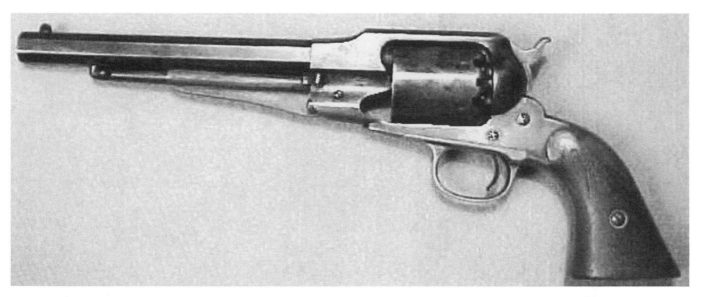

Remington .44 New Model with 8th Cavalry markings in the grip. (Courtesy: Kenneth McPheeters)

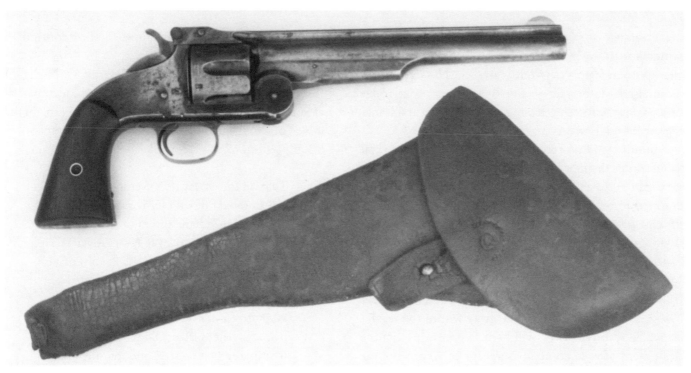

During the Civil War, Robert H. Young rose from the rank of private to captain before being mustered out in 1865. Two years later he was back in the army as an infantry lieutenant and proceeded to serve at various posts in the west. In 1873 he wrote to Smith & Wesson from Wyoming Territory complaining that the barrel of his No. 3 .44 American often poked his horse in the neck and asked if he could order a .44 with a 6-inch barrel. His American is illustrated here with its Civil War–style holster. (Courtesy: Lloyd Jackson)

of the three cartridge handguns undergoing field trial. Illustrating the potential ammunition supply problems this presented was an order from Col. Ranald S. Mackenzie, commanding the 4th Cavalry on a scouting expedition in Texas in June 1872: "Please have Capt. Comdg send to Concho, for me, five thousand rounds Smith and Wesson cartridges, five thousand Colt's metallic cartridges [for .44 Richards conversion] and ten thousand for the common Colt's [percussion Model 1860] army pistol."[71]

Another candidate completed initial testing in December of 1872, a newly designed solid-frame Colt centerfire .44. Compared with the S&W No. 3, the Colt offered

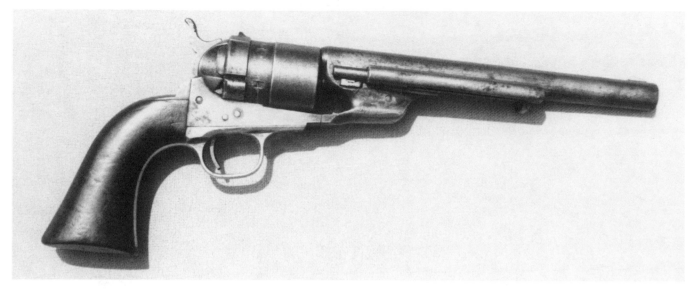

One of twelve hundred Colt M1860 .44 revolvers converted to .44 Colt centerfire for the army using the Richards system.

the advantage of fewer parts, better balance, easier disassembly for cleaning, and increased durability. These were all important factors to weigh against the No. 3's principal advantage of automatic ejection of all six empty cartridge cases at once by merely releasing the barrel latch and swinging the barrel downward.

In July 1873 Colt received an initial contract for eight thousand of the new weapons but in .45 caliber; deliveries began in November. This, the Single Action Army, was destined to be one of the most famous handguns of all times. Government contracts continued until 1890, with slightly more than thirty-seven thousand purchased for issue to the army, militia, post office, and other government agencies. Those procured for the army primarily served with cavalry regiments, but on May 20, 1882, General Order No. 56 expanded the use of revolvers within the regular army: "A 'revolver pistol' will hereafter form part of the equipment of each company sergeant of all arms of the service." These Colts were put up at the Springfield Armory in crates of fifty along with fifty screwdrivers, five each spare firing pins and rivets and main and other springs, plus sixty screws.[72]

The theft of government arms was a persistent problem. Occasionally arms of the early 1870s period are found with company markings applied to discourage theft, but this practice was not widespread and was halted by orders prohibiting the defacing of government property. The new Colt .45s were prime candidates for theft. Within the 8th Cavalry in 1876, Sgt. Graham at Fort Brown, Texas, was placed in charge of his company's Colts. When twenty were found missing, he blamed the loss on two deserters but as an investigation continued, the sergeant, too, deserted.[73]

In another incident, Corp. George W. Wylie of Company D, 7th Cavalry, appeared before a court martial at Fort Abraham Lincoln, Dakota Territory, to explain the loss of one of the new Colt .45s. The outcome is unknown but his testimony was recorded as follows:

> That on the lst day of November 1875 he was ordered out with his company during an alarm of Indians and in the gallop from Fort A. Lincoln to the Big Heart River D. T. His pistol, an improved Colts Revolver Cal .45 No. 5637, the property of the United States and for which Captain Thomas B. Weir 7th Cavalry is responsible was lost from his belt holster (Old pattern Remington belt holster) and that the loss was occasioned by no carelessness on his part. That upon his return to the fort he reported the loss. And that all due and diligent search was made for the lost pistol and that it could not be found.

The principal competitor to the Colt Single Action Army after its adoption into service was another No. 3 size S&W. This new handgun resulted from improvements made by Maj. George W. Schofield of the 10th Cavalry. One of his several design departures was in the barrel catch, which he mounted on the frame rather than on the barrel and for which he received patent protection in June of

Colt Single Action (#4698) with standard 7 1/2-inch barrel length. The gun's serial falls within the range of those thought to have been issued to Custer's 7th Cavalry before the Little Bighorn fight. (Courtesy: Dale C. Anderson)

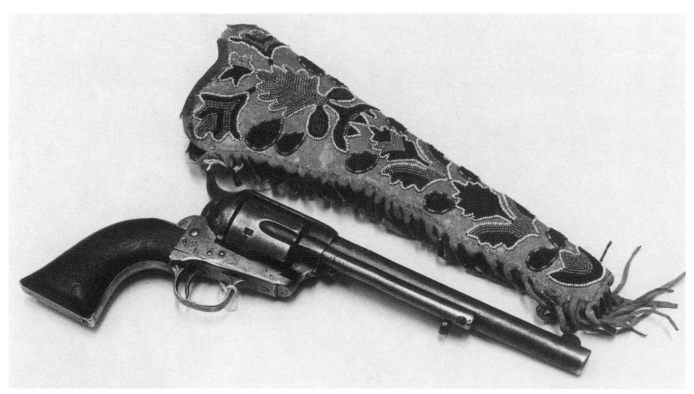

With its colorful beaded holster, this US-marked Colt Single Action (#4082) reportedly was purchased in the early 1900s on the Crow reservation from Curley, a former scout for Custer. (Courtesy: Roswell Art and Museum Center, NM)

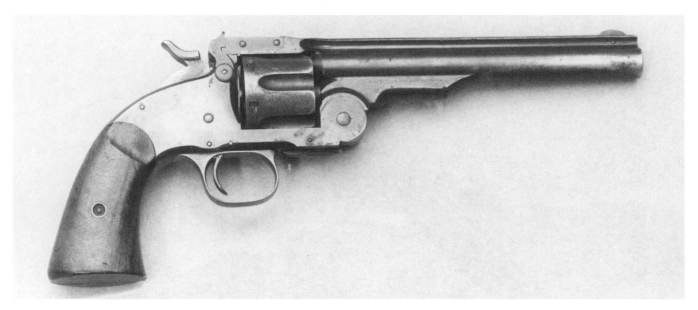

Ist Model S&W .45 Schofield (#112). (Photo by Hugo G. Poisson, courtesy Richard A. Bourne Co.)

A soldier photographed in Phoenix, Arizona Territory, holding a Springfield rifle and with a Schofield S&W and knife in his belt. He appears to be wearing buckskin moccasins and leggings. (Courtesy: Don Harpold)

1871. After various tests and other alterations, the army issued a contract for three thousand S&W Schofields on September 18, 1874, at a price of $13.50, which may have included a royalty of 50¢ per gun for Schofield, although the major claimed his invention was free to the government.

A problem for Smith & Wesson arose with the government's stipulation that the new revolvers chamber the .45 Colt round, for the S&W's cylinder was too short. Smith & Wesson offered a cartridge that would work with the Schofield's unique extraction system and give roughly comparable performance to that of the .45 Colt. But initially after the introduction of the Schofield into service, two different .45 revolver cartridges had to be issued until the army adopted a slightly less powerful .45 round suitable for both guns. Deliveries of the first Schofields took place in 1875; three more army contracts followed for a final total of about 8,005 delivered for issue to the regular army and militia. The later purchases incorporated minor changes in such components as the barrel latch, trigger, and base pin.

Sgt. Alfred Fosette of the 6th Infantry had a pair of Schofields sent from the factory to him at Fort Abraham Lincoln in Dakota Territory. When he found that the .45 Colt round would not chamber, he wrote S&W asking for fifty rounds noting his urgent need. "I travel every day through country infested with hostile Indians."[74]

Both the Colt and S&W Schofield had their advocates and the relative merits of each was cause for discussion in print and in face-to-face conversation. Returning again to the words of Capt. Michaelis, he reported in 1877:

> The experience of the past year has shown that the Colt's calibre .45 pistol is a reliable weapon. The Schofield Smith & Wesson revolvers used in the field, have not proved themselves acceptable to Cavalry officers. Of course their only claim to superiority over the Colt's, is founded upon their capability of automatic extraction. This feature... is attained with expense of simplicity of mechanism and strength.[75]

Those officers who purchased Schofields from the government for their personal use presumably disagreed with the captain's views. Furthermore, the government in 1878 and again in the early 1880s asked S&W for additional Schofields, but was told there weren't any available. As late as 1889 there apparently were still some in service with at least one company of the 4th Cavalry, but at an auction at Springfield in 1890, many were disposed of along with Hotchkiss, Lee, and Chaffee-Reese magazine rifles and carbines. During the Spanish-American War, some of these S&W .45s went to war with members of the Minnesota, Washington, and West Virginia national guards. During the turbulent year of 1877 in California, the army's Benecia Arsenal issued at least three hundred (possibly four hundred) Schofields to a San Francisco "Committee of Safety" to aid in controlling mob violence brought on by the national depression, unemployment, and anti-Chinese feelings.[76]

Maj. George W. Schofield received a lieutenant's commission in the 1st Missouri Artillery in October 1861 and at war's end was a brevet brigadier general for his service during such battles and campaigns as Champion's Hill, Vicksburg, and Atlanta. In 1866 he took a major's commission in the regular army with the black 41st Infantry, moved to the 10th Cavalry in 1870, and rose to lieutenant colonel with the 6th Cavalry in 1881 before taking his own life with one of his S&W revolvers on December 17, 1882.

Corp. E. A. Bode of the 16th Infantry offered insight into the officer's character:

> Major Schofield of the 10th Cavalry was a perfect gentleman, but the penny was his god. At one payday while I was on orderly duty for him, I had the pleasure to walk about ten or fifteen times to the different offices, all for thirty-five cents [extra pay]. As major at the fort [Fort Sill] he had nothing at all to do so he passed his time by experimenting in the improvement on pistols of which he had an interest.[77]

He showed less respect for the major as a result of a subsequent event when he encountered Schofield at the railroad station after escorting a quartermaster from Fort Sill.

> While there we had the misfortune to meet a certain major of our fort on his return from a leave of absence. He naturally took our accommodation instead of the stage to convey him there. This gentleman had nothing whatsoever to occupy his mind in the fort and had no duties except [when] the commanding officer was absent, in which case he took command for the time being. He generally passed his time with improvements of the pistol on which he already had a patent. While on this Caddo trip he engaged a colored woman as a servant and took her to

Sometimes thought to be Charles A. "Lonesome Charley" Reynolds, civilian scout for Custer and the 7th Cavalry who lost his life during the flight of Maj. Marcus Reno's battalion to what is known as Reno Hill. It may also be a Pvt. Henry M. Brinkerhoff who used the alias Charles H. Reynolds. Arms in this photo are a Smith & Wesson .45 Schofield revolver on the simulated fence and a Sharps carbine, probably one of those converted from percussion to .50–70 under a government contract of 1867 or '68. (Courtesy: Wyoming State Museum, Cheyenne)

Sill on government transportation, but subsequently made her work two months without compensation as the price of that trip. The gentleman took also the liberty to take freight, belonging to the post sutler, on government transportation, and without doubt received his share for it.

[On] our first day out [from Caddo] a hole got into one of the above mentioned sutler's freight boxes which gradually became larger and longer as soon as it was discovered that there were oranges in it. If the major did not get his share of them, we surely did, and it was not our fault that any reached the fort.[78]

Remington, Whitney, Hopkins & Allen (makers of Merwin & Hulberts), and Forehand & Wadsworth failed in their attempts to interest ordnance officials in their military size cartridge revolvers. Some nonstandard handguns of both British and American make did serve with officers of the frontier army as privately purchased weapons. In 1878 Colt introduced a double action version of the Single Action Army, and one of the first (#33) was a .45 with a 5 1/2-inch barrel presented to Capt. O. E. Michaelis, chief ordnance officer in the Department of Dakota. He was pleased with his gift and wrote: "All who have seen it pronounce the best revolver yet made. It is well-balanced and well-proportioned. I have asked for 100 to be issued to Cav'y companies for trials. The Colt's [Single Action] has been made the weapon of the 7th Cav'y by a regimental order."[79]

While posing for the photographer in Winfield, Kansas, this "doughboy" holds an S&W Schofield with an Army Model 1880 hunting knife suspended from his woven Mills cartridge belt. (Courtesy: Dr. John J. Kudlik)

Two sample M1878 revolvers eventually were tested at Springfield Armory but any possibility of adoption ended when during a test there were seven misfires out of one hundred attempts. "The liabilities to misfires arises from the necessity of making the mainspring so weak that its pressure may be overcome by the finger pulling the trigger," explained Col. James G. Benton at the armory.[80]

Some officers serving in the west purchased the '78 with their own money. Among the first to do so was Capt. E. W. Whittemore with the 15th Infantry in New Mexico Territory, who already owned a pair of double action Colt .38 Model 1877 Lightnings. He had seen an ad for the new revolver in *Army & Navy Journal* and in September 1878 ordered four .45s for himself and two other officers. One of these was Lt. Francis S. Dodge who in 1879 earned the

Medal of Honor for gallantry against Ute Indians. Lt. Henry M. Kendall campaigned with the 6th Cavalry against the Apaches and obtained a pair, while Capt. Robert H. Young between 1879 and 1884 purchased four, the last two with a 3-inch barrel.[81]

In 1883 Lt. Marion P. Maus purchased a new M1878 .45 with 7 1/2-inch barrel in Tucson but sent it to the factory when he found that the front sight was offset to the right. The defect was corrected and the gun was returned to the officer. Maus may have been carrying this .45 in 1886 when leading Apache scouts in pursuit of Geronimo's band, service for which he was awarded the Medal of Honor.[82]

The Colt .45 Single Action remained the standard army issue until withdrawn from service and replaced by Colt .38 double action revolvers with a swing out

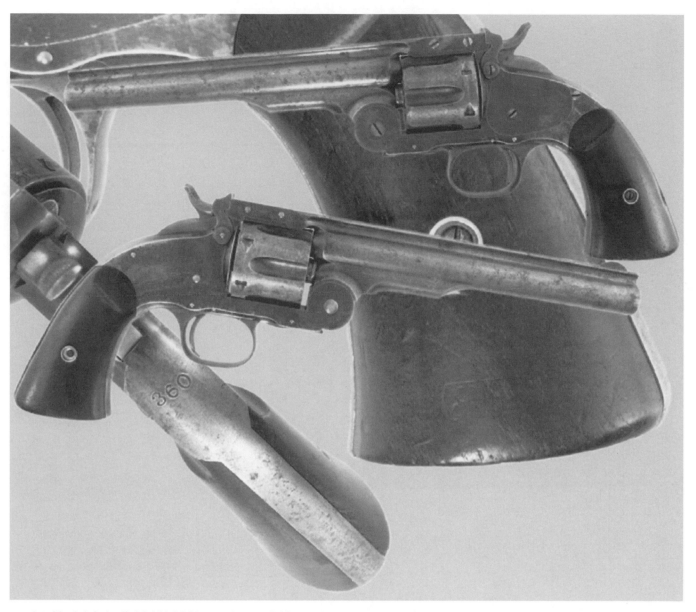

Ist Model Schofield (#1399) numbered 360 on the backstrap behind the hammer and issued in 1877 to a San Francisco "Committee of Safety." (Courtesy: Ron Paxton)

cylinder beginning in 1893. Those who doubted the effectiveness of the light 150-grain .38 bullet later were proved right when it failed to halt fanatical natives during the Philippine Insurrection of 1899–1902. As a result of the .38's weakness, obsolescent .45 Single Actions continued in service a while longer but with their barrels shortened from 7 1/2 to 5 1/2 inches. These are known by today's collectors as the Artillery Model, a modern designation derived from the issue of several hundred early examples to US artillery batteries during the Spanish-American War. In 1907 the army purchased its first .45 auto-loading pistol, the predecessor to the Model 1911 .45 which would serve our military personnel for more than a half century.

THE PLAGUE OF DESERTION

Desertion was a problem throughout the nineteenth century for the frontier army. When four deserters from the Ist Nebraska Veteran Volunteer Cavalry "took French leave" in February 1866, a listing of the accoutrements, horse gear, and arms they took with them included four Joslyn carbines at $30 each and four Remington revolvers at $20 apiece. Another miscreant was John Redmond, Company H, 23rd Infantry, who departed with a Springfield rifle, a gun sling, and sixty rounds of ammunition. He was captured and tried at Fort Laramie in December of 1876 and sentenced to be dishonorably discharged before serving three and one-half years at the military prison at Fort Leavenworth, Kansas.[83]

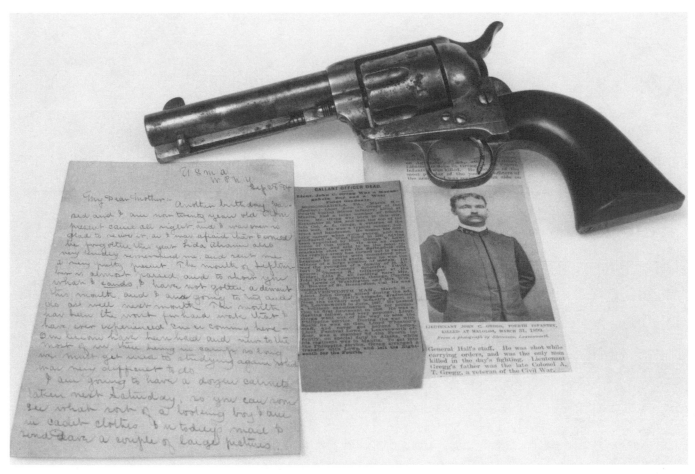

Before he graduated from West Point in 1887, Cadet John C. Gregg received this Colt .45 Single Action (#108640) from his father, Col. Aaron Gregg. The weapon stayed with him through his service in the west with the 16th Infantry. The regiment's rifle team had a tradition of superiority and Gregg in 1893 as a novice won the first place gold medal in a seven-day match at Fort Sheridan, Illinois. He continued to earn honors over the next several years and was described as "the most remarkable shot with the .45 caliber Springfield rifle the regular army has turned out in recent years." In 1899 with the 4th Infantry he was sent to the Philippines but there was fatally wounded by a sniper. (Courtesy: Dr. John J. Kudlik)

Pvt. William Sprague deserted from Camp Sheridan in Wyoming Territory, on May 15, 1888. He was apprehended a day later and was brought before a general court-martial. Charges against him were desertion, stealing government property, and losing accoutrements. The second specification charged he did "feloniously and forcibly remove, steal, and take away from an arm rack in the barrack room of troop M, 1st Cavalry, and convert to his own use one Colt's revolver, cal. .45, valued at thirteen dollars." The lost accoutrements involved one carbine screwdriver (valued at 24¢), a headless shell extractor (30¢), one meat can (39¢), a tin cup (17¢), one knife (8¢), one fork (8¢), one spoon (only 5¢), one pair of spurs (40¢), and a pair of spur straps (20¢) for a total value of $1.91. He was sentenced to reimburse the government $1.91, to be dishonorably discharged, and to be confined at hard labor for three years.[84]

Desertion sometimes provided a first sergeant with an opportunity to add to his private funds. If the deserter left without taking anything belonging to the government, the company records might show that he had stolen a gun, saddle, or horse for which he'd be charged. Corp. E. A. Bode of the 16th Infantry recalled that "there were very few first sergeants who did not make a false affidavit in the five years of [my] service [1877–1882]."[85]

A desertion in the late 1860s did serve a convenient purpose, providing a sergeant at Fort Richardson, Texas, with the means for clearing the 6th Cavalry's records.

> When I took charge of the company I
> found the Major carrying on his ordnance
> papers one Burnside carbine which he
> had been accountable for when in "the
> [Shenandoah] valley" with Sheridan, in

A high stakes poker game at Fort Riley, Kansas, in 1908 with Colt .38 double action revolvers and sabers ready at hand. (Courtesy: Pennell Collection, Spencer Library, University of Kansas, Lawrence)

1864, but which neither he nor anyone present had seen for years. An arm of any kind is harder to "drop" or "account for" than any other kind of property, and so it had been carried along for years as "on hand." [A recruit had deserted soon after his arrival] . . . and as he took no arms with him, of course I charged him up with the old "Burnsides." Looking over the invoices and receipts I had made out for him and his successor to sign, he [the major] noticed that the old carbine had been omitted and he remarked that perhaps I had forgotten it. "No, sir, it can't be found, and supposing the recruit who 'jumped' had taken it, he not knowing its worthlessness, I charged it to him" "Oh!"

said the Major, with a complicated wink, "I'm glad he didn't take a Spencer."[86]

In 1880 two 6th Cavalry troopers deserted with the intention of visiting some of the new mining camps in old Mexico. "They . . . sold their carbines and ammunition for thirty dollars each (probably to be sold the next day to Victorio's people for one hundred) and exchanged their .45 caliber revolvers for the .44's that civilians usually carried." Unfortunately they were killed by Victorio's Apache warriors near the Rio Grande after putting up a desperate fight. In another incident, forty-seven Colt .45s of Company D, 10th Cavalry, in Texas were found to be missing from storage in 1883. In a move not in harmony with usual procedures, Capt. A. S. B. Keyes, the troop commander, through his brother purchased replacement guns from Colt at his own expense of $512 to cover the loss.[87]

CHAPTER FIFTEEN

Hunters' Choices: The '73 Winchester and Others

For general hunting, or Indian fighting, I pronounce your improved
Winchester the boss. An Indian will give more for one of
your guns than any other gun he can get.
— William F. Cody, 1875[1]

The decades following the Civil War until the century's end were marked by the subjugation of Native Americans, the extermination of the once gigantic herds of bison, an expansion of national transportation and communication systems including the completion of a transcontinental rail line, the introduction into the Union of nine new western states, and the official closing of the frontier. With the exception of the short-lived Spanish-American War, there was no foreign conflict. It was an era of significant change in the firearms industry as well.

Gradually there developed increasing interest in the use of firearms for sporting purposes—hunting and target shooting both east and, as the frontier became less wild, west of the Mississippi River. As early as 1852 the Sacramento (California) Swiss Rifle Club was organized by Swiss miners and held its first large public shoot the next year. Eventually San Francisco had thirteen clubs affiliated with a national organization of target shooters, the Nationaler Schuetzen-Bund. The National Rifle Association was founded in 1871 by a small group of National Guard officers in New York with the stated purpose of encouraging marksmanship and promoting target shooting. In 1874

America for the first time participated in the international shooting match in Ireland.[2]

Some veterans of the Civil War had purchased arms from the government upon their discharge, an option made available to them under Army Ordnance Circular No. 13 dated June 5, 1865. The charge for any kind of musket was $6, a Spencer carbine $10, and any other carbine or a revolver $8. Others took advantage of the many government sales of surplus military goods. Such opportunities challenged the marketing skills of the commercial arms manufacturers.[3]

In search of gold, James Chisholm in 1868 headed for the Wind River valley in what today is Wyoming. His outfit included "a small hatchet and a butcher knife slung to my side, a Starr breach [*sic*] loader hanging from the horn of the saddle; a sack of flour, tea, coffee and bacon tied behind; a coil of rope; a tin cup, and an old peach can to boil water in." Presumably his gun was not one of the more common percussion Starr carbines but one of the 5,001 rimfire carbines that the government procured in 1865 near war's end which fired the .56–52 Spencer metallic cartridge since he wore a belt "studded with cartridges."[4]

Markings on the back of this studio cabinet card tentatively identify the holder of this muzzle loading target rifle as Adolph Stricker, probably a member of a German shooting club in the San Francisco area. The carte de vista was introduced in the late 1850s, a photo image on a card, so named because it was about the size of a calling card. The larger cabinet card appeared about a decade later, offering greater detail, and remained popular until shortly before World War I. (Courtesy: Lee A. Silva)

Another surplus Civil War carbine reportedly figured in the ill-fated effort by the James-Younger outlaw gang to rob the bank at Northfield, Minnesota, on the fall afternoon of September 7, 1876. From a second-story window, medical student Henry M. Wheeler with a breech loading percussion Smith carbine killed Clell Miller and shattered Bob Younger's elbow. Meanwhile, hardware store owner A. R. Manning seized a post-war Remington rolling block, possibly a sporting rifle, and killed Bill Stiles (alias Bill Chadwell) and wounded Cole Younger.[5]

Among the most popular of surplus Civil War long guns was the Spencer. During a roundup at Jabe More's ranch in Colorado in 1873, Jack Sheppard roped a stray Texas steer with the ZOZ brand to slaughter for beef. A quick shot failed to down the maddened animal and it

began a valiant struggle, placing the roper and his small mare in a tight spot. A dozen cowboys emptied their revolvers but failed to end the fray. Finally More rushed from his shanty with a Spencer rifle and "planted a .50 calibre ball right in the curl in the middle of [the steer's] forehead," ending the battle.

I never saw a man so cross as Jabe More was. "I'd have you know...that I don't want any strays 'mavericked' on my range. The foreman of the ZOZ wrote me to look after that steer and if you're wise you'll settle up for it in mighty short order. And there's another thing too, mister.... You oughter know by this time that you can't hardly do

Inappropriately dressed for a woodland hunt, the man seated at left holds a Spencer military rifle. Other guns include a Sharps carbine laid along the cabin's wall and another Sharps held by the man standing at right. A sign above the crude door proclaims "HOTEL HUNGRY" with another promising "POSSOM DINNER."
(Courtesy: Minnesota Historical Society)

a cattleman a worse mischief than go and spill blood close to where his cattle waters [*sic*], and send them all plumb crazy to fight and tear around.... The trouble with you is that you've got neither honesty nor manners about you."

This was mighty plain talk..., but he stood there with the Spencer in his hands and six shots still in the magazine.... Jack still had his [loaded] gun... and had always posed as a fighting man.... The way Jabe had planted that bullet... was discouraging and... Jack... apologized on the spot.[6]

Between 1868 and 1879 the War Department transferred some Spencer rifles and carbines to the state and territorial militias, including those of Arizona, Colorado, Iowa, Kansas, and Nebraska. Settlers in at least the first two territories were able to obtain some of these for self-

defense. The E. C. Meacham Arms Company of St. Louis was still advertising the Spencer .50 carbine at only $4 in their 1893 catalog, promoting it "For Coal Mine Strikers." One hundred cartridges with number six or eight shot at $2 made it "a good Farmer's Gun by using Spencer Shot Cartridges."[7]

Following the success of the brass frame Model 1866 Winchester, a more powerful repeater appeared in the form of the new model of 1873. Nelson King in August of '73, in correspondence with Colt, predicted "I can see nothing in the way of our making a cartridge suited both to your pistol and our rifle." However fewer than twenty of the new .44 Winchesters were shipped from the factory by year's end, in part because of a problem with cartridges in the magazine being detonated by the concussion of firing the gun. In a letter on October 31 of 1873 to the Colt company, Oliver Winchester wrote: "We have not yet perfected our center-fire cartridges, or rather we have not got through with the cap machinery, tools

Passed down through the family is this 1891 image of Bernard and Bertha Thorner and baby Eugene, photographed in El Paso. The Colt .44 Single Action and Bowie knife remain in the family although the fate of the M1873 Winchester carbine is unknown. A Colt and a '73 Winchester in .44–40 caliber was a common pairing in the west. (Courtesy: William T. Goodman)

and fixtures &c. for them." The hazard was eliminated by the substitution of the Milbank primer.[8]

The '73 incorporated a number of improvements as enumerated by the manufacturer. First and most significant was the new cartridge, retaining the .44 200-grain bullet but increasing the powder charge from twenty-eight to forty grains and the initial velocity from about 1,125 to 1,325 feet per second. Also, this new .44–40 centerfire cartridge could be reloaded, although that feature wasn't promoted until after the invention of a reloading tool by Winchester's son William in 1874. This was first announced in the 1875 catalog, "an advantage that will be appreciated by those at a distance from dealers in ammunition. Suitable tools for reloading are made by the Company."[9]

Another change was the substitution of iron in place of brass for the frame, side plates, butt plate, and some other parts. This lightened and strengthened the weapon. Continuing the use of a brass cartridge carrier block and lid for the cleaning rod opening in the butt plate avoided the impeding of movement of these parts by rust. A sliding dustcover over the opening in the frame in which the carrier block moved up and down kept out dirt and other debris.

When the '73 was introduced in the 1875 catalog, Winchester announced the '66 would be discontinued, but its announced death was premature. Persistent demand resulted in the sale of another 50,000 for a total of 170,000 M1866s which remained in the catalogs as late as 1898. During its own half century in production, the '73 totaled some 720,000 guns. In 1919 in a well-conceived marketing strategy, Winchester began using the phrase "the gun that won the west," referring most generally to

Hunting party in Clear Creek County, Colorado, in the 1890s. The rifles of choice appear to be M1873 Winchesters. A hammerless double-barrel shotgun lies against the wagon seat at left on the ground, the latter made more comfortable with the seats and backs of two chairs secured to it. (Courtesy: Denver Public Library Western History Department, neg. #F27472, CO)

the '73. Although the '73 would be offered in .38–40 caliber (1880), .32–20 (1882), and .22 (1884), about 80 percent sold were .44s. The availability of the ubiquitous Colt Single Action revolver in these first three calibers made the Colt and the '73 a most convenient matched set for the frontier user. The factory list price for a standard '73 rifle in 1874 was $50, $5 more than a '66, but the nation's economic depression between 1873 and 1879 saw the price drop to $28 for the '73, $24 for the '66, and $32 for the new Model 1876 by 1879.[10]

Even after the appearance of the improved Model 1892 firing the same .32, .38, and .44 ammunition as the '73 and the Model 1894 "thirty-thirty," the '73's popularity continued. One reason was its solid reputation and another may have been the ease with which the internal mechanism could be accessed by merely removing a side plate, as the following incident illustrates. During a skirmish with Indians, a Texas Ranger found himself in a serious predicament.

In reloading his Winchester after shooting it empty [George] Lloyd unfortunately slipped a .45 Colt's pistol cartridge into the magazine of his .44 Winchester and in attempting to throw a cartridge into his gun it jammed.... Taking his knife from his pocket [he] coolly removed the screw that held the side plates of his Winchester together, took off the plates, removed the offending cartridge, replaced the plates, tightened up the screw, reloaded his gun, and began firing. It takes a man with iron nerve to do a thing like that.[11]

Then as today, user endorsements often appeared in company promotions. The 1875 Winchester catalog included the following from W. J. Dixon of Stockville, Colorado. "I purchased one of your guns at Denver, a round barrel sporting rifle, set-trigger, No. 2,453. I

A dog sits patiently on top of the pack burro as his master is photographed with a '73 Winchester and a holstered revolver on the saddle pommel. (Courtesy: Museum of New Mexico, neg. #76511)

have owned Sharps,' Remington's, the Springfield Needle Gun, an English breech-loader, and several muzzle-loaders, and . . . for this country your gun is the best that I have tried."[12]

Thomas B. Evans described himself as a hunter at Antelope Station in Nebraska and expressed his delight with his early '73, #289. Of greater significance was another endorsement, from Fort McPherson in Nebraska by W. F. Buffalo Bill Cody.

> While in the Black Hills this last summer I crippled a bear, and Mr. Bear made for me, and I am certain had I not been armed with one of your repeating rifles, I would now be in the happy hunting grounds. The bear was not thirty feet from me when he charged, but before he could reach me I had eleven bullets in him, which was a little more lead than he could comfortably digest.[13]

Texas Ranger James Gillett recalled his '73 carbine as "a prized memento of the past." Soon after the '73 came on the market, Gillett and nine other rangers in Company D replaced their .50 Sharps carbines with the new .44–40

repeaters, paying $50 for a rifle or $40 for a carbine out of their wages. They had to purchase their own ammunition as well since the state only furnished cartridges for the Sharps at the time. Gillett purchased carbine #13401 "and for the next six years of my ranger career I never used any other weapon. I . . . killed almost every kind of game that is found in Texas, from the biggest old bull buffalo to a fox squirrel with this little .44 Winchester." After 1877, the ranger "carried a Winchester rifle or carbine, a Colt's .45 revolver, and a bowie knife."[14]

Other known former Texas Ranger carbines are #35112, #68208, and #68284. The last two guns probably were part of a delivery in September 1881 to the state of Texas of .44 '73s for the rangers—two hundred carbines and fifty rifles.[15]

Model 1873 #302678 was a .38 rifle with pistol grip, checkered stock, and set trigger, presented to Francis E. Warren by Lincoln County friends in July of 1890 upon his election as the first governor of the new state of Wyoming. Warren had been awarded the Medal of Honor during the Civil War before becoming a rancher. Other '73s of note included western artist Charlie Russell's rifle (#12919), outlaw Butch Cassidy's carbine (#64876), another carbine (#47629) associated with Pat Garrett and Billy the Kid, and Belle Starr's carbine (#296260). Not to be ignored are rifles attributed to Buffalo Bill Cody (#121153), cattleman Charles

A mule-drawn coach load of passengers in Indian Territory (Oklahoma) en route to Caldwell, Kansas, in 1887. The "shotgun messenger" is identified as Sheriff Todd, armed with a '73 Winchester rifle. (Courtesy: National Archives, photo #111-SC-87345)

Goodnight (#212488), and to the Dalton gang of outlaws (#132533). An engraved '73 rifle (#33669) was presented to a Kansas city marshal who later "went bad" and was captured after attempting to rob a bank in Medicine Lodge, Kansas, Henry Brown.[16]

However, the townspeople of Dodge City, Kansas, didn't select a handsome Winchester to show their appreciation for the work of lawman Joe Mason. As the Dodge City *Times* reported on September 15, 1877: "Policeman Mason was this week presented with a magnificent air gun which opens with a padlock. Mr. Mix has it on exhibition at the Long Branch."[17]

The last quarter of the nineteenth century saw a marked increase in hunting in the west for sport, both among those living beyond the Mississippi and among easterners and others venturing into the region for adventure. An expanding rail system and gradually diminishing threat from Native Americans certainly were factors. By the 1880s, gun manufacturers were devoting much of their production efforts to sporting rifles. The western hunter had numerous choices in type of game as well as of hunting rifle and caliber, whether it be a repeater or a single-shot.

Col. Richard I. Dodge, writing to sportsmen in the mid-1870s, recommended to the western hunter a good breech loading rifle of not less than .45 caliber. "The arrangement of sights and triggers is a matter of taste and habit." He objected to elevating sights and recommended the plain open "buck horn." His preference for a trigger mechanism was "the old-fashioned Kentucky double set trigger." He continued: "Some sportsmen use the single set and some few the French double set. With this latter the gun can only be brought to full cock after the trigger is set, which . . . gives occasion for numerous accidents and much bad language."[18]

Lever action Winchester repeaters in the form of the obsolescent but still popular Model 1866 and the improved Model 1873 had many devotees, but these fired what basically were revolver loads and lacked the longer range and hitting power of true rifle cartridges. When a resident of Grass Valley, California, wrote to the editors of *Field and Stream* in 1875 they advised him: "For your country the improved Winchester, the Model 73, is an excellent arm. Where long range shooting is desired, say up to 1,000 yards, we would suggest the single shot Remington, Sharps, or Whitney."[19]

Winchester had earlier recognized the need to expand its line and in 1876 introduced at the Centennial Exposition in Philadelphia what was commonly known as its Centennial Model. At first glance, it duplicates the Model 1873 in appearance except for its noticeably larger frame.

In December 1880 Sheriff Pat Garrett of Lincoln County, New Mexico Territory, took this .44 M1873 Winchester carbine (#47629) from Billy Wilson, one of Billy the Kid's associates. He also seized a Colt .44 Single Action (#55093) with which he later killed the Kid. (Courtesy: Robert E. McNellis Jr.)

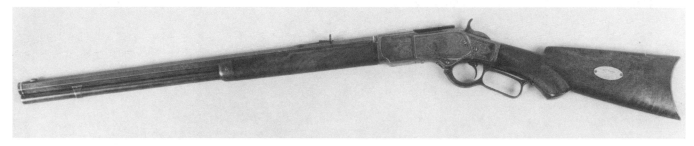

Engraved .44 Winchester M1873 rifle (#33669) presented to Kansas lawman—who later turned outlaw— Henry Brown. (Courtesy: Kansas Historical Society)

Buffalo Bill Cody with a '73 Winchester rifle shooting glass balls thrown by Johnny Baker at a 1901 rehearsal of his wild west show. The gun undoubtedly was a smoothbore firing shot rather than a bullet. (Courtesy: Denver Public Library, CO)

Stephen H. Meek, pioneer hunter and trapper, posed with an octagonal-barrel Remington or Whitney rolling-block sporting rifle. (Courtesy: Oregon Historical Society, neg. #19905, file 736)

The more powerful cartridges it chambered—.45–60, .45–75, and even .50–95—all found their advocates among hunters. Attempts to adapt the gun to fire the government .45–70 military cartridge failed when it was decided the toggle link action, developed by Smith and Wesson twenty years earlier, wasn't strong enough to handle the heavier 405- or 500-grain bullet.[20]

The Winchester firm explained its purpose in introducing the '76 thusly:

> The success attending the sale and use of Model 1873 and the constant calls from many sources, and particularly from the regions in which the grizzly bear and other large game are found, as well as from the plains where the absence of cover and the shyness of the game require the hunter to make his shots at long range, made it

desirable for the Company to build a still more powerful gun.[21]

The Model 1876 was the last of the lever action Winchesters to utilize the toggle link system but the first to offer a rifle better suited to longer range hunting than its predecessors. Total production numbered about 63,500 guns and essentially ended in 1888 except for a few hundred more assembled over the next decade. One unusual feature of the carbine version was the wooden forearm which extended virtually to the muzzle to enclose the entire magazine tube.[22]

An early Model 1876 to reach the frontier was one purchased by William A. Allen, later a Montana dentist. During a prospecting trip in 1877 to the Big Horn country, he mentioned his .45–60 Winchester and recommended it or its equivalent if one intended to tackle a grizzly bear. Montana cowboy J. L. Hill in 1883 "bought

Montana lawman John X. Beidler with a M1876 Winchester. (Courtesy: Montana Historical Society)

a Colt's forty-five six-shooter and a forty-five seventy-five Winchester [Model 1876]," thus becoming another customer who opted for the more powerful cartridge chamberings available in the '76. John Ringo was found dead outside Tombstone, Arizona Territory, on July 14, 1882, his body resting against a tree. Leaning beside the body was his .45–60 '76 Winchester (#21896); his Colt .45 Single Action (#222) was in his right hand and about his waist were two cartridge belts.[23]

One of the most famous hunters to appreciate the Centennial Model was Theodore Roosevelt. The future president while ranching in Dakota Territory owned three 1876s, two rifles and a carbine. The 1879 Winchester catalog made a special reference to the '76 in .50 caliber as its Express Rifle, noting with ninety-five grains of powder and

a 300-grain bullet it produced a muzzle velocity of 1,641 feet per second. The bullet's hollow point was filled with a copper cup, producing "a large, dangerous, bone-crushing, blood-letting wound with a prostrating shock." As much as Teddy Roosevelt admired Winchester rifles, he was less than enthusiastic about the .50 caliber version. "I...read...about killing antelopes at eight hundred yards with a Winchester Express, a weapon which cannot be depended upon at over two hundred, and is wholly inaccurate at over three hundred yards." The Winchester firm in describing the express rifle had not made any claim to its effectiveness as a long-range killer and in fact had stated it was intended "to meet the wants of the hunter who needs a weapon having absolute killing power but not necessarily long range."[24]

Theodore Roosevelt with a M1876 Winchester with a half-length magazine.

Outlaws rustling cattle and horses on the northern plains in the early 1880s were a problem and often received swift "frontier justice." Rancher Granville Stuart organized one of the vigilante bands which administered it at the mouth of the Musselshell River in Montana Territory in mid-1884.

> The rustlers of that day were a different class of men from the sneak thieves of today. They went in armed bands, took what they wanted by force, and defied arrest. It come to a showdown, fight or quit, and it was here that Granville Stuart showed the stuff he was made of. While lots of men went out of the territory for a trip and others sat in an office and said, "Go," Granville Stuart took his Winchester [Model 1876] 50–95 express in his hand and led the way, and he never asked a man to go ahead of him. That gained him the respect of all the cowpunchers.[25]

North of the US border, Winchester Model 1876 carbines entered service with the Canadian Northwest Mounted Police beginning in 1877. The guns met with substantial criticism, however. Commissioner Irvine

Royal Canadian Mounted Police with M1876 Winchester carbines.

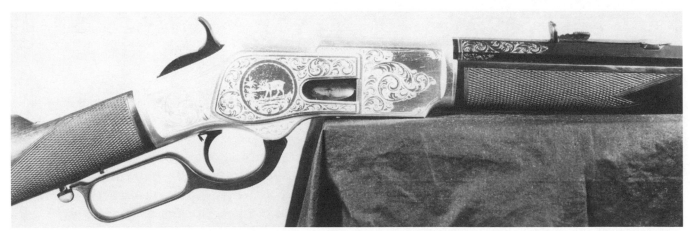

Winchester-engraved M1873 "One of One Thousand" (#18521), a gun with a colorful history. The original purchaser is unknown, but it was stolen by outlaw Teton Jackson, a rustler captured by Sheriff Frank Canton in 1885. The '73 was sold at auction by Sheriff Red Angus of Buffalo, Wyoming, to a sheep rancher, D. A. Kingsbury, who gave it to one of his herdsmen who traded it to Dr. W. A. Allen, a Montana dentist, for a lighter gun more suitable for use on horseback. Allen retained it until well into the twentieth century and eventually it was returned to the Winchester factory to be refinished. (Courtesy: Dr. Robert A. DePalma)

had considered them too frail to withstand the rough treatment they endured in police hands. Twenty years later, they were still in use and still being criticized. "It is quite impossible for men to make good practice with the Winchester and they constantly grow disheartened." "Accurate shooting with them is out of the question," another official complained. Superintendent John McIllree at Calgary described the guns in his command as "more or less honeycombed and sights not true."[26]

In an annual report for 1886, S. B. Steele, commanding D Division, wrote:

> The Winchester carbine has...proved to be too weak for the rough usage which it must necessarily receive...undergoing the rough work of a campaign. If a horse falls, with the carbine on the saddle, or a man is thrown with it in his hand, it is generally broken.[27]

The red-coated policeman had better success with his Enfield revolver, successor to those by Adams. Superintendent W. D. Antrobus in his report for 1887 called the former "in every respect a first-class arm, and it is very seldom that one gets out of order."[28]

Corp. John G. Donkin, at the time of his recruitment in the famed peacekeeping organization, noted that cartridge belts contained twenty Winchester and a dozen Enfield revolver cartridges. "We rode in the high peaked Californian saddle made by Main & Winchester in San Francisco." His eventual opinion of the issue Model 1876 Winchester carbines was not complimentary.

> The Winchester repeating carbine has been pronounced a failure. The sighting of these weapons is lamentably deficient in accuracy, even at 100 yards, and the limit of their range is 500 yards. The trajectory also is very much higher than any other military arm. The initial velocity is 1234 feet per second. At 1000 yards the remaining velocity is 610 feet.[29]

Although it was not the fault of the guns, cartridges made by the Dominion Cartridge Company for the Winchesters were officially described as "useless." Of 45,000 cartridges tried in different rifles at Calgary, all but 760 had to be forced into the chamber. American ammunition had to be imported to allow target practice. Some of the worse condition Winchesters could be discarded when two hundred Lee-Metford rifles were issued experimentally, but some of the '76 Winchesters remained in service with the Mounties as late as 1905.[30]

In 1874 the Winchester company inaugurated an innovative but perhaps ill-advised marketing tool. In the course of test firing each '73 sporting rifle, those barrels found to make a target "of extra merit" would be made up into guns with set triggers and extra finish and marked "One of One Thousand" and priced at $100. The next lower grade would be marked "One of One Hundred" and sold for a $20 premium. The promotion was dropped from the catalog in 1878, probably because it was felt that it wasn't wise to advertise that all barrels didn't shoot equally as well. However 136 One of One Thousand '73 rifles and 47 similarly marked '76s were shipped between 1877 and 1900 along with 7 One of One Hundred '76s. One of these '76s (#713) in late 1877 went to John Kelsey, who operated a stagecoach line and also served as a security guard for a Montana gambling establishment.[31]

Granville Stuart ordered several One of One Thousand 1873 rifles for himself and friends. Stuart had been successful as a gold miner before the Civil War and later established a ranching empire. He ordered his first two in October of 1874 and asked that they be "as nearly absolutely accurate as you can make them." He noted that the average Winchester couldn't compete with a Sharps or Remington in accuracy, but he considered them superior in "convenience."[32]

The guns didn't meet Stuart's expectations and he returned them as being no better finished than "your common ones." More significant was the fact that the heads of the cartridge cases were too thick and wouldn't allow the action to close properly. The Winchester firm replaced the guns and on July 26, 1876, Stuart sent $105.75 in payment for another "1 of 1000."

> It is indeed a beauty and the friend for whom I ordered it is in extacies [sic] over it and well may be, for if the Sioux should come a little further up this way it will be a mighty handy thing to have in the house. If poor Custer's heroic band had been armed with these rifles they would have covered the earth with dead Indians for 500 yards around.[33]

In 1879 Richard B. Townshend found himself "GTT" or "gone to Texas" from Colorado, there to purchase horses and mules and herd them to Leadville, Colorado. He undertook one trip into the brush to negotiate with a certain

Wyoming outlaw Teton Jackson. The saddle scabbard may hold his "One of One Thousand" '73 Winchester with its 28-inch barrel, four inches longer than the standard rifle length. (Courtesy: Dr. Robert A. DePalma)

Mr. Brown for the purchase of horses, traveling into an area known to be a no-man's-land where no law existed.

> I did not take my Winchester along. I now carried a new-model .45 [Model 1876] Winchester, an improvement on the old .44. If I was going to visit a band of outlaws this splendid A1 weapon might tempt somebody's cupidity, while against such odds, against such a crowd as I expected to find, I knew no weapon would give me any real chance. Of course, I wore my Colt, but every one did that.

Eventually it became clear that Mr. Brown would not be able to provide a bill of sale for the animals; they would be delivered "wet," just as they came across the Rio Grande. Townshend ended the negotiations without making a purchase, but the two men parted on friendly terms.[34]

In 1878 Winchester broke with its tradition of producing only those repeating arms which operated with the finger lever. In that year, it announced it had obtained the rights to manufacture a bolt action repeater designed by B. B. Hotchkiss. The gun underwent a thorough trial by the army and the chief of ordnance reported the weapon suitable for field trials in the hands of troops, commenting on its "strength, simplicity, and great effectiveness as a single loader." The reference to its use as a single-shot was not unexpected since the Springfield single-shot "trapdoor" was still the army's primary choice of a shoulder arm.

Although the operating principal was entirely different, several of the Hotchkiss's features were reminiscent of

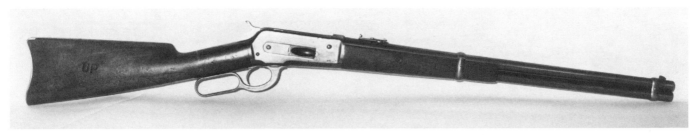

Winchester M1886 carbine stamped with the Union Pacific Railroad's "UP" in the butt stock. (Courtesy: Donald Snoddy, Union Pacific Railroad Company, Omaha, NE)

the post–Civil War Spencer. Both had a tubular magazine in the butt and each had a magazine cut-off, allowing the gun to be loaded and fired as a single-shot. About eighty-five thousand .45 Hotchkiss sporting rifles and carbines were produced by century's end, but the lever action Winchester arms remained the best sellers.

In August of 1886, Winchester began production of yet another lever action rifle, this one combining the design talents of John Moses Browning and William Mason. It eliminated the toggle action of its predecessors in favor of two vertical locking bars, making it possible to chamber longer and more powerful cartridges—first the .40–82 Winchester, the .45–70 Government, and .45–90 Winchester, followed by others including in 1888 the .50 Express (.50–110) and the smokeless powder .33 W.C.F in 1902 with a muzzle velocity of 2,300 feet per second. In all about 160,000 would bear the Winchester name.[35]

Theodore Roosevelt didn't wait long before he obtained one of the new Model 1886s, acquiring # 9205, a .45–90 with a half round barrel and half magazine. After the turn of the century he acquired another Model 1886 in .45–70 caliber, #125422. He noted:

> Now that the buffalo have gone and the
> Sharp's rifle by which they were destroyed
> is also gone, almost all ranchmen use some
> form of repeater. Personally I prefer the
> Winchester, using the new model [1886],
> with a forty-five caliber bullet of three hun-
> dred gains, backed by ninety grains of pow-
> der or else falling back on my faithful old
> standby, the [Model 1876] 45–75.[36]

Our twenty-sixth president expounded at some length on his views concerning the "proper" hunting rifle.

> There is an endless variety of opinion about
> rifles, and all that can be said with certainty
> is that any good modern rifle will do. It is

the man behind the rifle that counts after the weapon has reached a certain stage of perfection. One of my friends invariably uses an old Government Springfield, a 45-caliber with an ounce bullet. Another cares for nothing but the 40–90 Sharp's [sic], a weapon for which I myself have much partiality. Another uses the old 45-caliber Sharp's [sic], and yet another the 45-caliber Remington. Two of the best bear and elk hunters I know prefer the 32 and 38 caliber Marlin's [sic] with long cartridges, weapons with which I myself would not undertake to produce any good results. Yet others prefer pieces of very large caliber.

> . . . Each one of these guns possesses some excellence which the others lack, but which is in most cases atoned for by some corresponding defect. Simplicity of mechanism is very important, but so is rapidity of fire; and it is hard to get both of them developed to the highest degree in the same piece. . . . Flatness of trajectory, penetration, range, shock, and accuracy are all qualities which must be attained; but to get one in perfection usually means the sacrifice of some of the rest. . . . Other things being equal, the smallest caliber has the greatest penetration, but gives the least shock; while a very flat trajectory, if acquired by heavy charges of powder, means the sacrifice of accuracy. Similarly, solid and hollow pointed bullets have . . . their merits and demerits. There is no use of dogmatizing about weapons. Some which prove excellent for particular countries and kinds of hunting are useless in others.

> There seems to be no doubt, judging from the testimony of sportsmen in South

Original crate in which this .40–82 and four other M1886 Winchesters were shipped via Wells Fargo to H. J. Hagerman, foreman at John Chisum's South Spring Ranch & Cattle Company in Roswell, New Mexico Territory. Hagerman was a founder of the Denver & Western Railroad and he obtained the rifles for possible use if force was necessary to settle a railroad workers' dispute. (Photos by Steven W. Walenta, courtesy Ron Peterson)

Africa and in India, that very heavy caliber double-barreled rifles are best for use in the dense jungles and against the thick-hided game of those regions; but they are of very little value with us. In 1882, one of the buffalo-hunters on the Little Missouri obtained from some Englishman a double-barrelled 10-bore rifle of the kind used against rhinoceros, [Cape] buffalo, and elephant in the Old World; but it proved very inferior to the 40 and 45 caliber Sharp's [sic] buffalo guns when used under the conditions of American buffalo-hunting, the tremendous shock given by the bullet not compensating for the gun's great relative deficiency in range and accuracy, while even the penetration is inferior at ordinary distances. It is largely also a matter of individual taste. . . . I possessed a very expensive double-barrelled 500 Express, by one of the crack English makers; but I never liked the gun, and could not do as well with it as with my repeater, which cost barely a sixth as much. So one day I handed it to a Scotch friend, who was manifestly ill at ease with a Winchester exactly like my own. He took to the double-barrel as naturally as I did to the repeater, and did excellent work with it.

Personally, I have always preferred the Winchester. I now use a 45–90 [Model 1886], with my old buffalo gun, a 40–90 Sharp's [sic], as spare rifle. Both, of course, have specially tested barrels, and are stocked and sighted to suit myself.[37]

One Model 1886 user obtained his by a rather unusual method. Train robber Bill Cook reported that he had purchased four .45–90 Winchesters for $18 each from the factory, one for himself and the others for his brother Jim, Cherokee Bill, and Jim French. In 1894 Texas Ranger sergeant W. J. L. Sullivan captured several of Cook's men while the latter was absent. Sullivan retained one of the rifles and called it his "Bill Cook Winchester." In 1901 Sullivan was chasing a dog when his saddle slipped, his horse bucked him off, and he shot himself in the thigh with his cocked revolver, which he dropped. As he crawled unarmed toward a nearby house, he was threatened by a Durham bull which prompted him to wish he had his Bill Cook Winchester. The bull eventually ambled off, but the ranger's troubles weren't over. Now he found he was only a few feet from a coiled rattlesnake, but he managed to crawl around it to safety.[38]

In 1894 US Deputy Marshal Selden Lindsey shot outlaw Bill Dalton to death with a .38–56 Model 1886 Winchester. The bullet struck Dalton near the left nipple but did not exit the body. The marshal's faith in his

German-born Al Sieber with a M1886 Winchester. He was a cowboy, prospector, ranch manager, and served as Gen. Crook's chief of scouts during the 1883 Sierra Madre Campaign against Geronimo. (Courtesy: Phil Spangenberger)

Winchester was shaken and soon he discarded it because "he would not carry a gun that would not shoot through a man at 35 steps."[39]

It must have been the '86 to which Frank Canton referred when describing his employment by the Wyoming Stock Growers' Association during the Johnson County War.

> The best rifle we had in those days was the 45–70 Winchester, the 40–82 and the 38–56 magazine gun. The longest range for this gun was from six hundred to seven hundred yards. We were armed with this rifle and I presume [the "rustlers"] had the same kind of gun. But some man of their party had a rifle of larger caliber and greater penetration. The reports sounded

> to me like the old Sharps fifty-caliber that we formerly used on the plains and called the buffalo gun. This gun would hold up steady eight hundred yards and several times penetrated our breastworks, but did no particular harm.[40]

One Wyoming cowboy bought some hay-cutting machinery along with an old .45–70 1886 Winchester rifle. He sawed eight inches off the barrel and reduced it to carbine length. "It took me all winter to cut that barrel down, using a meat saw for the job."[41]

A scaled down version of the '86 appeared in 1892 as the successor to the famed Model 1873 and firing the same three centerfire cartridges as the '73—.32–20, .38–40, and .44–40, and later the .25–20. The '92 would have a production run of a half century and more than one million guns.

"Coyote Smith" on Deer Creek in Wyoming with a M1886 Winchester and a pair of antelope carcasses. (Courtesy: Wyoming State Museum, Cheyenne)

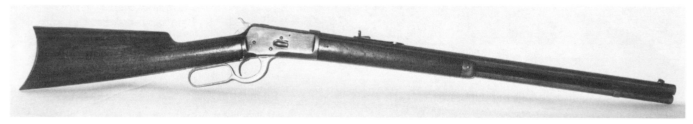

A Union Pacific Railroad Winchester M1892 rifle. (Courtesy: Donald Snoddy, Union Pacific Railroad Company, Omaha, NE)

As the popularity of various Winchester models grew, like the Colt name, that of Winchester overshadowed comparable quality guns by other makers. In 1881 efforts by panhandle stockmen to resist contamination of their herds by cattle from south Texas were known as the "Winchester quarantine." An unusual tribute to the Winchester came about 1888 when a group of men met in a small store to select the name for a post office. One of them suggested it be chosen based on the gun with the largest representation, hence the name—Winchester, Idaho.

In 1891, at every small settlement and post-office hitching rail in Wyoming, saddle ponies stood with a Winchester carbine in the scabbard. Every gun, whether rifle or carbine and regardless of make, was referred to as a "Winchester." As a matter of fact, the weapon may have been a Marlin, Savage, or any other make of arm.[42]

In making that comment, former Wyoming cowboy John K. Rollinson was accurate regarding almost a generic

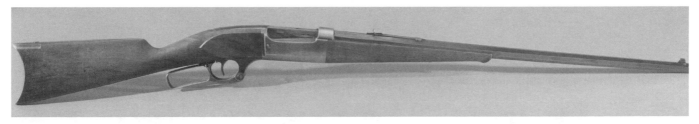

Model 1899 .30–30 Savage rifle, one of three that constituted Nevada's "execution machine," used only once, to execute Andrija Mirkovitch in 1913. The rifles were mounted in a steel framed hut and aimed at the condemned man, strapped in a chair. Only two of the rifles were loaded, but all three were fired at the same instant by a coiled spring mechanism set off when guards cut three strings. (Photo by Leland E. DeFord III, gun from Nevada State Museum, Carson City)

use of the Winchester name. He was in error in including the lever action hammerless Savage, however. The first sporting rifle to bear designer A. W. Savage's name was the Model 1895, a six-shot .30 repeater with a rotary magazine, the forerunner of the long-lived Model 1899.

The dominance of the Winchester, and the Colt, too, was reflected during Wyoming's cattle war in Johnson County. In April 1892 an invasion force composed mainly of representatives of the large ranchers and hired Texas gunmen set out to kill or drive out small ranchers and homesteaders. Some of the imported "invaders" were outfitted with the latest model Winchesters purchased by the stockmen's association. This fifty-six-man army met more resistance than it anticipated and was cornered at the TA Ranch south of Buffalo. The arrival of three troops of the 6th Cavalry ended the siege and when the invaders surrendered their guns, an inventory was prepared to permit their later return to their owners.[43]

Not all of the guns on the list can be identified as to model, but many can from serial numbers and calibers. Of the forty-five long guns tallied, thirty-eight were Winchesters and included seventeen Model 1886s, ten .44 Model 1873s, six '73s in .38 caliber, and three M1876s along with two .40 caliber Sharps and a shotgun. Most unexpected were three "Martini .44s" and a "Mart. .38." These last four rifles may have been Peabody-Martini single-shots made by the Providence Tool Company of Rhode Island. The thirty-nine revolvers listed consisted of one Webley .44, one .44 Smith & Wesson single action, and thirty-seven Colts. The latter included twenty-eight .45s (at least twenty-three were Single Actions), three .44 Single Actions, one .41 Single Action, and five Colt .38s and .41s of indeterminate model.[44]

The 1890s saw the introduction of smokeless powder to the sporting arms industry, first in shotgun shells and soon rifle and handgun ammunition. Not only were the distracting cloud of smoke and messy powder residue cre-

ated by black powder eliminated, but higher velocity and lower trajectory ammunition was possible. In 1895 Winchester was marketing seventeen smokeless powder loads. Some intended for use in guns designed for black powder cartridges offered no increase in velocity or penetration while others were intended for new models designed to accommodate smokeless powder ammunition with its higher pressures and improved performance. Winchester's lever action Model 1894, best known in .30–30 caliber, was just such an arm, the first Winchester repeating sporting rifle designed for smokeless ammunition. It went on to become the firm's most popular sporting rifle, with more than three million made by 1975.[45]

One of the first '94s produced, #1248, was owned by famed western artist Charles M. Russell who spent most of his life in Montana. Factory records indicate it was a .38–55 with several unusual features, a 22-inch barrel, checkered stock with pistol grip, and an uncommon two-thirds-length magazine. It was received in the warehouse in December 1894 but not shipped until December of the following year. These records also include an unusual notation that the shotgun butt was "1-inch short of regular." In 1907 Russell's wife, Nancy, gave the Winchester to a Brooklyn, New York, minister in appreciation for allowing use of the church for Charlie's first art exhibit on the East Coast.[46]

A far less distinguished '94 user was career outlaw Harry Tracy who died by his own hand in 1902 when finally cornered near Fellows, Washington, after a two-month manhunt. The Winchester .30–30 carbine found with his body reportedly went to the governor of Oregon. When lawman Joe LeFors interviewed convicted killer Tom Horn, the latter described his rifle as a .30–30 Winchester. LeFors asked him if it held up as well as a .30–40 and Horn said, "No, but I like to get close to my man."[47]

Close on the heels of the '94, Winchester introduced its Model 1895, another brainchild of designer John M.

A cabinet card image from a Leadville, Colorado, photographic studio. The prospector carries a small-frame double action revolver, perhaps an Iver Johnson. The burro's load includes skillet, coffee pot, and an 1894 Winchester with pistol grip butt stock. (Courtesy: Lee A. Silva)

With a '92 or '94 Winchester to ward off predators, a shepherd serenades his companion inside his sheep wagon. (Courtesy: Belden Collection, Wyoming State Museum, Cheyenne)

A varied array of long guns in this scene of a US Geological Survey party in Yukon Territory (1902). From left: a M1893 or M1895 Marlin, Winchester M1895 rifle, unidentified hammerless double-barrel shotgun, and a Winchester M1892 or M1894 carbine. The US marshal (second from left) holds a Colt Single Action Army with 7 1/2-inch barrel. (Courtesy: US Geological Survey, A. J. Collier neg. #171)

Browning. Although it was a lever action, its box magazine gave it a distinctive and easily recognized profile. It fired the new smokeless ammunition and when production ended about 1931, more than 425,000 had left the factory at New Haven.

The Arizona Rangers, who adopted the '95, were organized late in 1901 "for the protection of the frontier of this territory, and for the preservation of the peace and the capture of persons charged with crimes." To accomplish this goal, the force would consist of one captain, one sergeant, and "not more than twelve privates." In 1903 the force was enlarged to include a lieutenant, four sergeants, and not more than twenty privates. Before their dissolution in early 1909, 107 men wore the rangers' badge. They served during a period when Americans were introduced to such innovations as horseless carriages and flying machines. The Arizona statute originally organizing the unit specified that, if possible, officers and men were to be raised in the territory's frontier counties. Each ranger was to provide a suitable horse, "six shooting pistol (army size), and all necessary accoutrements and camp equipage." The government would provide provisions, ammunition, forage for horses, and "the most effective and approved breech-loading cavalry arms." These rifles were to be of the same make and caliber; the rangers were to pay for them out of their wages.[48]

The first captain of the rangers was Burton Mossman, a highly regarded former superintendent of the gargantuan Arizona Land and Cattle Company, but a man with a fiery temper. In 1896 he fought a duel with a Mexican captain, one shot for each man. His opponent missed with his shot from a German Luger; Mossman's aim was better for he wounded the captain in the shoulder with a slug from his Colt .45. His choice for a rifle for his ranger company was the lever action Model 1895 Winchester in .30–40 caliber, firing the same round as the army's newly adopted Krag-Jorgensen bolt action repeater. "We could always be sure the commanding officers at Fort Huachuca and Fort Apache would load us up with plenty of ammunition whenever we ran low." The '95 Winchester apparently remained in service with the rangers until their dissolution, although Ranger Chapo Beaty supplemented his with a sawed-off shotgun which he could shoot "from the hip like an automatic."[49]

Another lawman who selected the '95 was Charles A. Siringo, cowboy and later a Pinkerton detective. In 1899 he and W. O. Sayles were detailed to track down a band of robbers who had held up the Union Pacific Railroad at Wilcox,

Wyoming hunters with M1895 Winchesters. (Courtesy: American Heritage Center, University of Wyoming, Laramie)

Texas Ranger Walter Rowe with an 1895 Winchester. (Courtesy: George Jackson)

Wyoming. In Denver, Sayles and he each bought a .30–40 Winchester rifle.[50]

John Mahlon Marlin, a former Colt employee, in the midst of the Civil War launched his own gun-making business in New Haven. His name would grace a line of high quality lever action rifles and carbines which provided Winchester with strong competition. Marlin began with the production of a small .22 single-shot pocket pistol, then expanded into the revolver market about 1870. A few years later, Marlin took over the manufacture of single-shot Ballard rifles. The Marlin Firearms Company was formed in 1881 to continue Ballard production and to begin marketing its first lever action repeating rifle, designated later as the Model 1881, based on patents issued to Marlin, Andrew Burgess, and others.[51]

The M1881 Marlin closely resembled contemporary Winchester repeaters. It loaded through a port in the right side of the frame and with the 28- or 30-inch barrel length its tubular magazine beneath the barrel held ten cartridges. It was not an inexpensive gun by 1880s standards, with a list price of $32. It first was offered in .45 Government (.45–70) and .40–60 calibers. Marlin entered the rifle in the army's ordnance trials of 1881–82 and it performed well but no government orders were forthcoming. In .45–70 caliber, the '81 appealed to those hunters and others who wanted the advantages of a repeater capable of downing larger game and at longer ranges. The firm of Broadwater, Hubbell & Co. of Miles City, Montana, was advertising the rifle in March 1882 as "the New Buffalo Gun," although the northern herd would not survive much longer. Undoubtedly army officers shopping for a personal rifle looked carefully at a Model 1881 in .45–70 caliber.[52]

Perhaps it was an officer's gun which Pvt. Will Barnes of the 6th Cavalry carried when setting out on a hazardous night ride in 1882 through Apache country.

> I was riding a sure-footed, sensible cavalry horse, full of pep and speed, and I carried a Marlin repeating carbine [rifle], using government cartridges, and a forty-five Colt revolver. In my youthful enthusiasm, I felt myself capable of out-running, out-shooting, or out-generaling any bunch of Apache Indians in Arizona.[53]

Beginning in 1885, the Model 1881 was available in .32–40, .38–55, and .45–85 calibers as well. Subsequent models of lever action Marlins included that of 1888, which was lighter in weight and less expensive ($19.50) and chambered the popular .44–40, .38–40, and later the .32–20 cartridge

used in Winchester's Model 1873. The Model 1889, firing these same Winchester cartridges, broke from earlier Marlins and featured a side ejection system designed by L. L. Hepburn and proved to be the best selling Marlin rifle to that time, with about fifty-five thousand produced. It also was the first model to be offered in a short carbine length. The Marlin line was expanded with new models almost annually in the last decade of the century and in calibers from .22 rimfire to .45–90—models of 1891, 1892, 1893 (the first Marlin to accept smokeless cartridges), 1894, 1895, and finally 1897. Although Marlin lever action rifles never achieved the fame of their crosstown rival, Winchester, they offered the westerner and others high quality rifles for virtually any intended use.

In September 1898 when cattleman John H. Slaughter heard outlaw Albert "Peg Leg" Finney had been seen on his Arizona ranch, he and two companions set out to apprehend him.

> [We found him] laying down under a tree supposed to be asleep. So I walked up to him and took his Winchester rifle from near him and threw it about eighty feet back, it was the only gun I seen, until I told him that he was under arrest, and . . . he came up with a six-shooter in his right hand which was cocked and pointed his pistol at me. As he done so, I then shot him with my 45–85 caliber [Model 1881] Marlin rifle.

The former sheriff admitted Finney's revolver looked twice its size as he momentarily stared down its muzzle. "It was the closest call I ever had."[54]

In 1897 George Carrick from Illinois settled in Canada's Klondike region after he'd married an Indian woman. While fishing with two friends, he discovered gold in Bonanza Creek and in only a few days had extracted more than $1,200 worth from the stream. Similar discoveries led to the celebrated gold rush to the Klondike in 1898 which drew eager prospectors from the United States as well as Canada and elsewhere.

One outfitter in Edmonton, Alberta, published a "List of Articles Necessary for a Complete Outfit for a Klondyke [sic] Expedition." His suggested outfit totaled $224 worth of clothes, hardware, groceries, camping gear, and arms. Under the latter category, he recommended "One repeating rifle, 40–82, with reloading tools and 100 rounds of brass-shell cartridges, 1 large hunting knife, and an assortment of fishing tackle," weighing about forty

A goat hunter on Catalina Island, California, with an 1893 Marlin. (Courtesy: Lee A. Silva)

pounds at a cost of $29. Although he didn't specify a particular make of repeating rifle, either a Winchester Model 1886 or Model 1895 would have fit this description as would a Marlin Model 1895 lever action repeater, manufactured up until 1917.[55]

One advantage the Marlin provided over the Winchester lever action repeaters was its side ejection of empty cartridge cases, a feature introduced with its Model 1889. This arrangement facilitated the mounting of a telescopic sight on top of the frame. Such sights were known as early as the late 1600s and both Union and Confederate sharpshooters during the Civil War sometimes were armed with muzzle loading rifles, such as the Confederacy's English Whitworth, fitted with these aids.

A leading designer and maker of rifle telescopes was William Malcolm who began production in 1855 in Syracuse, New York. Typical magnification was 3x to 20x. His along with sights by such other makers as L. M. Moog gained acceptance among target shooters and by the 1870s among an increasing number of hunters in the west despite the cost, added weight, and susceptibility to damage in

rough country. One of Malcolm's best customers was dealer Charles Slotterbek of California who in a ten-year period in the 1870s and 1880s purchased more than 150 scopes.[56]

A letter published in *Shooting and Fishing* magazine from a resident of Cerro Gordo, California, testified:

> In ... 1865 ... I crossed the plains to the Rockies, carrying ... a Sharps rifle, .52-calibre linen cartridge [percussion].... fitted with a fine Malcolm telescopic sight. The following year found me, with this rifle, camped with a band of hunters and trappers in the Wind River Mountains, at that time a paradise for large game, and scalping Indians. The rifle itself, as well as the telescope, was something of a novelty in that region in those days, and much was the discussion as to the merits and demerits of the telescopic sight. Within a year ... every one of that little company ... had

Cooks at a US Geological Survey camp in Alaska. The two rifles at left are .22 Winchester M1890 slide action repeaters, designed by John M. and Matthew S. Browning, with production exceeding eight hundred thousand guns. Until the M1890's introduction, the Model 1873 was the only .22 Winchester repeater available. The '90 was popular as a shooting gallery gun as well as for hunting small game and casual target shooting. The rifle at right is a Marlin M1892 or 1897, forerunners of the Model 39 .22, popular throughout the twentieth century. (Courtesy: US Geological Survey, L. M. Prindle neg. #18)

fitted the best Malcolm telescopic sights to their muzzle-loading rifles. Years afterwards I met two members of that little band of hunters. They had discarded their muzzle-loaders and were equipped with Sharps rifles, model 1874, fitted with the best procurable telescopic sight.[57]

Beginning in 1883, Colt began marketing its own lever action repeating rifle, designed by Andrew Burgess. Buffalo Bill Cody obtained one, but production of the Colt-Burgess ceased a little less than two years after its appearance. Tradition says this was due to a gentleman's agreement between Colt and Winchester, but there is no documented evidence to substantiate this claim. More likely, Colt decided to concentrate its production and sales efforts on

another shoulder gun, a pump action magazine rifle, rather than compete with Winchester, Marlin, and Whitney-Kennedy lever action rifles.

Known as the Lightning and introduced in 1884, this new pump action Colt eventually was available in three frame sizes and in calibers from .22 to .50–95 Express. The gun met with mixed reviews. Some early guns were plagued by ejection problems and Deputy Sheriff J. G. Jacqurdin of Brownsville, Texas, in 1889 wrote the factory expressing his dissatisfaction with the two he had and asked if he could exchange them. In contrast, it probably was the Lightning rifle rather than the Burgess about which W. R. Thomas, captain of the Oakland, California, police wrote. The department had sixteen sixteen-shot (15-shot) octagonal barrel Colts and wanted twenty-four more. "[Winchesters] do not work well,

A moose for a surveying party's larder, perhaps killed with the Model 1893 or 1895 Marlin at left. (Courtesy: US Geological Survey, A. H. Brooks neg. #72)

This gentleman, tentatively identified as Charles Goodnight, holds a scope-mounted octagonal-barrel Sharps M1874 sporting rifle. (Courtesy: C. W. Slagle)

A westerner with a rare Colt Burgess carbine. (Courtesy: Herb Peck Jr.)

they catch and it is with great difficulty that the shells can be thrown out."[58]

One of the most elaborate of the Express Lightnings was an engraved .45–85, fitted with special sights and stock, and shipped in 1892 to Red Lodge, Montana. But despite the Colt name, advanced design, and variety of calibers, these guns didn't match the success of the various models of Winchester and Marlin rifles available at that time. Production ended in 1904.[59]

As repeaters came on the market in calibers suitable for any large game on the continent, single-shot rifles still had their devotees among hunters and target shooters. Between 1861 and 1873, five firms manufactured the single-shot rifle designed by Charles H. Ballard. Ball & Williams was the major producer during the Civil War with the majority of the guns going to fill military contracts for carbines and rifles, many for the state of

Kentucky. An ad in the February 11, 1865, issue of *Harper's Weekly* mentioned the use of Ballards by captains Medorem Crawford and James L. Fisk. These two in 1863–65 organized quasi-military escorts for immigrant wagon trains bound for Oregon and Washington; the guns were sold at journey's end.[60]

Postwar sales of sporting Ballards for hunting and target shooting initially were sporadic, despite the guns' reliability and the fact that early unadorned specimens were cheaper and simpler than such competitive repeating arms as the Winchester. One commendable feature of the sporting models was their dual ignition system. A swivel striker on the hammer allowed use of a rimfire metallic cartridge or the percussion ignition system by means of the nipple mounted in the breechblock.

One who considered a Ballard his "pet rifle" was geologist and explorer Clarence King. In 1872 his party gave

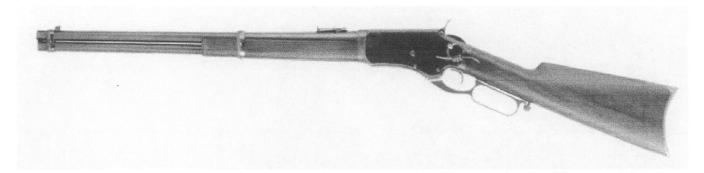

A .44–40 Whitney-Kennedy carbine stamped in the stock "No. 15/MO.PAC.RY." for Missouri & Pacific Railway. The line originated in 1849 as the Pacific Railroad and was the first rail line west of the Mississippi. It was reorganized in 1872 as the Missouri Pacific (commonly known as the MoPac) and in 1879 came under the control of New York financier Jay Gould who developed a system through Colorado, Nebraska, Arkansas, Texas, and Louisiana. (Courtesy: Dale H. Peterson)

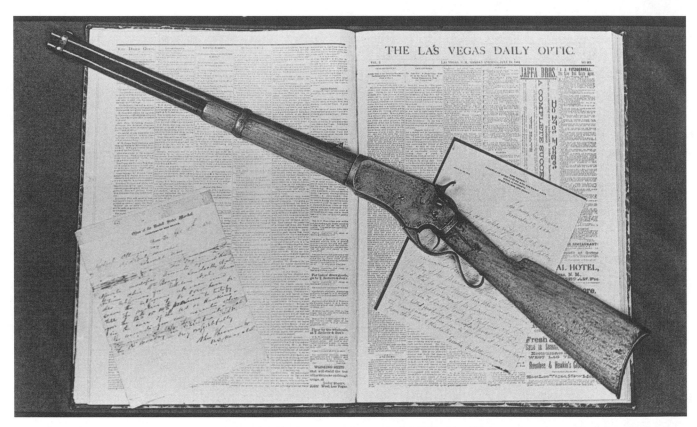

A .44–40 Whitney-Kennedy carbine (#808) given to a lawman by Billy the Kid, authenticated by the former's daughter. The Whitney Arms Company of New Haven produced an estimated fifteen thousand of these repeaters in carbine, rifle, and musket length in the 1880s. Those built using the light frame could be purchased in .32, .38, or .44 caliber while the heavier frame guns were offered in .40–60, .45–60, and .45–75 calibers as well as a few .50–90s. (Courtesy: Greg Martin)

chase to a large grizzly bear which retreated into its den. King with little hesitation had soldiers of the escort tie a rope around his legs and, armed only with his Ballard, he crawled into the almost lightless cave. Startled when they heard a single shot, the soldiers yanked King out, "nearly stripping him of his clothes and scratching and tearing him about the face and body about as badly (King always laughingly insisted) as the bear could have done." It turned out that King's bullet had entered the roof of "Caleb's" mouth, killing the giant bear instantly.[61]

A young doctor began practicing in Deadwood, Dakota Territory, but in the fall of 1877 moved to the Texas

Photographed in Indian Territory, the men are unidentified but the commonality of guns—Remington-Keene bolt action repeating rifles and perhaps Remington M1875 revolvers—suggests they may be peace officers or armed messengers. This was Remington's first bolt action rifle, with perhaps five thousand produced in the early 1880s. A magazine cutoff allowed the gun to be used as a single-shot, a feature found on the Winchester-Hotchkiss as well. (Courtesy: Lee A. Silva)

panhandle. "I carried an octagon-barreled Ballard rifle and a Colt's forty-five revolver, as the Sioux were still on the war path." En route he traded for a Sharp's carbine in place of his Ballard. "It had twice the range of the rifle and carried a larger bullet."[62]

A group of tourists from Montana in 1877 picked an inappropriate time to visit Yellowstone National Park's natural wonders, then still virtually a wilderness. They found themselves involved in the Nez Perces' desperate flight from Idaho and were captured and several of the party were murdered. One who survived the ordeal noted they had not been in a good position to resist. Two had Ballards but one had only three cartridges, two others had needle guns (Springfields probably), another a shotgun but only three shells and those loaded with fine birdshot, and the last a Henry, well provided with two hundred rounds. Two revolvers completed the whites' arsenal.[63]

In 1875 John Marlin along with Charles Daly and Augustus Schoverling acquired the manufacturing rights to the single-shot Ballard rifle from the defunct Brown Manufacturing Company, the former to oversee production while his associates promoted sales. Although the redesigned Ballard action showed little outward change, the action was strengthened and an internal extractor was added, eliminating the external extractor mounted beneath the barrel. The "automatic extractor" and "reversible firing-pin" were two features advertised in 1876. Under the Marlin name, the Ballard quickly gained increased prestige.[64]

As target shooting became increasingly popular after the Civil War, rifle clubs sprang up in many cities both east and west of the Mississippi. Sharps, Remington, Providence Tool Company (Peabody-Martini), and other prominent makers sought to fulfill

403

Three of the rifles are M1873 Winchesters but the gentleman at rear left holds a Colt Lightning pump action rifle. The small-frame revolver stuck in his waist belt may be a Harrington & Richardson or Iver Johnson top break double action. (Courtesy: Erich Baumann)

Denver Armory,
C. GOVE & SONS,

340 Blake Street, Denver, Colorado.

Carry the Largest Stock of Sporting Goods in the West. COLT'S PISTOLS, SHARP',S MAYNARD'S. WINCHESTER and BURGESS RIFLES ; COLT'S SCOTT'S, GREENER'S, WEBLY'S and FOX'S Breech-Loading Double Guns. Also, Single Breech-Loading Guns, Ammunition, Fishing Tackle, etc. Also Sole Agents of Colorado for the

BALLARD RIFLE.

Highest score on record. off-hand. 200 yards, made by C. Gove with a Ballard— 5-5-5-4-5-4-5-5-5-5-5-5-5-5—73 out of 75   Repairing a Specialty.   Send for Catalogue.

A September 1879 ad by Carlos Gove & Sons promoting Ballard and an extensive assortment of other arms.

Hunters at the JOD Ranch near Hugo, Colorado. From left: Matt Hamilik with a holstered large-frame S&W and possibly a Ballard in a saddle scabbard; Dave Henderson with a M1866 Winchester; Joseph E. Collier, founder of the Denver First Federal Savings and Loan, with a double-barrel shotgun; unidentified; and standing at right with a scoped Pacific or Montana Ballard rifle is Winfield Scott Stratton, a millionaire mine owner at Victor, Colorado, who became one of Colorado's leading philanthropists. Presumably the owl perched on the roof is stuffed. (Courtesy: Denver Public Library Western History Department, CO)

these shooters' needs with a myriad of target models. Some of these competitions were in the form of Schuetzen German-style off-hand matches. Use of specialized percussion Schuetzen rifles persisted into the late 1800s, but their users shot side-by-side with competitors firing single-shot breechloaders. The Marlin-Ballard No. 6 Schuetzen appeared in 1876 and remained in the Marlin line until 1890. Winchester made a Schuetzen-style version of its High Wall in the mid-1880s, and Stevens did the same within its Ideal target series introduced in the early 1890s.

In February 1883 Dr. C. M. Sinner, secretary of the Minneapolis Rifle Club wrote of another Marlin-Ballard target model, the No. 7 Long Range rifle.

> The nine Long Range Ballard Rifles now in our Club are giving the most perfect satisfaction. The highest yearly average and the greatest number of clean scores are made by the Ballard, although other first-class rifles are used.[65]

Hunters who wanted a single-shot rifle suitable for larger western game and shots at longer distances found various Marlin-Ballard models were well suited to their needs. The names given to certain models at the factory reflected the company's appreciation for western sales. One of the most popular of the large-caliber heavy barrel Ballards was the Pacific No. 5 with a hickory cleaning rod mounted beneath the barrel and available in calibers up to .50. The No. 1 3/4 hunting rifle introduced in 1877 or 1878 with double set trigger was designated the Far West Rifle. The Marlin Firearms Company catalog for 1882 noted in describing the fourteen-pound .45 Montana No. 5 1/2 hunting rifle: "This is a new style just introduced, suited to the Territory trade, where a heavy arm is required."[66]

Also available in a wide range of styles and calibers (from .22 to .50) were those hunting and target rifles manufactured by the Massachusetts Arms Company using Dr. Edward Maynard's design. While the firm was producing carbines on government contract during the Civil War, it also made some sporting arms, later succeeded by the Models of 1873 and 1882. (While all Maynards used

Poised and ready for anything, but safe in the photo studio of Fox & Symons, operating between 1885 and 1901 in Salt Lake City. The guns are a Marlin-Ballard Pacific and a Colt Single Action. A careful examination of the photo shows that the thimbles beneath the barrel to hold a cleaning rod on a Pacific model have been removed. (Courtesy: Craig Mossberg)

metallic cartridges, those of Civil War vintage used ones with a hole in the base to admit the flame from a separate percussion cap.) The Maynard action was uncomplicated—lowering the lever tipped the barrel downward for loading—and these rifles remained in production until the 1890s.

Among the features of the Maynard that the firm promoted was the gun's simplicity and the ease with which barrels could be interchanged, either rifled or smoothbore for use as a shotgun. Top of the line in their 1885 catalog was the Long-Range Creedmoor Rifle at $65 with fancy branch walnut stock, checkered pistol grip, and vernier and wind gauge sights with spirit level for precise target shooting. A testimonial in that catalog from E. P. Harris of Midland, Missouri, stated that with his .40 caliber Maynard with peep and globe sights he fired "17 consecutive 20 inch bull's eyes, at 500 yards, defeating at the same time a fine target muz-

zleloader with telescopic sights, made by [probably Nelson] Lewis of Troy, N.Y."[67]

Johnny T. Spaulding, a market hunter in the Black Hills in the mid-1870s, took a major toll on game animals around Deadwood. Modest though he was about his skill with his Maynard rifle, one witness saw him kill fifteen antelope on a single "stand" with fifteen shots. On a scouting expedition, he was cited as having dispatched an Indian at a range of at least five hundred yards.[68]

Far less expensive was the .22 caliber Maynard Improved Gallery Rifle priced in 1885 at $20 with a 20-inch barrel. At the same time, the company cautioned that:

Unscrupulous persons are, through circulars and newspaper advertisements, offering OLD DISCARDED GOVERNMENT CARBINES of the Maynard pattern as

A hunter's sturdy log cabin in the Black Hills, Dakota Territory. The elk antlers beneath the window support a Ballard rifle. (Courtesy: W. H. Over Museum, Vermillion, SD)

Target shooters at New Almaden, California, in 1885. Now a ghost town south of San Francisco, it was in an area in which mercury was mined for the gold and silver industry. The shooter at left holds a Springfield "trapdoor" rifle, the other men Ballard Pacific rifles. The target is a third class Creedmoor, generally used for offhand shooting at ranges up to three hundred yards. (Courtesy: Thomas N. Trevor)

The Denver Rifle Club Team, which in September 1899 won the Coors Championship Cup Contest at the Colorado Rifle Association's tournament. The single-shot target rifles from left include a M1885 Winchester, Ballard No. 8 Union Hill, Sharps Borchardt, and another M1885 Winchester. (Courtesy: John Dutcher)

Members of the New Braunfels (Texas) Schuetzen Verein pose at a bundes schiessen, or gathering of several rifle clubs, held at San Antonio, Texas, in June 1902. Their rifles are (from left, top row): Ballard Pacific, Stevens Ideal No. 44, Ballard Pacific, and perhaps another Ballard Pacific. Bottom row from left include: Stevens Ideal No. 44, Ballard Pacific, Stevens Ideal "Walnut Hill" No. 49 or No. 50, and Stevens Ideal "Schuetzen Junior" No. 52 with the butt plate removed. (Courtesy: Institute of Texas Cultures, San Antonio)

Handsomely attired and well-armed westerner with a Marlin-Ballard Pacific No. 5 rifle. (Courtesy: Idaho State Historical Society, photo #79-127.l)

genuine Maynard Central-Fire Sporting Rifles, at a very low price, and conveying the impression that the MASSACHU-SETTS ARMS CO. had failed.

Now this is to caution you and all others against buying such guns as they are simply old Cavalry Carbines, used during the late war, and which have been sold by the Government at a mere nomi-nal price. They have the twenty inch bar-rel and half inch bore, with percussion cap. So please don't be imposed upon, but send for our new price-list and circular for the only genuine MAYNARD SPORT-ING RIFLES AND SHOT GUNS.[69]

J. H. May was using a Maynard but apparently wasn't entirely satisfied with its performance. His letter dated

An April 1880 ad in which Carlos Gove of Denver promoted Ballard rifles. The cut is intended to represent either the Pacific or Montana model, each of which had a cleaning rod mounted beneath the barrel.

Maynard Model 1873 rifle with scope, used by Robert Hewley who hunted game for the Union Pacific Railroad. (Courtesy: Colorado Historical Society, neg. #F-32787)

September 5, 1877, to the Sharps factory from Wild Horse Springs near Fort Concho, Texas, stated: "I have been using last winter while hunting a 70 grain 40 cal Maynard, but would like to get a Sharps."

Although an increasing variety of civilian arms became available to the westerner, some acquired by one means or another examples of .50 and later .45 caliber Springfield "trapdoor" military rifles and carbines, some genuine and some fraudulent.

The Government had taken the old Springfield rifle [.58 rifle musket] and converted it into a breech-loading needle gun of very long range. It would carry a mile or more. I bought one from a soldier when they were first issued, and by cutting off about four inches of the barrel, I was able to retain it as a condemned

piece. I resighted it with peep sights, and it would shoot right where I held it; and I was a good shot.

Thus recalled William Breakenridge. In some instances, civilians were able to purchase guns directly from the army. General Order No. 9 and No. 103 dated February 5, 1874, and August 5, 1874, respectively, directed that at exposed frontier settlements in emergency situations ammunition and arms could be sold to settlers who didn't have the means to arm themselves otherwise.[70]

Henry Raymond, a bison hunter, in his diary entry for March 4, 1873, noted: "Bill brooks got shot at with needle gun, the ball passing through two barrels of water, lodging in outside Iron hoop." Brooks was an ex-marshal of Newton, Kansas, and escaped uninjured. [71]

Texas Ranger lieutenant John W. Baylor had a reputation as an outstanding marksman. He at first used a

Lower Main Street in Deadwood, Dakota Territory, in 1877. The wooden replicas of guns direct customers to Alexander D. and brother John McAusland's Creedmoor Gun Shop, next to the Big Bonanza Meat Market. The gun shop burned down not long after, along with much of the town's business district. (Courtesy: Montana Historical Society, Haynes Foundation Collection, neg. #H-130)

Winchester rifle, apparently a '73, but after his first Indian fight he concluded it was too light and discarded it for a .45–70 Springfield sporting rifle.

> He always used what he called rest sticks; that is, two sticks about three feet long the size of one's little finger. These were tied together about four or five inches from one end with a buckskin thong. In shooting he would squat down, extend the sticks an arm's length out in front of him with the longer ends spread out tripod-fashion on the ground. With his gun resting in the fork he had a perfect rest and could make close shots at long range. He always carried these sticks in his hand and used them on his horse as a quirt.[72]

In the 1870s, the operator of a Texas freight line armed his men with

> short, needle guns of 50 caliber that were ordered by Elmendorf & Co., of San Antonio, for me, at a cost of three hundred dollars a dozen. The gun was carried in a scabbard that was fastened to the driver's saddle mule, and when in camp, as a rule, it was placed against the left wheel of his wagon. The forty-five caliber six-shooter was carried in a scabbard on his cartridge belt, and if not, it always was in reach of his hand. The belt carried fifty rounds of cartridges for the needle gun and twelve rounds for the pistol. The guns ranged about eight thousand feet, and the

411

Springfield Sporting Breech Loading Rifle.

30 in. Octagon Barrel, Double Trigger, 45-70, 10½ to 11 lbs. 25 00
Springfield Breech Loading Musket, 32 in. Round Barrel, 45-70 .... 17 00
"   "   "   " 32 in. "   " 50-70 .... 15 00

In their 1884 catalog N. Curry & Bro. of San Francisco offered "sporting Springfields."

pistols about one thousand feet. I always carried about two thousand rounds of cartridges for the guns and about five hundred for the pistols.[73]

The short needle guns may have been cut down Model 1866 .50 Springfields, which the army began disposing of in the early 1870s not long after improved .50 Models of 1868 and 1870 became available.

One Wisconsin youth, new to the west in 1873, secured a job with a freight outfit as a "bullwhacker" in Wyoming Territory. He had outfitted himself with "a Derringer [sic] revolver, which was little better than a popgun." Although Henry Deringer Jr. died in 1868, his relatives continued the business in Philadelphia in the 1870s, producing .22 and .32 caliber pocket revolvers with a tip-up barrel similar to Smith & Wesson arms. This reference may have been to one of these revolvers.[74]

It was a proud day when the youth's boss confidently assigned him to duty as an outrider at least a thousand yards away from the ox train to watch for Indian signs.

I was well equipped with an army Springfield of large caliber, forty rounds in my belt, two Remington revolvers, and a butcher knife with a five-inch blade for the possibility of close quarters. I had a bottle of spring water and a saddlebag full of sandwiches of bread and fried bacon, and plenty of tobacco.[75]

However Springfield "trapdoor" .45 rifles or carbines were seldom sold by the National Armory, although "condemned" (obsolete) parts were. "Trapdoor" sporting rifles

and carbines advertised for sale by dealers from the 1870s forward in most instances were assembled using a mixture of such surplus parts and new components manufactured by the arms dealers. The quality and finish of such guns varied rather widely, with some showing superior workmanship. Both E. C. Meacham and San Francisco's N. Curry & Bro. were advertising pseudo-Springfield sporting rifles in 1883–84 with octagonal barrels; genuine armory-produced "trapdoor" military rifles had round barrels. The use of surplus parts in this manner caused national armory officials concern for some time, as a May 9, 1885, endorsement from Lt. Col. A. R. Buffington noted.

It has been a well known fact that obsolete and condemned parts of arms sold from time to time by proper authority, at this Armory, have been used by private Arms Corporations in the manufacture of arms, but it was not until 1882 that it was known so called Springfield arms were being manufactured.... [Restrictions on the sale of useable .45 breech parts existed after 1882 but it] appears most probable now private Arms Companies have machines and fixtures for the manufacture of all parts of Springfield arms [and] to obtain condemned parts by purchase is no longer relied upon and the arms are made entirely out of new material.[76]

The 1884 Curry catalog offered the "trapdoor" sporter with 30-inch octagonal barrel and double set trigger for $25, a handsome piece but not a bargain price considering a customer could procure a Model 1876 Winchester repeater for

Youthful Colorado hunters. The center boy holds a Stevens tip-up rifle, one of many produced from the 1870s to the 1890s in about fifteen different models and in calibers from .22 to .44. (Courtesy: Wade R. Lucas)

only $2 more from the same price list. One who wanted a .50–70 Springfield musket paid only $15, or $17 for a plain round barrel .45–70 "trapdoor" rifle.

Limited in production quantities but certainly not in quality were those lever action single-shot rifles designed by James H. Bullard, a former master mechanic at Smith & Wesson. The guns in both target and hunting style were marketed by the Bullard Repeating Arms Company during the early 1880s and 1890s in calibers from .22 to .50. Similar in appearance to the firm's single-shots and greater in number, Bullard lever action repeaters gained a reputation for the smoothness of the operating mechanism.

William A. Allen had been a blacksmith, express messenger, and ardent hunter before establishing a dental practice in Billings, Montana Territory, in the early 1880s. Demands on his service as a dentist had limited his hunting opportunities but in 1886 after a four-year hiatus he arranged a trip with friends. Some years before he had obtained a M1876 Winchester, but in describing his preparations for this trip he noted: "I grasped my faithful old friend, threw down the lever and surveyed the inside which gleamed like a mirror. It was my Bullard rifle, 45 calibre, eighty-five grains of powder, ten pounds weight and ten

shots. I seized my cartridge belt, my knife, a cold lunch and started out."[77]

On another occasion while hunting deer, Allen had a close encounter with a mountain lion. "Death had stared me in the face many times before in many different forms, and the old Bullard had never been found wanting."[78]

By the mid-1890s and continuing well into the next century, the J. Stevens Arms and Tool Company of Chicopee Falls, Massachusetts, was a leader in the production of single-shot sporting rifles. These ranged from the inexpensive .22 "Favorite" and "Crack Shot" boys' rifles to the Ideal series of high grade target rifles in a wide range of calibers and styles including "Ladies" models, the "Schuetzen Special," and the "Walnut Hill."

High quality single-shot sporting and target rifles by Whitney, Frank Wesson, and others also found their way into western dealers' inventories. Remington single-shot rolling-block rifles were major competitors to Sharps both on the bison killing grounds and among other hunters. The Remington involved the interaction of hammer and breechblock in a system that was simple to operate and strong. To open the breech, the shooter merely rolled the block backward and downward with the thumb, thus the

A westerner, perhaps from the northwest, with a Peabody carbine. Although the Providence Tool Company of Rhode Island sold some single-shot carbines and rifles commercially in the United States, much of their production went to fill foreign military orders. (The image is reversed in the photographic process.) (Courtesy: George Hart)

term "rolling block." In the closed position, the hammer blocked the breechblock in place. In the early 1880s the company added the Remington-Hepburn falling-block rifles. Winchester in 1885 brought out its first single-shot rifle, another of John M. Browning's designs, and would chamber it for a broad range of cartridges from .22 to .50. Perhaps eighty-five thousand or so of these so-called High Wall and Low Wall single-shots left New Haven before the end of the century. Not all were directed toward target shooters; plain versions in rifle and carbine lengths were available for the hunter.

In 1877 a party of prospectors headed for the Black Hills despite the threat posed by angry Sioux. Attacked by mounted warriors, a shot from Thomas Randall's .45–105 Remington rolling-block rifle was the first from the prospectors' defensive position. Beating off their attackers, the party turned back to organize and increase their number. About the same time, Brant Street when carrying mail between Deadwood, Dakota Territory, and Fort Laramie carried no arms other than a Remington rifle and a bag of cartridges, slung across the pommel of his saddle. When Indians jumped him and killed his horse, he took shelter in an arroyo and from there held off his attackers until they departed at nightfall.[79]

An undated but post-1884 ad for John P. Lower's Sportsmen's Depot at 377 Blake Street in Denver showed

Colorado hunting camp scene (1892). Rifles (from left) are a M1886 Winchester, a Remington rolling-block sporting rifle with tang sight, and a lighter M1873 Winchester. (Courtesy: Denver Public Library Western History Department, neg. #F13707, CO)

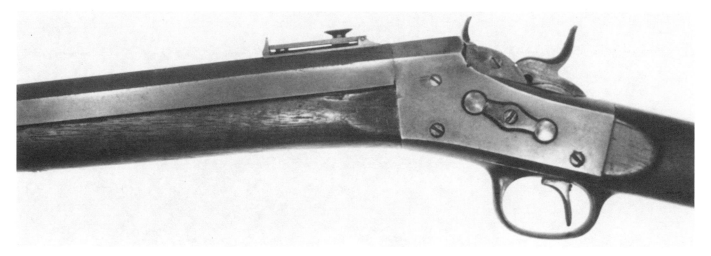

The stamping "NPRR" in the butt stock of this .44–77 No. 1 Remington sporting rifle may indicate ownership by the Northern Pacific Railroad. The rail line from Lake Superior to Puget Sound was chartered in 1864, but construction moved more slowly than did that of the Union Pacific and the project wasn't completed until 1883. (Courtesy: John A. Kopec)

the following prices, giving an idea of comparative costs of standard grade single-shot and repeating sporting rifles:

Ballard Pacific $30
Remington Hepburn .45–70 $27
Sharps Model 1878 Borchardt military style
    rifle $20
Colt "Lightning" pump carbine $25

Marlin .45–70 $32
Winchester .44 M1873 round barrel rifle $25

Rarely mentioned in personal accounts were the light, often inexpensive small-caliber rifles intended for use in acquiring rabbits or other small game for the cooking pot or to rid a henhouse of a raiding skunk or other unwanted predator. "Boys' rifles" was a term sometimes applied to such arms but they were also useful in adult

A .40 caliber Remington-Hepburn from Washington Territory. (Courtesy: Dennis C. Brooks)

Hopefully, for the sake of safety, the military-style Remington or Whitney rolling-block rifle upon which he was leaning was unloaded. (Courtesy: George Jackson)

Oliver J. Perry, Texas Ranger and city marshal of San Saba, Texas (1898–99). The Winchester .22 Model 1890 pump rifle is undoubtedly a studio prop. (Courtesy: George Jackson)

hands for informal "plinking" or target shooting. While trapping one winter, John Rollinson noted that he and his partner always carried a .22 rifle in hopes of bagging grouse. Riding fence lines, he and a companion were preparing dinner at a cabin when he asked about the chickens running loose. When asked to tell where he had seen them, he received a knowing smile.

> From a cigar box on a shelf, he produced a box of .22 cartridges, and from under the bed he brought out a Winchester repeater, loaded it, and started out-side.... "Them chickens you saw were sage hens. I guess you said it right when you called them my chickens, and as they are on my property, we will just go out and shoot some for our supper."[80]

Among the most common of these light rifles was the single-shot Belgian Flobert which used a dropping-block action similar to that of the Remington rolling-block design. E. C. Meacham Arms Company of St. Louis in their 1884 catalog offered these in .22 caliber beginning at only $2.25 and rising to $8.00 for a .32 rimfire model with checkered stock and a pistol grip. The catalog described these single-shots as being "a source of great amusement as a pastime for the ladies and other members of the home circle." James Van Horn, son of Capt. James J. Van Horn, received a .22 Flobert rifle for Christmas while at Fort Huachuca, Arizona Territory, in the late 1880s. Proud of his new possession, he approached a prairie dog village and fired at one of the rodents but missed as the animal dove into its burrow. Thinking to scare the animal out, the youngster thumped the mound with the butt of his rifle, only to splinter the stock.[81]

Members of the Hunters Club of 1875 of Brown County, Minnesota. The club purchased land near the Cottonwood River and called it "Yaeger's Ruh" (Hunter's Rest). The member seated at left holds a Stevens tip-up sporting rifle, perhaps the Expert model with half round and half octagonal barrel.
(Courtesy: Minnesota Historical Society)

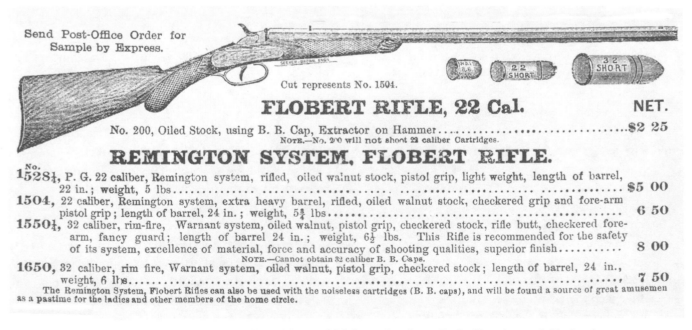

Send Post-Office Order for Sample by Express.

Cut represents No. 1504.

FLOBERT RIFLE, 22 Cal.

NET.

No. 200, Oiled Stock, using B. B. Cap, Extractor on Hammer..$2 25
NOTE.—No. 200 will not shoot 22 caliber Cartridges.

REMINGTON SYSTEM, FLOBERT RIFLE.

No.
1528¼, P. G. 22 caliber, Remington system, rifled, oiled walnut stock, pistol grip, light weight, length of barrel,
22 in.; weight, 5 lbs...$5 00
1504, 22 caliber, Remington system, extra heavy barrel, rifled, oiled walnut stock, checkered grip and fore-arm
pistol grip; length of barrel, 24 in.; weight, 5¾ lbs...6 50
1550¼, 32 caliber, rim-fire, Warnant system, oiled walnut, pistol grip, checkered stock, rifle butt, checkered forearm, fancy guard; length of barrel 24 in.; weight, 6½ lbs. This Rifle is recommended for the safety
of its system, excellence of material, force and accuracy of shooting qualities, superior finish...........8 00
NOTE.—Cannot obtain 32 caliber B. B. Caps.
1650, 32 caliber, rim fire, Warnant system, oiled walnut, pistol grip, checkered stock; length of barrel, 24 in.,
weight, 6 lbs..7 50
The Remington System, Flobert Rifles can also be used with the noiseless cartridges (B. B. caps), and will be found a source of great amusemen
as a pastime for the ladies and other members of the home circle.

.22 and .32 Flobert rifles offered in an 1884 catalog from E. C. Meacham of St. Louis.

The 1884 Meacham catalog also included .22 caliber tip-up "shooting gallery rifles" by J. Stevens & Co. beginning at $20 or Stevens "pocket rifles," essentially a pistol with an attachable metal skeleton shoulder stock, for $13.25. These latter single-shots were available in different size frames and barrel lengths; the option of interchangeable smooth or rifled barrels added to their versatility. The Hunter's Pet, for example, could be purchased in calibers from .22 to .44–40 and barrel lengths of up to twenty-four inches and with either target or hunting sights. G. O. Shields hunted and fished in the Rockies in 1881–82, sometimes with famed western photographer L. A. Huffman. Shields referred to his Hunter's Pet as "a light but very effective weapon."[82]

Artillery on the Frontier: Civilian and Military

As we had no soldiers on board coming down the river
we thought the Sioux would take advantage of it to attack us,
so we prepared for war. Three cannons were kept loaded with grape
for more than a week, while every man on board kept his
fire-arms loaded and ready for use at a moments notice.
— William J. Hays, 1860[1]

Throughout the nineteenth century, artillery in various forms saw service all over the west, and in civilian as well as military hands. When Lewis and Clark set out on their epic journey in 1803, they carried two blunderbusses of sufficient size to be mounted on swivels on the expedition's two pirogues. And from that time well into the 1870s, waterborne artillery continued to be popular. In 1811 an adventurous young attorney, H. M. Breckenridge, journeyed up the Missouri River with Manuel Lisa in a keelboat manned by twenty-two oarsmen. "There is ... a swivel [gun] on the bow of the boat, which, in case of attack, would make a formidable appearance; we have also two brass blunderbusses in the cabin." Such precautions, Breckenridge thought, were absolutely necessary in view of the hostility of the Sioux "who, of late had committed several murders and robberies on the whites." In 1812 Lisa's keelboat carried "howitzers" onboard in addition to the swivel. A newly constructed Pacific Fur Company post on the Columbia

River in 1813 was guarded by "a light brass four pounder." Alexander Ross's party, traveling down the Columbia River in 1814, kept threatening Indians at a distance with several shots into the woods from a three-pounder.[2]

Later Ross described the establishment of Fort Nez Perce: "Our weapons of defence [*sic*] were composed of four pieces of ordanance [*sic*] from one to three pounds beside ten wall pieces or swivels, sixty stand of muskets and bayonets, twenty boarding pikes, and a box of hand grenades." In 1834 Hill & M'Gunnegle of St. Louis advertised one-half- and two-pounder iron cannon "suitable for s[team?] boats and Indian Trade kept constantly on hand and for sale." An 1844 inventory of the trading post of Fort Chardon in Blackfoot country included two "three pd iron mounted cannon."[3]

The first steamboats ventured up the Missouri River in 1819, but only one got as far as Council Bluffs. Not for another decade did commercial steamboating on the Missouri begin in earnest. Nevertheless, in the

The pintle on this flintlock English blunderbuss allows easy mounting on a small boat or even in a wagon and use as a swivel gun.

June 25, 1819, edition of the St. Louis *Enquirer* there appeared a description of the river steamer *Western Engineer*. "The bow of the vessel exhibits the form of a huge water serpent, black and scaly, rising out of the water from under the boat, his head as high as the deck, darting forward, his open mouth vomiting smoke and apparently carrying the boat on his back." If this menacing-looking craft didn't intimidate Native Americans up the Missouri, the two swivel guns onboard presumably would. Throughout much of the 1800s, Missouri River steamboats often carried cannon with the dual purpose of firing salutes and intimidating any Native Americans who became too defiant.[4]

When the side-wheel steamer *Martha* plowed her way up the Missouri in 1847, a party of hostile Yankton Sioux attacked and gained access to the forward section of the boat, killing one deckhand. Unfortunately the vessel's light cannon "of about 2 1/2 inches caliber, mounted on four wheels" had gone belowdecks for repairs to its carriage. While the Indians were concentrated near the bow, the first engineer and a party of men were able to hoist the gun on deck and haul it into the aft part of the cabin. Capt. La Barge described the scene:

> I always kept in the cabin some powder and shot for use in hunting. I got the powder, but the supply of shot was gone. [Chief engineer] Grismore promptly made up the loss with boiler rivets and the gun was heavily loaded and primed, ready for action.... I lighted a cigar, and holding the smoking stump in sight of the Indians, told Campbell to tell them to get off the boat or I would blow them all to the devil. At the same time I started for the gun with the lighted cigar in my

hand.... The Indians turned and fled and fairly fell over each other in their panic to get off the boat.[5]

Although rarely seen in photos, cannon still were frequently onboard Missouri River steamboats throughout the 1860s and 1870s—and with good reason, since exchanges of gunfire between Indians and crews were not uncommon. In fact, one riverboat pilot complained he'd caught a cold after Sioux had shot out the windows of the pilothouse and rain had soaked him.[6]

Artist William J. Hays traveled down the Missouri in July 1860 onboard the steamer *Key West* and later wrote to his mother:

> As we had no soldiers on board coming down the river we thought the Sioux would take advantage of it to attack us, so we prepared for war. Three cannons were kept loaded with grape for more than a week, while every man on board kept his fire-arms loaded and ready for use at a moments notice.[7]

In 1865 the stern-wheel steamer *Bertrand* carrying groceries, mining supplies, and other goods sank just a few miles above where the Missouri River passes between Omaha and Council Bluffs. It's thought that it mounted a compact twelve-pound mountain howitzer for defense, although the piece presumably was off-loaded at the time of the sinking or soon afterward. Relics from the wreck site, some of which are exhibited at the DeSoto National Wildlife Refuge, include such items as artillery shells and primers, Maynard metallic cartridges and primer rolls, shot, bars of lead, percussion caps, molds, gunpowder kegs, and powder flasks.[8]

Those adventurers who chose to travel the frontier by land rather than by water used artillery about as often as their waterborne brethren. In one instance, an overland Texan expedition to New Mexico in 1841 was probably saved from Indian attack by its artillery piece:

> The fact that the Indians did not make an attack upon us, or attempt to steal our horses, was probably owing to the circumstance that they had seen our six-pounder. It is well known that the Camanches [*sic*] and other prairie tribes have the greatest dread of cannon, and can never be induced to approach within a mile of them. The story is told that a large party of Camanches [*sic*] attacked, many years since, one of the early Missouri expeditions journeying with a small cannon, loaded with grapeshot and rifle-bullets.
>
> So greatly did the savages outnumber the traders, that they felt confident of an easy and sudden victory, and impressed with this belief attacked them in a solid body, and with their usual yells. The traders calmly waited until they had approached within a few yards, when they let fly among them the unexpected shower of missiles. The gun was well directed, and sent a large number of the Indians tumbling to the ground. Those who escaped were so panic-stricken at the strange discharge, which carried such fearful destruction to their ranks, that they instantly wheeled and fled. . . . Overrating as they did the power of a cannon from the effect of this well-directed and fortunate shot, from that day to the present no p[art] of the tribe has ever dared attack openly any company fortunate enough to possess a fieldpiece. The fame of the big gun of the whites . . . has spread from the Camanches [*sic*] to the neighbouring tribes, and to such an extent has the story of its powers been magnified, that it is difficult to get any Indian within its utmost range.[9]

During the height of the California gold rush, some eager '49ers organized themselves into traveling units bound with almost military precision to rules of travel. The Sagamore and Sacramento Company of Lynn,

Massachusetts, adopted gray uniforms with silver braid and armed each member with rifle, revolver, and sheath knife. Their custom-made wagons were each drawn by four horses with silver-plated harness and a swivel gun protruded from the rear of each vehicle.[10]

From the 1840s to the 1860s, the standard field pieces in service with the frontier army were muzzleloaders, with smoothbore barrels or "tubes" of bronze. The six-pounder Model 1841 field gun, with a barrel alone weighing about nine hundred pounds, and the twelve-pounder Model 1841 field howitzer, with a tube weight of about eight hundred pounds, both used the same carriage. Smaller, lighter, and much more easily transported was the little twelve-pounder mountain howitzer. All these guns could fire three types of ammunition—solid shot, spherical case (a bursting hollow iron shell filled with lead balls), or canister (a tin cylinder filled with half-inch iron shot). In the six-pounder gun, the ranges of the three types of projectiles were about fifteen hundred, twelve hundred, and three hundred yards, respectively.

The little Model 1841 mountain howitzer was probably the most widely used artillery piece in the west. Its 220-pound, three-foot-long barrel weighed no more than a good size man and the gun could be pulled by one or two animals, depending upon the type of carriage used. It could also be disassembled and the tube carried on the back of a mule or horse while a second animal carried the compact carriage and a third the ammunition. Thus the gun could travel almost anywhere a horse or mule could go. Although able to shoot a standard twelve-pound solid shot, it often fired an explosive shell weighing about three pounds less or a canister round loaded with about 148 .69 caliber round balls. Elevated to five degrees and firing a shell, it had a range of about one thousand yards.[11]

Of French design, it first appeared in 1836 and was modified in 1840. Eventually about 430 mountain howitzer tubes would be produced. It was ideally suited for use in the west where roads were few and portability was critical and there was no threat from any counter-battery fire from an enemy's artillery. It proved to be a valuable weapon in Indian warfare where antipersonnel charges often broke up enemy concentrations.

In 1843–44 the diminutive western explorer John Charles Fremont—one detractor said he stood only about five foot, two inches tall—undertook his second expedition, to Oregon and California. "They have 12 two-mule carts, one light covered spring wagon for instruments and the daguerreotype apparatus, and a brass 12-pounder howitzer, managed by four of the men." Perhaps it was one of the light mountain howitzers, but whatever it was, the gun

The twelve-pound mountain howitzer could be pulled by one animal (above) or disassembled and packed on three.

had its own rather colorful tale. When Fremont requisitioned the piece Col. J. J. Abert of the Army Corps of Engineers directed Fremont to come to Washington to explain why a cannon was being taken along on a supposedly peaceful scientific mission. Fremont's wife intercepted the order in St. Louis after Fremont had set out for Westport. Fearing the delay this order implied, she sent it forward by steamboat but also sent another message to her husband by fast courier urging him to get underway quickly, thus insuring the cannon remained with the expedition.[12]

Topographer Charles Preuss, a frequent complainer, recalled the Fremont howitzer with some misgivings. "At a bad place the gun carriage of the howitzer broke, and it took time to repair it. If we had only left that ridiculous thing at home. . . . To travel with a powder magazine in one's wagon is no pleasure, especially when one has to light a pipe constantly." Eventually in January 1844 the freezing men abandoned the howitzer in the rugged California mountains.

Fremont's account of the party's reaction to the abandonment of the cannon conflicted with Preuss's. In his diary entry for January 29 of 1844, the leader wrote of the howitzer, "We left it, to the great sorrow of the whole party, who

were grieved to part with a companion which had made the whole distance from St. Louis, and had commanded respect for us on some critical occasions, and which might be needed for the same purpose again." It is said to have been recovered in 1861 by a man who ultimately sold it to some Virginia City, Nevada, residents where it was fired during Fourth of July and other celebrations. (For years it reposed in a corner of a dance hall in the city's National Guard Hall and eventually was set on a concrete base in front of a hotel in Glenbrook, Nevada.)[13]

The mountain howitzer won a loyal following during the Mexican War of 1846–48. During the siege of Mexico City, Lt. U. S. Grant won praise from Gen. Worth for his use of a mountain howitzer. Discovering a church which afforded an excellent vantage point, Grant with a voltigeur officer and men to work the gun disassembled it and carried it across several ditches chest deep in water and up to the belfry from which they shelled the enemy three hundred yards away with "marked effect."[14]

The guns traveled to the Rocky Mountains even earlier. In 1845 Col. Stephen Watts Kearny led five companies of the lst Dragoons, some three hundred men, on a journey from Fort Leavenworth to South Pass in the Rockies and back. Each man was armed with a carbine (probably a Hall), a saber, and a pistol and the outfit had two mountain howitzers which followed in the rear of the column. Many of the Indians encountered had not seen soldiers before. "Those who saw them were much struck with their uniform appearance—their fine horses—their arms and big guns [howitzers]." After the march had ended, Kearny noted that they had had but one serious accident, "which was that of a carbine being accidentally discharged by private Smith, of company G, when the ball shattered his right arm so much as to render amputation necessary." In December 1853 a squadron of the lst Dragoons under the command of Lt. Samuel D. Sturgis and Brevet Maj. James Henry Carlton left Albuquerque for an excursion to the ruins around Gran Quivira, New Mexico, trailing a twelve-pound mountain howitzer.[15]

Col. Joseph Mansfield's report on his inspection trip to the west in 1853–54 noted that within the Department of the Pacific there were sixteen six-pound brass field guns, twelve twelve-pound brass howitzers, six twelve-pound brass mountain howitzers, forty-seven sea coast guns, and three mortars. Totals for the Department of New Mexico showed one twelve-pound brass field howitzer, twenty twelve-pound brass mountain howitzers, two twenty-four-pound field howitzers, five six-pound brass field guns, three brass mountain howitzers, and one "Rifle Wall Piece."[16]

As Union and Confederate forces battled in the east, regular army units were pulled from stations west of the Mississippi even as hostilities between whites and Native Americans persisted. The task of quelling these hostilities fell largely to volunteer troops. In January of 1863, Col. Patrick E. Conner's California volunteer cavalrymen and Capt. Samuel W. Hoyt's infantrymen from Utah rendezvoused to strike a Shoshone village of seventy-five lodges along Battle Creek in Idaho. Many of the soldiers were incapacitated by frozen feet, but the force destroyed the village, killing an estimated 255 Indians, about 180 of whom were warriors. The two mountain howitzers that accompanied the infantrymen had to be abandoned in a snowbank prior to the engagement.[17]

Similar guns proved more useful in 1864, when Gen. Alfred Sully led a mounted force of more than two thousand volunteers from Sioux City, Iowa, up the Missouri River into Dakota Territory in an attempt to punish the Sioux. Fifteen steamboats supported him logistically while mountain howitzers made up his artillery contingent. The campaign was hard on men and horses, but these guns proved effective on various occasions. During a fight on July 28 they repeatedly dispersed groups of Indians.

The splendid discipline of the soldiers and destructive cannonading, would soon have decided the battle if the Indians had been concentrated or massed as the soldiers [were], but this was not their way of fighting; and while they had a solid body to shoot at they presented a very irregular line for a return fire.[18]

One of the most dramatic incidents involving the mountain howitzer occurred later the same year, when Kit Carson led a force of about four hundred New Mexico and California volunteers with two of the guns from New Mexico into the Texas panhandle. On the Canadian River near an abandoned trading post called Adobe Walls, the volunteers collided with more than a thousand Kiowa and Comanche warriors. In a desperate four-hour fight, only the artillery saved Carson's force from disaster. He later reported that had it not been for these howitzers, no white man would have left the valley of the Canadian alive.

Capt. Eugene Ware ran into a serious problem involving his mountain howitzer early in 1865, while he was escorting a stagecoach west toward Julesburg. Seeing smoke and Indians in the distance, he called a halt, and

inspected the artillery fully to see that everything was all ready for use; imagine my horror to find that the priming-wire had jolted out of its fastening and been lost. The priming-wire was an absolute necessity, because the cartridges were in thick flannel bags, and when rammed down they had to be opened, so that the friction primer would throw the fire down into the powder. This priming wire had to be pushed down through the vent into the flannel [piercing it] or the charge could not be exploded. A feeling of great horror ran over me as I vainly searched in the chest of the howitzer. Near us ran the telegraph line. I told one of the boys to climb up a pole, swing out on that wire hand over hand, and pull it down to the ground. With the aid and assistance of several, we finally got the wire swung down nearly to the ground, but not near enough. Thereupon, with an artillery hatchet, we chopped down a telegraph pole so as to give the wire more sag. We then cut the wire, and tying one end of it

Battery of twelve-pound mountain howitzers mounted on prairie carriages that accompanied Gen. Alfred Sully's expedition against the Sioux. At the July 28, 1864, battle of Killdeer Mountain in western North Dakota the army destroyed a large quantity of Indian stores. (Courtesy: State Historical Society of North Dakota)

to the rear of the coach we had the four horses pull on it until we got all the slack that could come from that direction. Then we pulled the other line and got all the slack that could come from the other, and we managed to get off two feet of wire and then put the wire together, and make a new connection. This took us nearly half an hour, but we got a priming-wire made out of this telegraph wire which was all right. We pounded it to a point on the iron tire of the howitzer, and were then ready to go ahead.[19]

During the same year, James Sawyers and Lewis H. Smith led a road-building train and a convoy of freight wagons from the Missouri River to Virginia City, Montana Territory. They had an army escort made up of two companies of the 5th US Volunteer Infantry—"galvanized Yankees" (Confederate prisoners of war who volunteered to serve in the west against the Indians)—and twenty-five men from the lst Dakota Cavalry. The escort had two twelve-pound mountain howitzers to counter any Indian resistance. Later the escort was reduced in size

with only a single mountain howitzer. On several occasions, "the gun which shoots twice" was put to effective use with exploding shells to disperse Indians with a burst or two over their heads.[20]

While army artillery on the frontier defended posts or fought in the field, it also had a ceremonial purpose—on one occasion with unexpected results. Two companies of the 2nd US Volunteers (more "galvanized Yankees"), were at Fort Zarah, Kansas, on the Santa Fe Trail when news of Lee's surrender reached the desolate post in April 1865. William Darnell was driving one of a convoy of six-mule government freight wagons approaching the outpost as the celebration began.

Dragging out their small brass cannons, they loaded them with a good charge of powder and crammed them to the muzzle with wet gunny sacks. As soon as the lead wagon of our train came within shouting distance ... the gunners pointed their cannons up into the air and fired. The firing alone possibly would not have frightened our mules, but when those gunny sacks hurtled up into the air, were caught by the

wind and opened up and then floating off, they were enough to startle the
dead.... The lead-wagon team ducked away
at a right angle and went stampeding across
the prairie.... The next shots following in
quick succession caused the next team to
follow suit. And no sooner had it left the
beaten track than the next and the next,
down the line.[21]

But by the mid-1860s, rifled artillery pieces with increased
range and accuracy were gaining prominence.

The close of the Civil War and the five years thereafter
brought about two notable changes in frontier artillery: a
wider issue of rifled pieces and the arrival of the Gatling
gun. But as advanced as they were, neither of these arms
completely displaced the older weapons. Bronze smoothbores remained much in evidence, especially the highly
regarded mountain howitzer. Joining the mountain gun
after the war was another bronze smoothbore, the twelve-
pounder Model 1857 gun-howitzer better known as the
"Napoleon." For frontier service it was on the heavy side,
having a six-foot tube weighing just over twelve hundred
pounds, but under certain circumstances it could be just
the right tool.

The most favored of the rifled pieces, officially
adopted in 1861, was commonly labeled the "Three-Inch
Ordnance Rifle." Built of tough wrought iron, its smoothly
contoured, six-foot tube weighed just over eight hundred
pounds, making it as easy to handle in the field as the
bronze six-pounder of 1841. (Because of its streamlined
appearance it was sometimes—and incorrectly—called
the "three-inch Rodman" or other similar name.) Another
iron piece, slightly longer and heavier than the Ordnance
model, was the three-inch Parrott rifle, a gun characterized by the reinforcing band around its breech. The tube
itself was cast iron, while the band was wrought. Under
the stress of lengthy combat the Ordnance rifle proved the
more durable of the two, but the Parrott was nonetheless
widely distributed and fairly well liked.

Capt. Eugene Ware left this description of a column
assembled near Julesburg in January of 1865:

the command...consisted of 640 cavalrymen. This was in addition to about 100
mule-wagons lightly loaded with rations,
corn, tents, and supplies. There was also a
herd of about fifty extra horses that were
fastened together close at the bit, and
driven by fours. There were also four

twelve-pound mountain howitzers, and two
light three-inch Parrott guns.

Later the same year, a section of three-inch Ordnance rifles
accompanied Col. Nelson Cole's column when it marched
against the Sioux in Montana and the Dakotas.[22]

Still, the popularity of the mountain howitzer continued unabated. Along the Bozeman Trail in 1866, as Indian
resistance to white presence intensified, Capt. Nathaniel
Kinney with sixty mounted men and one mountain howitzer rode out from Fort Phil Kearny to escort several trains
under threat of attack.

The famed Hayfield Fight in August of 1867 involved
the stubborn defense by a haying party attacked and
besieged by a superior force of Native Americans. Relief
came in the form of two companies and a howitzer.

Major Burrowes put a couple of Case
[exploding] shots into their mounted parties and scattered them. He thinks that but
for the howitzer he would have had all the
fighting he wanted before he got back, and
that the Indians had about 800 warriors
within reach when he got to the stockade.[23]

A similar defense took place the next day at the equally
well-known Wagon Box Fight not many miles distant from
the Hayfield site. Maj. Benjamin Smith led the relief force
and in his report noted: "I also took a Mountain Howitzer
and ten ox wagons, the citizen teamsters being armed."[24]

The following year, frontier scouts under Brevet Col.
George A. Forsyth withstood repeated Indian attacks at the
Battle of Beecher's Island on the Delaware Fork of the
Republican River in eastern Colorado. On September 17,
Forsyth sent out two messengers seeking relief from Fort
Wallace but two more the following night failed to get
through Indian lines. His message noted:

I am on a little island & have still plenty of
ammunition left. We are living on mule &
horse meat.... You had better start with not
less than 75 men & bring all the wagons &
ambulances you can spare. Bring a 6 pdr.
Howitzer with you. I can hold out here for
6 days longer if absolutely necessary but
please loose [sic] no time.[25]

Although sometimes effective, the practicality of taking artillery into the field was sometimes questioned. As a
teamster for the army, Billy Dixon recalled:

The compact mountain howitzer also served during the Modoc War of 1872–73 in northern California.
(Courtesy: National Archives, Signal Corps photo #111-SC-82562)

At Fort Harker [Kansas] was a lot of artillery that had been assembled there in 1867 by General Hancock for an Indian campaign. He found that dragging cannon here and there over the Plains in pursuit of hostile Indians was about as feasible as hitting a hummingbird with a brickbat. The Indians moved like the wind or shadows, and were too wary to come within range of artillery.[26]

During a period of Indian unrest in 1867, a traveler crossing the plains by stagecoach found an unusual defensive measure taken at one way station in Utah—a measure based on Native American wariness of artillery. "The old station-keeper had the hind carriage of a stage-wagon mounted with a section of large stovepipe, a caisson improvised out of a wheelbarrow, and the letters 'U.S.' painted on them in the largest possible style."[27]

Despite periodic complaints about the uselessness of artillery in Indian warfare, even such highly specialized pieces as mortars occasionally found a place there, their purpose to lob shells in a high arc. In April of 1873 a force

of roughly one thousand soldiers, civilians, and Indian scouts was fighting a band of fifty or so Modoc warriors strongly entrenched in the maze of caves and ravines in the lava beds near the California-Oregon border, described by some as "hell with the fires burnt out." To help drive them from their stronghold, the army brought in two mountain howitzers and four little twenty-four-pounder Coehorn mortars, named for the Dutch seventeenth-century inventor Baron van Menno Coehoorn. These probably were bronze Model 1841s with a tube only about sixteen inches long weighing about 160 pounds. The wooden base added another 130 or so pounds but four men grasping the handles on the bed could easily wrestle one into position. The Modocs endured their fire and the embarrassing war continued for another six weeks until a lack of food, water, and ammunition forced their surrender.

Depending upon the terrain encountered, artillery in the field could be difficult to haul, as during Nelson Miles's Montana campaign in 1876–77.

The country the fore part of the day was very hilly & full of steep ravines, which gave us lots of trouble to take out 12 lb.

Smoke from artillery or small arms firing black powder ammunition could quickly obscure the scene.

Rodman Gun [actually a Napoleon] along, which was drawn by 8 horses. Some times horses were unhitched and a whole co[mpany] would be pulling on a drag rope to get her up where the horses could get footing again.[28]

But when the Sioux gathered for attack, the gun proved its worth:

[We] opened fire upon a party on our right—toward Powder River—with spherical-case shell from our 12-pounder Napoleon gun, which spread consternation among them, and they were driven all along from the ravines and fled to the bluffs, as the shells went on their exploring expeditions, bearing more to the left each successive shot, until the whole ground in the bend between Powder River and Wolf Rapids on our left was commanded by our artillery.[29]

The presence of the famed rapid-fire Gatling gun in the post–Civil War west is well documented. Dr. Richard J. Gatling's first gun, patented in 1862, employed preloaded chambers, initially loaded with percussion-primed paper cartridges but later .58 metallic cartridges. The gun had its failings including a tendency to jam, but an extensive redesign, patented in 1865, proved to be a significant improvement. The Model 1865 was chambered for metallic cartridges in .50, .58, and 1.00-inch calibers, with either six or ten barrels. The army's initial order in August of 1866 was for fifty each of the .50–70 ten-barrel and six-barrel 1.00 caliber guns. Now the chamber was an integral part of each barrel, eliminating the problem of gas sealing, among others.[30]

Glowing comments following army tests were typical and by the mid-1870s, Dr. Gatling's gun was gaining a worldwide reputation for performance. The succeeding years brought various improvements in the feeding, traversing, and other systems. The last operational Gatling of the early era was the Model 1903, chambered for the .30–03 cartridge and three years later for the well-known .30–06 round.[31]

After the US Army's order for Gatling guns in 1866, it procured dozens more, sending a substantial number of them to posts on the frontier. By 1876, more than fifty of the crank operated weapons were in the west in all three calibers, with nineteen assigned to the Department of Texas alone. Fort Sully in Dakota Territory in 1867 had two .50 caliber Model 1865s on hand, which required frequent cleaning and storage under shelter. Two were still listed in post returns for 1891, although perhaps of an improved

A Gatling gun detachment of Company C, lst Nevada National Guard regiment. The soldier standing in front of the mounted sergeant holds an Accles Positive Feed doughnut-like magazine, introduced with the Model 1883 Gatling as an improvement over the gravity-fed cartridge loading system.

model. Personnel there in 1887 inventoried the contents of the 12 x 18 foot brick magazine building and found 25,001 Gatling gun cartridges plus 600 artillery shells, 38,000 rounds for rifles and carbines, and 4,400 .45 Colt cartridges. Gatling gun sizes ranged from the big six-barreled 1.00 caliber variant of 1866 to a little five-barreled "Bulldog" of 1877, which during one test fired an astonishing one thousand rounds in one minute, nineteen seconds.[32]

Immediately following the Civil War years, the army did not fully appreciate the Gatling's potential usefulness as an infantry weapon, but most often employed it as a piece of artillery to defend a fixed position such as a bridge or military installation on the frontier. Even though the army purchased nearly five hundred Gatling guns during the Indian war period, few were fired in anger. Ironically, the first use of a Gatling in the west appears to have been in a successful attempt by a 7th Cavalry escort to turn a stampeding herd of bison which was threatening a wagon train.[33]

In 1867 a new lieutenant of the 7th Cavalry was in charge of two Gatling guns which accompanied the escort for the Indian commissioners meeting with southern plains Indians at Medicine Lodge, Kansas. When he asked to allow his inexperienced gunners to practice with these guns, he was told he'd have to pay for the ammunition so the crews never did fire them. Custer in '67 left Fort Riley, Kansas, on a lengthy scout, leaving his wife Libbie in camp on a

little knoll. Rapidly rising flood waters threatened to sweep her tent away.

> As a last resort, a Gatling gun which stood near the entrance to the tent, and which from its great weight would probably withstand the force of the current, was hauled closer to the tent and ropes securely attached to the wheels; by these ropes it was proposed to fasten the ladies and the servant to the gun, and in this way, should the streams not rise too high above the knoll, their lives might be saved.[34]

In 1874 Gatling guns had a baptism of fire against Native Americans. On August 30 on the "staked plains" of west Texas, Lt. John Pope of the 5th Infantry used two Gatling guns to break up an ambush set for Col. Nelson Miles's force. Another column under Miles, this one led by Maj. William Price of the 8th Cavalry, also employed Gatling guns. One of Price's officers later wrote that on one occasion Price's force "was attacked by six hundred or seven hundred Indians, and he used his Gatlings with such excellent effect as to quite demoralize and drive off his savage assailants." In April of 1875, Lt. Richard Pratt of the 10th Cavalry was in charge of Cheyenne prisoners who had been selected for relocation from Fort Sill, Indian Territory (Oklahoma) to Florida. When they attempted to escape, they came under fire from a Gatling gun.[35]

To the north in 1874, the army authorized a reconnaissance led by Lt. Col. George A. Custer into the Black Hills, in part to investigate the rumors of gold discoveries. The Bismarck *Tribune* newspaper for June 24, 1874, described the organization of the expedition and mentioned the presence of a battery of three Gatling guns and one Rodman cannon commanded by 1st Lt. Josiah Chance. (The Three-Inch Ordnance Rifle, or so-called Rodman, was seldom used against the Indians.)

> The Gatling guns will fire 350 shots a minute, and are good for 900 yards. The ball used by the Gatling gun, is a trifle larger than the old Minnie rifle ball; the metallic cartridge is used. The cartridges are placed in a hopper and as a crank is turned, a rod is plunged into the end of the cartridge causing the explosion. The guns are ten barreled, consequently at each revolution ten shots are fired. Should [Lt.] Chance open on the red devils with one of these guns they would think the infernal regions had broken loose on them. Then imagine the effect should the Gatling guns with their rain of leaden hail, be supplemented by the unearthly shriek of a three-inch Rodman.[36]

On one occasion during the expedition, a band of antelope passed within a few yards of the column and despite orders, some men fired at them. One of the drivers with the Gatling gun battery "saluted the herd with his six-shooter" and his frightened four-horse team ran away, dragging the gun behind. Fortunately the team became bogged down in mud before the gun was damaged, but the driver was required to walk for the remainder of the day.[37]

Following the confirmation of gold by Custer's 1874 reconnaissance, white gold seekers made frequent attempts to circumvent the army's modest efforts to keep them out in recognition of Sioux Indian rights to the Black Hills. The 1st Infantry and 2nd Cavalry in the spring of 1875 were engaged in this task and encountered one of the largest groups of gold seekers, the Evans and Gordon party, and destroyed much of the miners' provisions and equipment. Sgt. John Cox of the 1st Infantry described the scene and mentioned that "from the ridge, frowned a gatling battery, ready to begin grinding out

death and destruction!" A year later, Cox participated in the disarming of the Sioux at Standing Rock Agency soon after Custer's defeat. As troops moved into position, "I caught a glimpse . . . of gatling batteries hurrying across the prairie in clouds of dust."[38]

Custer on his ill-fated final operation against hostile Indians in 1876 rejected the opportunity to include a battery of Gatling guns with his column, claiming they would only slow him down. Perhaps Custer's decision was influenced by his ego and his eagerness to make contact with the enemy first and clear his tarnished reputation. But the guns did weigh roughly one thousand pounds and the terrain ahead was rough. Also, the commander of the Gatling battery, Lt. William H. Low, had had difficulty in keeping up with the column. Whether the presence of any Gatlings would have affected the outcome of the battle on the Little Bighorn is merely a catalyst for discussion.[39]

Years later, Custer's personal orderly recalled,

> the Gatling guns was heavy to haul. The mules was already tuckered out completely from the scouting expedition under Reno. If Custer had taken the guns he'd had to march slow which ain't proper when you're plannin' a surprise attack on the hostiles. O' course, if he'd had them guns up on the hill he could've mowed down the Indians like hail mows down saplings but the idee is he could never've got 'em up thar.[40]

In July 1877 a Gatling gun was added to Col. Nelson Miles's force during his pursuit of the Nez Perce under Chief Joseph, but its role was not decisive. It did catch the attention of Pvt. William Zimmer of the 2nd Cavalry. "The steamer *Savannah* brought us some mail & a Gatling gun with men and horses. This is a new gun to me. It's a breech loader & a revolver. (There's a crank to it like an organ, but I think it will make rather louder music.)" This campaign also apparently saw the initial use of the new rifled breech loading Hotchkiss in Indian warfare. "The boys have been practicing with the little cannon. It's a nice little piece of furniture. It only weighs 400 lbs., & 4 horses which are used on it ought to be able to drag it anywhere."[41]

A year later, three .45–70 Gatling guns with the 1st Cavalry were deployed against the Bannocks and Paiute Indians. In this instance, their fire on the Indians' flank forced the Native Americans to retreat. Present was Lt. James H. Parker, who would become the army's foremost Gatling gun tactician and gained recognition directing their use during the Spanish-American War.[42]

Gatling gun mounted on an armored field carriage, present during a labor strike at Cripple Creek, Colorado (1903). (Courtesy: Denver Public Library, Western History Department, CO)

In 1875 the government chartered the light draft steamer *Josephine* to travel to the farthest navigable point on the Yellowstone River. Gen. James W. Forsyth of Gen. Sheridan's staff commanded the exploratory expedition with a company of the 6th Infantry as escort. A one-inch Gatling gun was dragged on board.

> This was a beautiful arm and when placed
> in position on the boiler deck of the boat,
> was enough to strike terror to the hearts of
> any Indians we might run against, as being
> "bad medicine" for them.... A crew was
> detailed to work the Gatling gun. A tree a
> mile away on the prairie served as a target,
> and it was struck repeatedly.[43]

The town of Lincoln in New Mexico Territory in July 1878 was the scene of a five-day battle between rival economic and political factions. The affair gained historic prominence because of the involvement of a buck-toothed youth born as Henry McCarty, then known as Kid Antrim, later by his alias of William Bonney, and during the last few months of his short life as Billy the Kid. The commandant at nearby Fort Stanton, the heavy

drinking Lt. Col. N. A. M. Dudley of the 9th Cavalry, arrived with about forty soldiers. He later reported he had taken with him "the Gatling Gun with 2000 rounds of ammunition, also the Howitzer with ample supply of ammunition." Dudley ostensibly was there to protect the town's women and children but he was strongly sympathetic to the Murphy-Dolan faction and refused to interfere when the McSween house was set ablaze. Neither of the two guns was fired.[44]

The presence of army regulars and a Gatling gun played a surprising role in the murder trial of Nebraska rancher Ira P. Olive. In the winter of 1878–79, hostility between cattlemen and legitimate homesteaders reached a flash point. Olive managed to win the election as sheriff and compelled some homesteaders to leave the country after he falsified charges against them. Two resisted when Olive and deputies tried to serve warrants on them and in a gunfight, the sheriff's brother was wounded. In retaliation, Olive and a posse arrested the homesteaders, took them to an isolated area, and murdered them, then burned the bodies.

Olive was brought to trial and the judge noticed that "the courthouse was rapidly being overrun by desperadoes and tough-looking cowboys, all packing six-shooters." It was understood "from grapevine sources" that if

Gunners of Battery E, 1st US Artillery, in South Dakota with a l.65-inch Hotchkiss gun (1891).
(Courtesy: Library of Congress)

there was a chance of Olive's conviction, they would shoot up the courtroom. Conviction was virtually assured by the agreement of one of Olive's gang to turn state's evidence and the judge requested military intervention to maintain order. On the morning of the scheduled unveiling of the surprise prosecution witness, the prosecutor delayed the proceeding by speaking for more than two hours before "we heard Uncle Sam's bugle blowing down the street. I think it was the sweetest music I ever listened to."

> On came the ninety-two regulars [9th Infantry] and deployed upon a vacant block diagonally across from the courthouse, ammunition was passed out and the gatling-gun squad stood ready for action.... I never saw so surprised and so quiet a crowd of men... as those cowboys were.... Trouble was all over.

Olive and one of his companions were found guilty and sentenced to life imprisonment. However, their convictions were overturned on a technicality by the Nebraska Supreme Court and they were freed.[45]

Trumpeter A. F. Mulford of the 7th Cavalry in 1877 observed one of the most unusual civilian applications of artillery.

> Considerable excitement was created... by the first appearance of one of the new Black Hills stages, or gunboats as we call them. They consist of a very heavy and large stage with a 2-pound [sic] Mountain Howitzer mounted on top. They also have twelve Winchester repeating rifles inside, with plenty of ammunition in little pockets near the windows, or rather port-holes. These stages run from Bismarck to the Black Hills, and despite all their arms and caution, are very frequently held up, by white as well as red devils, who rob the passengers and take valuables generally.[46]

An 1876 army report listed the various serviceable artillery pieces found at installations throughout the west between the Mississippi River and Rocky Mountains. Exclusive of those at Baton Rouge, Louisiana, the totals showed thirty-four three-inch rifles, forty-five twelve-pound bronze guns, seventy-eight twelve-pound mountain howitzers, and twenty-six iron or bronze six-pounders. Gatling guns listed were nineteen one-inch guns, thirty-four in .50 caliber, and one of the new .45s at Fort Concho, Texas.[47]

In 1876 the army purchased its first Hotchkiss 1.65-inch breechloader, a planned replacement for the muzzle loading twelve-pound mountain howitzer. Over the next twenty years, the army procured about fifty-six of the new mountain guns. It could be pulled or disassembled and packed on two mules or horses to accompany fast moving cavalry or a force campaigning in rough terrain.

Additional pack animals could carry seventy-two rounds of ammunition each. The gun's rifled barrel weighed 117 pounds, the carriage 220 pounds, and it could fire a shell two miles. Artillerists tested it in Dakota Territory in 1877 and an 1881 army artillery board called it "an excellent gun for mountain and Indian service." Its disadvantage was it was too small to employ a time fused shrapnel shell for effective air-bursts over an enemy. Four Hotchkiss guns of the lst Artillery participated in the last major encounter between whites and Native Americans, the unfortunate engagement of December 29, 1890, on Wounded Knee Creek in South Dakota.[48]

CHAPTER SEVENTEEN

Guns of the Native Americans

The marksmanship ability of Indians is woefully exaggerated.
A white man who can shoot at all is more than
a match for them as a class.
— Capt. O. F. Michaelis, 1879[1]

The sale of firearms to Indians east of the Mississippi was well established by French, Dutch, and English traders by the late seventeenth century. Complete pre-1700 examples of flintlock trade muskets are extremely rare, but based on archeological finds from Iroquois sites in the northeast, they are thought to have been light in weight with a slender barrel about fifty inches long with a round or octagonal breech and of .50 to .60 caliber. Indians generally preferred such light guns and in the 1690s, the English governor of New Netherlands rejected heavy English muskets as gifts for the Iroquois, preferring long, light Belgian guns from Liege. Ramsey Crooks of the American Fur Company in 1840 echoed the same sentiment when he wrote that "hunting Indians did not care to carry and use heavy guns."[2]

West of the Mississippi, guns were traded to the south and west by the French and English, sometimes through Indian intermediaries. French influence from Louisiana intermingled in Texas with that of Spain early in the eighteenth century both among Indians and Spanish colonials. The latter generally believed that French guns and other manufactured goods were superior to those made in Spain,

prompting a substantial commerce. In east Texas, for example, the Caddo and Wichita Indians eagerly traded horses and hides for French guns and other goods. These same tribes, along with the Tonkawas, found guns not only gave them a psychological advantage over their tribal enemies who lacked them, but were useful in hunting deer, which they did on foot.[3]

However the French trading of firearms to various Indian tribes on the plains caused concern among Spanish officials and colonists alike, as the Comanches and their allies grew in power. As an example of the French impact, the Comanche Indians in 1759 with French guns and assistance attacked an Apache mission west of San Antonio and easily repulsed Spanish troops which sought to retaliate. Eight years earlier Governor don Tomás Vélez Cachupín of New Mexico had warned:

> The greatest fear of the moment and for
> the future that one can conclude concern-
> ing the Comanche tribe is from their sup-
> ply and use of guns which they are
> acquiring, and which they are instructing

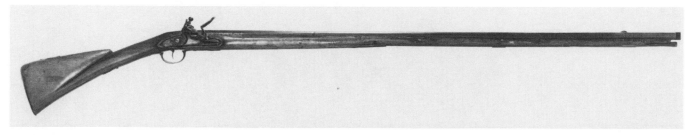

Mid-eighteenth-century French smoothbore trade gun of about .55 caliber with a 48-inch barrel. It's representative of the French trade guns available to Indians throughout much of that century. (Courtesy: Museum of the Fur Trade, Chadron, NE)

themselves with the handling thereof. With these weapons they will be greatly feared in this province.

As a compromise and recognizing the Indians' preference for firearms, Viceroy Gálvez at one point recommended that they be given inferior but gaudily decorated guns to decrease their effectiveness and at the same time come to rely more on the Spanish for powder, lead, and repair.[4]

However it was general Spanish policy to keep firearms out of Indian hands. The Shoshonis complained to Lewis and Clark in 1805 that the Spanish refused to let them have guns or ammunition on the grounds that they would kill each other. Indian agent Dr. John Sibley held a grand council at Natchitoches, Louisiana, in 1807 and presented Comanche and Tawakoni leaders from Texas with guns, saddles, and medals. If American traders would come to their villages on the Red River, they said, they could obtain horses, mules, and buffalo robes, but in exchange the Indians wanted guns, powder, and lead with which to fight the Osages.[5]

Between 1796 and 1822, the US government traded with Native Americans through a chain of "factories" or trading posts where guns, blankets, kettles, and many other items were sold at prices slightly above cost. In addition, American ships appeared off the northwest coast of North America in the 1790s and early 1800s. The firearms trade between the captains of these vessels and Indians of the region was a source of great concern to whites occupying Russian America. Sometimes these guns were turned on the Russians as in 1802 when the fort at Sitka in present-day Alaska was attacked by Tlingit Indians armed with British and American guns. More than four hundred Russian and Aleut inhabitants were killed and the fort was burned. When Governor A. Baranov complained to Americans, they laughed at him and "before our eyes [Americans] shamelessly trade powder, lead, pistols and muskets." Anxious to continue the trade in sea otter and

other pelts, in 1812 John Jacob Astor of the American Fur Company and the Russian-American Company agreed that firearms would not be traded to Indians in those areas occupied by the two firms. Soon the agreement lost any validity when the British took over Astoria.[6]

THE NORTHWEST GUN

Throughout the first seventy-five years of the nineteenth century, a common Indian firearm was what became generally known as the Northwest gun.[7] By the mid-1700s the general style of these guns was established and would persist with only modest changes. It was a light smoothbore musket, practical for conditions under which Indians used it. It could fire either a single ball or shot and using a single patched ball was capable of keeping the shots in a nine-inch group at ninety yards. Guns such as these plus powder and balls were eagerly sought in trade. In November 1812 on the Upper Missouri, Manuel Lisa, attempting to encourage the Arikaree Indians to hunt bison for his fur trading party, "promised 20 Loads Powder & Ball for each Cow."[8]

The barrel of the typical Northwest gun was octagonal at the breech but round from midsection forward; the bore was generally 24 gauge or about .59 caliber, at close range suitable for most of the larger game animals. There were exceptions to this caliber for in the 1850s, Henry Leman of Lancaster, Pennsylvania, made Northwest guns for the government in .60, .65, and .70 caliber. Precast balls of 30 gauge (.537 caliber) and 28 gauge (.55 caliber) were sold at many trading posts for use in these guns with a patch or wadding. The iron trigger guard was large, not to admit a gloved finger but rather to permit use of two fingers on the trigger, a feature requested by the Hudson's Bay Company as early as 1740. Barrel length in the 1700s often was forty-eight or forty-two inches, but thirty and thirty-six inches became popular in the 1800s. Whether known as a Northwest gun, fuke, fusee, Mackinaw gun, or fusil, one distinguishing

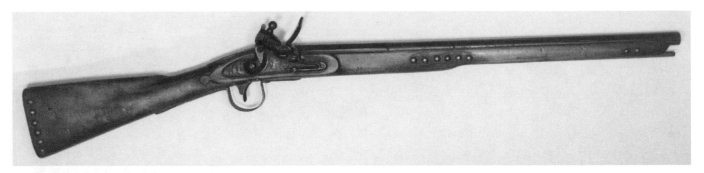

A cut down English Northwest gun by Parker, Field & Co. dated 1869. (Courtesy: Ralph Heinz and Fred Fellows)

characteristic was a brass dragon or sea serpent–like side plate inset into the left side of the stock opposite the lock.[9]

The most common Northwest guns are those of English or Belgian manufacture, but some American makers produced fusees. Henry Deringer in 1815–16 made the first documented American Northwest trade guns, 130 in response to a request from the US Office of Indian Trade for distribution through government trading posts after their supply of British trade guns was cut off by the War of 1812. In 1828 the American Fur Company ordered 580 Northwest guns with barrel lengths between thirty and forty-two inches from J. J. Henry's Boulton Gun Works near Nazareth, Pennsylvania. Fusees by Henry Leman of Lancaster were praised for their quality by an official of the American Fur Company in 1843, but Leman couldn't compete with the price of those made abroad and guns of American manufacture sometimes were rejected by Native American consumers.[10]

Jean Louis Berlandier in 1828 joined a Mexican scientific expedition into Texas as a botanist and zoologist. He spent the next several years traveling into the interior of Texas observing the flora, fauna, and the customs of the Indians he encountered there and gathering native artifacts. He later wrote of his travels and included numerous sketches made by him and under his supervision by Lino Sanchez y Tapia. Whether for convenience or because of careful observation, the guns which appear in these scenes are all long barreled pieces rather than ones shortened for ease of use on horseback. They can't be identified as Northwest guns, however he was precise in observing that among what he called the Chariticas (Arapaho Indians), they regularly acquired guns and ammunition from Anglo American traders but "to be good in their eyes, the guns must be British-made, and they reject all American ones." The warlike Comanches were well supplied with firearms but they, too, were selective:

A people they call the Aguajes, known as Pananes over toward New Mexico, bring their guns in from Canada. These weapons must be of English manufacture, and that is why the American traders sell them so few guns. But, to make up for that, they sell a good deal of ammunition.[11]

Despite frequent prejudice against American-made arms, between the mid-1840s and 1855, Edward K. Tryon of Philadelphia successfully bid on contracts with the Bureau of Indian Affairs to provide Northwest guns with 36-inch and 42-inch barrel lengths at $4.63 to $5.54 each and also delivered some to private trading companies such as Pierre Chouteau Jr. & Co. Government contracts specified that the Tryon guns be proof tested with two hundred grains of powder, two balls, and two wads. Some Tryon Northwest guns are found today with Belgian (Liege) proof marks on the barrel, which have been overstamped with stars to conceal the barrel's country of origin.[12]

Among English makers, one of the more prolific and highly regarded was Thomas Barnett of London. The remains of a Belgian-made fuke found in 1956 in a sand dune north of Rock Springs, Wyoming, bore the lock stamping "Burnett 1838." Its 42-inch barrel carried imitation Birmingham proof marks and Barnett's "TB" and star marking, presumably in an attempt to disguise its true origin. The American Fur Company directed that five hundred Northwest guns they ordered from a Belgian source in 1829 bear the Barnett name.[13]

Peter Skene Ogden in the northwest in 1824–26 was specific in a description.

[The] Indians had 4 Guns (Barnets) [sic] and although one had 1802 marked on the lock and another 1817 still they were in good order and appeared as if they were taken out of the store only a

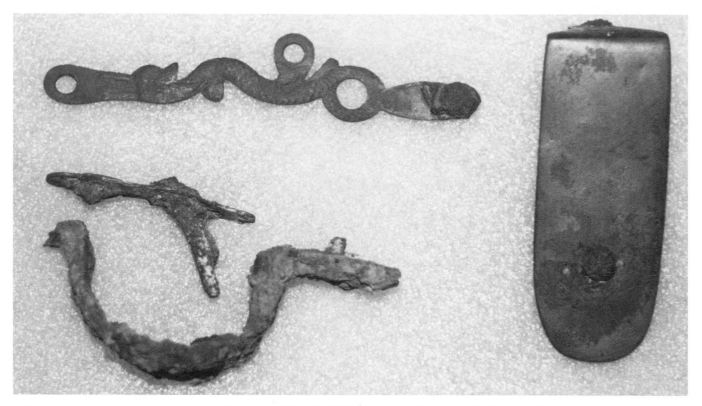

Northwest gun parts excavated at the site of Bent's Old Fort in southeastern Colorado. The brass butt plate and dragon or serpent side plate resisted corrosion far better than the iron trigger and guard.

few days since nor were they wanting in ammunition having procured it from the Americans.[14]

A letter from Sir George Simpson of the Hudson's Bay Company in 1821 indicated:

> The Trading Guns (marked Wilson) are not to be compared to those of "Barnets" [*sic*] made which the N W Coy. [North West Company] import, the Locks are badly finished, the Tumbler and Shear [sear] not properly tempered and the pan loses the Powder; the N W Locks are altogether better finished and bridled inside or the Tumbler covered.[15]

Although lacking in refinements, the Northwest guns were not cheaply made or of poor quality nor was the price determined by piling furs to the height of the gun. Indians generally were capable of recognizing the difference between a good and an inferior gun and were not reluctant to return the latter for a replacement. An agent of the American Fur Company in St. Louis complained to the New York office in 1832:

> The North West Guns are one of the articles most important in our business and our traders in general complain of those of this year.... The Stocks are a little too heavy, and not crooked enough—but the worst of it is that every stock [is] made of two pieces joined at the breech and this the Indians cannot endure.... Very often the Indians bring them back to be exchanged for better, or those who have them on credit will not pay for them.[16]

The Northwest gun was primarily intended for the Indian trade, but some trappers and other whites who wanted an inexpensive all-purpose gun procured them as well. Red River half-breeds along the Montana and Dakota border of Canada hunted bison with them and some Canadian ox-drivers on the Santa Fe Trail relied on these smoothbores as late as the 1840s. Isaac I. Stevens, superintendent of Indian affairs, in July 1854 met a party of Red River hunters on one of their twice yearly bison hunts for meat and hides, perhaps thirteen hundred men, women, and children in all. "The good conduct and hospitable kindness of these people impressed me very favorably.... The universal weapon is the short northwestern gun."[17]

American-made Northwest gun by H. E. Leman and so marked on the lockplate. It was discovered in Laguna Pueblo, New Mexico. (Photo by Steven W. Walenta, courtesy James D. Gordon)

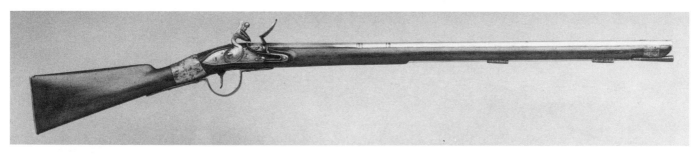

Samuel Allis's Northwest trade gun, unmarked as to maker but dated 1854 and with the Hudson's Bay Company fox in a circle stamp on the lockplate. Allis was a missionary who came to the Pawnee Indians in 1834 and lived with them near Genoa, Nebraska. (Courtesy: Nebraska State Historical Society, acc. #2460)

An English sportsman was similarly impressed by the performance of a Canadian companion during a mounted bison hunt.

> Before we would come up with him he had four buffaloes down, three cows and a calf, and yet he was using a single muzzle-loading flint-lock gun, called a trade gun, and costing in London seven and sixpence. His plan was as follows: The powder was in a bag carried on his belt and the bullets were in his mouth. He would put in half a handful of powder, and then drop in a wet ball, giving the gun a slap, to drive the ball home and the powder into the enormous pan, when he would lower the gun and fire at once, the muzzle being within a foot of the buffalo.[18]

Englishman John Long spent nearly twenty years in North America and described an accident which occurred in 1778.

> Some of the chiefs being desirous of seeing my Northwest guns, [and] I was obliged to open a case for their inspection.... Having

shewn [sic] them the guns, they loaded four, and laid them down by the cases, intending to try them; during the time they were thus employed I was busy in arranging the goods that had been displaced in getting at them; but as soon as I was at leisure, I took up one of the guns in a careless manner, not knowing it was charged, and snapped the lock, which most unfortunately shot off the ear of one of the chiefs.

Long was able to convince the angry chief that it was an accident and consoled him with presents. Long described the ear as "very large and handsome" and noted that the Indians prided themselves in having large ears.[19]

Another Long, Maj. Stephen H., led an exploring expedition to the Rockies in 1819–20. The smoothbore gun was preferred over the rifle by Indians, he noted, "the latter being too heavy for their use." He also noted among the "Omawhaws" their practice of tattooing themselves using dissolved gunpowder or pulverized charcoal.[20]

Charles Augustus Murray sailed from England in 1834 to North America where he traveled for several years, spending one summer with the Pawnee Indians. Later he made the following observation concerning their Northwest guns and the care they bestowed upon them.

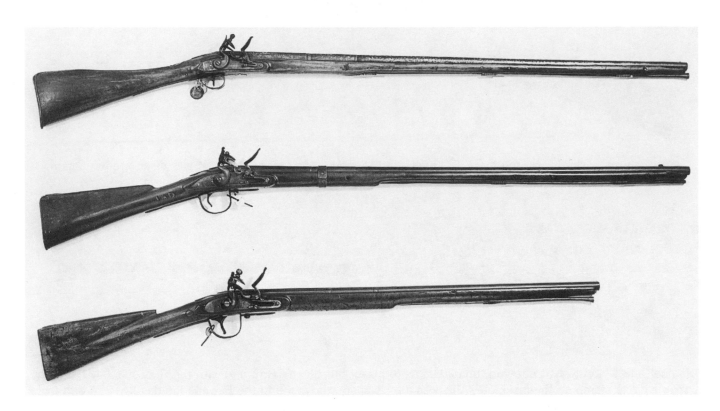

Left and right views of three smoothbore English flintlock trade guns,
from top to bottom: Chief's grade gun marked "MOXHAM" on the lock with
the British Board of Ordnance broad arrow stamp; Northwest gun by Ketland &
Allport branded on each side of the wrist "ID" with a broad arrowhead
between the letters, indicative of Canada's Indian Department;
Northwest gun by Barnett of London. The butt stock is stamped
"ID" for US Indian Department. Like the middle gun, it bears
the distinctive dragon or serpent side plate on the left.
(Photo by Steven W. Walenta, courtesy James D. Gordon)

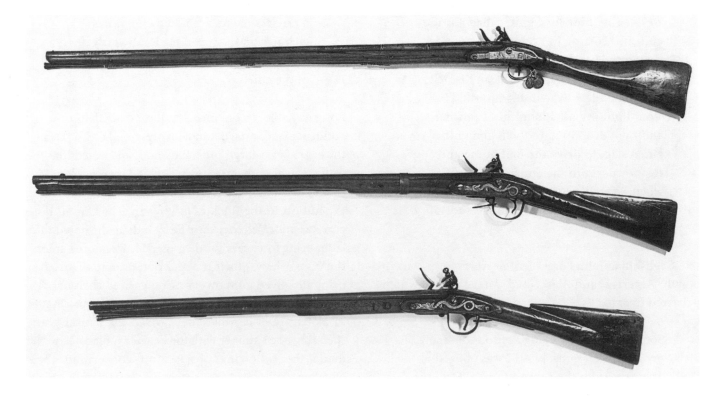

A weathered Harpers Ferry Model 1816 musket, converted to percussion and fitted with a hand-forged hammer. Crosses and stick figures decorate the stock and rawhide secures the forestock to the barrel. It was found in a cave in a bluff along the Colorado River near the Yuma Crossing, a site controlled by the Yuma Indians who cut off travel along the route to California during the Spanish colonial period. American scalp hunters, to whom the Mexican government paid Indian scalp bounties, later drove the Indians away, and the crossing was reopened for traffic during the California gold rush era until the Yumas regained control. (Photo by Steven W. Walenta, courtesy Jeff Hengesbaugh)

The Pawnees receive annually a certain number of guns, as part of the payment for the land ceded by them on the Kanzas [sic] river. These guns are light pieces manufactured at Birmingham, and cost about five or six dollars each. Some are tolerably good; but the Pawnees having but lately become acquainted with the use of firearms, soon destroy them, by examining, firing off powder, overloading, and other follies. Some they gamble away; and all that they do not either lose [sic] or spoil, they exchange with the Haitans and other predatory tribes in the West and South for horses; so that . . . very few efficient guns are to be found in the Pawnee village.[21]

A fight between Arikaree Indians and Gen. William Ashley's party of trappers in 1823 led to the temporary closing of the upper Missouri River to whites. Early that summer one of Ashley's men described a Ree village and its inhabitants. "There are probably seven hundred warriors; they are tolerably well armed, and possess some skill in the management of fire arms; about two thirds are armed with fusees, the rest with bows and arrows." Gen. Henry Atkinson's 1825 report of his negotiations with various tribes with whom he held council along the Missouri often echoed such observations of the well-established use of Northwest guns. "Well armed with fusees" or similar comments were common in his reports on the Pawnees, various Sioux tribes, Crows, Assiniboines, and others.[22]

Richard "Uncle Dick" Wootton as a young man of eighteen had his first encounter with hostile Comanche raiders after he signed on with a wagon train bound for Santa Fe in 1836.

A few of them had the old fashioned "fusees," but the most of them had bows and arrows and spears. What we called a "fusee" was a fire lock [flintlock] musket with a bore half as big as that of a small cannon, from which either slugs or ball could be shot, although not with any great degree of accuracy. The Indians used sometimes to shoot a copper ball from these guns. Where they got the copper I never knew, but I suppose it came from Old Mexico. They used both flint and steel pointed arrows, and the spears which they carried were long poles with bayonct shaped steel points, as long as a butcher knife.[23]

Henry Boller described one incident in 1858 along the Missouri River.

I was greatly amused at watching one of the Indians load his fusee. After a double handful of powder, he put in nine half-ounce balls one upon another, with a large wad of red flannel between each. The gun was literally loaded halfway up to the muzzle, and it seemed to me as if the safest place when fired off would have been directly in front.[24]

Of better quality were the flintlock smoothbore guns from the mid-1700s and on, sometimes described as "chief's guns." Although not true Northwest guns, these light fowling pieces sometimes displayed a form of serpent-like side plate. These English and American guns

Light French musket, representative of the trade in French arms among Plains Indians including the Comanches in the southwest. The pan, frizzen, and frizzen spring are old hand-forged replacement parts, probably a frontier repair. The stock shows extensive wear and at least two places where the barrel had been secured with wire. The muzzle is slightly flared, a feature some students of Native American culture theorize may be indicative of frequent pounding on the earth while dancing since dancing was such a common practice among many tribes. (Photo by Steven W. Walenta, courtesy Jeff Hengesbaugh)

Rather crude replacement barrel bands and pewter inlays in the stock of this French Charleville-marked musket indicate probable Indian use. (Photo by Steven W. Walenta, courtesy James D. Gordon)

generally were for the more discriminating Indian and sometimes were presented as gifts. Often these were fitted with a lightly engraved trigger guard and butt plate and a silver medallion inset into the wrist behind the barrel tang engraved with an Indian head or quiver and arrows. The locks were of superior quality but to facilitate the availability of ammunition their calibers were the same as those of Northwest guns.[25]

Even after Northwest guns in percussion form became available, among Indians in some areas of the United States and Canada, a demand for flintlocks persisted into the 1870s and later for in remote areas flints or flintlike silicates which could strike sparks would be more readily available than percussion caps or metallic cartridges. Apparently neither the American Fur Company nor the Pierre Chouteau Jr. & Co. ever ordered any percussion guns. Between 1856 and 1860, Henry Leman sold 7,500 Northwest guns to the federal government, and only 950 were percussion. These were priced at $6.25, a flintlock $6.50. In Canada, all the Hudson's Bay Company trade guns were flintlocks until 1862.[26]

The Northwest gun was a standardized form of smoothbore, but other smoothbores reached Indian hands. Single-barrel fowlers of both British and American make found their niche and by the late 1700s, British gun makers were producing flintlock double-barrel shotguns.

Doubles in both flintlock and percussion form were popular with sportsmen, but some entered Native American trade channels. Maj. Salmon Buell writing of the attack on settlers at New Ulm, Minnesota, by the Sioux in 1862 observed that many of the warriors were armed with "a heavy double-barreled shotgun, number ten or twelve bore, with very strongly reinforced barrel toward the breech, so as to shoot balls." The government had provided these smoothbores to the Sioux earlier for hunting bison and other large game, he said. A year later, the government purchased three hundred doubles from Poultney & Trimble of Baltimore for issue to Indians. Military smoothbore muskets also found their way into Indian hands by various means.[27]

BOW AND ARROW VERSUS THE GUN

In 1812–13, Indians on the Columbia River in the northwest had few guns, but like many other tribes they relied on bows and arrows. Hundreds of miles away in Texas, the situation was not much different a quarter century later and Big Foot Wallace claimed that in 1837 one well-armed American was a match for eight or ten Indians "with their bows and arrows and miserable guns; but now [1871], thanks to the traders, they are well furnished with good rifles and 'six-shooters,' and can hold their own, man for man."[28]

A trio of English trade guns, from top to bottom: A well-used Northwest gun with brass tacks and wire wrapping. The lock, converted from flintlock to percussion, is stamped "SARGANT BROTHERS 1850." Hudson's Bay Company single-barrel percussion trade shotgun, introduced in the 1890s by the firm to replace the Northwest gun. The barrel is marked "IMPERIAL No. 1." At bottom is undoubtedly one of the last Northwest guns produced, marked on the lock "Barnett London 1900." (Photo by Steven W. Walenta, courtesy James D. Gordon)

James Pattie of Kentucky embarked on a trapping expedition in 1827 into northern Mexico and what is now New Mexico. Some Indians the party encountered had never seen firearms and exhibited a mixture of terror and astonishment when they were demonstrated. Apaches, they found, relied heavily on the bow and arrow.

> They shoot this weapon with such force, that at the distance of 300 paces they can pierce a man.... Their second offensive weapon is a lance, fifteen feet long. When they charge the enemy they hold this lance with both hands above their head, and, at the same time, guide their horse by pressing him with their knees. Many of them are armed with firelocks, which, as well as the ammunition, have been taken in battle from the Spaniards, who never sell them any.[29]

At reasonable distances, the bow and arrow was an effective weapon whether used for hunting or in warfare.

It was fast firing, did not rely on ammunition available only from outside sources, and it produced no noise or position-revealing smoke. Its weight added little to the burden carried by an Indian pony and when running bison on horseback, the bow was easier to use than attempting to reload a gun. An American trader, Anthony Glass, kept a journal of his visit to Taovaya-Wichita villages on the Red River in Texas in 1808–9. He recorded: "I have seen an Indian with a Bow of the Boi' d Ark [bois d'arc or Osage orange] wood, the most Elastic wood in the world, drive an arrow entirely through a Buffalo with more force than a riffle [sic] would have sent a Ball."[30]

Some Indians developed a notable skill with bow and arrow. A young warrior visited an army camp in the late 1870s claiming to be a good shot with his bow. He was challenged by a promise of keeping every coin he could hit at thirty feet.

> He did better than we expected and we discontinued the coin shooting as a bad investment on our side. He was promised a square meal if he could hit a cap in the air.

443

A new cap was furnished willingly by a recruit who had been led to believe by us that the Indians were bad marksmen with bows and arrows. The cap was thrown up and we all thought he had lost, but a hole was found through the middle, to the great sorrow of the owner.[31]

Capt. William A. Thornton observed a similar demonstration in May 1856. A party of Mescalero Apaches arrived at Fort Stanton (New Mexico) and Thornton wanted to observe their skill with the bow and arrow. The target was a playing card pinned to a dry piñon post about five inches in diameter at a distance of sixty yards. The prize was $3 worth of tobacco. Eleven Indians fired five arrows each, some using borrowed weapons. Nine struck the post, two cut the card, and three grazed the post. All of the shots would have struck a man in the chest. The Indians' second effort was for a $10 cash prize with ten men firing three arrows each at fifty yards. Despite the gusty wind crossing the line of fire, ten arrows entered the post and four grazed it. Again, all arrows would have struck a man-sized target.[32]

A similar demonstration of Indian skill was entertainment for a group of civilian travelers in Nebraska in the 1870s. "[We had] them at a distance of fifty paces knock small coins from a stick placed in the ground, the coin inserted edgewise in the top end, the one striking the coin and knocking it from the stick being entitled to it." One of the observers recalled "it is surprising with what accuracy they can thus hit a small coin."[33]

Josiah Gregg observed life in the southwest throughout almost the entire decade of the 1830s. He was impressed with the alacrity with which an Indian chief could release his arrows, as quickly as Gregg was able to fire successive shots from his Colt Paterson revolver. "There is nothing strange in the rifleman's being able to hit his mark with his fine-sighted barrel; but the accuracy with which these savages learn to shoot their feathered missiles, with such random aim, is almost incomprehensible." He also noted that in the southwest Indians weren't the only ones to use the bow and arrow. Speaking of military forces in northern Mexico, he wrote:

> It is true that most of the regular troops are provided with English muskets, which... they are too ignorant to keep in order; but a great portion of the militia are obliged to use the clumsy old-fashioned *escopeta*, or firelock [miquelet] of the sixteenth century; while others have nothing but the bow and arrow, and sometimes the lance, which is in fact a weapon very much in use throughout the country.[34]

The *escopeta* to which he referred was a common weapon among Spanish frontiersman in northern Mexico in the seventeenth and eighteenth centuries and even beyond 1800. It was a crude but sturdy form of smoothbore flintlock, using a miquelet lock with an external mainspring. "The weapons most in use among the Pueblos are the bow and arrow, with the long-handled lance and occasionally a fusil. The rawhide shield is also much used, which, though of but little service against fire-arms, serves to ward off the arrow and lance." On another occasion, Gregg observed that both Indians and Mexicans often chased bison with the lance, "which, if the horse be well trained, is still a more expeditious mode of killing them than with the bow and arrow." An expert lancer would enter a herd, "and drawing up alongside, will pierce buffalo after buffalo until several are brought down."[35]

Frontiersman Uncle Dick Wooten recalled later in life:

> The mountain men always had a great advantage in fighting the Indians. While they were using the bow and arrow we had the advantage of being able to shoot a much greater distance than they could, and after they got to using guns, we could shoot more accurately and handle our guns a great deal quicker. To shoot with any accuracy whatever [when first using the rifle], the Indian had to have "a rest" for his gun, and he was always slow about "taking sight," while the mountain men all shot "off hand," and lost no time in "drawing a bead" on an enemy. At hunting game with the rifle the Indians were no match for the white hunters.... It was the habit of the Indian hunter, when using the rifle, to carry a couple of gun rods in his hand, and when he got ready to shoot at anything, down would go the rods on the ground in the form of the letter X. With one hand, the hunter held the rods together, while with the other he managed his gun, resting it between the two rods. Sometimes he could make a single rod answer the purpose, holding it with his hand in the same manner.... Of late years, they have learned to use them [rifles] to better advantage.[36]

In his account *Life Among the Apaches*, John C. Cremony noted the continued use of the bow and arrow in the late 1860s.

> The Apache will invariably add his bow and arrows to his personal armament, although he may be the owner of a Spencer [repeating] rifle and a couple of Colt's revolvers, with ammunition to suit. Whenever they design entering one of our military camps they invariably conceal, at some distance, firearms; so that they may appear innocent of designed enmity or their possession, but should occasion serve, they quickly manage to re-possess themselves of all their weapons.[37]

Col. Richard I. Dodge spent much of his career before and after the Civil War on the frontier. When he first went west, he noted "the Indians had little confidence in guns in a close fight. A whole quiver of arrows could be expended in the time it took to load and fire the gun once." He wrote in 1882 that if an Indian's gun was out of order or ammunition was scarce, one must turn to the bow. Also, "the young and the poor use the bow exclusively; those who possess firearms must use the bow occasionally."[38]

Arrow wounds could be difficult to treat. An army study of such injuries in the 1860s indicated that the average arrowhead was of soft hoop iron, from one-half to two inches long and from one-half to three-quarters of an inch wide at the base. Arrows averaged thirty to thirty-three inches in length. Hollywood films often show an arrow being withdrawn by pulling it free from the wound. In practice, such an act easily could separate shaft from head unless the wound was shallow, making the arrow point much more difficult to locate and extract. As Dr. Frank H. Hamilton wrote in an 1865 treatise on military surgery: "It must be fully understood that the [arrowhead] cannot remain without causing excessive suppuration, and perhaps death. It is so much the more dangerous than a ball, as it is usually larger and much more irregular upon its surface." There was less shock with an arrow wound than that of a bullet because of the former's lower velocity. However, if an arrow should become imbedded in a bone or beside it, it could become bent into a hook requiring surgery to remove.[39]

Turning again to Dodge's recollections, he wrote: "The war arrow has a short, sharp blade, like a lancet; the rear shoulders slope forward, forming barbs; their attachment to the shaft is very slight, as it is intended that the head shall remain in the wound, and kill eventually, if not immediately." Maj. Stephen H. Long confirmed the difference between hunting and war arrows more than a half century before Dodge. "The war arrow differs from that used for hunting, in having a barbed spear-head, very slightly attached to the wood, so that if it penetrates the body of an enemy, it cannot be withdrawn without leaving the point in the wound."[40]

INDIAN RIFLES

Versatile as the fusee and other smoothbores were, some Native Americans did prefer rifled guns despite their added weight. At the beginning of the nineteenth century, some makers of Pennsylvania-Kentucky rifles including Frederick Goetz of Philadelphia, Peter Gonter and Jacob Dickert of Lancaster, and others were producing rifles on government contracts for the Indian trade. Gun makers who would follow their lead included Henry Leman, J. J. Henry, and Henry Deringer Jr. The latter struck out on his own about 1806 after completing his apprenticeship and by 1809 was making proposals to the US Office of Indian Trade to provide rifles. A letter from John Mason of that office dated June 2, 1809, asked for a sample of what Deringer could provide at $12.50 each "compleat with charger, moulds, wiper" if fifty to one hundred guns were ordered. These were to be brass mounted, sixty balls to the pound (about .43 caliber), with a barrel between forty and forty-six inches long, "the whole finished in a neat strong & workmanlike manner." Mason added a cautionary postscript reminding Deringer that "part of the inspection to which the Indian rifles submitted is trial at the target."[41]

Mason liked Deringer's sample and directed his office's representative in Philadelphia "to make particular inquiry who Deringer is—as to his character as a workman & a man of punctuality." The response was favorable for on August 9, 1809, Mason ordered fifty rifles, the first of a series of contracts for Deringer rifles and smoothbore Northwest guns for the Indian trade. Succeeding orders between 1810 and 1812 totaled 568 rifles of 40 to 60 gauge (about .49 to .43 caliber) and with barrel lengths from forty-two to forty-six inches, packed ten guns to a box. Each rifle was to have a woolen case, an accessory that often accompanied both new trade rifles and Northwest guns, usually scarlet in color. Fifty-two of these guns were ordered "highly finished with stars or eagles on breech," presumably as chiefs' guns. Existing invoices up to 1820 include orders to Deringer for smooth bored rifles, both square (octagonal) and round barrel rifles, "rifles with star and thumb piece" decorations, gun worms, awls, brass pipe tomahawks, and beaver traps. Deringer produced Model 1814 and 1817 "common

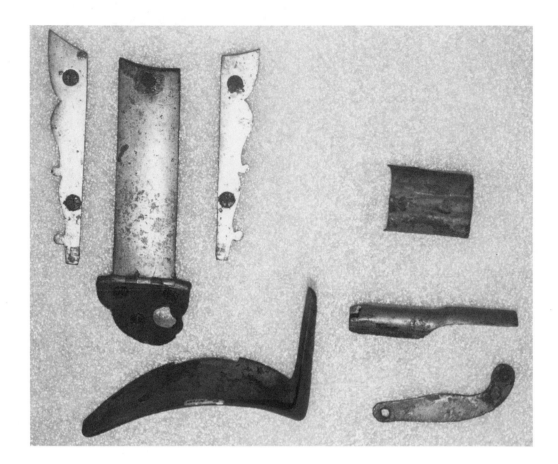

Found near Bent's Old Fort, brass components from a Deringer trade rifle—nose cap, ramrod thimble, lock screw plate, butt plate, and patchbox cover with Deringer name stamped inside.

rifles" and Model 1843 percussion boxlock pistols for the US military, but he may have produced more Indian rifles for the government than any other maker.[42]

Deringer continued to be a major supplier of Indian guns even after the Office of Indian Trade was abolished. In the 1820s, the government was forcing some eastern tribes to move westward. Compensation sometimes included a rifle for each adult male. This brought an order in 1826 for five hundred Deringer rifles for Creek Indians and one for one thousand in 1828 for Cherokees being displaced. Another purchase order in 1829 for a second one thousand Cherokee rifles was significant for it stated that half of the rifles could be percussion, the earliest known request for cap and ball Indian rifles. Choctaws requested Deringer rifles, and 550 were ordered, 200 to be percussion. When the guns arrived, however, the Native Americans asked the agent to replace the percussion guns with flintlocks. Choctaws on one occasion found that ten thousand pounds of gunpowder delivered to Fort Smith was of such poor quality it couldn't be used. It was a year before it was replaced.[43]

The year 1837 brought Deringer his largest order for Indian rifles, 2,750 at a time when contracts were also let to George W. Tryon for 1,000 rifles, Henry Leman for 500, and Jacob Fordney for 250. These Indian rifles were

strongly made, test fired with a half ounce (250 grains) of powder, two patched balls, and two wads, and they featured interchangeable lock parts. Meanwhile, Deringer occasionally was providing smoothbore Northwest guns on contract, although the government was importing many from Europe. His last known contract for fusees was for 385 in 1844.[44]

In addition to rifles, Deringer is known to have received at least one order for handguns for Indians, a request in 1835 for eighteen pairs of pistols, presumably flintlocks. These were destined for the Choctaw Light Horse, a semi-military troop composed of eighteen chiefs. These men were responsible for enforcing laws within the Choctaw Nation in Indian Territory (Oklahoma) following the tribe's forced relocation from Mississippi. Unfortunately no detailed description of these pistols exists; the order merely called for well-made, moderately priced "Light Horse pistols." The term generally meant a brass-mounted holster pistol with a pin-fastened full-stock and about a 9- or 10-inch barrel of about .56 caliber. The price was $9 each, in comparison with Deringer's usual charge of about $15 to $25 for his civilian percussion belt or dueler size pistols.[45]

Henry E. Leman of Lancaster remained a major producer of rifles for the Indian trade as late as the 1870s

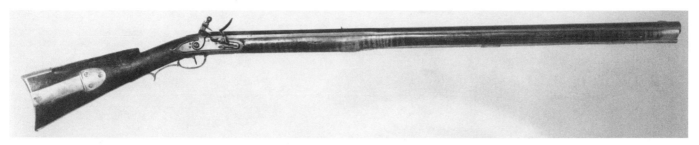

A .54 caliber flintlock by Christopher Gumpf of Lancaster, Pennsylvania, probably made under the 1807 government contract for rifles both for the army and as Indian annuity payments or for trade. (Courtesy: US Military Academy, West Point Museum, NY)

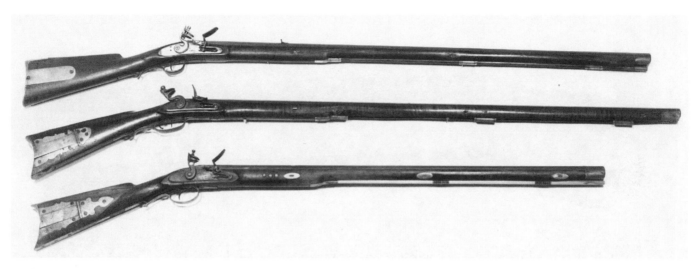

Typical flintlock Indian trade rifles (from top): English pattern by J. Henry (ca. 1830–40), Henry Deringer Jr., and Tryon (ca. 1850). (Courtesy: Museum of the Fur Trade, Chadron, NE)

Deringer trade rifle (ca. 1820s). The stock has been partially covered with leather and bears an Apache clan marking. (Courtesy: Arizona Historical Society, Tucson)

while filling orders for sporting guns as well. In 1850 he had thirty-four employees and a decade later the census showed this number had risen to sixty-two, a workforce which for the year ending June 1, 1860, had produced some five thousand guns. Guns from Leman's shop were highly regarded as several 1855 testimonials showed. Pierre Chouteau Jr. & Co. of St. Louis wrote: "Rifles manufactured by you for our Indian trade have always given entire satisfaction to our traders & the Indians." Robert Campbell, also of St. Louis, said he had "found no rifles

for the Indian trade that gave more general satisfaction than yours have done."[46]

Brass tacks often held the covering on trunks and fabric on furniture in the nineteenth century. They also sometimes decorated Indian rifles and smoothbores from at least the time of George Catlin's Indian paintings in the 1830s forward and possibly earlier. Such tacks were common trade items until at least the late 1870s. Actual placement of the tacks in gunstocks usually was done by the owner to suit his own taste, for religious or decorative purposes. Yet in

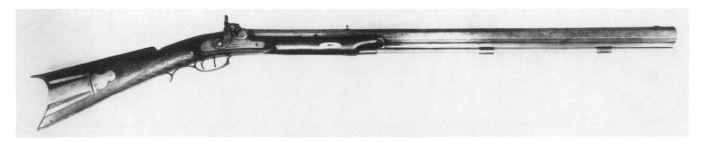

Heavy (almost thirteen pounds) halfstock .58 caliber rifle by Henry Leman, captured from Indians by later general John F. Reynolds during the war in 1856 with the Rogue River Indians in southern Oregon. The gun is more finely finished than a typical Leman trade rifle, with cheek piece, set triggers, checkered wrist, and a more elaborate patchbox cover. Reynolds was one of the leading Union generals during the Civil War but was killed by a sharpshooter at Gettysburg. (Courtesy: US Military Academy, West Point Museum, NY)

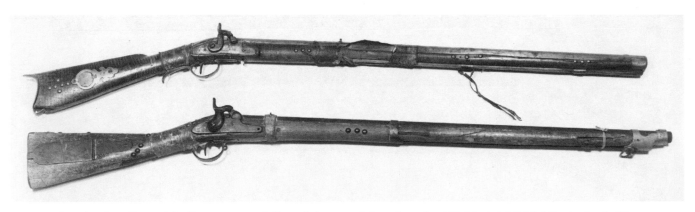

A pair of well-used Indian guns, a fullstock Leman (above) and a US Model 1841 Mississippi rifle. (Courtesy: Museum of the Fur Trade, Chadron, NE)

at least one instance trade guns were offered with tacks already installed. A newly constructed storehouse at Fort Atkinson (later renamed Fort Berthold) on the upper Missouri among the Mandans and Gros Ventres was described about 1859 as outfitted with shelves to display "blankets, knives, gaily ornamented bridles and fusees with their stocks profusely studded with brass tacks." One Sioux war chief known as Pawnee Killer in the 1870s was described as "six feet four, broad shouldered, and weighs 240 pounds avoirdupois. For every Pawnee Indian he kills a brass-headed tack is driven into the stock of his Winchester rifle, which now contains no less than 130. Hence the name conferred upon him."[47]

One traveler on the Missouri River in 1832–34 found that almost all the Mandans and Minatarees had guns. They decorated them with bits of red cloth on the brass ramrod thimbles, "and at the butt-end with brass nails. Besides the ramrod belonging to the gun, the Indians always carry another long ramrod in their hands, which they generally use." The Assiniboines, too, decorated their guns with "brass nails" and bits of red cloth, he observed. "Like all the Indians, they carry…a separate ramrod in their hand, a large powder-horn, which they obtain from the Fur Company, and a leather pouch for the balls, which is made by themselves, and often neatly ornamented, or hung with rattling pieces of lead, and trimmed with coloured cloth."[48]

Even if a gun were damaged, its components might be retained in use by an ingenious Native American. Shoulder gun stocks and barrels could be converted into pistols. A butt plate could be removed for use as a hide scraper or one could be made by flattening and sharpening a section of gun barrel. One chief's tobacco pipe bowl was described as having been made from an old gun barrel. "Mr. [James] Kipp had many similar bowls made by the smith, which he sold to the Indians for six dollars." (Kipp served as a fur company employee for almost a half century before retiring from the fur trade in 1865.) A New Mexico collector has a tomahawk with a handle made from a gun barrel.[49]

Improved firearms sometimes became objects of great interest to Indians unfamiliar with them. A party of soldiers about 1846 moved into Navajo country in the Chuska Mountains, summoning chiefs to talk peace. They became apprehensive when they soon were outnumbered by their Navajo escorts, but it then became obvious that the Native

A Caddo Indian with a fullstock percussion rifle, perhaps a Leman since the wood appears to have been artificially striped, as often was done by Leman workers. (Courtesy: Kansas State Historical Society)

Americans were most interested in trading. "They were very curious to examine our guns, and were astonished when shown the properties of a revolver. One of our men showed a watch, which excited great attention [and] on placing it to their ears they would start as from a snake."[50]

A decade later (1855), army Assistant Surgeon Jonathan Letterman carefully noted the Navajo culture in the southwest and then wrote:

> Some of them have fire-arms in addition to their usual weapons. We have seen some excellent looking rifles in the possession of some of them, bearing the name of "Albright," (of St. Louis, doubtless,) which the owners state were procured in the Territory of Utah. They have not been sufficiently accustomed to the use of these weapons to use them skill-fully, and at the present are much more formidable with the bow and arrow. They value fire-arms highly, and obtain them whenever an occasion offers.

Several others at the time confirmed that the Navajos found the Mormons to be a source of rifles.[51]

On one occasion in 1854 during his fifth western expedition, Capt. Charles Fremont's camp was invaded by fifty or sixty mounted Ute Indians, all armed with rifles and bows and arrows, and demanding knives, gunpowder, blankets, and other items. Fremont outwardly showed no concern and explained: "If they had any ammunition, they would have surrounded and massacred us, and stolen what they now demand, and are parlaying for."

> [Fremont] tore a page from his journal and . . . said: here take this, and place it

Brass tacks in profusion decorate this Bannock warrior's M1866 Winchester carbine, belt, and knife sheath. (Courtesy: Montana Historical Society)

against a tree, and at a distance near enough to hit it every time, discharge your Colt's Navy six shooters, fire at intervals of from ten to fifteen seconds—and call the attention of the Indians to the fact, that it is not necessary for the white men to load their arms.... After the first shot, they pointed to their own rifles, as much as to say they could do the same,... [then] I, without lowering my arm, fired a second shot, this startled them. I discharged it a third time—their curiosity and amazement were increased: the fourth time, I placed the pistol in the hands of the chief and told him to discharge it, which he did, hitting the paper and making another impression of the bullet. The fifth and sixth times two other Indians discharged it.... I had another one already loaded, which I dexterously substituted, and scared them into an acknowledgment that they were all at our mercy.[52]

James Kirker was one of the opportunists who traded guns freely to Native Americans on the southwestern frontier of the 1830s and 1840s. He apparently was cultured, educated, and certainly versatile. The Santa Fe *Republican* newspaper in December of 1847 described him as "the distinguished mountaineer and Indian slayer" and announced the opening of his hotel. He boasted of having taken 487 scalps in one decade and a member of a wagon train for which he served as a guide wrote of him as having been accused of scalping friendly Indians to collect bounties on scalps. His resume would have included experience as a

Plain English pistol with a flintlock marked "WHEELER & SON" and a 9-inch round barrel. Similar pistols frequently were imported and were popular in the western trade. The numerous tacks which decorate the stock indicate probable Indian usage. (Photo by Steven W. Walenta, courtesy James D. Gordon)

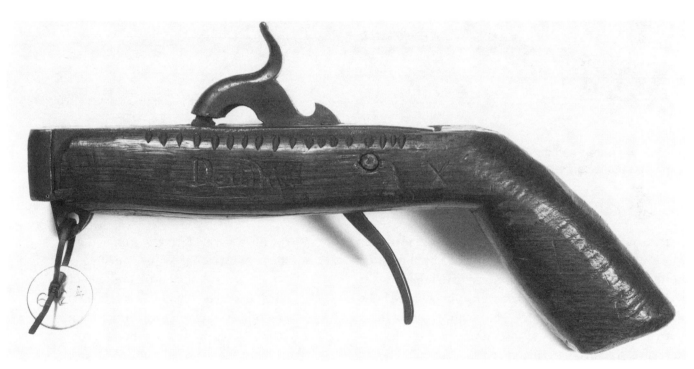

A crude wooden stock fitted to a Hall receiver, breechblock, hammer, trigger, and mainspring makes a simple pistol. The word "DEATH" is carved in the left side of the stock. (Photo by Steven W. Walenta, courtesy James D. Gordon)

privateer, guide, trapper, trader, merchant, miner, and army scout during the Mexican War—as well as gunrunner. A member of Doniphan's Missouri Regiment in 1846 described him as dressed in a fringed buckskin hunting shirt and breeches, heavy, broad Mexican hat, huge spurs, all embellished and ornamented with Mexican finery. He was armed with "A Hawkins [sic] rifle elegantly mounted and ornamented with silver inlaid on the stock . . . [and] a choice assortment of pistols and Mexican daggers."[53]

By 1834 Mexican authorities strongly suspected Kirker was one of the Anglo Americans who were engaged in contraband trade of guns and gunpowder with the Apaches and Comanches, in part under the guise of trapping and mining. He also was suspected of acting as a fence for

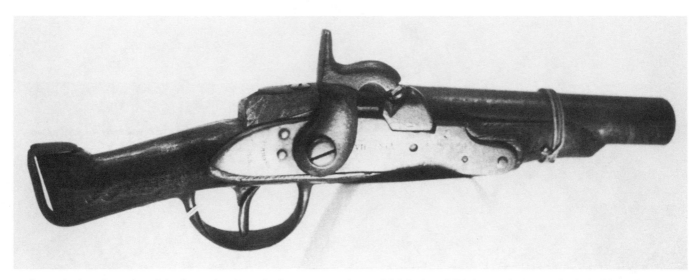

A crude but functional Indian pistol made from a cut down 1816-dated Richmond-made Virginia Manufactory musket. Its history is unknown but an old tag said it had been seized from an Indian named "Bad Heart" when he attempted to kill an Indian agent with it. (Courtesy: Dale C. Anderson)

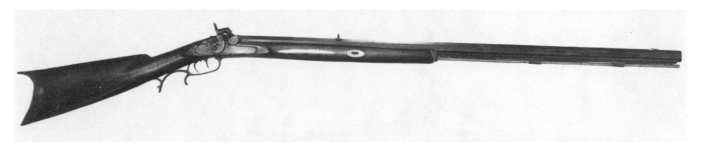

Iron-mounted halfstock .40 caliber rifle by T. J. Albright of St. Louis, similar to the type described by army assistant surgeon Jonathan Letterman who visited the Navajos in 1855. (Courtesy: Museum of the Fur Trade, Chadron, NE)

horses, mules, and other goods that Indians had stolen. Much of the killing and plundering done by Indians in northern Mexico and New Mexico Territory, authorities felt, was carried out by men equipped with arms obtained from Kirker and other gunrunners. The colonists, in contrast, often had only bows, arrows, lances, and various other crude defensive weapons. The situation reached such a crisis that in October 1834 in the state of Chihuahua, the sale of guns to rebel Apaches could be punished by death.[54]

IMPROVED INDIAN GUNS

During the 1850s and 1860s, the number and quality of firearms in the hands of western tribes gradually increased. Spencers, Sharps, and other breechloaders became even more common after the Civil War. One traveler in 1860 observed:

Amongst the prairie tribes are now to be found individuals provided not only with the old muskets formerly supplied to them, but with Yages [presumably Mississippi rifles], Sharp's breechloaders, alias "Beechers' Bibles," Colt's revolvers, and other really good fire-arms. Their shooting has improved with their tools: many of them are now able to "draw a bead" with coolness and certainty. Those who cannot afford shooting-irons, content themselves with their ancient weapons, the lance and bow.[55]

In a conversation in Santa Fe in 1866, frontiersman Kit Carson "freely admitted that a good many of the Ute Indians were better rifle shots than he was."[56]

A wagon train on the Bozeman Trail in 1863 encountered a band of about 150 Sioux or Cheyenne Indians, one of whom wanted to trade two horses for Robert Kirkpatrick's youngest sister, then not yet ten years old.

"Grey Wolf," a Winnebago chief, photographed in Sioux City, Iowa, about 1871 with a Henry repeating rifle. (Courtesy: Nebraska State Historical Society)

They succeeded in stealing three bridles and nine ox bows which they straighten out and make arrows of.... They were armed with all sorts of guns, some good breech loaders, some good muzzle loaders, shot guns cut off to 16 inches long, six shooters, pistols, horse pistols and a lot had old fusees [Northwest trade guns] not worth picking up. A great many had bows and arrows and spears.[57]

The Townsend train also had difficulties with Indians protesting the opening of the Bozeman Trail. A party of six men went back to look for a man seeking a stray cow. The search party when more than a mile away from the train was surrounded by about thirty warriors and a running battle began. The six reached safety with only one of their number wounded with an arrow in his back. The train was corralled hastily and many of its men took up a defensive position on a nearby hilltop where they could keep the Indians at a distance from the wagons. Some of the white men had Sharps and Henry breechloaders, but most of the Native Americans were reported as using bows and arrows. Eventually the Indians departed after their attempt to burn the train out by firing the grass failed.[58]

Henry repeaters were among those guns eagerly sought by Native Americans although procuring ammunition for those and other metallic cartridge arms could sometimes be difficult. In 1868 a group of men from St. Louis established a wood yard near Fort Union to

453

Baptiste Bayhylle (sp?) and Andrew Murray, Pawnee scouts under Luther North, with a Henry (left) and a M1866 Winchester rifle. (Courtesy: Nebraska State Historical Society)

provide fuel for steamboats on the Missouri River. A party of supposedly friendly Sioux visited their camp and the whites carelessly allowed their visitors to examine their Henry rifles. The visitors killed the entrepreneurs with their own guns.[59]

In late 1867, the government auctioned nearly twenty thousand surplus guns from its arsenal at Fort Leavenworth, Kansas. Colt revolving rifles; muzzle loading military rifles and muskets; Starr, Adams, and Whitney revolvers; and breech loading carbines by Burnside, Gallagher, Maynard, Merrill, Joslyn, and Smith were sold. It's logical that some of these arms eventually reached Native Americans through the course of either legal or illicit trade.[60]

Despite the increasing availability of large numbers of surplus military and other improved breechloaders, sturdy muzzle loading trade rifles—principally those by Henry E. Leman of Lancaster, Pennsylvania—remained in wide use.

Many such rifles between .45 and .55 caliber, were issued in the 1860s and 1870s along with percussion revolvers for hunting as annuity payments. Indians attending peace conferences in the late 1860s often requested and received guns and ammunition for this purpose. John P. Lower of Denver in 1876 was still advertising "Leman Indian Rifles" for sale at $12 to $15. The often quoted 1879 annual report of the army's chief of ordnance listed 410 guns which had been captured from Cheyennes and Sioux in 1877. Of the 160 muzzle loading rifles included, 94 were Lemans. Requisitions from agency traders in Montana in the early 1870s for ammunition and spare parts for .50 caliber Springfield needle guns, and both .36 and .44 caliber Remington and Colt percussion revolvers indicate the popularity of these arms as well among various tribes.[61]

Attempts by the army and others to limit the acquisition of improved arms and ammunition by Indians in the post–Civil War era varied in their effectiveness. On the

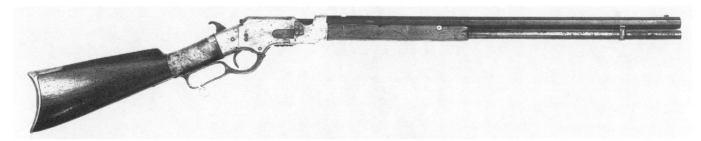

An unusual and primitive conversion of a very early M1866 Winchester rifle (#13097)—to a single-shot percussion muzzle loader! Apparently an early owner couldn't find a reliable source of ammunition or preferred an ignition system with which he was more familiar. The rifle was found on the Wind River Indian Reservation north of Lander, Wyoming, so it's probable the user was Native American. Another M1866 Winchester, a carbine, was found in the southwest and had been altered to percussion in similar fashion. The receiver had been cut on both sides just behind the barrel to allow access to a percussion nipple fitted into a plug secured in the chamber. (Photo by Steven W. Walenta, courtesy James D. Gordon)

Pueblo Indians photographed by Ben Wittick about 1883 in Santa Fe. The guns may be studio props—a double-barrel percussion shotgun and a Smith & Wesson No. 3 American or First Model Russian revolver. (Courtesy: Museum of New Mexico, neg. #65610)

A Blackfoot warrior before a tepee with a '73 Winchester carbine. His necklace or breast plate was made from a half-dozen serpent side plates from Northwest trade guns. (Courtesy: Wade Lucas Collection)

northern plains of Dakota and Montana, for example, sales by agency traders generally were closely monitored. On November 15, 1872, Special Indian Agent A. J. Simmons at the Milk River Sioux Agency, Montana Territory, informed traders that they were prohibited from trading breech loading arms and fixed ammunition of any sort on the reservation without his approval.

> The ordinary muzzle loading Indian trade rifle and ammunition for that character of arms may be sold during the ensuing year in quantities sufficient for hunting purposes, viz., rifles not exceeding twenty-four for the time above specified, powder twenty five and lead seventy five pounds per month at any one trading post, to

> Indians belonging to this Agency and receiving subsistence herefrom but in no case to any others.[62]

However an illicit trade in guns, ammunition, and liquor continued, driven by high profits. One example involved a trader by the name of Boucher who was illegally selling ammunition at his ranch ten miles from the Spotted Tail Sioux Agency in Wyoming Territory in 1876. Fearing this supply would fall into the hands of hostile Sioux, the commander at Fort Robinson, Nebraska, was directed to send an officer to seize all but fifty rounds of Boucher's ammunition and place it in storage.[63]

In 1873 Frank Herbert was with a government surveying party in western Nebraska when he was approached by an Indian who

Cut down percussion fowling piece marked "White & Bates" found on an Indian burial scaffold in 1905 near Forsyth, Montana. There is a shim between the barrel and the stock made up from part of an 1882 calendar and a newspaper. (Courtesy: Ralph Heinz and Fred Fellows)

"Big Jim," an Arapaho, with a Forehand & Wadsworth .44 New Model Army revolver. (Courtesy: Colorado Springs Pioneers Museum, acc. #A82-1-340)

457

The pitted and weathered condition of this Winchester M1866 carbine from the Crow Reservation in Montana indicates it may have come from a grave. The wrist and forearm are rawhide wrapped and the butt stock is decorated with brass tacks. Each side of the receiver is stamped with a cross representing the four directions. (Courtesy: Ralph Heinz)

offered me a scalp and a plug of tobacco for a six shooter I had. My six shooter had a brass handle and I kept it polished up and it shined very nice. It just took his fancy but I had no use for the scalp so I did not trade. The next day they came over to visit us, but their purpose was to buy ammunition. It was against the law to sell an Indian any cartridges but McMackin had some ammunition for the Spencer gun he had and showed an Indian the box. The Indian reached dwon [sic] in his shirt and pulled out a roll of bills tied up with a piece of rag. He slipped the band off and there was a five dollar bill in sight. He took it out and offered it to McMackin. McMackin shook his head no, as he caught sight of a twenty under it. The Indian took back the five and handed him two twenties. It was all the same to him. McKackin took that and gave him the shells. I walked away as I did not want to be a witness to that kind of business. I don't know whether the Indian had a Spencer gun or not, but they tried to get all the ammunition they could, and having plenty of money I think they got some. We had three thousand rounds, but it did not fit their guns, as ours were Needle, fifty caliber [Springfield .50–70 rifles, presumably].[64]

Billy Dixon earned a reputation as a buffalo hunter, but in the spring of 1867 at age fourteen he was hired as a government teamster. Arms issued to the drivers were "Sharpe's carbines, each carrying a linen cartridge, with which was used the 'army hat' cap. In addition, we were given a six-shooting Remington cap and ball pistol. These were the very latest arms." Strict orders had been given not to trade with the Indians, but the temptation was too strong. "I traded my old cap-and-ball six-shooter to an old Indian for three buffalo robes and other trinkets." When the wagon train reached Fort Harker, Kansas, "a rumor spread about what might happen to the fellows who traded firearms to the Indians. . . . The fine for a man who had sold a six-shooter would be fifty dollars, which was enough money to buy a whole lot of fun in those days." The arms were government property and the order came for the men to turn in their guns. Dixon was in a serious predicament, but a friend came to his aid, loaning him a revolver which was his personal property. Dixon turned in the borrowed gun and later gave his friend a replacement.[65]

As difficult and expensive as fixed ammunition sometimes was for Indians to acquire, they became quite resourceful in maintaining a supply. Gen. Phil Sheridan on April 7, 1877, wrote:

The Indians save every shell they fire, and pick up every one white men or soldiers throw away, and refill them as perfectly as is done by machinery, using a cut down percussion cap for the fulminator. In Col. [Ranald] McKenzie's [sic] last fight many shells of this kind were found, as well as one of the little instruments used in filling the shells. The Indians even use our cast off boxes for packing ammunition thus made.[66]

The silverwork and possible turtle shape fetishes suggest this M1866 Winchester may have been a Navajo weapon. (Courtesy: Roswell Art and History Museum, NM)

In 1873 during the second season of the joint American-British boundary survey of our country's border with Canada, a band of about thirty Assiniboine Indians visited the British camp, many armed with Winchester M1866 repeaters or sixteen-shooters (Henry rifles, perhaps). Capt. Albany Featherstonhaugh, assistant British astronomer, was somewhat surprised to find that the Indians were "particularly keen after matches," unaware that they used the match heads as substitutes for fulminate when reloading the rimfire cartridges used in their Winchesters.

Regardless of the arms with which they fought, Indians skilled in horsemanship preferred to fight cavalry on horseback rather than infantry for in the former situation the warriors had a significant advantage. Sgt. H. H. McDonnell of the 6th Cavalry recalled:

> With the enemy on terra firma they [Indians] were at a loss, for their tactics here would not avail them against a few determined dismounted men grouped together and presenting a firm front. It took our people a long time to find out that a dozen infantrymen with "long toms," [rifles] riding in a six-mule government wagon, were more dreaded by the Indians than a whole squadron of cavalry or rangers; but in the last days of Indian fighting or scouting this became the usual mode of arming and equipping parties of soldiers.[67]

A group of whites that passed through the Battle of the Little Bighorn site in 1877 was heartsick at seeing the bones and other marks of the engagement yet delayed an extra day to tour the field.

We started early, determined to make the rounds of the dead line occupied by the enemy. On the edge of Dry Creek, on the ridge and in the coulee, we found thousands of cartridge shells lying in piles, each pile showing clearly where each warrior was situated.... We made the round of the entire firing line, finding empty shells by the thousand, fifty calibre needle-guns [Springfields], Henry rifles .44, some Long Toms [*sic*?], Spencers, .56 calibre, Winchester 44–40 [Model 1873]. Bullets were also found that had not been shot, also round musket balls, buckshot, and some odd shells which I had never seen duplicated.[68]

A 1970 inventory of cartridge cases found at known Indian positions on the battlefield included:

969 .45 Government Carbine
380 .44 Henry rimfire (for the Henry or M1866 Winchester)
189 .50–70 Government
55 .56–56 Spencer
25 .45 Colt Government
21 .56–52 and .56–50 Spencer
19 .44–40 Winchester (for the new Model 1873 Winchester)[69]

In another example of the variety of Indian arms, when Texas Rangers in 1881 defeated a band of Apaches, they captured various items including "two Winchester rifles, one Remington carbine, one United States cavalry pistol [Colt .45 Single Action?], and one .40 double-action Colt's [.41 caliber Colt Model 1877 Thunderer].[70]

A Navajo "Mose," identified as "old Washie's boy," photographed about 1890. The revolver appears to be a Colt M1851 Navy, the rifle a '66 Winchester. (Courtesy: Museum of New Mexico, Ben Wittick photo #15939)

Although he didn't date the occurrence, Col. Richard I. Dodge cited the following incident:

A small party of Sioux once came into my camp, returning from an unsuccessful foray against the Pawnees. They were all well armed, but the leader particularly attracted my attention. He was a stalwart, ruffianly-looking fellow of about twenty-five, hand-somely dressed in buckskin. Across his saddle he carried a magnificent buffalo gun of the very best patent; on each side of his belt was a holster containing a beautiful ivory-handled Colt's revolver, and slung across his shoulder was a most excellent

field-glass. The rascal had been "in luck," killed some rich man on a hunt for pleasure, and secured his outfit.[71]

A cavalryman who served with the 2nd in Montana Territory, Pvt. William Zimmer, kept a diary and in 1877 wrote:

Some years ago when bows & arrows were principally used instead of the Remington & Sharps improved rifle, they used to bury them with the warrior, & even kill all the ponies he owned under the tree or scaffold where he was buried. As strong as an Indian['s] belief is, he don't [sic]

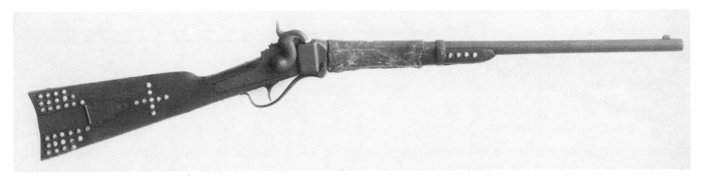

Sharps New Model 1863 percussion carbine (#83092) with brass tacks and a rawhide wrapped and sinew sewn forearm covering. The gun was found in the 1930s beneath the wooden floor of an adobe house that was being restored near the waterfront in Vallejo, California. (Courtesy: Ralph Heinz and Fred Fellows)

"Red Dog" with a Model 1874 Sharps sporting rifle.

461

Sharps .50–70 Model 1874 (#C,52489) shipped on June 18, 1873, to Edward English of Valeria, Iowa. In 1983 English's niece recalled that "the English boys did go west to hunt buffalo." The rifle is decorated with silver tacks and came from a private museum in Texas as a captured Indian gun, perhaps Comanche, Kiowa, or Southern Cheyenne. (Courtesy: Ralph Heinz)

Julius Meyer's "Indian Wigwam" store in Omaha, Nebraska. He recognized a market for Indian memorabilia while it was still readily available in the nineteenth century. "Indian, Chinese and Japanese Curiosities" the sign on his building proclaimed. (Courtesy: Nebraska State Historical Society, neg. #M163-7)

believe in sending many $50 rifles or ponies to that happy land.[72]

Since they obtained firearms from various sources, uniformity within any Native American group was lacking. In 1879 during the Sheepeater campaign in the Pacific Northwest, a band of nine men and twenty-eight women and children surrendered to Lt. W. C. Brown of the 1st Cavalry. Their firearms included one double-barreled shotgun, two muzzle loading rifles, two Henry rifles, and one each Sharps carbine, Springfield carbine, and Springfield "trapdoor" rifle.[73]

Custer's defeat at the Little Bighorn has a particular fascination for many today, in part because many details of what happened on that hot Sunday afternoon will always remain a mystery. Grass fires at the site in 1983 precipitated

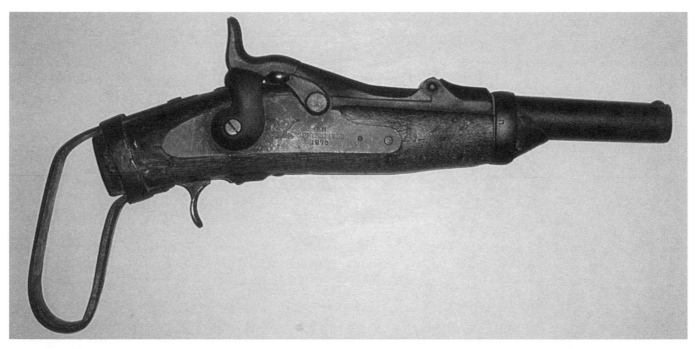

A Springfield Model 1873 rifle (#23905) manufactured in 1874 and converted into a classic example of an easily concealed Indian "blanket gun" with a crude iron pistol grip. (Courtesy: Gary L. Delscamp)

Maynard .50 carbine with brass tacks decorating the stock. Both sights are missing. (Courtesy: Roswell Museum and Art Center, NM)

further archeological fieldwork there in 1984 and 1985. In addition to metal arrowheads, the studies revealed the use of more than forty different makes and models of guns by Indian warriors there. Carbines and rifles by Starr, Smith, Winchester, Henry, Sharps, and Ballard along with .50 and .45 Springfield arms, various muzzle loading rifles and shotguns, and miscellaneous handguns apparently were among those present in Indian hands. However we must remember that a shell, cartridge casing, or perhaps even a gun could have been dropped by one of the curious individuals who visited the scene in the years soon after the battle.[74]

In the spring of 1877, a number of Sioux and northern Cheyennes in the Yellowstone country surrendered after Gen. Nelson Miles's success in the field and in negotiations. Pvt. Zimmer found that:

> It's quite a curiosity to go to the Quartermaster storehouse & see the different kind of firearms the Indians turned in. Some of the first ever invented, muzzle-loading shotguns & rifles with flintlocks, others with caplock, some old rifles with barrels

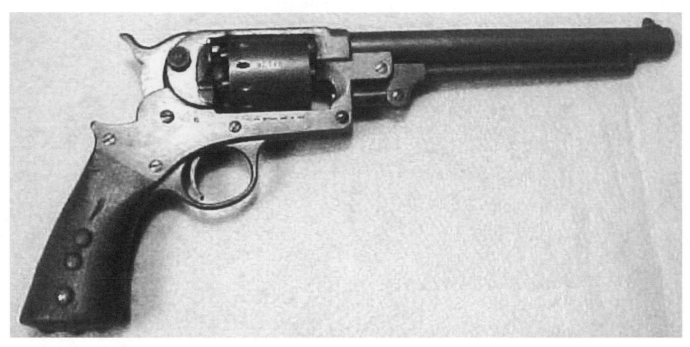

Nine brass tacks in the grip of this Starr .44 single action (#38426) may indicate former Indian ownership. (Courtesy: Kenneth L. McPheeters)

US-marked Colt .45 Single Action (#10372) missing the ejector rod and housing and decorated on each side of the one piece grip with a single brass tack. An early Montana rancher acquired the gun from an Indian in eastern Montana. (Courtesy: Ralph Heinz)

as large around as a chair leg & some as long as a school boy going on an errand.

Some of the shotguns probably were from the 117 or more which had been presented to the Sioux in 1867–68 by peace commissioners.[75]

During the final campaign against Geronimo and his renegade Apaches in 1886, Gen. Nelson Miles did all he could to see that no additional arms or ammunition fell into the enemy's hands. His General Field Order No. 7 issued at Fort Bowie, Arizona Territory, on April 20 included the following directive to his force: "To avoid ammunition getting into the hands of hostile Indians every

Its trigger guard slightly bent, museum records indicate this Colt M1860 .44 was picked up on the Little Bighorn battlefield. (Courtesy: Colorado Historical Society, acc. #H210-1m)

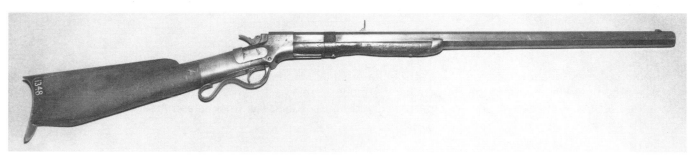

Many of the Indian firearms captured or turned in to the army in the 1870s were sent to the Springfield Armory for ordnance tests and examination conducted in 1879. Some eventually were transferred to the Rock Island Arsenal in the early 1900s. These photos, courtesy of the arsenal museum, illustrate a portion of that collection, some of which are on exhibition, including this well-worn Ballard rifle (#19723) captured in the southwest in the 1880s. (Courtesy: Rock Island Arsenal Museum, IL)

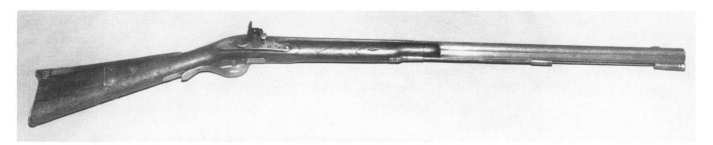

Harpers Ferry Model 1814 rifle, converted to percussion. The brass patchbox cover bears the crude engraving of a bird and perhaps a wolf. (Courtesy: Rock Island Arsenal Museum, IL)

cartridge will be rigidly accounted for, and when they are used in the field the empty shells will be effectively destroyed." Shell casings have been found which appear to have been pierced with a bayonet to render them useless to any Indian recovering them.[76]

Firearms were sometime given as gifts to Indian delegations visiting Washington DC. Although such presents and visits were usually extended toward tribes with peaceful intentions, criticism sometimes resulted. Peace medals, American flags, canes, white man's clothing, hair trunks,

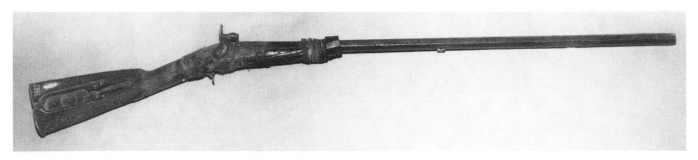

Rawhide strips help secure the lock and barrel to the stock of this assemblage of parts, a crude but operable weapon. The octagonal barrel was from a commercial sporting rifle and the rest of the parts from a Model 1841 Mississippi rifle dated 1851 and made at Harpers Ferry. It lacks a front sight and the rear sight is a crude improvisation. (Courtesy: Rock Island Arsenal Museum, IL)

A rare Morse breech loading carbine made at the State Military Works in Greenville, South Carolina, on machinery captured by Confederates from the Harpers Ferry Armory. Somehow it found its way into Indian hands. Holes in the butt stock indicate it once was decorated with tacks. (Courtesy: Rock Island Arsenal Museum, IL)

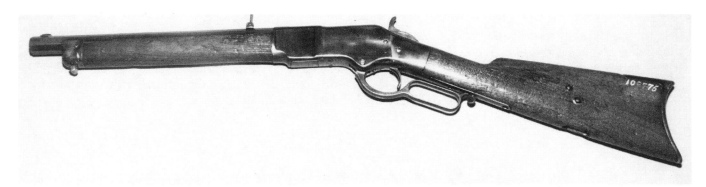

Winchester Model 1866 rifle (#109775). Its magazine tube is missing from beneath the barrel and its barrel was cut to thirteen inches. (Courtesy: Rock Island Arsenal Museum, IL)

Factory records indicate this M1866 Winchester rifle (#130775) was shipped on June 7, 1876; later it reached Indian hands. Fifty-four brass tacks decorate the stock. (Courtesy: Rock Island Arsenal Museum, IL)

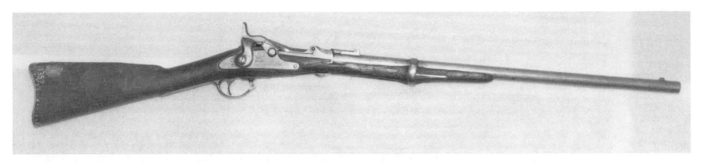

Springfield M1870 .50 rifle shortened for convenience. Wear on the underside of the forearm indicates it probably was carried extensively across a saddle. It reportedly was used at Little Bighorn.
(Courtesy: Rock Island Arsenal Museum, IL)

and other nonmartial items to many whites were preferable as presents to cement peaceful relations. The dozen or so Winnebago Indians visiting President John Quincy Adams in 1828 each received his choice of a musket, cutlass, or pair of pistols. "It was a curious spectacle to witness in such an apartment these destructive weapons, bristling as in a fight, and tossed from hand to hand by men of such powerful frame with the lightness and sport of children's gewgaws." President Andrew Jackson presented four pairs of pistols to delegates in 1832 and in 1846 President Polk gave a Winnebago chief a double-barrel shotgun "with silver plate and engraving" along with flask and shot pouch. A visiting Sioux in 1872 departed from a visit with President Grant with a Henry repeating rifle inscribed "from the President for Bravery & True Friendship."[77]

As mentioned earlier, guns sometimes were included in partial "payment" for land as to the Cherokee and other tribes forced to relocate west of the Mississippi. Arms and ammunition also sometimes were distributed as inducements to encourage participation at peace treaty negotiations. In the late 1860s, representatives of various central and northern plains tribes met with government officials at Fort Laramie. There commissioners distributed some surplus Civil War arms, as well as goods purchased from the post trader, Seth E. Ward & Co. Among the latter items were ninety-eight "Indian rifles" at $22.50 and $25 plus bulk powder, bar lead, and percussion caps—seventeen kegs (probably twenty-five-pound size) of powder at $20 per keg and 1,225 pounds of bar lead at 35¢ per pound. Other purchases included such noncontroversial items as combs, clothing, kettles, pans, needles, awls, cloth, blankets, plugs of tobacco, crackers, tea, and flour. The "Indian rifles" almost certainly were muzzleloaders, perhaps Lemans.[78]

During the closing moments of the 7th Cavalry's attack at the Battle of the Washita in 1868, Sgt. Ryan killed a dismounted warrior and then scalped him, saying to a friend holding his horse:

"John, here is the first scalp for M troop." I secured the [Indian's] rifle, which was a heavy muzzle-loading buffalo gun made at Lancaster, Pennsylvania [probably a Leman] and of the style issued to the Indians for hunting purposes. I also took a 44-calibre Remington revolver and a sheath knife.[79]

For years, whites and Mexicans alike in Arizona Territory and northern Mexico lived in fear of raiding Apaches under Geronimo. In 1877 twenty-five-year-old John P. Clum was the Indian agent in charge at the San Carlos Reservation. In April of that year, he and his Indian police captured the wily renegade and his band at Ojo Caliente. Clum described the confrontation.

I was watching Geronimo's face and particularly the thumb of his right hand, which was about an inch back of the hammer of his fifty-caliber United States Army Springfield rifle. . . . When five or six of my Apache reserves had emerged through the commissary doors, I noticed Geronimo's thumb creeping slowly toward the hammer of his rifle. My right hand was resting on my right hip, . . . and not more than an inch away from the handle of my Colt forty-five—all in accordance with prearranged plans rehearsed with Beauford and my original bodyguard of twenty-two Apache police. So when I discerned Geronimo's intent, I moved my right hand over until it touched the handle of my revolver. That was the second signal. Up came the rifles of Beauford and my twenty-two police,

John Clum's Apache Indian police at San Carlos Reservation. In May 1876 they received sixty .50 caliber Springfield rifles. (Courtesy: John D. McAulay)

Its barrel shortened, this Colt Model 1860 (#99671) was recovered at the Wounded Knee site. (Courtesy: Colorado Historical Society)

each one aimed point-blank at Geronimo or his most notorious followers. My eye was still on Geronimo's thumb. I saw it hesitate, just before it touched the hammer of his rifle. Intuitively, I knew that Geronimo had reconsidered; that he was my prisoner; that there would be no blood shed, unless we spilled it.

Clum retained Geronimo's Springfield rifle and it became a family heirloom. His police probably were equipped with the Model 1868 .50 Springfield rifles they had received in May of 1876.[80]

NATIVE AMERICAN GUNS IN ALASKA

Alaska was largely unexplored in 1867 when Secretary of State William Seward arranged for its purchase from Russia

Another witness to the Wounded Knee tragedy, a M1873 Winchester rifle (#143350A) taken from the body of a Sioux warrior by Charles Wesley Allen, editor of the Chadron (Nebraska) Democrat and a correspondent for the New York Herald. (Courtesy: Nebraska State Historical Society, acc. #6095-1)

for $7.2 million, a few cents an acre. The first official census (1880) tallied a few more than thirty-three thousand inhabitants, all but about five hundred being of Native American stock. The first official US reconnaissance of the region came in 1869 by Capt. Charles P. Raymond, but other expeditions followed. One of these to the Yukon Valley was led by Lt. Frederick Schwatka, 3rd US Cavalry, in 1883. Among the various Indian tribes observed—Tongas, Auk, Chilkat, Tangna, and others—their armament was typically a mixture of flintlock and percussion "Hudson Bay Company muskets" (Northwest guns probably), small bore double-barrel muzzle loading shotguns, and a sprinkling of older model repeating rifles including a few Henrys. Another observer found that as early as 1871 Alaskan Indians would "give the traders any price for such weapons as the Henry and Spencer arms.[81]

Lt. Henry T. Allen of the 2nd Cavalry, Gen. Nelson Miles's aide-de-camp, in 1885 led a remarkable twenty-five-hundred-mile seven-month Alaskan reconnaissance expedition which greatly expanded geographical knowledge of the area. He also reported on observations he made of some of the Indians.

> Bows and arrows are yet largely used by them [the Midnoosky Indians], though they are being rapidly superseded by the small-bore, double-barrel, muzzle-loading shotguns, of which there are two grades, one very inferior, the other good, with laminated steel barrels. Neither of them exceeds 5 or 6 pounds in weight. They fire out of these guns pebbles and bullets of lead or copper. The copper bullets are claimed by them to be superior to the lead ones for large game, such as moose and bear, for the reason . . . that the copper ones will always break the bones, while the lead ones will

not. The copper bullets in use on the Chittyna River are formed by hammering.[82]

Allen found a similar situation among the natives along the Koyukuk River.

> Many . . . are armed with old-fashioned rim-fire Winchester [1866] magazine rifles, caliber .44, which have been obtained, through the Eskimos, from whaling vessels. While possessing this gun, it is seldom that it can be utilized for want of cartridges. Besides these they have shot-guns, usually the single-barrel muzzle-loader, and bows and arrows.[83]

Yet despite Allen's observation of Winchesters, even as late as the 1880s, some flintlock Northwest trade guns were still in use in the more remote areas of Canada and undoubtedly Alaska as well. Several Hudson's Bay Company orders for the 1880–81 period included a total of seventy-three "flint NW guns 3 ?-foot" made by Hollis. A Hudson's Bay Company representative in 1955 wrote that the company had only ceased selling muzzle loading guns a few years before and those were last sold in Quebec. One authority stated that among some tribes in the Alaskan interior, smoothbore muzzleloaders remained the gun of choice until about 1914 as metallic rifle ammunition became more readily available from local traders.[84]

A US naval officer, Lt. George Thornton Emmons, in the 1880s and 1890s made extensive observations of the natives of southeast Alaska, particularly the Tlingits, while ashore on leave or official duty. He wrote that initially muskets plus a few pistols and brass blunderbusses apparently had came into their hands in the 1780s and 1790s, first from British traders, and then from Boston sea captains. The trade in sea otter and seal pelts was brisk,

Alaskan Indians in ceremonial dress. At left, a breech loading double-barrel shotgun and at right a flintlock Northwest trade gun. (Courtesy: Alaska State Library, Juneau)

and Russian efforts to halt that trade by these foreigners were ineffective.[85]

As in other remote areas of North America, Emmons found the Native Americans still using flintlock and percussion muzzleloaders in the mid-1880s. Accessories in their hunting bags included a powder pouch made of animal intestines with a mouthpiece of bone or wood. Often a wooden powder measure did double duty as a stopper. There also was a small double basket containing shot, a leather case containing bullets and wadding, plus a cap holder made of goat horn.

> To charge the pan of the flintlock, a bone tube for powder was carried suspended around the neck, and attached to the [trigger] guard by a string was a metal pricker to clean the touch hole or nipple. A convenient method of carrying caps was by fitting

them over corresponding lugs cut in a piece of leather which was tied to the guard. A thin, paperlike fungus growth, found in rotten wood, and shredded inner bark of the cedar served as wadding. When manufactured bullets were not to be had, pieces of lead or native copper were beaten into slugs, and these were often preferred for bear hunting.[86]

The Tlingits showed particular ingenuity when making shot. The mold was a piece of cedar wood, split partway in half like a pair of tongs.

> At the meeting of the upper edges, a groove extended the length of the split, [in which there were deep holes] at short intervals. [To make these holes] a small iron spike

Alaskan 1885 explorers Lt. Henry Allen (center), Sgt. Cady Robertson (right), and Pvt. Fred Fickett. The latter holds a Springfield .45 M1879 carbine. (Courtesy: Archives, Alaska and Polar Regions Department, University of Alaska at Fairbanks, acc. #72-164-1N)

with a narrow neck and a knob at the end, the size of the proposed shot, was put into the fire, and when sufficiently heated was placed between the halves of the mold to burn out the hollows. To run the shot, the halves of the mold were drawn together and lashed at the open end. The mold was held at a slight inclination and the molten lead ran down the groove to fill the holes through the openings.[87]

Tappan Abney traveled to Alaskan gold fields and a March 1902 issue of *Outing* magazine carried an article described Indian hunters he encountered.

The "A-C" [Alaska Commercial] company supplies them with the best of forty-five-seventy repeating rifles, which they carry in

brightly ornamented cases of caribou skin open at one end so as to be instantly drawn off in the presence of game. The older men cling to the long, single barrel trade smooth-bore, and bullets and caps are carried in an ornamented bag suspended in front by a strap around the neck, powder being carried in a horn at the side.[88]

GRADUAL PEACE ON THE PLAINS

Native Americans often lacked the means and perhaps the incentive to give their guns more than a minimal degree of care. Indian guns found today frequently reflect this as well as the hard use to which they often were put. Sights, if lost or damaged, might be crudely replaced if at all. The expense or shortage of powder or fixed ammunition often limited any opportunity for practice. Few Indians made use of such features as adjustable long-range sights when present on rifles they acquired and with little knowledge of such features as bullet drift and wind effect, it was uncommon for an Indian to acquire a marksman's skills at long range.

Under such circumstances, any incidents involving any display of marksmanship on the part of Native Americans warranted comment. Such was the case during the army's pursuit of the Nez Perce in 1877 as the latter sought to cross into Canada. A newspaper correspondent with Gen. O. O. Howard's force wrote of the battle at Clearwater:

> During the early part of the fight an Indian with a telescope rifle was picking off our men at long range with unpleasant rapidity...when one of Lieutenant Humphrey's men "drew a bead" on the rascal, and Lieutenant Humphrey now is in possession of the deadly weapon....At one point of the line, one man, raising his head too high, was shot through the brain; another soldier, lying on his back and trying to get the last few drops of warm water from his canteen, was robbed of the water by a bullet taking off the canteen's neck while it was at his lips.[89]

In a later dispatch, Howard noted:

> The fact of several hundred rounds of metallic ammunition being found in the hostile camp, it is rendered certain that the Indians are largely if not entirely armed with breech loading rifles of the following description: Henry, Winchester, U.S. Springfield carbine Cal. .45, U.S. Springfield Rifle, Cal. .45 and apparently some long range target rifles—name unknown.[90]

Another participant in the campaign, a 7th Cavalry trooper, later wrote:

> [Chief Joseph's warriors] also had a number of long range needle-guns, two of them being supplied with the most approved telescope sights. One of the rifles was a heavy Creedmore, such as is used by the most skilful [sic] shots in America on the celebrated ranges. No doubt it was one of these rifles that sent that bullet in the direction of General Sturges, during the

brief skirmish at the Gap in the Mountains, which caused him to lower his field-glass and step out of range.[91]

The unidentified target rifles, as well as reports of the use of explosive bullets by some of the warriors, may have been explained by an army doctor, Maj. Tilton, who participated in the campaign.

> I was disposed to doubt that the Nez Perces had any explosive balls, although several men insisted that they had been struck by them, as they distinctly heard the explosions....I...heard upon enquiry that in passing through Idaho they had made a raid upon a "ranch" of an Englishman who had hunted in all parts of the world, and who was well supplied with rifles and ammunition, and the Nez Perces had captured his outfit although he escaped....My attention having been drawn to the subject, I found that a citizen employee with the 7th Cavalry had explosive balls for use in hunting. The Winchester rifle ball was cast with a cavity of proper size to receive [a] .22 calibre cartridge at its apex.[92]

While recovering from wounds, Capt. Charles A. Coolidge told a reporter:

> One Indian sharp-shooter...took a position in the top of a cedar tree, eight hundred yards from the soldiers....Many a poor soldier bit the dust at the crack of his rifle. He was not discovered until near the close of the fight, when, seeing the enemy's rifles were being brought to bear upon him, he descended from his perch.[93]

Yellow Wolf was a Nez Perce who fought with Chief Joseph. He later recalled that his uncle had traded a yearling horse to some miners in Montana for a Winchester Model 1866 rifle, like one which he carried. His mother was with Looking Glass's family when the soldiers attacked and though the teepee was on fire, she saved his rifle and later disassembled it and hid it in her pack. "I was glad to see my rifle. My parents had bought it for me with one good horse. I now had my own sixteen-shot rifle for the rest of the war."[94]

Spencer carbine (#18529) captured on Chadron Creek, Nebraska, on October 24, 1878. By then an obsolete weapon, it may have been purchased by a Cheyenne from a trader. (Courtesy: Rick Vargas, Smithsonian Institution, neg. #93-4874, Washington DC)

Between 1876 and 1879, German-born Otho Ernest Michaelis, a bespectacled captain of ordnance, served as an observer in the Department of Dakota. In an official 1879 report he wrote of the typical Indian's ability as a marksman. "The marksmanship ability of Indians is woefully exaggerated. A white man who can shoot at all is more than a match for them as a class. They do not use elevated sights and hence at long range their aiming is guess work."[95]

Virtually any discussion of the variety and type of firearms used by Native Americans in the later 1800s turns to the survey the army conducted of captured or surrendered Indian guns, its results appearing in the 1879 annual report of the chief of ordnance. The arms had come primarily from northern plains tribes, the Sioux and Cheyennes. In analyzing the list, one must consider probable Indian efforts made to hide some of the best weapons, such as revolvers firing metallic ammunition, as the absence of Colt Single Action .45s and military model Smith & Wessons indicates.

Of 284 shoulder arms tallied, 160 were muzzleloaders. Those by Henry Leman predominated (94) while other names included J. P. Lower (10), Samuel Hawken and J. Henry & Son (6 each), and Henry Folsom & Co. of St. Louis (4). Somewhat surprising was the presence on the list of only two Northwest trade guns. Breechloaders included 49 .45 and .50 Springfields, 23 Spencers, 13 Sharps, a dozen .44 Winchesters, and four .44 Henry rifles, plus an assortment of single-shot carbines by Warner, Joslyn, Wesson, Ballard, Remington, Starr, Gallagher, Merrill, and Smith.[96]

Many of these long arms would have been considered unserviceable by an ordnance officer, with broken or worn stocks, faulty lock mechanisms, and missing or crude replacement sights. But many of these weapons even when worn "could be used by so enterprising an enemy as the American Indian." Some of these captured arms eventually were placed with museums, but the military surplus goods dealer Francis Bannerman Sons in their 1907 catalog advertised former Indian guns for sale at the rather high price of $20.[97]

Handguns were just as varied as to make but of 125 listed, all but one converted Colt and a .50 Remington single-shot were percussion. Colts represented the largest number (72) along with 37 Remingtons. The remaining dozen included Whitneys, Starrs, and one each of Manhattan, Pettengill, and Savage manufacture. During a commission discussion prior to the Treaty of Medicine Lodge concerning the issue of firearms, the military made no serious objection to providing the Indians with revolvers, useful for hunting bison.[98]

Contrasting with the 1879 report was an observation by Lt. Britton Davis of a band of Apaches in Arizona four years later.

> The party was armed, as in fact were nearly all the hostiles in Mexico, with the latest models of Winchester magazine rifles, a better arm than the single-shot Springfield with which our soldiers and scouts were armed. The Indians obtained their arms from settlers and travelers they killed, or purchased them from white scoundrels who made a business of selling arms, ammunition, and whiskey to Indians.[99]

However when Geronimo and his small band surrendered to Gen. Nelson Miles in 1886, thirteen guns were confiscated, mostly Springfield "trapdoors" and Winchester Model 1873s. One of the latter reportedly was Geronimo's, a .44 carbine (#2101) which bears an "R.M." stamping on the upper tang, probably a former Mexican government weapon acquired by the Apaches during one of their frequent skirmishes south of the Rio Grande.[100]

Winchester-armed Choctaw Lighthorse Police photographed in 1893 at Antlers, Indian Territory. (Courtesy: Phillips Collection, University of Oklahoma Library, Norman)

GUNS OF THE INDIAN POLICE AND SCOUTS

Another group of Native American firearms includes those provided to Indians serving as police on reservations in the last three decades of the 1800s. William F. N. Arny in 1872 organized an effective mounted Navajo police force and young John P. Clum, appointed as agent to the San Carlos Apaches in 1874, recruited a similar Apache body. The success of these forces encouraged Congress on May 27, 1878, to authorize the establishment of the US Indian Police Force. By November, Indian police served on about a third of the reservations, although at an initial salary of only $5 per month. Their duties included driving out squatters and livestock thieves, halting bootlegging, guarding the distribution of government rations, and arresting local troublemakers. In some instances, their native heritage and blood ties may have conflicted with these new responsibilities. However in 1882, forty agencies throughout the west had police, with a combined strength of 84 commissioned officers and 764 noncommissioned officers and privates.[101]

Within Indian Territory, now eastern Oklahoma, the primary police agency among the Five Civilized Tribes was the "light horse." On occasion they administered punishment such as whipping at a post, and they sometimes carried out the death sentence for serious crimes.

> Two Seminole "Light Horsemen" shot the condemned with Winchesters, shooting at a small white mark pinned over the heart . . . if a man was shot and lived over it, he was free. . . . A light-horseman was pointed out to me who had been condemned. His friends bribed two officers detailed to shoot. One of them shot too high, hitting him through he shoulder. The other one only half cocked his gun and cut his finger to the bone trying to fire. They cussed him for negligence . . . but they knew . . . the other one missed purposely so they chased him out of the country.[102]

Three Colt Single Actions and at lower left a .44 percussion Remington (or conversion thereof) in the hands of members of the Choctaw Lighthorse Police in Indian Territory. (Courtesy: Archives & Manuscripts Division, Oklahoma Historical Society, Oklahoma City)

Legislation enabling the creation of Indian reservation police contained no provision for arming them and rifles for policemen sometimes were borrowed from nearby army units. In one instance, a Mescalero Apache chief of police purchased ammunition for his men with his own money. In 1883 the US Interior Department purchased 639 nickel-plated Remington Model 1875 revolvers with a 7 1/2-inch barrel for use by Indian police. Examples of these single action handguns appear in photos taken at various reservations.[103]

In addition to these Remingtons was a batch of seventy-five Colt Single Action .45s with 5 1/2-inch barrels and blued finish ordered and delivered to the Pine Ridge Agency, South Dakota, in 1899. On April 8, Pine Ridge acting Indian agent Maj. W. H. Clapp wrote to the commissioner of Indian affairs and requested approval to replace the Remingtons which by now were "worn out and practically worthless." He noted that only a few days before, a policeman had been shot dead while attempting to arrest a man who knew the officer's gun to be out of repair. Clapp had received a quote from Colt for .38 double action revolvers at $12 each or the Single Action .45s at $10. He recommended the latter as being less expensive and less complicated. In a remarkably prompt government procurement action, the acting commissioner approved the request and the guns were shipped to government warehouse in New York City on May 26. Although government-purchased arms, these Colt .45s were pulled from Colt's inventory of civilian guns and were not US-marked. A recent Colt factory letter verifying gun #186399 confirmed

Sion Lewis, The Choctaw that was
Executed at Wilburton, I. T.
November 5th 1894.

Execution of Silan Lewis, a Choctaw convicted of murder, at Wilburton, Indian Territory, on November 4, 1894. As the Minnetonta (Minnesota) *News* reported the incident, Lewis was blindfolded, he knelt, and two men held his arms. Sheriff Pursely painted a cross just below his left nipple, then stepped back five paces and fired his Winchester. Although the body was spurting blood, Lewis lived for three minutes as the lawman held the dying man's nose and mouth shut to complete the execution. Perhaps the man at left with a '73 Winchester is Sheriff Pursely. (Courtesy: Archives & Manuscripts Division, Oklahoma Historical Society, Oklahoma City)

these features, indicated it was a blued .45 with a 5 1/2-inch barrel, sold to the "U.S. Government c/o U.S. Indian Agent" on May 26, 1899, and was one of seventy-five guns in the shipment.[104]

Also occasionally seen in photos of Indian police are examples of the Remington-Keene bolt action .45–70 magazine rifle. Although a contract hasn't been found yet, it's thought that five hundred of these went to the US Interior Department in 1880–81, stamped "U.S.I.D." on the left side of the frame. Apparently these guns weren't particularly popular and extractors caused some problems.[105]

Other Native Americans in government service were those who served as scouts, trackers, and auxiliaries—"wolves" in Plains Indian sign language. Some commanders had employed Indians before the Civil War, including Col. E. V. "Bull" Sumner's use of Delawares and Pawnees during his lst Cavalry's 1857 campaign against the Cheyennes. Even earlier, in 1839 Col. John Moore of the Texas Rangers led a force of sixty-three whites and sixteen Lipan Apaches in an attack on a Comanche camp. Use of Tonkawas, Nez Perces, Kickapoos, Crows, Winnebagoes, and members of other tribes persisted intermittently when the need for their skills arose. Two of the five companies of newly organized Arizona territorial militia in 1865–66 were composed of Native Americans—Company B of Maricopas and Company C of Pimas.[106]

Pvt. Hervey Johnson served in Dakota Territory with the 11th Ohio Volunteer Cavalry and in early 1866 mentioned one scout's bravery in a letter home.

"Little priest," and his squaw are now
attached to our company for messes. They

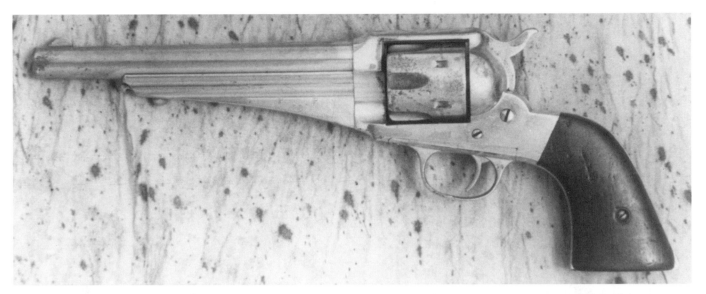

Nickel-plated Remington Model 1875 issued to Pine Ridge Indian Police and stamped "PR 36." (Courtesy: William Smith via Don Ware)

Nez Perce Reservation police photographed about 1885 at Salmon, Idaho. Three M1875 Remingtons are visible. The scratch across the face of two of the men may have been the result of an Indian custom indicating they later had "gone bad." (Courtesy: Phil Spangenberger)

are on their way from Fort Conner to the states on furlough. Priest is the chief of the Omaha scouts, a company of Indian soldiers who have been carrying mail across from [Fort] Laramie to Powder river. He was granted a furlough for distinguished bravery in a fight he had with the arappa-hoes [sic], where he fought one hundred indians alone. He had a Henry rifle (sixteen shooter). His clothes are full of bullet holes. He was not hurt himself.[107]

On July 28, 1866, Congress authorized the army to establish a corps of up to one thousand Indian scouts, to

Indian police at the Red Rock Otoe Reservation in Indian Territory (1894). All the long guns are .45–70 bolt action Remington-Keenes. (Courtesy: John J. Hays)

Remington-Keene–marked "U.S.I.D. 211" issued to "Fool's Bear," identified as a former Custer scout. (Courtesy: Roswell Art and Museum Center, NM)

receive the pay and allowances of cavalrymen. They could be discharged whenever the need for their services was over or at the discretion of the local department commander. Since the scouts were counted against the army's already insufficient total authorized enlisted strength, their numbers usually were far below the allowable maximum. For service during Gen. George Crook's 1872–73 winter cam-

paign in Apache country, Crook recommended ten Apache scouts for the Medal of Honor. A skeptical War Department rejected his recommendations, but he persisted and eventually prevailed.[108]

In Oregon to counter hostile Paiutes, two companies of scouts soon were enlisted under the new law of 1866, Warm Springs and Snakes. The former received up-to-date

Warm Springs Indian scouts during the Modoc War, armed with both Spencer and Sharps .50 carbines.
(Courtesy: Henry E. Huntington Library and Art Gallery, San Marino, CA)

Cheyenne and Arapaho scouts at Fort Reno, Indian Territory, with .45 Springfield "trapdoor" carbines.
(Courtesy: Archives & Manuscripts Division, Oklahoma Historical Society, Oklahoma City)

Apache scouts in uniform at San Carlos with Springfield carbines. (Courtesy: Arizona Historical Society, AHS #49,684, Tucson)

When taking to the field, Apache scouts such as these often replaced their uniforms with informal dress. (Courtesy: Smithsonian Institution, neg. #2494-A-2 [R], Washington DC)

Spencer carbines, while the latter had to be content with Harpers Ferry muskets, perhaps Model 1842s. In 1873 when Tonkawa scouts at Fort Griffin, Texas, were directed to exchange their Spencer repeaters for single-shot Sharps, they objected and even offered to purchase Winchester repeaters at their own expense if the army would provide the ammunition. They retained their Spencers.[109]

Among the most effective Indian scouts were those recruited by Maj. Zenas Bliss in 1870 from among descendants of Seminole Indians and escaped slaves. In 1873 Lt. John Bullis of the African American 24th Infantry took command. Sgt. Jacob Wilks, himself a former slave, served with the 116th US Infantry (Colored) during the Civil War and then enlisted in the 9th Cavalry. He had high praise for Bullis's men.

> Bullis' scouts were all Negroes from Mexico. A number of them were ex-slaves who before and during the war, had run off from their masters in Texas and got into Mexico, while most of them were sons of Negro parents who had been adopted into the tribe of Seminole Indians in Florida and went with a branch of that tribe into Mexico when driven from Florida [actually Indian Territory]. Many of these were part Indian. They all spoke Spanish; only a few of them, the Texas ex-slaves, spoke any English, and were considered to be the best body of scouts, trailers, and Indian fighters . . . in the Government service along the border. Their efficiency was due wholly to the skill and military genius of Lieutenant Bullis.[110]

During the eight years Bullis commanded them, they fought on both sides of the border and during twenty-eight expeditions in a dozen battles didn't lose a single scout in combat. They never numbered more than a half hundred at one time, but the scouts received four Medals of Honor. Three earned it in 1875 when they rescued Bullis after he was unhorsed while battling Kiowas and Comanches. In one remarkable demonstration of their tracking skills, Bullis and thirty-nine scouts trailed Mescalero Apache warriors for thirty-four days over 1,260 miles. The scouts were a highly effective mobile striking force, yet their families endured racial discrimination and government indifference to their request for reservation lands. The last sixteen Seminole scouts were mustered out of service in August 1912.[111]

Defense of the survey and track laying crews extending the Union Pacific rails west in the late 1860s was one of many operations performed by a battalion of Pawnee scouts led by their beloved Maj. Frank North (officially a civilian scout) with his brother Capt. Luther North as one of the company commanders. The first scouts were mustered in in January 1865 and armed with muzzleloaders, imported Enfield .577 rifle muskets if studio photos of the scouts can be relied upon. Two of the four companies received Spencer carbines just before the 1867 summer season. During the issue of these Spencers at Fort Sedgwick, Colorado, Capt. North examined them with care, test loading each one. Gen. Emery was present and questioned why North rejected some of the carbines, then took one of the guns in which a cartridge had stuck partway into the chamber.

> He took hold of the lever and gave it a quick jerk and the breechblock struck the rimfire cartridge with so much force that it exploded and the whole charge of powder blew out into his face. Fortunately he was wearing glasses and they saved his eyes, but the blood spurted from his face in streams. He had nothing further to say and left the scouts to select their own guns.[112]

The scouts soon put their Spencers to good use. In August, ten Pawnees under Lt. Isaac Davis were sent to the scene of a train derailed by torn up tracks near Plum Creek on the Platte River, but they retreated in the face of an overwhelming force. Maj. North and Capt. James Murie with thirty-some more scouts came to their aid. Newspaperman Henry M. Stanley of African fame described the scene.

> Music [Murie] formed his men in line, crossed a bridge and advanced upon them—carbines ready. The Cheyennes, one hundred in number, on seeing the Pawnees approach, gave a loud whoop, and discharged a perfect cloud of arrows at the little band, who kept steadily advancing on the double trot. When they were within one hundred yards of each other Music [Murie] gave the order to charge, which the Pawnees gallantly obeyed, using their Spencer rifles with terrible execution.[113]

On one occasion, Capt. Luther North demonstrated the precept that the appearance of a good defense

Frank Po_?, packer and chief of scouts, holds a Winchester M1873 rifle while posing with several of his Apache scouts and their Springfield carbines. (Courtesy: National Archives, neg. #111-SC-83732)

sometimes forestalled an attack by hostile Indians. In June 1870 he nearly drowned in the Niobrara River and two days later lost his gun. He became separated from the six cowboys with whom he was traveling and suddenly six Sioux dashed upon him out of the brush.

> My horse being about played out, I was afoot and it was nearly dark. Seeing a stick of wood about six feet long, I picked it out of the grass, and as the Indians came near enough, I dropped down upon a knee and pointed the stick at them. Thinking it was a gun, they scattered and turned back. I shouldered the stick and walked up the river in the direction the boys had gone; but each of several times the Indians charged, I knelt down as if to shoot. It was now quite dark, and coming to a point where they could see the cowboys starting [a] campfire, they took a couple of shots at me and rode off. I climbed on my horse, used the wooden "gun" to get a little more speed out of him and safely made the camp.[114]

In 1868 in Colorado, a farmer employed a similar ruse. "Dieterman's sister and daughter ran to where the German was working in a field near by. He stood off the Indians by pointing the handle of his hoe in their direction, making them believe it was a gun, and, in that way, covered [their] retreat to a neighbor's house."[115]

While serving with the 7th Cavalry in Kansas in '71, Sgt. John Ryan was a half mile away from camp attempting to capture a prairie dog, armed with nothing more than a spade and bucket. Shouts drew his attention to several comrades running toward him from camp with rifles in hand.

> I looked toward the bluffs... and saw about a dozen Indian warriors [riding] into plain view.... The men in camp had seen my predicament before I did, and immediately took steps to protect me. Quick as a flash I dropped to one knee and drew my spade up in front of me, as if I had a rifle and was going to fire, using knee and elbow for a rest. Suddenly these Indians came to a standstill.... I dropped my spade and made tracks toward camp; as fast as my legs would carry me.[116]

The Pawnee scouts in 1876 exhibited a surprising example of assimilation of white culture. While stationed at Sidney Barracks in Nebraska they organized a baseball team to play the white soldiers, often losing to the regulars, however. The scouts were mustered out for the last time the next year after a dozen years of intermittent service. One of the North family's prized possessions was a personal letter to Frank North from Gen. George Crook in which he praised the scouts' "soldier-like conduct and discipline" and calling it eloquent testimony to North's fitness as their commanding officer.[117]

Despite the invaluable assistance Indian auxiliaries often provided as scouts, trailers, intermediaries in surrender negotiations, or as fighters, not all commanders appreciated their services or trusted their reliability. When campaigning against the Chiricahua Apaches in the 1880s, Crook came under strong criticism from some for arming and employing Apache scouts. But as he explained to a correspondent with the Los Angeles *Times*:

> To polish a diamond there is nothing like its own dust. It is the same with these fellows [hostile Indians].... They don't fear the white soldiers... but put upon their trail an enemy of their own blood, an enemy as tireless, as foxy, and as stealthy and familiar with the country as they themselves, and it breaks them all up. The invention of the breech-loading gun and the metallic cartridge has entirely transformed the methods and the nature of Indian warfare.... They... now have the best makes of breech-loading guns and revolvers.... [The Chiricahua] knows every foot of his territory, and can live through fatigue, lack of food and of water which would kill the hardiest white mountaineer.[118]

Capt. John G. Bourke, aide to Gen. Crook, spent more than fifteen years on almost continuous duty in the west. At first he was a brash young 1869 West Point graduate, but he developed an absorbing intellectual interest in Native American culture and made voluminous field notes of his careful observations. He came to be called "Ink Man" by the Sioux and "Paper Medicine Man" by the Apaches and wrote extensively as he achieved a reputation as a leading Indian ethnologist. However his outspoken advocacy of Indian rights hampered his military career.

Crook began his spring 1883 campaign against hostile Chiricahuas in the Sierra Madre with almost one hundred Apache scouts from the San Carlos Reservation. Until 1890, Indian scouts were often clothed in obsolete uniform items. In that year, the War Department authorized a specific uniform for scouts which included a black felt fatigue hat decorated with a red and white cord. Bourke noted that issue uniform items often were reserved for ceremonial occasions and described those scouts in the 1883 campaign as wearing a calico shirt or army blouse and cotton drawers. If anticipating battle, they stripped to loincloths and moccasins and a scarlet headband to identify them as friendly. They were equipped with army Springfields and a waist belt holding forty cartridges and most carried a large knife, a canteen, an awl in a leather case to repair moccasins, tweezers to pluck their facial hair, and an identification tag. Again quoting Bourke, "knowing from past experience how important [his weapons] are for his preservation, [the scout] takes much better care of them than does the white soldier out of garrison."[119]

A brutal example of governmental perfidy was the treatment afforded sixty-five Chiricahua Apaches who had served faithfully as army scouts. After Geronimo's surrender, they were sent into exile to Florida along with the hostile warriors despite protests by some officers.

One other group of Native Americas who wore army blue resulted from the establishment of all-Indian units, Troop L of the first eight cavalry regiments and Company I of the 19th Infantry. This experimental effort began in July 1890, but eventually was deemed a failure, due in part to cultural differences. The last unit, Troop L of the 7th Cavalry, was inactivated in June 1897.[120]

"Wolf Voice and friend 1877 U.S. Army scouts" is the marking on the back of this cabinet card. The guns are a Spencer carbine (left) and M1873 Winchester.

Lt. Kislingbury of the 11th Infantry with Indian scouts at the Standing Rock Agency at Fort Yates, Dakota Territory, in 1877. He died in 1884 while on an expedition to the Arctic. Identifiable guns are all Springfield "trapdoors" except for two Winchesters (fourth from left and far right). (Courtesy: Minnesota Historical Society, neg. #36834)

A CAVEAT EMPTOR

The interest in Native American firearms among today's collectors warrants a word of warning. Many such weapons on the market are illegitimate, the recent handiwork of unscrupulous individuals anxious to increase the value of an already well-used gun. Some such attempts are so amateurish as to be laughable and are easily seen as what they are. Others are far more difficult to recognize. The addition of brass tacks is a common procedure, although many genuine Indian guns were never decorated in that manner. "Brass" tacks made today often are actually iron with a light plating. Whites and Native Americans alike found that wet rawhide tightly wrapped and sewn around a break in a gun stock produced a strong and durable repair when it dried and shrank. A few fakers today are quite skilled in attempting to duplicate the age, dirt, and wear that a legitimate nineteenth-century rawhide repair should exhibit. There is no easy guide to recognize a genuine Indian gun but when one is found, worn and battered though it often may be, it should be treasured as a relic of our nation's material culture, left in its original but honorable state.

The great danger of the future is not from
the red man's want of faith as much as
the indifference of our Government
to the plainest requirements of honor.
— Lt. John G. Bourke, 1877[121]

There are many humorous things in the world;
among them the white man's notion that he
is less savage than the other savages.
— Mark Twain, 1897

APPENDIX A

Opportunities to View Antique Firearms

There are numerous museums that exhibit guns of the type used in the nineteenth-century American west. I undoubtedly have overlooked many but listed here are some that have or are thought to have at least modest exhibitions of antique firearms. Before visiting, one must remember that exhibits change and galleries may be closed for renovation so one should contact the museum in advance to determine the current status and scope of any firearms exhibitions. Some museums have extensive collections but with many of the weapons in storage. Such museums sometimes are willing to make specimens in their study collections in storage available to serious researchers. Many of the museums listed also have informative web sites which can be accessed by entering the name of the museum in a search engine.

ARIZONA STATE MUSEUM, Tucson

BUFFALO BILL HISTORICAL CENTER,
Cody, Wyoming (A complex of museums of western art, firearms, and Native American culture.)

C. M. RUSSELL MUSEUM, Great Falls, Montana (Features Browning family collection as well as varied examples of eighteenth- and nineteenth-century firearms including a number of British double rifles.)

CHICKAMAUGA-CHATTANOOGA NATIONAL MILITARY PARK, Fort Oglethorpe, Georgia (Exhibits Claude Fuller collection of US martial arms.)

COLORADO HISTORICAL SOCIETY, Denver (Large collection although much of it in storage.)

COLORADO SPRINGS PIONEERS MUSEUM

CONNECTICUT STATE LIBRARY MUSEUM OF CONNECTICUT HISTORY, Hartford (Extensive Colt collection.)

DAUGHTERS OF UTAH PIONEERS MEMORIAL MUSEUM, Salt Lake City

FRAZIER HISTORICAL ARMS MUSEUM, Louisville, Kentucky

GENE AUTRY MUSEUM OF WESTERN HERITAGE, Los Angeles, California (Exhibits many historic guns once owned by individuals well-known in western history such as outlaw Frank James and others.)

J. M. DAVIS ARMS MUSEUM, Claremore, Oklahoma (Extensive and eclectic collection of guns in varying states of preservation.)

JIM GATCHELL MUSEUM, Buffalo, Wyoming (Closed in winter.)

GETTYSBURG NATIONAL MILITARY PARK, Gettysburg, Pennsylvania (National Park Service museum exhibits an outstanding collection of Civil War–era martial arms, both Union and Confederate.)

KANSAS MUSEUM OF HISTORY, Topeka

KENTUCKY MILITARY HISTORY MUSEUM, Frankfort

MISSOURI HISTORICAL SOCIETY, St. Louis

MISSOURI STATE MUSEUM, Jefferson City

MONTANA HISTORICAL SOCIETY, Helena

MUSEUM OF NEBRASKA HISTORY, Lincoln (Large collection in storage, only a portion on exhibition.)

MUSEUM OF THE FUR TRADE, Chadron, Nebraska (Closed in winter but exhibits an outstanding array of artifacts related to the fur trade, including Northwest trade guns and others. A "must see" for anyone interested in that aspect of frontier history.)

NATIONAL COWBOY HALL OF FAME AND WESTERN HERITAGE CENTER, Oklahoma City

NATIONAL FIREARMS MUSEUM, Fairfax, Virginia (Extensive National Rifle Association museum of both antique and modern arms.)

NATURAL HISTORY MUSEUM OF LOS ANGELES COUNTY, California

NEVADA STATE MUSEUM, Carson City

PALACE OF THE GOVERNORS, Santa Fe, New Mexico

PANHANDLE-PLAINS HISTORICAL MUSEUM, Canyon, Texas

REMINGTON ARMS COMPANY MUSEUM, Ilion, New York (Open only in summer but displays examples of most models of guns made in the firm's 189-year history.)

ROCK ISLAND ARSENAL MUSEUM, Illinois (Collection includes many arms surrendered by Native Americans.)

ROSWELL MUSEUM AND ART CENTER, New Mexico (Excellent exhibit of firearms as well as Native American artifacts.)

SAUNDERS MEMORIAL MUSEUM, Berryville, Arkansas (May be seasonal.)

SMITH & WESSON MUSEUM, Springfield, Massachusetts (Changing exhibits at S&W Shooting Sports Center, which sometimes include examples of pre-1900 S&W arms.)

SPRINGFIELD ARMORY NATIONAL HISTORIC SITE, Massachusetts (Major exhibit of US military arms.)

TEXAS A&M UNIVERSITY MUSEUM, College Station

TEXAS RANGER HALL OF FAME AND MUSEUM, Waco

US CAVALRY MUSEUM, Fort Riley, Kansas

UNION PACIFIC HISTORICAL MUSEUM, Omaha, Nebraska (Significant collection in storage but check for current status of exhibit before visiting.)

WEST POINT MUSEUM, West Point, New York

WOOLAROC MUSEUM, Bartlesville, Oklahoma (Features famed Phillips collection of Colts including numerous Patersons.)

WYOMING STATE MUSEUM, Cheyenne

Also, some arms collectors' associations offer a substantial number of excellent exhibits by members in addition to the hundreds of dealers' tables of merchandise for sale at their occasional weekend meetings. Many are open only to members and guests but among the foremost, which are available to the public for an admission fee, are the Maryland Antique Arms Collectors Association annual gathering in March in Baltimore and the May yearly meeting in Denver of the Colorado Gun Collectors Association.

Chronology

1798	Eli Whitney receives government contract for muskets and introduces partial interchangeability of parts.
1803	United States purchases Louisiana Territory from France for $15 million, doubling the size of the country.
1804–6	Lewis and Clark lead Corps of Discovery to Pacific Ocean and back.
1806	Lt. Zebulon Pike discovers what became known as Pike's Peak.
1808	Manuel Lisa establishes Missouri Fur Company.
1811	John H. Hall receives patent for breech loading gun design. Army contracts in 1817 for its first Hall rifles, which underwent field testing in the west.
1819	First paddlewheel steamer begins operation on Missouri River.
1820	Missouri Compromise prohibits slavery north of 36 degrees, 30 minutes. Maj. Stephen Long leads an army exploration to the eastern Colorado Rockies and characterizes the Great Plains as the "Great American Desert."
1821	Mexico gains its independence from Spain. William Becknell pioneers the Santa Fe Trail as a trade route from Missouri.

1822	William H. Ashley and Andrew Henry establish Rocky Mountain Fur Company. Joshua Shaw receives US patent on percussion cap, already in use in Great Britain as early as 1816.
1824	Jedediah Smith discovers South Pass through the Rockies.
1825	William Astor's American Fur Company begins purchasing rifles from John Joseph Henry of Nazareth, Pennsylvania, about this time. First annual fur trade rendezvous takes place. Brothers and gun makers Jacob and Samuel Hawken form a partnership in St. Louis.
1832	Nathaniel Wyeth party travels to Pacific Coast over what became the Oregon Trail, from Independence, Missouri, to Fort Vancouver, Washington. Congress declares all territory west of the Mississippi as Indian country.
1833	Army establishes first US Dragoon regiment of mounted troops.
1834	United States establishes Indian Territory in present-day Oklahoma, Kansas, and Nebraska. About half of this territory is abolished in 1854 to accommodate white settlers.
1836	Battle of the Alamo in San Antonio, Texas.

1837   Allen pepperbox pistols appear, the first American double action revolving firearms. Production of Colt firearms begins in Paterson, New Jersey, but ceases in 1842.

1840   Final fur trade rendezvous as trade shifts from beaver pelts to bison hides.

1842   Army adopts what would be its first percussion and its last smoothbore musket.

1843   Improved conditions on Oregon Trail allow travel the entire way by wagon.

1843–45   Capt. John C. Fremont leads three western exploring trips.

1844   Samuel F. B. Morse invents the telegraph.

1845   The United States annexes Republic of Texas. Dentist Edward Maynard patents a tape priming device for firearms.

1846–48   War with Mexico.

1847   Mormons led by Brigham Young reach the Great Salt Lake.
United States orders one thousand improved Colt revolvers, putting Sam Colt back in gun business.

1848   Gold is discovered in California.
Christian Sharps patents a breech loading rifle design.

1852   Wells, Fargo & Co. is established.

1854   Kansas-Nebraska Act opens that area to settlement; slavery question leads to violence.

1855   Army adopts new series of .58 caliber hand and shoulder arms using Maynard primer.
Rollin White patents revolver with a rear-loading rotating cylinder and licenses the patent to partners Horace Smith and Daniel B. Wesson.

1857   First Smith & Wesson revolver appears, a diminutive seven-shot .22.

1859   First major silver strike in the west, the Comstock Lode in Nevada.
Rush to gold fields in Colorado Rockies. "Pike's Peak Or Bust" becomes a slogan.

1860–61   Pony Express operates between St. Joseph, Missouri, and Sacramento, California.

1861   Transcontinental telegraph line is completed, making Pony Express obsolete.

1861–65   The Civil War.

1862   Confederate forces under Gen. H. H. Sibley are victorious at Valverde, New Mexico, but campaign later fails, leaving southwest in Union hands.
Homestead Act passes accelerating settlement of the west with offer of free land.
Sioux uprising in Minnesota.
Army receives its first seven-shot repeating Spencer rifles in December.
Henry .44 repeating rifles reach the market.

1864   Colorado volunteers massacre Native Americans at Sand Creek.

1865   Springfield Armory begins conversion of rifle muskets to breechloaders using system designed by Erskine Allin.

1866   Post–Civil War cattle drives begin from Texas.
James gang carries out its first robbery, at Liberty, Missouri.
Eighty men under Capt. William Fetterman are wiped out by Sioux on Bozeman Trail.
First repeating rifle to bear Winchester name appears.

1867   Armed with new breech loading Springfield .50 rifles, small bands of soldiers withstand attacks by large Sioux forces in Hayfield and Wagonbox fights.
United States purchases Alaska for $7 million, a move ridiculed by many.

1868   Custer's 7th Cavalry attacks Native Americans on the Washita River in present-day Oklahoma.
Battle of Beecher's Island, Colorado Territory, in which army scouts armed primarily with Spencers withstand repeated attacks.

1869   Nation's first transcontinental railroad completed.
        One-armed Maj. John Wesley Powell explores Colorado River and Grand Canyon.
        Women's suffrage act passed in Wyoming Territory.
        Rollin White patent on rear-loading revolvers expires.

1870   Smith & Wesson begins production of its first large-caliber revolver, the .44 Model 3, later known as the American.
        Commercial hunt for bison hides begins in earnest. By 1895, fewer than one thousand free roaming bison remained, although they once numbered in the millions.

1871   Indian Appropriations Act decrees federal government no longer will negotiate treaties with individual tribes.

1872   Yellowstone National Park is established.

1873   Joseph Glidden patents barbed wire.
        Colt introduces famed Single Action Army revolver, producing almost two hundred thousand by 1900.
        Winchester introduces an improved version of its Model 1866 rifle.
        Army adopts .45 caliber "trapdoor" Springfield, its primary shoulder arm for the next two decades.

1875   "Hanging Judge" Isaac Parker assumes his duties at Fort Smith, Arkansas.
        Silver is discovered at Leadville, Colorado.

1876   Custer's 7th Cavalry defeated at Battle of the Little Bighorn.
        James B. "Wild Bill" Hickok shot to death in Deadwood, Dakota Territory.

1878   Lincoln County War in New Mexico Territory, notable because of Billy the Kid's involvement.
        Colt Single Action Army revolver becomes available in .44–40 caliber, same cartridge used in Winchester's popular Model 1873 rifle.

1879   John M. Browning patents a dropping-block rifle action, which he sells to Winchester. Later Browning patents are incorporated in various Winchester rifle and shotgun models.

1881   Pat Garrett kills Billy the Kid.
        Gunfight near O. K. Corral, Tombstone, Arizona Territory.

1882   William F. "Buffalo Bill" Cody presents his first wild west show.
        Bob Ford murders Jesse James.

1883   Southern Pacific and Northern Pacific railroads are completed.

1886   Apache leader Geronimo surrenders for final time.

1886–87 Severe winter kills tens of thousands of cattle on northern plains.

1889   Oklahoma land rush; Guthrie becomes a town in one day.

1890   Battle of Wounded Knee, last major engagement of the Indian wars.
        Bureau of Census declares there is no more "free land" and frontier is closed.

1891   Colorado gold and silver rush at Cripple Creek.

1892   Army begins issuing Colt .38 double action revolvers, replacements for the .45 Colt Single Action.

1894   Army begins to replace .45 "trapdoor" Springfield with new .30 Krag-Jorgensen, a smokeless powder small-caliber repeating rifle.

1898   The Spanish-American War.

NOTES

CHAPTER ONE

1. David A. White, ed., *News of the Plains and Rockies 1803–1865* (Spokane WA, 1996), 1:123.
2. Ibid., 129.
3. Ibid., 124–29. Richard M. Clokey, *William H. Ashley— Enterprise and Politics in the Trans-Mississippi West* (Norman OK, 1980), 88–89.
4. Cecil Dryden, *Up the Columbia for Furs* (Caldwell ID, 1949), 43.
5. M. Catherine White, ed., *David Thompson's Journals Relating to Montana and Adjacent Regions 1808–1812* (Missoula MT, 1950), 148–49. Hiram Martin Chittenden, *The American Fur Trade of the Far West* (Stanford CA, 1954), 2:929.
6. *Museum of the Fur Trade Quarterly* (Spring 2003): 1.
7. Charles E. Hanson Jr., *The Plains Rifle* (Harrisburg PA, 1960), 6.
8. Charles E. Hanson Jr., "Trade Goods for Rendezvous," in *The Book of Buckskinning*, ed. William H. Scurlock, 5:70 (Texarkana TX, 1989).
9. White, *News of the Plains*, 1:367. Dale L. Morgan and Eleanor Towles Harris, eds., *The Rocky Mountain Journals of William Marshall Andrews* (San Morino CA, 1967), 71.
10. Charles E. Hanson Jr., *The Hawken Rifle, Its Place in History* (Chadron NE, 1979), 20, 29.
11. Ibid., 32–33.
12. Jack B. Tykal, "Etienne Provost and the Hawken Rifle," *Museum of the Fur Trade Quarterly* (Summer 1983): 2. Charles L. Camp, ed., *James Clyman, Frontiersman* (Portland OR, 1960), 316.
13. Hanson, *The Hawken Rifle*, 41. LeRoy R. Hafen, ed., *Pike's Peak Gold Rush Guidebooks of 1859*, vol. 9, *Southwest Historical Series* (Philadelphia PA, 1974), 168–69.
14. W. T. Hamilton, *My Sixty Years on the Plains* (Norman OK, 1960), 72. Dee Brown, *The Galvanized Yankees* (Lincoln NE, 1963), 202. John E. Parsons, *The First Winchester* (New York, 1955), 69.
15. A. C. Gould, *Modern American Rifles* (Boston MA, 1892), 40–41.
16. Elliott Coues, ed., *The Journal of Jacob Fowler* (Lincoln NE, 1970), 48.
17. Hanson, *The Hawken Rifle*, 23–24, 79. Hanson, "Trade Goods for Rendezvous," 79. James A. Hanson, "Percussion Fur Trade Guns," *Museum of the Fur Trade Quarterly* (Summer 2003): 7. Osborne Russell, *Journal of a Trapper* (Lincoln NE, 1955), 66. Hanson, *The Plains Rifle*, 76. Lawrence P. Shelton, *California Gunsmiths 1846–1900* (Fair Oaks CA, 1977), 215.
18. Granville Stuart, *Forty Years on the Frontier* (Cleveland OH, 1925), 1:33.
19. Russell, *Journal of a Trapper*, 66. George Wilkins Kendall, *Narrative of the Texan Santa Fe Expedition* (New York, 1850), 1:34, 52, 54.
20. Robert W. Frazer, ed., *Over the Chihuahua and Santa Fe Trails 1847–1848, George Rutledge Gibson's Journal* (Albuquerque NM, 1981), 66, 72.
21. Kendall, *Narrative*, 1:22, 190. Fayette Copeland, *Kendall of the Picayune* (Norman OK, 1943), 51–52.
22. Briton Cooper Busch, ed., *Alta California 1840–1842, The Journal and Observations of William Dane Phelps* (Glendale CA, 1983), 277. Josiah Gregg, *Commerce of the Prairies*, (Norman OK, 1954), 325
23. Hanson, *The Hawken Rifle*, 76–80.
24. Mike Stamm, *Horse Mule Grizzly Indian Buffalo Wrecks of the Frontier West* (Battle Mountain NV, 1997), 8.
25. Rufus B. Sage, *Rocky Mountain Life* (Lincoln NE, 1982), 38.
26. LeRoy R. Haven and Ann W. Haven, eds., *Rufus B. Sage His Letters and Papers 1836–1847* (Glendale CA, 1956), 2:210–11.
27. James Josiah Webb, *Adventures in the Santa Fe Trade 1844–1847* (Philadelphia PA, 1974), 116–17.
28. Exhibit caption, Missouri State Capitol, Springfield.
29. F. A. Wislizenus, *A Journey to the Rocky Mountains in the Year 1839* (St. Louis MO, 1912), 122–23.
30. Hamilton, *My Sixty Years*, 108.
31. Ibid., 30, 80. Frederick Law Olmsted, *A Journey Through Texas* (Austin TX, 1978), 74.
32. Louis A. Garavaglia and Charles G. Worman, *Firearms of the American West 1803–1865* (Albuquerque NM, 1984), 69. Jeff Long, *Duel of Eagles* (New York, 1990), 195, 379.
33. Hanson, *The Hawken Rifle*, 74, 76.
34. Webb, *Adventures*, 73.
35. Charles E. Hanson Jr., "Smoothbores on the Frontier," in *The Book of Buckskinning*, ed. William H. Scurlock, 4:124 (Texarkana TX, 1987). Charles E. Hanson Jr., "The Guns," in *The Book of Buckskinning*, ed. William H. Scurlock, 91 (Texarkana TX, 1981).
36. Dryden, *Up the Columbia*, 58.

37. Reuben Gold Thwaites, ed., *Early Western Travels 1748–1846* (New York, 1966), 6:97. Howard Louis Conard, *"Uncle Dick" Wootton* (Chicago IL, 1890), 55.
38. Dryden, *Up the Columbia*, 66. Osborne Russell, *Journal of a Trapper*, 17.
39. Hanson, *The Hawken Rifle*, 74–77.
40. Ibid., 74, 79. Norm Flayderman, *Flayderman's Guide to Antique American Firearms and Their Values*, 8th ed. (Iola WI, 2001), 338.
41. Washington Irving, *A Tour on the Prairies*, ed. John Francis McDermott (Norman OK, 1956), 93.
42. Charles Hanson Jr., "The Deringer Belt Pistol," *Museum of the Fur Trade Quarterly* (Winter 1982): 18–20.
43. *Contributions to the Historical Society of Montana* 3 (1900): 40, 47, 110.
44. Ibid., 18–19. John D. Duval, *The Adventures of Big-Foot Wallace* (Philadelphia PA, 1871), 16.
45. Kendall, *Narrative*, 1:237–38.
46. Hamilton, *My Sixty Years*, 7, 80.
47. Olmsted, *A Journey Through Texas*, 307–8.
48. *Museum of the Fur Trade Quarterly* (Summer 1987): 13–14.
49. Sage, *Rocky Mountain Life*, 50.
50. White, *News of the Plains*, 1:249, 255.
51. Lewis H. Garrard, *Wah-To-Yah and the Taos Trail* (Philadelphia PA, 1974), 193, 216.
52. E. M. Phillips, "A Paper of Flints," *Museum of the Fur Trade Quarterly* (Fall 1980): 4–5.
53. Charles E. Hanson Jr., "Lead in the Fur Trade," *Museum of the Fur Trade Quarterly* (Fall 1978): 8.
54. Charles E. Hanson Jr., "The St. Louis Shot Tower," *Museum of the Fur Trade Quarterly* (Fall 1967): 2–5.
55. Hanson, "Lead in the Fur Trade," 5–10.
56. *Museum of the Fur Trade Quarterly* (Winter 2003): 17.
57. Charles E. Hanson Jr., "Commercial Powder Horns," *Museum of the Fur Trade Quarterly* (Spring 1981): 6–8.
58. Ibid., 8–9.
59. Ibid., 9.
60. Charles E. Hanson Jr., "The Wooden Powder Keg," *Museum of the Fur Trade Quarterly* (Winter 1968): 9.
61. Kingsley M. Bray, "The Oglala Lakota and the Establishment of Fort Laramie," *Museum of the Fur Trade Quarterly* (Winter 2000): 4.
62. Allen Chronister, "The Fall of Fort McKenzie," *Museum of the Fur Trade Quarterly* (Fall 2001): 9–14.

CHAPTER TWO

1. White, *News of the Plains*, 3:391.
2. Michael L. Tate, *The Frontier Army in the Settlement of the West* (Norman OK, 1999), 317.
3. Ibid., 33, 37, 62.
4. John D. McAulay, *Rifles of the U.S. Army 1861–1906* (Lincoln RI, 2003), 10–11.
5. Garavaglia and Worman, *Firearms . . . 1803–1865*, 8.
6. Ibid., 13.
7. Francois des Montaignes, *The Plains*, ed. Nancy Alpert Mower and Don Russell (Norman OK, 1972), 23.
8. *Museum of the Fur Trade Quarterly* (Summer 1980): 9–11. Hanson, *The Hawken Rifle*, 70–71.
9. Samuel E. Chamberlain, *My Confession* (New York, 1956), 188.
10. John Flynn, "Reminiscences of Some Incidents in the Career of a United States Dragoon Between the Years 1839 and 1844" (unpublished manuscript, US Military Academy Library, West Point NY).
11. Percival G. Lowe, *Five Years A Dragoon* (Norman OK, 1965), 107.
12. U. S. Grant, *Personal Memoirs of U. S. Grant* (New York, 1894), 61.
13. Bobby J. McKinney, "Excavated Military Relics of the Texas Revolution and the Republic of Texas, 1836–1846," *Military Collector & Historian* 61, no. 3 (Fall 1999): 116.
14. *Collections of the Kansas State Historical Society 1913–1914* (Topeka KS, 1915), 13:26–27.
15. August Santleben, *A Texas Pioneer*, ed. I. D. Affleck (New York, 1919), 9.
16. Lt. Col. C. F. Smith to Assistant Adjutant General of the Army, 18 July 1860.
17. Ibid.
18. Charles Kenner, "The Origins of the 'Goodnight' Trail Reconsidered," *Southwestern Historical Quarterly* (January 1974): 393.
19. House Executive Document 89, *Sale of Arms and Ordnance Stores*, 42nd Cong., 2nd sess., 1871, serial 1511, 5.
20. White, *News of the Plains*, 4:136. Durwood Ball, *Army Regulars on the Western Frontier 1848–1861* (Norman OK, 2001), 30.
21. By General Order No. 55 of August 8, 1861, the lst Dragoons were redesignated as the lst Cavalry, the 2nd Dragoons as the 2nd Cavalry, the Mounted Rifles as 3rd Cavalry, and the lst, 2nd, and 3rd Cavalry as the 4th, 5th, and 6th Cavalry, respectively. The 7th through 10th cavalry regiments were created by Presidential Order of July 28, 1866.
22. R. C. Kuhn, "Early United States Ordnance Department Correspondence," *Texas Gun Collector* (May 1955): 5–6.
23. James S. Hutchins, "Major Thornton Goes West!" *Man At Arms* (June 2001): 30.
24. Ibid., 31–32.
25. Col. H. R. Craig to Ordnance Office, Washington DC, 19 February 1853. Arrott Collection, US Military Academy Library, West Point NY.
26. Hutchins, "Major Thornton," 42.
27. White, *News of the Plains*, 3:376–77, 393.
28. Ibid., 391.
29. Harold D. Langley, ed., *To Utah with the Dragoons and Glimpses of Life in Arizona and California 1858–1859* (Salt Lake City UT, 1974), 129–30.
30. Joseph Mansfield, *Mansfield on the Condition of the Western Forts 1853–1854*, ed. Robert W. Frazer (Norman OK, 1963), 39–41.
31. Ibid., 65–66, 196.
32. Ibid., 224, 231.

33. Ibid., 67.
34. Langley, *To Utah with the Dragoons*, 72–73.
35. Max L. Heyman Jr., *Prudent Soldier: A Biography of Major General E. R. S. Canby 1817–1873* (Glendale CA, 1959), 97–98.
36. Douglas C. McChristian, *An Army of Marksmen* (Fort Collins CO, 1981), 18–19.
37. Quotation from exhibit caption at Fort Kearney State Historical Park, NE.
38. Samuel P. Heintzelman, *Fifty Miles and a Fight*, ed. Jerry Thompson (Austin TX, 1998), 201.
39. McAulay, *Rifles of the U.S. Army*, 100.
40. Ibid., 90. Lawrence Kip, *Army Life on the Pacific* (New York, 1974), 56–57, 59.
41. John Salmon Ford, *Rip Ford's Texas* (Austin TX, 1963), 243.
42. Capt. John M. Elkins, *Indian Fighting on the Texas Frontier* (Amarillo TX, 1929), 95–96.
43. Kuhn, "Early United States Ordnance Correspondence," 6–7.
44. John D. McAulay, *Civil War Carbines* (Lincoln RI, 1991), 2:122–25.
45. Jerry Thompson, ed., *Texas & New Mexico on the Eve of the Civil War* (Albuquerque NM, 2001), 42.
46. Ibid., 54, 144.
47. Ibid., 42, 46, 52.
48. Ibid., 58, 59.
49. McCauley, *Civil War Carbines*, 2:23.
50. Thompson, *Texas & New Mexico*, 63–64.
51. Ibid., 82.
52. Ibid., 113–14, 140.
53. Ibid., 166–67.
54. Ibid., 167–68.
55. Ibid., 178–79.
56. R. B. Marcy to Col. S. Colt, 4 Oct. 1857.
57. Ibid.
58. James Larson, *Sergeant Larson 4th Cavalry* (San Antonio TX, 1935), 53.
59. Ibid., 73.
60. Ibid., 96–97.
61. Parker I. Peirce, *Antelope Bill* (Minneapolis MN, 1962), 27.
62. McAulay, *Rifles of the U.S. Army*, 61. Jacob A. Swisher, *Iowa in Times of War* (Iowa City IA, 1943), 159. Fred B. Rogers, *Soldiers of the Overland* (San Francisco CA, 1938), 58–59.
63. Marshall McKusick, *The Iowa Northern Border Brigade* (Iowa City IA, 1975), 38.
64. Donald F. Danker, ed., *Man of the Plains: The Recollections of Luther North, 1856–1882* (Lincoln NE, 1961), 13.
65. William R. Dunn, *I Stand by Sand Creek* (Fort Collins CO, 1985), 21.
66. Morse H. Coffin, *The Battle of Sand Creek*, ed. Alan W. Farley (Waco TX, 1965), 7, 24.
67. Ibid., 9.
68. Charles H. Springer, "Campaign Against the Sioux Indians While Lieutenant Commanding Company B, 12th Missouri Volunteer Cavalry."

CHAPTER THREE

1. Don Worcester, ed., *Pioneer Trails West* (Caldwell ID, 1985), 146.
2. Lansford W. Hastings, *The Emigrant's Guide to Oregon and California* (Cincinnati OH, 1845), 5:575.
3. Robert A. Murray, "Treaty Presents at Fort Laramie, 1867–68," *Museum of the Fur Trade Quarterly* (Fall 1977): 4.
4. Mary McDougall Gordon, ed., *Overland to California with the Pioneer Line* (Stanford CA, 1983), i. Susan Badger Doyle, ed., *Journeys to the Land of Gold* (Helena MT, 2000), 1:19. Gerald F. Kreyche, *Visions of the American West* (Lexington KY, 1989), 185.
5. Lillian Schlissel, *Women's Diaries of the Westward Journey* (New York, 1982), 132.
6. Thomas A. Rumer, ed., *This Emigrating Company, The 1844 Oregon Trail Journal of Jacob Hunter* (Spokane WA, 1990), 257.
7. Schklissel, *Women's Diaries*, 168. Webster, *Pioneer Trails West*, 146. Charles Ross Parke, *Dreams to Dust, A Diary of the California Gold Rush, 1849–1850*, ed. James E. Davis (Lincoln NE, 1989), 2.
8. James E. Potter, "Firearms On the Overland Trail" (unpublished manuscript, 1990), 9. John D. Unruh Jr., *The Plains Across* (Urbana IL, 1979), 410.
9. Emmy E. Werner, *Pioneer Children on the Journey West* (Boulder CO, 1995), 168. Brigham D. Madsen, *The Shoshoni Frontier and the Bear River Massacre* (Salt Lake City UT, 1985), 28.
10. Kendall, *Narrative*, 1:94.
11. Raymond W. Settle, ed., *March of the Mounted Rifleman* (Glendale CA, 1940), 301.
12. White, *News of the Plains*, 8:236. J. S. Holliday, *The World Rushed In* (New York, 1981), 114.
13. Holliday, *The World Rushed In*, 115. Anna Paschall Hannum, ed., *A Quaker Forty-Niner* (Philadelphia PA, 1930), 187.
14. Webster, *Pioneer Trails West*, 146. Holliday, *The World Rushed In*, 115.
15. Frazer, *Over the Chihuahua and Santa Fe Trails*, 65–68.
16. White, *News of the Plains*, 2:361.
17. William W. Slaughter and Michael Landon, *Trail of Hope: The Story of the Mormon Trail* (Salt Lake City UT, 1997), 48.
18. Will Bagley, ed., *Frontiersman: Abner Blackburn's Narrative* (Salt Lake City UT, 1992), 21.
19. Ibid., 140, 183.
20. Daniel W. Jones, *Forty Years among the Indians* (Los Angeles CA, 1960), 28.
21. Georgia Willis Read and Ruth Gaines, eds., *Gold Rush: The Journals, Drawings, and Other Papers of J. Goldsborough Bruff* (New York, 1944), 89. Stamm, *Horse Mule Grizzly*, 100–101.
22. Potter, "Firearms On the Overland Trail," 19.
23. Doyle, *Journeys*, 2:635.
24. Ibid., 1:127.
25. Ibid., 1:184.
26. Ibid., 1:335.

27. Sandra L. Myres, ed., *Ho for California—Women's Overland Diaries from the Huntington Library* (San Marino CA, 1980), 228.

28. Eugene D. Fleharty, *Wild Animals and Settlers on the Great Plains* (Norman OK, 1995), 220–21.

29. Briton Cooper Busch, ed., *Alta California 1840–1842*, 252–53.

30. Worcester, *Pioneer Trails West*, 144.

31. Hastings, *The Emigrant's Guide*, 143.

32. Read and Gaines, *Gold Rush*, 1170–71, 1173.

33. Ibid., 1173.

34. Ibid., 1173–74.

35. Ibid.

36. Ibid., 1174.

37. White, *News of the Plains*, 2:377–78.

38. Holliday, *The World Rushed In*, 52, 62. Hannum, *A Quaker Forty-Niner*, 191.

39. Ralph P. Bieber, ed., *Southern Trails to California in 1849* (Glendale CA, 1937), 5:169.

40. Gordon, *Overland to California*, 25, 57, 78.

41. Ibid., 37.

42. Ibid., 40.

43. Samuel L. Clemens, *Roughing It* (Hartford CT, 1872), 23–24.

44. Archer Butler Hulbert, *Forty-Niners, The Chronicle of the California Trail* (Boston MA, 1949), 36.

45. Lloyd W. Coffman, *Blazing a Wagon Trail to California* (Enterprise OR, 1993), 96.

46. Hanson, *The Plains Rifle*, 564–65.

47. Barton H. Barbour, ed., *Reluctant Frontiersman: James Ross Larkin on the Santa Fe Trail 1856–57* (Albuquerque NM, 1990), 89, 124–25.

48. Louis M. Bloch Jr., ed., *Overland to California in 1859* (Cleveland OH, 1983), 23.

49. E. F. Ware, *The Lyon Campaign in Missouri* (Topeka KS, 1907), 16–17.

50. Brigham H. Roberts, *History of the Church of Jesus Christ of Latter-Day Saints* (Salt Lake City UT, 1950), 7:509. Harry W. Gibson, "Frontier Arms of the Mormons," *Utah Historical Quarterly* (Winter 1974): 9, 11.

51. Joseph E. Brown, *The Mormon Trek West* (Garden City NY, 1980), 34, 87. Slaughter and Landon, *Trail of Hope*, 23. Gibson, "Frontier Arms of the Mormons," 11.

52. Gibson, "Frontier Arms of the Mormons," 11–12. Juanita Brooks, ed., *On the Mormon Frontier* (Salt Lake City UT, 1964), 1:210. John Browning and Curt Gentry, *John M. Browning, American Gunmaker* (Garden City NY, 1964), 1.

53. Juanita Brooks, *John Doyle Lee, Zealot—Pioneer Builder—Scapegoat* (Glendale CA, 1961), 98. J. H. Beadle, *Brigham's Destroying Angel* (New York, 1872), 66.

54. Daniel Tyler, *A Concise History of the Mormon Battalion in the Mexican War 1846–1847* (Glorieta NM, 1969), 113–14, 136. David L. Bigler, ed., *The Gold Discovery Journal of Azariah Smith* (Salt Lake City UT, 1990), 13–14.

55. White, *News of the Plains*, 8:241. Gibson, "Frontier Arms of the Mormons," 17–20.

56. Sir Richard F. Burton, *The City of the Saints and across the Rocky Mountains to California*, ed. Fawn M. Brodie (New York, 1963), 353–57. Gibson, "Frontier Arms of the Mormons," 23–25.

57. Burton, *The City of the Saints*, 354, 356. Anna Jean Backus, *Mountain Meadows Witness* (Spokane WA, 1995), 206. Gibson, "Frontier Arms of the Mormons," 23–25.

58. Granville Stuart, *Forty Years*, 1:122.

59. Burton, *The City of the Saints*, 13.

60. Ibid., 12–13.

61. Stuart, *Forty Years*, 1:191–92.

62. James E. Potter, "William Rotton, Nebraska Gunmaker," *Museum of the Fur Trade Quarterly* (Spring 1981): 1–5.

63. Ibid., 4–5.

64. John Q. Anderson, ed., *Tales of Frontier Texas 1830–1860* (Dallas TX, 1966), 216–17.

65. Doyle, *Journeys*, 1:114.

66. James E. Potter, "Firearms on the Overland Trails," *Overland Journal* 9, no. 1 (1991): 3.

CHAPTER FOUR

1. J. D. Borthwick, *Three Years in California* (London, 1857), 56.

2. T. H. Watkins, *Gold and Silver in the West* (Palo Alto CA, 1971), 280.

3. Valeska Bari, *The Course of Empire* (New York, 1931), 179.

4. Peter Browning, ed., *Bright Gem of the Western Seas* (Lafayette CA, 1991), 156.

5. Jessie Gould Hannon, *The Boston-Newton Company Venture*, (Lincoln NE, 1969), 30. Helen S. Giffen, ed., *The Diaries of Peter Decker Overland to California in 1849 and Life in the Mines 1850–51* (Georgetown CA, 1966), 3:255.

6. Peter Browning, ed., *To the Golden Shore* (Lafayette CA, 1995), 61, 89.

7. Ibid., 71, 165. Fayette Robinson, *California and Its Gold Regions* (New York, 1849), 86.

8. Joseph Henry Jackson, *Bad Company* (New York, 1939), xiii. Browning, *Bright Gem*, 136. Borthwick, *Three Years in California*, 119.

9. Mae Helen Bacon Boggs, *My Playhouse Was a Concord Coach* (Oakland CA, 1942), 56, 162.

10. Malcolm E. Barker, ed., *San Francisco Memoirs 1835–1851* (San Francisco CA, 1994), 253–55.

11. Ibid., 145.

12. A. P. Nasatir, ed., *A French Journalist in the California Rush* (Georgetown CA, 1964), 135.

13. Thomas D. Clark, ed., *Off at Sunrise, The Overland Journal of Charles Glass Gray* (San Marino CA, 1976), xvii, 144.

14. Browning, *To the Golden Shore*, 124.

15. George A. Root, ed., "The First Days Battle of Hickory Point," *Kansas Historical Quarterly* (November 1931): 31. "Memoirs of a Pioneer of Kansas," in *Collections of*

the Kansas State Historical Society, 1923–1925 (Topeka KS, 1925), 580.

16. Howard C. Gardiner, *In Pursuit of the Golden Dream*, ed. Dale L. Morgan (Stoughton MA, 1970), 15.
17. Ibid.
18. Ibid., 191.
19. George D. Dornin, *Thirty Years Ago—Gold Rush Memories of a Daguerreotype Artist* (New City CA, 1995), vii, 4.
20. Browning, *To the Golden Shore*, 121.
21. Bekeart, *Three Generations 1837–1949: Jules Francois Bekeart, A Gunsmith* (Oakland CA, 1949), 8.
22. Read and Gaines, *Gold Rush*, 126, 809.
23. Charles D. Ferguson, *The Experiences of a Forty-niner during Thirty-Four Years' Residence in California and Australia*, ed. Frederick T. Wallace (Cleveland OH, 1888), 211–12.
24. Nellie Snyder Yost, ed., *Boss Cowman: The Recollections of Ed Lemmon 1857–1946* (Lincoln NE, 1969), 3–4.
25. Rex W. Strickland, "Six Who Came to El Paso: Pioneers of the 1840s" *Southwestern Studies* (Fall 1963): 22.
26. William Perkins, *Three Years in California* (Berkeley CA, 1964), 296–97.
27. Ferguson, *The Experiences of a Forty-niner*, 185–86.
28. Ibid., 184.
29. Roger D. McGrath, *Gunfighters, Highwaymen, and Vigilantes* (Berkeley CA, 1984), 78–79.
30. Marvin Lewis, ed., *The Mining Frontier* (Norman OK, 1967), 65–66.
31. Ferguson, *The Experiences of a Forty-niner*, 190–91. Hannum, *A Quaker Forty-Niner*, 39.
32. Gardiner, *In Pursuit*, 209–10.
33. Ibid.
34. R. G. Badger, *Gold and Sunshine—Reminiscences of Early California* (Boston MA, 1922), 113.
35. Ibid., 173–75.
36. Ibid., 175–76.
37. Harry L. Wells, *History of Nevada County California 1880* (Berkeley CA, 1970), 121.
38. Ben C. Truman, *The Field of Honor* (New York, 1884), 108–9, 310–11, 313, 318–19, 326–28, 417.
39. Wells, *History of Nevada County*, 121–22.
40. Francis P. Farquhar, ed., *Up and Down in California in 1860–1864* (New Haven CT, 1930), 14, 89.
41. Ibid., 14.
42. Clemens, *Roughing It*, 295.
43. Maurice H. Newmark and Marco R. Newmark, eds., *Sixty Years in Southern California 1853–1913* (New York, 1916), 224.
44. R. E. Mather and F. E. Boswell, *Gold Camp Desperadoes* (Norman OK, 1993), 34.
45. Ibid., 347–48.
46. LeRoy R. Hafen, ed., *Colorado Gold Rush: Contemporary Letters and Reports 1858–1859* (Philadelphia PA, 1974), 274.
47. Ibid., 200. Vardis Fisher and Opal Laurel Holmes, *Gold Rushes and Mining Camps of the Early American West* (Caldwell ID, 1968), 98.
48. Barney Libeus, ed., *Letters of the Pike's Peak Gold Rush* (San Jose CA, 1959), 82–83.
49. William J. McConnell, *Frontier Law* (Chicago IL, 1924), 58–59.
50. William J. McConnell and James S. Reynolds, *Idaho's Vigilantes* (Moscow ID, 1984), 69–71.
51. Ibid., 78–79.
52. Anderson, *Tales of Frontier Texas*, 158–59.

CHAPTER FIVE

1. William A. Baillie-Grohman, *Camps in the Rockies* (New York, 1882), 410.
2. Morgan and Harris, *The Rocky Mountain Journals*, 246.
3. Charles Augustus Murray, *Travels in North America* (New York, 1974), 1:382, 455, 567; 2:65.
4. William Fairholme, *Journal of an Expedition to the Grand Prairies of the Missouri 1840*, ed. Jack B. Tykal (Spokane WA, 1996), 13–14, 54.
5. John I. Merritt, *Baronets and Buffalo* (Missoula MT, 1985), 93. Dave Walter, "Unsaintly Sir St. George Gore," *Montana Magazine* (November–December 1985): 58. James H. Bradley, "Sir George Gore's Expedition," *Contributions to the Historical Society of Montana* 9, (1923): 246–50.
6. Fleharty, *Wild Animals and Settlers*, 27, 235.
7. William Chandless, *A Visit to Salt Lake* (London, 1857), 6–7.
8. Ibid., 57.
9. Garavaglia and Worman, *Firearms . . . 1803–1865*, 303. Shelton, *California Gunsmiths*, 210.
10. John D. McAulay, *Civil War Pistols* (Lincoln RI, 1992), 7–8. "Miscellaneous News and Notes," *U.S. Martial Arms Collector and Springfield Research Newsletter* 62 (October 1992): 62–2.
11. Ibid., 297.
12. Frank Marryat, *Mountains and Molehills* (Stanford CA, 1952), 110–11.
13. Ibid., 133–34.
14. Stuart, *Forty Years*, 1:135–36.
15. J. S. Campion, *On the Frontier* (London, 1878), 10.
16. Ibid., 101–2.
17. Charles Alston Messiter, *Sport and Adventures among the North American Indians* (New York, 1966), 12.
18. Ibid., 215.
19. Ibid., 218, 225.
20. Ibid., 245.
21. John Mortimer Murphy, *Sporting Adventures in the Far West* (New York, 1880), 19–21.
22. Ibid., 31–33.
23. Ibid., 32.
24. Ibid., 33.
25. Baillie-Grohman, *Camps in the Rockies*, 13–14.
26. Ibid.
27. Ibid., 140–41.
28. Ibid., 142.
29. Ibid., 165, 270.
30. Ibid., 270.
31. Ibid., 410–11.
32. R. L. Wilson, *The Book of Colt Firearms* (Minneapolis

MN, 1993), 486–87. Lt. W. L. Scott to Colt Patent Fire Arms Mfg. Co., 18 January 1886. Connecticut State Library, Hartford.

33. R. B. Townshend, *A Tenderfoot in Colorado* (Norman OK, 1968), 5, 48.
34. Ibid., 11.
35. Ibid., 32.
36. Ibid., 50–52.
37. Ibid., 82–85.
38. Ibid., 95, 151–52.
39. Ibid., 217–19.
40. Ibid., 233–34.
41. Ibid., 13, 19–20, 95.
42. Ibid., 79, 82–83.
43. Ibid., 232–39.
44. Lincoln A. Lang, *Ranching With Roosevelt* (Philadelphia PA, 1926), 19.
45. Ibid., 63, 143.
46. Ibid., 171–72.
47. Ibid., 232–33.
48. F. J. Balentine, "Freund and Bro. Pioneer Gun Makers of the West," *Sharps Collector Association Report* (Summer 1994): 5–6.
49. Wingate, *Through the Yellowstone Park*, 39. F. J. Pablo Balentine, *Freund & Bro. Pioneer Gunmakers to the West* (Newport Beach CA, 1997), 45.
50. J. Marvin Hunt, ed., *The Trail Drivers of Texas* (New York, 1963), 2:586.
51. Bob L'Aloge, *Knights of the Sixgun* (Las Cruces NM, 1991), 143–45.
52. McGrath, *Gunfighters*, 192, 195–96, 236.
53. Newmark, *Sixty Years in Southern California*, 516.
54. Charles C. Lowther, *Dodge City, Kansas* (Philadelphia PA, 1940), 47–48.
55. *Winchester Repeating Arms Company Catalog*, 1 May 1879, 47–49.
56. J. S. Flory, *Thrilling Echoes from the Wild Frontier* (Chicago IL, 1893), 154.
57. Capt. R. G. Carter, *On the Border With Mackenzie* (New York, 1961), 350–51.
58. Garavaglia and Worman, *Firearms . . . 1866–1894*, 88.
59. *Winchester Repeating Arms Company Catalog*, 1 May 1879, 39.
60. *Spaulding-Haywood Arms Company Catalog*, n.d.
61. F. W. Gray, *Seeking Fortune in America* (London, 1912), 126–27.
62. Ibid., 127–28.
63. Ibid., 142–43.

CHAPTER SIX

1. Gerald R. Mayberry, "The End of the Line: The Last Days of the Sharps Rifle in Montana," *American Society of Arms Collectors Bulletin* (October 1992): 27.
2. des Montaignes, *The Plains*, 152.
3. Olmsted, *A Journey Through Texas*, 74.
4. Ibid.
5. Hamilton, *My Sixty Years*, 162.
6. White, *News of the Plains*, 8:32. Martin Rywell, *The Gun*

That Shaped American Destiny* (Harriman TN, 1957), 37.
7. White, *News of the Plains*, 8:33.
8. Ibid., 50. Olmsted, *A Journey Through Texas*, 289.
9. Wayne R. Austerman, *Sharps Rifles and Spanish Mules* (College Station TX, 1985), 70.
10. White, *News of the Plains*, 8:122.
11. Samuel Woodworth Cozzens, *Explorations & Adventures in Arizona & New Mexico* (Secaucus NJ, 1988), 226–27.
12. Rywell, *The Gun That Shaped American Destiny*, 39.
13. Alberta Pantle, ed., "The Connecticut Kansas Colony," *Kansas Historical Quarterly* (Spring 1956): 3–4.
14. "Letters of John and Sarah Everett 1854–1864," *Kansas Historical Quarterly* (May 1939): 144.
15. John Doy, *The Thrilling Narrative of Dr. John Doy of Kansas* (Boston MA, 1860), 18, 20.
16. Frank Sellers, *Sharps Firearms* (Dallas TX, 1978), 95. Phillip R. Rutherford, "More Kansas Sharps: The Rectification of a Seventy Year Old Error," *Gun Report* (May 1977): 12–13.
17. Thomas C. Wells, "Letters of a Kansas Pioneer 1855–1860," *Kansas Historical Quarterly* (February 1936): 165. "The Chicago Company and the Missouri River Pirates," *Kansas Historical Quarterly* (May 1947): 212.
18. Thomas C. Wells, "Letters of a Kansas Pioneer," 39.
19. Russell K. Hichman, "Lewis Bodwell, Frontier Preacher," *Kansas Historical Quarterly* (November 1943): 356. "First Free-State Territorial Legislature of 1857–'58," *Transactions of the Kansas State Historical Society* 10 (1908): 12.
20. Paul Buchanan, "John Brown's Colt Navies," *Man at Arms* (December 2001): 38, 43.
21. "A Buffalo Hunt," *Kansas Historical Quarterly* (May 1937): 203.
22. "Dr. Albert Morrall: Proslavery Soldier in Kansas in 1856," *Collections of the Kansas State Historical Society 1915–1918* 14:139.
23. Thomas F. Doran, "Kansas Sixty Years Ago," *Collections of the Kansas State Historical Society 1919–1922* 15:487–88.
24. Yost, *Boss Cowman*, 21.
25. Prentiss Ingraham, ed., *Seventy Years on the Frontier, Alexander Majors' Memoirs* (Chicago IL, 1893), 189–90, 192.
26. James E. Serven, *Conquering the Frontiers* (Los Angeles CA, 1974), 152.
27. James B. Gillett, *Six Years With the Texas Rangers 1875 to 1881*, ed. M. M. Quaife (New Haven CT, 1925), 21, 25, 56.
28. Mayberry, "The End of the Line," 31.
29. Ibid., 35–36.
30. Ibid., 34.
31. Philip Durham and Everett L. Jones, *The Negro Cowboys* (New York, 1968), 116.
32. *Sharps Collector Association Report* 10, no. 3, 18.
33. Edgar Beecher Bronson, *Cowboy Life on the Western Plains* (New York, 1910), 216.

34. William A. Allen, *Adventures with Indians and Game*, (Chicago IL, 1903), 157–58.
35. F. J. Balentine, "Two Shots Would Have Been Nice," *Sharps Collector Association Report* (Winter 1995): 2.
36. Robert Foster, ed., "Buffalo Guns in Texas," *Museum Journal* 12 (1970): 54.
37. *Sharps Rifle Company Catalog*, 1877.
38. Sellers, *Sharps Firearms*, 319–20.
39. Foster, "Buffalo Guns in Texas," 10.
40. Ibid., 12.
41. Ibid., 28.
42. Ibid., 35.
43. *Sharps Collector Association Report* (Spring 1994): 8.
44. Thomas C. Nixon to Sharps Rifle Company, 9 March 1880. Dr. Richard J. Labowskie Collection.
45. Michael A. Leeson, ed., *History of Montana 1739–1885* (Chicago IL, 1885), 86.
46. Sellers, *Sharps Firearms*, 314.
47. Ibid., 257. Foster, "Buffalo Guns In Texas," 71–72.
48. *Sharps Rifle Company Catalog*, January 1878.
49. Mayberry, "The End of the Line," 36. Sellers, *Sharps Firearms*, 260.
50. *E. C. Meacham Catalog*, St. Louis MO, 1884.

CHAPTER SEVEN

1. Olmsted, *A Journey Through Texas*, 75.
2. John J. Jenkins, ed., *The Papers of the Texas Revolution 1835 and 1836* (Austin TX, 1973), 6:514–15.
3. G. Maxwell Longfield and David T. Basnett, *Observations on Colt's Second Contract November 2, 1847* (Alexandria Bay NY, 1998), 3. Charles M. Robinson III, *The Men Who Wear the Star* (New York, 2000), 70–71.
4. Thomas W. Knowles, *They Rode for the Lone Star* (Dallas TX, 1999), 121.
5. Edwin Bryant, *What I Saw in California* (Minneapolis MN, 1967), 113–14.
6. Garavaglia and Worman, *Firearms . . . 1803–1865*, 100.
7. Kendall, *Narrative*, 1:209.
8. Mary Ellen Jones, *Daily Life on the Nineteenth Century American Frontier* (Westport CT, 1998), 83.
9. Garavaglia and Worman, *Firearms . . . 1803–1865*, 204.
10. C. C. Holloway, "San Antonio Letters of 1854–56," *Texas Gun Collector* (December 1954): 12–13.
11. Ibid., 12.
12. Stephen G. Hyslop, *Bound for Santa Fe* (Norman OK, 2002), 125–26.
13. Olmsted, *A Journey Through Texas*, 75.
14. Richard Ratenbury, "A Survey of Western Gunleather," *Persimmon Hill* (Spring 1991): 27.
15. Ibid., 29.
16. David Dary, *The Santa Fe Trail* (New York, 2000), 231–32.
17. Solomon Nunes Carvalho, *Incidents of Travel and Adventure in the Far West*, ed. Bertram Wallace Korn (Philadelphia PA, 1954), 85, 110. LeRoy R. Hafen, *The Overland Mail* (Cleveland OH, 1926), 98.
18. White, *News of the Plains*, 7:411, 413.
19. Joseph W. Snell, ed., "Diary of a Dodge City Buffalo Hunter, 1872–1873," *Kansas Historical Quarterly* (Winter 1865): 351, 354, 376.
20. Karen Holliday Tanner, *Doc Holliday: A Family Portrait* (Norman OK, 1998), 70. Clemens, *Roughing It*, 295.
21. Townshend, *A Tenderfoot in Colorado*, 115.
22. Robert K. DeArment, *Knights of the Green Cloth* (Norman OK, 1982), 343.
23. Charles T. Haven and Frank A. Belden, *A History of the Colt Revolver* (New York, 1940), 382.
24. *Sharps Collector Association Report* (Summer 1995).
25. Irving Howbert, *Memories of a Lifetime in the Pike's Peak Region* (Glorieta NM, 1970), 201.
26. Lt. J. E. B. Stuart to Sam Colt, 2 December 1859. Richard D. Hughes, *Pioneer Years in the Black Hills*, ed. Agnes Wright Spring (Glendale CA, 1957), 20.
27. Boggs, *My Playhouse*, 65.
28. Morris F. Taylor, *First Mail West* (Albuquerque NM, 1971), 85.
29. Herbert G. Houze, *Colt Rifles and Muskets from 1847 to 1870* (Iola WI, 1996), 78.
30. Art Phelps, *The Story of Merwin, Hulbert & Company Firearms* (Rough and Ready CA, 1992), 22.
31. James L. Mitchell, *Colt, A Collection of Letters and Photographs about the Man, the Arms, the Company* (Harrisburg PA, 1959), 96.
32. Hughes, *Pioneer Years in the Black Hills*, 50, 83.
33. Broadside, "An American Time Capsule: Three Centuries of Broadsides and Other Printed Ephemera," online Library of Congress exhibit.
34. John E. Parsons, *Smith & Wesson Revolvers* (New York, 1957), 76–78.
35. Charles Pate, e-mail message to author, March 11, 2004.
36. Parsons, *Smith & Wesson Revolvers*, 80–83.
37. Hughes, *Pioneer Years in the Black Hills*, 69.
38. Joe E. Milner and Earle R. Forrest, *California Joe* (Caldwell ID, 1935), 259.
39. Frederick Russell Burnham, *Scouting on Two Continents* (Garden City NY, 1926), 43. Charles A. Siringo, *Riatas and Spurs* (New York, 1927), 143.
40. William O. O'Neill to Colt Patent Fire Arms Mfg. Co., 6 December 1889.
41. Harold Hutton, *Doc Middleton* (Chicago IL, 1974), 179. Belvadine Lecher, director, Dawes County Historical Society Museum, Chadron NE, letter to author, September 22, 2003.
42. James H. Kyner, *End of Track* (Caldwell ID, 1937), 119–20.
43. J. Evetts Haley, *Jeff Milton—A Good Man with a Gun* (Norman OK, 1948), 29–30.
44. John K. Rollinson, *Pony Trails in Wyoming*, ed. E. A. Brininstool (Caldwell ID, 1941), 270, 287.
45. H. H. Crittenden, *The Crittenden Memoirs* (New York, 1936), 269–70.
46. Flayderman, *Flayderman's Guide*, 144.
47. Parsons, *Smith & Wesson Revolvers*, 85, 178.
48. Illustrated advertisement, *Man at Arms* (April 1996). Stan Nelson, "The Guns of Northfield," *Minnesota Weapons Collectors Association News* (December 2001): 12.

49. Mark Dugan and John Boessenecker, *The Grey Fox* (Norman OK, 1992), 75.

50. Gary Kangas, "The Guns of the Grey Fox," *Guns & Ammo Annual* (1991): 126–27.

51. Nyle H. Miller and Joseph W. Snell, *Why the West Was Wild* (Topeka KS, 1963), 332.

52. Frank Triplett, *The Life, Times, and Treacherous Death of Jesse James* (Chicago IL, 1970), 316.

53. Phelps, *The Story of Merwin, Hulbert & Company Revolvers*, 103, 105, 107, 112. Richard Rattenbury, "The Roosevelt-Merrifield Connection," *Man at Arms* (November–December 1982): 31.

54. Stan Nelson, "The Hopkins & Allen X-L No. 8," *Minnesota Weapons Collectors Association News* (March 1999): 10–12.

55. Foster, "Buffalo Guns in Texas," 80.

56. Corp. Thomas Schnepper to Colt Patent Fire Arms Mfg. Co., 14 October 1885. Connecticut State Library, Hartford.

57. Charles A. Siringo, *History of "Billy the Kid"* (Albuquerque NM, 2000), 133–37.

58. T. J. Stiles, ed., *Warriors and Pioneers* (New York, 1996), 285.

59. Henry F. Hoyt, *A Frontier Doctor* (Boston MA, 1929), 149.

60. Don Wilkerson, *Colt's Double Action Revolver Model of 1878* (Marceline MO, 1998), 34, 37, 40, 89, 153.

61. Ibid., 97, 153. John Boessenecker, *Badge and Buckshot* (Norman OK, 1988), 101.

62. Charles N. Cox to Colt Patent Fire Arms Mfg. Co., 13 May 1886.

63. Wilkerson, *Colt's Double Action Revolver Model of 1878*, 47.

64. Wilson, *The Book of Colt Firearms*, 337.

65. Parsons, *Smith & Wesson Revolvers*, 164.

66. Ibid.

67. Boessenecker, *Badge and Buckshot*, 235–37.

68. Dean F. Krakel, *The Saga of Tom Horn* (Laramie WY, 1954), 215.

CHAPTER EIGHT

1. *Winchester Repeating Arms Company Catalog*, 1871, 4.

2. Shelton, *California Gunsmiths*, 4.

3. Alson B. Ostrander, *An Army Boy of the Sixties* (Yonkers-on-Hudson NY, 1924), 102–3.

4. Parsons, *Smith & Wesson Revolvers*, 31.

5. Harold F. Williamson, *Winchester, The Gun That Won the West* (Washington DC, 1952), 28. *Winchester Repeating Arms Company Catalog*, 1871, 41.

6. *New Haven Arms Company Catalog*, 1865, 19.

7. Parsons, *The First Winchester*, 15. *New Haven Arms Company Catalog*, 1865, 24–25.

8. Henry Pickering Walker, *The Wagonmasters* (Norman OK, 1966), 88. Santleben, *A Texas Pioneer*, 45–46.

9. *Winchester Repeating Arms Company Catalog*, 1871, 4.

10. Parsons, *The First Winchester*, 68.

11. Garavaglia and Worman, *Firearms . . . 1866–1894*, 123. Boessenecker, *Badge and Buckshot*, 44.

12. Forest Crossen, *Western Yesterdays* (Boulder CO, 1967), 5:37.

13. Carlton Culmsee, *Utah's Black Hawk War* (Logan UT, 1973), 59–61.

14. Doyle, *Journeys*, 2:655.

15. Ibid., 698.

16. Henry B. Carrington, *The Indian Question* (Boston MA, 1909), 24.

17. James Willard Schultz, *Many Strange Characters, Montana Frontier Tales* (Norman OK, 1982), 96–97.

18. Luther S. Kelly, *"Yellowstone Kelly" The Memoirs of Luther S. Kelly*, ed. M. M. Quaife (New Haven CT, 1926), 26.

19. Dorothy Hoobler and Thomas Hoobler, *Photographing the Frontier* (New York, 1980), 153–54.

20. John Nicolson, ed., *The Arizona of Joseph Pratt Allyn* (Tucson AZ, 1974), 83.

21. Ibid., 83–84.

22. Charles A. Siringo, *A Texas Cowboy or Fifteen Years on the Hurricane Deck of a Spanish Pony* (Lincoln NE, 1950), 75.

23. William M. Breakenridge, *Helldorado* (Boston MA, 1928), 51.

24. Santleben, *A Texas Pioneer*, 79–80.

25. Austerman, *Sharps Rifles and Spanish Mules*, 237–38.

26. McAulay, *Rifles of the U.S. Army*, 58.

27. De B. Randolph Keim, *Sheridan's Troopers on the Borders: A Winter Campaign on the Plains* (Freeport NY, 1970), 17–18. House Executive Document 89, *Sale of Arms and Ordnance Stores*, 42nd Cong., 2nd sess., 1871, serial 1511, 15–16.

28. A. Roenick, "Railroad Grading Among Indians," *Transactions of the Kansas State Historical Society* (1904): 385.

29. Ibid., 385–86.

30. Dee Brown, *Hear That Lonesome Whistle Blow* (New York, 1977), 101.

31. Yost, *Boss Cowman*, 124–25.

32. Roy M. Marcot, *Spencer Repeating Firearms* (Irvine CA, 1983), 90.

33. Parsons, *The First Winchester*, xxxi. Marcot, *Spencer Repeating Firearms*, 112, 154–55.

34. Marcot, *Spencer Repeating Firearms*, 149.

35. Parsons, *The First Winchester*, 99.

36. Ibid., 59.

37. Capt. Henry W. Strong, *My Frontier Days and Indian Fights on the Plains of Texas* (Dallas TX, 1926), 24. *Winchester Repeating Arms Company Catalog*, 1875, 42.

38. Garavaglia and Worman, *Firearms . . . 1866–1894*, 129.

39. Frederick S. Dellenbaugh, *A Canyon Voyage* (New Haven CT, 1908), 11, 205.

40. The Hodges diary is in the possession of the Union Pacific Historical Museum. Herbert B. Nelson and Preston E. Onstad, eds., *A Webfoot Volunteer, The Diary of William M. Hilleary 1864–1866* (Corvallis OR, 1965), 152.

41. John C. Anderson, *Mackinaws down the Missouri*, ed. Glen Barrett (Logan UT, 1978), 11, 71.

42. Ibid., 77.

43. Allen, *Adventures with Indians and Game*, 40.
44. "A Stage Ride to Colorado," *Harper's New Monthly Magazine* (July 1867): 138, 144–45.
45. Garavaglia and Worman, *Firearms . . . 1866–1894*, 134.
46. A. J. Sowell, *Early Settlers and Indian Fighters of Southwest Texas* (Austin TX, 1900), 490–92.
47. Ibid., 544–45.
48. Lynne Rhodes Mayer and Kenneth E. Vose, *Makin' Tracks* (New York, 1975), 108.

CHAPTER NINE

1. Albert Marrin, *Cowboys, Indians, and Gunfighters* (New York, 1993), 172.
2. Laurence Iven Seidman, *Once in the Saddle* (New York, 1991), 17. Hunt, *The Trail Drivers*, ix–x. Jones, *Daily Life*, 166. Don Worcester, *The Chisholm Trail* (Fort Worth TX, 1980), 10.
3. J. Evetts Haley, *The XIT Ranch of Texas* (Norman OK, 1953), 3. Olmsted, *A Journey Through Texas*, 274.
4. James H. Beckstead, *Cowboying, A Tough Job in a Hard Land* (Salt Lake City UT, 1991), 7.
5. J. Evetts Haley, *Charles Goodnight, Cowman & Plainsman* (Boston MA, 1966), 186.
6. Seidman, *Once in the Saddle*, 27. Worcester, *The Chisholm Trail*, 12–14. Hunt, *The Trail Drivers*, xi.
7. Harry E. Chrisman, *Lost Trails of the Cimarron* (Denver CO, 1964), 66.
8. Joseph G. McCoy, *Historic Sketches of the Cattle Trade of West and Southwest* (Philadelphia PA, 1974), 128.
9. Hunt, *The Trail Drivers*, 24.
10. Gillett, *Six Years With the Texas Rangers*, 31. George Scarborough, *The Life and Death of a Lawman on the Closing Frontier* (Norman OK, 1991), 17.
11. Frank M. Canton, *Frontier Trails*, ed. Edward Everett Dale (Norman OK, 1966), 6–7.
12. Ibid., 11.
13. Hunt, *The Trail Drivers*, 910.
14. Ibid., 911.
15. Ibid., 912–13.
16. Chrisman, *Lost Trails*, 35.
17. Hunt, *Old Trail Drivers*, 341.
18. Stiles, *Warriors and Pioneers*, 135.
19. William French, *Some Recollections of a Western Ranchman* (New York, 1965), 164–65.
20. Hunt, *The Trail Drivers*, 625. Charles W. Allen, *From Fort Laramie to Wounded Knee in the West That Was*, ed. Richard E. Jensen (Lincoln NE, 1997), 1–2.
21. Bronson, *Cowboy Life on the Western Plains*, 42–43.
22. Hunt, *The Trail Drivers*, 485–86.
23. Siringo, *A Texas Cowboy*, 49. Durham and Jones, *The Negro Cowboys*, 89–90, 124–25. Lang, *Ranching with Roosevelt*, 286–88. Sara R. Massey, ed., *Black Cowboys of Texas* (College Station TX, 2000), 119–20.
24. Durham and Jones, *The Negro Cowboys*, 91–92, 96.
25. Larry McMurtry, *Lonesome Dove* (New York, 1985), 526.
26. Hunt, *The Trail Drivers*, 1006.
27. Pam Conrad, *Prairie Visions: The Life and Times of Solomon Butcher* (New York, 1991), 63–64.
28. E. C. Abbott and Helena Huntington Smith, *We Pointed Them North* (Norman OK, 1939), 40.
29. Laban S. Records, *Cherokee Outlet Cowboy*, ed. Ellen Jayne Maris Wheeler (Norman OK, 1995), 253.
30. Yost, *Boss Cowman*, 109.
31. Walt Coburn, *Pioneer Cattleman in Montana: The Story of the Circle C Ranch* (Norman OK, 1968), 131.
32. Edgar Beecher Bronson, *Reminiscences of a Ranchman* (Lincoln NE, 1962), 24–25.
33. Lang, *Ranching with Roosevelt*, 19, 63, 143.
34. Dee Brown and Martin F. Schmitt, *Trail Driving Days* (New York, 1952), 213.
35. Records, *Cherokee Outlet Cowboy*, 63–64.
36. Ibid., 122.
37. Hunt, *The Trail Drivers*, 260.
38. Abbott and Smith, *We Pointed Them North*, 24.
39. Ibid., 7.
40. Yost, *Boss Cowman*, 202–3.
41. Scarborough, *The Life and Death of a Lawman*, 69.
42. Con Price, *Memories of Old Montana* (Pasadena CA, 1945), 74–75.
43. Will C. Barnes, *Apaches & Longhorns*, ed. Frank C. Lockwood (Tucson AZ, 1982), 147.
44. Jeff C. Dykes, ed., *Recollections of Thomas Edgar Crawford* (Norman OK, 1962), 4.
45. Ibid., 10–11.
46. Ibid., 18.
47. Richard Harding Davis, *The West from a Car-Window* (New York, 1892), 15.
48. Stan Nelson, "Fanning the Hammer," *Minnesota Weapons Collectors Association News* (March 2001): 5.
49. Dykes, *Recollections*, 54–55.
50. Rollinson, *Pony Trails in Wyoming*, 199.
51. Davis, *The West From a Car-Window*, 143–44.
52. Ibid., 14–15.
53. Scarborough, *The Life and Death of a Lawman*, 100. Ed McGivern, *Fast and Fancy Revolver Shooting* (Chicago IL, 1957), 102.
54. Douglas Branch, *The Cowboy and His Interpreters* (New York, 1961), 26. William H. Forbis, *The Cowboys*, Time-Life "The Old West" Series (New York, 1973), 82.
55. Angie Debo, ed., *The Cowman's Southwest* (Glendale CA, 1953), 169.
56. Yost, *Boss Cowman*, 224–25.
57. Miller and Snell, *Why the West Was Wild*, 93.
58. George H. Tinker, *A Land of Sunshine, Flagstaff and Its Surroundings* (Glendale CA, 1969), iv.
59. Ibid.
60. Yost, *Boss Cowman*, 264–65.
61. Clifford P. Westermeier, "The Dodge City Cowboy Band," *Kansas Historical Quarterly* (February 1951): 4.
62. Ibid., 5.
63. Orlan Sawey, *Charles A. Siringo* (Boston MA, 1981), 22. Siringo, *A Texas Cowboy*, 75–76.
64. Sawey, *Charles A. Siringo*, 82.
65. Philip D. Jordan, *Frontier Law and Order* (Lincoln NE, 1970), 6–7. Alex E. Sweet and J. Armoy Knox, *On a Mexican Mustang through Texas* (London, 1905), 372.
66. Charles W. Harris and Buck Rainey, eds., *The Cowboy:*

Six-Shooters, Songs, and Sex (Norman OK, 1976), 64.

67. *The Abilene Chronicle*, 12 May 1870, 1. Miller and Snell, *Why the West Was Wild*, 200.
68. Miller and Snell, *Why the West Was Wild*, 482, 485.
69. Marrin, *Cowboys, Indians, and Gunfighters*, 112–13.
70. Chrisman, *Lost Trails*, 65.
71. Michael M. Hickey, *The Cowboy Conspiracy to Convict the Earps* (Honolulu HI, 1994), 83.
72. Watson Parker, *Deadwood, The Golden Years* (Lincoln NE, 1981), 204, 208.
73. Miller and Snell, *Why the West Was Wild*, 248.
74. Ibid., 252–53.
75. Haley, *The XIT Ranch*, 242–43.
76. Kenneth L. Holmes, ed., *Covered Wagon Women— Diaries and Letters from the Western Trails 1840–1890* (Glendale CA, 1988), 75.
77. Jordan, *Frontier Law and Order*, 18–22.
78. Ramon F. Adams, *The Best of the American Cowboy* (Norman OK, 1957), 115, 230.
79. Ibid., 210.
80. James H. Cook, *Longhorn Cowboy* (New York, 1942), 129–30.
81. Chrisman, *Lost Trails*, 95. Douglas D. Martin, *Tombstone's Epitaph* (Albuquerque NM, 1853), 28.
82. Richard W. Slatta, *The Cowboy Encyclopedia* (Santa Barbara CA, 1994), 139.
83. Canton, *Frontier Trails*, 15–16.
84. Bronson, *Reminiscences*, 210.
85. Breakenridge, *Helldorado*, 121.
86. Price, *Memories of Old Montana*, 34–35.
87. Clifford P. Westermeier, "The Cowboy in His Home State," *Southwestern Historical Quarterly* (October 1954): 225–26.
88. Ibid., 226–27.
89. Ibid., 227–28.
90. Abbott and Smith, *We Pointed Them North*, 210.
91. Ibid., 214.
92. Ibid., 219.
93. Sawey, *Charles A. Siringo*, 23.
94. Ibid., 82.
95. J. L. Hill, *The End of the Cattle Trail* (Long Beach CA, 1922), 100.

CHAPTER TEN

1. McGrath, *Gunfighters*, 5.
2. R. L. Wilson and L. D. Eberhart, *The Deringer in America* (Lincoln RI, 1985), 1:22.
3. Ibid., 222.
4. Rev. John Steele, *In Camp and Cabin* (Lodi WI, 1901), 229–30.
5. Boessenecker, *Badge and Buckshot*, 20–21.
6. Tristan Smith, *Arabia* Steamboat Museum, e-mail message to author, March 13, 2001.
7. Bronson, *Reminiscences*, 240–41.
8. McGrath, *Gunfighters*, 5.
9. John E. Parsons, *Henry Deringer's Pocket Pistol* (New York, 1952), 171.
10. Ibid., 92, 172.

11. Joseph G. Rosa, *The West of Wild Bill Hickok* (Norman OK, 1982), 123.
12. Garavaglia and Worman, *Firearms...1866–1894*, 269.
13. Canton, *Frontier Trails*, 118–19.
14. Doyle, *Journeys*, 2:653.
15. George D. Freeman, *Midnight and Noonday* (Norman OK, 1984), 121, 127.
16. Marc Simmons, *Ranchers, Ramblers & Renegades* (Santa Fe NM, 1984), 37–38.
17. Capt. John G. Bourke, *On the Border With Crook* (Glorieta NM, 1969), 70–71.
18. Ibid., 72.
19. Ibid., 72–73.
20. Clemens, *Roughing It*, 22–23.
21. Carter, *On the Border With MacKenzie*, 27.
22. Mitchell, *Colt, A Collection of Letters*, 95.
23. Miguel Antonio Otero, *My Life On the Frontier 1864–1882* (Albuquerque NM, 1987), 190–91.
24. Ibid., 118–19.
25. Ibid., 29–30.
26. Struthers Burt, *The Diary of a Dude Wrangler* (New York, 1938), 10.

CHAPTER ELEVEN

1. Henry E. Davies, *Ten Days on the Plains*, ed. Paul Andrew Hutton (Dallas TX, 1985), 14. James A. Hanson, "The Myth of the Wasted Meat," *Museum of the Fur Trade Quarterly* (Fall 1998): 3.
2. Harold H. Schuler, *Fort Pierre Chouteau* (Vermillion SD, 1990), 114–15. John E. Sunder, *The Fur Trade on the Upper Missouri, 1840–1865* (Norman OK, 1965), 17.
3. Kendall, *Narrative*, 78.
4. Ibid., 233.
5. Gordon A. Badger, "Recollections of George Andrew Gordon," *Collections of the Kansas State Historical Society* (1925): 497–98.
6. Sage, *Rocky Mountain Life*, 73.
7. Samuel W. Ferguson, "With Albert Sidney Johnston's Expedition to Utah, 1857," *Collections of the Kansas State Historical Society* (1912): 307.
8. Thwaites, *Early Western Travels*, 21:223.
9. Irene M. Spry, *The Palliser Expedition* (Toronto, Ontario, 1963), 71.
10. Francis Parkman, *The Oregon Trail* (Madison WI, 1969), 262–63.
11. White, *News of the Plains and Rockies*, 7:42.
12. des Montaignes, *The Plains*, 44.
13. Thwaites, *Early Western Travels*, 58. John R. Cook, *The Border and the Buffalo* (New York, 1967), 81–4.
14. Carvalho, *Incidents of Travel*, 113.
15. Stiles, *Warriors and Pioneers*, 88. R. L. Wilson, *Buffalo Bill's Wild West: An American Legend* (New York, 1998), 7. Davies, *Ten Days on the Plains*, 29–30.
16. Stiles, *Warriors and Pioneers*, 90.
17. Keim, *Sheridan's Troopers On the Borders*, 76. James McCague, *Moguls and Iron Men* (New York, 1964), 370–71.
18. Brown, *Hear That Lonesome Whistle Blow*, 145.

19. Fleharty, *Wild Animals and Settlers*, 255–56.
20. Keim, *Sheridan's Troopers*, 19–21.
21. Fleharty, *Wild Animals and Settlers*, 76.
22. C. Vance Haynes Jr., *General Custer and his Sporting Rifles* (Tucson AZ, 1995), 36.
23. Jim Zupan, "The Kansas Hunt," *Sharps Collector Association Report* 9, no. 3; 10, no. 1, 4. James A. Hanson, "The Myth of the Wasted Meat," *Museum of the Fur Trade Quarterly* (Fall 1998): 4.
24. Miles Gilbert, *Getting A Stand* (Union City TN, 1986), 2–4, 27. Wyman P. Meinzer, "Slaughter of the Ancients," *Texas Parks and Wildlife* (February 1988): 27.
25. Richard Irving Dodge, *The Plains of North America and Their Inhabitants* (Newark DE, 1989), 151.
26. Olive K. Dixon, *Life of "Billy" Dixon* (Dallas TX, 1914), 147, 152, 166.
27. Ibid., 181. Gerald R. Mayberry, "Buffalo Guns & Adobe Walls," *Sharps Collector Association Report* (Spring 1995).
28. Charles M. Robinson III, *The Frontier World of Fort Griffin* (Spokane WA, 1992), 55, 59.
29. Jeff Price, "After Fort Griffin," *Sharps Collector Association Report* 10, no. 3 (2004): 5.
30. Ibid., 4. Robinson, *The Frontier World of Fort Griffin*, 60–61.
31. Gilbert, *Getting a Stand*, 116–17.
32. Cook, *The Border and the Buffalo*, 127.
33. Ibid., 139, 161.
34. Ibid., 201–2.
35. Charles M. Robinson III, *The Buffalo Hunters* (Austin TX, 1995), 108.
36. Thomas T. Smith, ed., *A Dose of Frontier Soldiering, The Memoirs of Corporal E. A. Bode* (Lincoln NE, 1994), 108–9.
37. Gilbert, *Getting A Stand*, 194. Gerald R. Mayberry, "The Sharps Rifle In Frontier Montana," *Sharps Collector Association Report* 12, no. 3 (2002): 19.
38. Abbott and Smith, *We Pointed Them North*, 101–2.
39. Davies, *Ten Days on the Plains*, 14.
40. Fleharty, *Wild Animals and Settlers*, 263.
41. Ibid., 253.
42. Ibid., 255.
43. Ibid., 231. William Temple Hornaday, *The Extermination of the American Bison* (Washington DC, 2002), 466.
44. Gerald R. Mayberry "Buffalo Guns & Adobe Walls," *Sharps Collector Association Report* 2, no. 3 (1995). Richard J. Labowskie, "The Sharps Rifle and the Kansas Buffalo Hunt," *Sharps Collector Association Report* 9, no. 3 and 10, no. 1, combined issue (2003): 30–37.
45. Stan Anderson, "The Model 1874 Military Rifle on the Kansas Frontier," *Sharps Collector Association Report* 9, no. 3 and 10, no. 1, combined issue (2003): 23. Richard J. Labowskie, "The Sharps Rifle and the Kansas Buffalo Hunt," *Sharps Collector Association Report* 9, no. 3 and 10, no. 1, combined issue (2003): 30–37.
46. Gerald R. Mayberry, "Buffalo Guns & Adobe Walls," *Sharps Collector Association Report* (Spring 1995).
47. Gilbert, *Getting A Stand*, 1–2.
48. Charles Hanson Jr., "The Greatest Years of Hide Hunting," *Museum of the Fur Trade Quarterly* (Summer 1977): 3–4. Gilbert, *Getting a Stand*, 81. Gerald R. Mayberry, "Buffalo Guns & Adobe Walls," *Sharps Collector Association Report* (Spring 1995). Cook, *The Border and the Buffalo*, 229.
49. Gerald R. Mayberry, "Sharps Metallic Rifle Cartridges," *Sharps Collector Association Report* (Winter 1995).
50. Chrisman, *Lost Trails*, 27.
51. Ibid., 33. Charles Hanson Jr., "The Greatest Years of Hide Hunting," *Museum of the Fur Trade Quarterly* (Summer 1977): 9.
52. Gilbert, *Getting a Stand*, 144.
53. Records, *Cherokee Outlet Cowboy*, 73.
54. William E. Connelley, ed., "The Life and Adventures of George W. Brown," *Collections of the Kansas State Historical Society* 17 (1928): 120–21.
55. Gilbert, *Getting a Stand*, 146.
56. Ibid., 25–27.
57. Ibid., 28.
58. Ibid., 32.
59. des Montaignes, *The Plains*, 45.
60. Sellers, *Sharps Firearms*, 305. Charles Hanson Jr., "The Greatest Years of Hide Hunting," *Museum of the Fur Trade Quarterly* (Summer 1977): 4.
61. Fleharty, *Wild Animals and Settlers*, 63–65.
62. Ibid., 182–83.
63. Daniel Justin Herman, *Hunting and the American Imagination* (Washington DC, 2001), 241.
64. Ibid., 239, 242.
65. des Montaignes, *The Plains*, 44.

CHAPTER TWELVE

1. McGrath, *Gunfighters*, 71.
2. Olmsted, *A Journey Through Texas*, 74.
3. Carl P. Russell, *Guns on the Early Frontiers* (Berkeley CA, 1957), 67, 305.
4. Ibid., 71–72. Alexander Ross, *Adventures of the First Settlers on the Oregon or Columbia River* (London, 1849), 84.
5. Santleben, *A Texas Pioneer*, 12.
6. Ibid., 51–52. Fleharty, *Wild Animals and Settlers*, 219–20.
7. Flaherty, *Wild Animals and Settlers*, 220–21.
8. Lowther, *Dodge City, Kansas*, 115–17.
9. Fleharty, *Wild Animals and Settlers*, 171–73.
10. Joseph Howard Parks, *General Edmund Kirby Smith, C.S.A.* (Baton Rouge LA, 1954), 77, 90–91.
11. H. H. McConnell, *Five Years a Cavalryman* (Norman OK, 1996), 98.
12. Barnes, *Apaches and Longhorns*, 91.
13. Ibid., 15–16.
14. Martin Pegler, *Firearms in the American West 1700–1900* (Midsomer Norton, England, 2002), 22.
15. Edward J. McClernand, *With the Indian and the Buffalo in Montana, 1870–1878* (Glendale CA, 1969), 21.
16. Burnham, *Scouting on Two Continents*, 49.
17. Thomas Cruse, *Apache Days and After*, ed. Eugene Cunningham (Caldwell ID, 1941), 148–49.

18. McGrath, *Gunfighters*, 70–71.

19. Ibid., 71–72.

20. Exhibit caption, Missouri State Capitol, Springfield.

21. In 1931 Dodge loaned the shotgun and his revolver for display in a Los Angeles bank window to promote Stuart Lake's biography of Wyatt Earp.

22. Fred Dodge, *Under Cover for Wells Fargo*, ed. Carolyn Lake (Boston MA, 1969), 59–60.

23. Bronson, *Reminiscences*, 271–72.

24. McGrath, *Gunfighters*, 82–83.

25. Stuart, *Forty Years On the Frontier*, 223.

26. John Young Nelson, *Fifty Years on the Trail* (Norman OK, 1963), 188.

27. Joanna L. Stratton, *Pioneer Women—Voices from the Kansas Frontier* (New York, 1981), 199–200.

28. Townshend, *A Tenderfoot In Colorado*, 5.

29. Parsons, *The First Winchester*, 75.

30. Howard Ruede, *Sod House Days, Letters from a Kansas Homesteader 1877–78*, ed. John Ise (New York, 1937), 188.

31. John K. Rollinson, *Wyoming Cattle Trails* (Caldwell ID, 1948), 143.

32. Jim Herron, *Fifty Years on the Owl Hoot Trail*, ed. Harry E. Chrisman (Chicago IL, 1969), 218–19.

33. Glenn Shirley, *Six-Gun and Silver Star* (Albuquerque NM, 1955), 186–87.

34. Records, *Cherokee Outlet Cowboy*, 188.

35. Chrisman, *Lost Trails*, 110.

36. Floyd C. Bard, *Horse Wrangler* (Norman OK, 1960), 8.

CHAPTER THIRTEEN

1. Frances M. A. Roe, *Army Letters from an Officer's Wife 1871–1888* (New York, 1909), 76.

2. Hunt, *The Trail Drivers*, 799. Glenda Riley, *Women and Indians on the Frontier, 1825–1915* (Albuquerque NM, 1991), 116.

3. Cook, *The Border and the Buffalo*, 56–57.

4. Susan G. Butruille, *Women's Voices from the Oregon Trail* (Boise ID, 1993), 127. Schlissel, *Women's Diaries*, 220. Holmes, *Covered Wagon Women*, 4:40. Jeanne Hamilton Watson, ed., *To the Land of Gold and Wickedness* (St. Louis MO, 1988), 154.

5. Holmes, *Covered Wagon Women*, 201.

6. Schlissel, *Women's Diaries*, 133.

7. David Dary, *Entrepreneurs of the Old West* (New York, 1986), 263–64.

8. Baillie-Grohman, *Camps in the Rockies*, 376–77.

9. Marrin, *Cowboys, Indians, and Gunfighters*, 112.

10. Michele J. Nacy, *Members of the Regiment* (Westport CT, 2000), 28.

11. Martha Summerhayes, *Vanished Arizona* (Salem MA, 1911), 101–2.

12. Ibid., 117.

13. Ibid., 122–23.

14. Roe, *Army Letters*, 42–43.

15. Ibid., 76.

16. Patricia Y. Stallard, *Glittering Misery: Dependents of the Indian Fighting Army* (San Rafael CA, 1978), 135.

17. Fleharty, *Wild Animals and Settlers*, 199.

18. Glendolin Damon Wagner, *Old Neutriment* (Lincoln NE, 1989), 102.

19. Herman, *Hunting and the American Imagination*, 229.

20. Maureen Christensen, "A Gun in Her Hands, Women in Firearms Advertising, 1900–1920," *ARMAX, The Journal of the Cody Firearms Museum* 5 (1995): 18, 25, 27, 31.

21. Wingate, *Through the Yellowstone Park*, 43. Harold J. Cook, *Tales of the 04 Ranch, Recollections of Harold J. Cook 1887–1909* (Lincoln NE, 1968), 42–43.

22. Christensen, "A Gun in Her Hands," 18.

23. Ibid., 57, 69.

CHAPTER FOURTEEN

1. Carter, *On the Border With Mackenzie*, 175.

2. Nacy, *Members of the Regiment*, 5–6. Keir B. Sterling, "U.S. Army Contributions to American Natural Science 1864–1890," *Army History, The Professional Bulletin of Army History* (Summer 1997): 3.

3. Ami Frank Mulford, *Fighting Indians in the 7th United States Cavalry* (Bellevue NE, 1970), 92–93.

4. Ibid., 56–57.

5. John E. Cox, *Five Years In the United States Army* (New York, 1973), iii.

6. McConnell, *Five Years a Cavalryman*, 114.

7. Garavaglia and Worman, *Firearms . . . 1866–1894*, 28.

8. George A. Forsyth, *Thrilling Days in Army Life* (New York, 1902), 11, 13, 17.

9. Ibid., 69–70.

10. David L. Spotts, *Campaigning with Custer and the Nineteenth Kansas Volunteer Cavalry on the Washita Campaign 1868–69* (Los Angeles CA, 1928), 44–45.

11. Carter, *On the Border With Mackenzie*, 27, 174–75.

12. J. W. Vaughn, *The Battle of Platte Bridge* (Norman OK, 1963), 50–51.

13. McConnell, *Five Years A Cavalryman*, 102–103.

14. John M. Carroll, *The Black Military Experience in the American West* (New York, 1971), 336.

15. Jones, *Daily Life On the Nineteenth Century American Frontier*, 222.

16. William Loren Katz, *The Black West* (Garden City NY, 1971), 219.

17. John E. Parsons, *West on the 49th Parallel* (New York, 1963), 53, 74, 140.

18. Clive M. Law, *Canadian Military Handguns, 1855–1985* (Bloomfield, Ontario, 1994), 17, 24.

19. Raymond L. Welty, "Supplying the Frontier Military Posts," *Kansas Historical Quarterly* (May 1938): 167.

20. McAulay, *Rifles of the U.S. Army*, 106.

21. Garavaglia and Worman, *Firearms . . . 1866–1894*, 15.

22. *U.S. Martial Arms Collector and Springfield Research Newsletter* (April/July 2001): 3. R. Stephen Dorsey, *Guns of the Western Indian War* (Eugene OR, 1995), 150.

23. Franklin B. Mallory, "7th Cavalry Guns," *Military Collector & Historian* (Winter 1977): 163.

24. Sandy Barnard, *I Go with Custer* (Bismarck ND, 1996), 144.

25. Allen, *From Fort Laramie to Wounded Knee*, 9–10.

26. Harold H. Schuler, *Fort Sully, Guns at Sunset* (Vermillion SD, 1992), 118–19. McAulay, *Rifles of the U.S. Army*, 106, 114.

27. Albert J. Frasca, *The .45–70 Springfield Book II* (Springfield OH, 1997), 350. Smith, *A Dose of Frontier Soldiering*, 28.

28. Sherry L. Smith, *Sagebrush Soldier, Private William Earl Smith's View of the Sioux War of 1876* (Norman OK, 1989), 28. Wayne R. Kime, ed., *The Black Hills Journals of Colonel Richard Irving Dodge* (Norman OK, 1996), 53.

29. Davies, *Ten Days on the Plains*, 3, 102–3.

30. Herbert Krause and Gary D. Olson, *Prelude to Glory* (Sioux Falls SD, 1974), 12.

31. James Calhoun, *With Custer in '74*, ed. Lawrence A. Frost (Provo UT, 1979), 99.

32. Ibid., 13–14.

33. Ibid., 18–20, 25.

34. Ibid., 49.

35. Sandy Barnard, *Custer's First Sergeant John Ryan* (Terra Haute IN, 1996), 191.

36. Ibid., 204.

37. James S. Hutchins, ed., "Captain Michaelis Reports on Army Weapons and Equipment on the Northern Plains 1876–1879," *Man at Arms* (January/February 1988): 36. McAulay, *Rifles of the U.S. Army*, 137.

38. Dorsey, *Guns of the Western Indian War*, 64.

39. McAulay, *Rifles of the U.S. Army*, 139.

40. Peter A. Schmidt, *Hall's Military Breechloaders* (Lincoln RI, 1996), 85.

41. Hutchins, "Captain Michaelis Reports," 30. Douglas C. McChristian, *The U.S. Army in the West 1870–1880* (Norman OK, 1995), 115.

42. Hutchins, "Captain Michaelis Reports," 37. Garavaglia and Worman, *Firearms . . . 1866–1894*, 47.

43. McAulay, *Rifles of the U.S. Army*, 41.

44. Dodge, *The Plains of North America*, 131.

45. Thomas T. Smith, *A Dose of Frontier Soldiering*, 64–65. Don Rickey Jr., *Forty Miles a Day on Beans and Hay* (Norman OK, 1963), 221.

46. Hutchins, "Major Thornton," 45.

47. Merrill J. Mattes, *Indians, Infants and Infantry* (Denver CO, 1960), 151.

48. McChristian, *An Army of Marksmen*, 22.

49. Ibid., 23, 34.

50. Exhibit caption, Fort Kearney State Historical Park, NE. Mulford, *Fighting Indians*, 92.

51. Robert Wooster, *Soldiers, Sutlers and Settlers* (College Station TX, 1987), 151–52. McChristian, *An Army of Marksmen*, 46.

52. McChristian, *An Army of Marksmen*, 54, 66, 84.

53. Rickey, *Forty Miles a Day*, 104–5. Ray H. Mattison, *The Army Post on the Northern Plains 1865–1885* (Gering NE, 1962), 24.

54. Mattes, *Indians, Infants and Infantry*, 248–49.

55. Ibid., 249.

56. Ostrander, *An Army Boy of the Sixties*, 190.

57. Smith, *A Dose of Frontier Soldiering*, 47.

58. Ibid., 163.

59. Ibid., 46.

60. Ibid., 60.

61. Ibid., 94.

62. Garavaglia and Worman, *Firearms . . . 1866–1894*, 35, 38. Lawrence A. Frost, *Custer's 7th Cavalry and the Campaign of 1873* (El Segundo CA, 1986), 212. Haynes, *General Custer and his Sporting Rifles*, 49.

63. Frasca, *The .45–70 Springfield Book II*, 111, 115.

64. Albert J. Frasca and Robert H. Hill, *The .45–70 Springfield* (Northridge CA, 1980), 36. Frasca, *The .45–70 Springfield Book II*, 184–90.

65. Cruse, *Apache Days and After*, 120. James Pickering, "Marlins In the Apache Wars," *Man At Arms* (August 1996): 16–7. Foster, "Buffalo Guns in Texas," 51–52. Frasca, *The .45–70 Springfield Book II*, 187.

66. Frasca and Hill, *The .45–70 Springfield*, 114. Frasca, *The .45–70 Springfield Book II*, 213–14. Garavaglia and Worman, *Firearms . . . 1866–1894*, 53.

67. Capt. Leonard Y. Loring to Colt Patent Fire Arms Mfg. Co., 13 March 1882. Connecticut State Library, Hartford. Col. L. Wheaton to Colt Patent Fire Arms Mfg. Co., 6 April 1886. Connecticut State Library, Hartford. Lt. C. H. Rockwell to Colt Patent Fire Arms Mfg. Co., 18 February 1885. Connecticut State Library, Hartford.

68. McChristian, *The U.S. Army In the West*, 117.

69. Parsons, *Smith & Wesson Revolvers*, 79.

70. Ibid., 77–78. Robert Bruce, *The Fighting Norths and Pawnee Scouts* (New York, 1930), 54, 69.

71. Ernest Wallace, ed., *Ranald S. Mackenzie's Official Correspondence Relating to Texas, 1871–1873* (Lubbock TX, 1967), 95.

72. Edward Scott Meadows, *U.S. Military Holsters and Pistol Cartridge Boxes* (Dallas TX, 1987), 106. John E. Parsons, *The Peacemaker and Its Rivals* (New York, 1950), 22.

73. Rickey, *Forty Miles a Day*, 166.

74. Parsons, *Smith & Wesson Revolvers*, 93.

75. Hutchins, "Captain Michaelis Reports," 31.

76. *Springfield Research Newsletter* (October–December 1987): 2. Charles Pate, e-mail message to author, March 11, 2004. Charles W. Pate, "The San Francisco S&W Schofield Revolver," *Man at Arms* no. 3 (1996): 30–31.

77. Smith, *A Dose of Frontier Soldiering*, 41–42.

78. Ibid., 69.

79. Wilkerson, *Colt's Double Action Revolver Model of 1878*, 30.

80. Ibid., 31.

81. Ibid., 40.

82. Ibid., 60–61.

83. John D. McDermott, "Desertion in the Nineteenth-Century U.S. Army," *Nebraska History* (Winter 1997): 169. Paul L. Hedren, *Fort Laramie in 1876* (Lincoln NE, 1988), 210.

84. *Report of Findings*, General Courts Martial, Fort Keogh, Montana Territory, June 14, 1888.

85. Smith, *A Dose of Frontier Soldiering*, 38–39.

86. McConnell, *Five Years A Cavalryman*, 135.

87. Cruse, *Apache Days and After*, 69–70. John A. Kopec, "An Indian Wars U.S. Cavalry 'Cover-up,'" *Gun Report* (February 1978): 64.

CHAPTER FIFTEEN

1. *Winchester Repeating Arms Company Catalog*, 1875, 28.
2. Serven, *Conquering the Frontiers*, 151.
3. Marcot, *Spencer Repeating Firearms*, 89.
4. James Chisholm, *South Pass, 1868, James Chisholm's Journal of the Wyoming Gold Rush*, ed. Lola M. Homsher (Lincoln NE. 1960), 173.
5. Stan Nelson, "The Guns of Northfield," *Minnesota Weapons Collectors Association News* (December 2001): 10.
6. Townshend, *A Tenderfoot in Colorado*, 238–43.
7. Marcot, *Spencer Repeating Firearms*, 129.
8. Parsons, *The First Winchester*, 112. James D. Gordon, *Winchester's New Model 1873: A Tribute* (Grant CO, 1997), 2:639.
9. *Winchester Repeating Arms Company Catalog*, May 1879, 14.
10. Gordon, *Winchester's New Model 1873*, 1:341. George Madis, *The Winchester Book* (Lancaster TX, 1971), 195. Williamson, *Winchester*, 74.
11. Gillett, *Six Years with the Texas Rangers*, 224.
12. *Winchester Repeating Arms Company Catalog*, 1875, 26.
13. Ibid., 29.
14. Gillett, *Six Years with the Texas Rangers*, 21, 56–57. Gordon, *Winchester's New Model 1873*, 2:621.
15. Gordon, *Winchester's New Model 1873*, 2:605–6.
16. Ibid., 619–21.
17. Nyle H. Miller and Joseph W. Snell, "Some Notes on Cowtown Police Officers and Gun Fighters," *Kansas Historical Quarterly* (Summer 1961): 114.
18. Dodge, *The Plains of North America*, 129–31.
19. Williamson, *Winchester*, 68.
20. Madis, *The Winchester Book*, 201.
21. *Winchester Repeating Arms Company Catalog*, 1879, 18.
22. Madis, *The Winchester Book*, 230.
23. Allen, *Adventures with Indians and Game*, 43, 83. Hill, *The End of the Cattle Trail*, 76. Tanner, *Doc Holliday*, 196–97.
24. R. L. Wilson, *Winchester: An American Legend* (New York, 1991), 13–14. *Winchester Repeating Arms Company Catalog*, 1879, 19. Madis, *The Winchester Book*, 225.
25. Abbott and Smith, *We Pointed Them North*, 132.
26. Ronald Atkin, *Maintain the Right* (Toronto, Ontario, 1973), 266.
27. *The New West: Being the Official Reports to Parliament of the Activities of the Royal North-West Mounted Police Force 1888–1909* (Toronto, Ontario, 1973), 70.
28. Ibid., 125.
29. John G. Donkin, *Trooper and Redskin in the Far Northwest* (London, 1889), 12, 31, 229.
30. Atkin, *Maintain the Right*, 266–67,
31. Gordon, *Winchester's New Model 1873*, 2:384. Abbott and Smith, *We Pointed Them North*, 132. Williamson, *Winchester*, 72. Wilson, *Winchester: An American Legend*, 17.
32. Gordon, *Winchester's New Model 1873*, 2:384–85.
33. Ibid., 386–87.
34. R. B. Townshend, *The Tenderfoot in New Mexico* (London, 1923), 182.
35. Herbert G. Houze, "The Winchester Model 1886," *American Rifleman* (October 2003): 53–55.
36. Madis, *The Winchester Book*, 223. Theodore Roosevelt, *Hunting Trips of a Ranchman* (New York, 1926), 399.
37. Theodore Roosevelt, *The Wilderness Hunter* (New York, 1926), 370–72.
38. W. J. L. Sullivan, *Twelve Years in the Saddle for Law and Order on the Frontiers of Texas* (New York, 1966), 122, 234–36.
39. Harrell McCullough, *Selden Lindsey, U.S. Deputy Marshal* (Oklahoma City OK, 1990), 123.
40. Canton, *Frontier Trails*, 96–97.
41. Rollinson, *Pony Trails in Wyoming*, 394.
42. Williamson, *Winchester*, 102. Rollinson, *Wyoming Cattle Trails*, 270.
43. William B. Shugars III, "A Johnson County War Colt," *Gun Report* (October 1990): 20.
44. Robert A. Murray, "Arms of Wyoming's Cattle War," *Shooting Times* (July 1967): 42.
45. Christensen, "A Gun in Her Hands," 23.
46. Randy Saba, "'C.M.R.' 1894 Winchester," *Minnesota Weapons Collectors Association News* (January 2000).
47. Christensen, "A Gun in Her Hands," 23. Stan Nelson, "Harry Tracy's Outlaw Career," *Minnesota Weapons Collectors Association News* (Spring 1992): 10. Krakel, *The Saga of Tom Horn*, 52.
48. Bill O'Neal, *The Arizona Rangers* (Austin TX, 1987), ix, 185, 187.
49. Ibid., 4, 12, 48.
50. Siringo, *Riatas and Spurs*, 209.
51. William S. Brophy, *Marlin Firearms, A History of the Guns and the Company That Made Them* (Harrisburg PA, 1989), 145.
52. Ibid., 145, 147, 149. Garavaglia and Worman, *Firearms…1866–1894*, 197.
53. Barnes, *Apaches & Longhorns*, 73.
54. Allen A. Erwin, *The Southwest of John H. Slaughter* (Glendale CA, 1965), 260–61
55. James Blower, *Gold Rush* (New York, 1971), 2–3, 21.
56. Gould, *Modern American Rifles*, 80.
57. Ibid., 82.
58. Capt. W. R. Thomas to Colt Patent Fire Arms Mfg. Co., 2 October 1886. Connecticut State Library, Hartford.
59. Wilson, *The Book of Colt Firearms*, 505.
60. John T. Dutcher, *Ballard—The Great American Single Shot Rifle* (Denver CO, 2002), 30.
61. Bronson, *Reminiscences*, 352–53.
62. Hoyt, *A Frontier Doctor*, 40, 45.
63. Frank D. Carpenter, *Adventures in Geyser Land* (Caldwell ID, 1935), 98, 254.
64. Dutcher, *Ballard*, 87.
65. Ibid., 171, 249.
66. Ibid., 105, 155, 165.
67. L. D. Satterlee, "Maynard Breech-Loading Firearms

506

Catalog, 1885," 14 *Old Gun Catalogs* (Chicago IL, 1962), 2:35.

68. Hughes, *Pioneer Years in the Black Hills*, 100–101.
69. Ibid., 40.
70. Breakenridge, *Helldorado*, 41.
71. Miller and Snell, *Why the West Was Wild*, 53.
72. Gillett, *Six Years with the Texas Rangers*, 144.
73. Santleben, *A Texas Pioneer*, 115.
74. Howard R. Driggs, ed. *The Bullwhacker: Adventures of a Frontier Freighter* (Lincoln NE, 1988), 5.
75. Ibid., 73.
76. Frasca and Hill, *The .45–70 Springfield*, 183.
77. Allen, *Adventures with Indians and Game*, 256.
78. Ibid., 107.
79. Ibid., 36. Hughes, *Pioneer Years in the Black Hills*, 165n40.
80. Rollinson, *Pony Trails in Wyoming*, 47, 69.
81. Stallard, *Glittering Misery*, 135.
82. G. O. Shields, *Hunting in the Great West* (Chicago IL, 1890), 286.

CHAPTER SIXTEEN

1. Robert Taft, *Artists and Illustrators of the Old West 1850–1900* (New York, 1953), 43–44.
2. Dryden, *Up the Columbia*, 123. Thwaites, *Early Western Travels*, 6:31; 7:254. James A. Hanson, "The Keelboat," *Museum of the Fur Trade Quarterly* (Spring & Summer 1994): 18.
3. Ross, *Adventures of the First Settlers*, 216. Hanson, *The Hawken Rifle*, 74.
4. Kreyche, *Visions of the American West*, 78. Chittenden, *History of Early Steamboat Navigation*, 1:114.
5. Chittenden, *History of Early Steamboat Navigation*, 1:181–82.
6. Dr. John Kudlik, e-mail message to author, September 17, 2002.
7. Taft, *Artists and Illustrators*, 43–44.
8. Jennifer Stafford, museum technician, DeSoto National Wildlife Refuge, IA, e-mail message to author, September 17, 2002.
9. Kendall, *Narrative*, 1:143–44.
10. Hannon, *The Boston-Newton Company Venture*, 28.
11. Ibid., 25. Schuler, *Fort Sully, Guns at Sunset*, 120. Warren Ripley, *Artillery and Ammunition of the Civil War* (New York, 1970), 48–49, 367. Grant, *Personal Memoirs*, 96.
12. Effie Mona Mack, *Nevada: A History of the State from the Earliest Times through the Civil War* (Glendale CA, 1936), 81. des Montaignes, *The Plains*, xii–xiii.
13. White, *News of the Plains*, 7:37, 39. Mack, *Nevada*, 92–93.
14. Grant, *Personal Memoirs*, 106–9.
15. White, *News of the Plains*, 4:121–23, 159.
16. Mansfield, *Mansfield on the Condition*, 224, 231.
17. White, *News of the Plains*, 4:257–58, 326–27.
18. Frank Myers, *Soldiering in Dakota among the Indians In 1863–4–5* (Freeport NY, 1971), 15.
19. Eugene F. Ware, *The Indian War of 1864* (New York, 1960), 363–64.
20. White, *News of the Plains*, 3:346–47; 4:389, 392, 401, 525.
21. Dary, *The Santa Fe Trail*, 274.
22. Ware, *The Indian War*, 381–82.
23. Mattes, *Indians, Infants and Infantry*, 136–37.
24. Robert A. Murray, *The Army on the Powder River* (Bellevue NE, 1969), 29.
25. Mrs. Frank C. Montgomery, "Fort Wallace and Its Relation to the Frontier," *Collections of the Kansas State Historical Society 1926–1928* 17: 231.
26. Dixon, *Life of "Billy" Dixon*, 51.
27. A. K. McClure, *Three Thousand Miles through the Rocky Mountains* (Philadelphia PA, 1869), 144.
28. William F. Zimmer, *Frontier Soldier*, ed. Jerome A. Green (Helena, MT, 1998), 75.
29. *Annual Report of the Secretary of War*, 1876, serial 1742, 423.
30. Joseph Berk, *The Gatling Gun* (Boulder CO, 1991), 18–19.
31. Ibid., 16, 28.
32. *Outline Descriptions of the Posts in the Military Division of the Missouri, 1876*, reprint ed. (Bellevue NE, 1969), 260–64. Schuler, *Fort Sully, Guns at Sunset*, 120–21.
33. Berk, *The Gatling Gun*, 34.
34. Rickey, *Forty Miles a Day*, 99–100. George A. Custer, *Wild Life on the Plains and Horrors of Indian Warfare* (St. Louis MO, 1891), 72.
35. Berk, *The Gatling Gun*, 35. James L. Haley, *The Buffalo War* (New York, 1976), 127, 217.
36. Krause and Olson, *Prelude to Glory*, 11–12.
37. Calhoun, *With Custer in '74*, 25.
38. Cox, *Five Years in the United States Army*, 34, 98.
39. Berk, *The Gatling Gun*, 34–36.
40. Wagner, *Old Neutriment*, 126–27.
41. Zimmer, *Frontier Soldier*, 84–86.
42. Berk, *The Gatling Gun*, 38–39. Oliver O. Howard, *My Life and Experiences among Our Hostile Indians* (New York, 1972), 287, 404.
43. Gerald O. Kelver, ed., *15 Years on the Western Frontier 1866–1881* (Fort Collins CO, 1975), 53.
44. John P. Wilson, *Merchants, Guns and Money—The Story of Lincoln County and Its Wars* (Santa Fe NM, 1987), 177.
45. Mattes, *Indians, Infants and Infantry*, 240–41.
46. Mulford, *Fighting Indians*, 66. (In the 1870s, the Deadwood stage line used at least two armored stage coaches, the "Monitor" and "Old Ironsides" and presumably it was to these vehicles that Mumford referred.)
47. *Outline Descriptions of the Posts*, 260–64.
48. William E. Birkheimer, *Historical Sketch of the Organization, Administration, Materiel and Tactics of the Artillery, United States Army* (Washington DC, 1884), 296. Schuler, *Fort Sully, Guns at Sunset*, 121.

CHAPTER SEVENTEEN

1. Hutchins, "Captain Michaelis Reports," 36.
2. Charles E. Hanson Jr., "An Indian Trade Gun of 1680,"

Missouri Archaeologist (December 1960): 96.

3. Jean Louis Berlandier, *The Indians of Texas in 1830*, ed. John C. Ewers (Washington DC, 1969), 16.

4. Ibid., 13–14, 53. John L. Kessell, *Spain in the Southwest* (Norman OK, 2002), 237, 251, 272. Russell, *Guns on the Early Frontiers*, 300.

5. John C. Ewers, *Indian Life on the Upper Missouri* (Norman OK, 1968), 23. Dan R. Flores, ed., *Journal of an Indian Trader, Anthony Glass and the Texas Trading Frontier 1790–1810* (College Station TX, 1985), 24.

6. James P. Ronda, *Astoria and Empire* (Lincoln NE, 1990), 67–68, 85. George Metcalf, "A Mail Shirt of the Fur Trade Period," *Museum of the Fur Trade Quarterly* (Winter 1968): 2–3.

7. An outstanding collection of Northwest guns as well as extensive exhibits of other trade materials can be seen at the prestigious Museum of the Fur Trade in Chadron, Nebraska.

8. T. M. Hamilton, "Concluding Comments and Observations," *Missouri Archaeologist* (December 1960): 209. John C. Luttig, *Journal of a Fur-Trading Expedition on the Upper Missouri 1812–1813*, ed. Stella M. Drumm (St. Louis MO, 1920), 92.

9. Charles E. Hanson Jr., "Smoothbores on the Frontier," *The Book of Buckskinning*, ed. William H. Scurlock, 4:115–16 (Texarkana TX, 1987). Ewers, *Indian Life*, 38.

10. William H. Nevius, "The First American Northwest Trade Gun Part I," *Museum of the Fur Trade Quarterly* (Winter 1995): 9. Charles E. Hanson Jr., *The Northwest Gun* (Lincoln NE, 1956), 24, 31.

11. Berlandier, *The Indians of Texas in 1830*, 110, 119.

12. Charles Hanson Jr., "Tryon's Fancy Northwest Guns of the 1850s," *Museum of the Fur Trade Quarterly* (Winter 1983): 10, 13. Charles Z. Tryon, *The History of a Business Established One Hundred Years Ago* (Philadelphia PA, 1911), 21.

13. Charles E. Hanson Jr., "Locks From Indian Trade Guns of the 19th Century," *Missouri Archaeologist* (December 1960): 176. Ewers, *Indian Life*, 39–40.

14. E. E. Rich, ed., *Peter Skene Ogden's Snake Country Journals 1824–25 and 1825–26* (London, 1950), 43.

15. *Museum of the Fur Trade Quarterly* (Winter 1989): 12.

16. Ewers, *Indian Life*, 40.

17. Hanson, "Smoothbores on the Frontier," 118. T. M. Hamilton, "The Gunsmith's Cache Discovered at Malta Bend, Missouri," *Missouri Archaeologist* (December 1960): 151. Warren W. Caldwell, "Firearms and Related Materials From Ft. Pierre II (39ST217), Oahe Reservoir, South Dakota," *Missouri Archaeologist* (December 1960): 188. Isaac I. Stevens, "The Red River Hunters," *Report of Commissioner of Indian Affairs 1854* (Washington DC, 1855), 191–92.

18. Messiter, *Sport and Adventures*, 19.

19. Thwaites, *Early Western Travels*, 2:145–46.

20. Ibid., 15:78, 74.

21. Murray, *Travels in North America*, 269.

22. White, *News of the Plains*, 1:157, 210–15.

23. Conard, *"Uncle Dick" Wootton*, 41–42.

24. Henry A. Boller, *Among the Indians*, ed. Milo Milton

25. Quaife (Chicago IL, 1959), 31–32.

25. Hanson, "Smoothbores on the Frontier," 119–20.

26. James A. Hanson, "Percussion Fur Trade Guns," *Museum of the Fur Trade Quarterly* (Summer 2003): 7. *Museum of the Fur Trade Quarterly* (Summer 1995): 8–9.

27. Hanson, "Smoothbores on the Frontier," 124.

28. Duval, *The Adventures of Big-Foot Wallace*, 17.

29. Thwaites, *Early Western Travels*, 18:377.

30. Flores, *Journal of an Indian Trader*, 60.

31. Smith, *A Dose of Frontier Soldiering*, 127.

32. Hutchins, "Major Thornton," 45.

33. Flory, *Thrilling Echoes*, 19.

34. Thwaites, *Early Western Travels*, 20:122; 19:347.

35. Ibid., 20:66, 267.

36. Conard, *"Uncle Dick" Wootton*, 429–30.

37. John C. Cremony, *Life among the Apaches* (San Francisco CA, 1868), 189.

38. Richard Irving Dodge, *Our Wild Indians* (New York, 1959), 416–17.

39. Charles E. Hanson Jr., "The Deadly Arrow," *Museum of the Fur Trade Quarterly* (Winter 1967): 2–3.

40. Dodge, *Our Wild Indians*, 419. Thwaites, *Early Western Travels*, 15:77.

41. Charles Hanson Jr., "Henry Deringer and the Indian Trade," *Museum of the Fur Trade Quarterly* (Fall 1979): 5.

42. Ibid., 8–10.

43. Ibid., 11. Grant Foreman, *The Five Civilized Tribes* (Norman OK, 1934), 28.

44. Hanson, "Henry Deringer and the Indian Trade," 11. Tryon, *The History of a Business*, 21.

45. William H. Nevius, "Deringer's Pistols For the Choctaw Light Horse," *Museum of the Fur Trade Quarterly* (Spring & Summer 1994): 2–8.

46. Charles E. Hanson Jr., "Henry E. Leman—Riflemaker," *Museum of the Fur Trade Quarterly* (Winter 1984): 4, 7, 9.

47. Charles Hanson Jr., "The Deringer Belt Pistol," *Museum of the Fur Trade Quarterly* (Winter 1982): 21. Boller, *Among the Indians*, 90. Flory, *Thrilling Echoes*, 86.

48. Thwaites, *Early Western Travels*, 23:357; 22:389.

49. Ibid., 24:18.

50. Hyslop, *Bound for Santa Fe*, 355.

51. *Museum of the Fur Trade Quarterly* (Fall 1990): 13–14. Letterman is best remembered for his service during the Civil War reorganizing the army's medical service and greatly increasing its efficiency.

52. Carvalho, *Incidents of Travel and Adventure*, 158–61.

53. Hannum, *A Quaker Forty-Niner*, 185. White, *News of the Plains*, 8:236. Garavaglia and Worman, *Firearms . . . 1803–1865*, 52.

54. Ralph Adam Smith, *Borderlander, The Life of James Kirker, 1793–1852* (Norman OK, 1999), 50, 55.

55. Burton, *The City of the Saints*, 131.

56. Harvey Lewis Carter, *"Dear Old Kit," The Historical Christopher Carson* (Norman OK, 1968), 207.

57. Doyle, *Journeys*, 1:117.

58. Ibid., 152–53.

59. Parsons, *The First Winchester*, 68.

60. Wayne R. Austerman, "Maza Wakan For the Sioux," *Man at Arms* (January–February 1988): 20.

61. Charles E. Hanson Jr., "The Post-War Indian Gun Trade," *Museum of the Fur Trade Quarterly* (Fall 1968): 2, 6, 10.
62. Ibid., 7.
63. Ibid., 3.
64. Frank Herbert, *40 Years Prospecting and Mining in the Black Hills of South Dakota* (Rapid City SD, 1921), 32–33.
65. Dixon, *Life of "Billy" Dixon*, 30, 51–52.
66. John Fahey, *The Flathead Indians* (Norman OK, 1974), 313.
67. McConnell, *Five Years a Cavalryman*, 216.
68. Allen, *Adventures with Indians and Game*, 68–71.
69. Gordon, *Winchester's New Model of 1873*, 2:594.
70. Gillett, *Six Years with the Texas Rangers*, 209.
71. Dodge, *Our Wild Indians*, 424.
72. Zimmer, *Frontier Soldier*, 22–23.
73. George F. Brimlow, *Cavalryman out of the West* (Caldwell ID, 1944), 86.
74. Dick Harmon and Douglas D. Scott, "A Sharps Rifle From the Battle of the Little Bighorn," *Man at Arms* (January–February 1988): 12.
75. Zimmer, *Frontier Soldier*, 69. Austerman, "Maza Wakan," 20.
76. Nelson A. Miles, *Serving the Republic* (New York, 1911), 223.
77. Herman J. Viola, *Diplomats in Buckskins* (Bluffton SC, 1995), 106–8.
78. Robert A. Murray, "Treaty Presents at Fort Laramie, 1867–68: Prices and Quantities from the Seth A. Ward Ledger," *Museum of the Fur Trade Quarterly* (Fall 1977): 2–3.
79. Evan S. Connell, *Son of the Morning Star* (San Francisco CA, 1984), 187.
80. Woodworth Clum, *Apache Agent, The Story of John P. Clum* (Boston MA, 1936), 219, 222. McAulay, *Rifles of the U.S. Army*, 115.
81. *Compilation of Narratives of Expeditions in Alaska* (Washington DC, 1900), 323–46. Frank Oppel, *Tales of Alaska and the Yukon* (Secaucus NJ, 1986), 186.
82. Henry T. Allen, *Report of an Expedition to the Copper, Tanana, and Koyukuk Rivers in the Territory of Alaska in the Year 1885* (Washington DC, 1887), 132.
83. Ibid., 141.
84. *Museum of the Fur Trade Quarterly* (Summer 1995): 118. Russell, *Guns on the Early Frontiers*, 301. William E. Simeone, *Rifles, Blankets, and Beads* (Norman OK, 1995), 30.
85. George Thornton Emmons, *The Tlingit Indians*, ed. Frederica de Laguna (Seattle WA, 1991), 132.
86. Ibid., 130.
87. Ibid.
88. Oppel, *Tales of Alaska*, 98.
89. Mark H. Brown, *The Flight of the Nez Perce* (New York, 1967), 191.
90. Ibid., 195–96.
91. Mulford, *Fighting Indians*, 118–19.
92. Brown, *The Flight of the Nez Perce*, 412.
93. Ibid., 267.
94. Lucullus Virgil McWhorter, *Yellow Wolf: His Own Story* (Caldwell ID, 1940), 29, 77–78.
95. Hutchins, "Captain Michaelis Reports," 36.
96. Garavaglia and Worman, *Firearms . . . 1866–1894*, 370–71.
97. Ibid., 371.
98. Ibid. Jones, *The Treaty of Medicine Lodge*, 136–37.
99. Britton Davis, *The Truth about Geronimo* (New Haven CT, 1929), 59.
100. Gordon, *Winchester's New Model 1873*, 2:592.
101. Paul Knepper and Michael B. Puckett, "The Historicity of Tony Hillerman's Indian Police," *Journal of the West* (January 1995): 13–14, 18.
102. Frank Richard Prassel, *The Western Peace Officer* (Norman OK, 1972), 185.
103. Knepper and Puckett, "The Historicity," 14. Flayderman, *Flayderman's Guide*, 146.
104. John A. Kopec and H. Sterling Fenn, *Colt Cavalry & Artillery Revolvers* (Newport Beach CA, 1994), 177–78.
105. Flayderman, *Flayderman's Guide*, 161. Don Rickey to Bill Barnhart, 23 December 1974. Bill Barnhart to Don Rickey, 11 August 1975.
106. Thomas W. Dunlay, *Wolves for the Blue Soldiers* (Lincoln NE, 1982), 20, 30–31.
107. William E. Unrau, ed., *Tending the Talking Wire* (Salt Lake City UT, 1979), 319–20.
108. Ibid., 168.
109. Ibid., 44, 46, 72.
110. Carroll, *The Black Military Experience*, 339.
111. Fort Davis National Historic Site Web page, www.nps.gov/foda/. Jerry Thompson, *A Wild and Vivid Land* (Austin TX, 1997), 134.
112. Bruce, *The Fighting Norths*, 26. George Bird Grinnell, *Two Great Scouts and Their Pawnee Battalion* (Cleveland OH, 1928), 141–42.
113. Bruce, *The Fighting Norths*, 29–30. Henry M. Stanley, *My Early Travels and Adventures in America and Asia* (New York, 1905), 1:163.
114. Bruce, *The Fighting Norths*, 15.
115. Howbert, *Memories of a Lifetime*, 184.
116. Barnard, *Custer's First Sergeant*, 136.
117. Bruce, *The Fighting Norths*, 44, 60.
118. John Upton Terrell, *Apache Chronicle* (New York, 1972), 35–36.
119. William K. Emerson, *Encyclopedia of United States Army Insignia and Uniforms* (Norman OK, 1996), 187. John G. Bourke, *An Apache Campaign in the Sierra Madre* (New York, 1958), 33, 39, 40, 48.
120. "Warriors In Blue," brochure, Fort Sill National Historic Landmark and Museum, Fort Sill OK.
121. Joseph C. Porter, *Paper Medicine Man: John Gregory Bourke and His American West* (Norman OK, 1986), 64.

BIBLIOGRAPHY

BOOKS

Abbott, E. C., and Helena Huntington Smith. *We Pointed Them North*. Norman, OK, 1939.

Adams, Ramon F. *The Best of the American Cowboy*. Norman, OK, 1957.

Allen, Charles W. *From Fort Laramie to Wounded Knee in the West That Was*. Edited by Richard E. Jensen. Lincoln, NE, 1997.

Allen, William A. *Adventures with Indians and Game*. Chicago, IL, 1903.

Anderson, John C. *Mackinaws down the Missouri*. Edited by Glen Barrett. Logan, UT, 1973.

Anderson, John Q., ed. *Tales of Frontier Texas 1830–1860*. Dallas, TX, 1966.

Atkin, Ronald. *Maintain the Right*. Toronto, Ontario, 1973.

Austerman, Wayne R. *Sharps Rifles and Spanish Mules*. College Station, TX, 1985.

Backus, Anna Jean. *Mountain Meadows Witness*. Spokane, WA, 1995.

Badger, R. G. *Gold and Sunshine—Reminiscences of Early California*. Boston, MA, 1922.

Bagley, Will, ed. *Frontiersman: Abner Blackburn's Narrative*. Salt Lake City, UT, 1992.

Baillie-Grohman, William A. *Camps in the Rockies*. New York, 1882.

Ball, Durwood. *Army Regulars on the Western Frontier 1848–1861*. Norman, OK, 2001.

Barbour, Barton H., ed. *Reluctant Frontiersman: James Ross Larkin on the Santa Fe Trail 1856–57*. Albuquerque, NM, 1990.

Bard, Floyd C. *Horse Wrangler*. Norman, OK, 1960.

Bari, Valeska. *The Course of Empire*. New York, 1931.

Barker, Malcolm E., ed. *San Francisco Memoirs 1835–1851*. San Francisco, CA, 1994.

Barnard, Sandy. *Custer's First Sergeant John Ryan*. Terra Haute, IN, 1996.

———. *I Go With Custer*. Bismarck, ND, 1996.

Barnes, Will C. *Apaches & Longhorns*. Edited by Frank C. Lockwood. Tucson, AZ, 1982.

Barney, Libeus. *Letters of the Pike's Peak Gold Rush*. San Jose, CA, 1959.

Beadle, J. H. *Brigham's Destroying Angel*. New York, 1872.

Beckstead, James H. *Cowboying, A Tough Job in a Hard Land*. Salt Lake City, UT, 1991.

Bekeart. *Three Generations 1837–1949: Jules Francois Bekeart, A Gunsmith, Philip Baldwin Bekeart, His Son, Philip Kendall Bekeart, His Grandson—100th Anniversary of the Establishment in the Firearms Business in California April 1, 1949*. Oakland, CA, 1949.

Berk, Joseph. *The Gatling Gun*. Boulder, CO, 1991.

Berlandier, Jean Louis. *The Indians of Texas in 1830*. Edited by John C. Ewers. Washington, DC, 1967.

Bieber, Ralph P., ed. *Southern Trails to California in 1849*. 5 vols. Glendale, CA, 1937.

———. *Through Mexico to California*. Philadelphia, PA, 1974.

Bigler, David L., ed. *The Gold Discovery Journal of Azariah Smith*. Salt Lake City, UT, 1990.

Birkheimer, William E. *Historical Sketch of the Organization, Administration, Materiel and Tactics of the Artillery, United States Army*. Washington, DC, 1884.

Blaine, Martha Royce. *Pawnee Passage: 1870–1875*. Norman, OK, 1990.

Bloch, Louis M., Jr., ed. *Overland to California in 1859*. Cleveland, OH, 1983.

———. *Overland to California in 1859*. Cleveland, OH, 1990.

Blower, James. *Gold Rush*. New York, 1971.

Boessenecker, John. *Badge and Buckshot*. Norman, OK, 1988.

Boggs, Mae Helene Bacon. *My Playhouse Was a Concord Coach*. Oakland, CA, 1942.

Boller, Henry A. *Among the Indians*. Edited by Milo Milton Quaife. Chicago, IL, 1959.

Borthwick, J. D. *Three Years in California*. Edinburgh, 1857.

Bourke, John G. *An Apache Campaign in the Sierra Madre*. New York, 1958.

———. *On the Border with Crook*. Glorieta, NM, 1969.

Branch, Douglas. *The Cowboy and His Interpreters*. New York, 1961.

Breakenridge, William M. *Helldorado, Bringing the Law to the Mesquite*. Boston, MA, 1928.

Brimlow, George F. *Cavalryman out of the West*. Caldwell, ID, 1944.

Bronson, Edgar Beecher. *Cowboy Life on the Western Plains*. New York, 1910.

———. *Reminiscences of a Ranchman*. Lincoln, NE, 1962.

Brooks, Juanita. *John Doyle Lee, Zealot—Pioneer Builder— Scapegoat*. Glendale, CA, 1961.

———, ed. *On the Mormon Frontier*. Vol. 1. Salt Lake City, UT, 1964.

Brophy, William S. *Marlin Firearms, A History of the Guns and the Company That Made Them*. Harrisburg, PA, 1989.

Brown, Dee. *The Galvanized Yankees*. Lincoln, NE, 1963.

———. *Hear That Lonesome Whistle Blow*. New York, 1977.

———, and Martin F. Schmitt. *Trail Driving Days*. New York, 1952.

Brown, Joseph E. *The Mormon Trek West*. Garden City, NY, 1980.

Brown, Mark H. *The Flight of the Nez Perce*. New York, 1967.

Browning, John, and Curt Gentry. *John M. Browning, American Gunmaker*. Garden City, NY, 1964.

Browning, Peter. *To the Golden Shore*. Lafayette, CA, 1995.

———, ed. *Bright Gem of the Western Seas*. Lafayette, CA, 1991.

Bruce, Robert. *The Fighting Norths and Pawnee Scouts*. New York, 1930.

Bryant, Edwin. *What I Saw in California*. Minneapolis, MN, 1967.

Burnham, Frederick Russell. *Scouting on Two Continents*. Garden City, NY, 1926.

Burt, Struthers. *The Diary of a Dude Wrangler*. New York, 1938.

Burton, Richard F. *The City of the Saints and across the Rocky Mountains to California*. Edited by Fawn M. Brodie. New York, 1963.

Busch, Briton Cooper, ed. *Alta California 1840–1842, The Journal and Observations of William Dane Phelps*. Glendale, CA, 1983.

Butruille, Susan G. *Women's Voices from the Oregon Trail*. Boise, ID, 1993.

Calhoun, James. *With Custer in '74*. Edited by Lawrence Frost. Provo, UT, 1979.

Camp, Charles L., ed. *James Clyman, Frontiersman*. Portland, OR, 1960.

Campion, J. S. *On the Frontier*. London, 1878.

Canton, Frank M. *Frontier Trails*. Edited by Edward Everett Dale. Norman, OK, 1966.

Carpenter, Frank D. *Adventures in Geyser Land*. Caldwell, ID, 1935.

Carrington, Henry B. *The Indian Question*. Boston, MA, 1909.

Carroll, John M., ed. *The Black Military Experience in the American West*. New York, 1971.

Carter, Harvey Lewis. *"Dear Old Kit," The Historical Christopher Carson*. Norman, OK, 1968.

Carter, R. G. *On the Border with Mackenzie*. New York, 1961.

Carvalho, Solomon Nunes. *Incidents of Travel and Adventure in the Far West*. Edited by Bertram Wallace Korn. Philadelphia, PA, 1954.

Chalfant, William Y. *Cheyennes and Horse Soldiers*. Norman, OK, 1989.

Chamberlain, Samuel. *My Confession*. New York, 1956.

Chandless, William. *A Visit to Salt Lake*. London, 1857.

Chisholm, James. *South Pass, 1868, James Chisholm's Journal of the Wyoming Gold Rush*. Edited by Lola M. Homsher. Lincoln, NE, 1960.

Chittenden, Hiram Martin. *History of Early Steamboat Navigation on the Missouri River*. Vol. 1. New York, 1903.

———. *The American Fur Trade of the Far West*. Stanford, CA, 1954.

Chrisman, Harry E. *Lost Trails of the Cimarron*. Denver, CO, 1964.

Clark, Thomas D., ed. *Off at Sunrise, the Overland Journal of Charles Glass Gray*. San Marino, CA, 1976.

Clemens, Samuel L. *Roughing It*. Hartford, CT, 1872.

Clokey, Richard M. *William H. Ashley, Enterprise and Politics in the Trans-Mississippi West*. Norman, OK, 1980.

Clum, Woodworth. *Apache Agent: The Story of John P. Clum*. Boston, MA, 1936.

Coburn, Walt. *Pioneer Cattleman in Montana: The Story of the Circle C Ranch*. Norman, OK, 1968.

Coffin, Morse H. *The Battle of Sand Creek*. Edited by Alan W. Farley. Waco, TX, 1965.

Coffman, Lloyd W. *Blazing a Wagon Trail to Oregon*. Enterprise, OR, 1993.

Conard, Howard Louis. *"Uncle Dick" Wootton*. Chicago, IL, 1890.

Connell, Evan S. *Son of the Morning Star*. San Francisco, CA, 1984.

Conrad, Pam. *Prairie Visions: The Life and Times of Solomon Butcher*. New York, 1991.

Cook, Harold J. *Tales of the 04 Ranch, Recollections of Harold J. Cook 1887–1909*. Lincoln, NE, 1968.

Cook, James H. *Longhorn Cowboy*. New York, 1942.

Copeland, Fayette. *Kendall of the Picayune*. Norman, OK, 1943.

Coues, Elliott, ed. *The Journal of Jacob Fowler*. Lincoln, NE, 1970.

Cox, John E. *Five Years in the United States Army*. New York, 1973.

Cozzens, Samuel Woodworth. *Explorations & Adventures in Arizona & New Mexico*. Secaucus, NJ, 1988.

Cremony, John C. *Life Among the Apaches*. San Francisco, CA, 1868.

Crittenden, H. H. *The Crittenden Memoirs*. New York, 1936.

Crossen, Forest. *Western Yesterdays*. 5 vols. Boulder, CO, 1967.

Cruse, Thomas. *Apache Days and After*. Edited by Eugene Cunningham. Caldwell, ID, 1941.

Culmsee, Carlton. *Utah's Black Hawk War*. Logan, UT, 1973.

Custer, George A. *Wild Life on the Plains and Horrors of Indian Warfare*. St. Louis, MO, 1891.

Danker, Donald F., ed. *Man of the Plains: The Recollections of Luther North, 1856–1882*. Lincoln, NE, 1961.

Dary, David. *Entrepreneurs of the Old West*. New York, 1986.

———. *The Santa Fe Trail*. New York, 2000.

Davies, Henry E. *Ten Days on the Plains*. Edited by Paul Andrew Hutton. Dallas, TX, 1985.

Davis, Britton. *The Truth about Geronimo*. New Haven, CT, 1929.

Davis, Richard Harding. *The West from a Car-Window*. New York, 1892.

DeArment, Robert K. *Knights of the Green Cloth*. Norman, OK, 1982.

———. *George Scarborough: The Life and Death of a Lawman on the Closing Frontier*. Norman, OK, 1992.

Debo, Angie, ed. *The Cowman's Southwest, Being the Reminiscences of Oliver Nelson*. Glendale, CA, 1953.

Dellenbaugh, Frederick S. *A Canyon Voyage*. New Haven, CT, 1908.

des Montaignes, Francois. *The Plains*. Edited by Nancy Alpert Mower and Don Russell. Norman, OK, 1972.

Dillon, Richard. *Burnt-Out Fires*. Englewood Cliffs, NJ, 1973.

Dixon, Olive K. *Life of "Billy" Dixon*. Dallas, TX, 1914.

Dodge, Fred J. *Under Cover for Wells Fargo*. Edited by Carolyn Lake. Boston, MA, 1969.

Dodge, Richard Irving. *Our Wild Indians*. New York, 1959.

———. *The Plains of North America and Their Inhabitants*. Edited by Wayne R. Kime. Newark, DE, 1989.

Donkin, John G. *Trooper and Redskin in the Far Northwest*. London, 1889.

Dornin, George D. *Thirty Years Ago—Gold Rush Memories of a Daguerreotype Artist*. New City, CA, 1995.

Dorsey, R. Stephen. *Guns of the Western Indian War*. Eugene, OR, 1995.

Doy, John. *The Thrilling Narrative of Dr. John Doy of Kansas*. Boston, MA, 1860.

Doyle, Susan Badger, ed. *Journeys to the Land of Gold*. 2 vols. Helena, MT, 2000.

Driggs, Howard R., ed. *The Bullwhacker: Adventures of a Frontier Freighter*. Lincoln, NE, 1988.

Dryden, Cecil. *Up the Columbia for Furs*. Caldwell, ID, 1949.

Dugan, Mark, and John Boessenecker. *The Grey Fox*. Norman, OK, 1992.

Dunlay, Thomas W. *Wolves for the Blue Soldiers*. Lincoln, NE, 1982.

Dunn, William R. *I Stand by Sand Creek*. Fort Collins, CO, 1985.

Durham, Philip, and Everett L. Jones. *The Negro Cowboys.* New York, 1965.

Dutcher, John T. *Ballard: The Great American Single Shot Rifle.* Denver, CO, 2002.

Duval, John D. *The Adventures of Big-Foot Wallace.* Philadelphia, PA, 1871.

Dykes, Jeff C., ed. *Recollections of Thomas Edgar Crawford.* Norman, OK, 1962.

———. *The West of the Texas Kid: Recollections of Thomas Edgar Crawford.* Norman, OK, 1962.

Elkins, John M. *Indian Fighting on the Texas Frontier.* Amarillo, TX, 1929.

Emerson, William K. *Encyclopedia of United States Army Insignia and Uniforms.* Norman, OK, 1996.

Emmons, George Thornton. *The Tlingit Indians.* Edited by Frederica de Laguna. Seattle, WA, 1991.

Erwin, Allen A. *The Southwest of John H. Slaughter.* Glendale, CA, 1965.

Ewers, John C. *Indian Life on the Upper Missouri.* Norman, OK, 1968.

Fahey, John. *The Flathead Indians.* Norman, OK, 1974.

Fairholme, William. *Journal of an Expedition to the Grand Prairies of the Missouri 1840.* Edited by Jack B. Tykal. Spokane, WA, 1996.

Farquhar, Francis P., ed. *Up and Down in California in 1860–1864.* New Haven, CT, 1930.

Ferguson, Charles D. *The Experiences of a Forty-niner During Thirty-Four Years' Residence in California and Australia.* Edited by Frederick T. Wallace. Cleveland, OH, 1888.

Fisher, Vardis, and Opal Laurel Holmes. *Gold Rushes and Mining Camps of the Early American West.* Caldwell, ID, 1968.

Flayderman, Norm F. *Flayderman's Guide to Antique American Firearms and Their Values.* Iola, WI, 2001.

Fleharty, Eugene D. *Wild Animals and Settlers on the Great Plains.* Norman, OK, 1995.

Flores, Dan R., ed. *Journal of an Indian Trader, Anthony Glass and the Texas Trading Frontier 1790–1810.* College Station, TX, 1985.

Flory, J. S. *Thrilling Echoes from the Wild Frontier.* Chicago, IL, 1893.

Forbis, William H. *The Cowboys.* Time-Life "The Old West" Series. New York, 1973.

Ford, John Salmon. *Rip Ford's Texas.* Austin, TX, 1963.

Foreman, Grant. *The Five Civilized Tribes.* Norman, OK, 1934.

Forsyth, George A. *Thrilling Days in Army Life.* New York, 1902.

Frasca, Albert J. *The .45–70 Springfield Book II.* Springfield, OH, 1997.

———, and Robert H. Hill. *The .45–70 Springfield.* Northridge, CA, 1980.

Frazer, Robert W, ed. *Over the Chihuahua and Santa Fe Trails 1847–1848, George Rutledge Gibson's Journal.* Albuquerque, NM, 1981.

Freeman, George D. *Midnight and Noonday.* Edited by Richard L. Lane. Norman, OK, 1984.

Fremont, John C. *The Exploring Expedition to the Rocky Mountains.* Washington, DC, 1845.

French, William. *Some Recollections of a Western Ranchman.* New York, 1965.

Frost, Lawrence A. *Custer's 7th Cavalry and the Campaign of 1873.* El Segundo, CA, 1986.

Garavaglia, Louis A., and Charles G. Worman. *Firearms of the American West 1803– 1865.* Albuquerque, NM, 1984.

———. *Firearms of the American West 1866–1894.* Albuquerque, NM, 1985.

Gardiner, Howard C. *In Pursuit of the Golden Dream.* Edited by Dale L. Morgan. Stoughton, MA, 1970.

Garrard, Lewis H. *Wah-To-Yah and the Taos Trail.* Philadelphia, PA, 1974.

Gibbon, John. *Adventures on the Western Frontier.* Edited by Alan Gaff and Maureen Gaff. Indianapolis, IN, 1994.

Giffen, Helen S., ed. *The Diaries of Peter Decker Overland to California in 1849 and Life in the Mines, 1850–51.* 3 vols. Georgetown, CA, 1966.

Gilbert, Miles, ed. *Getting a Stand.* Union City, TN, 1986.

Gillett, James B. *Six Years with the Texas Rangers 1875–1881.* Edited by M. M. Quaife. New Haven, CT, 1925.

Gordon, James D. *Winchester's New Model of 1873: A Tribute.* 2 vols. Grant, CO, 1997.

Gordon, Mary McDougall, ed. *Overland to California with the Pioneer Line.* Stanford, CA, 1983.

Gould, A. C. *Modern American Rifles.* Boston, MA, 1892.

Grant, U. S. *Personal Memoirs of U. S. Grant.* New York, 1894.

Gray, F. W. *Seeking Fortune in America.* London, 1912.

Gregg, Josiah. *Commerce of the Prairies.* Norman, OK, 1954.

Grinnell, George Bird. *Two Great Scouts and Their Pawnee Battalion.* Cleveland, OH, 1928.

Hafen, LeRoy R., *The Overland Mail.* Cleveland, OH, 1926.

———, ed. *Colorado Gold Rush: Contemporary Letters and Reports 1858–1859.* Philadelphia, PA, 1974.

———, ed. *Pike's Peak Gold Rush Guidebooks of 1859.* Southwest Historical Series 9. Philadelphia, PA, 1974.

———, ed. *William B. Parson's Guidebook to the Gold Mines of Western Kansas.* Philadelphia, PA, 1974.

———, and Ann W. Hafen, eds. *Rufus B. Sage, His Letters and Papers 1836–1847.* Glendale, CA, 1956.

———, and Ann W. Hafen, eds. *The Diaries of William Henry Jackson.* Glendale, CA, 1959.

Haley, J. Evetts, *Charles Goodnight, Cowman & Plainsman.* Boston, MA, 1936.

———. *Jeff Milton, A Good Man with a Gun.* Norman, OK, 1948.

———. *The XIT Ranch of Texas.* Norman, OK, 1953.

Haley, James L. *The Buffalo War.* New York, 1976.

Hamilton, W. T. *My Sixty Years on the Plains.* Norman, OK, 1960.

Hanes, Bailey C. *Bill Doolin, Outlaw O.T.* Norman, OK, 1968.

Hannon, Jessie Gould. *The Boston-Newton Company Venture from Massachusetts to California in 1849.* Lincoln, NE, 1969.

Hannum, Anna Paschall, ed. *A Quaker Forty-Niner.* Philadelphia, PA, 1930.

Hanson, Charles E., Jr. *The Northwest Gun.* Lincoln, NE, 1956.

———. *The Plains Rifle.* Harrisburg, PA, 1960.

———. *The Hawken Rifle, Its Place in History.* Chadron, NE, 1979.

Harris, Charles W., and Buck Rainey, eds. *The Cowboy: Six-Shooters, Songs, and Sex.* Norman, OK, 1976.

Hastings, Lansford W. *The Emigrant's Guide to Oregon and California.* Vol. 5. Cincinnati, OH, 1845.

Haven, Charles T., and Frank A. Belden. *A History of Colt Revolvers.* New York, 1940.

Haydon, A. L. *The Riders of the Plains.* Chicago, IL, 1910.

Haynes, C. Vance, Jr. *General Custer and His Sporting Rifles.* Tucson, AZ, 1995.

Hedren, Paul L. *Fort Laramie in 1876.* Lincoln, NE, 1988.

Heintzelman, Samuel P. *Fifty Miles and a Fight.* Edited by Jerry Thompson. Austin, TX, 1998.

Herbert, Frank. *40 Years Prospecting and Mining in the Black Hills of South Dakota.* Rapid City, SD, 1921.

Herman, Daniel Justin. *Hunting and the American Imagination*. Washington, DC, 2001.

Herron, Jim. *Fifty Years on the Owl Hoot Trail*. Edited by Harry E. Chrisman. Chicago, IL, 1969.

Heyman, Max L., Jr. *Prudent Soldier: A Biography of Major General E. R. S. Canby 1817–1873*. Glendale, CA, 1959.

Hichman, William A. *Brigham's Destroying Angel*. Salt Lake City, UT, 1904.

Hickey, Michael M. *The Cowboy Conspiracy to Convict the Earps*. Honolulu, HI, 1994.

Hill, J. L. *The End of the Cattle Trail*. Long Beach, CA, 1922.

Holliday, J. S. *The World Rushed In*. New York, 1981.

Holmes, Kenneth L., ed. *Covered Wagon Women—Diaries and Letters from the Western Trails 1840–1890*. 4 vols. Glendale, CA, 1988.

Homsher, Lola M., ed. *South Pass, 1868*. Lincoln, NE, 1960.

Hoobler, Dorothy, and Thomas Hoobler. *Photographing the Frontier*. New York, 1980.

Horn, Tom. *The Life of Tom Horn, Government Scout and Interpreter*. Norman, OK, 1964.

Hornaday, William Temple. *The Extermination of the American Bison*. Washington, DC, 2002.

Houze, Herbert G. *Colt Rifles & Muskets From 1847 to 1870*. Iola, WI, 1996.

Howard, Oliver O. *My Life and Experiences among Our Hostile Indians*. New York, 1972.

Howbert, Irving. *Memories of a Lifetime in the Pike's Peak Region*. Glorieta, NM, 1970.

Hoyt, Henry F. *A Frontier Doctor*. Boston, MA, 1929.

Hughes, Richard D. *Pioneer Years in the Black Hills*. Edited by Agnes Wright Spring. Glendale, CA, 1957.

Hulbert, Archer Butler. *Forty-Niners—The Chronicle of the California Trail*. Boston, MA, 1949.

Hunt, J. Marvin, ed. *The Trail Drivers of Texas*. 2 vols. New York, 1963.

Hutton, Harold. *Doc Middleton*. Chicago, IL, 1974.

Hyslop, Stephen G. *Bound for Santa Fe*. Norman, OK, 2002.

Ingraham, Prentiss, ed. *Seventy Years on the Frontier, Alexander Majors' Memoirs of a Lifetime on the Border*. Chicago, IL, 1893.

Irving, Washington. *A Tour on the Prairies*. Edited by John Francis McDermott. Norman, OK, 1956.

Jackson, Joseph Henry. *Bad Company*. New York, 1939.

Jenkins, John J., ed. *The Papers of the Texas Revolution 1835 and 1836*. 6 vols. Austin, TX, 1973.

Johnson, Olga Weydemeyer. *Flathead and Kootenay*. Glendale, CA, 1969.

Jones, Daniel W. *Forty Years among the Indians*. Los Angeles, CA, 1960.

Jones, Douglas C. *The Treaty of Medicine Lodge*. Norman, OK, 1966.

Jones, Mary Ellen. *Daily Life on the Nineteenth Century American Frontier*. Westport, CT, 1998.

Jordan, Philip D. *Frontier Law and Order*. Lincoln, NE, 1970.

Katz, William Loren. *The Black West*. Garden City, NY, 1971.

Keim, De B. Randolph. *Sheridan's Troopers on the Borders*. Philadelphia, PA, 1870.

———. *Sheridan's Troopers on the Borders: A Winter Campaign on the Plains*. Freeport, NY, 1970.

Kelly, Luther S. *"Yellowstone Kelly," The Memoirs of Luther S. Kelly*. Edited by M. M. Quaife. New Haven, CT, 1926.

Kelver, Gerald O., ed. *15 Years on the Western Frontier 1866–1881*. Fort Collins, CO, 1975.

Kendall, George Wilkins. *Narrative of the Texan Santa Fe Expedition*. Vol. 1. New York, 1850.

Kessell, John L. *Spain in the Southwest*. Norman, OK, 2002.

Kime, Wayne R., ed. *The Black Hills Journals of Colonel Richard Irving Dodge*. Norman, OK, 1996.

Kip, Lawrence. *Army Life on the Pacific*. New York, 1986.

Knowles, Thomas W. *They Rode for the Lone Star*. Dallas, TX, 1999.

Kopec, John A., and H. Sterling Fenn. *Colt Cavalry & Artillery Revolvers*. Whitmore, CA, 1994.

Koury, Michael J. *Diaries of the Little Big Horn*. Bellevue, NE, 1970.

Krakel, Dean F. *The Saga of Tom Horn*. Laramie, WY, 1954.

Krause, Herbert, and Gary D. Olson. *Prelude to Glory*. Sioux Falls, SD, 1974.

Kreyche, Gerald F. *Visions of the American West*. Lexington, KY, 1989.

Kyner, James H. *End of Track*. Caldwell, ID, 1937.

L'Aloge, Bob. *Knights of the Sixgun*. Las Cruces, NM, 1991.

Lang, Lincoln A. *Ranching with Roosevelt*. Philadelphia, PA, 1926.

Langley, Harold D., ed. *To Utah with the Dragoons and Glimpses of Life in Arizona and California 1858–1859*. Salt Lake City, UT, 1974.

Larson, James. *Sergeant Larson 4th Cavalry*. San Antonio, TX, 1935.

Lass, William E. *From the Missouri to the Great Salt Lake*. Lincoln, NE, 1972.

Law, Clive M. *Canadian Military Handguns, 1855–1985*. Bloomfield, Ontario, 1994.

Lecke, William H. *The Buffalo Soldiers*. Norman, OK, 1967.

Leeson, Michael A. *History of Montana 1739–1885*. Chicago, IL, 1885.

Lewis, Marvin, ed. *The Mining Frontier*. Norman, OK, 1967.

Libeus, Barney, ed. *Letters of the Pike's Peak Gold Rush*. San Jose, CA, 1959.

Long, Jeff. *Duel of Eagles*. New York, 1990.

Longfield, G. Maxwell, and David T. Basnett. *Observations on Colt's Second Contract November 2, 1847*. Alexandria Bay, NY, 1998.

Lowe, Percival G. *Five Years a Dragoon*. Norman, OK, 1965.

Lowther, Charles C. *Dodge City, Kansas*. Philadelphia, PA, 1940.

Luttig, John C. *Journal of a Fur-Trading Expedition on the Upper Missouri 1812–1813*. Edited by Stella M. Drumm. St. Louis, MO, 1992.

Mack, Effie Mona. *Nevada, A History of the State from the Earliest Times through the Civil War*. Glendale, CA, 1936.

Macleod, R. C. *The North-West Mounted Police and Law Enforcement 1873–1905*. Toronto, Ontario, 1976.

Madis, George. *The Winchester Book*. Lancaster, TX, 1971.

Madsen, Brigham D. *The Shoshoni Frontier and the Bear River Massacre*. Salt Lake City, UT, 1985.

Mansfield, Joseph. *Mansfield on the Condition of the Western Forts 1853–54*. Edited by Robert W. Frazer. Norman, OK, 1963.

Marcot, Roy M. *Spencer Repeating Firearms*. Irving, CA, 1983.

Margo, Elizabeth. *Taming the Forty-Niner*. New York, 1955.

Marrin, Albert. *Cowboys, Indians, and Gunfighters*. New York, 1993.

Marryat, Frank. *Mountains and Molehills*. Stanford, CA, 1952.

Martin, Douglas D. *Tombstone's Epitaph*. Albuquerque, NM, 1953.

Massey, Sara R., ed. *Black Cowboys of Texas*. College Station, TX, 2000.

Mather, R. E., and F. E. Boswell. *Gold Camp Desperadoes*. Norman, OK, 1993.

Mattes, Merrill J. *Indians, Infants and Infantry.* Denver, CO, 1960.

Mattison, Ray H. *The Army Post on the Northern Plains 1865–1885.* Gering, NE, 1962.

Mayer, Lynne Rhodes, and Kenneth E. Vose. *Makin' Tracks.* New York, 1975.

McAulay, John D. *Civil War Carbines.* Vol. 2. Lincoln, RI, 1991.

———. *Civil War Pistols.* Lincoln, RI, 1992.

———. *Rifles of the U.S. Army 1861–1906.* Lincoln, RI, 2003

McCague, James. *Moguls and Iron Men.* New York, 1964.

McChristian, Douglas C. *An Army of Marksmen.* Fort Collins, CO, 1981.

———. *The U.S. Army in the West, 1870–1880.* Norman, OK, 1995.

McClernand, Edward J. *With the Indian and the Buffalo in Montana, 1870–1878.* Glendale, CA, 1969.

McClure, A. K. *Three Thousand Miles through the Rocky Mountains.* Philadelphia, PA, 1869.

McConnell, H. H. *Five Years a Cavalryman.* Norman, OK, 1996.

McConnell, William J. *Frontier Law.* Chicago, IL, 1924.

———, and James S. Reynolds. *Idaho's Vigilantes.* Moscow, ID, 1984.

McCoy, Joseph G. *Historic Sketches of the Cattle Trade of West and Southwest.* Philadelphia, PA, 1974.

McCullough, Harrell. *Selden Lindsey, U.S. Deputy Marshal.* Oklahoma City, OK, 1990.

McGivern, Ed. *Fast and Fancy Revolver Shooting.* Chicago, IL, 1957.

McGrath, Roger D. *Gunfighters, Highwaymen & Vigilantes.* Berkeley, CA, 1984.

McKusick, Marshall. *The Iowa Northern Border Brigade.* Iowa City, IA, 1975.

McMurtry, Larry. *Lonesome Dove.* New York, 1985.

McWhorter, Lucullus Virgil. *Yellow Wolf: His Own Story.* Caldwell, ID, 1940.

Meadows, Edward Scott. *U.S. Military Holsters and Pistol Cartridge Boxes.* Dallas, TX, 1987.

Merritt, John I. *Baronets and Buffalo.* Missoula, MT, 1985.

Messiter, Charles Alston. *Sport and Adventures among the North American Indians.* New York, 1966.

Miles, Nelson A. *Serving the Republic.* New York, 1911.

Miller, Nyle H., and Joseph W. Snell. *Why the West Was Wild.* Topeka, KS, 1963.

Milner, Joe E., and Earle R. Forrest. *California Joe.* Caldwell, ID, 1935.

Mitchell, James L. *Colt, A Collection of Letters and Photographs about the Man, the Army, the Company.* Harrisburg, PA, 1959.

Morgan, Dale L., and Eleanor Towles Harris, eds. *The Rocky Mountain Journals of William Marshall Andrews.* San Marino, CA, 1967.

Mulford, Ami Frank. *Fighting Indians in the 7th United States Cavalry.* Bellevue, NE, 1970.

Murphy, John Mortimer. *Sporting Adventures in the Far West.* New York, 1880.

Murray, Charles Augustus. *Travels in North America.* 2 vols. New York, 1974.

Murray, Keith A. *The Modocs and Their War.* Norman, OK, 1959.

Murray, Robert A. *The Army on the Powder River.* Bellevue, NE, 1969.

Myers, Frank. *Soldiering in Dakota, among the Indians, in 1863–4–5.* Freeport, NY, 1971.

Myres, Sandra L., ed. *Ho for California: Women's Overland Diaries from the Huntington Library.* San Marino, CA, 1980.

Nacy, Michele J. *Members of the Regiment.* Westport, CT, 2000.

Nasatir, A. P., ed. *A French Journalist in the California Gold Rush.* Georgetown, CA, 1964.

Nelson, Herbert B., and Preston E. Onstad, eds. *A Webfoot Volunteer, the Diary of William M. Hilleary 1864–1866.* Corvallis, OR, 1965.

Nelson, John Young. *Fifty Years on the Trail.* Norman, OK, 1963.

Newmark, Maurice, and Marco R. Newmark. *Sixty Years in Southern California 1853–1913.* New York, 1916.

Nicolson, John, ed. *The Arizona of Joseph Pratt Allyn.* Tucson, AZ, 1974.

O'Neal, Bill. *The Arizona Rangers.* Austin, TX, 1987.

Olmsted, Frederick Law. *A Journey through Texas.* Austin, TX, 1978.

Oppel, Frank. *Tales of Alaska and the Yukon.* Secaucus, NJ, 1986.

Ostrander, Alson B. *An Army Boy of the Sixties.* Yonkers-on-Hudson, NY, 1924.

Otero, Miguel Antonio. *My Life on the Frontier 1864–1882.* Albuquerque, NM, 1987.

Parke, Charles Ross. *Dreams to Dust.* Edited by James E. Davis. Lincoln, NE, 1989.

Parker, George F. *Iowa Pioneer Foundations.* Iowa City, IA, 1940.

Parker, Watson. *Deadwood, The Golden Years.* Lincoln, NE, 1981.

Parkman, Francis. *The Oregon Trail.* Madison, WI, 1969.

Parks, Joseph Howard. *General Edmund Kirby Smith, C.S.A.* Baton Rouge, LA, 1954.

Parsons, John E. *The Peacemaker and Its Rivals.* New York, 1950.

———. *Henry Deringer's Pocket Pistol.* New York, 1952.

———. *The First Winchester.* New York, 1955.

———. *Smith & Wesson Revolvers.* New York, 1957.

———. *West on the 49th Parallel.* New York, 1963.

Pegler, Martin. *Firearms in the American West 1700–1900.* Midsomer Norton, England, 2002

Peirce, Parker I. *Antelope Bill.* Minneapolis, MN, 1962.

Perkins, William. *Three Years in California.* Berkeley, CA, 1964.

Phelps, Art. *The Story of Merwin, Hulbert & Company Revolvers.* Rough and Ready, CA, 1992.

Porter, Joseph C. *Paper Medicine Man: John Gregory Bourke and His American West.* Norman, OK, 1986.

Prassel, Frank Richard. *The Western Peace Officer.* Norman, OK, 1972.

Price, Con. *Memories of Old Montana.* Pasadena, CA, 1945.

Read, Georgia Willis, and Ruth Gaines. *Gold Rush: The Journals, Drawings and Other Papers of Goldsborough Bruff.* New York, 1944.

Records, Laban S. *Cherokee Outlet Cowboy.* Edited by Ellen Jayne Maris Wheeler. Norman, OK, 1995.

Rich, E. E., ed. *Peter Skene Odgen's Snake Country Journals 1824–25 and 1825–26.* London, 1950.

Rickey, Don, Jr. *Forty Miles a Day on Beans and Hay.* Norman, OK, 1963.

Riley, Glenda. *Women and Indians on the Frontier, 1825–1915.* Albuquerque, NM, 1991.

Ripley, Warren. *Artillery and Ammunition of the Civil War.* New York, 1970.

Roberts, Brigham H. *History of the Church of Jesus Christ of Latter-Day Saints.* Salt Lake City, UT, 1950.

Robinson, Charles M., III. *The Frontier World of Fort Griffin.*

Spokane, WA, 1992.

———. *The Buffalo Hunters*. Austin, TX, 1995.

———. *The Men Who Wear the Star*. New York, 2000.

Robinson, Fayette. *California and Its Gold Regions*. New York, 1849.

Roe, Frances M. A. *Army Letters from an Officer's Wife 1871–1888*. New York, 1909.

Rogers, Fred B. *Soldiers of the Overland*. San Francisco, CA, 1938.

Rollinson, John K. *Pony Trails in Wyoming*. Edited by E. A. Brininstool. Caldwell, ID, 1941.

———. *Wyoming Cattle Trails*. Caldwell, ID, 1948.

Ronda, James P. *Astoria and Empire*. Lincoln, NE, 1990.

Roosevelt, Theodore. *Hunting Trips of a Ranchman*. New York, 1926.

———. *The Wilderness Hunter*. New York, 1926.

Rosa, James G. *The West of Wild Bill Hickok*. Norman, OK, 1982.

Ross, Alexander. *Adventures of the First Settlers on the Oregon or Columbia River*. London, 1849.

Ruede, Howard. *Sod House Days: Letters from a Kansas Homesteader 1877–78*. Edited by John Ise. New York, 1937.

Rumer, Thomas A., ed. *This Emigrating Company, the 1844 Oregon Trail Journal of Jacob Hunter*. Spokane, WA, 1990.

Russell, Carl P. *Guns on the Early Frontiers*. Berkeley, CA, 1957.

Russell, Osborne. *Journal of a Trapper*. Edited by Aubrey L. Haines. Lincoln, NE, 1955.

Rywell, Martin. *The Gun That Shaped American Destiny*. Harriman, TN, 1957.

Sage, Rufus B. *Rocky Mountain Life*. Lincoln, NE, 1982.

Santleben, August. *A Texas Pioneer*. Edited by I. D. Affleck. New York, 1910.

Satterlee, L. D., ed. *Ten Old Gun Catalogs*. Ann Arbor, MI, 1957.

———. *14 Old Gun Catalogs*. Chicago, IL, 1962.

Savage, William W., Jr., ed. *Cowboy Life: Reconstructing an American Myth*. Norman, OK, 1991.

Sawey, Orlan. *Charles A. Siringo*. Boston, MA, 1981.

Scarborough, George. *The Life and Death of a Lawman on the Closing Frontier*. Norman, OK, 1991.

Schlissel, Lillian. *Women's Diaries of the Westward Journey*. New York, 1982.

Schmidt, Peter A. *Hall's Military Breechloaders*. Lincoln, RI, 1996.

Schuler, Harold H. *Fort Pierre Chouteau*. Vermillion, SD, 1990.

———. *Fort Sully, Guns at Sunset*. Vermillion, SD, 1992.

Schultz, James Willard. *Many Strange Characters: Montana Frontier Tales*. Norman, OK, 1982.

Scurlock, William H., ed. *The Book of Buckskinning*. Texarkana, TX, 1981.

———. *The Book of Buckskinning*. Vol. 4. Texarkana, TX, 1987.

———. *The Book of Buckskinning*. Vol. 5. Texarkana, TX, 1989.

Seidman, Laurence Ivan. *Once in the Saddle*. New York, 1991.

Sellers, Frank. *Sharps Firearms*. Dallas, TX, 1978.

Serven, James E. *Conquering the Frontiers*. Los Angeles, CA, 1974.

Settle, Raymond W., ed. *March of the Mounted Riflemen*. Glendale, CA, 1940.

Shelton, Lawrence P. *California Gunsmiths 1846–1900*. Fair Oaks, CA, 1977.

Shields, G. O. *Hunting in the Great West*. Chicago, IL, 1890.

Shirley, Glenn. *Six-Gun and Silver Star*. Albuquerque, NM, 1955.

Simeone, William E. *Rifles, Blankets, and Beads*. Norman, OK, 1995.

Simmons, Marc. *Ranchers, Ramblers & Renegades*. Santa Fe, NM, 1984.

Siringo, Charles A. *Riatas and Spurs*. Boston, MA, 1927.

———. *A Texas Cowboy or Fifteen Years on the Hurricane Deck of a Spanish Pony*. Lincoln, NE, 1950.

———. *History of "Billy the Kid."* Albuquerque, NM, 2000.

Slatta, Richard W. *The Cowboy Encyclopedia*. Santa Barbara, CA, 1994.

Slaughter, William W., and Michael Landon. *Trail of Hope: The Story of the Mormon Trail*. Salt Lake City, UT, 1997.

Smith, Ralph Adam. *Borderlander, the Life of James Kirker, 1793–1852*. Norman, OK, 1999.

Smith, Sherry L. *Sagebrush Soldier, Private William Earl Smith's View of the Sioux War of 1876*. Norman, OK, 1989.

Smith, Thomas T., ed. *A Dose of Frontier Soldiering*. Lincoln, NE, 1994.

Sowell, A. J. *Early Settlers and Indian Fighters of Southwest Texas*. Austin, TX, 1900.

Spotts, David L. *Campaigning with Custer and the Nineteenth Kansas Volunteer Cavalry on the Washita Campaign, 1868–'69*. Los Angeles, CA, 1928.

Spry, Irene M. *The Palliser Expedition*. Toronto, Ontario, 1963.

Stallard, Patricia Y. *Glittering Misery: Dependents of the Indian Fighting Army*. San Rafael, CA, 1978.

Stamm, Mike. *Horse Mule Grizzly Indian Buffalo Wrecks of the Frontier West*. Battle Mountain, NV, 1997.

Stanley, Henry M. *My Early Travels and Adventures in America and Asia*. Vol. 1. New York, 1905.

Steele, John. *In Camp and Cabin*. Lodi, WI, 1901.

Stiles, T. J., ed. *Warriors and Pioneers*. New York, 1996.

Stratton, Joanna L. *Pioneer Women—Voices from the Kansas Frontier*. New York, 1981.

Strickland, Rex W. *Six Who Came to El Paso: Pioneers of the 1840s*. El Paso, TX, 1963.

Strong, Henry W. *My Frontier Days and Indian Fights on the Plains of Texas*. Dallas, TX, 1926.

Stuart, Granville. *Forty Years on the Frontier*. Vol. 1. Cleveland, OH, 1925.

Sullivan, W. J. L. *Twelve Years in the Saddle for Law and Order on the Frontiers of Texas*. New York, 1966.

Summerhayes, Martha. *Vanished Arizona*. Salem, MA, 1911.

Sunder, John E. *The Fur Trade on the Upper Missouri, 1849–1865*. Norman, OK, 1965.

Sweet, Alexander E., and J. Armoy Knox. *On a Mexican Mustang through Texas*. London, 1905.

Swisher, Jacob A. *Iowa in Times of War*. Iowa City, IA, 1943.

Sword, Wiley. *The Historic Henry Rifle*. Lincoln, RI, 2002.

Taft, Robert. *Artists and Illustrators of the Old West 1850–1900*. New York, 1953.

Tanner, Karen Holliday. *Doc Holliday: A Family Portrait*. Norman, OK, 1998.

Tate, Michael L. *The Frontier Army in the Settlement of the West*. Norman, OK, 1999.

Taylor, Morris F. *First Mail West*. Albuquerque, NM, 1971.

Terrell, John Upton. *Apache Chronicle*. New York, 1972.

Thompson, Jerry. *A Wild and Vivid Land*. Austin, TX, 1997.

———, ed. *Texas & New Mexico on the Eve of the Civil War*. Albuquerque, NM, 2001.

Thwaites, Reuben Gold, ed. *Early Western Travels 1748–1846*. 21 vols. New York, 1966.

Tinker, George H. *A Land of Sunshine: Flagstaff and Its Surroundings*. Glendale, CA, 1969.

Townshend, R. B. *The Tenderfoot in New Mexico*. London, 1923.

———. *A Tenderfoot in Colorado*. Norman, OK, 1968.

Triplett, Frank. *The Life, Times, and Treacherous Death of Jesse James*. Chicago, IL, 1970.

Truman, Ben C. *The Field of Honor*. New York, 1884.

Tryon, Charles Z. *The History of a Business Established One Hundred Years Ago 1811–1911*. Philadelphia, PA, 1911.

Tyler, Daniel. *A Concise History of the Mormon Battalion in the Mexican War*. Glorieta, NM, 1969.

Unrau, William E., ed. *Tending the Talking Wire*. Salt Lake City, UT, 1979.

Unruh, John D., Jr. *The Plains Across*. Urbana, IL, 1979.

Vaughn, J. W. *The Battle of Platte Bridge*. Norman, OK, 1963.

Viola, Herman J. *Diplomats in Buckskins*. Bluffton, SC, 1995.

Wagner, Glendolin Damon. *Old Neutriment*. Lincoln, NE, 1989.

Walker, Henry Pickering. *The Wagonmasters*. Norman, OK, 1966.

Wallace, Ernest, ed. *Ranald S. Mackenzie's Official Correspondence Relating to Texas, 1871–1873*. Lubbock, TX, 1967.

Wantland, Clyde. *Taming the Nueces Strip*. Austin, TX, 1962.

Ware, E. F. *The Lyon Campaign in Missouri*. Topeka, KS, 1907.

Ware, Eugene F. *The Indian War of 1864*. New York, 1960.

Watkins, T. H. *Gold and Silver in the West*. Palo Alto, CA, 1971.

Watson, Jeanne Hamilton, ed. *To the Land of Gold and Wickedness*. St. Louis, MO, 1988.

Webb, James Josiah. *Adventures in the Santa Fe Trade 1844–1847*. Philadelphia, PA, 1974.

Wells, Harry Laurens. *History of Nevada County California 1880*. Berkeley, CA, 1970.

Werner, Emmy E. *Pioneer Children on the Journey West*. Boulder, CO, 1995.

Werner, Fred H. *The Beecher Island Battle*. Greeley, CO, 1989.

White, David A., ed. *News of the Plains and Rockies 1803–1865*. 8 vols. Spokane, WA, 2001.

White, M. Catherine. *David Thompson's Journals Relating to Montana and Adjacent Regions 1808–1812*. Missoula, MT, 1950.

White, Richard. *It's Your Misfortune and None of My Own*. Norman, OK, 1991.

Wilkerson, Don. *Colt's Double Action Revolver Model of 1878*. Marciline, MO, 1998.

Williamson, Harold F. *Winchester, the Gun That Won the West*. Washington, DC, 1952.

Wilson, John P. *Merchants, Guns & Money*. Santa Fe, NM, 1987.

Wilson, R. L. *Winchester: An American Legend*. New York, 1991.

———. *The Book of Colt Firearms*. Minneapolis, MN, 1993.

———, and L. D. Eberhart. *The Deringer in America*. Lincoln, RI, 1985.

———, and Greg Martin. *Buffalo Bill's Wild West*. New York, 1998.

Wingate, George. *Through the Yellowstone Park on Horseback*. New York, 1886.

Wislizenus, F. A. *A Journey to the Rocky Mountains in the Year 1839*. St. Louis, MO, 1912.

Wooster, Robert. *Soldiers, Sutlers, and Settlers*. College Station, TX, 1987.

Worcester, Don. *The Chisholm Trail*. Lincoln, NE, 1980.

———, ed. *Pioneer Trails West*. Caldwell, ID, 1985.

Wright, Mike. *What They Didn't Teach You about the Wild West*. Novato, CA, 2000.

Yost, Nellie Snyder, ed. *Boss Cowman: The Recollections of Ed Lemmon 1857–1946*. Lincoln, NE, 1969.

Zimmer, William F. *Frontier Soldier*. Edited by Jerome A. Greene. Helena, MT, 1998.

MISCELLANEOUS GOVERNMENT DOCUMENTS

Allen, Henry T. *Report of an Expedition to the Copper, Tamana, and Koyukuk Rivers in the Territory of Alaska in the Year 1885*. Washington, DC, 1887.

Annual Report of the Secretary of War, 1876, serial 1742.

Compilation of Narratives of Expeditions in Alaska. Washington, DC, 1900.

Law and Order: Being the Official Reports to Parliament of the Activities of the Royal North-West Mounted Police Force From 1886–1887. Toronto, Ontario, 1973.

Outline Descriptions of the Posts in the Military Division of the Missouri Commanded by Lieutenant General P. H. Sheridan. Chicago, IL, 1876. Reprint edition, Bellevue, NE, 1969.

Report of the Commissioner of Indian Affairs 1854. Washington, DC, 1855.

The New West: Being the Official Reports to Parliament of the Activities of the Royal North-West Mounted Police Force 1888–1909. Toronto, Ontario, 1973.

UNPUBLISHED MANUSCRIPTS

Potter, James E. "Firearms On the Overland Trail," 1990.

PERIODICALS AND CATALOGS

American Rifleman
American Society of Arms Collectors Bulletin
ARMAX: The Journal of the Cody Firearms Museum
Army History
Contributions to the Historical Society of Montana
Gun Report
Journal of the West
Kansas Historical Quarterly
Man at Arms
Minnesota Weapons Collectors Association News
Missouri Archaeologist
Montana Magazine
Museum Journal [of the West Texas Museum Association]
Museum of the Fur Trade Quarterly
Nebraska History
Overland Journal
Persimmon Hill
Sharps Collector Association Reports
Shooting Times
Southwestern Historical Quarterly
Texas Gun Collector
Texas Parks and Wildlife
Transactions of the Kansas State Historical Society
Utah Historical Quarterly
Winchester Repeating Arms Company Catalog

INDEX

References to illustrations are in italics.

– INDEX –